THE RAILWAY-LOVER'S

COMPANION

The Railway-Lover'

"Railways have rendered more services, and have received
less gratitude, than any other institution in the land."

JOHN BRIGHT

EYRE AND SPOTTISWOODE (PUBLISHERS) LT

Companion

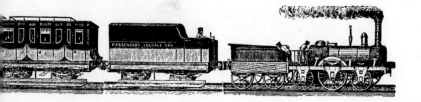

EDITED BY

BRYAN MORGAN

2 HENRIETTA STREET LONDON WC2

IN
MEMORIAM
W.M.

First published 1963
Copyright © Eyre & Spottiswoode 1963
Printed in Great Britain
by Billing & Sons Ltd., Guildford and London
Cat. No. 6/2485/1

Contents

5

PART IV: THE MASTER-BUILDERS

PART V: A NETWORK OF LINES

PART VI: SAFETY, DANGER AND DISASTER

PART VII: SERVICES AND SPECIALS

PART VIII: FOREIGN PARTS

PART IX: FACT AND FICTION

PART X: RAILWAY VERSE

List of Illustrations

THE ENDPAPERS

Tunbridge Wells Central Station, 1846 – the second station at
Tunbridge Wells on the South-Eastern Railway, which replaced
the original temporary terminus. From a lithograph by J. C.
Bourne. *Courtesy, Museum of British Transport, Clapham.*

Acknowledgements

Where the source of the illustrations has not been indicated,
please see page 553.

THE RAILWAY-LOVER'S

COMPANION

Introduction

This is not the first selection of railway writing to be published in Britain in recent years; but I think it is the second. Its predecessor was Stuart Legg's delightful *The Railway Book* (Rupert Hart-Davis, 1952); and here at the start I should thank Mr Legg for steering me towards a number of excerpts included in the present book.

The purpose of *The Railway-Lover's Companion* is, however, rather different. Mr Legg's anthology was one of brief excerpts and even anecdotes. But here we have attempted something more monumental, a Doric Arch of the railway age which should commemorate the drama and achievement – as well as some of the trivia – of one of the world's most tremendous revolutions. It is admittedly an arch built only from paper; but at least it is secure from vandalism.

I am no Hardwick, though; and however noble the plan with which we set out it has been modified by many factors – and most notably by the sheer bulk of railway writing. From semi-informed guesswork and scribbles on the backs of envelopes, I would hazard that the world literature of railways – in bound books alone – falls not far short of 250 million words. As a young man one could sit down to it with a few assistants, and one could die with it still unread and still expanding.

This literature, though, falls into several groups. There are the primary sources, the newsprint clippings of Hendon and the old companies' minutes. There are the secondary ones, the *Fifty Years of the South Staffordshire* type of book. Tertiary sources have titles like *Our Railway Age,* quaternary ones are called *Lines I Loved,* and most of the fifth class are *A Boy's Book of Trains.* Then one moves on to the magazine articles. . . .

This book has been assembled mainly from the third and fourth classes: in these are to be found the best of railway literature, since such books were written selectively and with love. But I would not claim that in my search for material I have exhausted even this corner of the bookshelves of Britain's railway history and description. For *Britain's* railway history it must be, since there proved no room in this book for more than a token showing of railroads overseas.

That history began seriously some 135 years ago, and has now reached a climacteric. Some see the railways of Britain – and of the world – as doomed: others believe that they are entering a phase of stripped-down renaissance. Rather than enter this controversy I have in general ended my selections with the twilight of the age of steam; but two things are certain. One is that, whatever technical advances the future holds, there will be little room in it for giant enterprises and comic failures, for glories and oddities. The other is that the individualities of Britain's railways have never been so widely appreciated as now when they are swiftly passing away.

There is a large and well-informed audience, in fact, for good writing about good and bad trains. Hence I cannot hope that all readers will endorse this selection of *railroadiana*. Subjects and styles, the balance of the solid and the charming – all these must in the end rely on personal taste. I believe, though, that the book has been shaped on certain principles.

Broadly, one can build an anthology in two ways: one can envisage a plan and then look for excerpts to fit it, or one can select pieces which one likes and then find a pattern for them. I have tried to compromise between these courses, with perhaps a bias towards the latter. But I would not claim that every piece reprinted here represents the best published account of a particular aspect or moment. For not only are a number of well-known sources (such as Osborne, Lambert and Marshall, Roscoe, Lewin, Lee and Bucknall) difficult to excerpt, but the editor is expected to provide varied fare. Mr A's *The Story of Britain's Railways* (1955) may seem to him better throughout than Mr B's *The British Railway Story* (1956); but the reader is entitled to both Mr A *and* Mr B.

Again, there are certain gaps where even a second-rate source may be appreciated – or so I persuade myself, if only to justify the fact that I have anthologized myself once or twice. And finally, whilst on the whole I have preferred to quote from bound books and "classic" writers, I have not hesitated to draw on unexpected authors and ephemeral sources when it seemed they had something special to offer. My only inflexible criteria were that each piece should seem good of its kind and should, for one reason or another, earn its place.

After the scissors came the paste-pot; and after the decisions of selection – of excerpting perhaps three times as much material as could be used – came those of arrangement. Would, for instance, a description of a French narrow-gauge line belong with one of an Irish narrow-gauge line or with one of a German main line? An editor should not justify his mental processes in too great detail, for it is the end-product which matters; but it may be useful to outline the system on which this book was finally arranged.

Its first section, then, forms an *hors-d'oeuvre*, a few comments on the mysterious fascination of railways. Then follows a weighty main course, which I think, needs a special comment.

Few technologies have been better documented than the development of Britain's railway system. Its first great reporter was Samuel Smiles; and whatever one's opinion of Smiles's ethical framework his prose style is a model of accurate engineering. Then – over a century later – Professor Jack Simmons brought the story to its latest (but still transient, for the Beeching Report has already modified several predictions) state of up-to-dateness in a book of which many paragraphs could almost be inserted into a Smiles *Life* with no sense of a violent change of style. This is not to suggest that the Victorian novelist used a "modern" diction or that the economic historian of today uses a "period" one. It is rather that the retailing of the railway story seems to engender a timeless economy of words and a classic discipline of ideas.

In the years between there have been published many dozen books under some such title as *A History of British Railways*. From those dazzling years when the first viaducts strode across fields unchanged since the Enclosures, up to the present age of doubt, each generation, each decade and almost each year seems to have needed a new summary of the railway story. But in this long shelf there is rarely reflected much sense of the gap of *feeling* which divides the ages of the past and present queens – of the technical, aesthetic and social revolutions which have rumbled behind Bourne and Frith and Pick, Stephenson and Stirling and English Electric, Midland and L.M.S. and B.R. The classic accounts of Britain's railway history are indeed to some extent interchangeable; and so in the key section of this book I have unfolded the story through only a few of those many pairs of observant eyes which have been focussed on it.

With the roadbed laid I turned to particular aspects of railways –

and first to the departments of the locomotive superintendent and
then of the civil engineer or architect. My fifth section – on
particular lines and systems – may seem brief; but there is a
surprising lack of good descriptions in this department. My sixth
may seem disproportionately long; but in a general work the
drama of the rare accident must take precedence over (for instance)
that routine of freight working which is so poorly represented
here or such miscellaneous subjects as railway docks. I think
Part VII explains itself; and Part VIII is all that remains of
the plan to make this a world anthology. Here I should add two
notes – to apologize for stressing my own predilection for narrow-
gauge journeys at the expense of such sagas as the building of the
Mont Cenis or the Canadian Pacific, and to acknowledge gratefully
that much of the Americana in this book has been culled *via* Botkin
and Harlow's splendid *A Treasury of Railroad Folklore*.

The last prose section is a miscellany of fragments which did not
fit elsewhere but which I could not exclude – fragments which all
cast light on the Great Railway Mystery. Among these are the only
fictional pieces included in this book – a lack which, perhaps,
requires more explanation than many of my inclusions.

We began with high hopes. Surely trains entered the English
novel with Mrs Gaskell, murmured to Trollope and sped past
Bennett and Wells and Priestley. Surely overseas they had wailed
in the background of Russian literature from Tolstoi to Pasternak,
rolled from Centerville U.S.A. to Bhowani Junction, and chal-
lenged Zola to the world's sole railway masterpiece. And, on a less
classic level, what of the lines which added their steamy menace to
Simenon and Greene or provided the overlooked clue in Sayers and
Christie, Freeman Wills Croft and Michael Innes? What too of the
originals of the *Titfield Thunderbolt* or that Orient Express which
bore the vanishing lady or the cinematic stars of *49th Parallel, Brief
Encounter* and *North-West Frontier*? What of *The Ghost Train*?

There is certainly no shortage of memorable journeys in fiction,
film and drama. But in almost every case which I analysed (even in
the one or two novels written by railway journalists) the journey
emerged as a background, a motif, or at most something subservient to the human characters and almost meaningless unless
one knew what *they* were at. With the possible exception of *La
Bête Humaine* one cannot extract pages in which the rails take over

as the sea takes over in Melville or Conrad or Masefield; and even the short-story writers have done less than justice to lonely waiting-rooms and sinister compartments. A collection of railway fiction would be a thing of rags and patches, with the pattern of each fragment lost through its having been torn out of context. And so fiction has only a token representation here.

The last section is a round-up of railway verse – *verse* since the romance of railways in their prime inspired no Shelley to a poetic equivalent of Turner's *Rain, Steam and Speed*. There is, indeed, no important poem in English which features the railway (nor, perhaps, any industrial subject) as more than an incidental setting or the subject for a sesquipedalian image; and from what I know of the French nineteenth century I doubt if there is one in any other language either. Of course Wordsworth cried "despoliation" in several wearisome sonnets and of course Tennyson earned his laurels with ordered odes on state occasions. But this is all pedestrian stuff.

The nineteenth and early twentieth centuries are hence typically represented here by two poets of magnificent badness (but there were worse . . .), by a hint of that folk-song tradition which sung loudest across the Atlantic, by one of the dozens of broadsides or broadsheets thrown up by the speculative element of the railway age, and by a handful of minor poems by major poets. In some of these latter the railway is still little more than a back-drop; but in others it forms the subject of the verse and is even viewed with a retrospective love.

In more recent times this has become the commonest stand-point. Railways have generally been more happily commemorated in their sunset, rather than their dawn or noonday, hours; and nostalgia is the note which chimes from the verse of the Georgians through the school of *Punch* to Mr Betjeman. In most of these *vers d'occasion* the sights have been set low; but they seem to me to communicate far more happily than do the contributions of the pylon school, written in the last years when railways could be equated with progress.

I should now explain some house-rules adopted in this book. In general I have tried to do the minimum of violence to the style of any of my victims, living or dead, even when this had led to –

for example – inconsistent capitalization. In one or two instances where misapprehensions might arise however (as when a comparatively modern source describes a line now closed) I have changed a few tenses – though without any guarantee that they will remain up-to-date: references to the Euston Arch were, however, so common as to constitute a special case. In many cases I have had to write in a few words to orientate an excerpt; and all these alterations and interpolations are indicated by square brackets.

Far more often, however, I have excised from an original half a line or half a chapter. A Victorian author proved prolix: a modern one passed tendentious asides: an "as we have already seen" was unseen in its new context: a general discussion was interlarded with passages of only specialist interest. All such cuts are marked by three small dots. . . .

Again, the titles of the prose excerpts differ in every case from any original book or chapter title. In most cases it was in any case necessary to invent a new headline; but even when the reshaping was minimal and the original title would have been apt it seemed fairer to both author and reader to make it clear that I was not necessarily presenting a verbatim transcript. For the verse, on the other hand, I have used the original titles wherever the poem was familiar and reproduced in its entirety.

It remains only to express some grateful thanks in addition to those offered in the formal list of acknowledgements to be found on page 551. Many of my friends and fellow-railway-lovers have helped with suggestions for this book or with assistance at its proof stage: notable among them were Messrs John Harris and John Antonakis. The Curator of Historical Relics for the Railways Board has advised on the illustrations, the public libraries service has carried out much valuable bibliographical work on my behalf, and I would particularly like to thank Messrs Cyril Cobbett and Jeremy Brooks for the introduction which made this book possible. It is hardly necessary to lay a garland on the buffer-beam of Mr John Bright-Holmes, the publishers' editor, without whose interest and aid with suggestions and facilities I would have worked a harder stint to produce a poorer result.

And that is enough of preamble. Mr Legg ended the introduction to *his* anthology with the image that the compilers had marshalled the train in the hopes that their passengers would enjoy the journey. I endorse that wish. But I am also reminded (as the after-dinner speakers say) of a conversation which took place in Ireland in the days when you could still travel on lines surviving on the strength of a train or two a week which ran whenever the complexities of market-days and holy days demanded it.

The timetable indicated that it would run from Bally-X to Kil-Y the day when I was there; but it seemed safest to check with the stationmaster. And "Sure it will leave," he said " 'T'will leave all right. 'Tis only the getting there that's in any doubt."

I hope that *The Railway-Lover's Companion* gets where it was planned to get. For now it is about to leave.

BRYAN MORGAN

London
 March 1963

PART I

The Enthusiasts

Watching the Trains go by

ROGER LLOYD

The curious but intense pleasure that is given to many people by the watching and the study of railway trains, their engines, and the detail of their organization is both an art and a mystery. It is an art because the pleasure to be had is exactly proportionate to the informed enthusiasm one puts into it. It is a mystery because, try as one will, it is impossible to explain to others exactly in what the pleasure consists. The connection between the sight of a railway engine and the quite deep feeling of satisfaction is very real for multitudes of people but it eludes rational analysis. You can perhaps say what it is about railways you enjoy most: but if somebody asks you why you should get any pleasure at all from what is no more than a handy method of conveying your person and your goods from one place to another, you can say, "Just because it is so", and then you have nothing further to add to that bald and very unconvincing remark. The pleasure of railway watching cannot be explained, but it can perhaps be communicated, and it can certainly be shared.

Generally "this strange madness", as somebody centuries ago accused Petrarch of possessing because he liked to travel about Europe more than to stay at home, is caught young; and once caught it is rarely lost while life lasts. My own memory, peering backwards through the years and cleaving the mists of time, comes to its terminus in 1915 with a little boy of ten or eleven who was much given to haunting the railway station at Whitchurch. It was the Shropshire Whitchurch where our home was. Unlike all the half-dozen other Whitchurches in England, the Shropshire Whitchurch is a place of considerable railway importance. It lies on the main line from North West to South West, between Crewe and Shrewsbury. From it the old Cambrian Railway, later of course part of the Great Western, takes its beginning, curves away to the right, and goes meandering sedately along its single track through the Welsh valleys. There is also a branch line from Whitchurch to Chester with a very few trains each way a day, all of which travel rather after the manner of an elderly tortoise. In those days they were mostly hauled by the old North Western o–6–o "Cauli-flowers", which panted furiously all the way and at night treated the beholder to grand firework displays.

Whitchurch station was incredibly ugly. But it was a good place for small boys all the same. It had two admirable features. The main line from Manchester and Liverpool to Shrewsbury and Hereford was very busy, and it was dead straight for a long way both north and south of the station. Trains which did not stop there did not hesitate either. They moved. Sixty miles an hour was slow dawdling for them. The other feature was an iron footbridge north of the station. It had lattice work sides, so that a small boy could look through the holes and down at the track underneath. To this bridge I regularly made my pilgrimage. That is to say I made it as regularly as I could contrive. But those were the days of the governess-cum-nurse era of social history. A child did not go for walks by himself. He was taken for walks; and there is a vast difference. My mother, who loathed everything to do with trains, rationed me. She would put up with the bridge once a week and for half an hour at a time; but the governess, though hating it just as thoroughly, was more pliable. She could be edged skilfully in the required direction on many of the occasions when we had really set out to walk in quite another.

Once on top of that bridge a rather murky but for me a most real heaven lay all about. If no trains were coming through there was the shunting in the Yard to watch. But trains were very frequent and they generally came very fast indeed, rushing at the bridge with a great roar, and crashing under it with a roll of thunder. I would stick my head as far through the iron lattice work as it would go and try to look right down the chimney. I never could, of course, but for long after there was a highly satisfactory smell of sulphur, and flying smuts which descended on one's clothes, and the tail lamp vanishing fast into the distance. To that bridge also I owe the fact that I discovered the right way to look at a freight train. It must be viewed from above the track, for then you can see what all the open wagons contain, and lose yourself in a maze of pleasant speculation about the extraordinary variety of goods which one freight train takes, and make guesses about where a particular wagon has come from and where it is bound.

Those of course were the days of the old "North Western", the

L.N.W.R. The trains were of mixed coaching stock, half of them the purple-brown and white of the North Western, and half the brownish red (as I think it was in those days) of the Great Western. The engines were mostly 4-4-0's, "Precursors" and "George V's", with the former heavily predominating. They seem very small now, and when the trains had more than a dozen coaches they often had to be double-headed; but small or not they could undoubtedly move. To be on the bridge as they fled beneath it was to savour in full measure the thrill of that speed. The one disadvantage was that there was no chance to read the engine's name as she flew under one's feet, nor yet the number of the engine shed to which it belonged, for that, painted on a white enamel circular tag, was then screwed to the lintel of the cab roof and could be seen only from behind. Most of the engines which took the expresses through Whitchurch belonged to Crewe or Manchester, while the slow trains were mostly drawn by Shrewsbury engines. But occasionally you got one from the Camden shed. There was moreover a special treat to be had sometimes, for the authorities at Crewe were fond of using the line to Shrewsbury to put new engines through their paces, so that if you were very lucky indeed you might get a sight of the prototype of a new class of engine – the very first "Claughton" perhaps – before anybody even at Euston had seen her. To learn these details you had to be on the station itself, and escorts were only forthcoming with difficulty. But from time to time somebody would feel kind and take me there; and sometimes there were guests to be met or seen off, and it could usually be arranged that these visits lasted longer than the strict requirements of the matter in hand.

It is now thirty-five years since I stood on Whitchurch station and I have never been there since. Yet I am surprised at how much I remember about it, and how much detail the slightest twitch of the cord of memory recalls. There was room in the station for three trains to stand at a time, for one of the two platforms was an island. A short spur led away from this platform to the tiny engine shed. It was not more than fifty yards away and it opened towards the platform, though you could never see more than a yard inside for there murk and darkness reigned. They kept not more than two or three engines there, an old North Western "Jumbo" perhaps and a couple of small tank engines, all with built-up chimneys. But there was always just the one engine of great resplendence. This was the Cambrian Railway's pride and joy, a new and gleaming 4–4–0. This particular engine used to take out the train for Machynlleth Junction which left somewhere about 4.30 in the afternoon. On the other side of the station was a short bay. The local to Chester always left from there – generally three elderly and grimy six-wheel coaches with an exceedingly decrepit "Cauliflower" at its head.

Whitchurch was a North Western station. The Great Western did not take over till Shrewsbury, and the Cambrian was allowed to use Whitchurch by courtesy rather than by right. This naturally did not much delight the Cambrian men, and their dependence and poor relation status was well rubbed into them. I had much sympathy for them then and I still have. The Cambrian never had a high reputation for speed or punctuality, and most of its engines and rolling stock looked as if they had been bought cheap off the nearest scrap heap. However they did have their one crack engine and train, and this was the 4.30 from Whitchurch, which I have already mentioned. Unfortunately for them it was timed to run in connection with a train from Manchester and Liverpool to Bristol which was due at Whitchurch at about 4.20. That train was not seldom late: sometimes it was three hours late. On these occasions the station authorities used to hold back the Cambrian, whereupon the driver used to protest vigorously in Welsh. No doubt the authorities deeply regretted the unfortunate necessity . . . and all the rest of the formula. But the trouble was that they always looked as though they were really rather pleased, and they grinned broadly as they gave the message, "The 4.20's running 40 minutes late, so you'll have to wait". There were groans from the guard, floods of vehement Welsh from the driver, and broad grins from the North Western men. On the whole Whitchurch was no bad station for a child to be initiated into the fascination of train watching. It offered plenty of variety – the one real criterion of excellence in a station – and a good deal of human interest. But it was a bit hard on my mother and the governess.

Still, I was all the time finding something worth much fine gold – a lifelong source of delight and fascination – and perhaps my mother realized that. If she did, I know very well she would have counted herself amply repaid for any boredom I made her suffer. A hobby which lasts as long as life does and does not stale as the years pass, and which can be pursued at any time and with negligible cost is at the least a subsidiary secret of joy. . . .

In Mr C. S. Lewis's brilliant book, *The Screwtape Letters*, the chief of the tempters, Screwtape, turns on his subordinate Wormwood, because Wormwood has allowed his human charge to be converted to Christianity at a deeper level than before and that at a time when Wormwood seemed to be doing rather well in his effort to edge him off the road that leads to God and into the road that leads to Hell. With diabolic prescience Screwtape puts his finger on what was the beginning of Wormwood's failure. He had actually allowed his charge to indulge a simple pleasure.

> How can you have failed to see that a *real* pleasure was the last thing you ought to have let him meet? Didn't you foresee that it would kill by contrast all the trumpery which you have been so laboriously teaching him to value? . . . The man who truly and disinterestedly enjoys any one thing in the world, for its own sake, and without caring twopence what other people say about it, is by that very fact forearmed against some of our subtlest modes of attack.

The pleasure of watching trains comes under the definition. That it is of no particular use to anybody does not in the least matter. We are not all Utilitarians or Pragmatists. The point is that it is satisfying and innocent, and it is morally good in the sense that it healthily occupies the mind, and so becomes a subsidiary and indirect cause of that self-forgetfulness which is at the root of all virtue. So the mothers whom we have bored when children are not without their reward.

from THE FASCINATION OF RAILWAYS *1951*

The Collector

ALVIN F. HARLOW

Rogers E. M. Whitaker stands unique among rail fans; he has an ambition – or to be more precise, he would like to ride over every mile of track on the North American continent. He knows that this cannot be accomplished as to track currently in use, for every little while another branch or small railroad is abandoned – the 12·7-mile Hooppole, Yorktown & Tampico in Illinois, for example, which [in 1952] folded its hands so suddenly and quietly that the world never noticed it. These abandonments annoy Whitaker as much as anyone of his placid temperament can be annoyed. He has been nibbling away at his hobby at odd moments for eighteen years, and at the last audit had racked up more than 400 railroads, big and little, and traversed some 900,000 miles of track, much of which he travelled in reaching other railroads which he wanted to add to his score.

Whitaker is one of the editors of that smart magazine, *The New Yorker*; a big fellow with a quiet, diffident manner which conceals a dogged persistence in getting what he wants. For some years past he has been dashing out of New York on week-ends – by plane since aviation became not too desperate an adventure – often to annex just one short railroad. For example, he recently flew to California to add the McCloud River Railroad (49·5 miles, Mount Shasta to Hambone) to his list, after hearing that it is soon to be dieselized. Like all dyed-in-the-wool rail bugs, he likes them in steam. His shortest single pickup for a cross-country flight was the Camino, Placerville & Lake Tahoe – 8 miles – in the Sierra foothills. During his vacations he really goes places, and may gather in short lines by the dozen. And in emergencies – for he has friends in rail circles who tip him off to sudden, rare opportunities – he may leave his desk in mid-week and rush off somewhere.

He has covered every major main line on the [North American] continent – including those in Canada and Mexico – though it took some doing in several cases, for what were once important arteries of travel, traversed by jaunty, busy passenger trains, now, in deplorably too many instances, know only the plodding tread of freight trains. Permission to ride on them isn't easy to obtain, and the ride is often somewhat of an ordeal when it is permitted. Some short lines which are "captive" roads, that is, owned by big iron, steel or copper companies, are simply inaccessible to the traveller, no matter what sort of plea he puts up; though Whitaker still ponders possible ways of reaching, wheedling or bringing pressure to bear – some of these days. . . .

He had a small but unexpected windfall once in the Northwest when he was cruising about there, picking up little rails; he heard of a two-mile branch of the Union Pacific which hadn't felt the pressure of wheels for months on end, but over which, two or three days later, an engine was to venture to bring out two flat-car loads of timber. He rushed by car to the division superintendent's office, explained his hobby, and the good-natured official gave the desired permission, though probably warning the train-crew privately to keep an eye on that fellow, as he might be a little off his rocker. That nameless little streak of rust was to Whitaker what the Bay Psalm-book is to a book collector; a poor thing intrinsically, but a jewel in its rarity.

Many of the little railroads which are Whitaker's chief objectives nowadays make a brave show in the *Official Guide*. It is not uncommon to find one occupying a quarter of a page in the *Guide* with its list of officers – President, Vice President, Secretary, Treasurer, Auditor, Superintendent, General Manager, Purchasing Agent, Traffic Manager and Master Mechanic, and then discover further down that the road is 7·6 miles in length and has only irregular freight service. The Southern Iowa, a freight-only line with 18 miles of trackage and Centerville and Moravia as its principal cities, spreads over more than a half-page of the *Guide* a map of a considerable portion of the Middle West, with the numerous lines which contribute to the S.I.'s traffic, and the statements, "Fast through service from all parts of the United States", and "Freight terminals on paved streets in the heart of the business sections".

Whitaker's smile over these immodesties is not merely tolerant, it is affectionate. He is all for these brave little pikes, which, like the old steam locomotive, so typify the hard-to-daunt American spirit, struggling against heavy odds to do its job, holding its head high, putting its best foot forward and contributing its bit, however small, to the functioning of the national economy.

There are dozens of midget railroads, one, two or three miles long, each functioning sturdily in its own little ant-hill. Name one, and the odds are in favour of Whitaker's being able to tell you about it, for he knows the *Official Guide* better than some preachers know their Bibles. There used to be a one-miler – but is no more – which bore the name, New York Central, Hudson River and Fort

Orange without tottering, extending from Castleton on the New York Central to a paper mill. There are others, too, which overload themselves with name; to mention only one, the Waco, Beaumont, Trinity and Sabine, whose 17·7-mile line touches none of those points but Trinity.

The railroads that Whitaker really loves are the little 5, 10, 20 and 30-mile pikes, many of which own no cars and use cast-off engines from bigger roads – sometimes owned, sometimes borrowed, permanently or temporarily, from a larger neighbour, frequently breaking down. The quainter they are, the better. One of the real peaks of enjoyment in Whitaker's travels seems to have been reached when, at the terminus of a little forest-and-swamp line in New Brunswick, the vehicle which met the train to receive the mail and express was a creaky wagon with a rough plank bed, drawn by a yoke of oxen.

Some of these little roads run mixed trains, some nothing but freights; some have alleged schedules, of others the *Guide* says, "Service irregular". They are quite prepared to violate their schedule – if they have one – when it's a matter of bread and butter to them. For example, let us say a certain one, as the Book shows, runs a mixed train on Tuesdays and Fridays. Whitaker flies down to some express plane stop in the Carolinas or Georgia, takes a train or two, maybe loses a night's sleep and arrives at the terminus on Tuesday morning, only to be told, "Well, y'see, the cotton mill wanted to make a carload shipment on Monday without fail, so we ran the train yesterday insteader today." And they think nothing of leaving a half or three-quarters of an hour ahead of the scheduled time.

All sorts of things delay and tie them up – wrecks, floods, landslides, washouts, breakdowns. Once Whitaker started out on a train just after there had been a fall of snow, and they weren't far out of town before they began bouncing on the ties. Stopping, they found that two rails had been removed, and the snow had prevented its being noticed. Whitaker never did find out who had removed them, but the on-the-spot surmise was the section men needed them somewhere else.

On some of these minor railroads in the South – not the extremely small ones, but the somewhat larger ones which still run passenger or mixed trains – one frequently finds a coach of late

Victorian make, with interior finish in fine cabinet work of the sort that isn't being done today; and more frequently an engine of the same period, the one which rail connoisseurs regard, in the matter of grace and beauty, as the Golden Age of locomotive building. And on a few roads such as the Aberdeen & Rockfish, the Georgia & Florida and others, one may find on the pilot one of those fiercely painted, sheet-iron cut-outs of an Indian in war dress, drawing a hostile bow.

For some little lines such as the twins, Louisville & Wadley and Wadley Southern, Whitaker's word is "gorgeous" – "from an antiquarian's standpoint, I mean," he explains. This is undoubtedly what Lucius Beebe means when he speaks of the Prescott & Northwestern in Arkansas as "indescribably beautiful". These two little roads running north and south from Wadley, on the Central of Georgia, are separate corporations, but with some mysterious umbilical tie by which they use the same rolling stock. The one mixed train performs a round trip over the 19·8-mile Wadley Southern in the forenoon, knocks off at Wadley for lunch, and then does the 10-mile L. & W. to Louisville and back in the afternoon. When something breaks down, they borrow from the Central of Georgia, under whose sponsorship they seem to be. The Wrightsville & Tennille and the Sandersville Railroad, near by, are in the same happy family of kinfolks.

Three weeks in succession Whitaker flew down to South Carolina to ride the 20-mile Buffalo-Union Carolina Railroad (now abandoned), but on the first tries, found that it wasn't going to run a train that week; nothing to haul, but was hopeful for next week. On his third trip he was lucky; they ran a train. This road had a nice brick depot at Union, but its locomotive was so asthmatic that when it had twelve gondolas of coal to haul to the cotton mill at Buffalo, it couldn't make the two per cent grade with the whole shipment, but had to take them up four cars at a time.

One of his toughest assignments was the Smoky Mountain Railroad (Knoxville to Sevierville, 30 miles). The first time he reached Knoxville, he was greeted with the news that there had been a flash flood on the line and half a mile of the track was covered with gravel; "be several days before we get it dug out". He gave them two months and flew down again. This time he found a surgical operation in progress. "Sorry, Mister," was the news. "One side

of our engine's broke down; be two or three days, maybe. . . ."
He flew back to New York, and came again the following week.
He felt an urge because the Smoky Mountain company was trying
to get permission to abandon its road (though the State Public
Service Commission wouldn't allow it). This time it was bad
flying weather, and he came down by train. Believe it or not, a
freight wreck made him four-and-a-half hours late in reaching
Knoxville, where he found that the Smoky Mountain had tooled
grandly out of town right on time, an hour and a half ago.

He sought a taxi and said, "I know you'll think I'm crazy, but I
want to catch that Smoky Mountain train," thinking he'd get at
least a piece of the ride.

The driver gave him only one startled look; seasoned taxicab
drivers have ceased being greatly surprised at anything. "Well, the
highway crosses the railroad twice between here and Sevierville,"
he said. "I'll do the best I can."

But at each crossing of the track, they learned from people in the
neighbourhood that the train had passed; it was almost setting a
record.

"Keep going," said Whitaker to the taximan. "I can ride back
to Knoxville on it, anyhow."

They reached the terminal at Sevierville, and there was the train,
the crew, greasy and sweating, labouring over what appeared to be
a leaky steam-chest. In fact, steam was escaping in several places.
They recognized him at once. It was too bad, the engineer said,
but they were having trouble again. Just barely did get here.

"How long will it take to make repairs?" asked Whitaker.

"Coupla hours, maybe."

"Going back to Knoxville today?"

"Yes, sir"; and then, with the hasty stipulation, "if we get this
thing fixed."

"Well, I'll ride back with you," said Whitaker.

"Here's my card," said the taxi driver, smiling. "Call me if you
need transportation."

But that time – wheezing, coughing, sputtering, clanking, leaking steam at every joint and seam, so that Whitaker expected any
moment to be the last, they finally won back to Knoxville and the
indefatigable collector added one more to his score.

On the little five- and ten-mile roads, especially in the South, getting passage on the freight trains, their only service, isn't hard. No ticket to be bought, of course, and no stipulated fare. "I declare, it's been so long since we had a passenger," the conductor may say, "I hardly know what it would be right to charge." Once in a while he solves the puzzle by saying, "Oh, shucks, let it go," and collects nothing at all. As for the crews on these little drags, their life is a bit monotonous, and they are pleased to have a passenger, especially one from New York, who has travelled far and wide. "Lunch? Sure, go and eat your lunch," they tell him. "We'll wait for you. There's the lunch wagon right over yonder; food ain't bad. Take your time. Don't worry; we won't leave you. Sure, it'll throw us a little late, but," with a grin, "we can make it up next trip."

Here is one of the chief joys of knocking about on those little Southern punkin-vines; no studied, from-the-teeth-out courtesy for policy's sake, but old-time, homespun friendliness that comes from the heart in a land that still hasn't quite forgotten how to live with serenity and content.

Whitaker can tell you of some railroad curiosities which few Americans will ever see; the Camas Prairie road, up in Idaho and Washington, with thirty-one trestles in 25 miles of track, covering only ten miles in an air-line, before it reaches the prairie; the 69-mile stretch of the old Carson & Colorado narrow gauge, in eastern California, north of Death Valley, which the Southern Pacific is keeping alive, as an official confessed, just because they are fond of it and its romantic past; the Nevada Northern which used to have all Japanese section hands, because it was hard to get white men to work in the desert – though the Japanese had to leave when the war came on; the Washington, Idaho & Montana, a 50-mile pike, of whose fourteen stations, eight are named Princeton, Harvard, Yale, Stanford, Vassar, Wellesley, Cornell and Purdue, this by the young engineers and rodmen who surveyed the line, honouring their own and their friends' alma maters, until it occurred to them that they were slighting the girls, upon which they added Vassar and Wellesley; of the Bellefonte Central on a Saturday afternoon, when half of the coach in which he rode was stacked to the ceiling with fibre boxes full of Penn State College students' soiled linen, going home to be washed; of the Western Maryland's big coal drags on its West Virginia division –

B

the former West Virginia Central Railroad – which climbs to 4,000 feet above sea level, the highest bit of track east of the Rockies – where you may at times see – like a horde of ants dragging a huge beetle – as many as ten big steam engines pushing and pulling a 100-car train of coal.

Whitaker began too late to ride on the Jupiter & Lake Worth, the "Celestial Line", on Florida's east coast, whose 8-mile track touched four stations – Jupiter, Venus, Mars and Juno; and he wasn't quick enough to catch the Bartlett Western in Texas, known as "the Road of the Apostles" before it was dismantled during the recent war. Its 23·2 miles between its termini, Bartlett and Florence, were studded with four stations named St Matthew, St Mark, St Luke and St John, and copies of the gospels of each of those reverend authors were affixed to the walls of the waiting rooms.

from A TREASURY OF RAILROAD FOLKLORE *1953*

The Modeller

E. BEAL

To be really happy in this world, says O. Henry, you must have "a little country where you don't live". I suppose that is the true purpose of any hobby – to provide just such a dream country; and with the miniature railway interest just such a country is provided.

Let there be no confusion, however, between this kind of thing and the "toy railway" idea. A miniature railway layout is a toy only in the manner in which a Rolls-Royce is a toy to the man who loves to drive it. But be it remembered that this miniature countryside and all that it contains is the product of your own creative genius and imaginative faculty, coupled with a minute knowledge of and adherence to real railway practice. You are not, for instance, ashamed of submitting your handiwork to the critical survey of a group of actual railway officials. In fact you would be rather proud to have such state visitors point out to you some deviation from correct procedure. It would be good both for your pride and for your somewhat pedantic scale sense. What you have found in your garnering of ideas and your studying of actual traffic conditions has indeed given you a new insight into the place of the railway in modern civilization. You have lavished upon your task the most careful experiment, your utmost artistic taste. For years you have taken periodic flights into "the little country where you don't live", carrying out detailed modifications and new reconnaissances. Here, repeatedly, with your layout, you have forgotten professional and business cares, the inclement weather, the unkindnesses of your friends, and have returned time and again to the bosom of your family refreshed in mind and body. If you are happy in the possession of sons of your own, your sojourns in this Arcadia have been a family holiday, and even your wife has lent a friendly word of guidance or criticism. To scores of visitors you have given pleasure, and in your perambulations and consultations you have come to know excellent folk whom otherwise you could never have known – people who are different entirely from all other acquaintances of your too-familiar world. Engaged with your simple tools and working diagrams, or trekking across railway yards in quest of guidance, you have repeatedly made astonishing discoveries and have learned more and more of another realm of human interest.

You recollect that week when you and the entire household revelled in the joys of nomenclature, when a terminal station required a name and competitive suggestions were volunteered. Finally the warfare centred itself around the alluring titles of Tillywhimpleton, Humphaughton (pronounced Humpton), and Dog's-body, the latter being finally adopted after euphonic elision to the sound of Doxby, the earlier spelling being retained. Or, if you have for long been engrossed upon the interest, you will have been amazed more than once by the vastness of its reaches. Maybe you began with a yard or two of completed track, only to find that you next required to push your inquiries into the whole realm of civil engineering, to find out the why and the wherefore of a hundred constructional gadgets hitherto taken as a matter of course. Train operation, time-table making, locomotive designing, signalling – all come within your purview. If you have gone with thoroughness into the task, your work may have brought you into actual contact with railway engineers and officials, and matters may culminate in your being fortunate enough to secure a "walking permit" from some London Traffic superintendent. There are no limits to the interest, and no boundaries to the range of design and application.

How peculiarly the railway is adapted to a man's instinct to make models will appear more and more in the course of time. The average member of the public has no notion whatever of the marvels, the ingenuities, the intricacies, and complexities of the traffic. The airway is not nearly so thrilling with wonder as the railway. A baffling network of intersecting tracks is no dull matter of mechanical calculation; it is the very poetry of the steadiness, the self-mastery, the unwavering accuracy of the human hand and brain. An express train, keeping the rails on a curve at 60 miles per hour is a perennial wonder. To model it in miniature, and to discover by some measure of experiment what it does involve may be one of the most engrossing of occupations. By far the most surpassing interest in modelling actual railway features is without doubt the perfection and intricacy of control.

The range of standard scales to which the enthusiast may work, regulated by the supply of commercial components and general accessories, is now so extensive that the most varied tastes are catered for. For the man who likes the open air there are the garden gauges; for the builder whose leisure is mainly restricted to periods of cold or wet weather there is the spare room or the outhouse. A garden layout may be planned with an indoor terminus and workshops under the roof of a disused greenhouse, the "pit" type of hothouse being ideally provided with its bench at the same grade as the ground level outside. If temporary conditions do not provide a building site, it is always possible to proceed indefinitely with the attractive task of modelling rolling stock and motive power for the smaller gauges on a table in the living-room of the house. One man I know, whose avocation is the Royal Air Force, and who has made some of the nicest small-scale models I have seen, carries out all his constructional work on an occasional table which in the evenings he brings into the drawing-room. Another ardent worker is a bed-ridden invalid. Elaborate tool equipment is not essential. One may instal a complete outfit of machines; one may work just as effectively in a smaller scale with a screwdriver, pliers, razor-knife, hand-drills, and an electric soldering iron.

from THE CRAFT OF MODELLING RAILWAYS *1937*

Romantic and Classic

L. T. C. ROLT

Of all man's mechanical inventions [the steam locomotive] remains the most evocative of power and speed, having been endowed with these attributes by generations of designers and craftsmen whose sole aim and consideration was perfection of function. Such a single-minded pursuit of fitness for purpose produced in locomotive design a quality of line and proportion which the poet Rupert Brooke described as a "calm, unpassioned beauty" and which occasionally, as in the 8-ft. single drivers of Patrick Stirling, achieved results which were virtually masterpieces of applied art. A future generation denied the spectacle of a steam locomotive in full cry will suffer a loss as great as we have suffered who have never seen a full-rigged ship with all her canvas set.

It was not necessary to be a sailor in order to appreciate the winged splendour of the sailing ship any more than we need a knowledge of anatomy to see the beauty of the human form. Similarly, we do not need to be engineers to appreciate the steam locomotive or the complex order and discipline of the railway system of which it is at once the focal point and moving spirit. In this the railway differs from most more recent mechanical inventions whose design and function are of a different order intelligible only to the technician; complicated machines which can fascinate the engineer as technical *tours de force,* but which lack that quality which appeals to our aesthetic sense and stirs the imagination of the layman. It is because the railway possesses this quality to a unique degree that all ages and conditions of men are numbered among its devotees. Schoolboys, businessmen, musicians, elderly clergymen and university professors – all the seven ages of man may sometimes be seen standing together at the head of a main-line platform to witness the departure of the "Royal Scot", the "Irish Mail" or the "Cornish Riviera Express".

The conflict between the Romantic and the Classic ideals, between the desire for individual freedom and the desire for order and discipline, is as old as man, and civilization itself is no more than a precarious balance between the extremes to which each

view can run. In varying proportions the same conflict is implicit
in the nature of each one of us, but railways appeal to both these
sides of our nature so that, in the love and study of them, the conflict is resolved or stilled. For the Romantic the speed and power
of the steam train epitomizes the freedom and romance of travel,
while the whole atmosphere of the railway is magic; the sulphurous
echoing gloom of a great station at night, with signal lamps and
other more mysterious lights glowing and flickering over the
intricate mesh of rails beyond the platform faces where steam
drifts and buffers clash; the hot summer's day somnolence of some
remote country station suddenly awakened to expectancy by the
single beat of a bell in the signal box; the whine of the wind in the
telegraph wires on a lonely upland section as we wait to watch the
passing of a northbound express. Yet at the same time the classicist
within us is aware that this romance is in fact the by-product of
order and discipline; that a great railway system is perhaps the
most elaborate and delicate, yet at the same time one of the most
successful, feats of organization ever evolved by man. The steel
rail is a symbol of disciplined movement, but that movement is
itself ordered and controlled by a complex human and mechanical
hierarchy which extends from the central control room to the
loneliest lineside signal box and which has made the railway the
safest form of transport ever evolved. The fact that railways
appeal so strongly to certain musical or academic minds is due,
I believe, to this blend of romantic freedom with classic order
which they present.

As a result of the headlong pace of the Industrial Revolution
and of the incidence of two world wars, the great age of railway
construction now seems to us more remote in time than in fact
it is. First hailed with wonder and eulogy, then taken for granted
or forgotten, railways have now assumed that place in history
where rediscovery and a fresh, objective appraisal become due.
We are learning to see with reopened eyes and new wonder the
magnitude of the work of such men as Brunel, the Stephensons,
Locke and Brassey. The bridges they built, standing fast today
beneath loads far in excess of those their designers ever dreamed
of, witness the greatness of their achievement. But even when their
last architectural work has crumbled to dust, England will still
bear their sign manual. The results of our diminished creative

powers are mostly ephemeral and, assuming that the world survives our vastly enhanced powers of destruction, we shall leave to remote futurity few memorials. But, like Silbury Hill or Offa's Dyke, the towering embankments or the great chalk defiles at Tring and Sonning will remain to prompt future archaeologists to ponder upon the wonders of the Age of Steam.

from LINES OF CHARACTER *1952*

The Old Great Western

W. A. TUPLIN

For the student or the lover of the locomotive, the Great Western [was] unique. At the end it had not the largest locomotives in Great Britain, nor the fastest trains, nor the British railway-speed record, but the locomotives associated with these distinctions all owed much to Swindon practice, which had been developed, not for the purpose of breaking records, but simply to meet anticipated operating needs with certainty and economy.

We who find fascination in examining the form and details of locomotives and their ability to do their work have had in Swindon a treasure indeed. We have seen a whole railway system laid on the broad 7 ft. gauge and upon it established a standard of railway speed that was barely equalled in the subsequent century. We have seen the gaunt shapelessness of many of the engines of that era replaced by pretty elegance in the time of Dean who nevertheless kept ahead of traffic needs. We have seen his beautiful single-wheelers moving swan-like with no visible means of propulsion on the level lines of Brunel's Great Way Round, the sturdy "Dukes" pounding with flashing cranks up the steep banks of the West Country and an endless variety of saddle-tanks working hard in every sphere.

We have seen the Swindon engine take on quite different forms devised by Churchward for power and speed, with hints from the New World and the Old. With tapered, domeless boiler, copper-capped chimney, thirty-inch stroke and gun-shot blast, they stood

out from all else in Britain and gradually we came to find them
everywhere on Great Western metals.

We have seen them fly through Reading with screaming whistle,
purring chimney and nimbly whirling rods on to the great sweeping curves of the Thames Valley and so to Bristol or West Wales.
We have seen the west-bound "Riviera" in full flight behind a
ten-wheeler gleaming in green paint, copper and brass, held in to
an easy "seventy" through the sylvan country of the Somerton
cut-off. We have seen them battle swiftly across Sedgemoor
despite Atlantic-born gales of wind and rain and at other times
flit at ease along the sun-scorched front at Dawlish, gathering
strength for the climb to Dainton.

On seaside branches in the west, we have ridden with scurrying
"forty-fives" and we have heard the mighty blasts of "thirty-ones"
in sulphurous murk beneath the Severn. The "Stars", "Castles"
and "Kings" have taken us from Paddington to Wolverhampton
with a rollicking zest that Euston never knew, and lesser Swindon
lights have completed our journeys to the northern corner of
Great Western territory. Behind "Bulldogs" and "forty-threes"
we have traversed the Vale of Edeyrnion and skirted the Mawddach estuary on the way to the Cambrian coast, while "Dean
goods" and "forty-eights" have taken us along the valley of the
romantic Wye. Everywhere we have heard the hard dry cough of
the industrious "panniers" on branch-lines or dock-sides with
passengers, coal or freight. They have toiled in dust and heat in
London sidings, prowled on obscure byways in the Black
Country, and burrowed chimney deep into blizzard-swept snow-
drifts high up on Arenig Fawr.

On nights when fog made even walking hazardous we have
travelled at speed behind Great Western drivers confident of a
siren-call and a brake-application on the approach to any caution
signal. In the brilliance of high summer we have crossed from
Brecon to Neath with the engine whistling to arouse sheep prone
on the unfenced mountain track.

As a background to these railway experiences we noticed the
spread of the Churchward standard classes, their multiplication in
replacement of older types, the demonstrations of their quality on
their own lines and others, and we came gradually to realize that
in them the Stephenson locomotive had been brought to ultimate

refinement. Commonsense compromise between theoretical ideals and practical possibilities had produced at Swindon a unique family of standard engines unsurpassed anywhere in fitness for purpose.

Shall we ever again see such distinction on rails? We fear; we doubt; we can scarcely hope.

from GREAT WESTERN STEAM *1958*

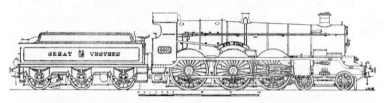

Journey into Childhood

C. HAMILTON ELLIS

Surely it was always summer when we made our first railway journeys! Only from later boyhood do we remember what fog was like at Liverpool Street, with the little North London engines puffing high-up and unseen, in and out of Broad Street next-door, and with the Westinghouse pumps of the Great Eastern panting so furiously amid the Plutonian murk close at hand; or what a rainy autumnal evening could be like at Cowlairs; or how the Thames Valley looked between Didcot and Oxford when there was naught but steel-grey water upon the drowned meadows. No, it was always summer! Sun shone on the first blue engine to be seen, a Somerset and Dorset near Poole; there was sunshine, most dazzling, on a Great Western brass dome; the sun shone on an extraordinary mustard-coloured engine of the London, Brighton and South Coast, seen, according to later detective research, by three-year-old eyes at Three Bridges, and he certainly shone upon the London and South Western!

. . . Everyone who has loved a train has had his favourite railway, the first one he ever saw, and mine was that magical South Western. Afterwards we had our false favourites: the London and

North Western because loving schoolfellows told us, with menaces, that it was the Premier Line, whatever that might mean; the Midland because it had red locomotives, and carriages which gave superlatively comfortable travel; the Great Western because it had achieved, on excellent authority, 102 miles an hour in 1904. But most of us went back to our old and various favourites, which sometimes, of course, belonged to that exalted trio. . . .

There was something very magnificent about the L.S.W.R. West of England express. It was much better than any ordinary train on other lines originating south of the Thames, for unlike its southern neighbours, the South Western took corridor trains seriously from the beginning of the century. In the middle was a dining car that advertised its presence by a clerestory roof considerably higher than anything else. The colour scheme was without parallel. While the upper panels were officially described as "salmon", and were rather like tinned salmon when quite new, they weathered into a terra-cotta brown after about a week. But to us, who knew and loved the South Western, it was above criticism. There was splendour even in the bright brass handrails inside corridor windows; the first-class carriages with their blue broadcloth and profusion of gold lace, even on the window straps and slings, were truly gorgeous, the brown plush seconds, which, like the firsts, could be identified from afar by their lemon-yellow window frames, were admirable, and the thirds, though dowdy, were solidly comfortable.

There at the head of the train was one of Dugald Drummond's express engines. No locomotive was more beautiful than a Drummond T.9 four-coupled in her glory of light green and rich lining-out. A thin film of clean grease covered her and was worked into a fascinating pattern that showed up in the sun like a watermark. Her brass safety-valve columns glittered, delicately as the crown of a Swedish bride, on her small shapely dome. She was a lovely thing!

Away we went, out into the green fields, which began at Raynes Park, through the heath of West Surrey, into Hampshire and past Farnborough with its prodigious new airship shed. More mysterious even than the anxious-looking airship which, on a red-letter day, might be butting into the wind overhead, was the line which here passed under ours at right-angles. It had odd signals with a round white spot on the red, and was, most surprisingly to uninformed youth, the Reading branch of the South Eastern and Chatham.

Then came Basingstoke and the Great Western, regarded as a quaint and exotic next-door neighbour, and then the rolling chalk. At Whitchurch was another of those mysterious lines crossing underneath. It was the Didcot, Newbury, and Southampton. At a remote age I painted a highly imaginative picture of a D.N. and S. train; I never forgave the line for turning out to be for all practical purposes, a branch of the Great Western after all! And so to Andover Junction. Now Andover was a very remarkable place indeed; it was the southern terminus of the Midland and South Western Junction Railway, of which the other extremity, improbably but truly, was Andoversford in the Cotswolds.

This was a small railway, with a poverty-stricken history, but under Sam Fay it had nevertheless grown into a model line from the passengers' point of view. It gave that rare thing, a really good cross-country service, for which, for better or worse, we nowadays seek rather in motor coaching circles. Cheltenham, where the M.S.W.J. terminated by virtue of running powers, had of course a main-line through service from Paddington. But if you chose your trains, travelling from Waterloo to Andover, and thence took the M.S.W.J. North Express, you could get to Cheltenham more quickly than by the Great Western with its wanderings round by Gloucester.

The Midland and South Western Junction trains were red, like those of the Midland, though it was a wholly independent line. Unlike those of the Midland, or the Great Western, or the South Western, its carriages all had electric light in its latter days, even the horseboxes, and Tyrrell's express engines, very neat, with the company's initials in flowery copperplate script on the tenders, were as good as those of many bigger companies. A great little railway! When the Great Western engulfed it in 1923, the result was not an improvement.

Beyond Andover, a new magic came into those long-ago journeys. We had entered Wessex, and something older than Wessex; the mysterious Plain was about us as we raced along high embankment or white chalky cutting. As Grateley flashed past, close to the railway there was a hill with a Celtic fort on the summit;

somewhere out on the Plain beyond the lonely Amesbury branch was Stonehenge – we called it simply The Stones – unmarred by gaunt hangar or mean hutment; as yet unprofaned by the heedless Motoring Many.

Then there was Tunnel Junction, with Sarum's spire showing over the skyline; there was the tunnel itself, followed by the violent reverse curves into Salisbury station. A little while before, the station curve had been the scene of one of the South Western's few major tragedies [but the] little boy who was I saw and remembered another railway accident at Salisbury, a very jolly one for the heartless onlooker.

The principal actors were a porter and an Adams 0–4–2 Jubilee engine. The porter was pushing a trolley, piled high with luggage, over the crossing at the eastern end of the station; the Jubilee was drifting in with the awful stealth of the light engine. Just when he had pushed the trolley so far, the porter saw the Jubilee. He was human. He fled.

Then the Jubilee took the trolley amidships. With one brief crunch it was gone. A buffer punched sweetly into a great trunk, a tuckbox exploded, a holdall ceased to hold and laid all before us. Neat suits, good jams and choice preserves, dainty millinery and masculine high boots rose in swarm from that riven hive. Into the station careered a vision of the *Jubilee Adorned*. A big picture hat crowned a lamp-iron; snowy lingerie blossomed in strange places, or danced a delicate rigadoon on a coupling rod.

There was a final tortured scream of brakes and wreckage in chorus, then all was still. Strong men, brows bent in horror, leaped down into that vale of tears and began to cram soiled and scattered finery back into split portmanteaux and scalped bandboxes. It was a great destruction. Doubtless much more followed, but at that point a Great Western train came clanking in. I had never before seen a locomotive with double frames and with so immense a brass dome, nor yet a train of carriages completely clerestoried. I turned my back on my first railway accident. . . .

Salisbury was where we left the express. With a fresh engine it disappeared into the unknown West. Later days brought experience of crimson Devon earth, of the magnificent climb from Seaton Junction to Honiton Tunnel, of the two Exeters, of Dartmoor and the great Meldon Viaduct, and of remote Padstow, a sort of railway Hy Brasil beyond the sunset. As yet we were for the local train, an amiable caravan serving all stations to Exeter, a train that should pause at Milborne Port, linger by Sherborne and dally with Sutton Bingham and Crewkerne, places which the express ignored save maybe to yell at their distant signals. Our local sat all leisurely in the bay until the express had cleared Wilton. A friendly train; its engine might be anything from a four-cylinder 4–6–0 (not Mr Drummond's most sparkling work) to an Adams veteran of the early 'eighties; its carriages had the faded gentility of an early Victorian parlour in the deep country, for there was buff velveteen in the first class and a delicious smell about it.

Where the express had raced, the local ambled; where the express had played something like Schumann's *Arabesque* on the railjoints, the local played a gentle pavane. It gave you time to study the outline of Wilton's great Italianesque church, the thatched roofs of Barford St Martin, the solemn line of the Downs and the lovely, lovely valley of the Nadder. And when at last we left it, there would be the same pony-trap with the same brown mare, the same ride to the same three-centuries-old house with the pomegranate tree on the south wall. There the trains were invisible, but if you woke in the small hours you had their occasional distant roar on the other side of the ridge for company, and in the daytime there was a glorious occupation crossing only half a mile away. On that crossing I learnt to flatten farthings into ha'pennies; there I learnt, without giving it a name, to recognize a Drummond T.9 as the most beautiful of engines at the age of two years and two months.

That was my journey on the London and South Western. Substitute for the grace of the Drummond engine the pride of a Claud Hamilton on the Great Eastern or the royal magnificence of a Johnson single on the Midland, or whatever; ring changes on the Cumbrian fells, the Welsh Marches, or where you will, and you have the rare delight of your own first journeyings. A smell encountered thirty years after can bring them back; so can noises, a few bars of music, certain lights on certain hills, or the spectacle of an ancient locomotive on a branch line.

from THE TRAINS WE LOVED *1947*

The Old Man and the Boy

CLIFFORD DYMENT

The room was full of model railway engines.

There were engines on the mantelpiece, where people usually had a clock and two rearing bronze horses; there were engines on wooden stands, where they usually had aspidistras; there were engines on wall brackets, tables, window ledges, shelves – everywhere I looked I saw small locomotives and carriages. If it hadn't been for the work-bench, and the scattered tools, and the treadle fretsaw, and the stacks of old magazines and books pushed against the walls I would have thought I'd walked into a toyshop.

I was standing close to a funny locomotive with a chimney like a factory's and a tangle of girders and rods surmounting its boiler: it looked like one of the machines used by road-menders for spreading tar, except that this engine was clean and decorated with stars at the points where its polished brass fittings reflected the gaslight.

"You've never seen an engine like that one, have you, Cliff?"

"No, Mr Belton."

"No, I was pretty sure that you wouldn't have."

"Why were you pretty sure, Mr Belton?"

"Because it was built a long time ago. Before you were born."

"How long ago, Mr Belton?"

"More than a hundred years ago. It was one of the first railway engines in the whole world. It was called the 'Puffing Billy'."

"Puff, puff, puff, puff," I imitated, moving my arms like coupling rods.

"That's it, lad," said Mr Belton. "That's why it was called the Puffing Billy – not many people had seen a steam-engine then, you see."

"Was the Puffing Billy the first steam-engine in the whole world?"

"No, it wasn't that. You see —' Mr Belton paused, gazing at me earnestly. "Would you like me to tell you about these old engines, lad?" He swept his arm around his room, taking in all the engines at one go.

"Yes I would, please, Mr Belton."

"You're sure? You wouldn't rather go back in the kitchen and read your comics?"

"No, Mr Belton."

"That's all right, then." A happy, relieved smile came into his face. "Well, there *had* been steam-engines before this Puffing Billy, but they'd been used for working the pumps that sucked water out of coal-mines, do you see? Here" – Mr Belton pointed an almost fleshless finger at a horizontal cross-arm above the net-work of steel over Puffing Billy's boiler – "this thing here is called a beam and that's why the olden-time engines were called beam-engines. One end of the beam was moved up and down by a piston in a cylinder and the other end also moved up and down and operated the colliery pump. Do you understand?"

I nodded.

"They were stationary engines – they stayed where they were built. Now the Puffing Billy – this one here – was one of these stationary engines fixed on wheels. The beam worked wheels instead of a pump. See?"

I nodded again.

"And so it ran along the rails. It was a stationary engine that got a move on, like." Mr Belton laughed. "Come here, son."

He tugged excitedly at my sleeve and pulled me a foot or two towards another old high-chimneyed engine with a string of wagons behind it. He pointed at some lettering on the boiler.

"Can you read that?"

I stared at the name, feeling my face go red. It was a long, hard word.

"Come on, lad!" Mr Belton encouraged, nudging me. "Show me what they learn you in school."

"Lo – co —" I spelled out. "Loco —"

"Right first time!" exclaimed Mr Belton delightedly, patting me on the back. "Locomotion! That's an old-fashioned word that means moving from place to place. A locomotive is a steam-engine that can travel from Nottingham to London. See?"

"Yes, Mr Belton."

There was a fluttering thrill in my inside because an old man like Mr Belton considered me grown up enough to talk with him about grown-up things.

"That was the first train in the whole world," Mr Belton said, laying his hand affectionately on *Locomotion* and the carriages behind it. "The very first train in the whole world! What do you think of that now?"

"The very first train in the *whole* world!"

"It was. It ran on the Stockton and Darlington Railway, in 1825. There was no Flying Scotsman then. No big stations like Crewe or Euston. Just fields and roads. If you wanted to go from one town to another you had to ride on a stagecoach."

"Stagecoaches were robbed by highwaymen," I said.

"They were, lad. And then this little train came along and changed everything, running from Stockton to Darlington and from Darlington to Stockton – the first public railway in the whole world."

His finger rested on the last of the carriages.

"But I haven't finished this model yet," he said with a sad fall in his voice. "There ought to be thirty-three wagons coupled up and I've only built twenty-nine so far. It's a lot of work, you know."

I nodded sympathetically.

"Come on here, son. Here's a train I *have* finished."

I followed him to a part of the room where one of his many models had a table all to itself. It stood on a proper permanent way, with a ballast of tiny stone chips between the rails, and the lovingly painted and burnished locomotive headed a procession of carriages got up as merry as roundabouts.

"There!" said Mr Belton with great pride. "The first passenger train in the whole world!"

"The first in the whole world?"

"Yes, boy. The Liverpool and Manchester Railway, 1830. That was the first *passenger* train, understand, because the Stockton and Darlington, although it carried passengers sometimes, was really a goods line. It was a proper Goose Fair when the Liverpool and Manchester ran for the first time, I can tell you. You can see how the carriages are all rigged out to look bright and gay. There were thousands of people present. There were flags. There was music. Why, even the Duke of Wellington was there!"

Mr Belton had described the occasion in such detail that I felt half sure he must have been present himself. If not, how could he have known what it was like?

"Were – were you there, too, Mr Belton?"

Mr Belton let out what was, for a sick man, a great guffaw.

"No, Cliff, I wasn't there. It was a bit before my time, you know."

He sat on a stool.

"I know I'm a crock, but I didn't know I looked such an *old* crock as that," he said.

He looked glum, and I wondered if I had offended him.

"Shall I go now, Mr Belton?"

"No, no, you needn't go, lad – unless you want to. Do you want to?"

"No, Mr Belton."

"Then you can stay a bit longer. Shall I go on talking to you about trains?"

"Yes, please, Mr Belton."

I waited for him to speak, but he remained silent, sitting bent on the stool and staring for a long time at the Liverpool and Manchester Railway's carnival of coaches. Then he said:

"Trains are wonderful things, lad. I'm glad they interest you. Some folk think I'm cracked, playing with trains at my age, but they don't understand. A railway isn't just carriages and a loco-motive and a permanent way. It's a sort of door. At any time you can open it and take to the road, turning your back on a home that's dreary and on a life that's a misery to you. Any time you fancy you can whizz off to a new home and a new life, in any place you choose. Whenever you're down in the dumps – just open the door. . . ."

"Now," said Mr Belton, getting up from the stool. "Tell me what you like doing most."

I thought, frowning. Was it eating apples? Or ice-cream? Or was it meeting Mother on Saturdays?

"Is it," asked Mr Belton coaxingly, "is it riding on trains?"

"I haven't been on many train rides," I answered truthfully. "The longest was when we came from Caerleon."

"Ah, that was the Great Western. It's not so bad, the Great Western, not so bad. But it's been up to some funny things in its time, has the G.W."

He pointed.

"That's a G.W. engine over there. See it?"

I walked to the spot he had indicated and saw a green engine with gold letters and lining on it.

"Not so dusty, eh?" Mr Belton said, joining me.

"It's topping, Mr Belton."

"Yes, it's not so dusty – for the G.W.R. In its day I suppose it was just about the most powerful express engine running."

"Was it really, Mr Belton?"

"Well, about. And the biggest."

"What, that little engine?"

"Yes, I suppose it was. The most powerful and the biggest."

"In the whole world?"

"Yes, in the whole world. . . ."

I gazed at the tiny green and gilt locomotive in wonder.

"Mr Belton."

"Yes, lad?"

"Why is it called *The Lord of the Izzles*?"

"You mean *The Lord of the Iles*," smiled Mr Belton.

He bent his long and narrow body in the middle as though he was a folding rule and peered closely at the name emblazoned on the engine's side.

"*The Lord of the Isles*," he read aloud thoughtfully. "That's funny, now you've made me think of it. There weren't any islands where that engine ran. Unless – unless it was the *British* Isles they meant. Yes, that must be it, Cliff – the British Isles. They meant to say that the engine was the Lord of the British Isles."

"The Lord of the British Isles!" I repeated, enjoying the march of sound and the pomp of meaning in the name.

"Just the sort of thing the Great Western would say!" snorted Mr Belton. "It was always a conceited line."

. . . He began to pace the room slowly, glancing affectionately at his models as he passed them.

"That's a nice engine – the old *Copper Nob* of the Furness Railway. *The Lion,* of the Liverpool and Manchester – it took me days, lagging that boiler with wood strips. There's Stephenson's *Rocket,* the most famous locomotive . . ."

". . . in the whole world," I joined in, boldly walking beside him.

He put his hand on my shoulder and grinned at me.

"And there's another old G.W.R. engine – the *North Star,*

which hauled the first passenger train out of Paddington in 1854. Yes, as I was saying, G.W.R. men have always been an amazingly conceited lot. And the most conceited of them all was a man named Brunel. Isambard Kingdom Brunel! What a name to go to bed with, eh? . . ."

"What company did you work for, Mr Belton?"

"I worked for the London and North Western, which is known as the Premier Line because it was the first main line railway . . ."

Mr Belton looked at me expectantly, a gleam in his eye.

". . . in the whole world!" I concluded, prompt on my cue.

"That's right, lad. At any rate, part of it was – the old London and Birmingham Railway from Euston to Curzon Street."

"But you don't work on it now, do you, Mr Belton?"

"No, lad, I don't."

"Didn't you like it?"

"Like it "

Mr Belton stared at me incredulously.

"Did I like it? I loved it – every minute of it. But I had to give it up because I was taken poorly. That's why I came here to Nottingham, you see, lad – to take a less tiring job on the Midland. . . ."

"I like being here with you, Mr Belton."

"And I like being here with you, Cliff. If you come often you could soon know as much about railways as me."

"I'd like to come often, Mr Belton."

"That's the spirit! How would you like to lend me a hand sometimes, eh?"

"You mean – help you when you're making engines and carriages?"

"That's right."

"Oh, yes, Mr Belton!"

"That's settled then. We'll say you're Assistant Mechanical Engineer, shall we?"

I nodded, thrilled.

"Now, before you take over your new duties," said Mr Belton, "I think you ought to inspect the motive power and rolling stock in our possession, don't you?"

"Yes, Mr Belton."

"Come on, then."

He caught me by the sleeve of my jersey and took me on a conducted tour of his collection.

"Most of what we've got is L.N.W.R. stock," he said, "because that's my favourite railway."

"Is that because it's the best railway?"

"Yes. Didn't I tell you it was the Premier Line? That means the first. Here's an early model – Allan and Trevithick's *Columbine* of 1845, the first of what was called the Crewe type of locomotive – here's *Jennie Deans*, one of F. W. Webb's engines – they were called Cauliflowers: yes, I thought that would make you laugh – Ramsbottom's *Lady of the Lake,* a pretty engine, that one – two more of Webb's: a Jumbo 2–4–0 and a Greater Britain compound 2–2–2–2 – and here's' – there was a grin in Mr Belton's voice – "and here's a nice pair of Bloomers."

I stared hard at the two engines he pointed out to me, red with bright brass domes and both exactly alike except that one had slightly larger wheels than the other. Why were they called Bloomers? There were two kinds of bloomers: one kind was often joked about by Mrs Belton – and these engines certainly bore no resemblance to them; it must be the other kind that was meant. . . .

"Do you mean they were mistakes, Mr Belton?"

"No, they weren't mistakes, Cliff. They were very good engines, very good engines indeed – worked the crack expresses. They were called Bloomers because, well, look at the wheels, son."

I looked.

"They're all exposed," continued Mr Belton. "Like the ladies' legs were when they wore trousers."

I thought how funny a lady would look wearing Sid Byron's bell-bottomed trousers, dribbling a tin down Carlyle Road.

"I didn't know ladies wore trousers," I said.

"They don't now," Mr Belton said. "They did once, though, in the olden days. I never saw them – it was long before my time. Still," he continued reflectively, "it's getting on for quite a while since I first joined the L.N.W.R. I was a proper nipper when I did that."

"Were you as old as me?"

"Just a wee bit older. I'd always wanted to be on the L.N.W.R. and as soon as I left school I went to Crewe station and got a job. I had my first long trousers on – talking of trousers – and a stiff celluloid collar and a trilby hat. I felt like a real toff. But all I was wanted for was making tea and running errands. But I moved up."

"Where to, Mr Belton?"

"The Corridor."

"The Corridor?" I repeated, puzzled.

"Yes. That was our name for the West Coast Express from London to Scotland – because in those days, you see, when I was a young man, corridors all the way through a train from beginning to end were a bit of a novelty. That was a fine train, I can tell you."

"Did it go at sixty miles an hour?"

"Sixty miles an hour? Faster – much faster! I say, lad – how would you like to come up on to the footplate with me – for a trip to the North? Eh?"

"On the Corridor?"

"Yes, on the Corridor."

"I'd love it, Mr Belton! I'd love it!"

"Up you come, then."

Mr Belton placed his hand under my elbow and eased me closer to him.

"Let's say our engine's one of Webb's 2–2–0's, a hundred and eighty pounds boiler pressure. See, the needle's showing a hundred and eighty pounds now and steam's blowing off at the safety valves. The platform inspector has blown his whistle and all we're waiting for is the guard's green flag. Are you looking out, fireman?"

"Yes, Mr Belton."

"Don't say 'Yes, Mr Belton'. Say 'Yes, driver'."

"Yes, driver."

"Did you say 'Right away, mate'?"

"No, Mr Belton."

"Fireman, you must say 'Right away, mate. . . .' "

"Right away, mate," I sang out.

"Right away it is! Regulator handle across the quadrant plate – just a few notches at first – cut-off at eighty per cent – we're moving! – four hundred tons of us are on the move out of Euston – gradually I open up a few more notches – easy does it – too much at one go causes wheel-slip – now it's full regulator and full cut-off for the Camden Bank! – up we go – fireman, look after that sanding gear – this is where we need it . . ."

"Right you are, driver," I called out.

"Incline here is one in seventy for almost a mile – up we tramp – engine panting, blowing out black smoke, spitting red cinders – up we plod, foot by foot – it's a stiff climb, is the Camden Bank – has to be, to clear the Regent's Canal – but here we are going through Camden Town and once past Camden Town the line's as level as a saucer of tea – Willesden Junction – now I can bring the cut-off back a few notches and we go lolloping along a treat – we're touching sixty as we go through the fields at Harrow – over sixty now – I can ease back the regulator – it's a picnic for footplate men, this line of Robert Stephenson's from London to Brum – fine grading, easy curves – he had to dig through millions of yards of rock and earth to make it so flat and good, though – passing Hemel Hempstead – now the engine's got hold of 'em – we're doing well over sixty, fireman – approaching Tring Cutting – rattling over the viaduct – Leighton Buzzard, Bletchley, Wolverton – now Roade Cutting – fireman, look out for Kilsby Tunnel . . ."

"Kilsby Tunnel ahead, driver . . ."

"Right you are, fireman – now we roar into Kilsby Tunnel – it took two and a half years to build this tunnel, fireman – it's as black as the inside of a Kodak – the smoke and the steam make you choke – see it swirling in the light from the fire-hole door – there's such a din I can't hear myself speak – screw up your eyes, fireman, and watch out for a pin-point of light in front – see it? – it grows bigger – soon we'll be out in the sunlight again – and here we are! rubbing our eyes – now it's as quiet as if a door had been shut to keep out the noise – and on we go, racing along the straight, leaning round curves, comfy as a car ride – Rugby, Birmingham – keep your eyes on the signals, fireman . . ."

"Right you are, driver . . ."

". . . and now we're running over the old Grand Junction section – all's fine until Madeley Bank – that's a three-mile pull at 1 in 77 – a longer cut-off and open regulator gets us up Madeley – and now a nice fall from the summit as we go coasting down to Crewe – good old Crewe! – and from Crewe there's the little hump of 1 in 135 to Acton Grange Junction and down to Warrington – nearly full cut-off up to Boar's Head now – Preston, Lancaster – and now we're on the stiffest section of the trip – the old Lancaster and Carlisle Railway's line up the Lune Valley, the Pennines to the east of us and the Lake District to the west – thirteen miles of steady climbing from Milnethorpe through Kendal to Grayrigg, then only a couple of level stretches near Low Gill and Tebay before we're on a gradient of 1 in 75 over Shap Fell – fireman, it's grunting and pounding and gasping higher and higher until our engine's up in the sky and we're dizzy and *praying* for the long float down to Penrith and Carlisle – we can't hold on a minute longer! – and we top the hill – just in time! – and we drift down, thanking God, towards Penrith, our fire low, pressure falling, regulator at the first port, cut-off back, until I put on the brakes outside Carlisle and here we are, fireman, tired and dirty, but almost in Scotland – open your nostrils wide, Cliff, draw in the bracing air and put your head back – can't you feel the brogue of the Highlands blowing into your face, eh?"

Having, with such delightful consequences, solved the mystery of the Beltons' front parlour I became a regular visitor to it, being taken on by Mr Belton, according to his promise, as Assistant Mechanical Engineer. I guarded the glue pot, to watch out for the moment when the slabs of inedible toffee turned to brown malodorous fluid; I held strips of metal in place while Mr Belton soldered them; I fetched templates and micrometers and files and screwdrivers; I handed him dies and taps and punches; I collected up and put away nuts and bolts and brass rodding and rivets; I cleaned paint brushes.

I enjoyed the responsibility of handling these tools and materials, but I enjoyed even more watching Mr Belton's hands and listening to his talk. Although poor health had made Mr Belton's fingers as knobby as a cane they possessed a workman's matter-of-fact competence; as grimy as a grate at their tips, their long nails were indispensable for levering up tongues of steel and copper and poking escaped components out of inaccessible hiding-places; and they made excellent tweezers for holding the heads of mettlesome bolts while the nuts were being screwed on and for nipping the ends of wires and pulling them through their appropriate holes. To manicure an artisan is to disable him.

As for talk, Mr Belton was my Homer. For hour after hour, sometimes in the day and sometimes in the evening, we sat in a

front room that shone with the glamour of the golden age and
shook with the triumphal march of legendary heroes. Enchanted
and entranced, I heard tales of feats, endurances, and giants: of the
crossing of Chat Moss, the conquest of Kilsby Tunnel, the Rainhill Trials, the Battle of the Gauges, the Railway Races; I heard of
Richard Trevithick who built the first practical railway locomotive,
of the primitives of John Blenkinsop and Timothy Hackforth, of
George Stephenson the pioneer and Robert Stephenson the
successful engineer, of John Ramsbottom the genius of Crewe, of
Thomas Russell Crampton who was not without honour save in
his own country. Except in moments of exaltation – and they were
not few – Mr Belton's narrative style was that of a Midland
plainsman, slow, honest, utilitarian. He spoke veritable prose, but
I heard veritable poetry – epics and sagas, fables and fantasies that
made me quake with the dark roll of drums and shiver with the
sensuous excitement of strings and flutes. My mind became a
roundhouse of knowledge. I learned what call-boys were, and
fire-droppers, and boiler-washers. I learned that at one time the
Midland Railway's trains used to arrive paradoxically at the Great
Northern's King's Cross Station. I learned why booking offices
were named booking offices, what Müller's Lights were, what
Castleman's Snake was. I learned that platelayers were called
plate-layers because in the early days of colliery lines rails were
made of wood and men were employed to lay metal plates on
them to give them greater durability; I learned that permanent
way is called permanent way to distinguish it from the imper-
manent way laid during the construction of a new railroad. My
mind became a bazaar of splendid technical arcana: flying junctions, ruling gradients, four-foots and six-foots, cross-heads and
shoes, blast pipes, superheater headers, soot blowers, gudgeon
pins, eccentrics, cranks. And as I went about the house and the
streets I recited the lovely lyrical lines that I knew by heart: the
Vale of Rheidol Railway, the Great North of England Railway, the
Swindon, Marlborough and Andover, the Newport, Abergavenny
and Hereford, the London, Chatham and Dover, the Kendal and
Windermere, the Preston and Wyre, the Burry Port and Gwen-
dreath Valley, the Highland, the Cornwall, the Taff Vale, the
Wirral, the Barry, the Birkenhead.

As I remember, we did an astonishing amount of work in that

best parlour in Carlyle Road, even though Mr Belton was a very sick man and had to visit the doctor every other day. On these doctor's days he and I set out from the house together in the early morning, in clear sunlight or chilling mists, keeping each other company and discussing our Enormous Project. This was the construction of a complete railway – not simply a series of immobile scale models such as we were building at present, but a *working* railway with locomotives operated by steam power, extensive rolling stock for passengers and goods, sidings, marshalling yards, tunnels, embankments, viaducts, bridges, and stations, with a practical signalling system and – as a romantic extravagance – equipment for the automatic collection and delivery of mailbags while the trains were in motion. We walked and talked, gazing at visions, until it was time for us to part, he to the surgery, I to school.

from THE RAILWAY GAME *1962*

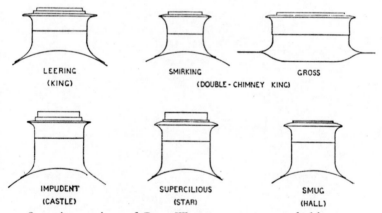

Some impressions of Great Western copper-capped chimneys.

PART II

The Making of Britain's Railways

Preview

MARJORIE WHITELAW

Railways have a perennial fascination. Big businessmen spend back-breaking weekends in North Wales relaying track for the tiny, archaic Ffestiniog railway, the stubborn line that would not die when British Railways abandoned it. Collectors pay fabulous amounts of hard cash for railwayana. Now that the Age of Aviation is in full sway over us, trains and their trappings have become Romance.

This was not the spirit in which they began. Trevelyan, the historian, has called railways "England's gift to the world" because it was here that engineers, by trial and error, first invented locomotives, found out how to lay track and operate a railway system and then, men of experience, went on to build railways over the world.

The possibilities of James Watt's steam engine had for long intrigued a number of experimenters, and one of these – the erratic genius in Cornwall, Richard Trevithick, succeeded in 1802 in building a steam-carriage which could be adapted for use on roads as well as on railways; but what worried a number of people at the time was that a locomotive engine could not draw heavy loads because the adhesion of smooth wheels to smooth rails would be so slight that there would be no traction.

In 1813 a Mr Blackett, the enterprising owner of a Newcastle colliery who had seen Trevithick's engine working in London, discovered by experiment that the weight of the engine was in itself enough to ensure traction, and proved the doubters wrong. About the same time the thirty-two-year-old George Stephenson, enginewright at the Killingworth collieries just north of Newcastle and already noted in the district as a good man with an engine, was absorbed in his own attempt to work out a machine for hauling coal cheaply from the pits to the river barges. Oddly enough, Stephenson already knew Mr Blackett, for his father had been a stoker at his colliery, and it was there, in 1781, that George had been born.

The elder Stephenson was a good workman, but times were

hard and his wages only 12s. a week. So none of the six children
went to school, and small George helped around the house until
he got his first job looking after some cows. When he was
fourteen he was, to his great joy, made assistant fireman to his
father, at 7s. a week. This was, he felt, a very large wage for so
little a boy, and in case the colliery owner agreed he hid whenever
his employer appeared. By seventeen, he was a full engineman and
earning more money than his father. He took his engine seriously,
and he spent most of his spare time pulling it apart and putting it
together again to see how it worked. He made models in clay of
every engine he could get described to him. And when he discovered that everything he wanted to know about engines could
be studied in books, he went to night-school to learn how to read.
He was then eighteen.

To make extra money, he turned his deft fingers to other trades
– cobbling and clock mending. At twenty-one he had earned a
fine reputation as an expert workman, and was sufficiently
established to marry; the next year, 1803, his only son, Robert,
was born. George had now risen a step or two, to brakesman, and
at this level he stayed for some years. Life grew a little grey: his
wife had died in childbirth, his parents were ailing and had to be
supported, England was at war with Napoleon. He thought of
emigrating to the United States but couldn't raise enough money
for the fare; instead, he went on working on more and more
engines.

His chance came when a new-fangled atmospheric pump at the
new Killingworth pit would not work. George was called in, and
he got it going. His reputation as an engine-doctor was made and
shortly afterwards he was offered the job of enginewright for the
Killingworth Colliery. He had already come a very long way; at
£100 a year, he was a made man. He had never dreamed of more
than that.

Self-help and hard work – these were the qualities, said the
Victorians a little later, which were for a deserving man the keys
to pious success, and George Stephenson's life was like a blue-
print illustration of this theme. These were indeed the years of
endurance and hard work and enterprise, with few apparent
possibilities and no glimpse of what lay ahead. But the small son
had to be taught and George went back to watchmending and

even tailoring in the evening to pay for Robert's schooling. George taught Robert practical mechanics and Robert, as he learnt mathematics in school, passed them on to his father in the evenings. For the rest of George's days, his life was complemented in this way by Robert's, and their work together had the force of complete unity. The more George learnt himself, the more he realized the value of real training for Robert, and he piled more on his own shoulders until he had enough money to send Robert to study for a time at Edinburgh University; no English university at that time taught science to men of modest purse.

George was also running over to Mr Blackett's colliery at Wylam from time to time to see how he was getting on with his engine. It had a lot of defects and George decided he now knew enough to try and build a better one for Killingworth, in which would be incorporated all the best features of all engines built to date. Ten months later he put it – his first – on the rails. At the end of the first year it was not exactly a howling success, for it went no faster than a horse and cost about as much to operate.

The whole idea of locomotives might have collapsed then and there, at least for a while, had it not been that people were complaining about the noise made by the steam escaping into the air with a hiss which terrified the horses. Stephenson decided to try running the steam out through the chimney which would also, he hoped, increase the draught. To his great content, it immediately doubled the power of the engine. He went to work to design a new, improved version and in 1815 produced what amounted to the prototype for the locomotives which ran Britain's railways for their first fifty or sixty years.

The piled-up stores of inventive energy were working like a yeast in the country. But each mechanical genius had to wait upon the work of others. In 1815 rails were still made of cast-iron and were being smashed to pieces by steam-engines. The malleable iron edge rail was not patented until 1820 – and then the way was opened.

But Edward Pease, the man who wanted to build the first public railway (for, so far, railways were operating only at the mines) saw it in his mind's eye as powered by horses, which would pull waggons on rails the 15-odd miles from the coal-rich Darlington to Stockton-on-Tees. Over the loud objections of

most of the merchants in the area, Mr Pease and his Quaker
associates raised funds and applied to Parliament for an Act. The
proposed line would pass near a fox covert owned by the Duke
of Cleveland; His Grace succeeded in having the Act thrown out
of Parliament. Mr Pease had a new line surveyed, avoiding the
Duke's fox holes, and made a new application to Parliament.

George Stephenson appeared on Mr Pease's doorstep soon after
the Act was passed, dying to try his hand at this job, bigger than
anything he had yet tackled. Mr Pease was impressed, and hired
him. Mr Pease had also been impressed by the fact that a horse
could pull ten times as much over rails as on the ordinary road,
but he had not thought beyond horsepower. He was made very
anxious by the vehemence with which George Stephenson cried
that he must have engines – and locomotive engines. For Mr
Pease, his cautious Quakers and indeed the whole public, informed
or ignorant, felt the question of steam locomotive power was
anything but proved. Most people rather liked the idea of fixed
engines which hauled the waggons with ropes and pulleys, and
George's insistence on locomotion merely shook his friends' confidence in his ability.

Mr Pease, however, finally made the journey to Killingworth to
see the Stephenson engines working, and was then persuaded.
An Amended Act was applied for, stating that locomotive power
would be used in addition to fixed engines and horses (for horses
were not to be abandoned). And, as an experiment, passengers
would also be carried, if indeed any could be found who would
buy tickets. Stephenson, the poor boy who had made good, was
appointed engineer at the greatly increased salary of three hundred
pounds per annum.

Since this was the first try at a public railway, there were a
thousand different questions to be decided, and one of these was
the gauge to be used. In the end this was based on the gauge of the
carts and waggons used locally and in the Killingworth colliery,
which averaged 4 feet $8\frac{1}{2}$ inches; and so the line and its equipment
was built. This was to cause one of the biggest battles of all time in
later years, when the various independent companies all wanted
to build their own gauge – the Great Western, indeed, tried out a
gauge as wide as seven feet. Stephenson, by then one of the very
few men with enough vision to see the possibilities of a national

network of railways, held out stubbornly for his own gauge. And so it stayed.

The Stockton and Darlington line opened in 1825 and to the intense surprise of absolutely everybody proved to be a whacking commercial success. Even the most optimistic of directors had not realized that the railway could carry coal to the coast for highly profitable export to London, nor had they realized the potential passenger traffic. Even more astounding, with the railway came expanded business between the two towns. Business, in fact, was so good there were frequent traffic jams, for the Act of this first railway provided that any person could, by paying the charges, put his own horses and carriage on the railway, and a number of competing passenger services were running simultaneously. At first passengers were pulled by horsepower, freight by steam-engines; but the freight trains became so frequent and so long that the passenger carriers took to hitching themselves on to the goods trains. Finally the railway company decided it would have to run its own railway line and, in a manner considered almost extravagantly foresighted at the time, built some special coaches for the increased passenger traffic.

Industry was mushrooming all over the country. Manchester, in the previous generation, had sprouted 200 factory chimneys pouring out smoke from 30,000 steam-powered looms. In Liverpool dock receipts had increased eight-fold, tonnage from 71,000 to over a million tons annually. But the only transport connection between the two cities remained the Duke of Bridge-water's canal. Manchester men were in a frenzy, waiting for deliveries from Liverpool: it sometimes took longer for a cargo to travel the 30 miles from Liverpool to Manchester than it did to get to New York. The canal owners sat back and watched the money roll in – they had a happy monopoly, and no imagination whatsoever.

A hundred and fifty leading citizens signed a statement that a new line was necessary and they requested the canal company to lower their rates and increase their service. The canal company loftily refused. The leading citizens therefore decided to build a railway and they offered the job to Mr George Stephenson.

The canal operators quickly opened a full-scale propaganda campaign against the railway and when Stephenson went out into

C

the country with his surveyors he had trouble. Time and time again he was driven off the ground by gamekeepers, by groups of farmers with pitchforks, by landowners with guns. The canal companies circulated anti-railway pamphlets over the country like a thick blanket of autumn leaves and paid the press for its support. The newspapers consequently generally spoke of the railways as a mere speculation, no crazier than the other projects of that crazily speculative period. In the 1820s you could invest in balloon companies which would carry passengers through the London air at forty miles an hour, or in coaching companies which were going to run coaches on relays of bottled gas instead of horses. Or you could lose your money in a railway run by steam. For by the time Stephenson's crazy idea of using steam locomotives got down to London it sounded as mad as the others. Stephenson had to appear as an expert witness before parliamentary committees; his Manchester sponsors begged him to conceal from Parliament his almost sacrilegious belief that locomotives could safely run at twenty miles an hour. If he did not bring his engine within a reasonable speed, they said, he would inevitably damn the whole thing and be himself regarded as a maniac fit only for Bedlam.

Stephenson was, in fact, unable to find any other engineer who would risk his reputation in supporting this idea of speed, and many engineers were definitely hostile. In spite of the satisfactory working of the Stockton and Darlington on a mixed horse-and-locomotive engine basis, in spite of his years of successful experience in all sorts of mechanical engineering, the locomotive engine was not yet believed. Even when Stephenson had almost finished the construction of the railway line, the directors had not yet made up their minds what they were going to use for power. Most of them favoured fixed engines, which would be stationed every mile and a half along the lines, and would propel the waggons by a system of ropes and pulleys. This plan was favoured over locomotive engines by a team of experts called in for consultation. Not a single professional man of any standing could be found to say a word for Stephenson's locomotives.

Stephenson hurled himself into battle and in the end, worn down by his stubborn refusal to take no for an answer, the directors agreed to stage a competition for the best locomotive, with a prize of £500 for the winner. There were certain specifications to be met and if, they said huffily, *if* any locomotive could be made which would meet these specifications, the railway would run on steam.

The great week of the locomotive competition at Rainhill was set for mid-October, 1829. Four engines were entered and it was as exciting and colourful as a horse-race. A stand was built for the ladies and thousands of people turned up to cheer their favourite. Stephenson's new, specially designed *Rocket* came at the bottom of the list. But one by one the others cracked up and the *Rocket* sailed through the tests, reaching at one point the impossible speed of thirty-five miles an hour. (One of the judges must have burst a blood vessel or two; he had firmly refused to believe that any vehicle was capable of moving faster than ten miles an hour.)

The *Rocket* and the Stephensons, father and son, were the sensation of the year. The Liverpool and Manchester Railway opened triumphantly with full acclaim and the presence of the Duke of Wellington on the 15th of September, 1830. The Railway Age had begun.

The new era brought the country the biggest programme of heavy construction it had known since the building of the great cathedrals and abbeys in the Middle Ages. The only earlier – and much smaller – parallel had been the canals, and the men who came to build the canals stayed to build the railways – the navigators, or navvies, the giants of British heavy labour and the most violent and savage body of men to be let loose on the countryside since Cromwell's wild soldiers. They were nomadic, homeless and ruthless; they lived sordid communal lives in turf huts on the site and, as the railway moved, they cut across the country like a horde of driver ants. Game disappeared from the most sacred preserves, gamekeepers were defied and villagers frightened. But they were demons for work. When George Stephenson went to France to build railways there, "Dieu", they would murmur, "Mon Dieu, que ces anglais travaillent . . ."

After the Liverpool and Manchester line had tried itself, it was more obvious that the railway had indeed come to stay. But for a number of reasons – supposed danger, certain discomfort – it was a long time before the upper classes deigned to give it their approval. Trains were all very well for commerce, but were declared to be rather "low" for the politer type of passenger.

When the aristocracy travelled, the servants went by train and the family in its own heavy lumbering coach. Finally the railways offered the fastidious traveller the privilege of setting his coach on top of a railway cart and joining the train thus. The Duke of Wellington travelled like this until his very old age in the 1850s.

The primeval four-wheeled first-class coach had three compartments, each containing six seats. Passengers at first were locked in at the station lest, through fear, they should open the door and throw themselves out. Second-class varied from railway to railway; sometimes closed in, sometimes with open sides above the waist. Third was normally an open waggon, sometimes even without seats. Nobody ever travelled third if he could possibly avoid it.

Under Gladstone's Railway Act of 1844, the companies were obliged to provide at least once a day third-class accommodation that would be weatherproof. Most companies interpreted this as stingily as possible. A "Parliamentary" carriage was a box with plank seats and with light let in through sliding shutters up near the roof. In bad weather the shutters were closed and the passengers sat in airless darkness.

In neither first, second nor third did anyone, for years, think of supplying plumbing and the embarrassment involved in taking a long train journey was something that had to be given careful thought. Establishing a trend, avant-garde railway plumbing came to Britain from American Pullman coaches.

The science of engineering, perhaps the most creative force in the nineteenth century, was born in the minds of humble men like Brindley, Telford and Stephenson, who filled the needs of their time like a hand in a glove. They were men of powerful imagination and sound judgement and stubborn will, and they fuelled these qualities with apparently boundless energy and physical toughness. Robert Stephenson, in surveying the London to Birmingham line, walked its length twenty times. Draughtsmen were expected to produce drawings continuously in twelve-hour day and night shifts, and navvies worked in gangs as large as eight hundred in twenty-four hour shifts around the clock, seven days a week.

The face of the country began to show more than surface change. Tunnels, viaducts, cuttings, bridges – in thirty years the railway engineers built more than 25,000 bridges alone, and this was more than all the bridges which had previously existed in the country.

For five years after her Coronation, Queen Victoria refused to trust herself to trains, although Prince Albert was a frequent traveller. Finally, one Saturday afternoon in June of 1842, the Great Western was informed, to its joy, that the Queen would like to return to London from Windsor by train on Monday morning.

Fortunately, the Great Western, one of the most imaginative of railways, had had the foresight to build a Royal Carriage some time earlier. It was ready and waiting at Slough on Monday morning in all its glory – lined, padded and tufted in pale blue satin, with hangings of blue and white. The Queen was charmed, and said so; the journey was a great success, and the Queen arrived triumphantly on time at Paddington at 12.25 on Monday. A large crowd awaited her and, when she stepped happily out of her pretty blue satin coach, she was greeted with the most deafening demonstration of loyalty in her experience.

The Railway Age had not only arrived, it had become Respectable.

from THE REVIEW OF THE HUNTING GROUP
OF COMPANIES *March 1958*

Liverpool to Manchester, 1830

ANON

Liverpool was never so full of strangers; they poured in during the last, and the beginning of the present, week from almost all parts of the three kingdoms, and we believe that through Chester alone, which is by no means a principal road to Liverpool, four hundred extra passengers were forwarded on Tuesday. All the inns in the town were crowded to overflowing, and carriages stood in the streets at night, for want of room in the stable yards.

On the morning of Wednesday the population of the town and of the country began very early to assemble near the railway. The weather was favorable, and the Company's station at the boundary of the town was the rendezvous of the nobility and gentry who attended, to form the procession at Manchester. Never was there such an assemblage of rank, wealth, beauty, and fashion in this neighbourhood. From before nine o'clock until ten the entrance in Crown Street was thronged by the splendid equipages from which the company was alighting, and the area in which the railway carriages were placed was gradually filling with gay groups eagerly searching for their respective places, as indicated by numbers corresponding with those on their tickets.

The large and elegant car constructed for the nobility, and the accompanying cars for the Directors and the musicians were seen through the lesser tunnel, where persons moving about at the far end appeared as diminutive as if viewed through a concave glass. The effect was singular and striking. In a short time all those cars were brought along the tunnel into the yard which then contained all the carriages, which were to be attached to the eight locomotive engines which were in readiness beyond the tunnel in the great excavation at Edge-hill. By this time the area presented a beautiful spectacle, thirty-three carriages being filled by elegantly dressed persons, each train of carriages being distinguished by silk flags of different colors; the band of the 4th King's Own Regiment, stationed in the adjoining area, playing military airs, the Wellington Harmonic Band, in a Grecian car for the procession, performing many beautiful miscellaneous pieces; and a third band occupying a stage above Mr Harding's Grand Stand, at William the Fourth's Hotel, spiritedly adding to the liveliness of the hour whenever the other bands ceased.

A few minutes before ten, the discharge of a gun and the cheers of the assembly announced the arrival of the Duke of Wellington, who entered the area with the Marquis and Marchioness of Salisbury and a number of friends, the band playing "See the conquering Hero comes". He returned the congratulations of the company, and in a few moments the grand car, which he and the nobility and the principal gentry occupied, and the cars attached to it, were permitted to proceed; we say permitted, because no applied power, except a slight impulse at first, is requisite to propel carriages along the tunnel, the slope being just sufficient to call into effect the principle of gravitation. The tunnel was lighted with gas, and the motion in passing through it must have been as pleasing as it was novel to all the party. On arriving at the engine station, the cars were attached to the *Northumbrian*, locomotive engine, on the southern of the two lines of rail; and immediately the other trains of carriages started through the tunnel and were attached to their respective engines on the nothern of the lines.

We had the good fortune to have a place in the first train after the grand cars, which train, drawn by the *Phoenix*, consisted of three open and two closed carriages, each carrying twenty-six ladies and gentlemen. The lofty banks of the engine station were crowded with thousands of spectators, whose enthusiastic cheering seemed to rend the air. From this point to Wavertree-lane, while the procession was forming, the grand cars passed and repassed the other trains of carriages several times, running as they did in the same direction on the two parallel tracks, which gave the assembled thousands and tens of thousands the opportunity of seeing distinctly the illustrious strangers, whose presence gave extraordinary interest to the scene. Some soldiers of the 4th Regiment assisted the railway police in keeping the way clear and preserving order, and they discharged their duty in a very proper manner. A few minutes before eleven all was ready for the journey, and certainly a journey upon a railway is one of the most delightful that can be imagined.

Our first thoughts, it might be supposed, from the road being so level, were that it must be monotonous and uninteresting. It is precisely the contrary; for as the road does not rise and fall like the ground over which we pass, but proceeds nearly at a level, whether the land be high or low, we are at one moment drawn through a hill, and find ourselves seventy feet below the surface, in an Alpine chasm, and at another we are as many feet above the green fields, traversing a raised path, from which we look down upon the roofs of farm houses, and see the distant hills and woods. These variations give an interest to such a journey which cannot be appreciated until they are witnessed. The signal gun being fired, we started in beautiful style, amidst the deafening plaudits of the well-dressed people who thronged the numerous booths, and all the walls and eminences on both sides the line. Our speed was gradually increased till, entering the Olive Mountain excavation, we rushed into the awful chasm at the rate of twenty-four miles an hour. The banks, the bridges over our heads, and the rude projecting corners along the sides, were covered with masses of human beings past whom we glided as if upon the wings of the wind.

Entering upon Parr Moss we had a good view of Newton Race Course and the stands, and at this time the Duke was far ahead of us; the grand cars appeared actually of diminutive dimensions, and in a short time we saw them gliding beautifully over the Sankey Viaduct, from which a scene truly magnificent lay before us. The fields below us were occupied by thousands who cheered us as we passed over the stupendous edifice; carriages filled the narrow lanes, and vessels in the water had been detained in order that their crews might gaze up at the gorgeous pageant passing far above their mast heads. Here again was a grand stand, and here again enthusiastic plaudits almost deafened us. Shortly, we passed the borough of Newton, crossing a fine bridge over the Warrington road, and reached Parkside, seventeen miles from Liverpool, in about four minutes under the hour. At this place the engines were ranged under different watering stations to receive fresh water, the whole extending along nearly half a mile of road. Our train and two others passed the Duke's car, and we in the first train had had our engine supplied with water, and were ready to start, some time before we were aware of the melancholy cause of our apparently great delay. We had, most of us, alighted, and were walking about, congratulating each other generally, and the ladies particularly, on the truly delightful treat we were enjoying, all hearts bounding with joyous excitement, and every tonge eloquent in the praise of the gigantic work now completed, and the advantages and pleasures it afforded.

A murmur and an agitation at a little distance betokened something alarming and we too soon learned the nature of that lamentable event, which we cannot record without the most agonized feelings. On inquiring, we learnt the dreadful particulars.

After three of the engines with their trains had passed the Duke's carriage, although the others had to follow, the company began to alight from all the carriages which had arrived. The Duke of Wellington and Mr Huskisson had just shaken hands, and Mr Huskisson, Prince Esterhazy, Mr Birch, Mr H. Earl, Mr William Holmes, M.P., and others were standing in the road, when the other carriages were approaching. An alarm being given, most of the gentlemen sprang into the carriage, but Mr Huskisson seemed flurried, and from some cause, not clearly ascertained, he fell under the engine of the approaching carriages, the wheel of which shattered his leg in the most dreadful manner. On being raised from the ground by the Earl of Wilton, Mr Holmes, and other gentlemen, his only exclamations were: "Where is Mrs Huskisson? I have met my death. God forgive me." Immediately after he swooned. Mr Brandreth, and Dr Southey, of London, immediately applied bandages to the limb. In a short time the engine was detached from the Duke's carriage, and the musician's car being prepared for the purpose, the Right Honorable gentleman was placed in it, accompanied by his afflicted lady, with Dr Brandreth, Dr Southey, the Earl of Wilton, and Mr Stephenson, who set off in the direction of Manchester.

The whole of the procession remained at least another hour, uncertain what course to adopt. A consultation was held on the open part of the road, and the Duke of Wellington was soon surrounded by the Directors, and a mournful group of gentlemen. At first it was thought advisable to return to Liverpool, merely dispatching one engine and a set of carriages, to convey home Lady Wilton, and others who did not wish to return to Liverpool. The Duke of Wellington and Sir Robert Peel seemed to favour this course; others thought it best to proceed as originally intended: but no decision was made till the Boroughreeve of Manchester stated, that if the procession did not reach Manchester, where an unprecedented concourse of people would be assembled, and would wait for it, he should be fearful of the consequences to the peace of the town. This turned the scale and his Grace then proposed that the whole party should proceed, and return as soon as possible, all festivity at Manchester being avoided. The *Phoenix,* with its train, was then attached to the *North Star* and its train, and from the two united a long chain was affixed to his Grace's

C*

car, and although it was on the other line of the rail, it was found to draw the whole along exceedingly well.

About half-past one, we resumed our journey; and we should here mention that the Wigan Branch Railway Company had erected near Parkside bridge, a grand stand, which they and their friends occupied, and from which they enthusiastically cheered the procession. On reaching the twentieth mile post we had a beautiful view of Rivington Pike, and Blackstone Edge, and at the twenty-first the smoke of Manchester appeared to be directly at the termination of our view. Groups of people continued to cheer us, but we could not reply; our enjoyment was over. Tyldesley Church, and a vast region of smiling fields here met the eye, as we traversed the flat surface of Chat Moss, in the midst of which a vast crowd was assembled to greet us with their plaudits; and from the twenty-fourth mile post we began to find ourselves flanked on both sides by spectators extending in a continuous and thickening body all the way to Manchester.

At the twenty-fifth mile post we met Mr Stephenson returning with the *Northumbrian* engine. In answer to innumerable and eager inquiries, Mr Stephenson said he had left Mr Huskisson at the house of the Rev. Mr Blackburn, Vicar of Eccles, and had then proceeded to Manchester, whence he brought back medical assistance, and that the surgeons, after seeing Mr Huskisson, had expressed a hope that there was no danger. Mr Stephenson's speed had been at the rate of thirty-four miles an hour during this painful errand. The engine being then again attached to the Duke's car, the procession dashed forward, passing countless thousands of people upon house tops, booths, high ground, bridges, etc., and our readers must imagine, for we cannot describe, such a movement through an avenue of living beings, and extending six miles in length. Upon one bridge a tri-colored flag was displayed; near another the motto of "Vote by ballot" was seen; in a field near Eccles, a poor and wretchedly-dressed man had his loom close to the roadside, and was weaving with all his might; cries of "No Corn Laws" were occasionally heard, and for about two miles the cheerings of the crowd were interspersed with a continual hissing and hooting from the minority. On approaching the bridge which crosses the Irwell, the 59th Regiment was drawn up, flanking the road on each side, and presenting arms as his Grace passed along.

We reached the warehouses at a quarter before three, and those who alighted were shown into the large upper rooms where a most elegant cold collation had been prepared by Mr Lynn, for more than one thousand persons. The greater portion of the company, as the carriages continued to arrive, visited the rooms and partook in silence of some refreshment. They then returned to their carriages which had been properly placed for returning. His Grace and the principal party did not alight; but he went through a most fatiguing office for more than an hour and a half, in shaking hands with thousands of people, to whom he stooped over the hand-rail of the carriage, and who seemed insatiable in their desire to join hands with him. Many women brought their children to him, lifting them up that he might bless them, which he did, and during the whole time he had scarcely a minute's respite. At half-past four the Duke's car began to move away for Liverpool.

They would have been detained a little longer, in order that three of the engines, which had been to Eccles for water, might have dropped into the rear to take their places; but Mr Lavender represented that the crowd was so thickening in upon all sides, and becoming so clamorous for admission into the area, that he would not answer for the peace of the town, if further delay took place. The three engines were on the same line of rail as the Duke, and they could not cross to the other line without getting to a turning place, and as the Duke could not be delayed on account of his keeping the crowd together, there was no alternative but to send the engines forward. One of the other engines was then attached to our train, and we followed the Duke rapidly, while the six trains behind had only three engines left to bring them back. Of course, we kept pace with the Duke, who stopped at Eccles to inquire after Mr Huskisson. The answer received was that there was now no hope of his life being saved; and this intelligence plunged the whole party into still deeper distress.

At Roby, his Grace and the Childwalls alighted and proceeded home; our carriages then moved forward to Liverpool, where we arrived about seven o'clock, and went down the great tunnel, under the town, a part of the work which, more than any other, astonished the numerous strangers present. It is, indeed, a wonderful work, and makes an impression never to be effaced from the memory. The Company's yard, from Saint James's Street to Wapping, was filled with carriages waiting for the returning parties, who separated with feelings of mingled gratification and distress, to which we shall not attempt to give utterance. We afterwards learnt that the parties we left at Manchester placed the three remaining engines together, and all the carriages together, so as to form one grand procession, including twenty-four carriages, and were coming home at a steady pace, when they were met near Newton by the other three engines, which were then attached to the rest, and they arrived in Liverpool about ten o'clock.

Thus ended a pageant, which, for importance as to its object and grandeur in its details, is admitted to have exceeded anything ever witnessed. We conversed with many gentlemen of great experience in public life, who spoke of the scene as surpassing anything they had ever beheld, and who computed, upon data which they considered to be satisfactory, that not fewer than 500,000 persons must have been spectators of the procession.

contemporary account quoted in THE RAILWAY AGE *by*
C. Bruyn Andrews 1937

Railways in 1843

W. M. ACWORTH

All the world knows that the Liverpool and Manchester Railway was opened in 1830, and that the Railway Mania occurred in 1846. The year 1843 marks the period of transition between these two points, and enables us to sketch the English railway system in a condition more nearly approaching a stable equilibrium than it has ever attained either before or since. A long and severe depression of trade, consequent on a series of bad harvests that culminated in the Irish potato famine and the Repeal of the Corn Laws, had brought railway building almost to a standstill, and had rendered it well-nigh impossible for projectors to obtain the money for new schemes.

But the main foundations of our railway system were already

laid, and with the exception of the Great Northern, and of course the Chatham and Dover, all the great companies were already in existence, or at least in embryo. The London and Birmingham had not yet united with the Grand Junction, the Manchester and Birmingham, and the Liverpool and Manchester to form the North Western, but passengers could travel from Euston, *via* Birmingham and Crewe, not only to Liverpool and Manchester, but to Chester, Lancaster, and Leeds as well. To the north-east they could travel as far as Hull and Darlington, though the Hull and Selby, the Great North of England with its 44¼ miles of line, the Clarence, the Brandling Junction, and half a dozen more, not forgetting the Stockton and Darlington, squabbled and fought over different corners of the territory where now the North Eastern reigns in undisputed sovereignty. The North Midland, the Birmingham and Derby, and the Midland Counties were on the eve of amalgamation into the Midland Railway – the "Great Midland", as it was considered that a company controlling no less than 130 miles of line had a right to be called. In the eastern counties too the first of the coalitions that have finally given us the Great Eastern was just taking shape. South of the Thames, the South Eastern was open to Folkestone; the Brighton line was finished, as was the South Western to Southampton and Gosport. The Great Western was running to Bristol and to Cheltenham, while the extension to Exeter was open beyond Taunton, and was fast approaching completion. There were also a good many lines scattered about England, from Hayle, Bodmin, and the Taff Vale, to that which was perhaps the most important of all, the Newcastle and Carlisle, but having no communication with the main railway system.

In all, some 1800 miles were open for traffic, and no great amount beyond this was under construction. The 1650 miles open at the end of 1841 had only been increased by 179 at the end of 1843. This latter year, however, saw the Parliamentary notices lodged for the Chester and Holyhead. In Ireland there was a railway from Dublin to Kingstown, and also a few miles in Ulster. In Scotland there were some local lines near Dundee, and direct communication was also open from Edinburgh to Glasgow, and on to Ayr and Greenock. But nine-tenths of the mileage was in England. The amount of capital authorized was about £70,000,000

and of this nearly £60,000,000 had already been spent. About
300,000 passengers were carried every week, and the total weekly
receipts from all sources were somewhat more than £100,000. For
purposes of rough comparison, it may just be mentioned that
today (1889) there are nearly 20,000 miles of line in Great Britain,
about seven-tenths of them in England and Wales, that the paid-up
capital exceeds £800,000,000, that the annual receipts are more
today than all the capital in 1843, and that the number of passengers
has increased more than forty-fold.

A General Railway and Steam Navigation Guide, bearing
already the familiar name of *Bradshaw* . . . had been for some time
in existence, and had just begun to appear regularly on the first of
each month; but, in spite of ample margins and wide-spaced
columns, it was necessary to insert much extraneous matter
relative to railways under construction and the price of shares in
order to eke out the thirty-two pages of which the slim pamphlet
was composed. . . .

Competent observers were, however, convinced that all the
lines it would pay to construct were already made. For instance,
it was gravely argued that the Lancaster and Carlisle (a line that in
fact paid enormous dividends for years before it was absorbed into
the North Western) would "prove a most disastrous speculation".
It was evident, said the wiseacres, that it could never have any
goods traffic; and as for passengers, "unless the crows were to
contract with the railway people to be conveyed at low fares",
where could they be expected to come from? The through traffic
could be conveyed almost as expeditiously and far more cheaply in
the "splendid steamships which run to Liverpool in sixteen or
seventeen hours from Greenock". As for the rival East Coast
scheme, "this most barren of all projects, the desert line by
Berwick", was even more fiercely assailed. "A line of railway by
the [East] coast", writes one gentleman, "seems almost ludicrous,
and one cannot conceive for what other reason it can have been
thought of, except that the passengers by the railway, if any, might
have the amusement of looking at the steamers on the sea, and
reciprocally the passengers by sea might see the railway carriages."

"The improvements that are constantly taking place in marine
engines and steam vessels," writes another correspondent, "are so
great that there cannot be a doubt but they will soon attain an

equal rate of speed to the present railway locomotives." For all
that, the East Coast route was strongly advocated, and an influen-
tial deputation, headed by Hudson and Robert Stephenson, had
an interview with Sir Robert Peel at the Treasury to solicit
Government assistance to the project. The construction of the
High Level Bridge at Newcastle, as a single line to be worked by
horses, was under consideration. Speaking of the proposed
Caledonian line from Glasgow and Edinburgh to Carlisle, the
Railway Times writes in January, 1843, that, if in any way the
present attempt should be rendered nugatory, the next ten years
will not see the commencement of a line to Scotland by the West
Coast. "Long before that time the route *via* the East Coast will be
completed, if its promoters proceed with the same spirit as heretofore; and, although ultimately there may be and must be *two*
distinct lines between the capitals of England and the North, it is
almost certain that, unless some great improvement takes place in
the making and working of railways, the present generation will
not witness the execution of both." The prophet's vision was so
far correct that the East Coast was open first, but it was only the
difference between July, 1847, and February, 1848. . . .

Not only was railway construction pretty much at a standstill,
but there were those who were persuaded that, though railway
building was a very good thing in its way, it was a thing that
already had been very much overdone. Here is what the *Athenaeum*
wrote on the subject in May, 1843: "With a view to the future, let
us glance at the facts as they now stare us in the face; in the first
place, look at the vicinity of London. Two railways – the Northern
and Eastern, and the Eastern Counties, to Cambridge and to
Colchester – are carried into the same district; both are unsuccess-
ful – one might have served all the purposes of both, and perhaps
neither is the line that should have been adopted. At all events,
one of the two is useless – total loss, say £1,000,000. Next, to the
westward, it is plain that one line should have served for the
Great Western and the South Western, as far as Basingstoke and
Reading – total loss, say £1,000,000. When going north, we have
two lines parallel with each other, the Birmingham and Derby,
and the Midland Counties, the latter of which should never have
existed – total loss, £1,000,000. Then Chester and Crewe, Manchester and Crewe, and Newton and Crewe, and Chester and

Birkenhead, three of them unprofitable, a total loss (without any advantage) amounting to £1,500,000. That the Manchester and Preston, and the Newton and Preston, and the Leigh and Bolton should co-exist in the same district, is a further absurdity, costing at least an unnecessary £500,000. No one acquainted with the country can for a moment admit that both the Manchester and Leeds, and Manchester and Sheffield should have been made as separate railways, at a loss of £1,500,000. Thus might good legislation have rendered to the country two essential services. The whole traffic at present existing might have been concentrated on the remaining lines by a judicious selection, so that they would have been rendered more profitable to the country, while these six millions would have remained for investment. With this money at its disposal, our Government might now have had the following lines for conveyance of mails, which it eminently wants, viz., a mail line from Exeter to Plymouth, and its continuation for the same purpose to Falmouth; a mail line to Ireland by way of Chester and Holyhead; and a mail line north to Scotland. These great lines would have been feeders to those which already exist, would have conferred great benefits on the country, and would have cost no more than has been already paid for partial communication."

The *Athenaeum* was not alone in hymning the blessings of State control. The *Artisan* for July points out that the railways of Belgium possess a great advantage over the railways of this country in the economy of their construction owing to the authority of Government, and further, "on the all-important point of safety, the system of State management, as exemplified in the railways of Belgium, far surpasses the railways of England". Convinced, however, that State control, whatever its abstract virtues, was alien to the English temperament, the writer goes on to consider whether there is no mean course available. "We turn to France, and find there is a system adopted which promises to secure the advantages of encouragement by the State with the independence of individual control."

We too can now turn to France, and, with the benefit of experience to guide us, can prove the pudding that the French people have had the privilege of eating for the last five-and-forty years. And today there can be but one opinion among those competent to judge, even those who are most dissatisfied with our

English railways, that the public, whether as passengers by first, second, or third class or as shippers of goods, either by *grande* or *petite vitesse*, are immeasurably worse served than they are in England. As for the system on which the French lines have been built – a system by which the Government guarantees dividends ranging from 7 to 13 per cent., and dare not call upon the companies to carry out obviously necessary extensions, lest it should in its turn be called on to make good its extravagant guarantee, while the companies, secure in the possession of a monopoly which yields them without effort an income far larger than even this guaranteed minimum, have no inducement to weight themselves with comparatively unproductive new lines – now that the *Artisan* is unfortunately defunct, it would be difficult to find for it one solitary supporter.

The entire unconsciousness even of the railway men themselves of the revolution they were working is nowhere better shown than in the different methods that were proposed for conducting the traffic. Practically the locomotive, as we have it today, capable of working up to 1000 horse-power, was already there. The multi-tubular boiler and the steamblast had long been in common use. But neither the public nor the specialists were convinced that the right system had been hit upon. To say nothing of a "patent aerial steam-carriage which is to convey passengers, goods, and despatches through the air, performing the journey between London and India in four days, and travelling at the rate of 75 to 100 miles per hour", all kinds of substitutes for locomotives were being sought for. One day the *Globe* reports that a "professional gentleman at Hammersmith has invented an entirely new system of railway carriage, which may be propelled without the aid of steam at an extraordinary speed, exceeding 60 miles an hour, with comparative safety, without oscillation, which will no doubt become the ordinary mode of railway travelling for short distances, as the railway and carriages may be constructed and kept in repair for less than one-fourth of the usual expense". Another day the Edinburgh and Glasgow Railway have, says a Scotch writer, "the discernment to employ Mr Davidson, a gentleman of much practical knowledge and talent", to construct for them an electro-magnetic carriage. The carriage, 16 feet long by 7 feet wide, was duly placed upon the rails, and "propelled by eight powerful electro-magnets about a mile and a half along the railway, travelling at the rate of upwards of four miles an hour, a rate which might be increased by giving greater power to the batteries, and enlarging the diameter of the wheels". "The practicability of the scheme is," we are assured, "placed beyond doubt," and its "simplicity, economy, safety, and compactness render it a far more valuable motive power than that clumsy, dangerous, and costly machine the steam-engine."

Then, again, Messrs Taylor and Conder, C.E., patented an ingenious system by which a carriage was to be drawn along the line "by the muscular power of the two guards who, as it is, constantly accompany it." The system, which is at the present moment in use for towing purposes on many German rivers, the Elbe for one, required that an endless rope should be laid along the line, and wound on to a drum which was attached to the carriage, and made to revolve by force, manual or mechanical, supplied from inside the carriage itself. Next Mr England, the engineer of the London and Croydon Railway, made a manumotive railway carriage, "very light and elegant in appearance, and capable of carrying seven or eight persons at the rate of 18 miles an hour". "We have no doubt," says a railway newspaper, "that these machines will come into general use, as they will effect considerable saving to the company in the expense of running an engine." Unfortunately none of these fine promises came to much. Mr England's manumotive carriage, under the more humble name of a trolley, is often employed on country lines to convey navvies or surface men to or from their work. And the endless rope and drum system is in some instances of unusually steep inclines used to let a train down into a station, but it can hardly be said to have revolutionized railway travelling. Mr Davidson, like many another inventor, was rudely checked by the cost of experiments and the stringency of the patent laws; and, after forty more years have been devoted to their improvement, electric railways are still hardly better than a scientific toy.

. . . The locomotive had, however, more serious competitors. The London and Blackwall Railway was worked by stationary engines, dragging the carriages with one wire rope for the up and another for the down traffic, each having a total length of about 8 miles and a weight of 40 tons. And on this line, among the first,

the electric telegraph was used, in order that the engineer at
Blackwall or Fenchurch Street might know when to begin to
wind up or let go his rope. The system in use was certainly most
ingenious. A down train, as it left Fenchurch Street, consisted of
seven carriages. The two in front went through to Blackwall; the
next carriage only as far as Poplar, and so on to the seventh, which
was detached at Shadwell, the first station after leaving Fenchurch
Street. As the train approached Shadwell, the guard, standing on
a platform in front of the carriage, pulled out "a pin from the
coupling at an interval of time sufficient to let the carriage arrive
at its proper destination by the momentum acquired in its passage
from London". The same process was repeated at each subsequent
station, till finally the two remaining carriages ran up the terminal
incline, and were brought to a stand at the Blackwall Station. On
the return journey the carriage at each station was attached to the
rope at a fixed hour, and then the whole series were set in motion
simultaneously, so that they arrived at Fenchurch Street at "intervals proportioned to the distance between the stations". On the up
journey the Blackwall portion of the train consisted of four
carriages, there being, so to speak, a "slip-coach" for Stepney and
another for Shadwell, and this seems to have been the nearest, and
in fact the only, approach to an attempt to deal with traffic between
intermediate stations. But the wear and tear was too much; there
were perpetual delays, owing to the rope breaking, and the cost
of repairs and renewals was something immense.

The Sunderland and Durham also was worked with a rope, at
first of hemp and afterwards of wire, as was . . . the Cowlairs
tunnel on the Edinburgh and Glasgow line. On other similar local
lines, such as the Edinburgh and Dalkeith, or the Dundee and
Arbroath, the carriages were still drawn by horses. In Ireland,
again, the continuation of the Dublin and Kingstown Railway on
to Dalkey, which was worked by atmospheric engines, was just
being opened for traffic, a speed of about 30 miles an hour having
been successfully obtained on several trial trips. It was proposed
to work the line from Exeter to Plymouth by water power. Water
power, however, was abandoned, and the atmospheric system
adopted, and this was so far at least a success, that on one occasion
the 8 miles between Exeter and Starcross were said to have been
covered at the rate of 70 miles an hour. . . .

Even where steam locomotives were employed, "the slowness to believe in the capabilities of the locomotive engine exhibited by the engineers of Great Britain is surprising . . ."

"The locomotive engine can climb the mountain-side as well as career along the plain." So wrote the *Athenaeum* in 1843, and so, in fact, it was proved in the next few years, when the Lancaster and Carlisle was carried over Shap Fell at a height of 915 feet above the sea, with a gradient of 1 in 75 for 4 miles, and the Caledonian climbed for 10 miles at a gradient of 1 in 80 to Beattock Summit, 1015 feet above sea-level. [But still] trains out of Euston and Lime Street, Liverpool, were hauled up by stationary engines, and the up trains through the Box Tunnel were assisted by a second engine behind. . . .

Though the *Athenaeum* said truly that the monumental lines of Stephenson and Brunel ought never to have been built in the style they were for the traffic of 1843, time has proved that, after all, the engineers were right, though they did not know it, and the philosophers were wrong. For to its splendidly straight and level track the North Western owes it that it can with ease keep abreast of the utmost efforts of its energetic rivals, the Great Northern and the Midland, in the race to Manchester; while the Great Western finds in the same circumstance ample compensation for the fact that its line to Exeter is no less than 23 miles further than the rival route. Meanwhile, the day of monumental lines was over, and the projectors of new routes were being compelled by the prevailing depression to cut their coats according to their cloth, and content themselves with schemes much more moderate than those with which they would have been satisfied a few years before. Unconvinced, however, that locomotives could climb gradients, they were still in search of contrivances scarcely less impracticable than the cogged wheels and movable legs of an earlier generation, in order to overcome their imaginary difficulties. One ingenious gentleman went so far as to suggest that, though the engine should have wheels to keep it on the line, the weight should be carried, and the driving power should be applied to rough rollers running upon a gravel road, maintained at a proper level between the two rails. By this method alone, he was convinced, would sufficient bite of the ground be obtained to enable a locomotive to draw a paying load up an incline. Another engineer proposed that on gradients steeper than 1 in 100 a second rail should be introduced, inside the ordinary one, on which the flange of the driving wheels, specially made rough for this purpose, might bite more firmly.

On the other hand, Lieutenant Le Count, R.E., of the London and Birmingham Railway, whose book is a mine of information in ancient history, writes as follows: "The want of adhesion, so much talked of, is found to be only nonsense, and, if there had been any, it would only be necessary . . . to connect a galvanized magnet with one or more of the axles to act on the rails, by which means, with the addition of only a few pounds, an adhesion equivalent to the weight of two tons would be produced at each axle, being capable also of acting or not at a moment's notice." Lieutenant Le Count was sceptical on another point also. The puny little "Goliaths" and "Samsons", with a boiler pressure of some 40 lb. as against the 140 to 180 lb. of today, were sometimes brought to a standstill by a fall of snow. But "the plans so often proposed", he writes, "of sweeping or scraping the rails will rarely be found necessary, much less the plan, seriously proposed and patented so late as 1831, of making the rails hollow and filling them with hot water in winter."

The tentative condition of the engineering knowledge of the time cannot be better exemplified than by a glance at a sketch furnished to the *Railway Times* in January, 1843, by an engineer as distinguished as Mr Crampton. This sketch "shows safety or reserve wheels not running upon the rails while the engine is

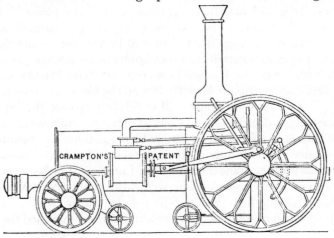

ordinarily at work, and not therefore liable to suffer. They are provided with deep flanches [sic], which act as a guide for the engine in the event of accidents. . . . It will be obvious", writes Mr Crampton, "that, should either axle break, the weight would be immediately supported by the reserve wheels, and the safety of the engine ensured." But there was another advantage, Mr Crampton thought: "By this arrangement I am enabled to place the boiler considerably lower than in the engines commonly used, which allows the use of much larger driving wheels, without endangering the safety of the engine, and also reduces the rocking and pitching motion to which engines having the centre of gravity placed high are continually subject." Such was the universally accepted ancient theory . . . [which] in 1847 led to Mr Trevithick building the famous old *Cornwall* with her boiler beneath the driving axle. Modern practice, however, has shown that engines with a high centre of gravity not only run more smoothly and are less hard upon the permanent way, but actually are safer in running round sharp curves at a high rate of speed.

Still, in spite of all these difficulties and hesitations, railways were steadily taking more and more hold of the public life and habits. In February, 1842, the *Morning Post* writes: "It is worthy of remark that Her Majesty never travels by railway. Prince Albert almost invariably accompanies the Queen, but patronises the Great Western generally when compelled to come up from Windsor alone. The Prince, however, has been known to say, 'Not quite so fast next time, Mr Conductor, if you please.' " His Royal Highness must have got pretty rapidly acclimatised, as in July, 1843, he came up from Clifton to Paddington within three hours. The Queen herself could not hold out much longer, and on June 18th, 1842, the *Railway Times* records: "Her Majesty made her first railway trip on Monday last on the Great Western Railway, and we have no doubt will in future patronize the line as extensively as does her Royal Consort. The Queen Dowager, it is well known, is a frequent passenger by the London and Birmingham Railway, and has more than once testified her extreme satisfaction with the arrangements of the Company. On Wednesday last Her Majesty Queen Adelaide went down by the South Western Railway for the first time *en route* for the Isle of Wight." Her Majesty returned a few days afterwards, and accomplished the 78 miles between Southampton and Vauxhall in one minute under the two hours – a run of which the South Western authorities were evidently not a little proud. And one must admit that they had a right to be so. It was not till July, 1888, that the present generation had a chance of getting to Southampton in so short a time. Not long afterwards, however, another "special" ran the distance in one hour and forty-six minutes. But the run must have been a pretty rough one, with little four-wheeled carriages loosely fastened together.

Queen Victoria apparently found a railway journey not as bad as she had fancied it, as on Saturday, July 23rd, she returned from London to Slough by the Great Western, "accompanied by his Royal Highness Prince Albert, their Serene Highnesses the Prince and Princess of Saxe Coburg Gotha, and a numerous suite". The Duke of Wellington took even longer to convert. It was not till August, 1843, that, being then in attendance on the Queen, he was compelled to take his first trip by rail to Southampton. On this occasion there were, it is reported, "the unprecedented number of eight specials (four each way) in addition to the ordinary traffic, twenty-seven trains in the day, including goods trains". Six weeks later there is this note: "We are glad to find that the Duke of Wellington's first trip on the South Western Railway, in attendance on Her Majesty, has reconciled his Grace to the new mode of travelling. Last week his Grace passed from and to Folkestone in one day by the Dover line."

But trains were not good enough even yet for foreign royalties. As late as July, 1843, the *Globe* translates from the French journal *Le Commerce* the following story of Louis Philippe: "When the King was intending to go with the Royal Family to his chateau at Bizy, he proposed to be conveyed by a special train on the railway as far as Rouen, and orders were given to this effect; but the Council of Ministers, on being acquainted with His Majesty's project, held a sitting, and came to the resolution that this mode of travelling by railway was not sufficiently secure to admit of its being used by the King, and consequently His Majesty went to Bizy with post-horses. This, it must be acknowledged, is a singular mode chosen by the Cabinet for encouraging railways." No doubt the frightful Versailles accident of the year before, in which fifty passengers were burnt to death, had something to do with this decision of His Majesty's ministers. It certainly gave rise to Sydney Smith's celebrated letter as to the necessity of sacrificing a bishop to secure the doors of the carriages being left unlocked. A correspondent of the newspapers, however, persisted that, "in spite of Socrateses, Solons, and Sydney Smiths, wise in their own conceit", locking in was right, while a second considered that the letter "showed a good deal of apparent prejudice, and something of irreverent and inappropriate wit, unbecoming a Christian minister". About the same time it is recorded that the Judges, sent down as a Special Commission to try some rioters at Stafford, went by special train from Euston. "It would appear, therefore," says the *Railway Times*, "that travelling by railway is not now considered beneath the dignity of the profession." On the other hand, Lord Abinger, presiding in the Court of Exchequer, said, "It would be a great tyranny if the Court were to lay down that a witness should only travel by railway. If he were a witness, in the present state of railways, he should refuse to come by such a conveyance."

Perhaps Lord Abinger and Louis Philippe's ministers might be forgiven if they were disciplined to accept "the present state of railways" as altogether satisfactory. Here is what Mr Bourne, a professed panegyrist of the new system, describes as a typical experience as late as the beginning of 1846: "It requires perhaps some boldness to claim for a mere piece of machinery, a combination of wheels and pistons, familiar to us by frequent use, any alliance with the sublime. Let the reader, however, place himself in imagination upon the margin of one of those broad dales of England, such for example as that of Barnsley in Yorkshire, of Stafford, or the vale of Berks, up each of which a great passenger railway is carried, and over which the eye commands an extended view. In the extreme distance a white line of cloud appears to rise from the ground, and gradually passes away into the atmosphere. Soon a light murmur falls upon the ear, and the glitter of polished metal appears from time to time among the trees. The murmur soon becomes deeper and more tremulous. The cloud rises of a more fleecy whiteness, and its conversion into the transparent air is more evident. The train rushes on; the bright engine rolls into full view; now crossing the broad river, now threading the various bendings of the railway, followed by its dark serpent-like body.

The character of the sound is changed. The pleasant murmur becomes a deep intermitting boom, the clank of chains and carriage-fastenings is heard, and the train rolls along the rails with a resonance like thunder.

"Suddenly a wagon stands in the way, or a plank, it may be, has been left across the rails; a shrill, unearthly scream issues from the engine, piercing the ears of the offending workmen, and scarcely less alarming the innocent passengers. Many a foolish head is popped out of the window, guards and brakesmen busily apply their drags, and the driver reverses the machinery of his engine, and exerts its utmost force, though in vain, to stop the motion. The whole mass fairly slides upon the rail with the momentum due to some sixty or seventy tons. Then comes the moment of suspense, when nothing remains to be done, and it is uncertain whether the obstacle will be removed in time. It is so; and the huge mass slides by with scarcely an inch to spare. Off go the brakes, round fly the wheels, the steam is again turned on, and the train rolls forward at its wonted speed, until smoothly and silently it glides into the appointed stopping-place. Then come the opening of doors, and the bustle of luggage-porters. Coaches, cabs, omnibuses, vehicles of every description, fill and rapidly drive off, until before ten minutes have elapsed the uncouth engine has slunk back into its house, and some hundred passengers, with their luggage, have disappeared like a dream, and the platform is once more left to silence and solitude."

Queen and Judges could please themselves as to whether they went by train or not. But for the mass of Her Majesty's subjects it was fast becoming a case of Hobson's choice. . . .

The forty coaches which had run daily through Northampton were all dead within six months of the opening of the London and Birmingham. Almost every week came a notice that some famous line of coaches had ceased to run. ...

Everyone has heard of the 2000 post-horses that used to be kept in the inns at Hounslow. As early as April, 1842, a daily paper reports: "At the formerly flourishing village of Hounslow, so great is now the general depreciation of property on account of the transfer of traffic to the railway, that at one of the chief inns is an inscription, 'New milk and cream sold here'; while another announces the profession of the chief occupier as 'mending boots and shoes'." "Maidenhead", writes an Old Roadster, "is now in miserable plight. The glories of 'The Bear', where a good twenty minutes were allowed to the traveller to stow away some three or four shillings' worth of boiled fowls and ham to support his inward man during the night, are fast fading away for ever. This celebrated hostelry is about to be permanently closed as a public inn." Here is a yet more important effect of railways, according to the *Berks Chronicle*: "The heath and birch-broom trade, which used to be of very considerable extent at Reading Michaelmas Fair, and from which many of the industrious poor profited, has fallen away to a mere nothing. When the dairymen had their cheese brought up the old road they used to load the wagons home with brooms; but now, since the mode of conveyance is changed to the railway, it does not answer the purpose of the dealers to pay the carriage for them by that mode of transit."

Nor were coachmen, innkeepers, and broom-cutters the only people who suffered from the change. The shopkeepers of Ashton-under-Lyne, Stockport, and other small towns round Manchester complained bitterly that their customers all went into Manchester to shop, and that they were left to sit idle. Canals had in some places fared no better. By the opening of the Manchester and Leeds line the value of the Rochdale Canal shares came down in two years from £150 to £40. The shares of the Calder and Hebble Navigation had been worth 500 guineas; they were now being freely offered at about £180.

On the other hand, new trades were springing up on all sides. One day it is recorded in a Liverpool paper that a Cheshire farmer has ceased to make cheese, and is supplying the Liverpool market with fresh milk, "conveying this nutritious article from a distance of over 43 miles, and delivering the same by half-past eight in the morning". Another day readers are startled to learn that wet fish from the East coast ports can be delivered fresh in Birmingham or Derby. A tenant on the Holkham estate bears witness to the advantage of a railway to the Norfolk farmers. His fat cattle, so he said, used to be driven up to London by road. They were a fortnight on the journey, and when they reached Smithfield had lost three guineas in value, besides all the cost out of pocket. As soon as the Eastern Counties line was opened he would send his cattle through by train in twelve hours. The farmers, in fact, seem to have taken kindly to the new order of things. For the great Christmas cattle market in 1843 the London and Birmingham brought up in two days 263 wagons, containing 1085 oxen, 1420 sheep and 93 pigs.

A good many of the notices remind us that the experience of the last few years is not the first revolution that the English agricultural interest has encountered and survived. Under the heading, "A New Trade in Darlington", the *Great Northern Advertiser* chronicles: "During the past month (November, 1843) vast numbers of sheep have been slaughtered by the Darlington butchers, and have been sent *per* railway to London." Here is a second from the same neighbourhood: "The 'Butter Wives' frequenting Barnard Castle market were not a little surprised on Wednesday se'nnight to discover that, through the facilities offered by the railways, a London dealer had been induced to buy butter in their market for the supply of the cockneys, and in consequence the price went up 2d. per pound immediately. This rise, however, did not deter the agent from purchasing, and 2000 pounds of butter were quickly bought, sold and packed off for the great Metropolis, where it would again be exhibited, and sold to the London retailers by five o'clock on Friday morning." And here is the result: "At a meeting of the Statistical Society a paper was read on the agricultural prices of the parishes of Middlesex.... The writer proceeded to say that the railway had greatly affected prices in the cattle market at Southall, and had occasioned much discontent among the farmers, who complained that, in consequence of the facility that it afforded for the rapid transfer of stock from one county to another, they had been deprived of the advantages which they formerly possessed from their proximity to London. Five hundred head of sheep and 100 head of cattle had upon more than one occasion been suddenly introduced into the market from the West of England, and prices had been proportionably forced down."

But, as a rule, on the great through lines, in 1843, everything except passenger traffic was a very secondary affair. The Great Western was earning £13,000 a week from passengers and only £3000 from goods. On the London and Birmingham the goods receipts were much the same, but the passengers returned some £15,000. On this latter line, for the first five months of its existence, the passenger receipts were about £130,000, while the total goods earnings were £2225 9s. 3d. On the South Western the proportion was six to one; on the Brighton more than seven to one; on the South Eastern more than ten to one. Even on the Midland Counties and North Midland, where nowadays passengers are far less important than goods and minerals, five-eighths of the whole receipts came from the "coaching" traffic. Of course there were exceptions; on a purely mineral line, such as the Taff Vale, the goods receipts were five-sixths of the total, while on the Newcastle and Carlisle they were two-thirds. Still, taking England as a whole, the goods traffic was only about a quarter of the total....

The express and through trains on the great lines, such as the Great Western or the London and Birmingham, were timed to run at something between 20 and 30 miles an hour. From London to Bristol, for example, 118 miles, the train took four hours and a quarter.... The 6 a.m. from Euston, described as "a quick train throughout", reached Liverpool, *via* Birmingham and Newton Junction (210 miles) at 4 p.m., and Darlington, *via* Derby and York, at 7 p.m. . . . The *Newcastle Courant* chronicles, as "a remarkable proof of the wonders of steam travelling", that Lord Palmerston's mare Iliona ran at Newcastle on Wednesday, and at Winchester on Friday. "The distance thus travelled was nearly 400 miles, and the time $32\frac{1}{2}$ hours, of which between nine and ten were spent in London. . . ."

These times would have been much faster had it not been for the long and frequent stoppages. There was a stoppage for refreshments at Wolverton, half-way from London to Birmingham, and another at Falkirk, on the 47-mile journey between

Edinburgh and Glasgow. When they were actually in motion, trains could go fast enough. We have already mentioned a run from Southampton to London at the rate of over 43 miles an hour. A special run from Liverpool to Birmingham with American despatches, 97 miles in 150 minutes, was scarcely slower, and the Grand Junction was a line more famed for dividends than for speed. Lord Eglinton's trainer, in order to be in time for a race, took a "special" from Manchester to Liverpool, 30 miles in 40 minutes. . . . Another "special" ran from Derby, 40 miles in 66 minutes, of which 16 were spent in three stoppages. A third, from Brighton to Croydon, 40 miles in 50 minutes. And there abundant proof that the light trains of those days (two smal coaches and a guard's van probably) could, if necessary, get along nearly as fast as our own ponderous expresses, which must be not unfrequently quite twenty times as heavy. . . .

It was a not uncommon custom, if any important person missed his train, to charter a "special" and start in pursuit. With good luck he might count on overtaking a train which had only had half an hour's "law", before it had got much more than half the distance between London and Brighton. On one occasion the Secretary of the London and Greenwich Railway, having missed the train, mounted an engine, and started in such hot pursuit, that he ran into the tail carriage with sufficient violence to break the legs of one or two passengers.

The *Edinburgh Chronicle* must take the responsibility of vouching the truth of the story that follows: "A gentleman, on urgent business in Glasgow, arrived at the Edinburgh station on Monday morning just as the 9 o'clock train had started. A special engine was engaged, and, starting at half-past 9 o'clock, overtook the train at Falkirk at 10 minutes past 10 o'clock, running the 23 miles in 40 minutes, 15 minutes of which time was occupied in stopping at three of the stations; the 23 miles were thus traversed in 25 minutes, being at the enormous speed of 55 miles in an hour." More remarkable yet is the statement of a correspondent of the *Railway Times*, who gives his name and address as "George Wall, Sheffield, 7th December, 1843": "I have frequently timed trains to 60 to 65 seconds to the mile, and on one occasion a train ran 3 miles in 53, 54, and 55 seconds respectively, giving an average of 54 seconds per mile, or $59\frac{1}{2}$ miles per hour. (*Sic* in original.

In fact it is 66⅔.) In this last case two other passengers marked the time, along with me, by our own watches, and we were all agreed." It perhaps helps us to understand why trains, which could travel on occasion as fast as this, were not timed faster in everyday working, to read that among the indispensable appliances on a railway were included tracks on which to convey broken-down engines, and also a suggestion that a trolley should always be attached in front of the engine, that it might be ready at hand to fetch assistance in case of a break-down.

But high speed was impossible over any long distance except when extraordinary preparations had been made beforehand. Even three years after this time it was looked upon as a remarkable feat that Mr Allport travelled from Sunderland to London and back – with relays of "specials" in waiting at Darlington, York, Normanton, Derby, Rugby, and Wolverton – 600 miles in 15 hours. Not only were the engines too small to run more than 20 or 30 miles without taking in water, but there were numerous spots where the permanent way was not wholly to be trusted. . . .

The Prince Consort was not the only person who protested against over-rapid travelling. The newspapers are full of complaints of dangerous speed. One correspondent suggests that notice boards shall be fixed all along the line, prescribing the due speed for each stretch, lest the engine-driver should be tempted to exceed the bounds of prudence. Another proposed to forbid all speed in excess of 20 miles an hour exclusive of stoppages, and "to insure this not being exceeded there should be a method adopted by which the engine would give notice of the same to every passenger, that they might report upon it. I am prepared to produce a plan by which this can be effected. The whistle might be blown (*i.e.*, utter a slight sound) at every *quarter* or *half-mile*, being worked by the driving wheel. And this arrangement would be attended with another advantage, viz., in a fog. It might then sound to its full power, giving not only notice of its approach, but some idea of the speed; and, if generally understood that the whistle of the down train sounded six seconds, whilst that of the up train uttered its note only three, there would be no mistake as to which train was approaching."

from THE RAILWAYS OF ENGLAND *5th edn. 1900*

The Mania and the Crash

JOHN FRANCIS

It was no ordinary time. The pulse of the people, fierce and excited, grew by what it fed on; and as every new project unfolded its prospects, it demanded a greater stimulus and a more extended action. If the ledger was then the bible of the people of England, and if gold was then truly their god, let it be remembered that nations have their fevers as individuals; that popular delusions take all forms and features; and that in a commercial country like Great Britain, it must ever take that which agrees most with the genius of the people. Let it be remembered, also, that the base, bad acts . . . were the work of the scum on the surface; that much of the trickery and treachery which prevailed was performed by men whose very avocation was to swindle, and that, had it not assumed this form, it must have taken some other, less public but not less pernicious.

The evil which was performed was not by the men whose names belong to our merchantocracy. In the heat of the moment they joined the crowd, and the throng carried them away. But it is due to many who sanctioned the lines which bore their names, to proclaim thus publicly and positively that they could not stay the iniquities they saw; that the majority always carry the day, and that the minority were generally composed of the good men and true, to whose names the faith of the shareholders was given. Mr Glyn expressly stated on one occasion that a particular minority, composed of London and Birmingham directors engaged in another line, were disgusted with the proceedings of the majority, but were powerless to prevent them.

These things must not be forgotten in extenuation, and allowance must be made for the frenzy which, when it seized on the nation, scarcely spared the few faithful in the city.

The gambling was as prevalent in the provinces as in the capital, but there was no method in their madness. In Leeds it absolutely raged. In no town throughout the country did it attain so fatal a form. In no town were men more easily duped by the falsehoods which it paid to promulgate. In lines known to be

95

worthless, in which no business was doing, if a rumour were judiciously spread that Hudson was after them, the Stock Exchange was in a ferment, and prices rose enormously, to the loss of the holder when the contradiction came. The same shares which were selling in London at £21, were sold in Leeds at £25 10s., and in one company where all the deposits were spent and the bill was rejected, were at £4 10s. premium. Lines which could not possibly pay more than three per cent, and which only promised five per cent in their prospectuses, were at a premium, and a price so heavy as completely to preclude all hope of paying so good a dividend as consols. In a third, the construction of which had, before the parliamentary committee, been proved to be next to impracticable, the shares were sold at £11 premium. While the Leeds and West Riding Junction, rejected by the legislative body, and with all its deposits expended, were freely bought at £7 10s.

The irritation was visible in the streets. The thoroughfares near the Stock Exchanges . . . were almost impassable. The purlieus were like fairs. Crowds of anxious brokers, and yet more anxious speculators, with earnest faces and excited minds, literally ran and rushed about the place. The cautious merchant and the keen manufacturer were equally unable to resist the speculation. It spread among them like a leprosy. It ruined alike the innocent and the guilty. It perilled many a humble home; it agitated many a princely dwelling. Men hastened to be rich, and were ruined. They bought largely; they subscribed eagerly; they forsook their counting-houses for companies: if successful they continued in their course, and if the reverse, they too often added to the misery of the homes they had already desolated, by destroying themselves. . . .

A return called for by the House of Commons of the dealers in railway undertakings, forms a very remarkable blue book. The noble who in the pride of blood and birth had ever held traffic in contempt, was there blazoned as a trader. The priest who at his desk prayed to be delivered from the mammon of unrighteousness, was there revealed as seeking in the city to sell his scrip at a premium. The lawyer, who, madly risking his money, sold the property of his client to meet his losses; the physician who perilled the savings of a life and the well-being of a family; the chemist who forsook his laboratory for a new form of the philosopher's stone; the banker who in the city and the senate denounced all speculation as illegitimate; the deacon of the meeting-house; the warden of the church; the Jew, the Quaker, the saint, the sinner, were all down in that huge condemning volume. There were nine hundred lawyers, and there were three hundred and sixty-four persons connected with the banking interest who subscribed contracts for above £2,000. One solicitor alone risked £154,000; one London banker was down for £240,000 and six country bankers for £100,000; nine others for £50,000; and seventy-seven more of that large and respectable body for £10,000 each. But this was legitimate compared with the fact that two hundred and fifty-seven "reverend" and "very reverend" clergymen signed their names to contracts, two of which were for £26,000, three for £20,000, six for £15,000, while the remainder were for sums varying from £15,000 to £2,000. There were one hundred and fifty-seven members of parliament, of whom one signed for £291,000, one for £250,000, one for £178,000, while the remainder were down for sums which must have influenced their feelings to a degree which might have influenced their votes.

It may thus be seen from most undeniable evidence that there has been no extravagance in the past description; and it is an unquestionable fact, that there was scarcely a family in England which was not directly or indirectly interested in the fortunes of the rail. But a change was coming. The day of triumph was over, and the night of trial was at hand.

On Thursday, 16th October, 1845, the Bank of England raised the rate of interest; and the effect was immediate. On that day men looked darkly and doubtfully at each other; on Friday there was a considerable cessation of bargains, and on Saturday the alarm commenced. The news passed from the capital to every province in the empire, that there was a panic in the share market. From London to Liverpool and from Liverpool to Edinburgh the intelligence spread. Money was scarce; the price of stock and scrip lowered; the confidence of the people was broken, and the vision of a dark future on every face. Advertisements were suddenly withdrawn from the papers; names of note were seen no more as provisional committee men; distrust followed the merchant to the mart, and the jobber to the Exchange. The new schemes ceased to be regarded; applications ceased to be forwarded; premiums were either lowered or ceased to exist.

D

Bankers looked anxiously to the accounts of their customers; bill brokers scrutinized their securities; and every man was suspicious of his neighbour. But the distrust was not confined to projected lines. Established railways felt the shock, and were reduced in value. Consols fell one-and-a-half per cent. Exchequer bills declined in price, and other markets sympathized. The people had awoke from their dream, and trembled. It was a national alarm. Words are weak to express the fears and feelings which prevailed. There was no village too remote to escape the shock, and there was probably no house in town, some occupant of which did not shrink from the morrow. The statesman started to find his new bank charter so sadly and so suddenly tried. The peer who had so thoughtlessly adventured, saw ruin opening to his view. Men hurried with bated breath to their brokers. The allottee was uneasy and suspicious. The provisional committee man grew pale at his fearful responsibility. Directors ceased to boast their blushing honours, and promoters saw their expected profits evaporate. Shares which the previous week were a fortune, were the next a fatality to their owner. The reputed shareholders were not to be found when they were wanted. Provisional committee men were not more easy of access.

One railway advertised the names and addresses of thirty – none of whom were to be heard of at the residences ascribed to them. Letters were returned to the post-office day after day. Nor is this to be wondered at, when it is said that on one projected line only £60 was received for deposits which should have yielded £700,000.

It was proved in the committee of the House of Commons that one subscription list was formed of "lame ducks of the Alley"; and that in another several of the directors, including the chairman, had also altered their several subscriptions to the amount of £100,000 the very evening on which the list was deposited, and that five shillings a man was given to any one who would sign for a certain number of shares.

An immediate change was felt in every market throughout England. In Liverpool the transactions were nominal. At Leeds, where four share marts and two hundred brokers had been maintained, the effect was similar; while at most of the small towns, the stock exchanges and the speculators shrunk into the littleness from which they sprung.

Nothing marked more decidedly the crisis which had arrived than the fact that every one hastened to disown railways. Gentlemen who had been buried in prospectuses, whose names and descriptions had been published under every variation that could fascinate the public, who had figured as committee men and received the precious guineas for their attendance, were eager to assure the world that they were ignorant of this great transgression. Men who a month before had boasted of the large sums they had made by scrip, sent advertisements to papers denying their responsibility, or appealed to the Lord Mayor to protect their characters. Members of Parliament who had remained quiet under the infliction while it was somewhat respectable, fell back upon their privileges when they saw their purses were in danger. There is no doubt that an unauthorized use of names was one feature of fraudulent companies and that amid a list of common names it was thought a distinguished one might pass unnoticed. The complaints, therefore, of those who were thus unceremoniously treated were just, but the great mass of denials emanated from persons who knowingly encountered the risk, and meanly shrunk from the danger.

It is the conviction of those who are best informed that no other panic was ever so fatal to the middle class. It reached every hearth, it saddened every heart in the metropolis. Entire families were ruined. There was scarcely an important town in England but what beheld some wretched suicide. Daughters delicately nurtured went out to seek their bread. Sons were recalled from academies. Households were separated: homes were desecrated by the emissaries of the law. There was a disruption of every social tie. The debtors' jails were peopled with promoters; Whitecross-street was filled with speculators; and the Queen's Bench was full to overflowing. Men who had lived comfortably and independently found themselves suddenly responsible for sums they had no means of paying. In some cases they yielded their all, and began the world anew; in others they left the country for the Continent, laughed at their creditors, and defied pursuit. One gentleman was served with four hundred writs. A peer similarly pressed, when offered to be relieved from all liabilities for £15,000, betook himself to his yacht, and forgot in the beauties of the Mediterranean the difficulties which had surrounded him. Another gentleman who, having nothing to lose, surrendered himself to his creditors, was a

director of more than twenty lines. A third was provisional committee man to fifteen. A fourth, who commenced life as a printer,
who became an insolvent in 1832 and a bankrupt in 1837, who had
negotiated partnerships, who had arranged embarrassed affairs,
who had collected debts, and turned his attention to anything, did
not disdain also to be a railway promoter, a railway secretary, a
railway director, or to spell his name in a dozen various ways.

By the suddenness of the crisis, the cunning of promoters and
provisional committee men fell upon themselves. They had
delayed answering applications until it was too late to make a
profit; they had meant to reserve a sufficient number to make their
own fortunes; but when they saw premiums give way to discounts,
when there was no price quoted for their scrip, when the public
looked shy and brokers would not look at all, they were most
liberal in issuing letters of allotment, and most unjust in demand-
ing payment. Those who had requested fifty shares expecting five
– about the proportion hitherto granted – found they were gra-
ciously allowed all they demanded. To pay would have been ruin.
Not to pay was to be involved in law.

Such was the melancholy close of the high hopes of the
memorable spring and summer of 1845.

from A HISTORY OF THE ENGLISH RAILWAY *1851*

The Battle of the Gauges

JACK SIMMONS

The railways had not been constructed to a single gauge. In the
early days several had been tried. The 4 ft. 8½ in. of the northern
coal lines, adopted in the days of horse traction, had been used by
the Stephensons for all the lines they were concerned with, and
it ruled without question throughout the North of England and,
with trifling exceptions, in Scotland. But as engineers began to
think about railways in the thirties, that gauge encountered its
critics. No doubt it had been found suitable, by long experience,
for horses working on colliery lines. That in no way proved its
fitness for the steam locomotive. If the gauge were somewhat

wider there would be more room, in the engine itself for its mechanism and in the vehicles it drew. There would be greater stability in running, and substantial economy in operation. These arguments were advanced most forcibly by the young I. K. Brunel and accepted by his employers the Great Western Railway, whose line was accordingly built, on Brunel's advice, to the gauge of 7 ft. The theory behind the adoption of this gauge was sound (though it missed its full effect through failing to provide greater height as well as greater width between the rails); and it impressed outside observers. Naturally, the lines connected with the Great Western adopted the 7 ft. gauge. But, away on the other side of London, the directors of the Eastern Counties Railway at once decided that their line must be built to a broad gauge too. Their engineer, John Braithwaite, thought that 7 ft. was too much. A compromise of 5 ft. was therefore determined on. The line was built to that gauge from London to Colchester and, by an associated company, to Bishop's Stortford. When the Irish trunk railways came to be established – very much more on the initiative of the State than in Great Britain – a gauge of 5 ft. 3 in. was adopted. It remains the standard in Ireland to this day.

Thus railways of three different gauges were under construction in England in the 1830s. Since neither Government nor Parliament had any conception of a railway system, the inconvenience of this multiplicity of gauges passed unnoticed until broad- and narrow-gauge lines began to arrive at the same point, as they did for example at Gloucester in 1845. Passengers then began to complain of the annoyance of having to change trains; traders of the damage that their goods sustained in transhipment. By this time the Great Western company and its allies were extending their lines far and wide – westwards into South Wales, northwards to Birmingham, Shrewsbury, and Chester, threatening even an invasion of Manchester. There was serious danger of a multiplication of points like Gloucester over half England and Wales. Only Parliament could avert that nuisance, by insisting on a national uniformity of gauge.

It was already too late. All that Parliament felt able to do – after an inquiry held at the very height of the speculation of 1845-46 – was to lay down that 4 ft. 8½ in. should be regarded as the standard gauge, to which all new railways should conform unless it

specifically permitted the use of a different one. This was obviously
a compromise, adopted under the conflicting pressures of two
powerful vested interests. But before it is condemned for its
feebleness, two things ought to be said. In the first place, even
though the imposition of a uniform gauge was evidently desirable,
that was asking more of Parliament than could realistically be
expected: for this crisis in the railway world coincided with the
bigger crisis in politics that arose from the repeal of the Corn
Laws. No stable Government, capable of so ruthless a policy,
could possibly be formed. Secondly, the working-out of this compromise proved better than it promised to be on paper. In effect
the spread of the broad gauge was now stopped. It advanced no
further to the north or east. Even within its own kingdom some
compromise was possible by the laying down of a third rail,
creating a "mixed" gauge, over which narrow- and broad-gauge
trains could both be worked. In the end the Great Western company came to feel the inconvenience of its unique position. Length
after length of its line was first "mixed" and then "narrowed",
until at last it was decided to do away with the 7 ft. gauge altogether, and it disappeared in 1892.

from THE RAILWAYS OF BRITAIN *1961*

Racing to Scotland

ROGER FULFORD

In this country the most celebrated railway races were those in 1888 and 1895. A traveller from London to Scotland had then – as of course he still has today – a choice of three routes. There was the line from Euston through Rugby and Crewe and up the north-west of England to Carlisle. There was the line from King's Cross through Peterborough and York along the north-east coast to Newcastle and Berwick. The third route followed a middle course from St Pancras. This route went past Sheffield and Leeds to Carlisle. For a number of reasons it was slower than the other two. But the wise traveller who did not wish to be hustled or crowded, and who was capable of enjoying the scenery after Leeds – easily the finest to be seen from any railway train in England – would (and even now should) use St Pancras. Today that line is largely reserved for goods trains and cattle trains. How silly to keep what is most beautiful for the unheeding eyes of sheep and bullocks. And to herd human beings along the humdrum routes to the east and the west.

Those routes – the east and the west – took about the same time to Edinburgh. They were therefore ideal for racing. Ever since the east coast route opened in the 1850s there had been constant rivalry. But warfare – open and declared – first broke out in the summer of 1888. In those days it took about 9 hours from London to Edinburgh by the east route and about 10 by the west. The racing began at the end of July and lasted until the middle of August. A train from Euston along the west route made the journey in 7 hours 38 minutes. That was nearly $2\frac{1}{2}$ hours quicker than before racing began, and three-quarters of an hour quicker than you could get to Edinburgh by the Mid-day Scot [in 1951]. The east coast route won the race – and it was a superb performance – by doing the journey in 7 hours $26\frac{3}{4}$ minutes. That was $1\frac{1}{2}$ hours speed-up as a result of racing and 10 minutes quicker than the Flying Scotsman in 1951. Honour satisfied, the railway companies agreed to a truce – $7\frac{3}{4}$ hours for the east; 8 hours for the west. But like many another truce it was uneasy. Seven years

later hostilities began again – this time much more exciting because
the race was run by night, and was fought out to Aberdeen –
almost 140 miles further than the race in 1888.

The struggle began in the middle of July, 1895, and here I
should explain why these races took place in high summer. The
reason for this was that the railway companies were fighting to
capture the sporting public going to Scotland for the grouse
shooting. If it is not offensive to the memory of these long-dead
sportsmen, I should say that they were the most valuable passenger
traffic on the English railways – a prize really worth winning. They
travelled with perhaps their wives – certainly a female companion –
plenty of servants, dogs, guns and luggage. Above all, they paid
their lavish way in golden sovereigns, and out of their own poc-
kets. . . . They were ideal railway passengers. They were not very
politely known in official railway circles as "The Grouse Traffic".

The race of 1895 began quietly, and the first person to realize
that it was on was a clergyman. On Monday, July 16th, the parson
was strolling round Euston station. He was startled to see huge
blue posters round the entrance which announced: "The 8 p.m.
from Euston will now reach Aberdeen at 7 a.m. – an acceleration
of one hour." The clergyman knew what was what, and he bustled
down the road to King's Cross. He arrived just in time to see a
high official of that railway, resplendent in top hat and with the
gleam of battle in his pince-nez, boarding the train for York,
where he was going to make arrangements for the east to answer
the challenge from the west.

One of the difficulties in arranging these races was that the
trains had to travel over the lines of several different companies.
From Euston you ran as far as Carlisle on the London and North
Western. From Carlisle you went to Aberdeen by the Caledonian
Railway – an outstandingly lovely line with brilliant, blue engines.
The King's Cross route was more complicated. The Great
Northern took you to York. There the North Eastern took over
to Edinburgh, and from Edinburgh the North British took on to
Aberdeen. Although the carriages ran right through from London
to Aberdeen, each change of company meant a change of engine.
The advantage to the west route of having only a single change of
company at Carlisle was considerable. To make up for this the
advantage of geography lay slightly with the east route.

A railway map shows that after Carlisle and Newcastle the two routes to Aberdeen converge – gradually but quite perceptibly. They finally meet at a place called Kinnaber junction – just beyond Montrose. From there they travel over the same line to Aberdeen. Whoever reached Kinnaber first had won the race. The man in the signal box at Kinnaber was a member of the *Caledonian* staff – a man whose sympathies were naturally with the west, and he had the crucial task of letting through the victor.

On July 22nd – that is, a week after the posters had appeared at Euston – the east coast route advertised that *their* train would reach Aberdeen at 6.45 – a quarter of an hour before the west. The authorities at Euston were rather modern in their ideas of warfare. They believed in a fierce thrust without any declaration of war. They accordingly said nothing but knocked 25 minutes off their time and slipped into Aberdeen at 6.35 – ten minutes before the east coast train. A week later the east coast advertised that their train would arrive at 6.25. Again the west coast authorities maintained a sphinx-like silence, but timed their train five minutes earlier. In fact the west coast train steamed into Aberdeen on July 30th at a minute to six – that is, 10 hours for the trip of well over 500 miles.

The west coast had, during this period of the race, a huge advantage. They could control their stopping time all the way to Carlisle. Nothing holds back a train's time more than stops in which luggage vans have to be cleared, nervous passengers shepherded on and off the train. The west coast trains stopped only at Crewe between London and Carlisle. The staff at Crewe did a magnificent job in clearing the vans and pushing on the passengers like greased lightning. One evening a porter, shepherding an old lady into a comfortable seat, was carried off to Carlisle. If the train "made" time between London and Crewe, the station master at Crewe got it away even if it was far in advance of its time.

The east coast could not do this so easily because after York the other companies – that is the North Eastern and the North British – insisted on keeping to the time-table. The North British – with the respect for authority which is perhaps a characteristic of the Scot – were absolutely maddening. On one occasion they held the east coast express back for nine minutes in Waverley station,

D*

Edinburgh. But by very tactful handling the authorities at King's Cross were eventually able to persuade these other companies to pay no attention to tiresome things like time-tables. Consequently when this was done there was a tremendous race on the night of August 15th. At Kinnaber the bell in the signal box rang to announce the arrival of the west train precisely one minute before it rang to announce the arrival of the east train. On the following night both bells rang together. The signal-man – and it will be remembered that he was a west man, a Caledonian servant – gave the road to the rival company. A really fine example of the sporting spirit shown throughout. Because it should not be overlooked that these races were a great strain not only on the drivers but on station and signal-box staff over both routes.

On the night of August 21st the east coast companies carried their train through in 8 hours 40 minutes. They were at Aberdeen at 4.40 a.m. The west coast train arrived $14\frac{1}{2}$ minutes later. On the following night the west coast, with a train stripped for racing, did the journey in the astonishing time of 8 hours 32 minutes. The race was over. Today the journey by either route takes something in the neighbourhood of 12 hours. As we compare these times we might say with the great Roman of old: "Oh, what a fall was there, my countrymen!"

During the height of battle some sharp things were said. Supporters of the west complained that the sleeping cars on the east were not heated and had no attendants. And they also complained that at Waverley station, Edinburgh, where there was just time for a snack, the eggs were always stale. Supporters of the east coast replied with a dirty thrust. They said that the arrangements on the west route for the engine to take up water while travelling were dangerous, and might cause an accident. This was dirty – really a blow below the belt, because the public were easily frightened and, ever since the days of Dickens, had believed that high speeds were the cause of smashes. The railway authorities did their best to counter this by issuing a statement that a speed of 70 m.p.h. was not enough to spill a cup of coffee and they argued that this was due to gyrostatic action which explained why a bicycle is steadier when ridden fast. . . .

But not all the public was convinced. There were the health bores who argued that increased speed meant increased vibration which was most wearing. Every train to Aberdeen, they argued, should include long stops so that passengers could have time to wash, and stroll along the platform, thereby restoring their shattered nerves and saving themselves hours of suffering. A gentleman actually wrote to the papers as follows: "I had to travel in a racing train and I reached Aberdeen in 10 hours. The oscillation was so great that I felt sick. Two of my servants *were* sick. A friend of mine only saved himself from sickness by a dose of brandy." Happy the traveller who had such an excellent excuse for a glass of brandy.

Night after night large crowds collected at King's Cross and at Euston to cheer the racers on their journey, and at each stop they were similarly encouraged. But the curious thing was that the companies never publicly altered their timetables and never openly admitted that a race was in progress. At a meeting of the North Western shareholders the chairman said: "There is no such *thing* as a race." He then added the cryptic comment: "But our company will not be last in it."

No doubt it is easy to say that the race to the north was pointless. Certainly the travellers who arrived at Aberdeen at 5 o'clock in the morning, and then had to wait two hours for breakfast, were not always enthusiastic. Yet it was a fine and spectacular advertisement for British railways. In a single night we doubly smashed the record (held by the Americans with their train from New York to Buffalo) for the fastest train in the world. It was a superb advertisement for the small engines of those days, for the rolling stock and for the permanent way. Above all, it was a tribute to the endurance and steadiness of British railwaymen. The highest speed of these trains has of course been exceeded in the twentieth century, but to have maintained such speeds for that distance, with the equipment then available, was an achievement which will never be surpassed.

from B.B.C. BROADCAST *July 1951*

North and South in 1889

E. FOXWELL and T. FARRER

The naturalist is still compelled to maintain that our railways south of Thames are, from the public point of view, quite another species from those to the north of that narrow stream. The traveller who cabs across from Waterloo to Euston, from Victoria to St Pancras, or from London Bridge to King's Cross, is in each case moving to a higher railway atmosphere, where the time-bills are meant to be taken in good faith, where the quality of the service is superb, and where we can rely on its being the rule, not the exception to carry out what has been contracted for. We say adieu (or *au diable*) to the "cheery stoicism" of that South-Western terminus, where incoming trains arrive at their own sweet time and place, to the subtle irony of the Brighton with its "fast" and very "limited" style, to the South Eastern with its fore-ordained chronic block in sight of port, to the Chatham with its hand-brakes; and we alight upon platforms of common sense, where efficiency is high, where only fares are low. Good-bye to the sportive tricks of southern complexity; now we come to stern simplicity, which merely says and does. Only the deeds are first class, though most of the passengers are third.

The southern lines form a group which must be called a different species if only because they are wanting in that essential characteristic *punctuality*. Of course there are good reasons – though bad excuses – for the fact, but the unpunctuality is none the less a monstrosity. Trains which never (well, hardly ever) throughout the year arrive decently near their time are maddening to everyone except the officials; there is no point in them, they have lost their savour, and are as different from the real article as a stale egg from a fresh one. Besides this lapse in regard to the crowning virtue, there are other reasons why the southern companies are justly unpopular. They pay very good dividends, yet charge exorbitant fares – what a contrast to the Great Eastern! But the *South Western* must be exempted from this particular reproach; it deserves peculiar respect for upholding universal and unconditional third class amid such demoralizing companionship, though its first and

second class fares are high. On the South Eastern we seem to hear
the old greeting of the highwayman, "Your money or your life";
for unless the victim be prepared to empty his purse he must
adjourn to the slow trains of that corporation, and life is not worth
living there. Then there is a feeling that in this part of England the
companies are leagued against the public, because here flourishes
the un-English system of "pooling" the receipts from traffic to
competitive places. Compare the number of express trains run between *e.g. Cambridge* and London by Great Eastern and Great
Northern with those enjoyed by Portsmouth or Dover; in the latter
case each company takes from its rival part of its motive to exert
itself, while the two northern companies, adopting the grosser
form of competition pure and simple, do the very best they can.
The result is that Cambridge has fifteen times as many third class
"express" journeys as either of the southern instances.

But we must not paint things blacker than they are. There is
something to be set off against all this abuse. In some respects the
southern companies put the northern ones to shame. Though their
trains run shorter distances than any, they are provided with the
best communication between passenger and guard – not with that
satirical "cord" which undulates so gracefully beneath the eaves of
the carriages on our leading lines. Again, it is on a southern line –
the Brighton – that we find the greatest advance in the lighting of
carriages. Not only on the Pullman cars, but in the third class of
its commonest suburban trains, the electric light is gradually
spreading, so that the smallest print may be read with ease.

Where the southern lines however most excel the northern ones
is in the matter of *Sunday* arrangements. They make the best of this
terrible day, not the worst, and deal with conflicting interests in a
sensible way. To a layman fond of fresh air there is great satisfaction in watching the volley of "cheap seaside" trains fired off by the
Brighton Company every Sunday morning (in summer) carrying
thousands of the "masses" out of London and alcohol to the
healthier air of Littlehampton, Bognor, Worthing, Brighton,
Eastbourne or Hastings. These trains are practically express, and
charge one-third the ordinary third class fare. The Brighton is the
largest benefactor in this respect, but similar praise is due to the
South Eastern and Chatham for their corresponding facilities to
Ramsgate, Margate, and the Kentish coast in general. The South

Western is very genial, for it starts a "cheap" train at the pleasant hour of half-past nine, and, running at 35 miles an hour inclusive, gives seven hours at Bournemouth before the equally quick return home. On Sunday these four southern companies show in their best colours, and offer a happy contrast to that gloomy dog-in-the-manger policy with which the northern lines disfigure the day.

No doubt these distinguishing traits, both good and bad, owe their existence in some measure to the intimate relation in which our southern companies stand to the Continental lines; in daily working partnership with them they cannot help adopting some of their ways and points of view. Unfortunately our southerners have failed to imitate their Continental brethren in that one point where they are most admirable, punctuality. From Mentone to Calais is 875 miles, but the through carriage will almost invariably arrive at Calais at its schedule time, and then on the remaining section of 100 miles to London the passengers will lose a quarter of an hour or more. We prefer "this direct simplicity of the French mind" to the pretentious promise which cannot be fulfilled. There are, of course, sufficient reasons why it is much harder for an ordinary English express to be punctual than for one on the Continent (*e.g.* third-class passengers, heaps of luggage, booking allowed at the last moment, the barbarity of the English custom-houses, and so on); at the same time unpunctuality is such a blot that wherever it occurs it obliterates all the good features of the service (for *finis coronat opus*), and disarms us of effective repartee.

Another good word may be thrown in for these unpopular companies, and that is to praise them for the plucky way in which they carry on their traffic during *fogs*. When an English railway is hard pressed it rises to the occasion and shows the stuff it is made of, and we are never so proud of our southern lines as during dense weather. Thus in the early weeks of January 1889, when for eight or nine consecutive days the fog was so thick at times that a pedestrian could not see the curb of the pavement on which he walked, it was a truly English experience to stand on the platform of such a station as Norwood Junction, and hear the Brighton expresses thunder through with not so much as half the length of a single carriage visible at once. The pluck and endurance exhibited by obscure *employés* whenever "fogging" is the order of the day are beyond words; an unappreciative public is whirled up to its office snug and warm, and prefers to expend its admiration on those scarlet-coated heroes who were lucky enough to receive a scratch in the Soudan and a paragraph in the London papers.

from EXPRESS TRAINS *1889*

The Last Main Line

JOHN PENDLETON

The traditions of fierce Parliamentary fighting in the early days of railway construction were revived in the session of 1891, when Sir Edward Watkin, one of the busiest and most versatile of men, not content with writing the *Life of Alderman Cobden of Manchester*, with discovering new coalfields, with buying Snowdon, with making arrangements for the erection of a new Tower of Babel, and with pegging away at his Channel Tunnel project, strove, on behalf of the Sheffield Company, to get sanction for the construction of the new trunk line to London. The railway, it was proposed, should be practically an extension from the southern terminus of the Manchester, Sheffield and Lincolnshire Railway at Annesley, to Nottingham, Leicester, Rugby, and Quainton Road, joining the Metropolitan Company's system, and getting direct access to the capital.

The line, estimated to cost six millions, would, it was urged, not only give important advantages to the industrial centres of Nottingham and Leicester, and open up much rural country, benefiting the agriculturist and the labourer, but would also provide a very necessary outlet for the traffic of the company from the great coalfield of South Yorkshire and East Derbyshire, and for the trade in fish and general merchandise that they had developed at Grimsby. Moreover, it was pointed out that the company, which had been obliged hitherto to "grin and abide" while handing their traffic to other companies, would now "obtain the unrestricted use of $42\frac{1}{2}$ miles of railway all round the metropolis and across the Thames into Kent and Sussex". It was a straightforward and apparently smooth and practicable scheme. The line threatened to interfere with no vital interest. At Nottingham it promised to do the work of a vigorous sanitary reformer and demolish a mass of old property that would be better razed to the ground. In various parts of the route it offered substantial help in business to those engaged in coal, iron, lace, hosiery, and leather.

Nor did it present any engineering difficulty, for with the exception of a tunnel 3,000 yards long south of Rugby the work of construction seemed likely to be easy. But opposition soon roused itself from slumber. In the heart of the country a protest was made by a baronet [who] emphatically declined to allow any railway within a mile of his mansion. The rival railway companies opposed the project; and the Great Northern Railway Company, holding that the Manchester, Sheffield and Lincolnshire Company were breaking the fifty years' agreement between the two companies..., showed persistent hostility to the scheme, fighting it tooth and nail in Committee. Quite apart from the ordinary railway rivalry, strong opposition sprang up. The intention was to make an ample terminus near Baker Street, between Euston and Paddington, to the west of Regent's Park. To get there it was calmly proposed that the line should cut through St John's Wood and skirt or dive beneath Lord's Cricket Ground. The residents of this part of London were indignant. The lovers of cricket throughout the country received a shock.

The Art colony held meetings and signed a petition against the Bill. Thirty acres of their precious land were to be converted into a railway depôt. The line, ruthlessly making its way by valuable residential property, was to be "a line for the conveyance not only of passengers, but of coal, manure, fish, and other abominations". Such vandalism was monstrous, and men of the fame of Mr Alma-Tadema, Mr J. MacWhirter, and Mr Briton Riviere, with many others more or less eminent, took part to protest against it....

In the world of cricket Sir Edward Watkin's audacity filled every player with amazement – some with rage. It was suggested that the railway magnate should be interviewed by W. G. Grace, that he should be confronted by Spofforth, the demon bowler; and that if he did not prove amenable to their persuasiveness, then, as a last resource, Briggs, the Lancashire cricketer – who, according to an amusing article in an evening paper, had been promoted, "owing to the accuracy of his aim", from a professional bowler to an officer of artillery and Dictator of England – should cripple the ruthless baronet. The menace to Lord's was looked upon almost as a national calamity. Everybody who took an interest in cricket, who had been at Lord's in sunshine and shower, or who had read about the wonderful bowling, and batting, and fielding there, hated Sir Edward Watkin, and was prepared, at any hazard, to protect the sacred ground.

The thought of steel rails running through it was repellent. Ballast and sleepers, Bessemer tracks and signal-boxes, banging waggons and the shrieks of engines seemed utterly alien to such a fine open space, hallowed by pleasant memories and by all that was best in cricket. The mind of many a player sped quite a century backward over the bridge of time, and recalled the early days of the Marylebone Club and the difficulty of obtaining the ground; how Thomas Lord, a sort of athletic jack-of-all-sport, bowled for the members of the club and secured a ground in Dorset Square; how the exorbitant rent drove the club to a new ground in North Bank Road, which was ultimately cut up for the Regent's Canal; and how, in 1814, the present site in St John's Wood was procured. So firm and fresh was the turf in Dorset Square that it was taken away and placed on the North Bank ground, and actually removed again to Lord's. . . . It was through this bulwark that the railway iconoclast intended to drive his engines. No such sacrilege had been contemplated since John Ruskin's wrath at the railway invasion of Derbyshire. There were people, indeed, who were inclined to apply the art critic's description of railway-making devastation to Sir Edward Watkin. They said he deserved to be seized by his own navvies and blown up by dynamite.

But, fortunately, no such fearful fate awaited him. Sir Edward Watkin, with the suavity which is one of his most conspicuous characteristics, soothed nearly all the indignant members of the club. He should be sorry indeed, he explained, to despoil such a cherished cricket-ground, and all he proposed to do was to take a narrow strip of the practice-ground, in compensation for which he was prepared to give the club the freehold of eight thousand yards of land near, to lease them four thousand yards, and to tunnel beneath the turf so carefully that there would be no inter-

ference with the play – nay, not a blade of grass would be disturbed. The ire of the club was appeased by the generous proposal;
but the artists remained obdurate, and the Great Northern persisted in their antagonism. Sir Edward Watkin did everything in
his power to propitiate the forces still against him. He was willing
to raise the question of the agreement with the Great Northern
when the line was completed. He was not averse even to an
alternative site for the terminus. But his diplomatic elasticity was
in vain. The Select Committee, after twenty-eight sittings, found
the preamble of the Bill not proved.

The cost of the Parliamentary proceedings was exceedingly
heavy, and some of the shareholders became uneasy as to the
amount they would be called upon to pay, though they were
scarcely so fluttered as certain proprietors of the South Eastern
Railway, for instance, who were once startled by the discovery
that "the solicitor's bill contained 10,000 folios, had occupied
twelve months in taxing before the master, and amounted to
£240,000"; or the shareholders who had to pay the bill after the
Stone and Ruby Railway fight, which was carried on through
sixty-six sittings in the session of 1839, renewed the following
session, and cost £146,000, the promoters being defeated after all.

Sir Edward was not disheartened. He told the shareholders in
July, 1891, that the railway decisions given during the session had
certainly been curious. Sanction had been given to the Lancashire,
Derbyshire and East Coast Railway, "as mad a scheme as was ever
presented to Parliament", and a great and prosperous concern like
the Manchester, Sheffield and Lincolnshire Railway had had its
Bill kicked out. But, he said, with a touch of defiance, the directors
were a stolid class of men who did not know when they were
beaten, convinced as they were that they were travelling on the
right line in the interests of 13,000 shareholders, and they proposed
to go forward with the Bill in the following session. Some of the
cricketers now took alarm again; and at a meeting of the Marylebone Club, Mr Denzil Onslow moved that the Bill should be
opposed at every stage of its progress, inasmuch as he believed
that the parting of any portion of the freehold at Lord's for the
purposes of the railway would be fraught with the greatest danger
to the interests of cricket. The resolution was rejected, however,
by a majority of the members, Sir Henry James reminding the

club that the company's proposals were very fair, and that they really had no *locus standi* in opposing the passage of the Bill.

The inhabitants of Marylebone, after the club had been propitiated, decided at a meeting held in January, 1892, to oppose the project on the ground that the railway would disturb the patients in the Samaritan Free Hospital, and in Queen Charlotte's Hospital, and, worse still, would dislodge 25,000 persons of the humbler classes from the neighbourhood. Sir Edward Watkin, however, went on with his scheme undismayed, and was able at a meeting of shareholders in Manchester the same month to announce that satisfactory arrangements had been made with those who at one time were opponents. In 1891 they heard a great deal about Lord's. It was the idea of an old friend of his that they were interfering with a cricket ground at Marylebone which belonged to the House of Lords. It was so called, he believed, because a man of the name of Lord kept a public-house there, and opened the back part of his premises many years ago for cricket, and it had gone by the name of Lord's ever since. The proprietors of the place were great people and great lovers of cricket. He liked the game himself very much, and would not do anything to damage so excellent an institution. They had made a settlement in a sensible manner, and Lord's were perfectly satisfied. And with regard to many of the landowners, they had come to a fair understanding and had got rid of opposition. They had also made a settlement with the Great Northern Company, under which the old agreement would be modified, and there would be a general interchange of running-powers and facilities with that company. The hon. baronet, jaunty and sanguine, now thought there was strong probability of getting the Bill through, and believed they might look forward with confidence to the new portion of their line paying six per cent.

The Bill came before the Committee of the House on March 21, 1892. The opposition was less formidable; but the promoters, ready for any emergency, were prepared with 159 witnesses. It was explained that the old fifty-year agreement with the Great Northern – an agreement prohibiting competition one with another – had been superseded by a working arrangement encouraging friendly and reasonable competition over each other's lines, and that the Great Northern were no longer antagonistic to the new line. Peace, it was also stated, had been made with those

who controlled Lord's Cricket Ground, and some other opponents
had been converted into friends. In London the line would begin
with a junction close to the West Hampstead Station on the
Metropolitan Railway, and terminate in the Marylebone Road.
The station would be fronted by a fine hotel, and at each side
would be a sixty-feet road giving access to the passenger platforms. A separate entrance would be provided to the goods
station, and the coal yard would be near the Portman Market, in a
situation where no objection could be taken to it. For a considerable distance in London the line would be in tunnel, but the
company were prepared to pledge themselves not to build over
the tunnel, and something like fifteen acres of land might then be
converted into a sort of boulevard.

The London County Council still looked askance at the project;
and the Art Colony in St John's Wood reiterated their dislike of
the line. . . . Mr Alma-Tadema protested against the railway
invasion, and maintained that the shake from traffic would interfere with good work; that when the artist sought to put a straight
line on the canvas the line would be crooked. Another painter,
residing at West Hampstead, said, in a sardonic vein, that the new
railway would give his neighbours a very good idea of what an
earthquake was like, the only difference being that while a natural
earthquake was soon over, the earthquake Sir Edward Watkin
proposed to work would be continuous.

Mr Bidder, Q.C., who held a brief for all the opponents, must
have had an intuitive misgiving that the opposition was likely to
be in vain, for he addressed the Committee in a remarkable speech,
declaring that the object of the Bill was not to accommodate the
towns and villages on the route of the proposed new line, but to
satisfy the ambition of the promoters to become a great trunk line
to London. It was, he said meaningly, to accomplish the deep-laid
ambitious schemes of one man – a man well known in the railway
world – whose hope and dream was to terminate his life by running a through carriage from the north to London, and from
London to Paris. The Channel Tunnel was part and parcel of Sir
Edward Watkin's dream; and he was now leading forward the
shareholders of the Manchester, Sheffield and Lincolnshire Railway to ruin in the wild belief that this great line would increase their
dividends. Mr Littler, Q.C., for the promoters, held that there was

no better pioneer and guide in railway matters than Sir Edward Watkin, and bluntly characterized Mr Bidder's utterances as "rubbish, and highly absurd". These speeches were made on April 18. The same day, the Committee having deliberated for half an hour in private, declared the preamble passed.

from OUR RAILWAYS *1894*

The Golden Years

C. HAMILTON ELLIS

Brief years, from the death of Queen Victoria to the outbreak of war in 1914, were proud years. In many respects they made up the railways' golden era. The railways had reached a high degree of efficiency, administrative and mechanical. They had a virtual monopoly of long-distance land transport, and the motor car being looked upon largely as a sport of the rich, no rivals feared it very much. Even the Hull and Barnsley paid dividends. It was a picturesque period. Enormous coal trains rumbled, and handsome expresses rushed about the country. Maintenance was high and locomotives were often painted in gorgeous colours. Senior officers still lived and worked rather like demi-gods in their respective spheres. The scale on which war would come, and kill the old world dead, was unforeseen. . . . While the electric tram caused anxiety, otherwise in transport the prospect was one of more and better motor cars for the minority who could afford them. (Locomotive engineers often loved them.) The aeroplane was a great excitement: it added something new to the wonders of applied science. Some cocked a speculative eye at Count Zeppelin's great airships, but that was because, in the Germany of 1913, they were running regular passenger services of a strictly limited sort. On the whole the railways felt safe – like most other people.

Now that the last of the great main lines were built, the most striking thing on the constructional side was the building of the Great Western cut-offs. . . . [For instance] Bristol had long been a bottleneck on the main Severn Tunnel route to South Wales. For some time after the completion of the Severn Tunnel the principal passenger service had continued via Chepstow. To cut out Bristol the longest of the new lines was authorized, the South Wales and Bristol Direct, with a length of 30½ miles from Wootton Bassett through Badminton to Patchway near Filton Junction. It was opened for passenger traffic on July 1, 1903, and shortened the time taken to Cardiff by half an hour. Further, it gave an alternative entry to Bristol and the West. . . .

Of what became the shortened route to the West of England and Cornwall, considerable sections had been in use for many years. Newbury had been reached from Reading right back in 1847, and Devizes via Savernake, in 1862. . . . As far back as 1883 there were authorized the Stert–Westbury line, leaving the Devizes line near Patney, and the Castle Cary–Langport line, the former of which would greatly shorten the Great Western distance between London and Weymouth, while the latter would turn this same line through Savernake and Westbury into an alternative line to the west. But the 14½ miles to Westbury were not open until 1900. . . .

July 1, 1906, was a fateful day. It was then that the Castle Cary–Langport line, which had got as far as Charlton Mackrell on July 1st of the previous year, was opened throughout and shortened the distance from Plymouth to Paddington to 225¾ miles, giving the Great Western a clear advantage over the London and South Western. Competition for the American traffic at Plymouth was in full swing, and had been much stimulated by the opening of Ocean Quay, Stonehouse, on March 14, 1904. Just before two o'clock in the morning the up South Western boat express left the road while passing at excessive speed through the severe curves at the east end of Salisbury station, colliding with the Fisherton Street Bridge girders, a down milk-empties train and a light engine. Destruction was tremendous; there was heavy loss of life, and all South Western traffic between the railway's eastern and western lines was blocked. It was fortunate from the public point of view that the last link to Langport was that day complete. It was peculiarly fortunate for the Great Western company, too, for on that same day, on the original main line to the west, a small but troublesome portion of Box Tunnel fell in. West of England expresses were not, however, officially routed via Castle Cary until July 2nd.

It was the real end of the Plymouth campaigning. The South Western had fought doughtily in spite of the Great Western grip on it at Exeter. Outflanked as it now was, its mortal misfortune at Salisbury seemed an unnecessarily cruel *dénouement*. In 1910, a working agreement in respect of Plymouth traffic finally brought to a close the last of the great prestige wars between British railway companies.

Yet the Great Western still was able to put out of joint the nose of its old enemy in the Midlands, the London and North Western. There came about what, save in the imagination of the late Sir Edward Watkin, was the most improbable alliance possible between two major British railways, the Great Western and the Great Central. . . .

What the Great Western wanted was a direct route to Birmingham and Merseyside, to place it on a more competitive footing than with the old line through Oxford. What the Great Central wanted was an alternative to the Metropolitan and Great Central Joint line out to Aylesbury, and another tap on outer suburbia. Jointly with the Great Central, the Great Western built a new line from Northolt Junction in the western London suburbs, to High Wycombe, the Great Central having at the same time constructed a spur from a junction on its old line near Neasden. This was in 1905. The spur from the old G.W. main line from Acton to Greenford had been completed in 1903, and thence to Northolt in the following year. North of Wycombe there was the old Wycombe Railway providing the joint route as far as Princes Risborough, and north of the latter place the joint line continued to Ashendon, whence the Great Central carried on by itself, to Grendon Underwood where the new line rejoined the existing one through Aylesbury. It was opened for goods on November 19, 1905 and for passengers on April 2, 1906. . . .

The Great Western completed the link between Ashendon and Aynho, with an interesting example of separate up and down locations and a flying junction at the latter place on the old Oxford and Birmingham line. Great Central expresses started running via Risborough on April 2, 1906. On May 1st of the following year the Great Western opened a short link between Uxbridge and Denham on the new line. The Ashendon–Aynho line was opened for goods traffic on April 4, 1910, and on July 1st, the Great Western began to run two-hour business expresses from Paddington to Birmingham, Snow Hill. The London and North Western was somewhat alarmed at this incursion on its preserves. Pending the Great Western opening, it had introduced its "City to City" service between London, Broad Street, and Birmingham, New Street, by virtue of its very close connection with the North London Railway. Since December, 1908, the North London had been officered by the North Western. The time taken was $2\frac{1}{4}$ hours, but it was evidently held at Euston that though the Great Western might attempt a two-hour run, no proper City man would bother to trek out to Paddington for the privilege when he could make the direct journey from Broad Street with, incidentally, the services of a travelling typist on the way. The "City to City" trains began on February 1st. On May 1st another typist with her necessary machine moved into the principal two-hour business service to and from Euston. The Broad Street trains, incidentally, called at Coventry and terminated at Wolverhampton.

Honours were about even. It was perfectly true that Broad Street was more conveniently situated to Mincing and other Lanes than was Paddington, and big business had not yet started to move west. The Great Western route was, and still remains, scenically the more agreeable of the two as a ride.

Meanwhile, Fishguard had come into something of its own as an ocean and Irish port, though it never became the great rival to Liverpool and Southampton for which the Great Western Railway had sanguinely hoped. The company inaugurated the Fishguard–Rosslare route to Ireland on August 30, 1906. On the other side, the Great Southern and Western Railway played up with a good service to Cork and some new, elegant, but curiously uncomfortable rolling stock; at least, so it was in the third class. Great Western main-line stock was generally very good. On August 15, 1907, the Great Western made what was for Wales a record non-stop run, from Cardiff to Fishguard, 120 miles. The Booth Line to and from South America used the port and the Cunard company sampled it also. The *Mauretania*, then the largest ship in the world, first called at Fishguard on August 30, 1909.

West Midland connections were capable of improvement on the Great Western. Two necessary links were between Honeybourne, on the old Oxford, Worcester and Wolverhampton line, and

Cheltenham; and what became the Birmingham and North Warwickshire Railway. Between the two there would be connection by the two Stratford-on-Avon branches, from Honeybourne (1859) and Hatton (1860). The Honeybourne–Cheltenham line was opened in three stages during 1904–6. A new line from Birmingham to Stratford had been projected in 1894, but the Birmingham and North Warwickshire, as built, had a different location, leaving the G.W.R. Birmingham line by a trailing junction at Tyseley, passing through a new station at Henley-in-Arden (hitherto at the end of a rather primitive branch where the locomotive took water from a canal aqueduct), and joining the Hatton–Stratford branch on a triangular junction at Bearley, having come in over a short section of the Bearley–Alcester branch (1876). Construction was begun in 1905, and the new route came into operation on July 1, 1908. Previously, on March 30th, the Great Western had opened a new station at Malvern Road, Cheltenham.

Two points may be noted in connection with the Birmingham and North Warwickshire Railway. The original Birmingham–Stratford line had been opposed by the Great Western. It got its Act, but was unable to raise the money. Its interests were acquired by the Great Western in 1899, and it was after this that the proposed line was re-routed, and the original plan for a separate terminus in Birmingham was cut out. Of more human interest is the fact that the great railway amateur, T. R. Perkins, who later achieved a lifetime's ambition by travelling over every public line in Great Britain, was a chemist in Henley-in-Arden, watched the line being built, and in its early days was fetched out of bed in the middle of the night to attend to people injured in an accident there. It was a very fortunate accident, for though damage was unusually severe, with the engine (*Mafeking*) destroyed, there were no fatalities.

There seemed at first to be little improvement to show for the South Eastern and Chatham merger. In May, 1902, the South Eastern had its last dig at London, Brighton and South Coast preserves by opening the Crowhurst–Bexhill line. A good thing in the same year was the linking of the Chatham to the South Eastern main line by the Bickley loop, followed two years later by the junction from Chislehurst to the Chatham main line. Apart from its usefulness, this layout is to this day and in all respects a remarkably beautiful junction, with sweeping flyunders amongst the green.

As for other lines in the south, the London and South Western Railway had quadrupled its main line out of London as far as Hampton Court Junction as early as 1885. Although it had nothing like the North Western and Midland goods traffic to cope with, its passenger traffic was formidable, especially in the Home Counties and in summer. Its widening was complete to beyond Basingstoke in 1905, with the up Southampton line coming in, across the up and down Exeter lines near Worting, by a very imposing flyover. Such junctions were numerous on, and a very praiseworthy feature of, the South Western system. Another very notable work in the South, carried out during the first decade, was the widening of the London, Brighton and South Coast main line to a point just north of Balcombe Tunnel, completed in 1910. A part of the scheme, which proceeded in stages, was the "Quarry Line" avoiding Redhill Junction, with the second Merstham Tunnel and a flyover north of this carrying the new line from the western to the eastern side of the old Brighton and South Eastern route between Croydon and Redhill.

To this time belong two very important works in the North East. Down the years Newcastle Central Station, with Dobson's and Prosser's magnificent buildings, had been terminal as far as through East Coast traffic was concerned, serving only the Wylam and North Wylam lines, and thence the Newcastle and Carlisle line, from its western end. All south–north traffic had to come in over the old Stephenson and Harrison High Level Bridge, which had but three tracks on its upper deck and a road below. Traffic over the famous multiple diamond crossing at the east end of the station was very congested. A new line was therefore built, diverging from the old East Coast route just west of Gateshead West and striking straight across the river on a second, purely railway high-level bridge, with four tracks, thence to enter Newcastle Central from the Newcastle and Carlisle end of the station. It was opened by King Edward VII on July 10, 1906, and the new crossing of the Tyne was named King Edward Bridge. A plain, massive, unadorned structure of lattice girders on stone piers, it was described soon after as being "not without a certain grandeur of its own."

Charles Harrison was the designer of this, and of the new Wear Bridge at Sunderland, opened in 1910. This was remarkable, not only for its single-girder span of 330 feet, but for its being a double-deck railway and road bridge, jointly built by the North Eastern company and the Sunderland Corporation. . . .

[Also in the North] the alliances and quarrels of the Great Northern and the Great Central had been going on for many years. In 1906 there were moves for a working agreement between the two companies, which might have developed into amalgamation, or something like it. This was successfully opposed, not only by the Great Eastern and Midland companies, but by the Board of Trade. Though still in a somewhat parlous financial state, under the management of Fay the Great Central achieved several important works. The railway had been a noteworthy dock owner from earlier years, indeed, whatever the virtues of the old Great Northern remark about picking the "Sheffield" out of the dirt, the latter company certainly had done something of the kind for the ancient borough of Grimsby. The fish and the timber came in, the coal went out. At the end of the first decade of this century, the Great Central had over a hundred acres of docks at Grimsby. Fish came first – the railway's fast fish services were excellent – but the outlet for Midlands and South Yorkshire coal was congested.

Some miles upstream from Grimsby, on the right bank of the Humber, was Immingham. There, under an Act of 1904, the Humber Commercial Railway and Docks Company purposed laying out docks and lines for coal shipment, to relieve Grimsby. Its powers were assumed, by agreement, by the Great Central, which Sam Fay was now shaking up to energetic measures of all sorts. Following the cutting of the first sod . . . in 1906, dock construction went on steadily and the great King's Dock was formally opened by King George V, accompanied by Queen Mary, on July 22, 1912. Ships had been using the dock since the middle of May, but this was an occasion of grand pomp. . . . Between Grimsby and Immingham the G.C.R. built something very like an American electric interurban line.

The feeding of coal to the Humber was a thing that engaged all the railways in South Yorkshire and the North Midlands. For marshalling coal trains, the Great Central in 1907 brought into use the great yard at Wath-upon-Dearne, precursor of other modern concentration yards worked by hump shunting. It was controlled by a system of electro-pneumatic route-indicating semaphores.

An important link in the Barnsley–Doncaster area was the Dearne Valley Railway, beginning at Brierley Junction on the Hull and Barnsley Railway and running south-east to join the Great Northern and Great Eastern joint line near Black Carr Junction, Doncaster. It had a spur to the Swinton and Knottingley joint line of the Midland and North Eastern, and four important colliery branches. Though its beginning was technically at Brierley Junction, from a traffic point of view it formed a continuation of a new line built by the Lancashire and Yorkshire Railway from Crofton, on its Wakefield–Goole line, to Shafton, south-west of Brierley. Traffic began from the L. and Y. to the Dearne Valley in May, 1905. The L. and Y.R. was the working company.

There was great enterprise in the Lancashire and Yorkshire Railway's approach to these parts, and the moving spirit in this lively, if austere-looking railway was Sir John Aspinall, perhaps the greatest of the engineer-managers, . . . He it was who, as general manager, was responsible for electrification in the Liverpool and Manchester areas. He it was who produced, on his railway, one of the best and most strictly punctual regional train services in the world. The London and North Western might utter specious slogans in its publicity, and the Midland was, in certain respects related to such various things as coachbuilding and scenery, *the Best Way*. The Great Eastern might issue curious maps which showed Liverpool Street to York as being what the Americans called "a Bee-line" and the South Western people might do the same sort of thing in respect of London and Paris: (theirs was indeed the pleasantest route, but by no means could it be called straight). The Lancashire and Yorkshire put out a poster showing a jovial bearded guard pointing to an enormous watch with obvious satisfaction – train in background – and the inscription *On Time!* It was the best direct claim made by any British railway on the credulity of its public. . . .

[Timings, however, were not impressive.] There had been times when British trains were easily the fastest in the world, quite apart from such jaunts as the "races" of 1888 and 1895, but at the end of the century the country was well behind both the United States and France, with only five bookings at over 55 m.p.h. start to stop, three on the Caledonian and two on the Great Northern.

In the fast-train revival which followed, the Great Western Railway took the lead, and some of its liveliest initial efforts were with special trains. On July 4, 1903, the 4–4–0 engine *City of Bath* (Dean/Churchward), hauling an extra train to which royal saloons had been attached, averaged 67 m.p.h. from the Paddington start to the Exeter pass (193⅝ miles via Bristol) and 51 m.p.h. thence to Plymouth North Road (52 miles) at 51 m.p.h. With ships of the American and German lines calling at Plymouth there arose intense competition between the Great Western and the South Western. The latter had the shorter route, 230·5 miles from Stonehouse Pool Junction, but much more heavily graded. In spite of the Great Western's severe gradients in Devonshire, from Whiteball Summit to Paddington was simply a romp. The Great Western also had an advantage at Exeter, where the South Western had to pass over its line between Cowley Bridge Junction and St David's and the South Western drivers had the mortification of being held at the former while the Great Western train went through, and at the latter simply because St Davids was St Davids. The South Western made an excellent run on April 3, 1904, with a 6 foot Drummond engine from Devonport to Templecombe and a 6 foot 7 inch one thence to Waterloo, which was reached in 243 minutes. Recklessness was not absent in respect of the Salisbury curves.

Some of the most striking running on both lines involved not the speed maxima but the magnificent tackling of uphill sections, even considering the lightness of the trains which were between 100 and 150 tons gross behind the tender. A South Western start-to-pass time, of 42 minutes on the 32½ miles from the dock junction to Okehampton, nearly all sharply uphill to Meldon summit on Dartmoor, was first-rate work, and averages of 50 m.p.h. and over were made between Devonport and Exeter. On May 9, 1904, the up Ocean Mail of the Great Western, 148 tons gross behind the tender, engine *City of Truro,* ran the 52 miles from North Road to Exeter, pass-to-pass, in just under 56 minutes, having climbed to Wrangaton summit, 14 miles 10 chains, in 16 minutes 41 seconds. Hemerdon bank, 3¼ miles long including 2¼ at 1 in 41 up, was polished off in just under four minutes; the longer Dainton bank was topped in the same heroic style. Average speed from the Exeter pass to the Bristol stop was just over 70 m.p.h. with a minimum of 62 while climbing to Whiteball and a maximum, according to Charles Rous-Marten, of just over 102 m.p.h. going down the other side. At Pylle Hill the train was lightened by one vehicle to 120 tons, and a fresh engine, Dean's 4–2–2 *Duke of Connaught,* thence covered the 118½ miles to Paddington in just over 99 minutes. . . .

As to timetable services, the Great Western's Cornish Riviera Limited Express, to give it its original full title, began running from Paddington to Plymouth without a stop during the summer of 1904. This, of course, was still by the old route via Bristol. It began a vogue for very long non-stop runs, which the widespread use of watertroughs made possible. They appealed to a public, the richer members of which were already discovering the roaring delights of the motor. By 1914 there were, of runs exceeding 100 miles without a stop, 41 on the London and North Western Railway, 33 on the Great Western, 22 on the Great Northern, 15 on the Midland, 8 on the North Eastern, 7 on the Great Eastern, and 4 each on the Caledonian, Great Central and London and South Western. That included all the ten largest British railways except the North British, as far as locomotive working went. The South Western it should be remarked, had no watertroughs. Of these runs the fastest were two on the Great Western at 59·2 m.p.h. on the 118·3 miles from Paddington to Bristol Temple Meads. Each of these trains, however, dropped slip carriages at Bath, which gave a time of 105 minutes for 106·9 miles – 61·1 m.p.h. Paddington to Plymouth North Road, 225·7 miles via Westbury, was the longest regular run still; speed, 54·8 m.p.h. . . .

In 1914 the fastest regular run in Great Britain was that of an evening train from Darlington to York, 44·1 miles in 43 minutes, or 61·5 m.p.h. This speed was equalled by a Great Central night mail and parcels train which covered the 22·6 miles from Leicester to Arkwright Street, Nottingham in 22 minutes. The London and North Western Railway had two up Birmingham trains which ran to Coventry, 18·9 miles, in 19 minutes, just under even time. There was great merit in high speed over short distances – very long non-stop runs had little real virtue, except at night. The Caledonian at one time and another had start-to-stop timings of

60 m.p.h. between Forfar and Perth, 32·5 miles, and the London and South Western had had a 60 m.p.h. timing, start to stop, between Dorchester and Wareham, a distance of only 15 miles. It was a point of honour among drivers to observe the public time-table, though the working timetable allowed 17 minutes – the sort of odd thing one sometimes found about the South Western.

In 1914, however, the Caledonian's Forfar–Perth run was down to 57·4 m.p.h.; next came the South Western's 57·2 m.p.h.; Basingstoke to Surbiton, and rather surprisingly the despised and lampooned South Eastern and Chatham came next, with a run at 56·8 m.p.h. between Tonbridge and Ashford, thus achieving, albeit over a very easy road, something faster than anything on the Midland and the Great Northern, the runners-up in the "55 and over" group. A plucky run was on the Highland Railway, 41·5 m.p.h. from Blair Atholl to Perth, 35·3 miles, which although downhill was severely curved and abounding in restrictions, and single track nearly all the way. . . .

Summing up, the great virtue of British railways was in the relatively high speeds of their ordinary trains, including certain of the outer suburban services and the short-distance inter-city and inter-urban services of areas like Lancashire. In comparable services, foreign railways frequently shone very dimly indeed.

from BRITISH RAILWAY HISTORY 1877–1947 *1959*

War and eAmalgamation

JACK SIMMONS

[The first world war shattered Britain's railways] as it shattered so much else of the world to which they belonged. It did not shatter them physically: the damage they suffered from enemy action was insignificant beside what was to come in the war of 1939–45. But it exposed them to intense strain, which for some of them became almost unbearable; and it destroyed many of the old assumptions on which their thinking had long been based.

A Railway Executive Committee, consisting of the General

Managers of the leading companies, had been formed by the
Government in 1912. Its task, in the event of war, was to co-
ordinate the services afforded by the railways, to make them as far
as possible into one system, as an instrument for meeting the
emergency. Under the authority of an Act of 1871 the Government assumed control of the railways immediately war broke out.
It made no attempt to administer them directly, working instead
through the Committee, which relied for the execution of the task,
in its turn, on the managements of the separate companies.

The burden falling on them was, necessarily, uneven. To some
it meant intensification of traffic, curtailment of supplies, the
interruption of many normal services and the frequent necessity of
providing abnormal ones: difficult conditions, especially as the
war dragged on into its fourth and fifth years, but still tolerable,
given ingenuity and good temper. To others the war brought
something like revolution. This is true of those that were in the
front line of defence, like the Great Eastern and the South Eastern
& Chatham. It is even more strikingly true of those that were
called upon to face wholly unprecedented military tasks. Two of
these may be mentioned, lying at opposite ends of Great Britain:
the London & South Western and the Highland.

No single railway company, large or small, made a greater contribution to winning the war than the London & South Western.
It had long been the pre-eminent military line, serving Aldershot
and Salisbury Plain; and from 1914 onwards Southampton became
the chief focus of communications between Britain and the Continent. Now the South Western not only controlled all the railways
of Southampton: it had owned the docks there since 1892. First
and last, during the four years of war, the company carried over
20 million soldiers – that is, some 13,000 a day; and 7 million
passed through Southampton docks. The use of Southampton
was facilitated by its exceptional position in the British railway
system. Its great advantage was that it could be reached from
South Wales, the North, and the Midlands by five separate routes,
without touching London: by Bath and Blandford, by Salisbury,
Andover, Newbury, and Basingstoke. The second and last of these
were main lines, double-tracked. The rest, however, were less well
equipped, having long stretches of single line. In the course of the
war all of them were used to the limit of their capacity. The South

Western alone was responsible for handling this vast traffic as it converged on Southampton. Its resources were stretched to their utmost limits; and the human strain placed upon the company's servants was correspondingly severe. It was made severer still because two of them held commanding posts in the Railway Executive Committee, whose work had necessarily to take precedence over the company's: the South Western's General Manager, Herbert Walker, presided over it, and his Assistant, Gilbert Szlumper, acted as its Secretary. The South Western company indeed deserved well of its country.

So also, in a different way, did the Highland. It provided the only railway access to two of the Grand Fleet's three bases, Cromarty Firth and Scapa Flow. In 1918 the materials for the huge minefield known as the Northern Barrage, stretching from the Orkneys to the coast of Norway, were assembled at Inverness and Dalmore, near Invergordon, many of them having been brought up by train from Kyle of Lochalsh, where they had been landed from American ships. No railway could have been less well adapted to the performance of this vital military function. The Highland main line between Perth and Inverness is mountainous, and as it moves on to Thurso it is again steeply graded and pursues a serpentine course. Three-quarters of this line of 280 miles was single, and it was inadequately furnished with sidings and loops. None of this reflects discredit on the company; for it must be remembered that it ran through a poor and thinly-populated country, carrying in peace-time a very sparse traffic for nine months in the year and a heavy one only during the short summer season. But what sufficed in peace was hopelessly inadequate in war. The company owned 150 locomotives. Within the first year a third of those were out of service and another third in pressing need of repair. The Railway Executive Committee arranged for the loan of 20 engines from other companies, and more followed later; but the shortage of rolling stock of all kinds – particularly goods wagons – remained acute throughout the war. Somehow, nevertheless, the traffic was kept going. Though it looked more than once as if there might be a complete breakdown, no such disaster occurred. It was on the Highland Railway, a thin and fragile thread, that the supplying of the Grand Fleet depended – and with it the naval security of Britain in the North Sea. That the

E

thread did not snap was owing, in large measure, to the tenacity and devotion of the railwaymen.

But even that tenacity and devotion would have been insufficient if the Highland company had not been assisted by the other railways further south. The war proved the value of such co-operation. When it ended it was clear that it would be very difficult for companies like the Highland to stand on their own ever again. How could they possibly raise the capital that would be needed for replacing their worn-out equipment?

Under state control, in time of war, the British railway system had been unified as it never had been before. The argument was now heard insistently that State control should not be abandoned; that this was the moment for the State to purchase the railways outright. The protagonists of nationalization were fiercely opposed by those who wished to return to the old ways. A coalition Government of Liberals and Conservatives could scarcely be expected to favour nationalization, but it recognized that it was not possible merely to put the clock back: if the railways were to return to private ownership, it must be on a new basis. In 1919, for the first time, a Ministry of Transport was established, inheriting the powers and duties in this field of the Board of Trade. It was headed by a tough Scotsman, Sir Eric Geddes, who had himself been a railwayman and devoted much of his abounding energy to working out a new plan for the railways.

As embodied in the Railways Act of 1921 it represented a great departure from previous practice. In the past amalgamation had been discussed by Parliament, but discussion had led to no legislative action. Now the initiative was taken by the Government, which applied a comprehensive, systematic, compulsory amalgamation scheme of its own. Leaving aside the Underground lines of London and certain very small and insignificant provincial companies, which were untouched by the Act, all the railways of Great Britain were now to be combined into four "groups", north-western, eastern, western, and southern. In this way 120 companies were reduced to four. One of these was based on a single existing company, the Great Western, with the addition of the Cambrian Railways and the series of small – though for the most part prosperous – lines in the Welsh Valleys. The other three were composite organizations. The biggest, the London, Midland

& Scottish, was based on the London & North Western, the Midland, the Lancashire & Yorkshire, the Caledonian, the Glasgow & South Western, and the Highland Railways. The new London & North Eastern included the three companies that had tried to amalgamate in 1909, the Great Eastern, Great Northern, and Great Central, together with the North Eastern, the North British, and the Great North of Scotland. The smallest of the four groups, the Southern, comprised the London & South Western, the London, Brighton & South Coast, and the South Eastern & Chatham.

The Act passed into law with little determined opposition. It came into effect on 1 January 1923. On that day the old British railway system, which had gradually evolved over the preceding century, passed away, and a new one took its place, conceived and managed on different lines.

A glance at a map of the four new companies will show two things: that each had the monopoly of a great territory, and that the four were very unequal in size. Competition did not disappear: it continued, for instance, between London and Exeter, London and Sheffield, Leeds and Glasgow. But the operation of the principle was now very much reduced. Great industrial kingdoms, like Lancashire and the South Wales coalfield, became dependent for their railway services almost entirely on a single company. The inequality in size between the groups resulted in part from the principle that, since the railways remained private property, none of the old companies could be dismembered. Artificially "equal" groups could not therefore be created; and the anomalies arising from the application of this principle must be accepted – even when they brought a "London & North Eastern Railway" into North Wales. Inequality of size was less important than inequality of economic power. The Southern company was not only the smallest. Its constituent companies had been particularly hard hit by the war, and two of them carried a vast and increasing suburban traffic into London, which it was painfully evident they could not handle. The London & North Eastern company was weaker still. In the twenties and thirties the north-east of England, its strong-hold, was one of the most grimly depressed areas in the country. It inherited a higher proportion of unremunerative secondary and

branch lines than any of the other three groups. Of its large con-
stituents the Great Eastern was poor through no fault of its own,
and the Great Central financially ramshackle. Even the Great
Northern, one of the strongest partners in the new corporation,
was in some ways singularly ill equipped. Whilst the other great
railways had quadrupled their tracks out of London – the London
& North Western for 60 miles, the Midland for 75 – the great
Yorkshire coal trains and the East Coast expresses had to jostle
one another on two tracks when they were hardly more than ten
miles from King's Cross.

The new managements faced considerable difficulties at the
outset in welding the amalgamated companies into one. This task
was hardest of all, without doubt, on the London, Midland &
Scottish. The London & North Western and Midland Railways
had been historic rivals. They were opposed to each other not
merely in an economic sense, as competitors. For nearly three
generations they had adopted – almost, as it were, by instinct –
opposite ideas and practices. Which would now prevail? After a
short interlude, during which the new company took its tone in
some respects from a junior partner, the Lancashire & Yorkshire,
it became plain that Midland notions had won, that Derby had
triumphed over Crewe. . . .

Many difficult problems, then, psychological as well as administrative, faced the managements of the four companies at the
outset. The two largest were hampered for some time, one by
internal dissensions, the other by poverty. It was the smallest, the
Southern, that showed the greatest enterprise, under the leadership of a remarkable man, Sir Herbert Walker. He had resigned
from the Railway Executive Committee in 1919 and returned to
his own company, the London & South Western. He became
General Manager of the new Southern Railway. On the South
Western he had been closely associated with the electrification of
the suburban lines in London, which was carried through its first
stage in 1915–16. He had no doubt that this was the solution to
the much larger problems of the Southern Railway, which was
subjected from the first to well-justified criticism of its suburban
services, not only in the press but in Parliament. Walker was
responsible for driving through a programme of electrification
that ultimately stretched far beyond the suburbs, in the old sense

of the term: perhaps it would be better to say that by 1939 it had
made suburbs of Chatham, Brighton, Portsmouth, and Alton,
with two or three trains up to London every hour of the day. This
gave the Southern Railway the biggest electrified suburban system
in the world. . . .

For the two northern companies, the 1920s were a time of consolidation, of working out the complex problems involved in the
new management, of bringing their services and equipment back,
as far as possible, to the standards of 1914. But times had changed
since 1914, and in one respect above all. Whereas then the only
serious competition the railways had had to meet had been that of
the electric tram, now the petrol-driven vehicle had made its way
on to almost every road in the country. The bus was a formidable
new rival to the railway; and the motor-lorry was as alarming a
competitor for freight traffic as the bus was for passengers. As we
have seen, the railways had begun with the advantage in this
struggle. But after the war they failed to pursue it. This was the
critical moment: for the war had shown the capabilities of petrol-
driven vehicles, and thousands of those who had handled them
then saw what could be done with them in peace-time. Within ten
years of the end of the war the railways had begun to lose ground
fast: in the towns and on rural branch lines to the bus, everywhere
to the lorry. Their reaction was painfully slow. They interested
themselves in a few bus undertakings, especially after 1928, when
their legal powers to do so were enlarged; they started to consider the closing of a few notoriously unremunerative branches.
And that was all. They seemed helpless spectators of their own
defeat.

This ingloriously defensive attitude of mind can be understood, in the light of the past and of their current economic difficulties. Labour problems caused them increasing anxiety in these
years. Even in war-time, in 1917, there had nearly been a railway
strike. There was one in fact in September 1919, and a coal strike
(which, in the days of steam haulage, was almost as serious for the
railways) a year later. The General Strike of 1926 hit the railways
very hard indeed; and here, as in other industries, it left behind it
a legacy of ill will between management and men.

These strikes were accompanied by a steep rise in costs: a rise
that helped, indeed, to cause them and was, in its turn, made

steeper by them. This did not hit the railways alone; but whereas other commercial concerns were free to raise prices as they saw fit, passing on the burden to the consumer, the railways were severely limited, by the legislation of the past hundred years, in their freedom to raise fares and rates. Both were increased, while the railways were still under the control of the Government, in 1920; but no further general increase took place until 1937. The railways thus found themselves in a doubly unpleasant position: undercut by the cheaper and more flexible motor-vehicle on services that were being run at a loss, and at the same time prevented from recouping themselves by increasing rates and fares on the services in which they still enjoyed a strong position.

All this was bad enough in the twenties. With the slump of 1929–31 it grew very much worse. Now there was nothing for it but defensive action, of a drastic kind. . . . 1,240 miles of line were closed in 1923–47. It was the beginning of an effort to tackle the problem; but only the beginning. As for any vigorous drive to win back the lost traffic from the roads by new methods, that seems to have been scarcely considered.

One ultimate solution to this problem was indicated in these years by a great change brought about in the control of passenger transport in London. In 1929 the Underground group of companies and the London County Council put forward a joint scheme for the co-ordination of transport services. Though it was rejected by Parliament, another plan, with a similar end in view, was eventually embodied in an Act of 1933. This established a London Passenger Transport Board, which was entrusted with the biggest transport monopoly yet created in this country: a complete monopoly of both road and rail passenger transport in the London area, excluding only that of the mainline railways. . . .

The London Passenger Transport Act of 1933 was an example of the co-ordination of road and rail transport at the command of the State [but it] could not bring itself to issue other directives of the same kind in these years. Confronted with the fierce competition between road and rail . . . it stood aside, hesitating to intervene. It gave a little help to the railways: as in 1935, when it made available to them a loan of £30 million to enable major works of reconstruction and electrification to be undertaken. But on the main question, of the relationship between road and rail in the transport system of the country as a whole, it had no leadership to offer. Here was a refusal to accept responsibility quite as deplorable as that of the Governments in the early days of the railways a century earlier. Morally, it was worse: for whereas in the 1830s and 1840s *laissez-faire* was the orthodox policy expected of Governments in this country, in the 1930s that policy was clearly outmoded. In fact, the Government refused to intervene not from any devotion to the principle of *laissez-faire* but from timidity. . . .

In 1938 the four companies began concerted pressure on the Government to give them freedom to fix their own rates and fares. As they put it in their popular campaign, they were asking for a "Square Deal". They were justified in arguing that the existing system was antiquated and unrealistic; justified, too, in pointing to the many services they had rendered to the country in the past and in claiming that their weak economic position was hampering their ability to render similar services in the future. In 1939, as war approached (with all the demands it was certain, once again, to make on the railways), there were signs that their arguments were making some headway. But the Government had reached no decision in the matter when war broke out.

The story of the British railways in these years is not an entirely sombre one. If they were on the defensive, and fighting on some fronts a losing battle, they yet had some fine achievements to their credit, worthy of comparison with those of their great days. The Southern could show the greatest triumph, in its electrification; but it had other claims to distinction too. It did more than any of the other companies in the rebuilding of stations. The architectural style it adopted was depressing, involving the relentless and unimaginative use of ferro-concrete, but the new stations – Surbiton, Richmond, Ramsgate, Hastings, and many more – offered accommodation and facilities greatly superior to the old. The Southern was almost alone in building new railways in these years: the Ramsgate and Lewisham loops, for example, the Wimbledon–Sutton line, the Chessington branch. And finally, in 1936, in collaboration with the Chemin de Fer du Nord, it inaugurated the train-ferry service between London and Paris, which has proved a most profitable investment.

If the Great Western's effort in these years was less striking,

that was in part because it started in better order, less urgently
needing improvement. It had led the way in developing automatic train control . . . and it now extended the installation to the
whole of its main lines. It was the only one of the four companies
to make widespread use of diesel railcars. . . . It effected two
improvements in its main route to the West Country, which
enabled express trains to "by-pass" Westbury and Frome stations.
In September 1932 its up Cheltenham Spa Express was accelerated
so as to run from Swindon to Paddington at an average speed of
71·4 m.p.h. This was the fastest schedule in the world.

The most spectacular efforts of the London & North Eastern
company were also in the realm of speed. In 1935–37 it introduced
a series of streamlined express trains that gave Newcastle, Edinburgh, Leeds, and Bradford a substantially faster service to and
from London than any they had known before. And in 1938 one
of the locomotives built for these trains, *Mallard*, attained a speed
of 126 m.p.h., the highest authenticated speed that has ever been
reached by a steam locomotive. . . .

The London, Midland & Scottish Railway looked, more than
any of its fellows, to the United States for an example. This was
proclaimed in its very terminology. On this railway, as on no
other in Britain, the Chairman was also "President of the Executive". Among the Vice-Presidents was a distinguished man of
science, Sir Harold Hartley. Under his direction the company
embarked on a programme of research, with modern laboratories
at Derby (opened in 1935) and a testing station for locomotives,
established jointly with the London & North Eastern company,
at Rugby. The London, Midland & Scottish pursued very much
further than either of the other "composite" companies the strict
standardization of its equipment, especially in signalling and
locomotives. It too went in for high-speed trains, putting on a
fine express to run between London and Glasgow in 6½ hours.
The London, Midland & Scottish also interested itself, to a much
greater extent than the other three companies, in the development
of air services within the British Isles, from 1934 onwards; an
intelligent attempt to "tame" a potentially dangerous competitor.

from THE RAILWAYS OF BRITAIN *1961*

World War Two

C. HAMILTON ELLIS

Travel was cheerless during the second German war – by recollection worse than it had been during the Kaiser's bloody adventure. All really fast services vanished abruptly, many ordinary trains were withdrawn. Things remained most nearly normal on what had been the London, Brighton and South Coast system, where the electric Brighton "fasts", making their familiar, monotonous *klickeradoms* of 52 miles in one hour, were suddenly found to be the fastest trains in Great Britain. Coaches became more crowded than in the memory of many years, and during the weeks until hooded lamps and chinkless blind arrangements could be improvised, passengers sat through the long roaring hours in a dim, ghostly glimmer of blue light, recalling H. G. Wells's description of travel inside the Moon. Marshalling of wagons in the great yards, indeed all train and locomotive movements, were very difficult, and throughout the war was carried out with devotion and extraordinary ability, subject, during successive phases of the war, to the attacks of the German Air Force and the unpiloted missiles of the last year. . . .

Traffic continued along the routine lines arranged for war conditions until the break-through on the western front and the fall of France in the summer of 1940. The retreat and the evacuation through Dunkirk (Code name: Operation Dynamo), entailed the most wonderful emergency service ever organized in the history of British railways. It began on May 27, 1940, and for getting the returning troops away from the south-eastern ports to reception centres inland, the four companies furnished a pool of 186 rakes of coaches. Normal services in the south east were drastically cut and in some cases entirely suspended for the duration of the operation. Redhill Junction on the old Brighton and South Eastern lines, for instance, became a concentration point for this traffic on its way to diverse parts of the country. During the evacuation it was closed to public traffic. Off overloaded and battered ships came the men, thousands of men, hundreds of thousands of men; Englishmen, Scotsmen, Welshmen, Irishmen;

with them came a peppering of Frenchmen, Spahis, Senegalese, even some indignant Germans. There were sound men, wounded men, men who had swum out to the ships naked and still were almost so; they were dirty men, famished and dog-tired; they staggered into the trains and fell instantly asleep on the faded jazz-pattern plush and on top of each other. The movement went without delay, without hitch, without incident; the Southern Railway moved the trains off much as it moved them off from Margate and Brighton on August Bank Holiday, or from London Bridge any day. Voluntary workers fed them as they went. They ate, drank and slept again, and the trains took them far into and across the country. There could be no emergency time-table; the train movements were directed from Control by telephone. In those days while Dunkirk lay under the inky pall of its oil fires and the Stukas dive-bombed the beaches, while Calais had its last desperate siege, the British railways quietly moved away from the coast 620 trains, carrying more than 319,000 exhausted soldiers. Then, in the south east, routine wartime traffic was resumed. In the history of emergency train operation, it was an epic. . . .

Damage to railways was considerable, yet chancy. Fairly obvious efforts to destroy the elevated railway through Central London, from Blackfriars to Snow Hill, caused most damage in the City about St Pauls and north thereof. On the other hand, later in the war, when a "Baedeker" raid was carried out on York . . . the old walled city suffered little; the Minster stood where it did, and the most spectacular results were the burning of the station with a night Scotch express in it, and severe damage to a running shed, where a locomotive had a direct hit and was destroyed. Unexploded aerial mines, a feature of the earlier phases of aerial bombardment, caused much anxiety. It was somewhat unnerving to the most courageous and devoted of signalmen to have one hanging on to the box by its parachute cords. Fires caused by oil- and incendiary-bombs did tremendous damage in various places, especially in the dock areas. In all these raids there was the constant danger of blockage by fallen aircraft, in addition to the bombing. . . .

It is clearly impossible . . . to chronicle all the major incidents of aerial bombing on railways. The worst periods were during 1940–41, and 1944–45 when flying bombs from France and rockets from the Low Countries reopened an air offensive which in the meantime had been sporadic. A few specimens must suffice.

Of bombing effects, as both sides in the war were well aware, the most serious was the stoppage and delay of traffic. Marshalling yards were always targets for piloted bombing; not only could large numbers of wagons be destroyed, but a well-placed bomb on the hump throttled all movement for a while. More lasting delays were achieved by bridge destruction. Late in 1940, three arches of a brick viaduct carrying two electric and two steam lines into Liverpool Exchange, on the L.M.S., were destroyed. A temporary steel structure was built for the electric lines. Replacement of the permanent bridge was going on when a second attack destroyed most of the work. . . .

Most curiously, some of the worst damage of this kind was by chance. On April 19, 1941, a parachute mine brought down the Southern Railway's Southwark Street Bridge, carrying eight roads. This cut the through London line, Blackfriars–Snow Hill, and was very serious. The through roads were temporarily restored during May and June; the bridge was permanently rebuilt by December, 1942. In May, 1943, the railway connections at Brighton were attacked in a mid-day raid. A bouncing bomb, that had gone through three buildings, exploded against Rastrick's great viaduct, 80 feet high above the London road, and brought down a pier and two arches. A temporary span was installed in a month and the bridge completely restored in four months.

Entirely random bombing achieved some unpleasant flukes. In 1944, pilotless flying bombs demolished a bridge at Coborn Road on the main Great Eastern line, and the track and decking of the local lines over Charing Cross Bridge. Another of these destroyed an underbridge immediately in front of a Kent Coast express of the Southern Railway. The train rushed into the gap and was wrecked with heavy loss of life. The thing was reported in the papers as a bad railway accident, with cause unstated.

Running sheds, naturally, were often attacked; 484 locomotives were damaged but only eight had to be written off, generally a consequence of broken main frames. The engines proved extraordinarily tough. Vehicles were naturally more vulnerable; 637 carriages and 2,685 wagons (excluding those not owned by the railway companies) were destroyed. Underground effects of

bombing were sometimes severe. Two separate incidents blocked
the Great Central line tunnel near St John's Wood. A narrow
passage with interlaced tracks was opened two months later, and
the double-track tunnel restored about 11 months after the event.
In May, 1941, St Pancras was heavily bombed, with two bad
explosions in the vast vaults under the main station. One damaged
and filled the tunnel to the Metropolitan lines at King's Cross. In
rapid repair, interlacing was used here also. Traffic was resumed in
the main station a week later. Of many other station casualties, one
recalls a slice being taken out of Cubitt's roof on the departure
side of King's Cross, and an unusually bloody business at Middles-
brough, where the Gothic iron roof was brought down and a
train wrecked by a stick of bombs falling along the station.

In East Kent the Southern Railway was further under constant
fire from shore batteries on the French side, and Dover Priory
station was heavily damaged. South-eastern England was not in-
frequently the scene of trains being shot up by lone raiders.
"Train busting" had a strong sporting appeal to the armed airman.
Both sides delighted in it.

Damage to railway property through air attack was estimated at
about thirty million sterling. It was most extensive on the London
and North Eastern, structurally most serious on the Southern, and
very bad on the London Transport lines having regard to their
limited extent. All the deep-level underground stations were
equipped with three-tier bunks for all-night shelterers. Sanitation
was by a form of water carriage under air pressure. The scene and
the atmosphere after dark, with traffic still moving, beggared
description. Before the outbreak of war, London Transport had
equipped all the under-river tunnels with flood gates which could
be instantly closed, but there was a terrible disaster at Balham
through flooding by broken water mains and sewerage. Sloane
Square Station on the District line, which had just been rebuilt,
was destroyed early in the war, but the conduit carrying the West
Bourne across the tracks was fortunately undamaged.

During the 1914–18 war, the early, slow-moving tanks had been
transported from works to ports on crocodile wagons by special
goods train. The ancient technique had been to manoeuvre the
tank on from one side and edge it laboriously round by the
differential working of its tracks. In this second war armoured

divisions had to be moved about, and a special type of train was provided. It consisted of anything up to nine wagons ("warflats") each capable of carrying 50 tons, with a ramp wagon each end for loading or unloading the tanks under their own power, they running on to the train in procession. The train was completed by sufficient coaches for the unit and a stores van.

During October–December, 1942, the North African campaign entailed the running of 440 special troop trains and 680 special freight, chiefly to Clyde and Merseyside. Altogether, between September, 1939, and August 11, 1945, 538,559 special trains were run, of which 258,624 were troop trains and 279,935 special freights. The latter category might carry anything from stores to ammunition and armour. There was a major explosion at Soham, L.N.E.R., arising out of a fire on an ammunition train, and the George Cross was awarded to Driver B. Gimbert and posthumously to Fireman J. W. Nightall who hauled the train out of the station in an attempt to reach the open country.

In spite of a limited number of tank wagons, there was enormous movement of petroleum and petrol spirit over the railways, and though this was somewhat relieved by the construction of pipelines after May, 1941, in the first month after invasion of the Normandy beaches, 1,579 petroleum specials were run – a record. Each train consisted of 25 tank wagons containing approximately 100,000 gallons.

For the invasion of France in June, 1944, Southampton was chosen as the main embarkation point. In the second half of 1944, from D-Day to the end of the year, 14,763 special freight trains were run wholly in connection with the invasion. Troop traffic was at its peak in the six days June 14–20, 1944, with the movement of some 99,000 men in 271 special trains.

Ordinary passenger traffic the companies carried as best they could. First-class accommodation was withdrawn from suburban trains on October 6, 1941. Crowding varied in different areas. Through East Coast expresses had been severely cut; now they were of caravan length and often quite incredibly crowded, with corridors jammed, with men and women sleeping propped up in gangways and lavatories. By comparison some other lines were fairly normal and comfortable. Passengers were confronted with notices asking them if their journeys were really necessary.

Pleasure motoring had vanished, except among those, never absent even under the gravest emergency, who knew how to *work a fiddle*. This of course was to have unfortunate repercussions after the war. Many were those who, swaying for hours through the darkness in some crammed long-distance train, vowed that if ever they emerged from this they never would use a railway again.

Ordinary freight and mineral traffic was likewise congested and subject to delay. An immense tonnage of coal was diverted from coastal shipping to the railway. During 1941, the peak year, 10,034 coal trains were despatched from the north east and the Midland coalfields. There were difficulties because the bottom-unloading steel hopper wagons of the north east could not be dealt with in the southern counties. Requisitioned wagons of old type and sometimes in doubtful repair had to be used instead. After some troubles there was an improvement in the turnround of wagons and barges, and this was maintained with F. J., afterwards Lord Leathers, wise and experienced in coal, at the Ministry of War Transport. It was unfortunate that the London and North Eastern company's scheme for electrifying the Manchester, Sheffield and Wath lines, with their enormous coal traffic, had been begun too late and was suspended with the outbreak of war. This line with its heavy gradients and its frightful old Woodhead Tunnels formed a serious bottleneck for traffic east and west across the North Country.

The motive power position was not easy. First, about a hundred old Dean goods engines were requisitioned from the Great Western for the use of the War Department overseas. They were handy engines, proved in the previous war and able to go anywhere on fairly light duties. In lack of them the Great Western was helped out by the L.M.S. and L.N.E. Railways with 80 engines. Lending of this sort continued during the war years. The companies handed over 343 locomotives to the Government, mostly steam but some diesel from the L.M.S. and Southern Railways. When Germany attacked Russia, and the Persian railways became suddenly an allied lifeline, 92 heavy goods from the L.N.E.R. and 43 from the L.M.S. were converted for oil burning, chiefly at Swindon and Eastleigh, and sent out. Persia, indeed, with its ferocious conditions and rather desperate standards of maintenance, became a locomotive graveyard. There already, were old

Austrian and Swedish engines, displaced by electrification. Everything was worked until it wore out or was destroyed by accident,
then more were demanded. For home traffic Sir William Stanier's
standard L.M.S. mixed-traffic and goods engines had priority of
construction; later, in 1942, for both home and overseas service,
new classes were designed and built for the Ministry of Supply, and
a large number of American engines also saw service on British
railways before being shipped overseas.

There was always the danger of the large electrified network of
the Southern Railway being put out of action by heavy bombing
of power stations, and a pool of old steam tank engines was formed
to work a substitute steam suburban service in the event of this
happening. Fortunately, power station damage was comparatively
slight. A fluke bomb went down the north track of Durnsford
Road Power Station, Wimbledon, and damaged part of the boiler
installation, but the electric service was maintained on all lines.

from BRITISH RAILWAY HISTORY 1877–1947 *1959*

Up to Date

JACK SIMMONS

When VE-day arrived Britain's railways could feel justifiably
proud of the part they had taken in one of the greatest military
operations in history.

It stretched their capacity to the uttermost . . . their physical
condition when the war ended was frankly deplorable. And almost
at once, before they had had time to repair any of the damage they
had suffered or to consider their position and policy in the post-
war world, they found themselves at the centre of a political storm.
At the general election held immediately after the war ended a
Labour Government was returned to power, committed to the
nationalization of the railways.

Its policy was carried out in the Transport Act of 1947, under
which the railways were compulsorily purchased by the State and
placed under the management of a newly-created body, the British
Transport Commission. At midnight on 31 December 1947, the

old railway companies and the London Passenger Transport Board ceased to exist, and a State system took their place. . . .

The first and most obvious change [was] in management. Though they were all now "British Railways", under common ownership, they could not be run as a single unit. The old companies had been split up, for operating purposes, into "divisions" or "sections". A similar arrangement would clearly have to be adopted for the new and much bigger organization. It was announced that in future the railways would be divided into six Regions – or seven if we include the London area, which continued to be managed as a transport unit on its own. Three of these Regions were based, roughly, on the arrangements adopted in 1921 [but] the former London & North Eastern system was split into three parts. Its English lines were divided into an Eastern and a North Eastern Region. Finally – the one part of these arrangements that could be called a great innovation – Scotland was constituted a Region of its own, the lines of the former London, Midland & Scottish and London & North Eastern companies north of the Border all falling under the control of a Chief Regional Officer in Glasgow.

The new Commission faced a task of formidable difficulty. Its first business was to put the railways on their feet again, in both a material and a moral sense. As we have seen, they had never fully recovered from the strain placed on them in the first World War. They had suffered much worse in 1939–45; and their recuperation had been hampered by the protracted controversy over their future in 1945–47. Now it was the duty of the Commission to restore their efficiency: a pressing duty, too, for the public expected to see quick results.

No great duty of this kind could have been undertaken in more discouraging circumstances. The Commission was instructed from the outset that its services must be made to pay for themselves. But that, for the moment, was an impossible ideal. The first thing to be done was to re-equip the railways, to repair the damage they had sustained during the war and to overtake the arrears of maintenance. This in itself was a big job; for money was scarce, prices were rising, and the necessary materials were hard or even impossible to get. In spite of all these difficulties, the old companies had made a stout start on the task in 1945–47. The Commission took over their work and gradually managed to speed it up.

From the outset of the new *régime* it was clear that something more was needed than a restoration of what had gone before, in 1939 or in 1914; that the place of the railways in the economy and society of Great Britain as a whole needed reconsideration. If they were to play their proper part in the life of the country – still more, if they were ever to make ends meet – three things were essential. They must be freed of the ancient commercial restrictions that had hampered them so severely in the past; they must be allowed to concentrate, as far as possible, on those tasks to which they were best suited; and their equipment and operation must be completely overhauled and brought up to the standards of the mid-twentieth century.

The Act of 1947 had not done very much to give the railways the "square deal" asked for by the old companies in 1938. A change in this direction was attempted by the Transport Act of 1953, which allowed the railways a much increased freedom to adjust their charges. Henceforward they were obliged to publish only their maximum rates for freight traffic; below that level the British Transport Commission was to be freed to fix rates that competed with those of other forms of transport. A considerable administrative reorganization also took place, with the object of diminishing the close central control over the Regions that was a feature of the Act of 1947. The powers of the former Chief Regional Officers were increased to approximate much more nearly to those of the General Managers of the old companies. . . .

No one who looks at British Railways dispassionately can fail to sympathize with the management's desire to apply its resources to the work that the railways can perform best and to rid itself of the liability to maintain services that are, and must remain, unremunerative. Again this was not a new policy. The old companies had addressed themselves to the closing of branch lines, and by so doing they had effected considerable economies. The Commission carried this policy a long step further. Between 1948 and 1959 it closed 2,944 miles of railway, either to passengers or to all traffic.

A careful investigation was undertaken at the same time of every station on the whole system, considered as a commercial asset; and this led to the closing of a large number, on lines that otherwise remained open. Such a reduction in the number of wayside stations effects a double economy: by reducing, or altogether eliminating, the costs of running the stations themselves and by assisting the movement of through traffic, unimpeded by stopping trains.... In 1956 the British Transport Commission closed to passengers, at a single stroke, no less than 27 stations on the old Caledonian main line between Glasgow and Aberdeen. All the villages served by them were on bus routes. . . .

This negative policy, of ridding British Railways of unprofitable commitments, has to be seen as part of something positive: a policy of improving, at every point, the services they can offer with best effect. Some such improvements were put in hand very soon after the Transport Commission was formed. It carried through the old London & North Eastern's plans of electrification. . . . In East Anglia, the introduction of the "Britannia" locomotives made possible an express service between London, Ipswich, and Norwich of a quality that under earlier managements would have been quite unattainable.

Much bigger ideas were then being worked out. At the beginning of 1955 the Commission announced a plan of long-term development. It began by admitting that "British Railways today are not working at full efficiency", and attributed this shortcoming chiefly to "their past inability to attract enough capital investment to keep their physical equipment fully up to date". Starting from this premiss, the Commission set out the case for undertaking an expenditure of £1,200 million on "modernization and re-equipment". It pointed out that, in any event, nearly half this sum would have to be found in order to maintain the existing services and the plant they demanded. Rightly arguing that it was out of the question to undertake merely this expenditure, for so limited a purpose, it went on to set out a scheme of large-scale planned development under four main heads: improvement of track and signalling; replacement of steam by electric or diesel traction; modernizing of passenger rolling-stock and station facilities; and – the biggest item of all, estimated to cost £365 million – the recasting of freight services, especially through the fitting of continuous brakes to all wagons. . . .

The plan has run into technical difficulties, as any large scheme of the kind is bound to do. It has been handicapped by rising costs,

and by financial restrictions imposed by the Government. . . . The
Commission [which was itself dismembered in 1963] originally
estimated that the work would not be completed until 1970.
That statement may well turn out to be optimistic.

We are seeing at the moment what amounts to a revolution – no
less – in the operation and equipment of the British railways: a
modernization far more drastic than any of them has ever under-
gone in the past. For precedents one must look to the Continent,
to railway systems that were damaged much more heavily than
Britain's in the second World War, like those of Italy, Holland,
and France.

Britain's railways are an enduring monument of the age of her
greatest power. They are now being adapted to serve the needs of
a society very different from that in which they were first planned.
It is a fascinating study to see how much of the past has survived
into the present, how the past is influencing and moulding even
the great "modernization" now in progress.

from THE RAILWAYS OF BRITAIN *1961*

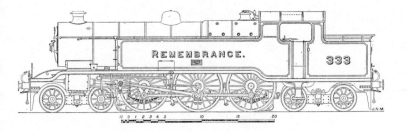

PART III

Men and Machines

"PUFFING BILLY."

The Pioneers

SAMUEL SMILES

Railways, like most other important inventions, had very humble beginnings. The first railway, properly so called, consisted of a rude line of wooden or iron rails, laid down for the easier guidance of waggons in which coal was hauled from the pit to the shipping place. This germ of the modern railroad, planted by some unknown hand, grew to maturity gradually and slowly. Progress, in this as in almost all branches of mechanics, was effected through the exertions of many; one generation entering upon the labours of that which preceded it, and carrying onwards their improvements.

There is, doubtless, a vast difference between the old road track, on which pack-horses carried the main traffic of the country down to a comparatively recent date, and the modern railroad worked by powerful locomotives; yet the change was effected by comparatively easy stages. From an early period the growing trade and commerce of the country demanded constantly increased facilities for the transport of heavy articles. This was especially necessary in the mining districts, where it is to be observed that nearly all the modern improvements in road-making have had their origin. The prime object of all the improvements made in the road was, so to diminish friction by increasing the smoothness of the surface, that the haulage of the coal-waggons by horses should be rendered as easy as possible. With this object, wooden rails were first laid down by one Mr Beaumont between his coal-pits, near Newcastle, and the staithes by the river side. On these a large loaded waggon could be drawn by one horse. This was as early as the year 1602. The same mode of transport was shortly after generally employed in the principal colliery districts. Old Roger North thus describes them, as they were laid down in the neighbourhood of the Tyne, in 1676:

"Another remarkable thing is their *way-leaves*; for when men have pieces of ground between the colliery and the river they sell the leave to lead coals over their ground, and so dear that the owner of a rood of ground will expect 20*l*. per annum for this leave. The manner of the carriage is, by laying rails of timber from the colliery down to the river exactly straight and parallel, and bulky carts are made with four rowlets fitting these rails, whereby the carriage is so easy that one horse will draw down some four or five chaldron of coals, and is an immense benefit to the coal merchants."

A century later (in 1770–1772) the same roads were found in general use by Arthur Young, an intelligent traveller. The road-way was little improved, but the works on which the road was formed were sometimes of a formidable character. Speaking of the waggon roads near Newcastle, Mr Young observes: "The coal-waggon roads, from the pits to the water, are great works, carried over all sorts of inequalities of ground, so far as the distance of nine or ten miles. The tracks of the wheels are marked with pieces of wood let into the road for the wheels of the waggons to run on, by which means one horse is enabled to draw, and that with ease, fifty or sixty bushels of coals."

An intelligent French traveller, named Saint-Fond, who visited Newcastle in 1791, speaks in terms of high admiration of the colliery waggon-ways, as superior to everything of the kind that he had seen. He describes the wooden rails as formed with a rounded upper surface, like a projecting moulding, and the waggon wheels as being "made of cast-iron, and hollowed in the manner of a metal pulley," that they might fit the rounded surface of the rails. The economy with which the coal was thus hauled to the shipping places was strongly urged upon his own countrymen, as an inducement to them to adopt a similar mode of transit.

Similar waggon roads were laid down in the colliery districts of Scotland at a comparatively early period. At the time of the Scotch rebellion, in 1745, a railway existed between the Tranent coal pits and the small harbour of Cockenzie, in East Lothian; and a portion of the line had the honour of being selected as a position for General Cope's cannon at the battle of Prestonpans.

In these rude wooden tracks we find the germ of the modern railroad. Improvements were gradually made in them. Thus, at some collieries, thin plates of iron were nailed upon their upper surface, for the purpose of protecting the parts most exposed to friction. Cast-iron rails were also tried, the wooden rails having been found liable to rot. The first iron rails are supposed to have been laid down at Whitehaven as early as 1738. This cast-iron road was denominated a "plate-way", from the plate-like form in which the rails were cast. In 1767, as appears from the books of the Coalbrookdale Iron Works, in Shropshire, five or six tons of rails were cast, as an experiment, on the suggestion of Mr Reynolds, one of the partners; and they were shortly after laid down to form a road. In 1776, a cast-iron railway, nailed to wooden sleepers, was laid down at the Duke of Norfolk's colliery near Sheffield. The person who designed and constructed this coal line was Mr John Curr, whose son has erroneously claimed for him the invention of the cast-iron railway. He certainly adopted it early, and thereby met the fate of men before their age; for his plan was opposed by the labouring people of the colliery, who got up a riot in which they tore up the road and burnt the coal staith, whilst Mr Curr fled into a neighbouring wood for concealment, and lay there *perdu* for three days and nights, to escape the fury of the populace. In 1789, Mr Wm. Jessop constructed a railway at Loughborough, in Leicestershire, and there introduced the cast-iron edge-rail, with flanches cast upon the tire of the waggon wheels to keep them on the track, instead of having the margin or flanch cast upon the rail itself; and this plan was shortly after adopted in other places. In 1800, Mr Benjamin Outram, of Little Eton, in Derbyshire, used stone props instead of timber for supporting the ends and joinings of the rails. As this plan was pretty generally adopted, the roads became known as "Outram roads", and subsequently, for brevity's sake, "tram-roads". From this time the use of tram-roads rapidly extended, until at length they were generally adopted in the mining districts.

The progress of railways was, indeed, such that the canal interests became somewhat uneasy respecting them. The Duke of Bridgewater, when congratulated by Lord Kenyon on the successful issue of his scheme, made answer, with farsighted shrewdness, "Yes, we shall do well enough if we can keep clear of these d—d tram-roads – there's mischief in them!" It will be observed, however, that the improvements thus far affected had been confined almost entirely to *the road*. The railway waggons still continued to be drawn by horses. The gradual improvements made in the rail, by improving the firmness and smoothness of the track had, indeed, effected considerable economy in horse power; but that was all. What was further wanted was, the adoption of some mechanical agency applicable to the purpose of railway traction.

Unless some such agency could be invented, it was clear that railway improvement had almost reached its limits. Inventors and projectors, however, presented themselves in numbers, and various schemes were proposed. One suggested the adoption of sails, supposing that the waggons might be impelled along the tram-ways like ships before the wind. But the most favourite project was the application of steam power on the high-pressure principle, for the purpose of railway traction.

Solomon de Caus, who was shut up for his supposed madness in the Bicêtre at Paris, seems to have been the first to conceive the idea of employing steam for moving carriages on land as well as ships at sea. Marion de Lorme, in a letter to the Marquis de Cinq-Mars, dated Paris, February, 1641, thus describes a visit paid to this celebrated madhouse in the company of the English Marquis of Worcester: "We were crossing the court, and I, more dead than alive with fright, kept close to my companion's side, when a frightful face appeared behind some immense bars, and a hoarse voice exclaimed, 'I am not mad! I am not mad! I have made a discovery that would enrich the country that adopted it.' 'What has he discovered?' asked our guide. 'Oh!' answered the keeper, shrugging his shoulders, 'something trifling enough: you would never guess it; it is the use of the steam of boiling water.' I began to laugh. 'This man,' continued the keeper, 'is named Solomon de Caus; he came from Normandy four years ago, to present to the King a statement of the wonderful effects that might be produced from his invention. To listen to him, you would imagine that with steam you could navigate ships, move carriages; in fact, there is no end to the miracles which, he insists upon it, could be performed. The Cardinal sent the madman away without listening to him. Solomon de Caus, far from being discouraged, followed the Cardinal wherever he went with the most determined perseverance, who, tired of finding him for ever in his path, and annoyed at his folly, shut him up in the Bicêtre. He has even written a book about it, which I have here.'" It appears that the Marquis of Worcester was greatly struck by the appearance of De Caus, and afterwards studied his book, portions of which he embodied in his "Century of Inventions". The Marquis is also said to have entertained the idea of moving carriages by steam power, but never embodied it in any practical form.

Savery, the Cornish miner and engineer, who did so much to develop the powers of the high-pressure engine, also proposed it as a method of propelling carriages along ordinary roads. But he took no practical measures with the view of carrying out his suggestion. The subject was shortly after, in 1759, introduced to the powerful mind of James Watt, by Dr Robinson, then a young man studying at Glasgow College. "He threw out," says Watt, "the idea of applying the power of the steam-engine to the moving of wheel-carriages, and to other purposes; but the scheme was not matured, and was soon abandoned, on his going abroad." Watt, however, afterwards, in the specification of his patent of 1769, gave a description of an engine of the kind suggested by his friend Robinson, in which the expansive force of steam was proposed as the motive power. It also appears that other inventors were in the field about the same time; for, in a letter written by Dr Small to Mr Watt on the 18th of April, 1769, it is stated that "one Moore, a linendraper of London, had taken out a patent for moving wheel-carriages by steam"; but no steps were taken to reduce the invention to practice. Watt again, in his patent of 1784, described a similar engine to that indicated in his first patent, specifying the mode of applying steam to the moving of wheel-carriages. The plan proposed by Watt, although a curiosity at the present day, bears the impress of his original mind. The boiler was to be of wooden staves hooped together with iron; the iron furnace inside the boiler, and almost entirely surrounded with water; the whole being placed on a carriage, the wheels of which were to be worked by a piston, the reciprocatory action being converted into a rotatory one by toothed wheels and a sun and planet motion. The cylinder was to be seven inches in diameter, the number of strokes sixty per minute, and their length one foot. The carriage was to carry two persons. But no such carriage was ever built, Watt being too busily occupied with the perfecting of his condensing-engines to proceed further with his proposed locomotive.

The first actual model of a steam-carriage, of which we have any written account, was constructed by a Frenchman named Cugnot, who exhibited it before the Marshal de Saxe in 1763. He afterwards built an engine on the same model, at the cost of the French monarch. But when set in motion, it projected itself onward with such force, that it knocked down a wall which stood in its way; and its power being considered too great for ordinary use, it was put aside as being a dangerous machine, and was stowed away in the Arsenal Museum at Paris.

An American inventor, named Oliver Evans, was also occupied with the same idea; for in 1772, he invented a steam-carriage to travel on common roads; and in 1787, he obtained from the State of Maryland the exclusive right to make and use steam-carriages. The invention, however, never came into practical use.

It also appears that in 1784, William Symington, the inventor of the steam-boat, conceived the idea of employing steam power in the propulsion of carriages; and in 1786 he had a working model of a steam-carriage constructed, which he submitted to the professors and other scientific gentlemen of Edinburgh. But the state of the Scotch roads was at that time so horrible, that he considered it impracticable to proceed further with his scheme, and he shortly gave it up in favour of his project of steam navigation.

The first English model of a steam-carriage was made in 1784, by William Murdoch, the friend and assistant of Watt. It was on the high-pressure principle, and ran on three wheels. The boiler was heated by a spirit lamp; and the whole machine was of very diminutive dimensions, standing little more than a foot high. Yet, on one occasion, the little engine went so fast, that it outran the speed of its inventor. . . . One night, after returning from his duties in the mine at Redruth, in Cornwall, Murdoch determined to try the working of his model locomotive. For this purpose, he had recourse to the walk leading to the church, about a mile from the town. The walk was rather narrow, and was bounded on either side by high hedges. It was a dark night, and Murdoch set out alone to try his experiment. Having lit his lamp, the water shortly began to boil, and off started the engine, with the inventor after it. He soon heard distant shouts of despair. It was too dark to perceive objects; but he shortly found, on following up the machine, that the cries for assistance proceeded from the worthy pastor of the parish, who, going towards the town on business, was met on this lonely road by the hissing and fiery little monster, which he subsequently declared he had taken to be the Evil One *in propria persona*. No further steps, however, were taken by Murdoch to embody his idea of a locomotive carriage in a more practical form.

Towards the end of the last century, the adoption of rail and tram-roads, worked by horses, had become general in the colliery and mining districts. There could be no doubt as to the great economy secured by this mode of moving heavy loads, as compared with the ordinary method of haulage on common roads. As trade and manufacturers were extending with great rapidity, Watt's invention of the steam-engine having given an immense impetus to industry in all its branches, it was proposed to extend the application of railroads to the transit of merchandise and goods from town to town, especially in those districts where canals were not considered practicable. . . .

In 1801 this idea was taken up by Dr James Anderson of Edinburgh, who proposed, in his "Recreations of Agriculture" the general adoption of railways, worked by horse power, to be carried along the existing turnpike roads. Dr Anderson dilated upon his idea with glowing enthusiasm. "Diminish carriage expense but one farthing," said he, "and you widen the circle of intercourse; you form, as it were, a new creation, not only of stones and earth, and trees and plants, but of men also, and, what is more, of industry, happiness, and joy." The cost of all articles of human consumption would, he alleged, be thus reduced, agriculture promoted, distances diminished, the country brought nearer to the town, and the town to the country. The number of horses required to carry on the traffic of the kingdom would be greatly diminished, and a general prosperity would, he insisted, be the result of the adoption of his system. Indeed, said he, "it is scarcely possible to contemplate an institution from which would result a greater quantity of harmony, peace, and comfort, to persons living in the country, than would naturally result from the introduction of railroads."

That the same idea was taking hold of the more advanced minds of the country, is further evident from the fact, that in the following year (1802) Mr Edgeworth urged the adoption of a similar plan for the transit of passengers. "Stagecoaches," he said, "might be made to go at six miles an hour, and post-chaises and gentlemen's travelling carriages at eight – both with one horse; and small stationary steam-engines, placed from distance to distance, might be made, by means of circulating chains, to draw the carriages, with a great diminution of horse labour and expense."

While this discussion was going forward, Richard Trevethick, [*sic*] a captain in a Cornish tin-mine, and a pupil of William Murdoch's – influenced, no doubt, by the successful action of the model engine which the latter had constructed – determined to build a steam-carriage adapted for use on common roads. He took out a patent, to secure the right of his invention, in the year 1802. Andrew Vivian, his cousin, joined with him in the patent – Vivian finding the money, and Trevethick the brains. The patent was dated the 24th March, 1802, and described as "A grant unto

Richard Trevethick and Andrew Vivian, of the parish of Cranbourne, in the county of Cornwall, engineers and miners, for their invented methods of improving the construction of steam-engines, and the application thereof for driving carriages, and for other purposes". The steam-carriage built by Trevethick on this patent, presented the appearance of an ordinary stage-coach on four wheels. It had one horizontal cylinder, which, together with the boiler and the furnace-box, was placed in the rear of the hind axle. The motion of the piston was transmitted to a separate crank-axle, from which, through the medium of spur-gear, the axle of the driving-wheel (which was mounted with a fly-wheel) derived its motion. It is also worthy of note, that the steam-cocks and the force-pump, as also the bellows used for the purpose of quickening combustion in the furnace, were worked off the same crank-axle.

This was the first successful high-pressure engine constructed on the principle of moving a piston by the elasticity of steam against the pressure only of the atmosphere. Such an engine had been described by Leopold, though in his apparatus the pressure acted only on one side of the piston. In Trevethick and Vivian's engine, the piston was not only raised, but was also depressed by the action of the steam, being in this respect an entirely original invention, and of great merit. The steam was admitted from the boiler under the piston moving in a cylinder, impelling it upward. When the motion had reached its limit, the communication between the piston and the under side was shut off, and the steam allowed to escape into the atmosphere. A passage was then opened between the boiler and the upper side of the piston, which was pressed downwards, and the steam again allowed to escape into the atmosphere. Thus the power of the engine was equal to the difference between the pressure of the atmosphere and the elasticity of the steam in the boiler.

This first steam-carriage adapted for actual use on common roads, was, on the whole, tolerably successful. It excited considerable interest in the remote district, near to the Land's End, where it had been constructed. Being so far removed from the great movements and enterprise of the commercial world, the ingenious inventors determined upon exhibiting their machine in the metropolis, with a view, if possible, to its practical adoption for the purpose intended. In furtherance of this object, they set out with the locomotive to Plymouth, whence a sea captain, named Vivian, was to convey it in his vessel to town. Coleridge relates, that whilst the vehicle was proceeding along the road towards the port, at the top of its speed, and had just carried away a portion of the rails of a gentleman's garden, Andrew Vivian descried ahead of them a closed toll-gate, and called out to Trevethick, who was behind, to slacken speed. He immediately shut off the steam; but the momentum was so great, that the carriage proceeded some distance, coming dead up, however, just on the right side of the gate, which was opened like lightning by the toll-keeper. "What have us got to pay here?" asked Vivian. The poor toll-man, trembling in every limb, his teeth chattering in his head, essayed a reply – "Na-na-na-na-" – "What have us got to pay, I say?" "No-noth-nothing to pay! My de-dear Mr Devil, do drive on as fast as you can! nothing to pay!"

The carriage safely reached the metropolis, and was there publicly exhibited in an enclosed piece of ground near Euston Square, where the London and North Western Station now stands; and it dragged behind it a wheel-carriage full of passengers. On the second day of the performance, crowds flocked to see the machine; but Trevethick, in one of his odd freaks, shut up the place, and shortly after removed the engine. While in the metropolis, he secured the support of Lord Stanhope, Davies Gilbert, and other distinguished men. Sir Humphry Davy took much interest in the invention of his countryman, and writing to his friend David Geddy, in Cornwall, shortly after the machine had reached town, he said, – "I shall hope soon to hear that the roads of England are the haunts of Captain Trevethick's dragons – a characteristic name." It was felt, however, that the badness of the English roads at the time rendered it next to impossible to bring the steam-carriage into general use; and thus, after having been successfully exhibited as a curiosity, it was abandoned by Trevethick as a practical failure.

In the year following the exhibition of the steam-carriage, a gentleman was laying heavy wagers as to the weight which could be hauled by a single horse on the Wandsworth and Croydon iron tram-way; and the number and weight of waggons drawn by the horse were something surprising. Trevethick very probably put the two things together – the steam-horse and the iron-way – and proceeded to construct his second or railway locomotive. The idea, however, was not entirely new to him; for although his first steam-carriage had been constructed with a view to its employment on common roads, the specification of his patent distinctly alludes to the application of his engine to travelling on railroads. In 1804 he proceeded to construct a locomotive after an improved plan for this special purpose; and in the course of the same year it was completed, and tried on the Merthyr Tydvil Railway in South Wales. On the occasion of its first trial, the engine succeeded in dragging after it several waggons containing ten tons of bar iron, at the rate of about five miles an hour. The boiler of this engine was cylindrical, flat at the ends, and constructed of cast-iron. The furnace and flue were inside the boiler, within which the single cylinder, of eight inches in diameter, and four feet six inches stroke, was immersed upright. As in the first engine, the motion of the wheels was produced by spur-gear, to which was also added a fly-wheel on one side. The waste steam was thrown into the chimney through a tube inserted into it at right angles; but it will be obvious that this arrangement was not calculated to produce any result in the way of a steam blast in the chimney. In fact, the waste steam seems to have been turned into the chimney in order to get rid of the nuisance caused by throwing the jet directly into the air. Trevethick was here hovering on the verge of a great discovery; but that he was not aware of the action of the blast in contributing to increase the draught, and thus quicken combustion, is clear, from the fact that he employed bellows for this special purpose, and at a much later date (in 1815) he took out a patent which included a method of urging the fire by means of fanners.

Although the locomotive tried upon the Merthyr Tydvil Railway succeeded in drawing a considerable weight, and travelled at a fair speed, it nevertheless proved, like the first steam-carriage, a practical failure. It was never employed to do regular work, but was abandoned after a few experiments. Its jolting motion champed up the cast-iron road, which was little calculated to bear so heavy a weight – though it was very light as compared with modern engines – and it was consequently dismounted from its wheels, and the engine was subsequently fixed and used to pump one of the largest pumps on the mine, for which work it was found well adapted.

Trevethick was satisfied with merely making a few experiments with his steam-carriage and engine; and, being a volatile genius, fond of new projects, he seems to have thought no more of the locomotive, but left it to take care of itself. Yet his machine, although unfitted for actual work, was a highly meritorious production, and its invention may be said to constitute an important link in the history of the mechanism of the steam-engine.

Trevethick having abandoned the locomotive for more promising schemes, no further progress was made with it for some years. An imaginary difficulty seems to have tended, amongst other obstacles, to prevent its adoption and improvement. This

F

was the supposition that, if any heavy weight were placed behind
the engine, the "grip" or "bite" of the smooth wheels of the
locomotive upon the equally smooth iron rail, must necessarily be
so slight that the wheels would slip round upon the rail, and, consequently, that the machine would not make any progress. Hence
Trevethick, in his patent, recommended that the periphery of the
driving wheels should be made rough by the projection of bolts or
cross-grooves, so that the adhesion of the wheels to the road might
be secured. This plan was adopted in Trevethick's engine tried on
the Merthyr Tydvil Railway, and its progress must therefore
necessarily have been a succession of jolts, very trying to the cast-
iron plates of the colliery tram-road.

Following up the presumed necessity for a more effectual
adhesion between the wheels and the rails than that presented by
their mere smooth contact, Mr Blenkinsop, of Leeds, in 1811, took
out a patent for a racked or toothed rail laid along on one side of
the road, into which the toothed-wheel of his locomotive worked
as pinions work into a rack. The boiler of his engine was supported
by a carriage with four wheels without teeth, and rested immediately upon the axles. These wheels were entirely independent of
the working parts of the engine, and therefore merely supported
its weight on the rails, the progress being effected by means of the
cogged-wheel working into the cogged-rail. The engine had two
cylinders instead of one, as in Trevethick's engine. The invention
of the double cylinder was due to Matthew Murray, of Leeds, one
of the best mechanical engineers of his time, Mr Blenkinsop, who
was not himself a mechanic, having consulted him as to all the
practical arrangements of his locomotive. The connecting-rods
gave the motion to two pinions by cranks at right angles to each
other; these pinions communicating the motion to the wheel
which worked into the toothed-rail.

Mr Blenkinsop's engines began running on the railway extending from the Middleton collieries to the town of Leeds, a distance
of about three miles and a half, on the 12th of August, 1812. They
continued for many years to be one of the principal curiosities of
the neighbourhood, and were visited by strangers from all parts.
In the year 1816, the Grand Duke Nicholas (afterwards Emperor)
of Russia observed the working of Blenkinsop's locomotive with
curious interest and expressions of no slight admiration. An engine

dragged behind it as many as thirty coal-waggons at a speed of about three miles and a quarter an hour. These engines continued for many years to be thus employed in the haulage of coal, and furnished the first instance of the regular employment of loco-motive power for commercial purposes.

The Messrs Chapman, of Newcastle, in 1812, endeavoured to overcome the same fictitious difficulty of the want of adhesion between the wheel and the rail, by patenting a locomotive to work along the road by means of a chain stretched from one end of it to the other. This chain was passed once round a grooved barrel-wheel under the centre of the engine; so that, when the wheel turned, the locomotive, as it were, dragged itself along the railway. An engine, constructed after this plan, was tried on the Heaton Railway, near Newcastle; but it was so clumsy in its action, there was so great a loss of power by friction, and it was found to be so expensive and difficult to keep in repair, that it was very soon abandoned. Another remarkable expedient was adopted by Mr Brunton, of the Butterly Works, Derbyshire, who, in 1813, patented a locomotive contrived to go *upon legs!* But the engine never got beyond the experimental state, for, in one of its trials, it unhappily blew up and killed several of the bystanders. These, and other similar contrivances with the same object, projected about the same time, show that invention was actively at work, and that many minds were now anxiously labouring to solve the important problem of locomotive traction upon railways.

But the difficulties contended with by these early inventors, and the step-by-step progress which they made, will probably be best illustrated by the experiments conducted by Mr Blackett, of Wylam. . . .

The Wylam waggon-way is one of the oldest in the north of England. Down to the year 1807 it was formed of wooden spars or rails, laid down between the colliery at Wylam – where old Robert Stephenson had worked – and the village of Lemington, some four miles down the Tyne, where the coals were loaded in keels or barges, and floated down the river past Newcastle, thence to be shipped for the London market. Each chaldron waggon was originally drawn by one horse, with a man to each horse and waggon. The rate at which the journey was performed was so slow that only two journeys were performed by each man and

horse in one day, and three on the day following, the driver being
allowed 7d. for each journey. . . .

Mr Blackett was the first colliery owner in the north who took
an interest in the locomotive engine. He went so far as to order
one direct from Trevethick to work his waggon-way, about the
year 1811. The engine came down to Newcastle; but, for some
reason or other, perhaps because of the imperfect construction of
the waggon-way as compared with the weight of the engine, it
was never put upon the road. Mr Blackett eventually sold it to a
Mr Winfield, of Gateshead, by whom it was employed for many
years in blowing the cupola of his iron-foundry.

Mr Blackett had taken up the wooden road in 1808, and laid
down a "plate-way" of cast-iron – a single line, with sidings. The
waggons continued to be drawn by horses; but the new iron road
proved so much smoother than the former wooden one, that one
horse, instead of drawing one chaldron waggon, was now enabled
to draw two. Still determined to make the experiment of working
his plate-way by locomotive power, Mr Blackett, in 1812, ordered
another engine, after Trevethick's patent, which had yet two
years to run. He also resolved to employ the rack-rail and toothed
driving-wheel, like Blenkinsop's, and he had the road altered
accordingly. The locomotive was constructed by Thomas Waters,
of Gateshead, who executed the work for Trevethick on commission. This engine was of the most awkward construction
imaginable. It had a single cylinder six inches in diameter, with a
fly-wheel working at one side to carry the cranks over the dead
points. The boiler was of cast-iron. Jonathan Foster, the Wylam
engine-wright, who superintended its construction, described the
machine to the writer as having "lots of pumps, cog-wheels, and
plugs, requiring constant attention while at work". The weight of
the whole was about six tons. When completed, it was conveyed
to Wylam on a waggon, and there mounted upon the wooden
frame supported by four pairs of wheels which had previously
been constructed for it. A barrel of water, placed on a rude frame
supported by other two pairs of wheels, served as a tender. After
a great deal of labour, the cumbrous and unsightly machine was
got upon the road. But the engine would not move an inch! When
the machinery was set in motion, Jonathan Foster says, "She flew
all to pieces, and it was the biggest wonder i' the world that we

were not all blown up". The useless engine was taken off the road and sold; and Mr Blackett's efforts were thus far in vain.

He was still, however, desirous of testing the practicability of employing locomotive power in railway traction, and he determined upon making yet another trial. Accordingly, he proceeded to build another engine under his own and Jonathan Foster's inspection, in the Wylam workshops. The new engine had a single eight-inch cylinder, was fitted with a fly-wheel, and ran on four instead of eight wheels: the driving-wheel on one side being cogged, in order to enable it to travel in the rack-rail. This engine proved more successful than its predecessors. Although it was clumsy and unsightly, it was found capable of dragging eight or nine loaded waggons down to the shipping place at Lemington. Its weight was, however, too great for the road, and the cast-iron plates were constantly breaking.

Although this new locomotive was considered by Mr Blackett to be an improvement upon horse traction, its working was by no means satisfactory. It crept along at a snail's pace, sometimes taking six hours to travel the five miles down to the loading-place. It was also very apt to get off the rack-rail, and then it stuck. On these occasions, the horses had to be sent out to drag on the waggons as before. The engine itself, constructed by incompetent workmen, often broke down; its plugs, pumps, or cranks got wrong; and then the horses were sent out to drag it back to the shop. Indeed, it at length became so cranky, that the horses were very frequently sent out following the engine, to be in readiness to draw it along when it gave up: and at length the workmen declared it to be "a perfect plague".

Mr Blackett did not obtain any credit amongst his neighbours for these expensive experiments. Many laughed at his machines, regarding them only in the light of costly crotchets – frequently quoting the proverb of "a fool and his money". Others regarded them as absurd innovations on the established method of hauling coal; and pronounced that they would "never answer".

To some, indeed, they were the cause of considerable apprehension and alarm.

A story is still current at Wylam, of a stranger who was proceeding one dark evening down the High Street Road, as the "Black Billy" (for so the locomotive was called) was seen advancing, puffing and snorting its painful and laborious way up from Newburn. The stranger had never heard of the new engine, and was almost frightened out of his senses at its approach. An uncouth monster it must have looked, coming flaming on in the dark, working its piston up and down like a huge arm, snorting out loud blasts of steam from either nostril, and throwing out smoke and fire as it panted along. No wonder that the stranger rushed terrified through the hedge, fled across the fields, and called out to the first person he met, that he had just encountered a "terrible deevil on the High Street Road".

Notwithstanding the comparative failure of his locomotive thus far, Mr Blackett persevered with his experiments. About 1813, he took out a patent, in the name of William Hedley, his viewer, for a frame on four wheels on which to mount the locomotive engine. One of the first experiments which he made with this frame was, to test the adhesion of the smooth wheels of a carriage, properly weighted, upon the smooth rails of the road. Six men were placed upon the frame, which was fitted up with windlasses attached by gearing to the several wheels. When the men were set to work the windlasses, Mr Blackett found that the adhesion of the wheels on the smooth rails was sufficient to enable them to propel the machine without slipping. Having then found the proportion which the power bore to the weight, he demonstrated by successive experiments that the weight of the engine would of itself produce sufficient adhesion to enable it to drag after it, on a smooth tram-road, the requisite number of waggons in all kinds of weather. Thus was the fallacy which had heretofore prevailed on this subject completely dissipated, and it was satisfactorily proved that rack-rails, toothed-wheels, endless chains, and legs, were alike unnecessary for the efficient traction of loaded waggons upon a moderately level road.

from THE LIFE OF GEORGE STEPHENSON *1857*

The Rainhill Trials

O. S. NOCK

The building of the *Rocket* and its successful running in the Rainhill trials may well be considered as the great turning point in early locomotive history. Until then the old "puffers" had trundled along at low speeds over short distances. Even the 20-mile main line of the Stockton and Darlington had extended them to their limit, and for a time the resolute optimism of George Stephenson was hardly supported by the day-to-day work of his engines in the hauling of the coal trains. His vision of a railway network covering the whole country needed some solid backing in greater and more sustained steaming capacity, and greater freedom of running. It is, of course, easy to lay down such desiderata ... but the Stephensons, father and son, while sufficiently aware of the operating difficulties on the Stockton and Darlington, chose to take a broader view. While Timothy Hackworth struggled to keep things going on the line with the limited equipment available in the repair sheds at Shildon, George Stephenson had more particularly in mind the future motive power requirements of the Liverpool and Manchester. It was perhaps inevitable that in after years Hackworth felt that he had received the "rough end of the stick": that he pulled the Stephenson chestnuts out of the fire only to receive a very public rebuff at Rainhill. Although one would not go so far as to say that a feud developed between the two families, the Hackworths and Stephensons were henceforth keen rivals instead of allies. ...

The *Royal George*, built by Timothy Hackworth at Shildon in 1827 was the largest and heaviest engine to be constructed at that time; it provided the power needed for working the coal trains by use of a much larger boiler than any Stephenson himself had so far built, and by having six wheels coupled. But the large boiler in itself did not provide the entire answer. Hackworth increased the steaming capacity by arranging the flue from the fire-box to the chimney in the form of a U, instead of a single large pipe, and so presented an increased area of flue tube in contact with the water. It is also generally agreed nowadays that Hackworth was the inventor of the blast pipe as we know it today – a narrowing cone, through the nozzle of which the exhaust steam passes at high velocity and creates an intense draught on the fire....

Outwardly the wheels were perhaps the most distinctive feature of the *Royal George,* and although the design was nothing more than an ingenious make-shift to suit the manufacturing facilities at his disposal, Hackworth's design remained standard on the Stockton and Darlington freight engines for the ensuing twenty years. In the *Royal George* the wheels were 4 ft. in diameter. There were no lathes in the Shildon shops large enough to turn up the rims when the wheels were fixed on the axles, and so Hackworth made the wheels in two parts. The inner portion including the boss was made in cast-iron, and as large as the lathe would take; this "centre" was trued up, and then the outer section was fitted, and trued to the inner portion, the two sections being held together by a series of wooden keys. A beautiful example of Stockton and Darlington six-coupled goods engines having the Hackworth type of plug-wheel has been preserved, and now stands on a pedestal in Darlington station. This is the *Derwent,* which was built by Alfred Kitching in 1839.

Another unusual feature, common to the *Royal George* and to later Stockton and Darlington coal engines was that the fire-door was at the chimney end of the boiler. This was made necessary on the *Royal George* by the U-shaped flue, which started from the fire-box, ran the length of the boiler, and returned again to the chimney. As a result these Hackworth engines had to be provided with two tenders; one, on which the fireman rode, was propelled ahead of the engine, while the second, with the driver, was in the conventional position between the engine and the train. It is extraordinary to realize that locomotives of this type were built down to the year 1846, and that some were still in regular service on the Stockton and Darlington Railway at the time of the Jubilee celebrations of 1875.

The success of the *Royal George* emboldened Hackworth to enter the competition staged by the directors of the Liverpool and Manchester Railway in opposition to his friends and associates the Stephensons. The circumstances were enough to daunt the boldest and most determined of pioneers. As engineer and manager of the Stockton and Darlington Railway he was not a free agent. The designing of the engine for the competition had to be done in his spare time, and although the Company allowed him to erect the engine in the Shildon shops it had to be done at his own expense. The boiler was made at Bedlington Ironworks, the cylinders were cast at Stephenson's works. Some of his suppliers were late with their deliveries, and the erection of the engine was done hurriedly in order to reach Rainhill in time for the trials. Before the actual competition there was little opportunity for any thorough testing, and a few midnight runs on the level stretch of the line near Aycliffe were all that was possible in the time. As a courageous piece of pioneer locomotive construction Hackworth's *Sans Pareil* can have few equals. But before coming to the special features of this brave little engine some reference is needed to the test conditions imposed by the Liverpool and Manchester Railway.

The conditions were stated in a circular issued from the Railway Office, Liverpool, on April 25th, 1829. They included a number of general provisions, such as safety valves, springs, and so on, plus the important one that the engine must "effectually consume its own smoke". The maximum weight of the engine only, with a full complement of water in the boiler, was not to exceed 6 tons, though a lighter engine was preferred. If the engine exceeded $4\frac{1}{2}$ tons in weight it was to be carried on six wheels. The working steam pressure in the boiler was not to exceed 50 lb. per sq. in., and in such conditions certain train loads were specified for a speed of 10 m.p.h. according to the weight of the engine itself:

F*

a 6-ton engine was required to haul 20 tons; a 5-ton engine, 15 tons, and so on. . . .

The running ground chosen was a stretch of level track on the Manchester side of Rainhill bridge. The test length was $1\frac{3}{4}$ miles long, but this included one-eighth of a mile at each end for starting and stopping. The central portion of $1\frac{1}{2}$ miles was to be covered at full speed. To simulate service conditions as far as possible each competitor was required to make ten return trips over the course in rapid succession. Thus a total of 30 miles would be covered at full speed, and this was approximately equal to a run from Liverpool to Manchester. After the test was completed more fuel and water was to be taken on, and ten more return trips made. There were no facilities for turning, and so half the runs over the measured $1\frac{1}{2}$ miles were made with the competing engines propelling their trains. . . .

Four steam locomotives were entered for the prize, and one horse machine. In addition to the *Rocket* and the *Sans Pareil,* there was the unconventional *Novelty,* entered by the Swedish inventor, Ericsson, in conjunction with John Braithwaite. [This] had a vertical boiler and the necessary draught for rapid steam raising was provided for by a set of mechanically worked bellows. There was only one cylinder, fixed almost vertically above the rear pair of wheels. The fourth locomotive, the *Perseverance* built by Mr Burstall was quite outclassed, and took little or no part in the competition. Robert Stephenson, his father, and [Joseph] Locke regarded the *Novelty* as their most serious rival, and Vignoles in his eye witness account of the trials records that: "the machinery was of much more finished workmanship than Stephenson's engine, and when it was brought to view burnished with copper and dark blue paint, it evoked universal admiration". The *Novelty* was certainly the popular favourite. The local newspapers eulogised it as "exhibiting by its beauty and compactness the very *beau-ideal* of a locomotive"; and when on a preliminary run without any load it swept past the Rainhill grandstand at 23 m.p.h. it became more than ever the favourite. But Locke and George Stephenson looked on critically, and when on the return trip the bellows failed and the *Novelty* came to stand in mid-course George Stephenson turned to Locke and said, "Eh mon, we needn't fear yon thing, it's got no goots!"

The *Rocket* was an exceedingly simple and straightforward engine. Unlike the earlier Stephenson machines and Hackworth's *Sans Pareil*, it had but a single pair of driving wheels, with a pair of carrying wheels underneath the driver's footplate. The really novel feature was the boiler. To promote rapid evaporation by increasing the hot surfaces in contact with the water the flue from the fire-box to the chimney was split up, so that the hot gases of combustion instead of passing through one large pipe passed through a nest of much smaller ones. Nicholas Wood's drawing shows twenty-five flue tubes. This arrangement, adopted at the suggestion of Henry Booth, gave Robert Stephenson some anxious moments in the constructional stages. . . .

The opening day of the test may be described in the words of Vignoles:

First day, October 6th, 1829 (Tuesday)

Place: Manchester side of the Skewbridge at Rainhill, on the level of one and three quarter miles, on which each competing engine was to make ten double journeys, or thirty-five miles in all, rather more than the distance between the two towns. Vast numbers of people were present. The "Rocket" first to try: it drew 12 tons 9 cwt. at exact rate of ten miles four chains per hour; without load it ran eighteen miles per hour. Its velocity was very unequal, and it did not at first thoroughly consume its own smoke.

For precise details of the actual performances we may turn to Nicholas Wood's account. The running was timed to the last second, and the logs of the two experiments, representing the journey from Liverpool to Manchester and back, include notes of the instant at which water was taken, the engine was oiled, the pistons greased, and so on. The *Rocket* performed with complete reliability, and her two trips gave the following results for the 30 miles covered at full speed: first experiment, average speed 13·4 m.p.h.; second experiment, 14·2 m.p.h. On examining the details of individual runs it was found that the 1½-mile stretches in the eastbound direction were invariably done faster than the corresponding westbound runs. The carriages were being propelled in the westbound direction and it would certainly seem that the resistance to motion was greater in this method of working.

Nicholas Wood felt that too much notice should not be taken of
the performance when propelling, as no train would ordinarily be
worked in this way. He accordingly took the average of all the
eastbound runs made by the *Rocket,* and these gave a speed of
15 m.p.h. But in any case the requirements of the "ordeal", as it
was called, had been fulfilled, without making any allowance for
the abnormality of propelling, and it remained to be seen how the
other competitors would fare.

Next came the *Sans Pareil.* It was duly weighed before starting
on any run, but when found to scale 4 tons 15½ cwt. it was at once
realized that one stipulated condition had not been complied with
– namely that if a competing engine weighed more than 4½ tons it
should be carried on six wheels. On consideration the judges
determined to put the engine through its trials, and if its performance was satisfactory some recommendation might be made
regarding its claim for the prize. The *Sans Pareil* started well, and
at first her speeds averaged much the same as those of the *Rocket*
with the same variation between eastbound and westbound
running. But then Nicholas Wood writes: "In traversing the
eighth trip to the west, the pump that supplies the boiler with
water got wrong, which, checking the supply, the water in the
boiler got below the top of the tube, and melted the leaden plug,
inserted for the purpose of preventing accidents in such a case and
put an end to the experiment." And of the *Sans Pareil* Wood says
no more. . . .

In the meantime the *Novelty* had been putting up some spectacular, if erratic performances. She was dogged by numerous
small failures, and never completed a single series of trials.
Vignoles writes of October 10th.

> It was three o'clock when the "Novelty" was again fit to run,
> and her performance also was not deemed competitive. She
> drew a total weight of 10 tons 6 cwt. and one quarter, inclusive
> of her own weight. I rode on the engine and carefully timed her
> performance. She went her first distance at seventeen and a half
> miles per hour, and then discarded the load for a wagon full of
> forty-five passengers, which she whirled along at upwards of
> thirty miles an hour.

Charles Fox, who afterwards built the Crystal Palace, was a

spectator, and used to say he could never forget the look on Robert Stephenson's face as the *Novelty* shot by the *Rocket*. Really, however, Stephenson had nothing to fear, and on his second series of runs, while maintaining a comfortable margin in hand over the stipulated speed it was evident that the *Rocket* was far from being pressed to its utmost. On the eastbound runs, over the measured 1½ miles, he had averaged 14·4, 15·1, 17·0, 12·7, 14·8, 15·4, 14·6, 16·7, and 16·6 m.p.h. on nine successive runs; but on the last he opened out, and with the full test load he put up an average speed of 24·1 m.p.h.

From one cause or another neither the *Sans Pareil* nor the *Novelty* completed a single set of trials, and the judges naturally awarded the prize to the Stephensons and Henry Booth. This outcome left Ericsson and Hackworth very disappointed men. Ericsson was annoyed that mechanical failures of a really minor kind had prevented his engine from staying the course, when it was so obvious that it could have fulfilled the conditions. Right up to the end the *Novelty* remained the popular favourite, and further trials were continued on the Liverpool and Manchester line. On December 17th, 1829, Ericsson wrote to Braithwaite:

> We have been at work steadily the whole day, and everything has gone extremely well. . . . We went at various speeds during the day, sometimes with and sometimes without passengers, and the steam was kept up in wonderful style.
>
> The engine did not exceed two hundred and sixty strokes per minute, not quite forty miles an hour; and I am confident that if I dare trust the *force pump* at such a rate I could have done *one mile in one minute*!
>
> As the engine passed on in its velocity the spectators cheered in a glorious manner. I will send the particulars of more experiments tomorrow.

Forty miles per hour in 1829: railway travel was certainly progressing!

from THE RAILWAY ENGINEERS *1955*

Patrick Stirling

O. S. NOCK

Patrick Stirling was a Scot born and bred, who from 1853 to 1866 was Locomotive Superintendent of the Glasgow & South Western Railway.

Stirling brought to the Great Northern Railway in 1866 a style in locomotive lineaments that for simple, austere beauty has never been surpassed. On the Great Northern, and before that on the G. & S.W.R., his engines were domeless. The line of the boiler was unbroken between the chimney and the huge brass casing that enclosed the safety valves just ahead of the cab. Stirling's brother James and his son Matthew both followed the cult of the domeless boiler; but the engines of James on the South Eastern Railway, and of Matthew on the Hull & Barnsley, could not compare for sheer elegance with those of Patrick. The Great Northern express engines of 1870–1895 were not merely handsome to look at. They have a special claim to be remembered in that they hauled the fastest trains operated in the country at that time. The Great Western, still working much of its passenger mileage on the broad gauge, had long dropped out of the lead, and the Great Northern had quite a number of trains keeping start-to-stop averages of 52 to 54 m.p.h.

Patrick Stirling used single-wheelers to the exclusion of all other engines on the crack trains. He once likened a coupled engine to "a laddie runnin' wi' his breeks doon"; and although he built a large class of admirable 2-4-os that on any other line would undoubtedly have been graded as "express passenger", there are no recorded instances of them getting a turn at the Scotch expresses, the fast Leeds trains, or the Manchesters. Like all his fellow engineers of that time, Stirling was responsible not only for designing, building and repairing locomotives; he was responsible for running them as well, and in one respect he had very pronounced views. His inflexible rule was "One train, one engine". Where other companies countered exceptional loading or inadequate engine-power by double-heading, Stirling stood firm; his great single-wheelers were judged to be good enough for anything the traffic department cared to put behind them.

And what engines they were! Stirling built two varieties of these supremely beautiful engines: a very simple, austerely-styled 2–2–2, with 7 ft. 7 in. driving wheels, and the 8 ft. bogie type, with outside cylinders and the running plate carried high in a sweeping curve so as to display in full the graceful action of the connecting rod in following the long piston stroke of 28 in. It is no exaggeration to say that the Stirling 8 ft. bogie singles were, in outward appearance, the most distinctive locomotives to appear on any British railway. It is indeed fortunate and fitting that the first of them should be preserved and exhibited in the Railway Museum at York. But the Stirling singles were no mere showpieces. They were absolute greyhounds, and when speeds of 70 m.p.h. were relatively rare on other lines they ran at 75 and even 80 m.p.h. with the fast Great Northern expresses.

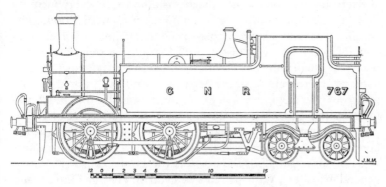

Stirling never ceased to be a Scot in outlook. . . but he absorbed to the utmost the traditions of the Great Northern Railway. There were then no retirements at the age of 65. Stirling continued in full harness until his death in 1895, in his 76th year. Age had not wearied his spirit nor his enthusiasm, and when the second great railway race broke upon the Great Northern in 1895 one finds him telling his district superintendents that "we can never allow" the North Western to draw ahead of them, and to be sure and put the men concerned on their mettle. Stirling's death marked the end of an era. Ending were the days of six-wheeled coaches and non-corridor trains. The twentieth century was not far upon its turbulent course before his domeless-boilered engines were little more than a memory. Yet, as with Fletcher on the North Eastern, the spirit of Stirling lingered at Doncaster. His successor, Henry A. Ivatt, told the men: "I am following in the footsteps of a very great engineer, and whatever changes I have to make I will see to it that you have plenty of steam."

from STEAM LOCOMOTIVE (B.T.C.) *1958*

Richard Moon

C. HAMILTON ELLIS

For thirty years, from 1861 to 1891, a very eminent personage commanded, dominated and oppressed the London and North Western Railway Board, its officers, its officials, its every member down to the junior porters and van boys. Sir Richard Moon, as he became, was not the type of chairman one encountered on all sorts of railways, which was just as well for some people. He was at once able, incorruptible and one of the most terrifying personages in Victorian private business. He it was who had purged the old company of many office holders, from the amiable and much too mild Francis Trevithick to the buccaneering Mark Huish. He had, it seems, most of the cardinal virtues – who dare say that at the bottom of the pile there was not humility of a sort? But kindness was not apparent. With the possible exceptions of his successive general managers, William Cawkwell and Sir George Findlay, and of Francis Webb, his chief mechanical engineer, those who knew him were almost mortally afraid of him. He it was who had taken a slackly knit railway company, all too obviously the product of amalgamation, and had welded it into a supreme power of its kind, a totalitarian corporate state in nineteenth-century capitalism, which persuaded its clients, and which had no gentle compunction about political dictation to its servants. No railway stood more highly than the London and North Western in public opinion, which was critical of railway companies. The North Western was indeed a Premier Line, even though one of its expressed reasons for that claim – descent through amalgamation from the venerable Liverpool and Manchester Railway – might not be entirely sufficient.

Moon's appearance was in keeping with his character. He was a man with rocky brows above cold, small, fierce eyes, a strong cranium, a strong nose, and a mouth like a steel gin. He was born into an era when his every gift, his every talent, were of sorts which the ruling class appreciated, consequently he became eminent in the new ruling class, that of the Victorian technocracy. He was essentially British, and essentially English at that. He was no more comparable to his American contemporaries such as Vanderbilt and Gould than Wellington was comparable with Talleyrand and Fouché.

from BRITISH RAILWAY HISTORY 1877–1947 *1959*

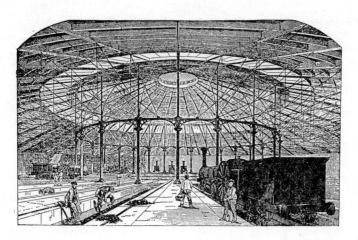

Henry Ivatt

G. GIFFARD JACKSON

Patrick Stirling was succeeded by H. A. Ivatt, who came to the Great Northern from the Great Southern and Western – Ireland's chief railway.

He was faced with a problem at the outset – the trains had grown beyond the power of the eight-footers. What was to be done?

Ivatt had no fixed ideas on the point of locomotive design. From the first he realized that conditions on an English railway,

noted for its speed, were very different to what he had been used
to. Like a wise man he took time to think, meanwhile providing
for the heavier loads by re-building with bigger boilers as many of
the eight-footers and the 7 foot 6 inch "singles" as possible. Outwardly the greatest change Ivatt made was the introduction of a
dome on a railway which had not seen one since its earliest days,
when a few engines, built by private builders, possessed this usual
locomotive fitting.

Then at length Mr Ivatt was ready, and he produced three new
types – all of them good and one being a startling novelty.

This was the first "Atlantic", whose wheel formula is 4–4–2.
This "Atlantic" was a much bigger engine than had been seen on
the Great Northern, and from the first she did good work.

She appeared in 1898 and the following are her principal
dimensions. The cylinders were placed outside, slightly inclined,
with dimensions $18\frac{3}{4} \times 24$ inches; coupled wheels 6 feet $7\frac{1}{2}$ inches
in diameter, the boiler was 14 feet $8\frac{1}{2}$ inches long, heating surface
1442 square feet, and a working steam pressure of 175 lbs. per
square inch was used. The total weight of engine and tender came
to just within 99 tons. The number given to this new departure in
British practice was 990, and it was rendered exceptionally interesting to locomotivists by bearing a name, "Sir Henry Oakley",
after a famous general manager of the line.

For some time Mr Ivatt was content to watch the performances
of his new model, but whilst doing so he turned out several
batches of very useful 4–4–0s, which, whilst considerably bigger
than any four-coupled engines the G.N. had possessed, were not
of striking design. . . .

Then, convinced that Stirling did not cling to the "single"
without good reason, Ivatt determined to see what could be done in
that direction. The result was one of the finest single drivers we
have seen on British metals. This was his famous "266" class, which
will go down to history as the "last of the 'singles' "; with the
completion of the order for twelve in 1901, no further single drivers
were built on the Great Northern, or any other British railway.

Stirling had gone back to the 2–2–2 type, with 7 ft. 6 in. drivers.
Ivatt followed him with his new "singles", but he used a much
bigger boiler and added a leading bogie. . . .

The inside cylinders of the "266" class were 18×26. The engine

and tender scaled rather more than 88 tons. The fine appearance of
this model was somewhat spoiled by placing the dome on the first
ring of the boiler barrel, instead of over the driving-wheels, but, of
course, this had no effect on the fine work which the twelve of
them did. . . . The later engines had some slight variations, but in
all essentials they followed the pioneer engine of their class.

These machines put up a good fight for the single-wheeler, and
again we may say that had loads consented to remain stationary
their numbers would have been greatly increased, since in first cost
and running they were considerably cheaper than the "Atlantics".
Unfortunately, loads were still increasing very rapidly, and in 1901
Mr Ivatt realized that, despite all he could do, the day of the
favourite type of express engine on the Great Northern, and on
most other railways, was indeed past. So no more "singles" were
ordered, and the type which had built up speed records for this
famous railway was gradually withdrawn from the best expresses,
though it is only right to say that "266" and her sisters were
retained on some of the lightest and fastest for many years.

from THE BOOK OF THE LOCOMOTIVE *1924*

Churchward's Classics

W. A. TUPLIN

Much of the distinction of Great Western locomotive practice in
the twentieth century is due to G. J. Churchward, a cautious
locomotive engineer of much experience. Like most others who
attain managerial positions he had a strong instinct for planning
for his future. Born at Stoke Gabriel, near Totnes, he entered the
service of the South Devon Railway and, with its absorption by the
Great Western became a member of the staff of that system. With
successive promotions he soon began to see himself as the
Locomotive Superintendent of the Great Western and so, while
learning all he could about the building, running and repairing of
locomotives he kept his eyes open for bright young men whom he
could hope to collect when he was in a position to appoint staff of
his own.

Even though an engineer may be inventive himself, it is extremely valuable to have subordinates who are similarly gifted; it
may be easier to pick and choose among other people's ideas than
to produce one's own, and it is certainly easier to treat them with
the remorseless criticism that is necessary if weaknesses are to be
eliminated.

After about the year 1890, it was merely a matter of arithmetic
for Churchward to see that, unless he slipped up somewhere, he
could expect to be in charge of the Great Western Locomotive
Department from 1902 (Dean's retiring date) to 1921 (his own
retiring date). He planned to make those nineteen years as restful
as possible. No position of such responsibility can ever be really
restful because of the normal jungle-warfare of industrial life. In
any large organization of any type, departmental heads keep a
wary eye on each other in the incessant battle for more power and
this may be nearly a full-time occupation. If a big job is to be
worth having at all, the technical necessities must be so completely covered that they are not a worry. The manager gets staff
to do the internal work reliably without much supervision by per-
suading them that what is good for him is good for them and he
can then concentrate on coping with the enemies from without.

Churchward recognized that the Great Western locomotive
stock in the 1890s was a collection of oddities – picturesque perhaps but still oddities – and that something better in every way
was going to be needed between 1902 and 1921. At the end of that
period indeed, something quite different from the steam locomotive might be required. Even before 1900, electric locomotives
were running on railways, the petrol engine was used in road
vehicles, and the gas turbine was being discussed. What might
another twenty years bring?

Churchward must have considered questions of this sort but
guessed that if anything was going to supersede the steam locomotive as a haulage agent on railways, it would probably take at
least twenty years to develop it into entirely practical form. What
he was sure about was that he was not going to do the developing.
His job was to give the Great Western reliable locomotives with
the least risk or trouble for himself and that demanded that he
should not use any device or design that had not already been
thoroughly tested by somebody or other. He was wedded to the

very sound engineering principle of using other people's experience and he declined to lose time, money or sleep on trying to make sense out of revolutionary ideas however bright. He kept an inquiring eye on locomotive practice all over the world with the idea of combining the best from everywhere as a basis for the next generation of Swindon locomotives. The ideal for him was to have done all his experimental work while Dean was there to take the responsibility and, soon after his own acceptance of the head position, to bring out new standard designs that he could claim as his own, to cover Great Western needs until 1921. What happened after that was for someone else to worry about.

Churchward's appointment as Locomotive Superintendent in 1902 thus marks the great turning point in Great Western history. He quickly developed at Swindon standard locomotives markedly different in appearance from any others in Great Britain and of an excellence that was tardily equalled but never surpassed. He may perhaps be called the greatest locomotive engineer since Stephenson, but even that does not make him into the supernatural mechanical genius that some of his admirers are ready to assume him to be. The truth is that Churchward locomotives include no important feature that had not been previously used by someone or other, for what Churchward did was to sort out from well-tried practice the features that would best suit Great Western needs and then to make them work.

Something fairly drastic had to be done to unify the Great Western locomotive stock for it is no serious exaggeration to say that there were hardly half-a-dozen engines exactly alike. For example, it is said that there were twelve different designs of bogie in the eighty Dean "singles" which were of a standard type, as the G.W.R. had understood standardization at that time. Quite clearly a more rigorous policy was required. . . .

The advantages of reducing the locomotive stock to the smallest possible number of classes and of making components interchangeable between different classes are so great that such standardization had clearly to be the main characteristic of new locomotive practice for the Great Western Railway. But a stock of some 3,000 odd locomotives cannot be replaced overnight and Churchward realized that some fifteen or twenty years might elapse before the new standard engines could form the bulk of the

company's stock. Obviously the new engines had to be designed
to do what would be required twenty years ahead, so far as that
could be foreseen.

In designing the future standard engines, Churchward com-
promised between rash experiment and perpetuation of old
methods. He accepted the broad principle of the steam locomotive
but proceeded to design it with more open-minded care than had
ever been used before. Far from indulging in entirely novel ideas
he tried nothing that had not already had some success on the
G.W.R. or elsewhere, although in size, shape and detail his first
locomotives were as different from their Swindon predecessors as
could be imagined.

The results achieved in the experimental engines were so grati-
fying that the principles embodied in them were adopted with
little modification in standard designs that even over 25 years later
were superior to their British contemporaries. This, of course, has
often been pointed out, and it is natural to assume that the admirable qualities of Churchward locomotives are attributable entirely
to their design. In actual fact, the credit must be divided between

(1) excellence of basic design;
(2) excellence of detail design;
(3) excellence of materials used;
(4) excellence of workmanship;
(5) intelligence and enterprise in handling on the road;
(6) high standard of maintenance in service.

It would obviously have been foolish to allow the overall performance of the locomotives to be vitiated by imperfection in any
one of these respects and as Churchward had control of all of them
he was able to ensure that every department concerned kept up to
the mark. On some railways in more recent years, the organization
is such that those responsible for (1) and (2) have no official control
over the other matters and the results achieved usually suffer from
the effects of the normal interdepartmental enmities.

Churchward started out with the big advantage that he himself
could decide all major issues at every point in the locomotive's
career from conception to final decomposition. With his position
assured in that respect he had no need to assume the unreasoningly
autocratic manner that some other locomotive engineers of the
period are understood to have affected. In the drawing office he

allotted different men to specialize on different components of the locomotive. On questions of manufacture, officials from the works were consulted while the opinions of shed superintendents and locomotive inspectors were sought on matters concerned with the daily running of the engine. He himself, with experience in every branch, could reach a sound decision on any point after hearing the views of the specialists and was usually able to convince all concerned that it was indeed sound. In the exceptional case he had the authority to enforce the decision and this eliminated the loss of time and effort that always results from reluctance to co-operate in a joint effort. It must have taken more than persuasion to get the running-shed staff to agree to the multiplication of the 4-cylinder engines with their buried valve-gear.

You will sometimes hear an engineer say pathetically "All engineering design is at the mercy of the junior draughtsman', and truly designs are to be seen that confirm that remark to the hilt. It was not so with Churchward. Every detail was examined and criticized before a design was approved and the result is seen in the elemental simplicity of the major and minor components of Swindon locomotives. Nowhere does one see fussiness, flourishes or fads as any such puerility that may have raised its head in the first stage of a design was ruthlessly swept away. It was first decided just what each component had to do, it was then designed to do just that at minimum total cost in material, manufacture and maintenance. If it looked crude or inelegant to some Victorian designer, that was unfortunate but it was not altered on that account.

Whilst the practice of discussing design in collaboration with representatives of all departments concerned is obviously advantageous, it must be admitted that it does not always have the maximum possible effect. One reason is that no single representative of a department is certain to know every detail of what occurs in it. For example, two long-established details of Swindon practice – smokebox-regulator and screwed-in piston-rods – were adopted by Stanier on the L.M.S. but were abandoned there because they could not be made to work satisfactorily. Evidently some uncommunicated detail of "know-how" made all the difference between success and dissatisfaction.

Another reason is that the enginemen learn to cope with a

difficulty till they cease to be worried by it and after a time no complaint or suggestion for improvement in the matter ever reaches the Chief Mechanical Engineer. An example is the continued laborious use of the flap-plate as a fire-door on Great Western locomotives, when something far less fatiguing is easily practicable.

Churchward early decided that fewer than a dozen classes of locomotive would cover all Great Western needs. Starting at the large and spectacular end of the range, what type of express passenger locomotive would be required for the next twenty years? Looking at what was being done in America, thinking of the steep gradients in some parts of the Great Western main lines, anticipating increase in train loads in conjunction with the higher speeds that the G.W.R. was contemplating, he selected an outside-cylinder 4–6–0 with a grate area of about 27 sq. ft. and twenty-three years later, nothing better for the same purpose had been seen in Great Britain. Ten major dimensions for each of six projected classes of locomotives were laid down in a document prepared in the year 1901 to define the design programme for the new standard engines, and except for the development of 4-cylinder engines for the fastest trains, and the addition of three other classes incorporating standard major components, remarkably little departure has ever been made from this scheme in Great Western locomotive practice.

The immediate aim was to produce a few designs of boilers, cylinders, connecting rods, valve gear and wheels which all the standard engines would eventually use and to try them out in experimental engines. Actual service would suggest ways of improvement (it always does) and when satisfactory results were achieved, the new designs would be accepted as standards and very strong resistance shown to any further suggestion for modification. It is here that great willpower is required by an engineer intelligent enough to see that improvement is always possible. Having reached a satisfactory design he must say to himself, in the interest of the great economies effected by standardization, "We will make no change for at least ten years." The distinction of Churchward's work on the G.W.R. was that in a period of about three years, intensive effort produced designs far in advance of those to be found elsewhere, and of a nature that permitted long-term standardization to be started with confidence. . . .

Not many personal details have been published about Churchward but it can be said that whilst he was held in high regard by his assistants, he was not the supernatural deity that some fervent admirers of his locomotives are apt to assume him to be. A photograph reproduced in the *Railway Magazine* at the time of his retirement in 1922 shows a dignified scholarly veteran whilst one that appeared in the *Locomotive Magazine* for January 14, 1922, depicts him as a sporty gent with a startling black moustache. Stories from those who worked for him tend to support the suggestion that he was a multiple personality. He could choose men for jobs and get the best out of them; he was in fact a leader. Churchward bore himself with dignity when the occasion demanded it but more often his manner was hearty and he could talk to labourers in language that they easily understood. He threatened to resign when the General Manager questioned the cost of Swindon locomotives. He was known to speak slightingly of one of his assistants in the presence of juniors. In short he had a full share of human frailties and that his work made history was merely incidental to its success in earning him a living by holding down a big job on the Great Western Railway. . . .

Churchward continued to live at Swindon after his retirement and was a frequent visitor to the works. Not in his lifetime or even for long afterwards, were any substantial departures made there from his methods and so his old age was not sorrowed by any suggestion that he was being out-moded. On the contrary, the successes of Swindon engines in locomotive-exchanges led to the adoption by other British railways of features that had come to be regarded as peculiar to Churchward and so began one of the brightest periods in the history of British locomotive performances.

So it was that Churchward could maintain a gratified interest in Swindon and its locomotives even when responsibility for them had passed from him and so it happened that when walking from his home to the works on the foggy morning of December 19, 1933, in the seventy-fifth year of his age, he was run down and killed by a train on the main line.

from GREAT WESTERN STEAM *1958*

The Heyday of Steam

O. S. NOCK

For the railways of this country the end of the century was also a milestone in their history. The art of locomotive engineering was rapidly approaching a vital system of cross roads, and viewing the events of the years 1900 to 1910 in retrospect it seems that some engineers – among them, too, some of the most eminent men of the day – were not sure which way to go. The Drummond 4–4–0, now seen in its full maturity on the London and South Western, and on the Highland, can be taken as a typical embodiment of all that was best in nineteenth-century practice: a robust chassis, simple cylinder and valve design, with ample passages for the flow of steam, and a good boiler, easily fired. The South Western earned the nickname of the "Greyhounds" while of the Highland "Small Bens", a Scottish driver once told Hamilton Ellis "Yer mither could driver her, ay, and get sixty oot o' her." But certain of the basic features of the design that made it so simple and so successful precluded any enlargement. The slide valves were placed between the cylinders, and the cylinders were between the frames. Dugald Drummond had already used certain artifices in construction, at which some engineers looked askance, in order to obtain the port areas he needed for free running, and yet the increasing weight of trains clearly demanded larger and more powerful locomotives. The way in which various engineers tackled the problem of getting enhanced power forms an absorbing study. It was a time when locomotive superintendents still had a fairly free hand, and the lines they took in many cases reflected the personalities of the men themselves.

The direct successors of Dugald Drummond on the Scottish railways had an essentially sound basis on which to work; these successors were Matthew Holmes on the North British, and John Farquharson McIntosh on the Caledonian. There was actually a period of five years on the latter line between the Drummond and the McIntosh regimes, when John Lambie was locomotive superintendent; but the express locomotives he built were little more than repetitions of the Drummond type, with slightly altered boiler mountings. It has been suggested, too, that the influence of Hugh Smellie was also discerned in the Lambie engines. He was the chosen successor to Drummond, but died only a few months after his appointment. He had built for the Glasgow and South Western a class of very fine 4–4–0 locomotives, and some details of the valve setting of those engines may have been incorporated in future Caledonian designs. But it is with McIntosh that we are now concerned. One might broadly classify locomotive men of that day into those whose interests lay in engine design, in running, and in works matters. A blend of all three was necessary in order to hold down any job of major responsibility, but it is noticeable that many men naturally tended to lay emphasis upon the particular branch of the service in which the larger part of their earlier experience had been gained. McIntosh was essentially a running man. He had been a driver, and a locomotive inspector, and had lost an arm in a footplate accident; and immediately upon taking up the post of locomotive superintendent in 1895 he set himself the task of producing a real "driver's engine".

The Drummonds were excellent engines, but the Caledonian men had found that if they were thrashed up the banks they tended to run short of steam. This, of course, was exactly in accordance with Drummond's intentions – the engines were so proportioned that they couldn't be thrashed. Johnson did just the same on his Midland 4–4–0 engines. Although the process of thrashing extracts a thrilling performance out of a small engine it usually results in a disproportionately high consumption of fuel, and worse still causes heavy maintenance charges on the boiler. But McIntosh wanted more power, and he got it by building engines to the basic Drummond layout, but with much larger boilers. At first he was outstandingly successful. There were mighty few engines of 1895– 1900 vintage, if any, that could have run trains of 170 to 200 tons over the 117·8 miles from Carlisle to Stirling in two hours, or less; the first engine of the new class, No. 721, was named *Dunalastair,* and very soon that name was a household word among locomotive men and enthusiasts alike. From the first series of 1896 McIntosh went on, and built bigger and bigger "Dunalastairs", but on reaching the fourth series, although the total heating surface was 1,615 sq. ft., compared with the 1,028 sq. ft. of a Drummond, and boiler pressure had been increased from 150 to 180 lb. per sq. in., the cylinder diameter was only one inch larger – 19 in. against 18 in. of the Drummond. In consequence one could not get true expansive working when running hard, and the McIntosh engines were accordingly extravagant on coal.

The climax so far as boiler design on the Caledonian was reached in 1903 when two huge 4–6–0 locomotives with no less than 2,523 sq. ft. of heating surface were built at St Rollox works. But by that time McIntosh and his Caledonian locomotives had already become something of a legend. They rejoiced in one of the most beautiful liveries that ever adorned a steam locomotive; they ran hard, kept excellent time, and looked massive and modern, while conforming to the best British traditions of simplicity and neatness in outline. . . .

The influence of McIntosh's work was profound. Following the race to the north in 1895 enthusiasts looked eagerly for any signs of the revival of the racing in the following year, and even if there was no racing, as such, those who travelled through the summer nights and clocked the running of the Tourist express between Carlisle and Stirling were usually well rewarded. With loads of 150 tons and more the "Dunalastairs" were night after night making times nearly as fast as those of the race, but with nearly double the load. One of them starting from Carlisle – almost at sea level – passed Beattock summit, 1,015 ft. up, and 49¾ miles from the start in 52¾ minutes. Charles Rous-Marten, the leading railway journalist of the day, wrote enthusiastic articles in *The Engineer* and elsewhere, and the obvious success of the "Dunalastairs" started a fashion among locomotive engineers for big boilers. Even before McIntosh himself had built his big 4–6–0s of 1903, the Great Northern, throwing to the winds the small domeless boiler traditions of Patrick Stirling, had produced a locomotive that by the sheer girth of its boiler caused an out-and-out sensation in 1902. Until 1903, however, McIntosh himself had not felt it necessary to go beyond the old traditional bogie 4-coupled express engine of the 4–4–0 type for the heaviest passenger work.

from STEAM LOCOMOTIVE *1957*

Nigel Gresley

O. S. NOCK

During the difficult years of the 1914–1918 War, when no new
locomotive-building on any scale could be undertaken, H. N.
Gresley had been working on the arrangement of conjugating the
valve gear so that only two sets of motion would be needed for a
three-cylinder engine. By this method all the rods could be outside
and accessible, and the advantages of three-cylinder propulsion
could be realized without the extra complication of three sets of
gear. On the Great Western only two sets were used on the four-
cylinder engines, though it is a simpler matter to work four sets
of valves from two gears. In the years immediately following the
war Gresley had tried out his new layout on heavy freight and
mixed-traffic engines, so that by 1922 it was sufficiently tried to be
incorporated in the new "Pacifics". When, after grouping in 1923,
Gresley became Chief Mechanical Engineer of the new London &
North Eastern Railway, his Pacific design was adopted as the new
standard. At first the actual valve movements were conventional,
with short travels and consequently restricted port openings, but
as a result of trials against Great Western "Castle" class engines in
1925 some important though simple alterations were made to the
gear, and the performance of the Gresley "Pacific" was brought
into the very top flight.

Throughout the nineteen-twenties, however, the locomotives
of the L.N.E.R. were handicapped by the relative slowness of the
express train schedules. The huge, amalgamated system took some
little time to settle into its stride, and this unsettled period was
followed by the slump years of 1929–1931. But Gresley was not the
man to be content with a rather poor second place. At that time
the Great Western was far ahead of the other British companies in
speed and the quality of locomotive performance. How far Gresley
was personally responsible for spreading the germs of speed fever
that gripped the Northern lines from 1932 onwards it is not
possible to say; but of one thing there was no doubt – he provided
the L.N.E.R. with the tools for the job, at a most opportune time,
when railway prestige was low and competition from long-distance

road coaches intense. No ordinary measures would avail in such circumstances. It was a case of all or nothing.

And so, on a raw November morning in 1934, a special train of four coaches, headed by the Pacific engine 4472 *Flying Scotsman,* went out of King's Cross as if shot from a gun. Two hours 32 minutes later that train was at rest in Leeds – 185½ miles in 152 minutes. The same afternoon, with the load increased to six coaches, the special returned to London in 157½ minutes. On the long racing descent from Stoke tunnel towards Peterborough an average speed of 97·4 m.p.h. was maintained for 3½ miles, and a peak of 100 m.p.h. was registered in the dynamometer car. Well might the railway world speculate as to what was afoot! The next demonstration came in March 1935, this time with a "Super-Pacific", No. 2750 *Papyrus.* In one day a six-coach special of 217 tons was taken from King's Cross to Newcastle, 268¼ miles, in 237 minutes, and brought back the same day in 231¾ minutes. The latter was equivalent to an overall average speed of 69½ m.p.h., but this time the Stoke bank produced the truly sensational maximum speed of 108 m.p.h. It was a Great Western engine, the *City of Truro,* which had hitherto been considered to hold the British speed record – approximately 100 m.p.h., reached on a run with an Ocean Mail special some thirty years earlier – but now the honours had definitely passed to the L.N.E.R.

There were now definite prospects of a big acceleration to New-castle. The runs of *Papyrus* showed that a standard "Super-Pacific" could do it, though in trying for a record maximum speed on the return journey the engine was worked extremely hard. While the normal point at which steam is cut off in the cylinders when running at high speed is at 15 per cent of each piston stroke, *Papyrus* was working at 32 per cent cut-off at over 100 m.p.h. For regular high-speed working, as distinct from the haulage of the heavy ordinary trains, Gresley designed a special class of "Pacific" engines – the ever-memorable "A4" type, streamlined both inside and out. The most amazing point about the Silver Jubilee express, which inaugurated a four-hour service between London and New-castle in the autumn of 1935, was perhaps not the speed with which the engine and train were designed and built at Doncaster, nor yet the breath-taking speed made on the trial run to Grantham on 27 September, but the fact that the first streamlined engine,

Silver Link, went into regular service on the new train when no more than three weeks out of the Doncaster shops, and for a whole fortnight ran the Jubilee in both directions, five days a week, without the slightest trouble. There were, indeed, *no* teething troubles with these engines – the finest possible tribute not only to Gresley's overriding direction, but to the detail design, to the workmanship and to the handling of the engine on the road.

from STEAM LOCOMOTIVE (B.T.C.) *1958*

Rolling Stock

C. HAMILTON ELLIS

Back in 1874, the ordinary British railway carriage was four- or six-wheeled. The Metropolitan Railway used non-bogie eight-wheelers, a type built experimentally by the Great Western as far back as 1852 (the "Long Charleys"); the latter company had a solitary bogie first class running on the Paddington–Birkenhead line; the Great Northern had a design for a bogie composite, but did not carry it any further. There were, except on the exclusive Pullman cars, no corridors, lavatories, radiator heating, or any artificial light save that of the primeval oil-pot in the roof on ordinary main-line carriages. The District, Metropolitan, North London, and Lancashire and Yorkshire, however, used coal gas in collapsible holders, carried in oblong roof boxes of clerestory shape on the London underground lines, and in the guards' vans on the others. Two gas-jet globes was the allowance in a Metropolitan or District first class, and a gushing contemporary account described the result as so brilliant as to destroy all suggestion of travelling underground.

The roofs were of plain camber shape, nearly flat and equipped with luggage rails in the oldest carriages. The curved, three-cornered window, another relic of ancient road practice, was still to be seen, but had become unfashionable in the 'sixties. First class was of the ordinary type, with three well-cushioned seats each side, divided by headrests and elbows. The latter were usually fixed, so it was not possible to fold them up and stretch out when the train was lightly loaded at night, otherwise, first-class travel was by no means bad. Second-class compartments had the seats thinly padded and covered with corded velveteen or American cloth, and often two compartments had to share one oil-pot lamp, occupying a half-moon hole cut in the top of the intervening partition. The third-class compartments were generally mean, wooden, and with partitions carried barely to shoulder height. This assisted general sociability, and also favoured the wandering minstrel on an excursion train or the travelling evangelist trying to save souls by the way.

Brakes were often hand-operated, and dependent on vans marshalled at strategic intervals along the train. Certain lines used early types of continuous brakes, chiefly mechanical in principle. . . . Of power brakes – pneumatic, vacuum and hydraulic – the Westinghouse air system was most promising, and gave a very good showing on a Midland train at the famous Newark brake trials during June 1875. . . .

In the early 'seventies, extra travelling comfort could be had at a price. For wealthy invalids, the South Eastern Railway had built, as far back as 1860, a carriage with a movable bed and a fully equipped lavatory, and during the middle 'sixties, various companies began to provide family carriages, available on payment of a certain number of first- or first and second-class fares. Usually there would be comfortable armchair- or cross-seats for the Governor and Mamma, and less easy ones along the sides for their brood and for poor Miss Jones. Adjacently there would be a lavatory, complicated in equipment and floral in decoration, and beyond that a very small second class where John and Mary Anne sat in readiness to assist Master and Madame on the journey or at its end.

The very first British sleeping carriage, apart from invalid coaches and such makeshifts as twin sticks and a cushion placed between the seats, was a six-wheeler built by the North British Railway in 1873, for the East Coast night expresses. It was designed very much on family saloon lines, for it was considered that such intimate things as sleepers would be chiefly in demand by large family parties travelling together. . . .

This *lits-salon* type of sleeping berth persisted on certain British railways into the 'eighties, side-by-side with the American Pullman type, in which bedclothes were provided from the beginning.

Pullman parlour cars appeared on the Midland Railway in 1874 along with the sleepers. They, likewise, were completely American except in their reduced dimensions, with a long general saloon furnished with pivoted easy chairs, one or two private compartments similarly equipped, lavatories and Baker hot-water heaters. . . .

From the beginning, it had been possible to serve meals in the Pullman cars to passengers who ordered them in advance. The food usually arrived in baskets, but there were facilities for serving hot meals previously cooked and kept warm. In 1879, however, a Pullman car called *Prince of Wales* was placed in service on the Leeds expresses of the Great Northern Railway, and this contained a fully equipped kitchen, being thus the first real dining car in Great Britain. Passengers rode in it all the way, and paid a halfcrown Pullman supplement for so doing, in addition to the price of meals.

Apart from the Pullman cars, there appeared in 1878 and 1881 respectively two types of bogie sleeping car with the berths in compartments having lavatory access through side corridors. . . . [The latter] formed in many important particulars the prototype of the modern British sleeping car. There was a side corridor throughout, in this example crossing over in the middle through a steward's pantry. All the berths were arranged in compartments, longitudinally at the ends but otherwise across the car, and there were no upper berths. The crossover corridor was supposed to secure a good balance. Ventilation was by ordinary droplights and by the deep, boxlike clerestory which was for so many years characteristic of the Great Western. . . .

Following this corridor sleeper on the Great Western, in 1882 the Great Northern Railway designed the first British side-corridor ordinary coach, a six-wheel first class for the East Coast Joint Stock. It had four compartments, each containing four seats. One was for ladies only, and had its own lavatory adjoining; there was a "gents" at the other end. There were as yet no gangway connection between carriages; the first diner passengers travelled all the way in the same car. In 1888, a very similar Great Northern corridor coach design was brought out for third-class passengers, having five compartments. These two classes remained the standard for the East Coast Scotch expresses until the end of the century, with a few important exceptions.

G

Great improvements had been made in the dimensions of passenger compartments. In 1875, the Midland had fixed on 6 ft. as the minimum distance between partitions of a third-class compartment, and had discarded the very objectionable low partitions at the same time upholstering the seats. First-class compartments varied from about 7 ft. to 7 ft. 6 in. between partitions.

During the 'eighties, bogie coaches appeared in increasing numbers on the best express trains of various railways in addition to the Great Western and the Midland, notably on the London and South Western, Manchester, Sheffield and Lincolnshire, North Eastern, and even on the despised and lampooned South Eastern, whereon the veteran Richard Mansell built them for the Dover Continental expresses. The Great Northern and the London and North Western were much more suspicious of the bogie coach. The former remained enamoured of its standard six-wheelers, while building a few eight-wheel non-bogie carriages. The North Western for long had its style cramped by an old short traverser at Euston. From the middle 'eighties onwards it built many eight-wheel carriages with the outer axles mounted on Webb's radial trucks. Webb claimed that these ran more smoothly and more steadily than bogie carriages, but his celebrated radials were prone to treat their passengers to sudden lurches at disconcerting moments. What was wanted at that time was a combination of Clayton's beautiful twelve-wheel Midland coaches and the North Western's magnificent permanent way. . . .

Provision of lavatories, with or without corridor access, now began to be more common on British express trains, though many lines continued to confine it to the first class. Some companies, notably the Cambrian, Caledonian and North British, were much concerned to ensure that the new lavatory carriages seated the same number of passengers per compartment as their predecessors. So the lavatory doors were padded, and hinged seats were placed in front of them. For sensitive people, especially ladies, it was a horrifying arrangement.

The 'eighties also saw gradual adoption on certain lines of oil gas for lighting, the illuminant being carried in cylinders under the frames and used in fish-tail or, in the very best stock, in Argand annular burners. Stroudley on the Brighton from 1881 onwards, and Clayton on the Midland, made considerable use for some time of electric light, with storage cells charged, like the gas cylinders, at suitable times and places. The light, however, was little brighter than gas and much less steady; the old carbon-filament lamps were fragile and unreliable, and the batteries uneconomically heavy.

While dining service was at first provided exclusively by the Pullman cars, from the late 'eighties onwards several railway companies began to provide their own dining cars, notably the London and North Western, which never used Pullmans. Some very handsome twelve-wheel diners, for first-class only, were built by the Manchester, Sheffield and Lincolnshire Railway in 1888 ... and were operated by it jointly with the Great Northern Railway between Manchester and King's Cross via Retford.

But the most important contribution to dining-car services, after the original Pullman service on the Great Northern, was that of James Holden on the Great Eastern Railway in 1891. For its Harwich Continental service, this company put on a first and third-class dining-car train, which was also notable in that it was one of the first two sets of coaches in the country, apart from Pullmans, to be interconnected by covered gangways. There was a four-compartment first-class side-corridor coach, then a dining-saloon to seat eighteen, with a kitchen at one end, and to complete the set, a third-class side-corridor coach with five compartments, one of which had a table and tip-up seats. All were six-wheelers; the middle vehicle had the sides bulged out to give greater elbow room to the hungry diners who had survived the crossing from Holland without permanent prostration, and a clerestory roof. Cooking and lighting were by oil gas. If not an immensely imposing sort of train, it was nevertheless a very noteworthy one and provides a landmark in the history of passenger amenities. The short-bodied dining saloons were later greatly enlarged and mounted on six-wheel bogies, in which form they gave useful service for many years. A curiosity about the third class was that its "ladies only" compartment had lavatory access only, and was cut off from the main corridor.

In the same year of 1891, the Great Western built what is generally regarded as the prototype of the modern British corridor train. It consisted of five vehicles, all mounted on Dean's four-wheel bogies, which had four-point suspension by pendulum links with the central pin acting as a guide only. There was a guard's brake and luggage van, a third class, a first, a second and a brake third. All the four passenger-carrying vehicles had oil-gas lighting. clerestory roofs and the sides bulged out between the flat doors in a style known on the Great Western as the "bay window" type. Men's and women's lavatories were separate, at opposite ends of the carriages. Side corridors were used except for the smoking compartments, which had open passageways with cross seats on each side, as in a diner.

The flexible bellows connections between carriages were at one side instead of centrally-placed, which meant that the train had to remain permanently marshalled as a block set. This gangway arrangement persisted for several years on Great Western corridor stock, and is retained to this day for Travelling Post Office carriages, which ply on regular and invariable routes. For passenger stock, of course, it had awkward results when a vehicle was turned on a triangular junction in the normal course of operations.

The Great Western corridor train, after some experimental runs, went into regular service between Paddington and Birkenhead in 1892 and was an immediate success. It did not include a dining car; the corridors were intended simply to give complete lavatory access and to enable the guard to patrol the whole train while running. He held the key to the gangway connections which he kept locked to prevent third-class passengers from moving into superior quarters on the quiet. The credit for having produced the typical British express train of later years may therefore be shared jointly by the old Great Eastern, with its York Continental, and the Great Western with its Birkenhead Corridor, both built in the same year.

A most interesting feature of the Great Western train was its system of passengers' communication. On most British railways at that time, this was a very weak point, in spite of the periodic incidence of criminal attacks and assaults in isolated compartments. The commonest arrangement was the rigging of a cord through eyelets outside the carriage, on the gutter rail. This communication cord was coupled between the carriages, with a good deal of slack, and operated a gong or a whistle on the locomotive. In the van, the other end of the cord was wound on a sort of winch with a large wheel rather like a ship's. It had been devised on the North Eastern Railway and generally applied on railways north of the Thames from 1869 onwards. This served its purpose after a fashion, but using it in sudden emergency was an awkward business. The passenger faced with abrupt murderous attack, or a girl at the mercy of a ruffian, had to remember quickly which was the right side of the rapidly moving train, open the window, grope upwards for the elusive cord and pull in several feet of slack before anything happened. Sometimes the cord stuck or broke, and nothing happened at all. In a bad smash on the Great Western (Shipton, on Christmas Eve of 1874) a passenger, previously becoming alarmed at the violent motion of his carriage, leant out of the window to get at the cord and was thrown through it on to the grass by a violent lurch. He was unhurt, saved by the accident of an accident, for the train turned over immediately after, with heavy loss of life.

On the Great Western corridor train just described, electric bells were provided in all compartments, by which the guard could be summoned from his van. Outside the carriages, in the same place as the usual cord, there was a wire, which on being pulled, made a partial application of the automatic vacuum brake. This, of course, is the principle of the present arrangement, with a tight chain inside the carriages and an external disc or semaphore indicator at the end. It was officially approved and generally adopted on all main-line British and Irish railways from 1899 onwards, being applicable to either the Westinghouse or the vacuum automatic brake. On open electric stock, a turncock in the air-pipe serves the same function.

Long before this, the much maligned southern lines had done far more enterprizing things than the northern companies in the cause of emergency communication, using various electrical systems. The best was Stroudley and Rusbridge's patent electric arrangement on the London, Brighton and South Coast, operated by a pull-out knob in a conspicuous position on the compartment partition. It survived on the older Brighton carriages right into the nineteen-twenties.

From the early 'nineties onwards, corridor coaches were employed to an increasing extent on the best expresses. On the West Highland trains of the North British, and on the American boat expresses of the London and South Western, central corridors

were employed, without end gangways. The South Eastern
Railway, in 1892, had a train of first-class drawing-room cars built
in America by the Gilbert Car Manufacturing Company of Troy.
They were of Pullman type, with open platforms at the ends, but
previously, on the London, Brighton and South Coast in 1889,
Pullman cars with closed vestibules had made their appearance on
the Brighton Limited trains. In 1897, the South Eastern Railway
had built in England a really magnificent eight-car centre-corridor
train, very much on American lines, with closed vestibules and
flexible connections throughout. There was a first-class drawing-
room with a first-class pantry car, a second class and five third
class including the brake thirds at the ends. The underframes were
composite, with the solebars of steel, there were Gould automatic
centre-couplers between the coaches, electric lighting with dyna-
mos and closed-circuit hot-water heating with a stove to each
vehicle. There were clerestories over all the passenger sections,
but on the brake thirds the luggage compartments had plain roofs,
with raised lookouts for the guard, giving an up and down effect
and spoiling the appearance of what was otherwise the finest complete train in the country. This American Car Train, as it was
called, was placed in service on the Charing Cross–Hastings service, but the incalculable British public did not take to it. The
train suffered the same luke-warm reception as had the Midland
American trains of the 'seventies. It was complained that the
carriages were too warm, or too draughty, or that they afforded
no privacy. These objections came rather oddly from a public
which, on the South Eastern, had been using some of the poorest
third-class stock in the country. Nevertheless, the cars were dispersed and taken over by the Pullman company, which used them
singly on various trains.

Dining-car trains for all classes of passenger, initiated as we have
seen by the Great Eastern Railway, made their appearance on the
Anglo-Scottish expresses of the Midland, East Coast and West
Coast companies in 1893, though at first only the West Coast
Joint Stock provided complete corridor trains. An excellent
feature of the East Coast expresses, which were of Great Northern
design, was the provision of a separate kitchen car, six-wheeled
in this case, marshalled between the first- and the third-class diners,
thus providing centralized cooking and, in the passenger quarters

relative freedom from the greasy odour of different viands being prepared together in a confined space. The Midland and West Coast companies used twelve-wheel dining cars with kitchens included....

Passing reference has already been made to periodic progress in the heating and lighting of carriages. As far back as 1843, hot-water heating, or rather the admission of air preheated by a closed circuit hot-water coil with a small boiler under the vehicle, had been devised by Perkins (of steam gun notoriety) and installed in the London and Birmingham Railway's royal saloon, but at the beginning of our period and for many years after, the flat hot-water tin on the floor was the only apparatus available to prevent ordinary passengers freezing on winter journeys. The tins left much to be desired; when freshly installed they induced heat-ache in the feet, when they cooled they became a useless clutter on the floor. At one stage in the history of British fashion, boots with gutta-percha soles came into favour. These stuck to the carriage footwarmers, and left their wearers effectively birdlimed. In 1880, on the London and North Western, F. W. Webb introduced tins containing sodium acetate. Heated in a boiling vat on the platform, this liquified, and on solidifying again it gave out the heat it had previously absorbed, continuing to do so for as long as any of the salts remained uncrystallized. One could give new life to the expiring footwarmer by giving it a violent shaking, and even on a long night journey it was good for several hours.

On the old Pullman cars ... the American Baker heater was in use, somewhat resembling the ordinary greenhouse apparatus, with a small oil-fired boiler and hot-water pipes making a circuit of the car. The West Lancashire, as already remarked, used steam heat with a boiler in the van from 1879 on. Another glimmer of things to come was seen in the late 'eighties, when the Caledonian Railway diverted the exhaust steam from the locomotive's Westinghouse brake pump to heat radiators in the carriages. It was a makeshift; the flexible connections between the carriages were made out of hosepipe which had become too worn to serve more serious purposes. In it, however, was the main principal of modern heating by low-pressure steam.

On the Glasgow and South Western Railway at the same time, there was a very clever heating system operated on the something-for-nothing principle. Above the flame of the carriage lamp there was a small wrought-iron boiler, serving a closed pipe circuit incorporating a sort of heat reservoir under one of the seats. If the lamps were unlit, the passengers remained cold. From the 'nineties onwards, direct steam heating from the locomotive boiler, through a reducing valve, came into general use, though the flat tin foot-warmer died hard on secondary services, and lasted longer still on the once-popular slip carriages. The early corridor trains just des-cribed were among the first to provide low-pressure steam heating.

The old pot-lamps, burning rape oil, were abominable things, and provided little light even when, as on the Great Western, two were provided in each compartment. The burner was of the most primitive type and could not be regulated once it was alight. If the wick was too high, it smoked atrociously; yet, with the motion of the carriage, it tended to shake down in its narrow holder and go out. The only attractive thing about the pot lamp was the spectacle of its installation. It was a two-man job. One went along the platform with a barrowload of the lamps, already lighted, in racks. His colleague walked along the roof of the train. At each com-partment, they would stop, the man on the roof would pull the wooden plug out of the lamphole, the man on the platform would toss up a lighted lamp, which was instantly caught and dropped into place. The operation was extraordinarily quick and beautifully dextrous.

Oil-gas lighting originated with the system introduced in Prussia by Julius Pintsch, and appeared in England on the St John's Wood branch of the Metropolitan Railway in 1876. The Great Eastern Railway took it up two years later, and thereafter this, and the somewhat similar arrangement of Pope, came into widespread use. The pressure at burner was 84 lb. per sq. in. and the gas was carried between the frames in cylindrical reservoirs which contained, when fully charged, a 40 hour supply. Trouble over the discharge of waste from the Pintsch gas plant at Stratford, Great Eastern Railway, resulted in James Holden adopting it as a locomotive fuel during the 'nineties and nineteen hundreds, this being the first large-scale use of liquid fuel for motive power purposes on a British railway.

As already recorded, the first use of electricity for train lighting, on any railway in the world, took place under Stroudley on the London, Brighton and South Coast in 1881. In October the drawing-room car *Beatrice* was equipped with a 32-cell Fauré battery and twelve Swan lamps. Two months later a four-car Pullman train was similarly equipped. A much better arrangement, of Stroudley's own devising, appeared in 1883, using a belt-driven generator in the van, with accumulators. Elsewhere, the North British Railway in 1882 and the London and North Western in 1884 experimented with steam-driven generators mounted on the locomotive, but for a decade Stroudley's was easily the best arrangement. The modern system, with a small generator under each coach, charging accumulators, was originated by J. Stone in 1894 (single battery) and 1896 (double battery). Oil gas died hard. The Welsbach incandescent mantle gave it new life and new light, more brilliant than that of the early electrical installations. Improvements in the latter, coupled with several serious fires following accidents to gaslit trains, brought gas into increasing disfavour. . . . Smaller railways were the first to go in for electric light exclusively, for example, the Great Northern of Ireland; London, Chatham and Dover; London, Tilbury and Southend; and North Stafford.

In the 'nineties, the best main-line stock was noteworthy for its elaborate construction and decoration. Dining- and sleeping-cars built at Wolverton Works by the London and North Western were conspicuous with the most ornate brass handrail arrangements at their end entrances. Saloon carriages for the various royal trains were often flamboyant in style, but in this there was nothing new. As the nineteen-hundreds advanced, there was a strong reaction, particularly marked in the case of the East Coast Joint Stock. Woven wire seats, some of them abominably uncomfortable, but recognized as much more hygenic than the old buttoned-in cushions, enjoyed an increasing vogue. Except on the Midland Railway, the clerestory was used less and less in new stock. When well-designed, its appearance was admirable and its qualities in ventilation and daytime lighting was undoubted. On the other hand it was a complicated arrangement, and keeping it clean was a problem, for which reason many railways, including the North Western, employed it only for dining, sleeping and saloon carriages, whereon it could be given special attention.

End entrances, instead of side doors, began to be used on long-distance ordinary coaches, as well as on Pullmans, diners and

G*

sleepers, and some of the finest examples of the end-door coach built during this period were those introduced by the North-Western in 1907 for the American boat specials, and for the famous 2.0 p.m. Scots expresses. After many vicissitudes, the stock of the Pullman company finally changed hands and came under the exclusive control of an all-British concern, the Pullman Car Company. In 1908 this undertaking placed in service on the London, Brighton and South Coast Railway the first Pullman cars proper to be built as such in Great Britain, forming the celebrated *Southern Belle,* successor to the old Brighton Pullman Limited trains. In 1910 two Pullman buffet cars appeared on the extension line trains of the Metropolitan Railway, a veritable godsend to various old bar-proppers who could now drink their way happily home on the midnight train from Baker Street after other places had closed. The buffet car, however, was considerably older than this; the first train bars, complete with handsome pictures of the highest saloon-lounge standard, had made their appearance on the Great Central Railway when that line opened its London extension. In 1914 the Pullman car re-established itself in Scotland, where it had not been seen since the withdrawal of the Highland sleepers *Balmoral* and *Dunrobin* in 1907. The new cars, employed on the Caledonian and on the Highland Railway south of Avie-more, included dining cars catering for both first- and third-class passengers and for the beautiful Callander and Oban line, a very handsome Pullman observation car called *Maid of Morven.*

An interesting mechanical innovation in carriage design was Gresley's articulated arrangement, whereby adjacent coach bodies rested on a single bogie. It was first applied in 1907, in the course of re-building old six-wheel and non-bogie eight-wheel coaches, but was later very extensively employed on all kinds of new vehicles. Also in 1907 a very fine pair of royal saloons was built, one by the Great Northern and the other by the North Eastern, in which the first use was made of electric cooking on a British train. Cooking, however, was not exclusively by electricity. In-direct heating combined with ventilation was another interesting feature, anticipating in a simple form the much more elaborate air-conditioning of modern times.

from THE TRAINS WE LOVED *1947*

The Twilight of Steam

GEOFFREY FREEMAN ALLEN

September 27th, 1935, determined the future of British railway
motive power for the next twenty years, though even when the
afternoon's remarkable exploits were splashed over the country's
newspapers next morning it is doubtful whether many railwaymen
fully appreciated their significance.... It will suffice here to remind
anyone who has forgotten the exact date that this was the occasion
on which the L.N.E.R. and its Chief Mechanical Engineer, Nigel
Gresley, unveiled Britain's first fully streamlined high-speed train,
the "Silver Jubilee", in a dazzling demonstration from King's
Cross to Grantham, during which the 76·4 miles to Peterborough
were tossed off in 55 minutes, 25 successive miles were run at an
actual speed of 100 m.p.h. or more and a maximum of $112\frac{1}{2}$ m.p.h.
was touched, setting up a new British rail-speed record. . . .

It was the first real challenge of diesel traction that had evoked
the "Silver Jubilee". In 1932 the Germans pioneered the application of the diesel engine to high-speed rail traction in the "Fliegende
Hamburger" of the German State Railway, a two-car streamlined
multiple-unit that within a year was being scheduled to run daily at
an average of 77·4 m.p.h. – and to travel at up to 100 m.p.h. *en
route* – over the 178 miles between Berlin and Hamburg. The flier's
success was prompt and in the ensuing years up to 1939 the German State Railway developed a network of similar diesel-electric
multiple-unit services between their principal cities, some of them
even more smartly timed; the "Fliegende Kölner", for example,
was timed at an average of 83·1 m.p.h. over the 157·8 miles from
Berlin to Hanover and then at an average of 82·3 m.p.h. over the
109·7 miles from Hanover to Hamm. A year before the "Silver
Jubilee's" inauguration, the U.S. diesel revolution had been spec-
tacularly initiated by the early "Pioneer Zephyr" diesel streamliner
of the Chicago, Burlington & Quincy Railroad and the "City of
Portland" of the Union Pacific.

These developments were not lost on British railwaymen, particularly the authorities of the L.N.E.R., who fell to planning a
similar high-speed inter-city service for this country. Gresley first

sought an estimate from the builders of the German diesel multiple-units of the performance that could be expected from similar stock and power plant between King's Cross and Newcastle. With a three-coach unit seating 140 passengers, replied the Germans, and taking into account the permanent speed restrictions along the route, a time of $4\frac{1}{4}$ hours was feasible – but not less. A series of tests with existing, unstreamlined 4–6–2s of his own design confirmed Gresley's conviction that steam could improve on this target schedule, thereby enhancing its initial advantage to a British railway of burning home-mined coal rather than more expensive imported oil. The "Silver Jubilee" and the "A4" Pacific were born and by their instantaneous success justified Gresley's faith in British locomotive engineering skill.

They did more than that. Since the war we have learned how deeply the achievements of the Gresley "A4" Pacifics and the "Silver Jubilee" impressed the managements of the pre-war "Big Four" – the L.M.S., L.N.E.R., G.W.R., and S.R. A tight grip had to be kept on the purse-strings, with the result that, shunting locomotives apart, every British experiment with diesel traction up to that time had been a rather half-hearted tinkering with a prototype, never a full-scale experiment with a number of standard units. Now, when diesel traction seemed to be posing a challenge difficult to overlook, here was eagerly accepted evidence that far cheaper steam locomotives, burning home-mined coal that was plentiful and manned by first-class labour that was not difficult to recruit, could more than match diesels for speed and reliability. Moreover, the "A4's" daily mileage on the "Silver Jubilee" was in the range of what, even today, seems to be considered in some quarters of British Railways a reasonable utilization of a fair-sized main-line diesel. With the exception of the Southern, which cherished plans to extend its already large network of electrified lines, the railways of this country thankfully kept their trust in steam.

The late 1930s were the heyday of the British steam locomotive, from the viewpoint of high speed express passenger haulage, and the outbreak of war in 1939 cut short even more impressive developments. The L.M.S., which in 1937 had entered in the streamliner stakes its "Coronation Scot", running the 401·4 miles between Euston and Glasgow in $6\frac{1}{2}$ hours each way daily, aimed to raise more of its Western Division expresses to this speed standard. The "Coronation Scot" was a light train of only 297 tons' tare weight, whereas the average express weight on the London–Glasgow main line was nearer 450 tons, so that the L.M.S. intentions presupposed some high-capacity locomotives for their fulfilment.

In 1938, therefore, under the direction of the railway's Chief Mechanical Engineer, Sir William Stanier, plans were drawn up for a huge streamlined 4–6–4, even more massive than the "Coronation" 4–6–2s of his design that were by then in command of the principal Western Division expresses. It would have been a four-cylinder, 119-ton locomotive with, by British standards, a very large boiler pressed as high as 300 lb. per sq. in., and a mechanical stoker in its heavy eight-wheel tender to enable the fireman to extract the highest possible rate of steaming when maximum effort was needed; for one of the designer's chief aims was to produce a locomotive that would rival electric traction in its capacity for rapid acceleration and swift uphill work with heavy loads.

What this fascinating design might have achieved if the war had not intervened, unhappily, can be no better than guessed from the amazing 1939 exploit of one of Stanier's "Coronation" 4–6–2s, ... freshly modified with a double chimney and blastpipe. With a twenty-coach test train of 610 tons the Pacific was set at the tough obstacles of Shap and Beattock banks on a trip from Crewe to Glasgow and back. Going north, No. 46234 averaged 56½ m.p.h. throughout the 31½ miles from near sea-level at Carnforth to Shap summit and stormed over both Shap and Beattock (which is approached by ten miles graded at between 1 in 69 and 1 in 88 up) at a minimum of 30 m.p.h. Coming back, with an admittedly easier approach to Beattock summit from the Glasgow side, it was still an exciting performance to hustle twenty coaches over the top at 62 m.p.h., and equally so to average 44 m.p.h. on the seven miles at a mean 1 in 125 from Clifton up to Shap summit, which was breasted at 38 m.p.h.

Equally impressive designs were being draughted on the other side of the country. To haul the heaviest L.N.E.R. Anglo-Scottish expresses at streamliner speed Gresley was engaged in elongating his 4–6–2 type into a three-cylinder 4–8–2 with an even higher nominal tractive effort than Stanier's 4–6–4 (45,700 lb. as against 42,850 lb.). An improved "A4", too, was on the drawing-board, with increased tractive effort secured by a higher boiler pressure; this was needed because the L.N.E.R.'s three streamlined expresses – the "Silver Jubilee" and the later London–Edinburgh "Coronation" and London–Leeds and Bradford "West Riding" – had so captivated the public that the management was anxious to add another coach or so to their formation. Construction of both 4–8–2 and "super-A4" was about to begin when war broke out and the plans were shelved. Sir Nigel Gresley, unfortunately, died two years later and his successors at Doncaster soon made it plain that his ways were not theirs.

On the Southern Railway steam locomotive development continued into the war years. Here bigger power than the "Lord Nelson" 4–6–os, which were still the largest passenger engines the railway owned right up to 1939, had for years been in demand to work increasing loads on the main lines from London to Kent and the West Country, but two Pacific schemes of the 1930s had been condemned as too heavy in axle weight for the Southern's track and bridges. The limits laid down by the S.R. Civil Engineer for the routes to Kent were, in fact, more stringent than those on any other principal main line in the country, but they constituted a challenge ideally matched to the man who took over as Chief Mechanical Engineer of the S.R. in 1937, O. V. S. Bulleid. For Mr Bulleid, who had previously been Gresley's assistant at Doncaster, is probably the most adventurous engineer any British railway has had in command of its locomotive affairs in this century.

Bulleid's answer to the problem was his "Merchant Navy" and lighter "West Country" and "Battle of Britain" 4–6–2 classes, all three-cylinder designs, which combined a high-capacity, extremely free-steaming boiler working at 280 lb. per sq. in. with a multitude of novel ideas to save weight, including a chain-driven valve gear; thereby he achieved a powerful locomotive that would pass the Civil Engineer's scrutiny. Unorthodox as the Bulleid Pacifics were, they were far from being the limit of their designer's inventiveness, They were followed by the extraordinary double-ended "Leader" o–6–6–os, embodying yet more revolutionary ideas that the 1948 nationalization of British railways deprived of development, for the new overlords of the mechanical world decided to break up the "Leaders" while they were still dogged by not unexpected teething troubles. Bulleid's intention in the "Leader" was to devise a steam unit with the same performance and ready availability for use (by virtue of being double-ended) as an electric locomotive; by carrying the whole weight of the locomotive on driving wheels he hoped to enhance its acceleration through improving adhesion, while another innovation – the use of sleeve valves instead of the more usual piston valves – should have helped by bettering cylinder performance. These were two major features of a design that incorporated a host of ingenuities. The 1948 change in railway management forestalled another Bulleid scheme, to equip one of his "Merchant Navy" 4–6–2s with a complicated piece of apparatus to condense the exhaust steam from the cylinders and re-use it as boiler feed water, thereby economizing in fuel and increasing the output of the boiler.

Only on the Great Western . . . was there no apparent evidence of steam locomotive development as the 1939 war fell on the country, and it was not until peace came that Swindon produced plans for a new 4–6–2 design, which was unhappily frustrated by post-war restrictions on capital expenditure. It was, however, anything but discontent with steam that preserved the *status quo* in the G.W. locomotive world. In the first two decades of this century the genius of its great engineer Churchward had given the G.W.R. such a lead in British locomotive design that, following its translation by Churchward's successor, Collet, into the bigger four-cylinder "Castle" and "King" 4–6–0s, Swindon evidently considered perfection had been achieved. . . .

After the war we had not long to wait for portents of a change of mood. It is true that some steam locomotive classes of earlier years, notably the four-cylinder G.W. "Castles" and the three-cylinder Bulleid 4–6–2s, were multiplied in considerable numbers. It is also notable that the L.N.E.R., pursuing Gresley's "big engine" policy in broad outline but dissenting in detail, gave birth to new classes of three-cylinder 4–6–2s, the "A1s" and "A2s", that were still issuing from the works well after the 1948 nationalization. But the appearance of the new L.N.E.R. Pacifics was coupled with an announcement that these two types were to be the largest of a range of ten standard classes, each one for a different grade of work, to which it was intended by degrees to reduce the company's entire locomotive stud through scrapping of old designs and new construction. A similar scheme, involving eleven types, was published by the L.M.S.

At the same time as these steam standardization programmes were revealed, however, both the L.M.S. and the L.N.E.R. disclosed also that they proposed to adventure with diesel traction for main-line work. The L.M.S. scheme at least resulted in the appearance of prototypes, the 1,600 h.p. "twins" Nos. 10000 and 10001 and the 825 h.p. branch line type, No. 10800, but the much more ambitious L.N.E.R. programme of twenty-five 1,600 h.p. units for express haulage on the East Coast route was pigeon-holed after nationalization. . . . The S.R., on the other hand, was allowed to proceed with its more modest batch of three, Nos. 10201–3. Meanwhile the G.W.R., individual as ever, was devoting its attention to the use of gas turbines for rail traction.

One reason for this change of affection will be a vivid memory of many – the acute post-war coal shortage. It reached its peak in 1947, when on some lines the truncated timetables were barer of trains than they had been even in the dimmest days of the war; even such time-hallowed aristocrats as the "Cornish Riviera Express" and the "Mid-day Scot" were missing at different times of that gloomy year. Matters gradually improved, but owing to the increased demands of other home consumers and of the export trade, the railways never regained the supply of good quality steam coal that they had taken for granted before 1939. . . .

There were other important post-war changes that affected the railways' attitude to the steam locomotive. Post-war full employment in the country at large, with other industries frantically outbidding each other in the quest for skilled labour, dimmed the attraction of security as a selling-point of service with the railway. Motive-power depot staffs dropped below establishment and locomotive maintenance, fallen to a very low ebb during the war, showed no signs of recuperating. The post-war intake of enginemen, too, did not have the quality of the staff before the war in all too many cases. Unlike other railways in Europe, those of Britain were relegated to the rear of the industrial queue for capital investment, so that new construction of motive power had now to be concentrated on its cheapest form – steam; and to suit the conditions in which they found themselves, the new chiefs of British Railways' locomotive engineering opted for steam without frills – a simple, sturdy series of standard designs that any engineman would soon get the feel of, which would not be faddy about the coal they were given to burn and which would have the widest range of use.

Only two of the new classes were described as specifically for passenger or freight, and not mixed-traffic use. One was a three-cylinder express passenger Class "8P" 4–6–2, and in the event only one engine of this type, No. 71000 *Duke of Gloucester*, was ever built. The other was a two-cylinder Class "9F" heavy-freight 2–10–0, which in practice has proved one of the most versatile and well-loved of all types. . . .

There was to be no more of the practice of some railways in the past, who would create a new design for very special needs, and rely on the outdated types they displaced for secondary work. The guiding policy behind the B.R. standard designs was to produce locomotives that would switch from passenger to freight and back to passenger, and from a main to a secondary line and back, all in one day's work if need be. In other words, to turn out machines that could be adapted to any work offering and therefore kept in traffic as near continuously as is possible with a steam locomotive, rather than machines to which the work had to be adapted, so that their range of usefulness was limited.

It was these mixed-traffic types – the Class "7" and "6" 4–6–2s, the Class "5" and "4" 4–6–0s, the Class "4", "3" and "2" 2–6–0s, the Class "4" 2–6–4 tanks and the Class "3" and "2" 2–6–2 tanks – on which work was concentrated after nationalization, for the "Big Four" had left the railways reasonably well provided with pure express and heavy-freight power. Within the limits necessary to keep the engines to a size and weight passable by Civil Engineers on the widest number of routes, particular attention was paid to the provision of a boiler of high steam-producing capacity when maximum effort was needed, but on the other hand, the firegrate and boiler were designed so that the standard locomotives would be sparing of fuel when lightly loaded. . . .

The appearance of the standard locomotives, with their high running plates, set a new and not universally appreciated style for this country, but this was a compromise between the traditional

British locomotive outline and the practical need to make working parts as accessible as possible. . . . The best known and one of the most successful of them is the Class "7" 4–6–2 – the "Britannia". When it first appeared many commentators were surprised that it had only two cylinders, whereas three or four had been favoured for almost all the six-coupled tender engines of similar size designed in the two previous decades. Here again the engineers were concerned to achieve simplicity, ease of maintenance and economy; they calculated that the provision of a third cylinder would add about £1,000 to construction costs, 3½ tons to the engine's weight and a disproportionate increase in maintenance expenses, since an inside cylinder and its gear are more bothersome to attend to than one outside the frames. They maintained that a locomotive working at 25 per cent cut-off – that is, with steam admitted to the cylinders for 25 per cent of the piston stroke and propelling by expansion for the remainder – in two cylinders is no less efficient in terms of haulage performed for fuel consumed than one working on 15 per cent in three or four cylinders. Moreover, they held that the advantages of three- or four-cylinder propulsion in better balance of reciprocating masses and avoidance of damaging hammer-blows on the track when the engine is at speed were not so great as some past engineers had proclaimed. The "Britannias", therefore, demonstrated in many features a reversal of trends in big-engine design prior to 1939, and in their quest for simplicity and economy reflected the post-war railway financial and labour situation in which steam was making a last-ditch fight for survival.

from BRITISH RAILWAYS TODAY AND TOMORROW *1959*

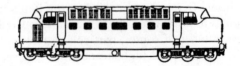

PART IV
The Master-Builders

Order out of Chaos

CHARLES DICKENS

The first shock of a great earthquake had, just at the period, rent the whole neighbourhood [of the Camden Hill cutting] to its centre. Traces of its course were visible on every side. Houses were knocked down; streets broken through and stopped; deep pits and trenches dug in the ground; enormous heaps of earth and clay thrown up; buildings that were undermined and shaking, propped by great beams of wood. Here, a chaos of carts, overthrown and jumbled together, lay topsy-turvy at the bottom of a steep, unnatural hill; there, confused treasures of iron soaked and rusted in something that had accidentally become a pond. Everywhere were bridges that led nowhere; thoroughfares that were wholly impassable; Babel towers of chimneys, wanting half their height; temporary wooden houses and enclosures, in the most unlikely situations; carcasses of ragged tenements, and fragments of unfinished walls and arches, and piles of scaffolding and wildernesses of bricks, and giant forms of cranes, and tripods straddling above nothing. There were a hundred thousand shapes and substances of incompleteness, wildly mingled out of their places, upside down, burrowing in the earth, aspiring in the air, mouldering in the water, and unintelligible as any dream. Hot springs and fiery eruptions, the usual attendants upon earthquakes, lent their contributions of confusion to the scene. Boiling water hissed and heaved within dilapidated walls, whence also, the glare and roar of flames came issuing forth; and mounds of ashes blocked up rights of way, and wholly changed the law and custom of the neighbourhood.

In short, the yet unfinished and unopened railroad was in progress; and, from the very core of all this dire disorder, tailed smoothly away upon its mighty course of civilization and improvement.

But, as yet, the neighbourhood was shy to own the railroad. One or two bold speculators had projected streets; and one had built a little, but had stopped among the mud and ashes to consider further of it. A brand-new tavern, redolent of fresh mortar and size, and fronting nothing at all, had taken for its sign The Railway Arms; but that might be rash enterprise – and then it hoped to sell drink to the workmen. So, the Excavators' House of Call had sprung up from a beershop: and the old-established ham and beef shop had become the Railway Eating House, with a roast leg of pork daily, through interested motives of a similar immediate and popular description. Lodging-house keepers were favourable in like manner, and for the like reasons were not to be trusted. The general belief was very slow. There were frowzy fields, and cow-houses, and dunghills, and dustheaps, and ditches, and gardens, and summer-houses, and carpet-beating grounds, at the very door of the railway. Little tumuli of oyster shells in the oyster season, and of lobster shells in the lobster season, and of broken crockery and faded cabbage leaves in all seasons, encroached upon its high places. Posts, and rails and old cautions to trespassers, and backs of mean houses, and patches of wretched vegetation, stared it out of countenance. Nothing was the better for it, or thought of being so. If the miserable waste ground lying near it could have laughed, it would have laughed it to scorn, like many of the miserable neighbours.

from DOMBEY AND SON *1846*

The Navigators

JOHN FRANCIS

The "navigator" is necessary to the rail. He is an important portion of this new system of political economy. He risks life and limb to form the works which we admire. He braves all weather, he dares all danger, he labours with a power and a purpose which demand attention. For years he was disregarded by those who, availing themselves of his strength and skill, left him, when his daily task was done, to his own pleasures and his own resources. Rude, rugged, and uncultivated, possessed of great animal strength, collected in large numbers, living and working entirely together, they are a class and a community by themselves. Before the time of that great duke who called inland navigation into existence, this class was unknown; and in the works which bear witness to his forethought, the "navigator" gained his title. The canal manias which ensued created a demand and increased the body; the great architectural works of the kingdom continued it; and when the rail first began to spread its iron road through England, the labourer attracted no attention from politician or philosopher, from statistician or from statesman; he had joined no important body, he had not made himself an object of dread. Rough alike in morals and in manners, collected from the wild hills of Yorkshire and of Lancashire, coming in troops from the fens of Lincolnshire, and afterwards pouring in masses from every country in the empire; displaying an unbending vigour and an independent bearing; mostly dwelling apart from the villagers near whom they worked; with all the strong propensities of an untaught, undisciplined nature; unable to read and unwilling to be taught; impetuous, impulsive, and brute-like; regarded as the pariahs of private life, herding together like beasts of the field, owning no moral law and feeling no social tie, they increased with an increased demand, and from thousands grew to hundreds of thousands. They lived but for the present; they cared not for the past; they were indifferent to the future. They were a wandering people, who only spoke of God to wonder why he had made some so rich and others so poor; and only heard of a coming state to hope that there they might cease to be railway labourers. They were heathens in the heart of a Christian people; savages in the midst of civilization: and it is scarcely an exaggeration to say, that a feeling something akin to that which awed the luxurious Roman when the Goth was at his gates, fell on the minds of those English citizens near whom the railway labourer pitched his tent.

"A perfect dread," said one witness before a committee of the House of Commons, "was on the minds of the people of the town near which the railway labourer was expected." Nor was it, until this period, when they became an element of the power of England; when their numbers made them feared by the rich who avoided them, and a curse to the poor who associated with them, that the Chadwicks of the nineteenth century could compel the attention they deserved.

The inquiry instituted by parliament elicited information which surprised some and revolted all. The mode in which they herded together was melancholy; and if the homes of the people be an index to their civilization, the home of the railway labourer was significant enough. They earned high wages, and they spent them. They worked hard, and they lived well. The waste of power which their daily labour necessitated, was supplied by an absorption of stimulant and nourishment perfectly astounding. Bread, beef, bacon, and beer, were the staple of their food. They drank ardent spirits if they had money, credit, or craft to procure it; for "there was not an atom's worth of honesty among them". They devoured as earnestly as they worked; they drank whisky by the tumbler, and called it "white beer": and they proved what open air and hard labour would do in the disposal of their food. They were in a state of utter barbarism. They made their homes where they got their work. Some slept in huts constructed of damp turf, cut from the wet grass, too low to stand upright in; while small sticks, covered with straw, served as rafters. Barns were better places than the best railway labourer's dwellings. Others formed a room of stones without mortar, placed thatch or flags across the roof, and took possession of it with their families, often making it a source of profit by lodging as many of their fellow-workmen as they could crowd into it. It mattered not to them that the rain beat through the roof, and that the wind swept through the holes. If they caught a fever, they died; if they took an infectious complaint, they wandered in the open air, spreading the disease wherever they went. In these huts they lived; with the space overcrowded; with man, woman, and child mixing in promiscuous guilt; with no possible separation of the sexes; in summer wasted by unwholesome heats, and in winter literally hewing their way to their work through the snow. In such places from nine to fifteen hundred men were crowded for six years. "Living like brutes, they were depraved, degraded, and reckless. Drunkenness and dissoluteness of morals prevailed. There were many women, but few wives; loathsome forms of disease were universal. Work often went on without intermission on Sundays as well as on other days."

"Possessed of all the daring recklessness of the smuggler," says Mr Roscoe, . . . "their ferocious behaviour can only be equalled by the brutality of their language. It may be truly said their hand is against every man's, and before they have been long located, every man's hand is against theirs. From being long known to each other, they generally act in concert, and put at defiance any local constabulary force; consequently crimes of the most atrocious character were common, and robbery without any attempt at concealment was an every-day occurrence." Attention was rarely paid to the day of rest, excepting to make it a day of debauchery. Many of them lived in a state of intoxication until their money was spent, and they were again obliged to have recourse to labour, to the loan ticket and the truck system.

The dread which such men as these spread throughout a rural community, was striking; nor was it without a cause. Depredation among the farms and fields of the vicinity were frequent. They injured everything they approached. From their huts to that part of the railway at which they worked, over corn or grass, tearing down embankments, injuring young plantations, making gaps in hedges, on they went, in one direct line, without regard to damage done or property invaded. Game disappeared from the most sacred preserves; game-keepers were defied; and country gentlemen who had imprisoned rustics by the dozen for violating the same law, shrunk in despair from the railway "navigator". They often committed the most outrageous acts in their drunken madness. Like dogs released from a week's confinement, they ran about and did not know what to do with themselves. They defied the law; broke open prisons; released their comrades, and slew policemen. The Scotch fought with the Irish, and the Irish attacked the Scotch; while the rural peace-officers, utterly inadequate to suppress the tumult, stood calmly by and awaited the result. When no work was required of them on the Sunday, the most beautiful spots in England were desecrated by their presence. Lounging in highways and byeways, grouping together in lanes and valleys, insolent and insulting, they were dreaded by the good, and welcomed by the bad. They left a sadness in the homes of many whose sons they had vitiated and whose daughters they had dishonoured. Stones were thrown at passers-by; women were personally abused; and men were irritated. On the week day, when their work was done, the streets were void of all save their lawless visitors and of those who associated with them. They were regarded as savages; and when it is remembered that large bodies of men armed with pitchforks and scythes went out to do battle with those on another line a few miles off, the feeling was justified by facts. Crime of all description increased, but offences against the person were most common. On one occasion, hundreds of them were within five minutes' march of each other, ere the military and the magistrates could get between them to repress their daring desires.

Their presence spread like a pestilence. Tempted by the high wages they received, the hind left his master to join them. Occasionally the inhabitants of the district received the labourer as a lodger, and paid for it in the impurity of character and conduct it engendered. The females of his family left their home to join the wild encampment, and were in their turn left by those who had betrayed them. Their boys aped the vices of men. They fought, smoked, swore, and reeled along the streets at an age when, in other classes, they are scarcely left by themselves. The "navigators", wanderers on the face of the earth, owning no tie and fearing no law; "were", said the Rev. St George Sargent, "the most neglected and spiritually destitute people I ever met; ignorant of Bible religion and Gospel truth, infected with infidelity, and prone to revolutionary principles."

from A HISTORY OF THE ENGLISH RAILWAY *1851*

Railways and Landscapes

MICHAEL ROBBINS

It may seem a curious thing, at first sight, that the railway slipped so easily into the landscape of Britain. In the earliest days, awe was excited by the stupendous scale of the great engineering works; but then it could be seen that the sweeping horizontal line of embankment and viaduct consorted quite well with the existing pattern of tidy field and hedgerow. The wayside station, with its neat station house, two sidings, four railwaymen's cottages, and attendant inn, fitted snugly into its surroundings; the level crossing, with its keeper's single-storied dwelling, that was visible for miles across the Fens was certainly no worse in its looks than the contemporary farms and cottages. So it happened that, in the early age, it was only in the mountains that much opposition was raised in defence of what would now be called the natural ameni-ties. The *locus classicus* is Wordsworth on the Kendal & Winder-mere Railway:

> Is there no nook of English ground secure
> From rash assault?

he thundered. (Later he was pleased to discover that railway labourers could be gentle and pious men.) Ruskin became very angry indeed: "I detest railways. Your railway has cut through and spoiled some of the loveliest bits of scenery in the country." And again: "Now, every fool in Buxton can be in Bakewell in half an hour, and every fool in Bakewell at Buxton; which you think a lucrative process of exchange – you Fools Everywhere."

But in fact the English landscape was not ruined by railways. At certain places there may be two views about particular pieces of line: at Dawlish, where the Great Western runs between the town and the sea; on Ludgate Hill, where a bridge is set in the foreground of the view of St Paul's cathedral from the west, though it does not block the view from Fleet Street; on the Thames at Charing Cross; near Southwark cathedral; at Conway, where the castle is shaved by the Chester & Holyhead line; or in Edinburgh, where the approach from the north and west to the best-sited station in the two kingdoms runs at the foot of Princes Street gardens. Nor did much that was historically valuable perish in the process of building the railways. It is true that what was left of Northampton castle, the castle of Berwick-on-Tweed and St Pancras priory at Lewes disappeared; but a diversion saved Maiden Castle at Dorchester, and a Roman pavement under the long Great Central viaduct at Leicester has been preserved with special care. On balance, archaeology has gained far more from railway excavation than it has lost; and where amenities have been spoiled, it is more often (as above Miller's Dale station, on Ruskin's favourite stretch between Buxton and Bakewell) the industries and settlements that have followed rather than the railway itself which are to blame.

Even a hundred and more years ago, few voices were raised against railway builders on the grounds that natural beauties or amenities were being destroyed. There were, it is true, plenty of proprietors who used some such argument to screw more money in compensation from the companies; but when the argument had served its turn, and the money was paid, most of them continued to dwell quite happily on their ravaged domains. A few cases of pertinacious opposition, with violence, there certainly were. A well-known diehard was the Earl of Harborough, who offered strenuous and successful opposition to the line proposed for the Midland's Leicester and Peterborough railway across the grounds of his seat at Stapleford Park in Leicestershire; so for over forty years, until a more complaisant proprietor agreed to a realignment which was brought into use in 1892, Midland trains had to traverse a sharp and awkward curve at Saxby. But there was not nearly so much of this kind of thing as some modern accounts might suggest. More often the railway was cheerfully accepted as an element in the scenery.

In 1842, for example, when the railway between Leicester and Derby had been open for only two years, Mr Thomas Potter wrote in his description of Charnwood Forest: "From this point, too (the summit of Long Cliff), the trains of the Midland Counties Railway may be observed, almost uninterruptedly, from Sileby to Derby, and form a pleasing object darting across the grand panorama." The author of Murray's *Handbook for Surrey* could write in 1865 of the view from the North Downs behind Reigate:

"The railway lines from Redhill to Dorking, from East Grinstead to Three Bridges, and from Redhill far on the way to Brighton, are visible from this point; the wreaths of white smoke that float above the deep foliage of the Weald marking the progress of the trains across the old country of the Iguanodon and the Plesiosaurus." It seemed perfectly natural to those antiquaries, who had no special interest in the intruder. White smoke against green countryside – they liked the look of it.

George Eliot wrote on the same theme, more explicit and more imaginative:

> Our Midland plains have never lost their familiar impression and conservative spirit for me; yet at every other mile, since I first looked on them, some sign of world-wide change, some new direction of human labour, has wrought itself into what one may call the speech of the landscape. . . . There comes a crowd of burly navvies, with pickaxes and barrows, and while hardly a wrinkle is made in the fading mother's face, or a new curve of health in the blooming girl's, the hills are cut through, or the breaches between them spanned, we choose our level, and the white steam-pennon flies along it.

One reason for this general acceptance at the time must have been that in the years since 1760 many of the country districts in England and Scotland had already been subjected to sweeping changes in their scenery. The process of enclosure by Parliamentary act led to minor landmarks being destroyed wholesale, little woods and coppices being uprooted, and small fields thrown together into large ones, which left the land in the counties most affected looking as though it had been newly shaved. The growth of hedge timber and the healing hand of time since then have made it difficult to imagine what an upheaval there was. Turnpike roads had been driven straight (or comparatively straight) from town to town, dividing fields and properties in what seemed a ruthless manner. The road from Northampton to Kettering, for example, ran straight without turning aside to a single village for eleven miles, until it came to Broughton. Then canals had been built, sometimes straight, more often following the contours of the land round the minor hills until more important features forced them into a tunnel or on to an embankment like the Grand

Junction's at Wolverton or the magnificent aqueduct across the Dee valley at Pontcysyllte in Denbighshire.

Thus the construction of the railways, plunging with great gashes across the countryside as they often did, was not something quite outside the experience of the eighteen-thirties and forties. More important, the manner of doing it was, in the formative years, worthy of great public undertakings. The works of the great engineers of that period were austere, massive, imposing. They had a kind of Roman grandeur; they did not look either cheap or vulgar. The whole railway system was something more than a commercial transaction; it was a public improvement. The buildings were always decent, sometimes imposing, sometimes romantic. The bridges and viaducts were well built, solid, sometimes elegant; the tunnel-mouths were finished to suggest classic majesty or Gothic gloom. . . .

The railway has taken its place in the landscape with all the other artificial elements that man has put there: fields, hedges, farms, roads, canals. It has taken its place because it fits in – it rarely dominates in any view – and because, unlike the airfield which must obliterate existing features to create its shaven emptiness, the railway etches in fresh detail to the scene. It rarely jars and usually pleases.

from THE RAILWAY AGE *1962*

The Architecture of Railways

CHRISTIAN BARMAN

The age of English railway building is not the only episode in the architectural history of the world that the historians have neglected, but it certainly is among the most important of them. It is important not only because it includes many works of uncommon power and distinction, but more especially because it contains in itself a complete epitome of the architectural movements of nineteenth-century England. More than all the churches and town halls and private houses, more than any other buildings of whatever kind or type, the great and varied collection of buildings erected by the railway companies can help us to understand the architecture of the Victorian age, to grasp its purpose and meaning, and to give it its proper place among the most exciting achievements of Atlantic man.

Like the bulk of nineteenth-century architecture, it is an architecture of revolution. It is only now when we can look back from a comfortable distance that we begin to see how tremendous was the upheaval that shook the country at that time. Other revolutions – Oliver Cromwell's, for example – have left a permanent mark on the habits of life of our society, but in the perspective of the centuries they appear as short-lived disturbances that did not radically alter its structure. The continuity of leadership was not really broken; the settled order was shaken but not destroyed. They were revolts rather than revolutions, a rising up, not a turning upside down. But when we talk about the Industrial Revolution we use the word to describe a process immeasurably greater in depth and scope. For in this revolution a social structure that had stood secure for centuries was gradually demolished and another and different structure arose in its place. Railway architecture reflects very faithfully the origin and growth of this alternative structure. It is the architecture of the new people, the people without culture who built the foundations of the new epoch out of the rubble that was all that was left of the old.

Our national architecture bears the mark of two other revolutions of this kind. The first was when Roman leadership had collapsed and the Anglo-Saxon folk developed the new Christian culture of the Middle Ages; the second when Catholic leadership went down under the Tudors and the culture of the humanist arose to take its place. The new leadership class was struggling then to find expression in the architecture of Oxburgh and Haddon, of Layer Marney and Hampton Court. It was an architecture of action and adventure to which the vivid interplay of violence and compromise, of excitement and restraint, has given a special character utterly different from that of earlier and later buildings. The architecture of Tudor and Elizabethan England is the archi- tecture of the new ruling class feeling its way to power. It is a remarkable thing about the English genius that the climate of revolution should bring forth its choicest fruits; our classical moments did not as a rule show us at the top of our form. Today we look on those years as a golden age. . . .

But the time came when the new leaders in their turn faced failure and abdication. They fought their enemies at home and abroad; they narrowly escaped defeat in India; on the other side of the Atlantic they were routed by a colonial tobacco planter who laid the foundations of an alternative leadership in that part of their rich domain. They were attacked from above and below, from right and left, from front and rear.

The typical member of the new leading class was a man who had worked with his hands and taught himself the hard way. Of course there were exceptions. Armstrong had been a solicitor, and the power-loom and the reaping machine were both invented by clergymen. While Fairbairn, who with Robert Stephenson de- veloped the revolutionary designs for the Conway and Britannia tubular bridges, was working as an apprentice to a colliery mechanic, he would put in a few hours every evening cutting pit timbers to eke out the family income. After that he got down to his daily time-table; arithmetic on Mondays, history on Tuesdays, algebra on Thursdays, geometry and trigonometry on Fridays. Many, like Bramah, started life as agricultural labourers; others had been carpenters, weavers, blacksmiths (like Matthew Murray), millwrights, clock repairers (Huntsman, the first to produce cast steel, was one). Arkwright was once a hairdresser and Fox, inventor of the planing machine, a butler in a country vicarage.

The men who invented and built our railways were of this same type. How do we describe them? The term "working class", which seemed so obviously appropriate to every kind of Victorian writer from Smiles to Ruskin, is not well suited to these modern times. . . . Moreover, to say that the builders of the railways were working-class people would not be altogether accurate. Perhaps the best way of describing them is to call them craftsman-inventors. They knew little about the arts of life and many of them did not want to know. "Classics may do very well," says John Thornton's proud mother in *North and South*, "for men who loiter away their lives in the country or in colleges; but Milton men ought to have their thoughts and powers absorbed in the work of today." And the work of today made heavy demands on the men whom her son, himself one of them, described as "the great pioneers of civilization". Most of them, like Brindley, Arkwright and Stephenson, hardly had time to learn to read or write. But these above all were the men who, grasping the new reins of power in this interval of momentous change, stamped a new physical aspect on nineteenth-century England.

The railway builders had their tradition of craftsmanship in stone and brick and timber, and they also had a newly acquired skill in the handling of iron and the building of machines. The architectural environment in which they were brought up had habituated them to the great humanist patterns of thought and expression. Moreover, architects educated in the humanist tradition were employed on many of their enterprises. And so it comes about that we find in their work a fascinating mixture of engineering design and vernacular architecture strengthened here and there with an infusion of high architectural skill. Its virtues were the virtues of the people who made it, but the language in which those virtues found expression is often derived from the language of the humanist age. It would perhaps be more correct to say that it derived from a number of languages, for, like most architects of those days, the railway builder took his pick from the idiomatic wealth of the pre-revolutionary style not only of his own country but of many others. There is no greater eclectic than the self-educated. But to be an eclectic means living on capital, and the capital of humanist culture could not be expected to last for ever. The old traditions maintained their hold for about a quarter of a

H

century after the birth of the steam railway, and it is into that quarter of a century that the golden period of railway architecture is compressed. There is nothing quite like this mixture anywhere else in our architecture, for the seventeenth century upheaval which was so like the Industrial Revolution had provided its builders neither with a new subject matter comparable to the steam railway nor with a new technique like the technique of iron buildings. It is the many subtle combinations of old and new diction that give to the railway style its characterful uniqueness. In that short period something was produced the like of which we shall not see again.

The men who built our railway stations had three important things to think of. The first was to build practically and strongly, to satisfy Wootton's first two conditions of firmness and commodity. Their buildings had a job to do, and this job must be done in a sound, workmanlike manner. In the typical station house the job was a straightforward and familiar one; elsewhere, as in the cantilevered verandas and in the great train sheds, it was a novel and adventurous job requiring new kinds of skill and often a high degree of confidence and pluck. This kind of problem is a typical engineer's problem, involving mainly physical factors and only incidentally concerned with human ones. There are great spaces to be bridged and covered, and the spaces must be encumbered with the fewest possible supports. Not since the days of the great cathedrals had the constructor of buildings been faced with such a challenge.

The second thing these designers had to consider was the relation of their work to the prevailing visual environment. The craftsmen and engineers who made our railways were not themselves men of culture, but they understood and respected the great humanist tradition. They did not want their iron machines or their iron structures to offend against this tradition; they preferred that their work should be well received by the environment in which it was placed. It was inevitable that the assumption of power by a new social class should involve many breaks with the past; but the new leaders had no desire to break unnecessarily and indeed all their work shows how earnestly they strove to maintain a sense of continuity. Their buildings were often strange and curiously shaped, but the people who designed them did their best to show that they could fit in and belong.

There was also a third problem to which the railway builders paid much attention. They were constructors, they were guardians of a great tradition, but they were at the same time the leaders and organizers of the greatest adventure in the world. For that is how the railways of England were regarded not only by their creators but by the more thoughtful of their contemporaries. These men were out to conquer space, they were out to establish civilization in a new dimension, not only in their own country but throughout the world. They sought to express this sense of leadership in their architecture. The humanist culture had placed a high value on the idea of leadership. Its architects had known how to project that idea in terms of building. They had also been busy working on another idea, the idea of military victory. Vanbrugh's great composition in honour of the victory of Blenheim had been followed on the other side of the Channel by a long, systematic exploitation of the same theme under Napoleon which went on until his eclipse at Waterloo was celebrated by the building of the finest classical bridge in the world. The railway builders knew, as everybody knew, that the day of great military victories had passed; but they also knew that another very different sort of victory was at hand. Napoleon has left bigger arches than Stephenson, but he never left a grander one. In the triumphal porticoes of Euston and Birmingham, of Newcastle and Huddersfield, the sense of conquest over nature's forces is even more apparent than is the dominant position attained by those who had laboured to bring that victory about.

The functional adventure of railway station architecture is concerned with the design of shelters for passengers and trains. These shelters started from humble beginnings. The earliest of them unmistakably belong to the tradition of country craftsmanship that Mr Lewis Mumford has dignified with the title *eotechnic age*. Passengers on the London and Birmingham railway waited under sheds that might have been built to serve for cattle or wagons on a prosperous farm. It was the obvious precedent; the agricultural entrepreneur of the eighteenth century and the railway builder of the nineteenth followed one another in the same line of descent.

But there is always a temporary look about these simple wooden shelters; it is as if those who built them knew they were dealing

with an invention whose full development was certain to be so
tremendous that it was useless for them to try to forecast what it
would be like. One of the most fascinating contrasts of this age of
contrasts is the one between the simplicity of the improvised train
shelters at the London and Birmingham terminal stations and the
splendour of the lofty monuments that guard the entrances. The
contrast struck many people at the time. Some were puzzled;
others clearly felt that the builders had made themselves ridiculous.
Pugin could see no virtue in "the colossal Grecian portico" or
gateway, one hundred feet high, for the cabs to drive through, and
set down a few feet further, at the fourteen-inch brick wall and
sash-window booking-office. "This piece of Brobdingnagian
absurdity," he says, "must have cost the company a sum which
would have built a first-rate station, replete with convenience, and
which would have been really grand from its simplicity. . . . The
London gateway could not shelter a porter; while the Birmingham
entrance was so unsuitable for its purpose that the company have
been obliged to erect various sheds right up to the large columns,
and tack on a brick house, to make it at all available for its intended
purpose. These two gigantic piles of unmeaning masonry, raised
at an enormous cost, are a striking proof of the utter disregard
paid by architects to the purposes of the building they are called
upon to design; and many thousands have been fairly thrown away
on every line in the erection of show fronts, and inconsistent and
useless decoration." There was nothing humble about Pugin, and
it was difficult for him to understand the humility of a designer
who realized that the job of planning a big metropolitan station
was better left until it was possible for a fully developed railway
to be studied in action.

Brunel at Bath and Bristol (1841) was the first to give serious
architectural treatment to the train shed of which the wooden
station at Lime Street, Liverpool, and the iron station at Euston
(1836) were the rough and simple prototypes. Perhaps it was inevitable that his fine roof trussses and elegant glazing should be so
strongly inspired by our church building idiom; they grew out of
the earlier barn shelters just as the church roofs themselves had
done many centuries before. Pugin, who bitterly criticized Brunel's
gothic masonry details, had no fault to find with his Gothic roofs.
The Gothic Revival produced few carpentry roofs as good as that

of the Bristol station, which is still in existence today. But the building of carpentry roofs could not go on for long. The iron roof was real engineering. Within a few years the railways were to find in John Dobson of Newcastle an architect who was not only worthy of their opportunities for imaginative large-scale planning but capable also of answering the structural challenge of the broad train-hall roof.

Dobson (1787–1865), greatest of all railway architects, was an architect of the finest and most developed type – planner, engineer and man of affairs as well as a sensitive designer. As an engineer, Dobson is usually credited with the first development of the kind of vaulted roof that is constructed with arched ribs of rolled malleable iron, the precursor of rolled steel.

It is in the great roofs of the middle of the century, of which Dobson's, with its three fifty-five foot spans, was the first, that the architecture of the English railway station reaches its highest moment of functional adventure and discovery. But by the side of this stream of major building there ran a smaller current whose claims to our interest is of a very different kind. It was only at the most important stations that big train shelters were needed. For the thousands of smaller stations some form of passenger shelter was usually enough. . . . The practical thing to do was to attach some sort of platform covering to the station building. But the traditional form of lean-to shedding was liable to be a nuisance, for the columns were sure to get in the way of carriage doors. The columns must be set back from the platform edge and the roof must be cantilevered out over them. Sometimes the whole of the roof was bracketed out from the building, and the columns dispensed with altogether. At the busier stations the roof was continued beyond the buildings to protect the whole length of the platform, or the greater part of it. The light and graceful structures of cast-iron, timber and glass that were built for this purpose are known among railwaymen by the Portuguese word *varanda*. They are found up and down the railway lines of England, in every corner of the island, and the astonishing thing is that no two of them are alike. That the woodwork detail should vary even from station to station on the same line is understandable. The delicate hanging valances, for example, were built up of short lengths of board cut out and scalloped by hand two at a time, and the carpenters must have had tremendous fun competing against each other in the working out of new and original patterns. What is much more remarkable is that the ironfounder's repetitive processes should have so far failed to obtrude themselves, that everywhere the cast-iron columns and brackets should show a similar profusion of individual design. It has been said that the abounding fertility of invention shown by English vernacular designers of the eighteenth century is shown at its best in their furniture, and more particularly in their chairs. Our railway stations, too, were lavishly enriched by it, but the full story of the English railway veranda, like the story of the English chair, is still waiting to be told.

The strictly functional problems were not always confined to the structure. They came up in the planning of the buildings, too. There were the waiting rooms, the booking hall, the refreshment rooms, the offices for the station staff; sometimes living quarters for the station staff and offices for the management of the line and perhaps for that of the whole company were also needed. These rooms had to be arranged in the right relation to each other; good circulation must be provided through a properly articulated plan. But here the architect was on familiar ground. All his life he had been planning buildings for many different purposes in just this kind of way. There were not many big functional problems in planning that could be said to be peculiar to railway buildings. But there certainly were a few such problems, and one of them at least has left its mark on railway architecture down to the present day.

For one reason or another, it was sometimes desired to introduce a great hall into the station plan – not the long, open-ended kind of hall that sheltered trains, but an enclosed concourse forming part of the habitable station building. From this concourse the passengers would move in and out of the booking offices, waiting rooms and refreshment rooms. In the course of the twentieth century the outer concourse (which has to be distinguished from the inner concourse beyond the ticket barrier) has come to be accepted as a standard element in the plan of the big modern station. In the nineteenth century the idea was exuberantly demonstrated in P. C. Hardwick's Great Hall at Euston (1849) and quietly dropped by most railway managements after that.

No doubt this Great Hall with its sixty-one foot wide coffered ceiling was an extravagance – one of those extravagances that, like the elder Hardwick's portico outside, were to cause much worry to their owners in succeeding generations. And there were only a few years left before the great crisis of the 'fifties. When that crisis had passed, and railway development started to go forward again, the companies were no longer able to indulge in those architectural flourishes that Pugin had held up to ridicule as "colossal" and "sublime". Instead of concourse blocks like Euston's standing up above the rest of the station like the auditorium of a concert hall, they built smaller halls that fitted into the building with the other public rooms and were therefore incapable of being expressed in the general exterior shape. . . .

In the nineteenth century station the architects' attempts to develop the quality of sociability are usually of far greater interest than his expression of functional plan forms. Our thousands of smaller stations express this idea of sociability clearly and very delightfully. Their designers seem to have been anxious above all to demonstrate that railway people were ordinary human beings and that their buildings were meant to be lived in. The quality that Mr Trystan Edwards calls architectural good manners is seen in their homely window treatments, their cosy domestic roofs and chimneys. With their porches on the front and their verandas on the back, they developed into a station house type of structure that is exclusively English, as English as the high, stone-kerbed station platform on which they stand. Some were two-storey blocks with staff living quarters. There might, for example, be a house for the station master on one side and one for the head porter on the other; such a station was Needham Market (1844) designed by Frederick Barnes, the Ipswich architect. But the single storey building is commoner. The style is mostly some variety of Italian, as it was called, that useful and flexible style to which contemporary writers used to refer as "the railway style". . . .

It was probably by David Mocatta (1806–1882) in his charming Brighton Station (1841) that the Italian manner was finally established as the accepted railway tradition for the busy decade that lay ahead. . . .

Mocatta was a pupil of Sir John Soane. But there were others who clearly passed on the inspiration at second hand – Sir Robert

Smirke, for example, who in his turn taught Sancton Wood and Dobson. Sir William Tite and Charles Fowler were trained in the office of David Laing, another of Soane's pupils. Tite, architect of the Royal Exchange, built a number of fine stations including Carlisle Citadel; and Henry Roberts, who later worked for a time in the office of Sir Robert Smirke, and was appointed joint architect for London Bridge station, was one of Fowler's pupils.

There is only one other railway architect in the great humanist tradition who gave to the small country station the same meticulous study as Mocatta, and that is Francis Thompson of Derby. Like Mocatta, he was responsible for large stations, too; his great buildings at Derby and Chester (the Derby one disappeared long ago) were among the best in the country. He avoided using big columns just as Mocatta did, but his sense of grandeur was keener; he was more deeply imbued with the tradition of Hardwick and Smirke. As architect to the North Midland Railway he designed a number of stations along the line between Derby and Sheffield. There is probably no better small station in the East Anglian gabled style than Ambergate, and Wingfield is an example in the strict classical manner that is unequalled anywhere. . . .

A few years later came Thompson's designs for Chester and Bangor and for the intermediate stations on the Chester and Holyhead line. A characteristic feature developed in these later stations is the cantilevered platform veranda contained between two little terminal blocks projecting out from the station building. On this line Thompson also designed the architectural approach structures to the Britannia tubular bridge near Bangor, for which John Thomas (1813–1862), the architect sculptor, provided the sculpture.

Mr J. M. Richards, who has written more understandingly about railway architecture than any other living critic, suggests that the steam railway was an object of terror and that it was the architect's business to persuade the public that this frightening creature was not as dangerous as it looked. His picture of the railway builder behaving like a nature photographer who camouflages himself as a small tree contains a good deal of truth, but it is not the whole truth. The insistence on conformity, on being a good mixer, that is so conspicuously present in railway architecture is more than the conciliating manner assumed by a man who knows that his physical aspect is frightening or repulsive. It is the feeling of the self-made leader that, no matter how big or important his job may be, no matter how strange and unorthodox the methods whereby he must seek to accomplish it, the continuity of humanist culture is to be taken for granted; the possibility of breaking it is not seriously to be thought of.

The most ambitious of all these attempts to live up to a great humanist environment was that which was made at Liverpool. The City Corporation, conscious of their responsibility as custodians of Elmes's St George's Hall, insisted that the Grand Junction Railway company's Lime Street station must harmonize with the architecture of that superb building. They had had the good sense to appoint as their architect John Franklin (d. 1855), one of the ablest architects ever employed by an English municipality, and his station design (completed 1839) proved so popular that he was invited also to build the Birmingham terminus at the other end of the line. Franklin, who designed the Great George Street and Pembroke Place Chapels and the Crescent Chapel, Everton, did a great deal for Liverpool. But Lime Street was an unlucky station. It was always having to be enlarged or rebuilt. The church of SS Simon and Jude, which stands at the end of the deep cutting outside the station, was taken down, moved and rebuilt stone by stone three times to make room for successive enlargements. Franklin's building did not last many years. And by the time the third station was built the City Corporation had forgotten all about Elmes's masterpiece. Perhaps it was just as well. Even if they had wished to do so, it is doubtful whether at that time they could have found an architect capable of manipulating that ample classical idiom. As for the London & North Western Railway,

H*

which had absorbed the Grand Junction, it never quite recovered from the effects of its great venture at Euston which had left it with a marked leaning to austerity. Besides, by the time the new Lime Street was built (1879) the railways were no longer thinking about their humanist environment. They had gone back to the plain standardized shedding with which they had started – the shedding concealed behind the great monuments at each end of the London and Birmingham line, the shedding that was to reach a new low level of banality in the twentieth century station at Waterloo.

Some of the best architects – and notably Tite himself – made their finest contributions to railway architecture not in the Italian manner but in the Gothic. Thompson, for example, designed a Gothic station for Conway. The most ambitious of all Gothic railway buildings is, of course, Sir George Gilbert Scott's St Pancras station and hotel (not the iron train hall, previously designed by Barlow, the engineer). The peculiar interest of this building (1876) lies in the almost pathological intensity with which Scott concentrated in its design all those deeply cherished architectural themes that the Government had prevented him from using in his greatest work, the Foreign Office building in Whitehall, completed twenty years before. The story of Scott's desperate frustrations . . . need not be repeated here. "It would have been a noble structure," was his own comment on his original Foreign Office design, "and the set of drawings was perhaps the best ever sent in to a competition, or," he adds, "nearly so. . . . I designed windows suited to all positions, and of all varieties of size, form and grouping; doorways, cornices, parapets and imaginary combinations of all these, carefully studying to make them all thoroughly practical, and suited to this class of building. I did not aim at making my style Italian Gothic; my ideas ran much more upon the French, to which for some years I had devoted my chief study. I did, however, aim at gathering a few hints from Italy, such as the pillar-mullion, and the use of differently-coloured materials and of inlaying; I also aimed at another thing which people consider Italian – I mean a certain squareness and horizontality of outline. This I consider pre-eminently suited to the street front of a public building. I combined this, however, with gables, high-pitched roofs and dormers."

Smarting under the memory of his rejected competition design, Scott in designing his great combined station and hotel building was mainly interested in taking his revenge on the shade of Palmerston. Here was a chance to show the country how great was the treasure it had lost. Scott's description of the Foreign Office building might equally well be applied to St Pancras, except for the "Italian squareness and horizontality" to which he came to attach less importance in later years. Scott acknowledges the violent division of opinion on the merits of his station. "This work," he wrote in his diary, "has been spoken of by one of the revilers of my profession with abject contempt. I have to set off against this the too excessive praise of it which I receive from other quarters. It is often spoken of to me as the finest building in London; my own belief is that it is possibly too good for its purpose, but having been disappointed, through Lord Palmerston, of my ardent hope of carrying out my style in the Government offices, and the subject having been in the meanwhile taken out of my hands by other architects, I was glad to be able to erect one building in that style in London."

It was not to be expected that the prophets of the Gothic Revival should look approvingly on Railway Gothic. For years they had been urging architects to study the use of gables and pointed arches, but as one Gothic station went up after another they did not like what they saw. It was not for that kind of Gothic that they had pleaded with a degenerate nation. Like Voysey and le Corbusier in more recent times, they had not been trying to start a new fashion, they had been searching after an idiom that they could regard above all others as an honest projection of the structural idea in buildings. They thought medieval architecture was different from every other kind in that it was more closely and faithfully expressive of this idea. And so they held up medieval buildings to their contemporaries as a lesson in clear, practical thinking. As few of these contemporaries felt any desire to think they received them as a lesson in stylistic design. It was the last thing the teachers had wanted.

There were many places in England where the prevailing environment made Gothic the most sociable of styles. But Gothic was more than that: it was becoming respectable. By the end of the eighteen-forties, the eyes of many railway companies had been opened to the social prestige attaching to the architecture of the medieval castles and the great Tudor houses, and of those Oxford Colleges that had received their approaches with such haughty contempt. Citadel station (Carlisle), built in 1848, is our finest piece of railway architecture in the sixteenth century collegiate manner; it is incidentally, one of the few stations in the country with a first-rate block of platform buildings built on an island platform under the broad (and depressingly mediocre) iron roof. But it is rather in the smaller Gothic stations like Tite's at Windsor with its Royal porch and waiting room (1850) and William Tress's Battle station (1852) that this emphasis on good manners is seen in its clearest and most attractive form. Here were buildings obviously fitted for the best circles. The social projection of the railways was directed mainly to their immediate neighbours, but in such architecture as this they could show that they were never at a loss even when those neighbours were the highest people in the land.

But the railway builder's interest in the old leadership class did not go very deep. They knew that they themselves were the representatives of the new leadership, and they intended that their buildings should properly announce the greatness of their position. To do this, their architects used a number of hieratic devices with varying degrees of success. There was, for example, the tower. The Italian *campaniles* of the Middle Ages had filled many pages in the sketch books of architects travelling in that country. . . . But the first towers used by railway architects were not mere symbols; they served the same practical purpose as the tower-chimneys of the great waterworks. The eighteen-forties were the years of the atmospheric railways on which the trains were worked by a piston moving along a pipe laid in the middle of the track. The system was adopted in 1843 for the Croydon and Epsom railway and in the following year Brunel, who had argued against Stephenson before the Parliamentary committee on the Croydon and Epsom Bill, adopted it for the South Devon railway. In each of the three engine houses on the Croydon and Epsom line – at Forest Hill, Norwood and Croydon – the chimneys became a prominent part of the general station design. The company showed a commendable desire to safeguard local amenities. "They determined," says a contemporary newspaper account, "to give their chimneys an architectural character, and to relieve their baldness by the addition of proportions and decorations which have hitherto belonged almost exclusively to the bell-towers of the early Gothic churches. And," continues this account, "as, in the opinion of the promoters of this scheme, beauty is as cheap as deformity, they have taken another step in the right direction, by a resolution to construct the station and engine houses in the style of the half-timbered manor houses of the Middle Ages." The projection of the social idea could not be carried further. The architects were Raphael and Arthur Brandon, and there is enough left of their buildings today to show how successful was their handling of this delicate task.

In these buildings, as in Brunel's Italian stations along the South Devon coast, the architects seized on the functional form of the chimney and used it as a vehicle for the expression of hieratic ideas. . . . But most station towers were built for their own sake. There was no stationary steam engine at London Bridge or Colchester to give the graceful Italian towers a functional job to do. In Lewis Cubitt's gay and dashing Dover station (1844) the business of hieratic symbol making is carried to such a point that the tower becomes the most important part of the design. Dover is, of course, exceptional; there is no other station quite like this. But there are a great many stations in which towers and turrets are skilfully used on a smaller site. Tite's wholly English turret at Carlisle Citadel is a particularly happy example.

But the most characteristic and the most effective hieratic symbol in railway architecture was not the tower but the classical column, and, above all, the group of columns as arranged in either of the two great traditional patterns of colonnade and porch. Most of the cast-iron colonnades supporting station roofs and platform verandas are elongated variations of the classical types. They vary considerably in quality; Dobson's at Newcastle are among the best. One architect only, Matthew Digby Wyatt (1820–1877), tried seriously to develop a first-class cast-iron column that owed nothing to the humanist tradition. Widely travelled in France, Italy, Sicily and Spain, he had been Secretary of the Royal Society of Arts executive committee for the Great Exhibition, superintendent of works for the building of the Crystal Palace, and, with Owen Jones, responsible for the Fine Arts Section of the Exhibition. His treatment shows a close acquaintance with the Saracenic architecture of the Mediterranean countries and of India. The reason for Wyatt's choice of idiom is obvious. What makes his Paddington station (1854) so remarkable is that the whole of the train hall structure is treated as a single design. It is a unique work of art, remarkable for many qualities but above all for a unity of architectural treatment that is not to be found in any other iron station. His detail flows freely and fluently from the ridge of the great elliptical arches with their six graceful crossings down the long lattice girders to the octagonal pillars of the well-spaced colonnades. It would have been impossible within the classical tradition to attack every point of the engineering structure in this way. Wyatt's friendship with Brunel, the engineer, is said to have sprung from their common interest in the Great Exhibition. It was a brilliant partnership; artist and engineer were never to work together in quite the same lively and imaginative way again.

Long before Paddington was built, the classical portico had established itself as the hieratic symbol most suitable for expressing the highest social values. Buildings like Elmes's St George's Hall, Smirke's British Museum and Basevi's Fitzwilliam had shown what could be done with it. Even the architects of important churches could no longer rely on a tower alone to suggest the special quality of their buildings; the Gothic Revival people were doing their best, but the effect was seldom as strong as they would have liked it to be. For the railway architect who had to give his design a sense of high dignity and importance the portico was the obvious form to use. And so it comes about that high over all the railway buildings of the first decades we see looming the three splendid porches of Euston, Newcastle and Huddersfield. As a true portico attached to the front of a building this last (1847) is unequalled anywhere. This remarkable design has been generally ascribed to H. Stansby, father of the architect of the two little lodges in front of the Euston portico (1870); but signed drawings preserved at Euston establish it beyond a doubt as the work of James Pritchett, senior (1788–1868) – another James, a son, practised at York – and his son Charles. The elder Pritchett was for fifty years architect to the Earls Fitzwilliam, and carried out much work in the neighbourhood of Wentworth. Among many notable contributions this gifted family made to the architecture of the North, Huddersfield station is certainly the finest. The long façade terminating in pavilions linked to the central portico by Corinthian colonnades is fortunate, too, in its siting: it can really be seen as it should be seen, which cannot be said of many of our great station buildings.

Dobson, who inspired but did not design the Newcastle portico as we now see it, had absorbed the grand tradition in the office of Sir Robert Smirke, but Vanbrugh was another powerful influence. Newcastle central station is his acknowledged masterpiece; the circumstances in which this building came to be finished by another hand makes it also a memorial of one of the great personal tragedies in our architectural history. Dobson, when he was working out the design for the York, Newcastle & Berwick and the Newcastle–Carlisle railways, foresaw inevitable developments and combinations in railway operation and planned his station accordingly. The directors made him reduce the size of his building. The walls were half-way up when they decided to transfer their head office from York to Newcastle; enlargements had to be hurriedly improvised and the great portico had to be omitted. It was added many years later, during Dobson's last, fatal illness, by Thomas Prosser, the architect of Leeds (1869) and York (1877) stations. The design is manifestly inferior to Dobson's own; no wonder an obituary notice speaks of his "grief and disappointment" as he lay dying. The place of Newcastle Central in English railway architecture is great and assured; with Dobson's own portico it would have stood in the front rank with the best of all our public buildings.

The railway builders were moved by the spirit of the conqueror, and nowhere is this spirit more clearly visible than in the portico at Euston. Marching southward for their attack on London we can see that they understood the greatness of their mission. And so when finally they had invaded the greatest city in the world they built the portico at Euston to proclaim as a memorial their victory to posterity. For this portico, though designed in the manner used for porches attached to buildings, is by virtue of its starkly isolated position a genuine military *arc de triomphe*. But Hardwick's portico is more than a conqueror's gateway, more than a great hieratic porch: it is also the first attempt to apply to the exterior of a railway station the monumental screen treatment as developed by Soane and Adam. . . .

The screen front had suggested itself naturally and indeed, inevitably at Paddington (1837), where the façade of the station had been contrived out of the arches of a bridge, and Tite in his little Nine Elms station (1838) at Vauxhall was using a regular arcaded treatment that is more fully developed in the long screen façades of Cambridge (1845) and Lewis Isaac's Holborn Viaduct (1873), the original pattern for the London Electric Railway's arcaded fronts of the end of the century. At Euston, the screen is made up of seven free-standing blocks linked by high cast-iron railings and gates, and it is clear that the great propyleum was intended by the architect to be seen as the central incident in this long horizontal composition. The same building-up of a screen out of separate blocks is seen in a different form in Franklin's Lime Street (Liverpool) station; here the connection is established by a plain building front with engaged Corinthian columns.

The conquest of London was an event unique in railway history. Other great stations were built, but the circumstances of their building never again reached this sense of high occasion. A few – they are remarkably few – were inspired by reasons of personal aggrandisement; Monkwearmouth, for example, seems to have been designed to commemorate the election of George Hudson, the Railway King, as Member of Parliament for Sunderland. Lime Street, Liverpool, sprang from another kind of motive. But the enlightened control of building development by a local authority, too, was a rare occurrence. The commonest reason for building a station in the grand manner was the successful marriage of competing railways. P. C. Hardwick's Great Hall at Euston is a monument to the amalgamation of three of the earliest companies into a new unit, the London and North Western, and the partnership between this new company and the old Midland Counties railway; at Newcastle Central three companies were planning to enter into joint operation; Chester was built by five different railways that at the time of building agreed about nothing except the necessity of a common station; Bristol and Huddersfield also were joint ventures. If anything could be more peculiarly English than the incidents in railway history that are recorded in these buildings, it is the manner of their recording. Many little railway companies, often fiercely competitive, divided the country between them. It was Victorian individualism in its most vigorous form. And when two or more of these railways got together and composed their differences it was a matter for solemn rejoicing. Their energies, which had been wasted in competition, would now be husbanded and pooled in the interests of a single purpose and policy. This was what progress meant. One can almost see the grizzly fighters celebrating after years of exhausting conflict: "Let us shake hands and build something!" Great architecture may be the result of many different kinds of moments and moods. When it testifies to a hard-won partnership between proud and obstinate opponents the occasion gives it a special kind of impetus; its strength is the strength of the wills that were subjugated in the interests of a shared adventure, of a new and exciting common task.

As one watches the railway builders' projection of the idea of function and the idea of sociability it becomes clear that these two ideas have continued to occupy their minds down to the present day. There are still practical problems of planning and structure to be dealt with, and the quality of good manners in buildings, though it has been often neglected, is once again taken seriously as it must be by a country that calls itself civilized. But the hieratic idea, the idea of leadership, could never be as important again as it had been in those glorious early years. You cannot go on celebrating the same victory for ever. The triumphal gateways and porticoes had done their job, and it was time to pass on to other things. In all the best buildings after 1850 – and this is true of English architecture in general and not only of that of the railways – the classical column was laid aside under the new inspiration of Barry and Pennethorne. A generation later it was rediscovered by architects like Gribble and Brydon, and from that time down to the second outbreak of war in 1939 the architecture of the revolution was to flow in a constantly broadening stream of pointlessness and vulgarity.

from AN INTRODUCTION TO
RAILWAY ARCHITECTURE *1950*

The Railheads of London

JOHN BETJEMAN

The study of railway stations is something like the study of churches. It can be turned into archaeological detection work. For piscina, read cast-iron lamp bracket; for arcading, read girder construction; for transepts, read waiting-rooms; for hangings, read tin advertisements. Then with very little practice anyone with an eye for detail can date the objects inspected.

Picture a disused platform of a rather forgotten station, let us say South Hampstead, the first station after Euston ($2\frac{1}{2}$ miles) on the old L.M.S. electric line to Watford. It opens late and shuts early and few people seem to use it. When I was a boy we called it Loudon Road and the booking office building stood, as it still stands, looking rather like a small mid-Victorian brick Vicarage, harmonizing happily with the Gothic fancies of this lilac-shaded part of St John's Wood. I should think from the style of architecture it was built in the late 'seventies by which time enough platforms had been constructed at Euston to make it possible for the London & North Western to run an enlarged suburban service. I have never departed from nor alighted at South Hampstead. . . . I prefer to imagine the station. I like to think that it contains the various fittings of a former age for which my eye is always on the watch when I use an unfamiliar station. Perhaps there are some very old tickets in the booking office – a first-class return to Chalk Farm (which would mean going down to Euston and coming back again) would probably be printed with "Loudon Road" and the letters L.N.W.R. Under the treads of the stairs to the platform there may be those tin advertisements saying IRON JELLOIDS, IRON JELLOIDS, IRON JELLOIDS in blue on an orange ground, insisting, as one ascends, on the weakness of one's heart and its need for the stamina which those pills supply. Still in imagination, I walk right down to the end of the platform to the oldest lamp standard, a graceful thing on twisted columns with, perhaps, a six-sided glass cage for the gas-burner and the name of the iron foundry where it was made at the base of its column. Against the station wall there may be tin signs for MAZAWATTEE TEA and the still-familiar black and blue splodge of STEPHEN'S INK on a white ground. And, of course, there will be those two old friends VENO'S LIGHTNING COUGH CURE and DR J. COLLIS BROWNE'S CHLORODYNE.

Then what waiting rooms may there not be! Gothic Revival cast-iron grates in which no fire has been lighted since the days when a mountain of glowing coal warmed the early-morning pin-striped bottoms of city gentlemen who used this station as the preliminary part of a journey from Boundary Road to Euston, thence by steam train on the inner circle from Euston Square to Aldersgate. . . . The walls of the waiting room will be green. The lighting gas. There will perhaps be a framed collection of photographs, "Beauty spots" of the L. & N.W.R. – Killarney; Sackville Street, Dublin; Blarney Castle (the L. & N.W. always liked to give the impression that it owned all the Irish railways); George's Landing Stage, Liverpool; Bettws-y-coed; Warwick Castle. These

will be in sepia with gilt lettering on the wooden surround. Then
there will be a framed looking-glass in which it will be impossible
to see all one's face at once because painted on the surface are the
words IDRIS TABLE WATERS and a long maiden in clothes rather
like a water lily holding in her hand a sparkling glass of IDRIS.
These are but some of the delights I imagine there may be at
South Hampstead.

The serious scholar of London railway stations will make the
historical approach. I unfold the map of my *Bradshaw's Railway
Companion for 1841* [and] notice that there were fields beyond
Regent's Park and Pentonville and Islington and Hackney.
Bethnal Green was in London, Stratford was not. South-east of
Bermondsey and south of Walworth there were still fields between
terraces and squares, fields that in two years were to be filled with
either Italianate merchants' houses amid laurel shrubbery or with
rows of two-storey artisans' dwellings. Chelsea and Brompton and
Kensington still had separate personalities. No railways dared to
invade the centre of London. Westminster was even more sacred
than the City. There they are on the map, little pink lines, pushing
tentatively towards the heart of the metropolis.

These early stations, you must remember, are part of the
Georgian age. They are stately but not sumptuous. They are
spreading but not soaring. They suggest coaches pulled by iron
horses. They are merely another sort of posting inn, not something private, railed off and of another world, which railways
have now become. They are the stables of the iron horses and they
blend naturally with the drays which clatter over cobbles towards
them and the carriages which are unloaded from them and pulled
away by horses to the noblemen's houses of Mayfair. Euston
(1837), London Bridge (1838), Paddington (1839) are still on their
original sites. Philip Hardwick's magnificent Doric Arch of
granite (1837) at Euston originally had two lodges flanking each
side and was visible from the Euston road; the outer pairs of these
have been destroyed. It was the gateway not only to all the
country houses of the North, but also to a new age. The little iron
sheds of the station behind it, so ridiculed by Pugin, are rather an
anti-climax. Successive generations have treated this noble arch
scurvily and its glory has been hidden by the Euston Hotel. As an
essay of the Greek Revival, I consider the arch even now, almost

shorn of its lodges, the noblest thing in London, nobler even than St Pancras church or the British Museum or the Hyde Park Screen. Only one building rivalled it and that was Rennie's Waterloo Bridge. The L.M.S. made determined efforts to remove Euston Arch altogether. British Railways will probably succeed in doing so.*

London Bridge, now a shattered collection of girders and temporary-looking platforms, has little to show of the old terminus of the Greenwich Railway, that remarkable line carried on 878 brick arches, which was merged with the South Eastern and Chatham. There is a spacious dignity, created by white brick walls and an arching roof, about the Terminus part of the station whence trains depart over a loop line via the Crystal Palace (Low Level) and Norwood to Victoria, through Italianate stations and brick cuttings and sudden elevations from which one may see the brick Italianate houses of Ruskin's South London, the prehistoric monsters of the Crystal Palace Park and perhaps glimpse Sherlock Holmes hiding amid the laurels, lamp posts and ivy-clad clinker of a merchant's private drive.

The severe nine-arched entrance of Paddington has disappeared entirely, though the space in front of where it stood, now under glass, is still known as "the lawn". But two others of these six early stations survive. Nine Elms, erected in 1838 by Sir William Tite (architect of the Royal Exchange) as the terminus of the South Western Railway, may be found standing, classic, stuccoed

* As, of course, they have—*Ed.*

and deserted, amid the gasworks, goods yards and factories of that
district where strikes seem often to originate. There are no passengers and the more important goods yards seem to be in another
part of Nine Elms, so that this building and its platforms are an
early station survival. I know of no more complete example
except Philip Hardwick's great arch at the old and disused
terminus in Birmingham of the London to Birmingham Railway.

A smaller London station of this period is now out of reach of
the public. It is the Blackwall terminus of the old London and
Blackwall Railway. Those frequent and quite empty trains of the
Blackwall Railway ran from a special platform of Fenchurch
Street. I remember them well. Like stage-coaches they rumbled
slowly past East-End chimney pots, wharves and shipping,
stopping at black and empty stations, till they came to a final halt
at Blackwall station, a handsome building in white brick and
Portland stone, from an Italianate design by Sir William Tite.
When one emerged there was nothing to see beyond it but a
cobbled quay and a vast stretch of wind-whipped water, over one
of the broadest tidal reaches of the Thames.

There may be, among the bomb damage, some remains of
Bricklayers' Arms Station (1840), long demoted, like Nine Elms,
to a goods depot. Bricklayers' Arms was known as the "West End
Terminus" of the South Eastern Railway and marks probably the
first and last time the Old Kent Road has been described as the
West End of London. It was a classic structure.

Somewhere, too, among arches, goods yards and stables down a
side street off Shoreditch one may still be able to find remains of
the old Terminus of the Eastern Union Railway (1839) which was
designed by Sancton Wood. It was the precursor of Liverpool
Street and its architect was a pupil of Sir Robert Smirke and like
his master a bold classicist. He designed the palatial Roman
terminus of Kingsbridge, Dublin (1845), with its twin cupolas,
and Leinster Square, Paddington, and part of Hyde Park Gardens.

By the 'fifties, the old coaching view of railways was out of date.
They were establishing an architecture of their own and as keenly
as Tractarians and Evangelicals they joined in the Battle of the
Styles, Classic v. Gothic. On the whole the Classic style won.
Euston, long a pioneer in railway architecture, set the tone with
the Euston Great Hall which was completed in 1849. It was the

joint design of old Philip Hardwick and his son Philip Charles
Hardwick. Never had there been and never has there been since
in England so magnificent a piece of railway architecture. . . . It is
still possible to note its double staircase, its rich ceiling, its
figured consoles supporting the ceiling and carved by John
Thomas, who made the figures and bosses in the Houses of
Parliament. At the top of the staircase, is the room for the Shareholders' General Meetings, an untouched specimen of Roman
Revival of the late 'forties. This sumptuous hall and offices set the
fashion for railway architecture. Even the chairs of waiting rooms
and desks in the offices had a Roman grandeur about them, executed in oak and mahogany, solid and heavy as a Christmas dinner.
To compare with Euston, there is nothing. Other lines as they
built their termini and chief suburban stations went in for classic,
but the classic style preferred was that of the French Renaissance.
It may be seen in those stations of the 'sixties, Charing Cross,
Cannon Street, Broad Street, Farringdon Street, Aldersgate,
Highbury, Bow, Camden Town, and it even survived into the
next decade when Holborn Viaduct Station was built.

The architect of Charing Cross and Cannon Street was Edward
Middleton Barry, a son of Sir Charles, the architect of the Houses
of Parliament. Edward's masterpiece is undoubtedly the Charing
Cross Hotel (1864). I know few pleasanter meeting places than the
first floor of that building. A broad staircase leads to corridors
done in the manner of Sir John Soane, unexpectedly Graeco-
Roman when there is also much French Renaissance about the
exterior. On this floor is the suite of rooms I call "the club". There
is a smoking room with bar attached and billiard room adjoining
and one can walk on to a balcony, drink in hand, to survey the
crowds and trains of the station below. There are horse-hair seats
in the smoking room, a bookshelf with a set of Shakespeare and a
guide to the Southern Railway, and one has the place to oneself,
while all around in stately dining rooms, private luncheons are
being held by old-fashioned boards of directors, the Ouse
Catchment Board, the Blackwall Tunnel Company, the Tower
Hamlets Development Society, the United Kingdom Union of
Persecuting Protestants. Much of this activity used to occur at the
Cannon Street Hotel (1866) designed by the same architect. The
station itself at Cannon Street is a far finer building than that at

Charing Cross which has been deprived of its original semi-circular roof. Barry's towers and cupolas at the river opening of Cannon Street compare well with Wren's steeples and blend this great structure into the steepled outline of the City.

The only time the Great Western went in for Classic in a big way was when it employed Philip Charles Hardwick to design the Paddington Hotel in the 'sixties. The dining room here with its curving caryatids, probably by John Thomas, was almost up to the standard of Euston's Graeco-Roman office buildings. Just before the Hitler war this dining room, or "Coffee Room" as it was called, was ruined by being streamlined with plywood in a jazz-modern manner, so that it is now like any semi-smart new restaurant. The Great Western otherwise has been fairly loyal to Tudor, a style which it first adopted at Temple Meads, Bristol, and still employs there. The only nearly untouched examples of a Tudor station on the London to Bristol line which survive are Shrivenham and Box. . . .

The richest Gothic station is, of course, St Pancras (1868). The enormous iron and glass roof with a clear span of 240 feet, 100 feet high and 700 feet long, makes the trains and platforms below it look like a model railway. It was designed by P. W. Barlow, the Civil Engineer. The tie beams that hold it are below the station and form a roof for the enormous vaults, which are under the whole area of the station. The hotel which is attached to the station, but not related to it, is by Sir Gilbert Scott. Ferguson much objected to it. "There is no proportion between the shed and its uses, and everything looks out of place, and most of all the Gothic mouldings and brickwork, borrowed from the domestic architecture of the Middle Ages, which thrusts itself between the gigantic iron ribs of the roof."

. . . The hotel is now, alas, offices. But the splendid intertwining double staircase of ironwork survives (in the well of this there used to be a Turkish kiosk for coffee) and the huge Arthurian style wallpapers are to be found here and there. The refreshment rooms have all been jazzed and only the station booking hall remains as an untouched Scott interior. Alongside St Pancras is the Midland goods station whose brickwork is undoubtedly the best in London. Sir Gilbert, like his grandson Sir Giles, was always interested in brick and stonework and for the goods station he had bricks specially made of varying sizes. You may see in the screen wall of the building (with its exquisite iron grilles) that the bricks grow smaller as they go higher, giving an effect of solidity to the wall.

Of the exterior of the hotel I am myself enamoured. The clock tower has always seemed to be a highly picturesque outline and the rows of middle-pointed windows along the whole curving sweep achieve an effect of unity with diversity. As a practical plan for an hotel, the building is appalling. But as an exercise in scale and the skilful use of brick and stone it is unsurpassed in railway architecture. All other Midland stations in London are an anti-climax, as though the company had ruined itself on St Pancras and had to be content with mere wooden sheds and brick booking hall for the rest of the system. Fenchurch Street, which it took over from the London, Tilbury and Southend Railway, is a humbler affair more in the manner of (and but a few years later than) the Great Northern Railway terminus of King's Cross.

This building, which Ferguson describes as the more successful and pleasing "plainer sister" of St Pancras, is entirely the work of the engineer Joseph Cubitt. It was built in 1851 and the materials are white brick, glass and iron. The purpose at once is plain. One great semi-circular archway is for departure, the other beside it is for arrival. Between them on the main front is appropriately placed a clock tower. A colonnade of brick arches runs along the base of this front, between vast brick buttresses, and acts as a shelter for those awaiting their carriages. The booking office is on the departure side of the building and opposite this is a crescent-shaped hotel in a simple white-brick and stone, classic style. Office buildings balance this on the arrival side of the station. The coherence of the design is now much hampered by an underground station and by shops which hide its truthful simplicity from the Euston Road. Ruskin said in the *Seven Lamps of Architecture*, "Better bury gold in the embankments than put it in ornaments on the stations. . . . Railroad architecture has, or would have, a dignity of its own, if it were only left to its work. You would not put rings on the fingers of a smith at his anvil." He must surely have approved King's Cross, though he makes no specific mention of it. . . .

King's Cross started no new style, except at different stations on its own line beyond London. The nearest approach to it, other than Fenchurch Street, is Liverpool Street which was built in the 'seventies. It is civil engineer's Gothic, rather than architect's Gothic, and none the worse for that. The Gothic-style iron pillars support many-vistaed arcading, the flattened arch of the roof is crenelated on its own hanging edge and many mouldings and capitals in ironwork are to be found by the careful observer. Indeed, on a foggy evening, when those pear-shaped arc lamps used to hang down low from the roof, casting a purplish-white light, Liverpool Street had quite a resemblance to an ancient abbey.

The last large station to be built in London was Marylebone (1899) for the Great Central Railway. Its buildings are of hard pink midland bricks with yellow terra-cotta dressings and all in Flemish Renaissance style. They look like a public library from Nottingham which has unexpectedly found itself in London. . . . The weakness of the Great Central for gorgeous decorations in its carriages did not extend to stations; but its luxury is commemorated in Colonel Edis's gorgeous Great Central Hotel on the Marylebone Road. This entirely dwarfs the quiet terminus behind it.

There is no doubt that Marylebone set a new tone to London railway architecture. Henceforward something more tasteful than the flimsy wooden constructions was considered suitable for suburban stations. The L. & N.W.R. employed the noted domestic architect Gerald Horsley in 1901 to design stations at Harrow and Pinner in a style half-way between that of a bank and a medium-sized country house. Harrow, with its tower, was remarkably successful. Termini were thought to be ornate in the wrong sort of way, too like the Louvre and not enough like Michael Angelo. So there were the great rebuildings in an Edwardian monumental Renaissance manner starting with the L.B. & S.C. in 1908 at Victoria. The most ponderous effort of all was Waterloo with its twenty-three platforms and vast, useless entrance arch, approached by flights of steps unlike Euston, symbolical of nothing. Baker Street by Charles W. Clarke was a quieter rebuilding for the Metropolitan Railway in the neo-Georgian style (1914). Its refreshment rooms are still untouched. The most charming of all the Edwardian and neo-Georgian Renaissance stations is the entrance to Charing Cross Underground by H. W. Ford (1913). Marble columns in restaurants, stained glass, thick and crinkly, and adorned with wreaths, Turkey carpets, bronze or beaten copper electroliers, mahogany screens with panels of bevelled glass, plaster-work in the baroque manner, external sculpture in the manner of Sir Hamo Thorneycroft as at Waterloo – all these are characteristic of the last age of Railway Architecture. Redecorations in this manner went on in nearly every station. The hotel at Liverpool Street sustained such refittings and even at the St Pancras Hotel a dining room was redecorated in a "Georgian" style.

Such is the stylistic development of the London railways until the dismal grouping and the even more dismal eclipse of all individuality which has now occurred. But just as in a church architecture is not so important as the worship which goes on there, so in railways the associations of a station and of a line are part of its beauty. The personality of most stations in London survives, even through British Railways, and will continue to do so until everyone in England is exactly the same as everyone else.

Waterloo is the "services" and race-goers' station – for "Pompey", "Soton", Aldershot, Epsom, Ascot. It has a rather high-class suburban connection. Civil Servants who have reached C.M.G. and knighthood stage find it near Whitehall and convenient for Esher and in pine-clad Southern Electric suburbs their wives play cards with wives of rich city gentlemen. The humbler Civil Servant uses the Metropolitan and moves outwards beyond to Rickmansworth and Northwood as his salary increases. . . .

The flashiest of all suburban travellers are those who travel daily from Victoria by first-class Pullman trains to Brighton. Indeed, Brighton so dominates Victoria Station that though continental trains depart from its South Eastern Section, though many of the inner London suburbs are served by puzzling loop lines which start here and end at London Bridge, Victoria is the station of what moneyed leisure is left in London. Though it is meant to be associated with the South Coast and summer holidays, the sea is not what one associates with those who use it regularly. They do not look as though they took a winter dip in the English Channel. Warm flats, television, cocktail cabinets and bridge seem to be more in their line.

What a contrast is Liverpool Street! Here those extraordinary, cramped and uncomfortable Great Eastern carriages are drawn out above the East End housetops to wide acres of Essex suburb, two-storey houses, flat recreation grounds, strange chapels of strange sects, the well-trodden commons on the fringes of Epping Forest. Here workmen's trains run early in the morning. Here the old London sulphur smell pervades and even red bricks receive a black coating. Dense streets of Tottenham, Wanstead, Leytonstone, Barking, Edmonton, you are the real London and you form a barrier between the town and the unspoiled country of East Anglia! So many trains carry your patient passengers in and out of the black cathedral of Liverpool Street that expresses to Harwich, Yarmouth and Norwich seem slow at starting and ending for fear, no doubt, of knocking into one of these hundreds of suburban trains. Fenchurch Street has the same quality as Liverpool Street and so has London Bridge. . . .

I do not know what to say of Cannon Street. Of all the stations of London it is my favourite, so echoing, so lofty and so sad. Whoever used it and who uses it now? Holborn Viaduct was the great station for hop-pickers on their journey to Kent. But Cannon Street is too stately for that sort of thing. It is much less important than London Bridge at which most of its trains stop. Perhaps the people of Bromley, that lonely high-class suburb in Kent, love Cannon Street as I do.

There is one station, however, which hardly anyone uses at all – Broad Street, which is given over to ghosts of frock-coated citizens who once crowded the old North London trains from the steam suburbs of Highbury, Canonbury and Camden Town. Often do those sumptuous L.M.S. electric trains swing across the North London suburbs on that smooth, useless, beautiful journey to Richmond. At no time of day have I known it impossible to find a seat in their spacious carriages. And the frock-coated ones are dead and gone like the rolling stock which carried them, their houses have been turned into flats, their gardens built over by factories. The North London was the last line to use wooden-seated third-class carriages as it did on its Poplar branch (now closed), the last line in London to run no trains during church time on a Sunday morning, and within living memory the General Manager of the line refused to allow Smith's bookstall on Broad Street to sell any vulgar-looking papers. Still the trains run,

through haunted gas-lit stations, on the most revealing railway
journey London can provide.

The main line platforms of King's Cross are all expresses and
Civil Servants bagging the first-class sleepers to Scotland, their
fares paid for them out of our taxes. I do not like it, despite its
noble architecture. It is a station, like Euston, that those few of
us who are not Civil Servants will associate with injustice. But
these dim suburban platforms at King's Cross to which trains
come puffing up from the inner circle, are still Victorian London.
Here runs much uncomfortable rolling stock to Barnet and
Hatfield, climbing slowly to Finsbury Park. All the money is spent
on streamlining those L.N.E.R. expresses in the main station.

St Pancras is a station apart, a Royal Station. . . . There is a
suburban service, but it is of no importance. I have the impression
that St Pancras is still the aristocratic route to Scotland. Gun-cases
and fishing-rods go north with tweed-clad lairds, salmon and game
returning in the guard's van without them. I have little doubt that
British Railways will do away with St Pancras altogether. It is too
beautiful and too romantic to survive. It is not of this age. Euston
has stolen its trains but not its atmosphere. Except for that concealed platform where the Irish mail leaves of an evening, there is
no personality left about the trains from Euston. To the Irish,
Euston is the chief of English stations. Even lesser stations on the
line are written on their minds for I know of an Irish Peer who
woke up during a Wagner Opera at Covent Garden and exclaimed:
"Just like Willesden Junction!"

Except for Broad Street, Marylebone is the quietest station.
Only two expresses leave it in a day, the "South Yorkshireman"
and the "Master Cutler." There is hardly room for more and the
suburban service to Buckinghamshire seems like an after-thought.
I have never met anyone who has used one of the Marylebone
expresses, but lately I had the pleasure of coming into Marylebone
on a semi-express which stopped at Brackley. We rushed through
late Victorian cuttings and under bridges of glazed brick, nearly
merging with the Metropolitan. When I reached London I found
I was one of fifteen passengers.

Paddington has the strongest personality of all the larger London
stations. Its passengers are nearly all country people. There is the
one exception, a large contingent of South Welsh who seem always

to be travelling in trains. There is a lessening section of old-fashioned people, too poor now to travel first, who come up on the cheap day fares from Wiltshire and Gloucestershire to visit the Army and Navy Stores. Relations from further west stay a night or two at the Paddington Hotel. There are some Oxford dons and at holiday times more schoolboys than on any other line. Add to them a final section of commuters who have transformed Newbury and Maidenhead, Reading and Henley into suburbs of London.

I am aware that this attempt at the atmosphere of London stations is sketchy. Sketchy and no doubt unfair, for there must be many to whom King's Cross and Euston are charming places and others who detest Cannon Street, St Pancras and Liverpool Street as I do not. To them I apologize, but if I have caused them to think of these stations as places with the strong personalities that only those who use them can know, I will have achieved my object. To me they are people, and people have sides to their characters that they reveal to some and not to others.

from FIRST AND LAST LOVES *1952*

Temple Meads Station

JACK SIMMONS

Though almost all great stations afford terminal facilities for some trains, few of those in the provinces are termini and nothing else. Such termini are to be found: Glasgow (Central and St Enoch), Inverness; Swansea, Norwich, and Hull; Liverpool (Lime Street and Exchange), Manchester (London Road and Central). But the characteristic large provincial station is different. Either it is a junction for through trains, like York, Carlisle, or Crewe; or it is a station that serves primarily as a terminus but also affords through facilities, like Edinburgh (Waverley) or Aberdeen. To the student of railway history the most interesting are those that have been built up from separate units on adjacent sites, owned by different companies: Bristol (Temple Meads) for example.

Brunel had no hesitation in designing the first station in Bristol as a terminus, for it was the end of the broad-gauge Great Western Railway. It was by no means complete when the Bristol–Bath section of the line was opened in 1840; the last rail was laid only half an hour before the first train left that morning. The building was finished within the next few months, and most of it is still in use. The offices comprise a stone building in the Perpendicular Gothic style. The train shed contains two platforms (nos. 13 and 15 today) with siding accommodation between them, covered with a wooden hammerbeam roof of the medieval kind: 72 ft. in span, and so wider than that in Westminster Hall. This splendid shed is [now] the grandest monument surviving from the early years of the Railway Age.

It was not until 30 June 1841 that through trains began to run between Bristol and London; and by that time another railway had been opened, the first section of the Bristol & Exeter line as far as Bridgwater. This company, however, had no station of its own at Bristol. Its line ran in at right angles to the Great Western's, and a curve had therefore to be constructed to enable Bristol & Exeter trains to be manoeuvred into the Great Western station. The Bristol & Exeter company built its own station in 1845, though its offices, in the Jacobean style (still to be seen on the right of the modern station approach road), were not completed until 1854. For through trains from the west to London an "express platform" was built on the curve, but it was not invariably used for such trains: the down Flying Dutchman of 1862 ran to the end of the curve and then backed into the Bristol & Exeter station.

Meanwhile a third railway had arrived, to share the Great Western station at Temple Meads: the Bristol & Gloucester, opened in 1844 and swallowed up by the Midland company in the following year. The Midland was determined to carry its narrow gauge into Bristol, and after much legal argument with the Great Western it succeeded in doing so in 1854.

Here, then, was a strange tangle: three railways operating in two stations, adjacent but at right angles, with separate booking-offices (there was even one on the express platform) and with track of two different gauges – all on a site a good mile away from the centre of the city, to be reached only by a series of inconvenient lanes. A scheme for cutting a new "Victoria Road" through them was authorized in 1847 and then deferred indefinitely through the ratepayers' opposition. Another plan, put forward in 1861 and backed by the Great Western company, for extending the railway system to a new central station in Queen Square was rejected by a narrow majority of the City Council. This failing, the three companies fell back on the idea of a new joint station at Temple Meads. It was fulfilled with unbelievable slowness. Four years passed before Parliamentary sanction for the scheme was secured, ten before work was begun, 16 before it was finished and opened in its entirety on 1 January 1878. The new station was entered by a rising approach road and booking office in the acute angle between the original station and the curve, on which the new platforms were placed. Architecturally, the work continued Gothic in character, the embellishment being entrusted to Sir Matthew Digby Wyatt, who had acted in a similar capacity with Brunel at Paddington in 1851–1854. The station did duty without substantial change until it was much extended, on the side away from the original buildings, in the early 1930s.

At Temple Meads it is thus possible to study railway architecture of four different dates and to see very plainly on the ground how a modern layout may be determined by past history.

from THE RAILWAYS OF BRITAIN *1961*

York Station

JOHN PENDLETON

The travellers' terminus at York in the coaching days was the "Black Swan" in Coney Street; and the mud-splashed vehicle, four days out from town, caused considerable sensation as it rolled up to the inn door and deposited its passengers, their joints stiff and their stomachs empty with their last stage of riding, for which luxury they paid twopence halfpenny per mile. The new and the old modes of locomotion are nowhere so accentuated as at York. The city is grey with antiquity. You could imagine, sauntering through Micklegate Bar, with its crests and curious figures, that the hands of the clock had been put back two hundred years at least, that the fever of the Revolution of 1688 had just died away, and that "Danby, after dashing at the head of a hundred horsemen into York and giving the signal for a rising in the north", had ridden proudly home again, conscious that he had done something to quicken the king's flight.

Outside the weather-beaten walls, in which "the moss is weaving its tapestry", there is today a dash of another sort – the wield of a force far more powerful than fearless Danby's – the dash of the locomotive. The great station, with its bold sweep of main line and ample sidings, accommodates more than two hundred trains daily from the "Flying Scotsman" to the humblest stopper that crawls out Seamer way "to watch the corn grow". There is no station more interesting than that of York. With its handsome hotel, it is a gentleman among stations. It seems almost to take its proportions from the grand old minster close by. It is lofty and spacious; handsome so far as a railway station can be, and attractive from its brightness, its light lines, and the harmoniousness of its colouring. A modern novelist has made a picture of life at York Station the appropriate opening to his interesting story; and certainly there is no platform that affords more scope for the student of character. There is a flavour of London about the group of business men who have come down by the East Coast express, and are taking their five-course dinner in the refreshment-room; but there is little of the intense hurry, or of the grind of town, in evidence here. There is a crowd at the refreshment-counter, another by the bookstall, and a shoal of people on the long, curving platform. But they are altogether different in stamp from the surging crowd that rushes to catch the morning train into the City.

The stately dignity of York is alien to hurry; if it hurries at all, its quickened step and bustle are associated rather with pleasure than with trade. In summer and autumn it is the halting-place of a multitude, full of the anticipation of enjoyment, on their way to the seaside – to Scarborough with its spa and music, to Filey with its spray-flecked brig and sea-bird colony of Speeton, and to Bridlington with its fine old harbour and new promenade and boating paradise. Later it is thronged with hunting-men, and there is the rattle of horse-boxes in the sidings. At Convocation the platform is crowded with bishops and clergy; and it was at one time a fine sight to see the great, manly form of Archbishop Thomson, moving giant-like among the crowd.

from OUR RAILWAYS *1894*

The Royal Albert Bridge

L. T. C. ROLT

We may appreciate how much Brunel benefitted from his experience at Chepstow when he confronted the far greater task of bridging the Tamar. Here, the river to be crossed is 1,100 ft. wide and 70 ft. deep at high water, while the Admiralty required a headway of 100 ft. Forced to abandon his original idea of a timber structure, he prepared two tentative designs, one of four spans and another with a single immense span of 1,000 ft. Both were discarded, the first on account of the difficulty of sinking so many piers in deep water and the second on the score of expense. Finally he determined upon two main spans of 465 ft. each which would involve only one deep water pier.

The formation of this central pier was Brunel's greatest problem, for soundings showed that it would be necessary to go down through sand and mud to a rock foundation no less than 80 feet

below high water level. He decided to try the idea of using a cast
iron cylinder as a coffer-dam within which a masonry pier could be
built. In 1848 a trial cylinder 6 ft. in diameter and 85 ft. long was
made, towed out to the site between two hulks equipped with
special tackle, and lowered into the Tamar. When its bottom end
had sealed itself, the water was pumped out and no less than 175
borings were made through the mud into the rock below. From
the information so obtained Brunel was able to make a model of the
invisible rock showing its exact geological nature and its profile.
Finally, in January 1849, the mud was excavated down to the rock
and a small piece of masonry constructed to demonstrate the practicability of the scheme. At this juncture the Cornwall Railway Company suspended operations for three years owing to lack of capital.

When it was eventually decided to proceed, the need for economy had become paramount and Brunel reported as follows to
the Board of Trade: "This bridge had been always assumed to be
constructed for a double line of railway as well as the rest of the
line. In constructing the whole of the line at present with a single
line of rails, except at certain places, the prospect of doubling it
hereafter is not wholly abandoned, but with respect to the bridge
it is otherwise.

"It is now universally admitted that when a sufficient object is to
be attained, arrangements may easily be made by which a short
piece of single line can be worked without any appreciable inconvenience. . . . This will make a reduction of at least £100,000." So
the Saltash bridge was built for a single line only and remains so to
this day.

The great cylinder, 35 ft. in diameter at the base, which Brunel
designed for constructing the underwater portion of the central
pier was a most ingenious piece of apparatus which embodied experience which he had gained in his youth in the sealing of the
Thames tunnel breaches. It was actually a tube within a tube, the
former incorporating a diving bell within which the masons
worked. This was kept clear of water by pumps and ventilated by
means of a pipe which extended from the top of the dome of the
bell to the full height of the outer cylinder. But the influx of water
into this inner working compartment could never be great because
the annular space, 4 ft. wide, between the inner and outer cylinders
was sealed and pressurized, the same "pneumatic apparatus" being

used for this purpose as had been previously employed at Chepstow. By this device only the workmen clearing the mud in the annulus as the cylinder descended had to work under air pressure. The masons in the central chamber were spared this inconvenience; also the necessity of passing all the material for the pier through air lock doors was avoided. The lower edges of this great double cylinder were shaped to fit as closely as possible the profile of the submerged rock as it had been plotted three years before.

The cylinder was built on the river bank, floated off on the tide, guided to the site by pontoons and lowered into position in June 1854. By February 1855 it had reached the rock, some difficulty and delay having been caused by the presence of dense beds of oyster shells in the mud through which it had to sink. The rock was intensely hard greenstone trap which proved extremely difficult to work. Moreover, unsuspected springs burst through fissures which taxed the powers of the pumps to the utmost. However, all these difficulties were overcome and by the end of 1856 the great pier had been completed to the temporary cap which would receive the ends of the main trusses. The cylinder, which now encircled the pier, had done its work. Brunel had designed it in halves with an eye to its eventual removal, so it was now speedily unbolted and towed ashore.

While the pier was building, the first of the main trusses was taking shape on the Devon shore. Its principle was exactly the same as that of the main span of the Chepstow bridge, and apart from its vastly greater size it differed from it only in detail. Whereas the tubes of the Chepstow bridge are for practical purposes straight, being only very slightly arched for the sake of appearance, the Saltash tubes are arched to an extent equal to the fall of the suspension chains. Again, instead of the circular section used at Chepstow the Saltash tubes are oval, being 12 ft. 3 in. high and 16 ft. 9 in. broad. Brunel's purpose in depressing the tubes into ovals was that their breadth was thus made equal to that of the bridge platform below so that the suspended chains would fall vertically. This was an improvement on the Chepstow bridge where the chains are inclined. Other design details were modified to suit the different circumstances. At Chepstow owing to the restricted site and to the fact that the Wye navigation could not be obstructed for more than a single tide, Brunel had designed a truss whose different portions could be quickly raised separately and assembled aloft. The Tamar, on the other hand, allowed more room for manoeuvre, while as the bridge was in two spans the question of obstruction did not arise. He therefore designed the Saltash trusses to be prefabricated complete on the shore and floated bodily into position.

There was one feature of these trusses which must have saddened their designer. This was that the tension chains which were used on this, his last bridge, rightly belonged to his first. They had been bought by the Cornwall Railway from the Clifton Bridge Company when that most unfortunate concern again stopped work for lack of funds in 1853. Obviously they cannot have been of sufficient length to equip both the Saltash trusses. But their makers, the Copperhouse Foundry of Hayle, were near at hand to provide additional links and to adapt them to their new purpose. How long it must have seemed to Brunel since, as a young man filled with enthusiasm by his first important commission, he had travelled down to Hayle to see these very links tested by an hydraulic press.

The weight of each truss complete was over 1,000 tons so that their floating was no mean undertaking. Brunel had obtained valuable experience not only at Chepstow but also at the Menai where he had assisted Robert Stephenson to float the tubes of his great Britannia bridge. But this did not fill him with any false confidence; on the contrary he planned the whole operation with meticulous care down to the smallest detail. Nothing was to be left to chance or to the hurried improvization of the moment. In his notebooks we find the pencilled notes which he jotted down as he brooded over the problem, thus : . . .

Floating
Signals. Numbers to distinguish tow lines. The order is given and flags for the order seem to be the best. Numbers about 30 in. high on placard, standards or poles and flags of about the same size with a stiffening rod . . .
Signals by flag:
Heave in – red.
Hold on – white.
Pay out – blue.
Waved gently means gently.
Waved violently means quickly.

The pontoons were built at Plymouth and launched sideways into the river. They were virtually floating tanks designed so that water could be rapidly let into or pumped out of them in order to vary their draught. The truss had been built parallel to the river bank and two docks just wide enough to admit the pontoons were cut beneath each end. The plan was that when the pontoons had floated the truss they would be guided into position by cables, each bearing a number for signalling purposes, attached to crabs on the shore and on ships which would be anchored in the Tamar. Every move was carefully rehearsed and printed instructions issued to all those taking part.

The day fixed for the floating, September 1st 1857, was brilliantly fine and the whole neighbourhood was en fête. Church bells pealed, flags hung from every house in Saltash, a general holiday was declared and from all the country round the people flocked to see the wonder performed until every field and vantage point on both banks of the Tamar was crowded to capacity. Out in the river the five naval vessels under the command of Captain Claxton lay ready at their moorings. Beyond their field of operations the water was packed with crowded, flag-bedecked craft. In the morning the expectant throng watched the pontoons being manoeuvred into position, two in each dock and the cables attached. As the tide rose the water was pumped out of the pontoons and at a quarter past one there sounded a murmur like the sudden sighing of a wind as the great truss lifted slightly and the thousands of awestruck spectators whispered "she floats".

At this moment, like the conductor of an orchestra, Brunel moved to his place upon a platform mounted high in the centre of the truss. Directly above him were his signallers, standing ready with their numbers and flags. He had insisted that the whole operation must be carried out in complete silence and his wishes had been widely publicized. Consequently, no sooner had he taken up his position than there fell a dramatic stillness like that which follows the tap of a conductor's baton, and every eye in the vast crowd was strained towards the distant figure of the engineer. Numbers whose purport was unintelligible to the crowd were displayed; flags flickered and then the huge truss swung slowly and majestically out into the Tamar. "Not a voice was heard", wrote an eye-witness. " . . . As by some mysterious agency, the tube and rail, borne on the pontoons, travelled to their resting place, and with such quietude as marked the building of Solomon's temple. With the impressive silence which is the highest evidence of power, it *slid*, as it were, into its position without an accident, without any extraordinary mechanical effort, without a 'misfit', to the eighth of an inch."

Just as the time of high water came at three o'clock, the ends of the tube were secured in their positions on the piers from which they would be raised by hydraulic presses as the masonry was built up beneath them. As soon as the truss was safely in place the tension was broken. A band of the Royal Marines struck up "See the conquering hero comes" and Brunel stepped down from the platform to the accompaniment of a storm of cheering. It was a moment of triumph which must have sweetened the bitter memory of the atmospheric disaster. But not one of the thousands of west-countrymen who cheered themselves hoarse that day realized that their tribute was also a valediction, that their hail was also a farewell.

It was Brunel's chief assistant, Brereton, who superintended the floating of the second Saltash span in July 1858 and who saw the work through to its successful completion in the following spring. When Prince Albert, as Lord Warden of the Stanneries, travelled down from Paddington to open the Royal Albert Bridge in May 1859 amid fresh scenes of wild enthusiasm, the last link in the broad gauge route to the west was completed. Wrote the ballad monger:

From Saltash to St Germans, Liskeard and St Austell,
The County of Cornwall was all in a bustle,
Prince Albert is coming the people did say
To open the Bridge and the Cornish Railway.
From Redruth, and Cambourne, St Just in the west
The people did flock all dressed in their best.
From all parts of England you'll now have a chance
To travel by steam right down to Penzance.

But the engineer was not there. No flags flew, no bands played, no crowds cheered when he took his first and last look at the completed bridge. He lay on a specially prepared platform truck, while one of Gooch's locomotives drew him very slowly beneath the pier arches and over the great girders. For his railway career was ended. Broken by the last and the most ambitious of all his schemes – his great ship – Brunel was dying.

from ISAMBARD KINGDOM BRUNEL *1957*

The Britannia Bridge

H. SHIRLEY SMITH

A long list of failures made Stephenson and Fairbairn realize that the main task before them was to devise a structure with a stiff enough deck; the arrangement and form of the cables were of secondary importance. The bridges were required to carry the Chester and Holyhead railway over the Conway river and the Menai Straits; the latter bridge derived its name from the Britannia Rock in the middle of the crossing. Stephenson's first proposal was to build two cast-iron arches of 350-foot span, because he realized that an arch was much more rigid and therefore better suited to heavy railway traffic than the suspension type. The arches were ruled out, however, as they could not provide the clear passage 100 feet high throughout the crossing demanded by the Admiralty. Stephenson then evolved the idea of a wrought-iron tube through which the trains would run and which would be supported from cables above it. The recent production of wrought-iron plates and sections for shipbuilding contributed to this design. Stephenson discussed the matter with his father . . . who thought the idea sound. Small-scale models of tubes of circular, elliptical, and rectangular section were made and tested to destruction at Fairbairn's works; and Eaton Hodgkinson, the mathematician, was called in to assist in interpreting and applying the results to the full-size design.

Stephenson had from the start been somewhat sceptical about the need for chains or cables at all, except for use temporarily to assist in erection, if the tubes were assembled *in situ*. Fairbairn, too, considered them unnecessary, but Hodgkinson wanted to retain them. An alternative method of erection, however, was to float the tubes into position on pontoons and then lift them up bodily into place. When Fairbairn also backed this method it was agreed to adopt it and to dispense finally with any chains or cables. Meanwhile, however, the masonry piers had been built up to the height required for the towers of a suspension bridge. This was now no longer necessary, but the towers were retained; the fine aesthetic appearance of the bridge is therefore to some extent accidental. As to the shape of the tubes, there was serious difference of opinion between Hodgkinson and Fairbairn; probably in order to overcome difficulties in manufacture of circular sections, Stephenson finally decided to have them made rectangular. Before erection, the first tube for the Conway bridge was supported at the ends only and tested by running 300 tons of ballast wagons inside it. This load caused a deflection of only 3 inches and confirmed the accuracy of the design and calculations.

The bridge was opened to traffic in 1850 after Stephenson had himself driven the last one of the 2,000,000 rivets, which is kept white-painted to this day. It has never given any cause for anxiety or required more than the normal maintenance, in spite of the ever-increasing weight of traffic. The Britannia bridge has four continuous spans, two of 230 and two of 460 feet, whereas the longest wrought-iron girder previously built had been but 31 feet 6 inches. Such was the magnitude of the advance that Stephenson and Fairbairn made. In effect they designed the first plate girder bridge, the forerunner of the tens of thousands of bridges of this most useful type which can be seen on railways all over the world today.

The building of bridges of unprecedented span is always a heavy strain on the engineers responsible. At the opening of the Menai [road] suspension bridge, Telford wanted to cut ceremony to a minimum. To him it was a matter of thanksgiving that the sleepless nights and long days of worry and anxiety were over; his friends who came to congratulate him found him on his knees. Stephenson too, records that "at night he would lie tossing about seeking sleep in vain. The tubes filled his head. He went to bed and got up with them." It is only by virtue of the single-minded application to their work of men like these that such masterpieces can be achieved.

from THE WORLD'S GREAT BRIDGES *1953*

1*

The Woodhead Tunnel

O. S. NOCK

With the Sheffield and Manchester line commencement of the
work was at first delayed by lack of funds. Vignoles, characteristically, had already taken a number of shares himself; he induced
some of his relatives to do the same, and it might well have seemed
strange for the engineer to canvass many business houses in the
City of London with a view to their becoming shareholders. Yet
so Vignoles did, and when some of the Manchester subscribers
began to grow apprehensive of success and gave up their holdings
Vignoles went to the stage of buying up large quantities of the
depreciated shares. It seemed as though his whole existence was
wrapt up in this railway. Unlike other speculators of the Mania
period his motives appear to have been solely the furtherance of
the company's well-being. In 1838 he was duly selected as
engineer-in-chief for the construction of the line, and with his
usual zeal he threw his whole strength into the job. A large staff
and labour force was engaged, and operations were commenced
at the Manchester end. In profile the line can be likened to a huge
gable, having its apex at the point where the railway was carried
in a tunnel under the Pennines. And what a tunnel! At that time
only two major tunnels had been driven in the construction of
railways in England; of these the notorious Kilsby was 2,425
yards long, while Box, on the Great Western was 3,230 yards.
Yet out in the wilderness of Woodhead Moor the Sheffield Railway was to pass through a tunnel 5,300 yards long, blasted from
the millstone grit of the Pennines.

Vignoles seems to have realized that here was his great opportunity, by carrying through this tremendous work to put himself
alongside the greatest engineers of the day. To his zeal was added
immense confidence in himself, which, however, a small minority
of the directors did not share. . . . Vignoles had something of the
Brunellian touch about him, in the way everything he did had to
be done in handsome style – one might almost say regardless of
cost. He took a beautiful country house at Dinting Vale, and
brought his younger children there from London; a resident tutor

was engaged, and with all at first going well on the railway it seemed at last that his star was really in the ascendant. Work had begun on the Woodhead Tunnel, though here his estimates seem to have omitted to include any accommodation for the workmen. Even today there are many stretches where there is no human habitation in sight, and when Vignoles got to work in 1838 the entire countryside was depopulated. Then, when the problem presented itself, he urged the directors to provide tents for the workmen. Difficulties were arising in other ways. Some of his opponents on the board took quite uncalled-for liberties when visiting the tunnel works, giving instructions to individual employees, and even countermanding the orders Vignoles had previously issued. There seems little doubt that such tactics were used deliberately, knowing that with his fiery temperament he would rise to the bait. He did, and there were many cases of strained loyalties. Nevertheless, Vignoles's enthusiasm still carried him along, and when his eldest son came of age, in August 1839, the event was signalized by great festivities at his home at Dinting Vale. The entertainment was on the most lavish scale; all the gentry for miles around were invited, and with them, of course, the directors of the company and the principal officers. A month later the shadows began to close in upon Vignoles.

It was about this time that he began to feel the financial strain of the 1,402 shares he held in the company, with a liability upon them of £140,000. Accordingly, after taking advice of two of his firmest friends among the Sheffield section of the board, he went with them to see Lord Wharncliffe, the Chairman, and to explain the circumstances. He asked to be relieved of at least some of the liability. The matter was referred to a meeting of shareholders in October 1839, at which meeting Lord Wharncliffe said in respect of Vignoles's holdings: "This gentleman, in August 1837, being very anxious that the threatened break-up of the company should be avoided, thought fit to buy up this vast number of shares and distribute them to his various friends in small apportionments, under a guarantee that they should not be called upon to pay up. . . ."

A committee of directors appointed to deal with the matter met Vignoles next day, and after a long conference a compromise was agreed upon, that the engineer should forfeit all the shares he had bought, and thus lose the money he had paid for them in the first place. But beyond that, Lord Wharncliffe promised, no further claim would be made upon him or his friends who held shares. This was a blow sufficiently heavy, involving a loss of some £10,000, but, of course, it also compelled his resignation from the post of engineer. But, he thought, it put his friends in the clear. The worst, however, was to follow. The Board refused to confirm the arrangements between Lord Wharncliffe and Vignoles; the Manchester section were determined to enforce their rights to the uttermost, and appealed to law. The case went against Vignoles, with the result that not only was he faced with a personal loss of £80,000, but, as he wrote in his diary for January 15th, 1841:

> a great number of my friends will be utterly ruined, and the rest either cruelly embarrassed or obliged to go through the *Gazette*! Considering in what way I could assist some of them to meet the cruel pressure that will immediately be put on them. Half distracted at the frightful prospect before us all!
>
> Good God! that men whom I had served so faithfully, and for whose railway I had done so much, should act like this!

That Vignoles never flinched under the terrible results of his zeal to help the Manchester and Sheffield line, and continued his professional work with undiminished vigour and skill is a tribute to a great personality. In appraising the present developments on that line, the completion of the third Woodhead Tunnel, and the inauguration of electric traction, one cannot but think back wistfully to the crushing misfortune suffered by the first engineer-in-chief.

Lord Wharncliffe, and most of the Sheffield Section of the directors had resigned when their agreement with Vignoles was not ratified; and it was no more than natural that the reconstituted Board should invite Joseph Locke to become engineer-in-chief. He found that his predecessor had let the work in small contracts to small men. Locke's biographer tends to exaggerate the confused situation that had developed in the early stages of the boring of Woodhead Tunnel; but the new engineer managed to secure the services of Nicholas Wood as contractor-in-chief for the tunnel, and against Vignoles estimate of £98,000 Locke told the directors it would cost at least double! Due to a lack of funds the tunnel was in any case to be made for a single line of rails only. . . . [So] in

1839 Joseph Locke quickly brought his clear brain and superb organizing skill to the great task of boring the first Woodhead Tunnel. His biographer tells us that the job of getting supplies forward was as bad as supporting the Crimean army before Balaklava! The contractors built shops of their own; sometimes the men were paid in food, and they camped in huts, quickly run up with loose stones and mud, and thatched with heather. They slept upon improvised truckle beds, twenty together. It was a tremendous task. The tunnel was driven from two portals and five intermediate shafts, though no technical description of the work has survived. Driving in from the open hillside at the Woodhead portal the rocks are hard gritstone and sandstone at first, but then comes a thick slanting layer of that most treacherous of rock formations – shale. Although there is no direct evidence it would seem certain that serious trouble with rock falls occurred; in any case during the six years it was under construction the first Woodhead Tunnel claimed the high casualty list of 28 killed, 200 seriously injured or disabled, and 450 lesser accidents.

Eventually it took six years to complete, and on December 20th, 1845, it was ready for the Government Inspection, by General Pasley. The execution of the work was first class, though against the naked rock-faces the castellated portals looked rather grim. At the western end the effect was heightened by some grotesque gargoyles over the entrance! General Pasley said that it was one of the finest pieces of engineering he had ever seen, and it was opened for traffic just before Christmas 1845. The short-sightedness of the original decision to have a single tracked bore was apparent before the line had been open two years! And while the engineering work to build a double line tunnel in the first place would not have been greatly more difficult in 1847 the railway embarked upon the costly job of boring a duplicate tunnel alongside the older one, and this took a further five years to complete. The original cost borne by the railway was thus very much greater than would have been the case if a double-line tunnel had been driven in the first place. Moreover, the two single line bores were to bring troubles of their own later. Towards the end of the Second World War deterioration became evident. Maintenance was never easy, due to the volume of traffic and the restricted space available, and eventually the situation grew so serious, that in 1946 the drastic step was taken of giving the engineer absolute possession of each tunnel alternately over a period of nine months, so that repair work could proceed night and day. The consequent delays were so serious, however, and the volume of repair work needed so great, that eventually the London and North Eastern Railway engineers had to give up the task and recommend the building of an entirely new tunnel.

In view of the early history of the original tunnels, it is of particular interest to compare the relative estimates made for the new work in 1947. Three alternatives were considered:

(a) to build one new single line tunnel and repair one of the old ones;

(b) to build two new single tunnels;

(c) to build a new double-line tunnel and abandon the old ones completely.

This last course proved the cheapest of all, according to the 1947 estimates, while the cost of building two new single-line tunnels was estimated at 43 per cent more than that of building one double-line bore. Against Locke's original estimate of 1839, £200,000 for one single-line tunnel, and presumably £400,000 for the twin bores eventually built, the actual cost of the new double-line tunnel completed in 1954 came out to £4,250,000. By this staggering amount has the cost of railway construction increased in a hundred years!

from THE RAILWAY ENGINEERS *1955*

The Severn Tunnel

C. HAMILTON ELLIS

Two abortive Bills had been introduced to Parliament before the Severn Tunnel Railway Act was passed in 1872, and the work was placed in the hands of John Hawkins, who was appointed consulting engineer, with Charles Richardson, as engineer-in-charge. The lower Severn is not as other rivers, and to the tunnel builders it presented problems in excess of the usual ones attending underwater tunnelling. At the site it was two miles wide, with abnormal tidal differences (e.g. 50 feet at the mouth of the Wye below Chepstow). The bottom was irregular. For a mile and a half out from the Gloucestershire shore it was level and composed of hard marl (the English Stones) which became uncovered at half-ebb. On the Monmouth side was a corresponding shelf (Lady Bench) extending half a mile out to the reef called the Gruggy. Between the two, came the Shoots, 400 yards wide with a maximum depth of 95 feet at spring tide high, and a current of 10 knots at the ebb. It was decided that the tunnel should fall on a gradient of 1 in 100 from each side, to pass under the Shoots at a depth of 30 feet below rock bottom. This would give a length, portal to portal, of 7,942 yards, rather more than 4½ miles. Total length of the new line would be seven miles from Pilning, on the Bristol and South Wales Union line, to Rogiet on the South Wales line. To explore the strata, a 200 foot shaft, 15 feet wide, was sunk at Sudbrook on the Monmouth side. By August, 1877, this was done and 1,600 yards of drainage heading had been excavated on an upgrade through the Pennant sandstone under the river. This was known as the Old Shaft. Tenders were invited for the construction of the tunnel, but the three received were all rejected, and in the meantime contracts were awarded for the sinking of shafts, to Rowland Brotherhood (Hill Shaft and Marsh Shaft on the Monmouth side) and Oliver Norris (Sea Wall Shaft, Gloucestershire). By the summer of 1879 the heading from Old Shaft was nearly two miles long and within 138 yards of a heading which Norris had built under the river-bed from Sea Wall Shaft. A second, higher heading was excavated from Old Shaft, and it was this that, on October 16, 1879, tapped a powerful spring of fresh water, so powerful indeed, that it was far beyond the capacity of the pumps. In 24 hours, with all the pumping machinery going, the Big Spring had conquered. Old Shaft was filled up to river level. On that day, October 17th, [Sir Daniel] Gooch was at the opening of the Midland Railway's Severn Bridge at Sharpness. He wrote: "There was a large gathering, and of course a feast. The day was cold and very uncomfortable. Yesterday at the Severn Tunnel we struck a strong feeder of water on the heading under the land on the Welsh side, which is more than our pumps can manage, and we are drowned out until we can get more power." What he did not record, or what, at any rate, Lady Gooch did not allow into the published excerpts from his journals, was that the accident put him in a rather embarrassing position. At the "feast", unaware of what was going on below ground and confident that in six weeks time the headings would have met, he cordially invited his fellow guests, and the Midland people, to visit the tunnel works, when they could walk under the river through the headings, adding a gentle warning that the walk might be "rather wet".

Fortunately, the men working in the heading had been able to escape, but the workings presented a most dreary scene. They were not cleared until early in December, 1880. Meanwhile, at Gooch's instance, Hawkshaw had been placed in command of the job of clearing and continuing the works. He stipulated that he should be allowed to engage a single contractor. This was agreed, and T. A. Walker, who had tendered for £948,959 in 1877, and had been turned down with the others, was accepted. He took over the desolate works on December 18, 1879, and wrestled with the water for the ensuing year. Hawkshaw prepared new plans, and rapidly. To avoid risks he deepened the level under the Shoots by 15 feet, increasing the western gradient to 1 in 90 to allow for this. But nothing practical could be done on the Monmouth side until the workings had been pumped out. A new pumping shaft was sunk at Sudbrook. The men at work at the time of the flooding had naturally got out in a great hurry. There was an iron water-gate which could have held the flood in the upper end of the heading, but they had left it open. The first thing necessary was to shut it. Diver Lambert, a highly skilled, taciturn man, strongly courageous, undertook to do so. He went down into the profound black deep of Sudbrook Old Shaft, using the common diving equipment of the period with a long air pipe, and then made his way, very slowly up the heading, amongst all the wreckage of abandoned labour. He penetrated the heading to within 30 yards of the iron door, trailing his air pipe, which was continually threatened over several hundred yards with stoppage or cutting against the abandoned equipment. Lambert had to return, and had moreover to gather up 270 yards of his air pipe as he walked. The nightmare expedition had been in vain.

Now at that time Fleuss was demonstrating his diving equipment, which depended on a reservoir of compressed air, and was therefore free of pipes and pumps, in the Westminster Aquarium. Hawkshaw called him in and he was sent down to the bottom of Sudbrook Old Shaft. After some investigations, Fleuss said flatly that he would not walk through that heading and shut the gate if he were offered £10,000. Be it considered that the walk, and the operation, would be in total darkness. So Lambert volunteered to make the walk with Fleuss's apparatus. Fleuss was at first very unwilling to allow this, but consented after long argument. Lambert practised with the equipment, then made the walk and shut the gate. In the west heading, a wall was built up against the Big Spring, and was completed early in January, 1881, while new and more powerful pumping machinery was installed. Building of the tunnel proper was begun at the Gloucestershire end. Late in April, water came rushing into the nascent tunnel. It was salt water, and clearly came from the estuary and not from some unsuspected spring. A hole was located in the depression called Salmon Pool. It was stopped from above. One of the men engaged on locating it did so by being sucked into it, but fortunately he was pulled out by the others. The hole was plugged with loose and bagged clay alternately, in large quantities.

On October 10, 1883, the Big Spring came again on the rampage and flooded what was built of the tunnel. Two days later there was on top of this a high tide of almost unprecedented enormity. While the spring delivered its unwelcome supply of fresh water at a rate of about 30,000 gallons a minute, the brackish water of the flood tide poured down the shafts. A boat was hurriedly lowered into the abyss to rescue 83 men from the rising water. One was drowned. Lambert's services were again engaged, the spring was blocked and the water pumped out.

On October 27, 1884, Gooch wrote: "I went this morning to the Severn Tunnel. Lord Bessborough met me there before lunch, and we inspected the surface work, and after lunch went below. It fortunately happened that the headings were just meeting, and by the time we had finished lunch the men had got a small hole through, making the tunnel open throughout. I was the first to creep through, and Lord Bessborough followed me. It was a very difficult piece of navigation, but by a little pulling in front and pushing behind we managed it, and the men gave us some hearty cheers."

In the same passage from his journal, Gooch gave the flow of

the Great Spring at that time as "about 7,000 gallons per minute."
A new side heading was driven to take the flow of the spring,
which was then walled off. The tunnel proper became relatively
dry. On September 5, 1885, Gooch took a party through the
tunnel by special train from Rogiet. Soon after this the spring, so
optimistically walled off, burst through again, blowing large pieces
out of the new brick tunnel lining. There was no alternative to
abandoning the idea of walling off the spring and installing
pumping machinery which could carry the entire flow and discharge it at surface into the Severn. Some was used by the engines.
Hawkshaw's permanent pumps could deal with the water at the
rate of 38,000,000 gallons daily, but they were augmented to have
a potential of 66,000,000 gallons in the 24 hours. The Tunnel had

been somewhat altered from the original plan. The cutting was lengthened at the west end to provide material for new sidings at Rogiet (afterwards called Severn Tunnel Junction). As we have seen already, the depth below the bottom of the Shoots was increased by 15 feet and the gradient towards the "Welsh" end was increased to 1 in 90. The final length, portal to portal, reduced in the manner described, came to 4 miles, 628 yards. The middle level under the river was 12 chains long. From beneath its eastern end a 5 foot drainage culvert was put in, leading to the main Sudbrook shaft, and above this, immediately below the tunnel itself, a 9 foot ventilation tunnel, connected with fans at Sudbrook. The tunnel lining, 27 inches thick, contained about 77,000,000 bricks and 37,000 tons of cement.

On January 9, 1886, a coal train was worked through the tunnel on its way from Cardiff to Southampton via Bristol and Salisbury. It was not, however, until September 1 that regular goods traffic began, following completion of the pumping engines and the installation of a big Guibal fan for ventilation. The six main pumping engines at Sudbrook were beam engines, each having 10 foot stroke and 5 feet 6 inches diameter cylinders. The ventilating equipment was overhauled in 1924, with the installation of a fan of 27 foot diameter, with a capacity of 800,000 cubic feet a minute. On November 17, 1886, the tunnel was inspected and passed by Colonel Rich for the Board of Trade, and on December 1st it was opened for all traffic. . . .

It cannot be said that the Severn Tunnel has been a joy for ever to its owner. To this day, the expense of keeping it dry and properly ventilated is immense, and apart from the interest of traversing the longest under-water tunnel in the world, its passage cannot be described as particularly pleasant. A giant Severn Bridge, or the long-proposed Severn Barrage, carrying road and railway tracks, would be far more agreeable and certainly less troublesome. Yet until one or other of these comes to be built, the tunnel will remain as a monument to the vision of Sir Daniel Gooch and the patience and skill of Sir John Hawkshaw; to the courage and devotion of those who built it. Diver Lambert's heroic walks through the flooded workings remain a classic event in the history of railway construction.

from BRITISH RAILWAY HISTORY 1877–1947 *1959*

PART V

A Network of Lines

East Coast to Scotland

O. S. NOCK

For me, after many years of travelling into Scotland, no route, either road or rail, can compare with that of the *Flying Scotsman*: the astonishing beauty of Berwick revealed suddenly as the train comes over the cliffs at Scremerston; the final majestic sweep of the Tweed; the three great bridges, each a masterpiece of its day – and as the train slows down and enters upon the loftiest of the three, Robert Stephenson's Royal Border Bridge, the passenger by the *Flying Scotsman*, surveying this fair scene and watching his motoring friends below crossing the Royal Tweed Bridge with their eyes more intent on the traffic lights at the north end than on the scenery, has, as J. J. Bell once aptly expressed it, "the advantage of the eagle over the sparrow."

The London and North Eastern Railway erected two attractive signposts at the actual point where the railway crosses the Border some 2½ miles north of Berwick. Though not quite such a "no man's land" as Solway Moss, it is a lonely spot high on the cliffs and beneath the slopes of Lamberton Moor. From this quietly impressive entry into Scotland the railway soon turns inland to cut across the hinterland of the St Abbs country, and then mounts to the summit, 385 feet above sea-level, near Grantshouse station, and in a fold of Penmanshiel Moor. From a short tunnel the most severe incline between London and Edinburgh brings the train swiftly down to the sea again at Cockburnspath, and a broad panorama opens out across the Firth of Forth. The most dramatic glimpse is reserved for the driver and fireman – that first sight of the Bass Rock, standing just off the shore well beyond Dunbar. There are several such thrilling first glimpses on the railways of Great Britain that can be seen only from the engine. There is one of Lincoln Cathedral seen when approaching from Sleaford and an equally beautiful one of Salisbury from the western approach; and each successive time I am privileged to travel in the engine cab I look out for the Bass Rock more eagerly than ever, for the great rock never looks the same twice running, and there is always some combination of brilliant colour or intense light and shade to add a rare charm to the wide seascape. So we ride on over historic ground: Dunbar, Prestonpans, to the point where Edinburgh can already be seen far ahead, lying smokily beneath the heights of Arthur's Seat and the Salisbury Crags.

from SCOTTISH RAILWAYS *1950*

Express to the West

CECIL J. ALLEN

Though for many years past, back into London & South Western days, an express had left Waterloo for the West of England at about 11 a.m., it was not until 1927 that the Southern Railway introduced the title of "Atlantic Coast Express" for this service – the Southern "ACE", as it has sometimes been called. Like its neighbour, the 10.30 a.m. "Cornish Riviera Limited" from Paddington, the "Atlantic Coast Express" in peacetime was one of the most multi-portioned trains in the country. Nine different sections were included in the formation.

Next to the engine was the Ilfracombe portion, consisting of two third-class brakes and a composite coach between. This was followed, in succession, by composite brakes for Torrington, Padstow, Bude and Plymouth. After these the restaurant cars – first-class and kitchen car with open third-class car – could be classed as a "portion", for they were detached at Exeter. Then followed composite brakes for Exmouth, Sidmouth, and for stations between Salisbury and Exeter, the last-mentioned detached at Salisbury. In the days of the keenest competition between the L.S.W.R. and the G.W.R. for the traffic to and from the West of England, the predecessor of the "Atlantic Coast Express" was regarded as being a Plymouth train, with a connection for Ilfracombe; but the opening of the G.W.R. Westbury route enabled the latter company to accelerate its Plymouth services to such a degree that the S.R. fell into the background as a route from London to Plymouth, and the Ilfracombe section of the train then assumed the major importance.

On its peacetime schedule, through nine months of the year the

"Atlantic Coast Express" was booked to leave Waterloo at 11 a.m., and to make its first stop at Salisbury at 12.26 p.m. – 83·8 miles in 86 minutes. Although the provision of water-troughs on this route has often been mooted, and years ago Dugald Drummond, then Locomotive Superintendent of the L.S.W.R., even went to the length of fitting some of his tenders with water-scoops, the troughs never materialized. For reasons of water alone, therefore, it has never been possible to run non-stop from Waterloo to Exeter, though the Salisbury stop is desirable for more reasons than locomotive requirements merely, as important connections are made here. Through locomotive running has been tried from Waterloo to Exeter, but a change of engine at Salisbury is preferred, and this is now the invariable practice.

West of Salisbury the locomotive running is some of the most exciting in Great Britain. Nowhere else in the country are such high speeds run relatively to the severity of the profile. The route is particularly well aligned and there is practically no limit to maximum speeds; in consequence the drivers make the utmost use of the falling gradients, in order that the impetus so gained may help them on the succeeding ascents. In the westbound direction, speeds of over 80 m.p.h. are frequently attained at Gillingham, Sherborne, Axminster, Honiton and at Broad Clyst (between Sidmouth Junction and Exeter). The stiffest task set the locomotives in this direction is the ascent of Seaton bank; beginning just to the west of Axminster, this rises for $1\frac{1}{2}$ miles at 1 in 100, then for $4\frac{1}{2}$ miles at 1 in 80, and finally for $\frac{3}{4}$ mile at 1 in 132 through Honiton tunnel to the summit at the latter's western portal, $153\frac{1}{2}$ miles from Waterloo.

At Salisbury, on the peacetime schedule of the "Atlantic Coast Express", the rear coach was detached and went forward with a stopping train that followed at 12.38 p.m. The main train left for the West at 12.31 p.m., and was booked to run the 75·8 miles to Sidmouth Junction in 83 minutes. Here the Sidmouth and Exmouth coaches came off the rear of the train; a tank engine of the 0–4–4 type collected them and worked them to Tipton St Johns, continuing from there to Sidmouth with the Sidmouth coach, due at 2.23 p.m., while another 0–4–4 tank worked the other coach through Budleigh Salterton to an arrival in Exmouth at 2.46 p.m. The express itself was booked to leave Sidmouth

Junction at 1.58 p.m., and to run the 12·2 miles into Exeter
Central in 14 minutes. Arriving at 2.12 p.m., the "Atlantic Coast
Express" had come down from Waterloo in 3 hours, 12 minutes.

Here a general break-up of the train occurred. The restaurant
cars were detached from the rear, and the remaining coaches were
divided into two parts. A Mogul backed on to the Ilfracombe and
Torrington sections, and left with these coaches at 2.18 p.m.,
reaching Barnstaple Junction 62 minutes later. Ten minutes before
this, a Great Western Railway "slow" from Taunton had put in an
appearance at Barnstaple with the through Ilfracombe coach off
the "Cornish Riviera Limited"; this the "Atlantic Coast Express"
added to its formation, while leaving the Torrington coach behind.
From Barnstaple Junction, the Ilfracombe train then continued
over some of the steepest main line gradients in Great Britain,
climbing for $3\frac{1}{4}$ miles at 1 in 40 to Mortehoe, and finally dropping
for $2\frac{1}{4}$ miles at 1 in 36 down into Ilfracombe. This popular coast
resort, 226·5 miles from Waterloo, was reached at 4.6 p.m., eight
minutes after the Torrington coach had arrived at its destination.

The three remaining portions of the "Atlantic Coast Express"
left Exeter in company at 2.25 p.m. for Okehampton, usually with
a three-coach corridor set added to the Waterloo–Plymouth coach.
At Okehampton the Padstow and Bude coaches were detached,
for the journey over the North Cornwall line, and it was not until
5.36 p.m. that the former ran into Padstow, 259·7 miles from
Waterloo, after completing the longest daily through journey on
Southern metals. The Bude coach, parting company with the
Padstow portion at Halwill, reached Bude at 4.54 p.m. At Meldon
Junction, where the Plymouth and Padstow lines separate to the
west of Okehampton, after passing over a high lattice steel
viaduct, the train attained the greatest altitude reached on the
Southern system, which is 950 ft. above sea level.

A striking feature of the working of the Plymouth portions of
Southern trains from London is the way in which they almost box
the compass in the course of their journeys. Through Exeter they
run for a short distance over G.W.R. metals between St David's
station and Cowley Bridge junction, where trains from Waterloo
are travelling due north; through North Road station at Plymouth,
which is joint G.W.R. and S.R. property, they are running east;
but before reaching Plymouth Friary they have turned due west

again. Moreover, twice in succession, both at Exeter St David's and Plymouth North Road, they meet the G.W.R. expresses from Paddington to Plymouth travelling in the opposite direction! In peacetime, the Plymouth coach of the down "Atlantic Coast Express" comes to rest in Friary terminus, 234 miles from Waterloo, at 4.19 p.m.

In the height of the summer season, two daily down services were needed to carry the traffic, at 10.35 a.m. to Ilfracombe, Torrington, Bude, and Padstow, and at 11 a.m. to Sidmouth, Exmouth, and Plymouth. On Saturdays the two branched out into no fewer than *eight* complete restaurant car trains between 10.24 a.m. and 12.5 noon – at 10.24 and 10.35 a.m. to Ilfracombe, 10.40 a.m. to Padstow, 10.54 a.m. to Bude, 11 a.m. to Plymouth, 11.45 a.m. to Sidmouth and Exmouth, 12 noon to Exeter, and 12.5 p.m. to Salisbury and all stations from Axminster onwards. Similar arrangements were in force in the opposite direction. . . .

from TITLED TRAINS OF GREAT BRITAIN *1946*

Cambrian Profile

L. T. C. ROLT

One of the earliest railway recollections of my childhood is of standing on the platform at Three Cocks Junction and watching a long Cambrian train drawn by two locomotives come rolling into the station bound for the Mid-Wales line. Although I lived nearby at Hay on the very border of Wales, this was my first sight of the Cambrian, for the station at Hay was served by the Midland line from Hereford and by the less frequent trains of the Great Western's Golden Valley branch. Now, seeing the unfamiliar green coaches and black locomotives bearing the insignia of the Cambrian – the red dragon of Wales and the English rose entwined – I felt that I had entered a foreign country.

The Cambrian was indeed a line of character, of a strong Welsh character, and I am glad that I am old enough to have seen it before its identity was lost in the Great Western. The Cambrian was itself a consolidation of a number of smaller undertakings of which the first to be opened, was the Newtown and Llanidloes Railway in 1859. Because of its splendid isolation from the rest of the railway system, the two engines bought for the opening of the line had to be hauled to Newtown by road, but the fact that one of them was named *Milford* reveals the aspirations of the promoters. They believed that their railway would become a section of the Manchester and Milford and dreamed rosy dreams of the rich industrial freight of South Lancashire rumbling through Newtown *en route* for the port of Milford Haven. But alas for their hopes, the M. & M. never reached Llanidloes, let alone Manchester or Milford, remaining a small local line west of the great central mountain massif of Wales. At this time the railway promoters stood upon the marches of Wales like the advance guard of an invading army probing an enemy's defences, and the Manchester and Milford was only one of the assaults which the mountains defeated as they defeated the invading armies of the past. From Shrewsbury and from Craven Arms the West Midland, Shrewsbury and Welsh Coast and the Bishops Castle Railways both set out confidently westwards only to waver and fall back like the ruled roads of the Roman before them. Behind these venturesome and often ill-fated reconnaissance units stood the main army, the great interests of the Great Western and the London and North Western, powerful rivals manoeuvring for advantage, courting and being courted, but reluctant to commit their own forces.

Out of this complexity of railway politics, of scheme and counter-scheme, the lines destined to form the Cambrian Railway finally emerged: the Oswestry and Newtown; the Newtown and Machynlleth, the Aberystwyth and Welsh Coast; the Oswestry, Ellesmere and Whitchurch, the Wrexham and Ellesmere and the Mid-Wales Railway. The promoters of these lines received little or no support from their great neighbours even when they sought it, otherwise there might have been no Cambrian Railway. As it was, the Cambrian was essentially a Welsh enterprise in its conception, construction and operation despite the fact that its main line extended through Shropshire to the borders of Cheshire at Whitchurch, and that it made its headquarters at Oswestry in the English march. Its main business, too, was to serve local Welsh interests although, in its heyday, the Cambrian co-operated extensively with its neighbours in running through coaches to the

Welsh coast during the holiday season. In this connection the Cambrian seems, curiously enough, to have been on less intimate terms with the Great Western, who finally absorbed it, than with any of the other lines with which it connected, an anomaly which the timetables continued to reflect long after the Cambrian had ceased to exist. Great Western trains over the Cambrian section connected as of yore with the L.M.S. at Whitchurch and the L.N.E.R. at Wrexham, thus perpetuating bygone Cambrian associations with the L. & N.W.R. and the Wrexham, Mold and Connah's Quay. On the contrary he would be an optimistic, determined and infinitely patient traveller who would attempt to enter Cambrian territory from the Great Western Shrewsbury–Chester line by changing stations at Wellington or Wrexham, or even via Gobowen and Oswestry. There might be sound reasons for this, but it was pleasant to imagine that Oswestry continued stubbornly to preserve a certain autonomy in face of the might of Paddington.

The contractors responsible for building the greater part of the Cambrian main line were Thomas Savin of Llwynymaen and the redoubtable David Davies of Llandinam, acting at first as partners and later separately. The construction of the lines along the valley of the Upper Severn may have been straightforward enough, but the building of the coast line by Savin and of the Newtown and Machynlleth by Davies were very different propositions which entitle both men to a place in any catalogue of Welsh worthies.

While the other railway engineers still stood upon the march and aired their paper schemes, it was David Davies who conquered the Montgomeryshire uplands and first brought the sound of the locomotive whistle to West Wales. It was a considerable engineering feat. From its junction with the Newtown and Llanidloes at Caersws the line climbs 273 ft. to its summit and then falls no less than 645 ft. to the levels of the Dovey at Machynlleth. To overcome such a difference of level in mountainous country with comparatively few major engineering works and a ruling gradient no steeper than 1 : 52 was a fine achievement. Where other engineers planned to overcome the highland barrier by means of long tunnels, Davies avoided tunnelling. Instead, on the summit at Talerddig his line passes through a defile 120 ft. deep hewn through the solid rock which makes a more impressive gateway to

western Wales than any tunnel. It is as though Davies in his pride
scorned to burrow under his native mountains but chose to carve
them like a sculptor despite the additional work involved. In fact,
however, the great cutting at Talerddig was a canny stroke on the
part of the contractor, for from it he drew the building stone for
the other works on the line including the fine viaduct over the
Twymyn stream near Cemmaes Road. In 1863 the opening of the
line was fittingly celebrated when a long double-headed train
forged out of Machynlleth with 1,500 passengers bound for
Newtown. The great David Davies himself travelled on the
leading locomotive accompanied, we read, by the Marquis of
Blandford "playing *See the Conquering Hero Comes* on a cornet-
a-piston". That was long ago, but we can still admire the work of
David Davies as our train . . . blasts its way up the long bank to
Talerddig Top. We may also admire the smartness with which
traffic, relatively dense in the holiday season, is handled over this
tortuous and heavily graded single-line route. Although upon a
much smaller scale it is comparable with the working of the old
Highland main line between Perth and Inverness.

In striking contrast to the hill-climbing feats of David Davies,
but no less a tribute to the boldness of its builder, Thomas Savin,
is the section of the Cambrian coast line from Dovey Junction to
Barmouth. Dovey Junction itself is a unique station in that it
possesses no road access whatever. Set in the midst of the salt
marshes of the Dovey estuary where the counties of Montgomery,
Merioneth and Cardigan meet, it is intended solely for passenger
exchange. I have often felt tempted, out of curiosity, to book a
ticket to Dovey Junction. On the south side of the estuary the
marshes extend to the sea coast, but on the north the hills rise
sheer from the shore. Consequently, from Gogarth Halt, the first
stop west of Dovey Junction, to Aberdovey the Barmouth line is
carried on what is virtually a sea wall. And such are the indenta-
tions of the shore line that there can scarcely be a straight rail
length in four miles. As the train proceeds along this tortuous
track at a remarkably smart pace the flanges squeal in protest at
the endless succession of reverse curves. Occasional outcrops of
rock force the line into short tunnels or cuttings which present
the curious appearance of having been deliberately contrived like
those on a child's toy railway.

North of Aberdovey the hills recede for a space, only to force the railway to the edge of the sea once more between Tonfanau and Fairbourne. Here, descending almost sheer to the rockstrewn and storm-swept shore of Cardigan Bay, they set the railway builder a task as formidable as that of traversing the central table-land. Near Llwyngwril the rails are perched upon a ledge in the rock high above the sea and it is not surprising to learn that the indomitable Savin employed seamen to cut his roadbed where previously only seabirds had found a foothold. Hereabouts, on New Year's Day, 1883, the evening train from Machynlleth ran into a landslip in the darkness and although, mercifully, the train remained precariously on its ledge, the locomotive *Pegasus* and its crew plunged to destruction on the rocks below. Fifty years later a second accident occurred at the same point for the same reason and with the same tragic consequences. Now, at the point where the cliff rises most precipitously, a rock shed protects the line from falls in the same manner as snow sheds guard the trans-Alpine railways from the avalanche.

The promoters of the Cambrian coast line originally planned to span the estuary of the Dovey between Ynys-Las and Aberdovey, but after sounding the shifting depths of sand they decided that discretion was the better part of valour. But at the second barrier, the Mawddach estuary, the railway takes the plunge, striding boldly across the sands and shallow seas from Barmouth Junction into Barmouth. The footway over this great bridge has inciden-tally given to Barmouth an esplanade which commands a magnifi-cent prospect of sea and mountain. At the southern approaches to the bridge the fine sand, whipped up by the wind, drifts over the rails like snow, while on more than one occasion in its history Barmouth Junction has been almost engulfed by gale-driven tides. During one great storm, passengers and staff were marooned all night while the water lapped the platform faces, their vigil shared by the cattle and sheep which had sought refuge there. At the Barmouth end the bridge has a swinging span, although the railway itself destroyed the need for such provision by speedily killing the once extensive coastal trade to the small quays and creeks of the Mawddach.

From Barmouth the coast line continued northward to tap the Portmadoc slate trade, to join the old North Western at Afon Wen

and to terminate at Pwllheli. Yet once it had much higher ambitions. Porthdynlleyn on the northern coast of Lleyn was to have
been at once the Ultima Thule and El Dorado of the Cambrian,
a flourishing port for Anglo-Irish traffic. But in this race for the
Irish trade the Cambrian was no match for the great North
Western, straddling the Menai Straits and advancing upon Holyhead. So Porthdynlleyn remained undisturbed and forgotten, a
small group of cottages and a single inn set on the brink of the sea
and accessible only by a steep track down the flank of the headland
beneath which it shelters.

from LINES OF CHARACTER *1952*

On Cambridge Platform

ROGER LLOYD

Cambridge station has two features, one absolutely unique, and
one nearly so. There is no other station in the British Isles of comparable importance which has only the one through platform.
You enter it, and you expect to see the platform on the other side
after the traditional manner, but instead you look out upon a sea
of railway lines and there is absolutely no other platform except
the one on which you stand. As this has to serve the need of both
up and down trains, and as very often both an up and a down train
use the same platform at the same moment, there is some very
pretty and dexterous intricacy of working to see. The second and
nearly unique feature is that in only one other station, Carlisle,
could one see every day the engines and trains of quite so many of
the old companies. Here I fully expect (for it is sadly usual) that
somebody will write to tell me how wrong I am. But I cudgel my
brains in vain to think of another station, Carlisle always excepted,
which was used by no less than four of the old mainline companies. When I was an undergraduate it was still a Great Eastern
station. But the Great Northern regularly used it for its trains from
King's Cross via Hitchin; the North Western had perhaps half-a-
dozen trains a day to and from Bletchley; and the Midland drove
a single line to it from Kettering by way of Huntingdon. Thus

there were engines and the rolling stock of these four railways to be seen, so that this station was very prodigal in its variety.

What is more, there was one hour in the twenty-four when you had the comings and goings of all four railways within slightly less than sixty minutes, and this hour was the very convenient one of 3.30 to 4.30 in the afternoon. At 3.30 the consciousness of the station was plainly directed towards the arrival of the train to London from Norwich and Ely; and a whole series of traffic movements began which the fact that this important train was shortly due had set in motion. First of all the new engine backed out of the sheds at the north end and moved slowly down to the tiny bay at the south end, where relieving engines always waited for their trains. Nearly all the trains to and from London changed engines at Cambridge; and they still do. In those days the old Great Eastern 4-6-os, with their enormous cab roofs, took the fast main line trains. Nowadays they call them B 12s, and they are rather *passée*. But during the last war they served their country with conspicuous success. An engine was wanted which was powerful enough to pull a long and heavy ambulance train, but light and short enough to run on practically all lines. These elderly B 12s were just what was wanted; for they weighed only 63 tons and they had a tractive effort of 21,969 pounds. So after the invasion of Normandy in 1944 many of them were taken away from Cambridge and Ipswich and were to be found all over the country, each one with its own ambulance train, which it pulled to its destination wherever it might be. I came across one of them in the little Great Western station at Winchester, and I should think it must be the only 4-6-o which has ever traversed the little branch line between Winchester and Didcot. I wondered when I saw it pulling out its ambulance coaches full of American wounded whether it was the same one that I used to see years ago come slowly down the length of Cambridge station and wait for the Liverpool Street express.

But to return to Cambridge, no sooner was the relieving engine safely stowed out of the way in its bay than a train of four of the old clerestory six-wheeled coaches of the Great Eastern came round the tremendous curve from Mildenhall, and poured out its passengers and parcels in a tearing hurry. It was standing where the express must come to rest and it had not long to get clear.

K

Most of its passengers and parcels were for London, but some always walked the five yards across the platform to the bay where the four o'clock for Bletchley was waiting. Its coaches were still chocolate and white (they gradually changed to red while I was at Cambridge) and it might be pulled by a 2-4-2 tank engine or else by a "Precursor". It was always a well-filled train. Schoolboys going home to villages with exciting names like Old North Road and Lord's Bridge used it, and there were always plenty of people making for Bedford or Birmingham. The really long-distance travellers to Lancashire or Scotland went by the 6.20 to Bletchley where they caught a train which got them to Crewe at about eleven o'clock at night. One of the "Precursors" which haunted Cambridge in those days was *Sirocco,* [and if she] was on the train that day one went up and inspected her all over and greeted her like an old friend. But even as one was doing it there was that indefinable stir on the platform which always heralds the approach of an express, and is set in motion by the wiseacre who keeps his eye on the appropriate signal and murmurs to a friend, "She's signalled," and who is always over-heard, and suitcases are picked up and everybody takes one step forward or two to the side as though that mystic and instinctive drill somehow helped to get a better seat in a train not yet in sight. We all do it, however irrational. That meant it was time to get back to the very centre of the platform, opposite the booking hall. That was the exciting place, and the peculiar arrangement of Cambridge station made it so. I have said that Cambridge has one and only one platform to serve the needs of both up and down traffic. It is long enough for two full-length trains, one for London and the other for Norwich, to stand tail to tail at the same moment at the same platform. But an up and a down train often arrive within a few minutes of each other, and when they do it is obviously impossible for either to travel the length of the platform by the platform line. So at the centre of the station there is a cross-over.

This particular London train was followed soon after by a train from London, and therefore it always used the cross-over. So one took care to stand at a point just a yard to the south of the actual centre of the crossing. You heard the train before you saw it; the driver generally whistled as he crossed the River Cam a mile away. Then up she came, headed by her blue Holden engine, going fast –

far too fast, as it always seemed, to get over that crossing safely. It must have been a point of honour with those Cambridge drivers to take it as fast as they dared. I have seen them do it scores of times, and never without a second's holding of my breath. Always the thought came, "He'll never get over it at this speed," but he always did. The train came fast down the track. She arrived at the points, and did a quick jerking lurch as the bogies took them. Then all those heavy wheels thudded and crashed over the diamond centre, and the coach wheels followed suit, their normal common time rhythm broken into an unbarred syncopation; and it always seemed to me, and still does, the most satisfactory of noises, only comparable for joy with the roaring blast of one of the old Southern Railway "Paddleboxes". . . . There the train was, at rest at last, but one could never see the engine that had brought it, for it came off at Cambridge, and the Cambridge firemen never wasted a second in uncoupling their engines, running them back to the shed, and getting away to their tea. They never left time to walk the length of the train.

It was now about 4.14, and so far as I can remember the train from London was due at 4.25; but before it came in something much more interesting was due – the Midland branch-line train from Kettering. But exactly where it would arrive was always rather a gamble. If the train to London got smartly away, there was just time to nip the little Midland train in over the central crossing on the heels of the express before the train from London arrived and claimed that same crossing. But there was also an empty bay at that time of day at the north end, and often they brought the Midland in there. But it was pleasantest when it followed the express over the crossing into the orthodox plat-form, for as it took the points it repeated all the thuds and bangs of the express, but *pianissimo,* as it were a faint echo. It was not possible to watch both the 4.20 from Kettering and the 4.25 to Norwich, but my own choice was for the Midland train every time. The 4.25 was simply a duplication of the express which had just left for Liverpool Street. But the 4.20 from Kettering was an exceedingly individual little train. Normally it had just the two coaches – very elderly Midland, but of that company's best vintage. The train had meandered its slow way through a succes-sion of villages with intriguing names like Raunds, and had arrived at Cambridge by way of Huntingdon. It was nearly always drawn by what was even then nearly, if not quite, the oldest class of engines in regular service in Britain, the Kirtley 2-4-0. They had two of them at Kettering, and they treated them as working museum pieces should be treated; they kept them clean and they polished their brass parts till they shone. But the gaze of the beholder was at once riveted not on the brass but on the phenomenal height of the chimney. The cab, too, seemed minute; and such of its roof as there was, which was not much, seemed designed to protect the front parts of a dwarf. But the man who often drove it was no dwarf: far from it, he was something of a giant, and he seemed to have great difficulty in tucking his head under that cab roof. I remember him still, an elderly man with long and streaming white moustaches, looking like a taciturn but venturesome pirate of the railway age. He and the old Kirtley engine were working out their declining years together, but the engine lasted longer than he did. They have all been scrapped now, but before the war there were just two left, and one of them was always on the Kettering to Cambridge run, but, alas! with a different and a much less decorative driver. . . .

By this time, the London and Norwich trains have both gone, the Midland has backed out into the yard, and *Sirocco* has departed to Bedford and Bletchley. On the main platform a local to Liverpool Street is standing with a "Claud Hamilton" at its head. But there is still one more sight to behold before we call it a day and go off to tea. I said at the beginning that Cambridge was the only place where you could see the engines of no less than four of the old companies, and so far we have only seen three. But a signal at the south end is down and the points are set for the bay near the flour mill, and there she comes, the 4.40 from King's Cross and Hitchin, with its authentically Great Northern teak coaches, and headed by one of the Ivatt 4-4-2 [class which were] in their heyday – 1902 to 1910 – the most famous express engines in the country but already superseded and relegated to local running from places like Hitchin. But I have a very deep personal affection for those engines for it was on one of them that I rode on the footplate for the first time. There was a certain Hitchin driver who seemed to tolerate importunate undergraduates, and if I happened to be about when he brought a train in he would invite me into the cab and let me stay there while he took the engine out into the yard to do a little shunting and to be turned at the turntable. If he happened to be on the 4.40 when I was there I always missed my tea, but it was worth it.

Such was the rich menu of one hour's station sauntering at Cambridge. It was fun all the year round, but best of all in early December on a fine day. The light gradually faded and dusk had come when the platform ticket was handed to the collector at the barrier. And there waiting was the Ortona bus – a green double-decker with solid tyres and no roof, to take me back through the lit streets of Cambridge to college, and a firelit room high up under the rafters and muffins by the fire for tea, and afterwards a long session in an arm-chair with the Holy Roman Empire or the Congress of Vienna.

from THE FASCINATION OF RAILWAYS *1951*

City and Suburban

JACK SIMMONS

No one wishing to travel from London to Rochester would normally think of beginning his journey at Fenchurch Street. Few people, indeed, except those who commute from South Essex, think of Fenchurch Street at all, for it is among the obscurest and most inconvenient of London stations. Yet to anybody interested in the history of railways, and the wider life of the past 150 years with which it is involved, the trip offers a most rewarding way of spending half-a-guinea and a leisurely afternoon.

The obscurity and inconvenience of Fenchurch Street station are beyond argument. The nearest station on the Underground is Tower Hill. By the church of St Olave, Hart Street, you mount a flight of steep steps and find yourself in front of the station, its *façade* sliding away from you at an oblique angle. If you are elderly or happen to be carrying any substantial luggage, your troubles are not over: for another flight of steps, longer and equally steep, awaits you, running from the booking office to the platforms. Broad Street is the only other London terminus that is approached in this uncomfortable way. All the rest are either built on a level with the road (like King's Cross and Victoria) or provided with gently-sloping ramps (like Liverpool Street and Waterloo). There was no room for anything of that kind at Fenchurch Street. As it is, the building is wedged as tightly as possible between its neighbours. A ramp would have to project out into the front of the station; and the forecourt is so poky that six cars and a van make a crowd in it.

Arrived at the top of the steps, you find there are four platforms only. From a railwayman's point of view, the most awkward of all the London termini to work is probably Marylebone. It too has only four platforms; but – much more tiresome – the tracks narrow down to two just outside and then plunge into tunnel. This strictly limits the number of trains that can be worked into and out of Marylebone station. Fenchurch Street is superior. Its four tracks are continued as far as Stepney East. It is possible to work as many as 175 trains into the station and out of it in the course of the 24 hours. On the other hand the platforms are extremely narrow, and – again owing to the confined site – they cannot be widened. It is no easy matter for the station staff to pass through the 25,000 people who are estimated to use it between 4 p.m. and 7 p.m.

All this springs directly from the station's history. It was originally built as the terminus of the London & Blackwall Railway, a line that ran to the East India Docks, enabling passengers to arrive in London very much more quickly than they could do if they had to continue their steamer journey by Greenwich Reach and the Pool. When the railway was opened, in 1840, it ran only to a terminus at the Minories. In the following year the line was carried further west, to Fenchurch Street. Although this extension was only a quarter of a mile long, it was an important quarter of a mile: for it brought the line within the limits of the City of London – much to the disgust of many citizens, who opposed it by every means in their power, on social as well as economic grounds. The original Fenchurch Street station was rebuilt in 1853 to the designs of George Berkeley, who was responsible for the present *façade,* and it has been further modified since, though never essentially altered.

The London & Blackwall line was a curiosity. At first it was operated by cable traction and had no connection with any other railway. Then, step by step, it became involved in the affairs of a new company, promoted jointly by itself and the Eastern Counties Railway: the London, Tilbury & Southend Railway. That company never owned a London terminus. When its line was opened as far as Tilbury in 1854, its trains ran both to Bishopsgate (the predecessor of Liverpool Street, half a mile further to the east) and to Fenchurch Street; but from 1858 onwards they used Fenchurch Street alone. The guest company soon became far more important than its host. In the twentieth century the electric tram and the motor-bus killed the Blackwall traffic, and the line ceased to carry passengers altogether in 1926. By contrast the Tilbury and South-end business grew steadily: with the growth of Southend as a watering-place and dormitory for London, the building of Tilbury Docks (begun in 1882), the gigantic industrial development of South Essex since the first World War and the mass immigration that has accompanied it – to make of Dagenham, for example, a town of 120,000 people. As early as 1912, when the great Midland Railway absorbed the London, Tilbury & Southend, it undertook to electrify the line. . . .

So much history must be understood if the interest of this journey is to be clear. The line runs out of Fenchurch Street over the East End roof-tops, throwing off branches on the down side to the goods stations at Haydon Square and Whitechapel, and passing the sites of two closed stations, Leman Street and Shad-well. At Stepney East (a station still very much in use) the Blackwall line diverged. Its path can still be seen immediately behind the station on the up side, though most of the track has been removed. Access to Blackwall is now needed only from the north, and this is provided by an easterly "chord" to the junction. A mile further on, at Gas Factory Junction, the line makes a three-pronged fork: one arm goes off on the down side to Bow Road, to join the main line out of Liverpool Street; a second burrows steeply down on the up side to a junction with the North London line; whilst our Southend line bears round in a curve to the east, nosing its way beneath the great gas-holders. The scarlet electric trains of London Transport have now begun to appear coming up from Whitechapel and the District line and running side by side with the Southend trains right on through Barking to Upminster.

The stations at Bromley and Upton Park still have an old-fashioned look about them, with the Tilbury company's initials worked into an elaborate iron monogram in the brackets supporting the roof. It is just beyond East Ham that you first become aware of the great upheaval that the Tilbury line is going through under the British Railways modernization scheme.

Barking is the meeting-place of three lines: that on which we are travelling is joined by one from St Pancras on the down side; and the Tilbury and Southend lines diverge at the eastern end of the station. The junction has always been a peculiarly busy one, and difficult to work because the intensive services on the District and Fenchurch Street lines were constantly interrupted by the crossing of trains running between St Pancras and Tilbury. No regular passenger trains have run on this route for many years – they have terminated at East Ham or Barking. But the boat trains for Tilbury docks all travel over this route; and, much more important, it is used by some 80 goods trains a day. Every one of them has had to cross the District and Southend lines on the level. In 1956 work began on a complete remodelling of the junction, providing for a flyover to carry the St Pancras line across the rest, so enabling trains from Tilbury to enter Barking station on the up side and pass over to continue their journey to St Pancras without causing any obstruction.

The passenger trains from Barking to St Pancras make a great circuit round north-east London, *via* Leytonstone, Walthamstow, and Kentish Town. This is a kind of service, through outer London, that was common in Victorian days but has now usually been abandoned by the railways to the buses – like the corresponding services on the Ceinture in Paris. The others of the same sort that survive have nearly all been electrified: those from Broad Street to Willesden and Richmond, for example, or the South London line from Victoria to London Bridge. This one still seems to pay its way, with nearly 30 trains in each direction running on weekdays, and a substantial Sunday service too.

The Southend and Tilbury lines now diverge. At once, on the Tilbury train, you are in a quieter atmosphere, though "modernization" is with you here too, in the building of the great new marshalling yard at Ripple Lane. On the down side is the Becontree Estate of the London County Council; on the other, over the

marshes, the Thames. Another minute or two, and there are the
two gigantic pylons, nearly 500 ft. high, taking electricity across
the river; beyond them Dagenham Dock and the Ford Motor
Works. It is a weird, lunar landscape, particularly in a November
mist with these huge shapes emerging, the stillness broken only
by the hooting of the engine or of an occasional passing ship. No
sharper contrast between the old and the new can be imagined
than what one sees here: for the old villages, like Rainham and
Wennington, survive, built up to the edge of the high ground
(though its rise may not be more than ten or fifteen feet); below
them the marshes, stretching away for a mile or more, flat as a
billiard-table, to the river. Here they form an immense rifle range.
(One remembers John Rhode's ingenious story "The Elusive
Bullet", in which a traveller on the railway was killed by a stray
shot as the train was passing this point.) At Purfleet the line begins
again to serve industry. The great chalk pits have been worked for
centuries past; and one of the earliest railways in the south of
England was in operation here – with horse-power only, of
course – before 1807. The West Thurrock Marshes now bear a
great Industrial Estate, whose buildings tower over the medieval
parish church, standing till lately in solitude.

The next station, Grays, is a small junction, with a single line
coming in on the down side from Romford and Upminster. Its
buildings on the up side were damaged in the second World War.
They have now been entirely replaced by a pleasant, simple new
block in which timber and glass predominate. The down-side buildings of the mid-Victorian period remain. The contrast between the
two, facing each other across the rails, is piquant and instructive.

The train is now approaching Tilbury. A mile beyond Grays the
lines of the Port of London Authority branch off on the up side:
the Docks are under its control, and it has its own railway system.
This is the route taken by the boat trains for the liners sailing
from Tilbury. But – once again because of the smallness of Fenchurch Street station – they leave London from St Pancras. Ships'
funnels and masts now loom up, almost on top of the Town
station at Tilbury. The last mile, on to the Riverside station,
reminds one of the stretch between Calais Ville and Maritime.
There is a triangular junction, with an engine shed in the middle;
and the train stops at the terminus.

K*

Its platforms are singularly bleak. Behind them, however, is a
large station building, of a kind unusual in this country, for it
dates from the 1920s, when little work of the sort was being
undertaken here (though much in the United States), and is one
part of a double building, the other half belonging to the Port of
London Authority. The architect was Sir Edwin Cooper, who had
already built the Authority's imposing offices in Trinity Square
E.C. From the outside the two parts are closely similar: substantial
blocks of neo-Georgian brick, crowned by slightly different cupolas.
Internally, the railway station is a big, bare hall, with a metal
cantilever roof: the Port of London Authority's half is differently
treated, with brick columns and a plastered vault, which make it
warmer – and were certainly more costly. The station has to
provide for all the multitudinous requirements of international
traffic: buffets (still carefully separated into first and second class,
even on the British Railway notices), post office, *bureau de change*. It
serves the Swedish Lloyd steamers for Gothenburg, and until very
recently it was the point of departure for the weekly Batavier boat
to Rotterdam – the last successor of Mrs Gamp's "Ankworks
Package".

The Riverside station fulfils another purpose as well, for 19
hours in the day. It provides the landing stage for the ferry over to
Gravesend. The original interest of the railway in Tilbury arose
from the idea of operating this ferry, a particularly valuable prize
then owing to the popularity of the Rosherville Gardens, on the
shore between Gravesend and Northfleet. The London, Tilbury
& Southend Railway was from the first empowered to operate a
ferry service. The present steamers (now about to be replaced)
were built to its orders – *Rose* as far back as 1901, *Catherine* in 1903,
Edith in 1912. They have the stately appearance that all ships of
their time, even the smallest, derive from their tall, slender funnels;
and they bustle across the Thames at intervals of a quarter of an
hour. The journey is never without interest, from the shipping
on the river, the lights and half-lights of the atmosphere, the
huddled "townscape" of Gravesend in front. It is at this point,
too, that the river holds the memory of the climax of *Great
Expectations*.

The Town Pier at Gravesend is a ramshackle affair. It was put
up in 1834 by the Corporation of the town, which sold it in what

seems to have been a somewhat corrupt manner to the London,
Tilbury & Southend Railway exactly half a century later.

To reach the Central station, for the last stage of the journey
on to Rochester, you go straight up the High Street. (Can there
be a narrower High Street in England? It offers room for one car
at a time.) The station lies below the level of the ground, and on
the south side it preserves its original building of 1849: a charming
structure, still entirely Georgian in character, with a colonnade in
front, sheltering a room with a three-sided bay window looking
on to the platform, this central block flanked by two two-storey
"pavilions". There have been some later alterations. A canopy,
resting on iron columns, masks the colonnade, and the bay
window is occupied by a cigarette kiosk. But it is easy to strip
these additions away in one's mind, and one is left with a perfect
country-town station of the early Railway Age.

Just over a mile to the east of Gravesend station the railway
begins to run along the bank of a canal. This is the Thames &
Medway Canal, which was opened with pomp in 1824. The canal
was a disastrous failure, but its directors showed exceptional
astuteness when in 1844 they decided to establish a railway, under
their own control, to run beside it. The line was opened in 1845.
The canal company had one great asset: the tunnel running eastwards from Higham, which when it was built was the second
longest in the country ($2\frac{1}{4}$ miles) Any competing railway that was
to run from Gravesend to the Medway would either have to bore
a second tunnel of similar length, or make a long detour. Those
were unthinkable notions: this line was therefore bound to command the traffic.

The canal company laid the railway on the towing-path, with
one of the rails projecting over the bed of the canal and supported
on a frame. Railway and canal traffic could thus continue to use
the tunnel at the same time. This arrangement lasted only nine
months. In November 1845 the canal ceased to be worked through
the tunnel. All traffic was then suspended until 1847, when a
double-track railway was opened, built on the bed of the canal,
which had been filled in. Meanwhile, in 1846, the canal company
had been bought up by the South Eastern Railway.

To the traveller, one tunnel is much like another. But this one
has an odd feature. After running through it for nearly a mile from

Higham, the train suddenly comes out into a great well, fifty yards across, open to the sky, and then plunges at once into tunnel again for another mile and a quarter. When the canal barges were being worked through the tunnel in its early days, it was found almost impossible for them to pass in the total darkness. This great shaft was therefore opened up, to afford a crossing-place for them in daylight.

As the train emerges at the south end of the tunnel, the line swings away on a sharp curve. On the down side at this point is the old Frindsbury canal basin: the southern terminus of the canal, where it joined the Medway. The train now stops at Strood: a junction from which one line runs south, up the Medway, to Maidstone, the other swinging east over the river into Rochester. Immediately south of the station another line comes in from the west, crossing the Maidstone railway by an overbridge. This is the old main line of the London, Chatham & Dover company, from Victoria and Swanley Junction.

The history of the remaining mile of line into Rochester is a complicated and extraordinary one, providing a visual demonstration even now of the almost incredible absurdities that railway competition could lead to in this country. The East Kent Railway was given powers in 1853–1855 to build a line from Strood through Rochester to Canterbury and Dover. It appeared to be a natural continuation of the South Eastern system. However, by the time the line was completed in 1861 the two companies had quarrelled bitterly; the East Kent had transformed itself into the London, Chatham & Dover and had acquired, with pertinacious ingenuity, a route of its own to Victoria station in London. Henceforward for nearly 40 years the South Eastern and the "Chatham" indulged in murderous warfare all over Kent.

Now that it had independent access to London, the Chatham company had no intention of passing its traffic to and from the South Eastern. It had its own station serving the village, which it called "Rochester Bridge", and the line from the bridge to Strood carried nothing but a single goods train a day. Such amenities were all very well between the two companies. The public suffered, and in 1876 a public-spirited Mayor of Rochester, Mr Toomer, took legal action to force the companies to resume an effective service, for passengers as well as goods. He was successful; whence the short line between Strood and the junction was known ever afterwards as the Toomer Loop.

But this was not the end of the story, by any means. In 1881–1888 the South Eastern took powers to build its own line from Strood into Chatham, crossing the Medway by a second bridge only a few yards north of the existing one belonging to the London, Chatham & Dover. The new line reached Rochester in 1891 and Chatham in the following year. Its stations in both towns were badly sited, and it was a hopeless economic proposition from the start. In 1899 the two companies – at last – formed a Working Union. One consequence of this was a gradual reconsideration of the competing lines they had built in the past, and in 1911 the South Eastern line into Chatham was closed. Both bridges, however, continued in use; a junction was put in east of the river from the South Eastern to the Chatham line, and this enabled the Toomer Loop to be closed. But Mr Toomer's spirit still ranged abroad. In 1919 the South Eastern bridge was badly damaged in a fire. His Loop was hastily put into order again, and traffic was resumed over it until 1922. Five years later, when the old Chatham railway was realigned, straighter than before, to run on to the South Eastern bridge, the Chatham bridge was closed. But even then the story was not quite ended: for in June 1942 the bridge was once again overhauled and strengthened, to serve as a substitute for the railway or the road bridge in case either should be put out of action by bombing. It was not, however, used for that purpose, and it is now again derelict: still to be seen on the up side, as the train crosses the river to run on a long viaduct into Rochester station.

from THE RAILWAYS OF BRITAIN *1961*

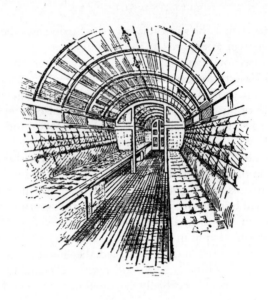

Tuppenny Tubes

C. HAMILTON ELLIS

In 1884, there was an Act for what became London's first deep-level electric railway – the first of the "tubes" as we know them. At the time, cable traction was intended. The passing of this Act is interesting, as the Parliamentary technique went back to that of George Stephenson's days, when everything depended on what sort of an account the engineer gave of himself and the project during the Committee stage. Harking back to the Tower Subway, this had been built by Peter Barlow, helped by James Henry Greathead, a South African who had been a pupil of his and invented the improved tunnelling shield bearing his name. Greathead it was who contracted to build the Tower line. Greathead it was whose evidence piloted the Act safely through. The oddity is that Greathead, who was to become famous for his technique in tunnelling, moved in on what was to be the City and South London Railway as an exponent of cable-haulage, which Andrew Hallidie had successfully introduced to San Francisco and which had made its first appearance on Highgate Hill in this same year of 1884.

The original Act was for a two-tunnel cable subway line between termini at the north end of London Bridge and the Elephant and Castle, respectively, to be called the City of London and Southwark Subway. . . . A northern terminal station was built at No. 46, King William Street, close to the Monument. The line passed down the course of Swan Lane, under the river, and thence down Borough High Street and Newington Causeway to its first intended terminus at the Elephant. Tunnelling began late in 1886 and continued steadily through the next year, when an Act was obtained for continuing the line to Stockwell. To avoid the payment of easement fees the line followed the streets throughout. The practice was continued in all subsequent tube lines, without prejudice to the very considerable depths to which some of them penetrated. Contracts had been placed for the cable-haulage equipment when the company began to have second thoughts. Another, more considerable electric line, the Bessbrook and Newry, had been opened in Ireland in 1885 and was working very satisfactorily. C. E. Spagnoletti, Telegraph Superintendent to the Great Western Railway, and one of the ablest electrical engineers of his time, was called into consultation. In 1888, a contract was placed with Mather and Platt of Salford for locomotives and other electrical equipment. The generating station and works were established at Stockwell, the second intended terminus, whence there was rail access to the tunnels by a steeply inclined plane with cable haulage. Late in 1889, an experimental train of a locomotive and two coaches was run between the City end and the Borough. The locomotive, like all those subsequently used on the City and South London Railway, as it was to be called, was a four-wheeler with the motor armatures mounted directly on the axles. Under the formula of later days it was describable as Bo, for the axles were not coupled. An alternative design, not carried out save in a model, had the motors mounted inside the body with cranks and crossed connecting rods, the wheels still being uncoupled. In both projected and actual design, the entire body took the form of a deep clerestory with the two enginemen's heads and shoulders in the "clere" part. The original coaches have often been described, and to anyone who experienced them they were unforgettable.

To fit the 10 foot 6 inch diameter of the tunnels (the term "tube" had not yet been coined, though this was a true tube railway) the cars were only 6 feet 10 inches wide. As there was no scenery, and the conductor was to call out the names of the stations, narrow top lights were all the windows at first considered necessary. The cars were heavily stuffed inside; it was inevitable that the travelling public would call them "padded cells". The rail gauge, as in all subsequent London underground lines, was 4 feet 8½ inches, though the dimensions of the rolling stock suggested a much narrower gauge.

In 1890 an extension to Clapham Common was authorized, together with the change in the railway's name and an increase in capital. On November 4th, of that year the line was passed by Major-General C. S. Hutchinson, with Major Cardew as electrical adviser. On that same day the line was formally opened by the Prince of Wales, afterwards King Edward VII, and the Duke of Clarence. Together with the Lord Mayor and the Sheriffs, the Princes were taken through the tunnel to Oval, and thence to a ceremonial luncheon at Stockwell, whose rather forbidding streets were gaily beflagged. There was a workmen's supper in the evening.

The company was cautious against a premature public opening. No railway like this had ever been run before; a failure might have done incalculable damage. Regular working began on December 18, 1890. There was charged a universal fare of twopence, with entry by turnstiles. Though this was in strict fact the original, "Twopenny Tube", the term was to be the nickname of the later, much more advanced Central London Railway. There were many oddities about this first London tube. Where it passed under Swan Lane to the old Swan Pier the right of way was so narrow that the tunnels were placed one above the other. As King William Street Station, planned for a cable line, sited east-to-west to dodge easement, had a single terminal road with platforms on both sides, this entailed the extremely steep falling gradient of 1 in 14 on the southbound line as it wove into position under the northbound. Leaving King William Street, the trains took a steep, sharply curved and somewhat alarming dive into the city's basement. Access to the stations was by hydraulic lifts from rather nicely ornate, pavilionesque buildings at street level. Stockwell, where there was a double crossover and of course a junction to the works ramp, was the first of the railway's stations to have two roads and an island platform in a single tunnel. This was subsequently copied, as the line extended, at Clapham Common, Angel and Euston. Signalling was mechanical, with a special arrangement of Spagnoletti's lock-and-block apparatus. Electric automatic signalling was not to come to the line until after the 1914-1918 war, when it was due for complete rebuilding.

From the first, the City and South London Railway was a great success. It worked admirably, though the lighting was extremely bad to start with, both in the electrically-lit cars and in the stations and tunnels where, owing to short supply of current, gas and oil lamps were used for a while. The week-day service was on a five-minute headway; Sunday trains did not come until April 5, 1891. Average daily user during 1890–1891 amounted to 15,000 passengers. . . .

King William Street terminus was awkwardly arranged and had other limitations. In 1893, powers were obtained for its replacement by a new line leaving the old one north of Borough Station and passing via London Bridge to the Bank and Moorgate. This was opened on February 25, 1900. On June 3rd, the southern extension to Clapham Common was opened. Subsequent extensions during the present century were from Moorgate to the Angel, Islington (November 17, 1901), and thence to Euston on May 12, 1907. These completed the line in its original form. As is well remembered, the railway was almost entirely rebuilt to take standard Underground rolling stock between 1921 and 1924, and now, as part of London Transport's Northern line, may be said to extend from Morden to Camden Town. The Morden line, at any rate, is a natural projection of the old Clapham Common line, but north of the Camden Town Junctions we come into the Hampstead and Highgate lines, constructed during the present century.

As for the old King William Street line, it was given over to complete disuse. Many years later, pieces of the old mechanical signalling equipment, including semaphores, were still in position. Fortunately a cannibalized version of locomotive No. 1 is in the Science Museum, South Kensington, and one of the original "padded cell" cars is at York. A second locomotive, built by Crompton, was kept as a relic at Moorgate, Metropolitan Line, for some time, but was damaged beyond repair by fire during the Hitler War.

Especially in view of the great numbers of passengers carried, the City and South London was a fortunate railway. It had one collision and two lift falls in its earlier days, both without fatality, but in 1892 a passenger fell off a leading car platform, where the conductor, in exchange for a trifle, had been in the most improper habit of taking people to "watch the engine". The unfortunate passenger was cut up in the tunnel and the horrified conductor fled into hiding. The year before there had been a fatal lift accident at Oval Station, through an impatient passenger trying to get into a lift that was already going up. The gate was not quite shut, there being then no gate-control. In the shemozzle the liftman was unable to stop the lift at once; the passenger fell on the floor and the girder over the shaft gate cut off his head. These two gruesome events were isolated in a long history of safe working. . . .

A focal point of the inner West London suburbs was Shepherd's Bush, and in the 'nineties it could not be regarded as well served. There was Uxbridge Road Station on the West London Railway, with the old Outer Circle service to Broad Street and Mansion House. There was the Middle Circle, Aldgate to Mansion House. There was the London and South Western's Gunnersbury–Kensington line. There were the buses heading into London up Notting Hill. Here clearly was an opportunity for promotion of a tube.

There were two schemes in 1890. The London Central Subway unsuccessfully promoted a line from Shepherd's Bush to Gower Street via Oxford Street. The Central London Railway, proposed an electric line from Bayswater along below Oxford Street, thence to King William Street in the City and to a junction with the City and South London. Its sponsors included (Sir) Ernest Cassel, (Sir) Richard Farrant, and certain mining interests. Its opposers were numerous and very formidable. Forbes and Watkin both went into action, for the proposed line cut right across the Inner Circle. The Metropolitan, which long ago had intended the extinction of the bus, argued that buses could handle all the user along such a route; further, its Counsel asserted that additional powers would have to be sought to work the line by steam, "the only motive power which at present can with any efficiency be used upon railways". Other enemies of the scheme included the Vestries, the City Corporation, the Dean and Chapter of St Paul's and the Gas Light and Coke Company. . . .

In mid-July the Bill was thrown out by the Lords, but an improved scheme for a line from Shepherd's Bush to a terminus near Cornhill, introduced in the next Session, was luckier, and received the Royal Assent on August 5, 1891. A contract was placed with the Electric Traction Company, formed to this end, for the equipment of the line and the purchase of land. . . .

An extension from the Bank to Liverpool Street was authorized in June, 1892, but about four years later there was trouble with the Great Eastern and the North London and the line was not completed for some years, what there was of it being meantime used for car sidings. While construction was going on, another deep-level line was promoted – the City and West End – to run from Hammersmith to Cannon Street. This was successfully opposed by Forbes, who half-promised a deep-level "express" line of the District. He said that until the Central London were a going concern, the sanctioning of another electric line would be premature. The exemplary behaviour of the City and South London was presumably something in the Far East about which no man knew.

Greathead proposed using electric locomotives, one at each end of a train and working together from one controller. But the Board of Trade objected, on the grounds that it was undesirable to have power cables running through the coaches. Instead, rather large locomotives were designed for working singly at the heads of the trains. Thirty-two of them were built, and as they weighed 42 tons each, and as, owing to the disposition of the motors, rather a high proportion of that weight was unsprung, there was incipient trouble from vibration. The engines were based rather on those of the Baltimore and Ohio type but were in one piece, on bogies, giving the wheel arrangement Bo-Bo. The Americans consisted of four-wheel motor units articulated together in pairs. In both cases the cab was central, with sloping bonnets fore-and-aft.

Cars had gated platforms, as on the City and South London, but they were much larger and more comfortable, similar in lateral dimensions to the present standard tube car. The trimly upholstered seating, too, was excellent, partly transverse and partly longitudinal, as it is today. With clerestory roofs and a style of painting similar to that of the London and North Western Railway, adorned with the company's coat of arms (a quartering of the arms of the City of London and of the boroughs of Holborn and St Marylebone, and of the County of Middlesex) the new carriages looked far more important and railwaylike than those of the City and South London, or the more fairly comparable, but hideous, Waterloo and City. With the imposing, but short-lived bogie locomotives, the Central London could produce quite a train. Seven cars was the full formation.

Horace Parshall, the company's electrical engineer, had designed the engines, which were built by the General Electric Company and supplied by British Thomson-Houston. Ashbury and Brush built the cars. Lifts were American, by Spragues. In the Shepherd's Bush power station the generators were driven by six 1,300 h.p. Corliss engines, and current was supplied to a central conductor rail at 550 volts d.c. The permanent way was peculiar. It consisted of 100 lb. bridge rails on longitudinal sleepers with cross-transoms supporting the conductor rail and, on one side of this, a boarded whitewashed catwalk for men walking the track. For there was no filling between the rails. One looked down into a dark gulf, bounded only by the bilge of the tube, and even more deterrent in aspect than the "suicide pits" of later years, which it probably inspired. This same "hollow way" distinguished the City and South London, which, however, used T rails instead of the bridge type. When the Liverpool Street extension ultimately came, be it added, bull-head rail keyed into chairs made its appearance. It was also used at points and crossovers.

Signalling was mechanical, with control by Spagnoletti's lock and block. The starting signals were semaphores, while the homes and outer homes gave their indications by moving coloured spectacles. One of the many striking features of this new and much improved tube railway were the glittering locking frames at the platform ends. Track circuiting, it may be remarked, was introduced in 1912.

On June 27, 1900, London's first "modern" deep-level railway was opened by the Prince of Wales. . . . Half an hour later the royal train left for Shepherd's Bush, and on arrival there was the customary cold collation and champagne-bath in a big marquee. It was a glorious opening.

Without doubt, the Central London was a great success. Serving as it did the fashionable West End, with fine-sounding stations like Bond Street and British Museum, it caught the public fancy in a way that the City and South London, in its rather drab district, and the gloomy little Waterloo and City, had not. There were always gags to be interpolated in Gilbert and Sullivan operas. In 1900, *Patience* introduced Archibald Grosvenor, the metamorphosed aesthete, as a Tuppenny-Tube Young Man.

All was not smooth, however. The big locomotives gave serious trouble owing to their unsprung motors, inducing a degree of rail corrugation that made the vibration worse than ever. Then there was a bad fire at Notting Hill Gate. When the Fire Brigade arrived, its commanding officer was earnestly warned to defer his waterworks until it should be certain that all current was cut off. But promptitude was his watchword; as he remarked: "When we're called we take charge." Certain high-tension cables were still alive, and the fire had melted their leaden casings. The sudden descent of quenching water was answered by a roar of outraged electricity.

Of the offending locomotives, three were rebuilt as geared engines with their weight reduced to 31 tons. But they had to go, all but two which were retained for shunting about the carsheds. There were also two steam 0–6–0 tank engines, with Holden oil-fuel burners for working underground in the small hours with ballast trains, when the current was cut off. They lasted until 1923. The 32 condemned electric camels were replaced, at a cost of £63,000, by 64 motor coaches, following an examination by a Board of Trade Committee. Evidently, the B.O.T. was satisfied that control circuits were not the same as power cables.

In its first year, the Central London Railway carried just under fifteen million passengers, and paid 2½ per cent. By 1910, two years after a western extension to Wood Lane, its annual user was about 40,500,000 passengers. Working conditions were not very good at first; the motormen worked a 60 hour week without meal-breaks, taking sandwiches in the cabs with them and being handed occasional mugs of tea by the signalmen.

The motor coaches having replaced engine haulage, there was

no more trouble; the line was, of its day, a model tube. It never succeeded, as was at one time intended, in making of itself a circular railway with a southern line via Hammersmith, Piccadilly, the Strand and Fleet Street, with a spur to Gunnersbury, but the Liverpool Street extension, making very useful contact with the Great Eastern and Metropolitan as well as getting an important City terminal, was opened in July, 1912, and the western extension from Wood Lane to Ealing followed in 1920. From the first, the Central London trains set a new standard of underground railway comfort as to the seating. For many years they were much better in this respect, not only than the old steam Metropolitan and District trains, but also as compared with the electric successors of these and with early tube cars on lines built during the present century – the Piccadilly, the Bakerloo and the Hampstead and Highgate.

With the successful working of the Central London Railway, the deep-level underground electric line had truly arrived, and in one form or another doubtless will continue for as long as great cities continue. The line's reception was favourable. It was a tremendous improvement on the Metropolitan, still steam-worked and very little changed since the 'sixties. *Punch* published a happy cartoon of sweet little *Fairy Electra* riding on a sort of sparkling Catherine wheel, waving a minatory wand at a hideous demon with a smoking chimney hat, and remarking that now people had seen her, she fancied his days were numbered.

from BRITISH RAILWAY HISTORY 1877–1947 *1959*

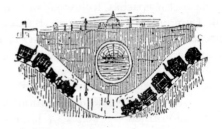

Irish Extension

L. T. C. ROLT

[By 1951] the Tralee and Dingle [only came] to life on the occasion of the monthly cattle fair in Dingle. Through the courtesy of Coras Iompair Eireann I was able to make a footplate trip on one of these cattle specials and it proved the most unforgettable railway journey I have ever made or am likely to make.

The narrow-gauge metals run into the yard of the broad-gauge station at Tralee, but the passenger station is situated some little distance away and consists merely of a single platform. The late Robin Flower knew this station in the days when it was alive. "To the little station of the Dingle line," he wrote in *The Western Island,* "the country people come at the tail of a market-day with their motley purchases; you forget London and Dublin, all the cities of the earth, and with Gaelic faces and Gaelic voices about you stand in the gateway of an older and a simpler world." But those country people that he knew come no more and the dead station wears a sadly dilapidated air. But it was here that we found our train awaiting us, a long string of drab grey cattle wagons with locomotives 1T and 8T at their head and a bogie brake van bringing up the rear. Even this van had been adapted to carry more cattle, the guard being relegated to a small section at the brake end where he was protected from too intimate an association with the livestock by a crude waist-high partition. Ahead of us stretched the thirty-one miles of mountainous road, its running surface rust-dulled by a month's disuse, and as there [were then] only three platelayers at work on the whole length I found myself wondering what unsuspected defects, subsidences or obstructions might be lying in wait for us. But such pessimistic reflections were soon forgotten in the excitement of departure. Owing to the lack of coaling facilities combined with small bunker capacity, every available space on the two locomotives was stacked with fuel. Briquets were piled on the front footplating and along the tank tops, while most of the fireman's side of the cab was occupied by a heap of coal consisting mostly of slack which the wind was soon to whip into our eyes. Cab accommodation was on this account more than usually restricted, but I managed to tuck myself out of the way at the back of the footplate on the driver's side of the leading engine. As whistle answered whistle and with a clank of coupling rods the two locomotives drew slowly away in a cloud of steam from open cylinder drain cocks, I experienced a feeling of excitement and suspense such as I have never known before on rails but only in a car setting out upon some unknown and difficult trials course. There was the same sense of adventure, the same sense of special preparation in the piles of fuel on the locomotives, and the same feeling that, special preparation or no, anything might happen before the journey was over. I knew that before now the unexpected had happened in the shape of the failure of water supply sources *en route* or brake failures due to leaking vacuum pipe connections on the train. Nowhere are fully operative vacuum brakes so necessary and so peculiarly reassuring as on the Tralee and Dingle.

The line sets out from Tralee in a prosaic and unassuming fashion which gives no indication of the excitements to come. It describes a semi-circle round the outskirts of the town, crossing the streets by a series of gated crossings, passes the terminal basin of the disused Tralee canal, and then swings westwards over the marshy estuary of the River Lee. The dykes of this tidal river have been broken down and it is hereabouts that the waters are apt to invade the track. On occasions of high spring tides, trains have had to wait for as long as three hours for the flood to subside, while more venturesome and less patient drivers have had their fires put out. Happily, on this occasion the tide was out, but the soft ooze and the pools of water which lay between the sleepers told their own story.

At Blennerville the railway joins the road which it follows in true tramway style as far as Castlegregory Junction, and accompanies more or less closely all the way to Dingle. This first section was reminiscent of the Arigna branch of the Cavan and Leitrim, the railway following the undulations of the road and occasionally swinging across in startling fashion from one side to the other. There were the usual scenes of alarm and excitement when horses or straying livestock were encountered. Some of the latter seemed bent on suicide but were deterred by cries, whistles and wild gestures from both ends of the train. The scenery, however, was incomparably finer already than anything on the Arigna branch. On our left marched the dark peaks of Slieve Mish, part of that spine of the Dingle peninsula which our train was soon to cross. To the right was the wave-whitened arc of Tralee Bay with Fenit Harbour opposite and the distant prow of Kerry Head beyond. Ahead of us there rose a majestic group of peaks, their colour varying from a forbidding black to hyacinthine blue with distance and the magical vagaries of a constantly changing, sea-reflected light. Most distant and peer of them all was Brandon, the mountain of St Brendan, soaring almost sheer from the sea to a height of over 3,000 ft.

At Castlegregory Junction where we reached the end of the first section from Tralee there was a pause while both engines took on water from a stand-pipe lagged against frost with straw ropes and while their crews imbibed liquid of a darker and stronger character at the neighbouring bar. Of the six miles long branch line which continued along the shore of the bay to Castlegregory only the roadbed now remains, for the village it served is so small that it did not yield sufficient traffic. The layout of the junction is peculiar, there being one long platform and a bay which was used by the branch trains. By means of a middle loop, both up and down main-line trains drew into the same platform. Although it is, or was, the most important station on the line, Castlegregory is simple and primitive in character like the rest of the stations on the T. & D.

By the time the tank of the train engine had been filled, both safety valves had lifted with a deafening roar of escaping steam. We needed a good head of steam, for the easy run along the shore of the bay was over and we must now cross the peninsula from shore to shore. We stood at the foot of the celebrated Glenagalt Bank, certainly the most formidable gradient in Ireland and probably unsurpassed in length and severity anywhere in the British Isles. Once more whistle answered whistle, two regulators were opened, two smoke stacks simultaneously erupted smoke and steam like miniature volcanoes and to the accompaniment of the slow, syncopated rhythm of two locomotives labouring in full gear we set out to climb from almost sea-level to a height of 680 ft. in less than four miles. Officially the gradient for most of this distance is 1 in 30/31, but it looked to me to be steep enough to

force many a car down to third gear, and my driver stoutly maintained that parts of it were as steep as 1 in 25.

Soon after leaving Castlegregory the line crossed from side to
side of the deep little valley of a mountain stream by a viaduct set
upon a most acute semi-circular curve. This looks disconcerting
enough, particularly when descending the bank, yet in fact it
represents an improvement upon the original route which was
even more steeply graded and acutely curved and was abandoned
as a result of an accident. The remains of the original stone viaduct
still stand, and my driver, with a blissful disregard for my peace
of mind, shouted above the roar of our exhaust as he pointed out
with a blackened finger the precise point where the engine of a
mixed train from Dingle plunged from the rails into the stream
50 ft. below. The driver had lost control on the gradient and,
with his two companions on the footplate, paid for his mistake
with his life. So did a number of pigs in the vans which followed
the engine, but fortunately the coupling of the passenger coach
at the rear of the train parted and it remained precariously suspended on the edge of the viaduct.

Beyond this horseshoe curve the railway works its way round
the edge of a steep bluff where it is already high above Tralee Bay,
turning as it does so due south into the mountains. Here a signal
at danger appeared silhouetted against the skyline; but in response
to a long and urgent blast of the whistle the arm dropped and we
pounded on over a road crossing, the engine crews waving to the
old lady who had to come out of her lonely cottage to open the
gates. There was now a deep valley on our right, and far ahead I
could trace the road and the railway climbing in close company up
the bare mountainside towards the valley watershed on the high
skyline which marked the summit of the pass. There was something most moving and dramatic in the contrast between the
silence, the solitude and the vast scale of this landscape which
made our train seem so puny a thing and the fiercely sustained
sound and fury of our two locomotives as they pitted their
strength against the unrelenting gradient. Like some long grey
slug whose horns were pillars of smoke and steam the train
crawled slowly but surely upward until at last we ran into the
shallow cutting which marked the summit, regulators were eased
and the tumult died away. It was to Gleann na nGealt, to use the

true Gaelic spelling, that according to legend, all the mad folk of Ireland once flocked to drink the magical waters of a spring which had the power to restore their ruined wits. The site of this spring, far below in the glen, was pointed out to me before we entered the summit cutting which translated us from one scene to another as quickly as a doorway from room to room. One moment we had been pulling hard on the grade with Tralee Bay still visible to the north, and the next we were descending equally steeply with steam shut off, vacuum brakes hard on and the highlands of the southern side of the peninsula upon either hand. Occasionally the uplands on our left parted to reveal distant glimpses of Dingle Bay and the mountains of the Waterville peninsula beyond.

The gradient of this western approach to the pass is not so continuous. It descends for two miles to Glenmore platform, but the next two miles to Emalough consist of a series of ups and downs almost worthy of a roller coaster, and our progress over this section was indeed as wild a ride. It was enlivened the more by a certain lack of co-ordination between our two locomotives. My companion on the pilot engine was a Tralee and Dingle driver of long standing whereas his mate on the train engine had had less experience of the road. The latter was a large and jovial individual· who seemed to be imbued with the spirit of adventure and whose motto appeared to be "ignorance is bliss". Long before we had reached the foot of an incline and before my driver had released his brake, he would decide that it was time to put on steam to "rush" the next ascent. With a sudden roar of exhausting steam from just behind our cab we would find ourselves urged briskly forwards towards the bottom of a dip which invariably seemed to consist (in my recollection at least) of a sharp curve on a high embankment. Glancing back somewhat nervously at such moments, I would see his face, grinning from ear to ear, framed in the circle of his cab spectacle, while behind him the long swaying string of cattle vans came snaking round the curve, the last vehicles still on the steep descent while we were already climbing hard. To add a further spice to these hazards there were numerous encounters with straying sheep. The technique here was to scare them into safety by suddenly opening the cylinder drain cocks, but there were several near misses.

From Emalough there is an almost continous descent at 1 in 29 into Gleann an Scail where the Irish hero Cuchulainn fought his legendary battle with the giant and the earth is littered with the rocks which they hurled in their combat. Here we made our second stop for water at Annascaul Station, a crossing place and the end of the section from Castlegregory Junction. The labours of our hard-working engines were by no means over yet, however, for at Annascaul we faced a second long climb to a summit near Garrynadur platform whence the line again falls at 1 in 29 for over a mile to Lispole. The Tralee and Dingle might have been deliberately engineered to deter all but the most nerveless and unimaginative of passengers, for the lofty Lispole viaduct is situated just at the foot of this frightening declivity. Moreover, my knowledge that it was once the scene of another serious derailment and that the strength of the structure is now in some doubt was hardly reassuring as we thundered down the bank in a succession of gravity-urged bursts of speed punctuated by brief and violent applications of the vacuum brake. However, the train ground to a standstill just short of the viaduct where the pilot was uncoupled to run light over the bridge, there to await the rest of the train. . . . As I moved away from our train on the footplate of the pilot and we rumbled on to the viaduct, I must confess that I wondered with a slight qualm whether we should meet again, or whether it would be a case of "gone before but not forgotten". But we were soon happily reunited on the other side.

Five more undulating miles of track, mostly beside the road, brought us to the last descent to the terminus with the stone finger of Dingle pier pointing into the land-locked harbour directly ahead. Here between the sea and the peaks of Croaghkearda and Connor spread the roofs of the most westerly town in Europe; for from Dingle it is but a little way by mountain road to Dunquin, the harbour for the Great Blasket where the islanders speak of America as their next parish. The train slowed, passed under the roof of the station, and came to a creaking halt beside the single platform. We had come to the end of the road.

from LINES OF CHARACTER *1952*

London Extension

JOHN BETJEMAN

It is my delight to travel by suburban steam trains in London. I have waited half an hour in the echoing and unfrequented half of Aldersgate station for the rare and nearly empty steam trains to grind up the slope from Moorgate on their way to the Midland and Great Northern suburbs. I have sat in the gaslit compartment of a Great Northern train here, with the ghosts of Carrie and Charles Pooter, Murray Posh, Mr Padge and Eliza's husband and Jerome K. Jerome's Harris and seen from the window mysterious arcades of sidings which are something to do with that goods line the Great Western runs to Smithfield.

I have gone by steam from Liverpool Street to Chingford and from Liverpool Street to Palace Gates, changing at Seven Sisters in order to do so. And at that high-up wooden junction I have crossed the little bridge to the lonely platform where the train from North Woolwich waits to take me through West Green and Noel Park to its countrified forgotten terminus. And walking thence over municipal grass I have climbed the slope to Ally Pally and there seen the summer evening sunlight catch the steeples and water towers of North London.

Who are the passengers on such unfrequented lines? Who are they who for so long, to quote E. V. Lucas, have

> peered from a third class "smoker"
> Over the grimy waste of roofs
> Into the yellow ochre?

They are certainly not those who must use steam because they have to, living in Tilbury or Southend and feeling obliged to arrive at Fenchurch Street. The people who use the lines I mention could perfectly well take the dull Tubes or duller buses. Looking at them, I think they must be seekers of peace and creatures of habit loyal to the glorious pre-grouping days and aware that the personalities of the old railways still survive in suburban stations which have been spared rebuilding in concrete. "I've always used the line and my father did before me. Now that there's not so much for me to do in the office I find I can comfortably catch the 5.11 from Moorgate to Cricklewood."

All this is a prelude to the most exciting and unknown of London's steam suburban lines to survive – the West London Extension Railway. It is not mentioned in *Bradshaw*. But it *is* mentioned at the end of the green Southern time-table and is printed in different type from the rest of the tables so as to show it is independent. This line runs from Clapham Junction to Addison Road (for Olympia). The trains are few and irregular, and they start at different times on different days of the week, like times of services when the vicar is without a curate, except that on W.L.E.R. there are no Sunday services. A porter at Waterloo told me that two old ladies own the line and that they have refused to sell out to British Railways and that they receive 1/6 for every train which crosses their bridge over the Thames from Battersea to Lots Road. So glorious a story cannot be true, but I like to believe it.

Let me recommend a visit to the most northerly and the least used of all the platforms on Clapham Junction, that flimsy collection of cast iron, glass, wood and brick set among so many shining rails. Let it be where the rails are least shiny, on a weekday when the W.L.E.R. is working at about 4.30. Not a soul will be on the platform. Suddenly an antique engine will be seen riding over brick arches among the Battersea chimney pots and then curving in towards the platform, dragging a trail of London and South Western rolling stock. Surprisingly the train is crowded. Perhaps they are people who work at Cadby Hall, perhaps Civil Servants from that hideous new barrack near Olympia. They dismount slowly and are let out one at a time by the ticket collector down dark stairs into Clapham.

The train which goes back through Battersea, over the Thames with the best possible view of Battersea Reach and down stream to Westminster, is empty except for you and me. The interior woodwork is grained to look like oak: sepia photographs of Parkstone and Sidmouth adorn the walls: the seating arrangements are rather like the top of a tram. We hurtle through a land of docks and canals at great speed. Willow herb rises on the ruins of Chelsea and Fulham station as we flash past its dismantled platforms. Soon West Brompton is upon us in a brown brick cutting and here we are, slowing down into that neglected waste of platforms which was once to be the great station of West London, the Paddington, St Pancras, Victoria and Willesden of all first- and second-class passengers: KENSINGTON (Addison Road), more recently named Olympia. The whole journey took eight minutes. Never did man move so far in London so fast in recent years. There is no one to collect our tickets. Two late typists board our train for the last journey of the day back to Clapham.

In one of those tall Italianate streets, which are not quite Kensington and not quite Fulham, I can picture a tall four-storey semi-detached house. All the other houses in the road have been turned into flats. The district has "gone down". But this house alone retains its privacy, though the windows are dusty and some of the blinds have stuck. Here live the two old ladies, the proprietors of the West London Extension Railway. Now as we leave Addison Road they will be having tea, and it is pleasant to think that as our train crossed the bridge from Battersea they received one-and-six towards their cakes and jam.

from PUNCH *25 August 1954*

Farewell to a Branch

R. C. ROBERTSON-GLASGOW

It is said [in 1961] that British Railways are losing £300,000 every day. No doubt we ought to be disturbed by this colossal information. No doubt we should also be ashamed that our country ended her financial year in the red by some £390,000,000. Mr Micawber would certainly not have approved.

But what touches the heart more deeply is that our Railways are losing at least one more Line every year; one more unpunctual but peaceful journey; one more chance for the faithful and solitary traveller to watch the scenery of his countryside; to watch it without the rivalrous insanity of some car-driver who seems to want to exchange the beauty of this world for ambiguous orchestration in the next.

On the slow single-liner, the best views were to be had at the unadvertised stop. There was the lane on the left winding up to the farm: the stream on the right, flowing between willow-trees. Farm and stream may have been commonplace to those who lived there; but they were magical to the passing spectator, who had time, while the engine recruited its strength and the signalman his wits, to frame a short story about that farm.

But there was one advertised stop that remains most particularly in my memory. It was at a small station, little more than a Halt, in Scotland, now just a name in deceased *Bradshaws*. In a meadow that almost invaded the track there was a single-storeyed stone cottage. On the gate, written in enormous letters, was the notice, "Beware of the Dog". But I never once saw the considerate owner or his dangerous dog. Perhaps they were always asleep.

Yet, I have one accusation against the train that dawdles through the meadows. The views from it of any game are incurably inconclusive. There is a cricketer coming out to bat; ruddy with optimism, or like one that on a lonesome road doth walk in fear and dread. There is a cricketer walking back from batting, with head bowed, or jaunty with feigned jocularity. But never once have I seen a batsman being bowled; only an umpire or two picking up the bails without surprise or enthusiasm.

It is the same at golf. As you sit by the window, you never see a master-stroke played to the green, or a curly putt holed. They are always walking after their ball, with the eternal egotism of the golfer. As to football, it is sure to be Half-Time.

No matter. I can still make an imaginary journey in a ghost train on my favourite single-line. It will be spring: the silver birches will be in their glory: the lambs will be running to a meal of reassurance. The elderly engine will puff with triumph at arriving rather against odds and expectation. Jimmy, the unofficial porter, will take my suitcase, and his fee. But Jimmy has moved on, to where money has no more meaning.

from SUNDAY TIMES *16 April 1961*

PART VI

Safety, Danger and Disaster

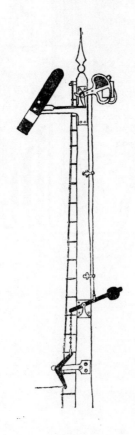

L

Signalling grows up

RICHARD BLYTHE

Illiteracy was the great problem in bringing forward signalling systems at the rate made possible by new inventions. The engineer Brunel observed to a Parliamentary Select Committee in 1841 that the greater number of signalmen could neither read nor write – a convincing reason why the electric telegraph, invented a few years earlier, did not come into general use very rapidly. W. W. Tomlinson, in his history of the North Eastern Railway (which adopted telegraphs in 1846), says there was a great deal of difficulty in teaching staffs to use the equipment. Only one stationmaster between York and Milford Junction was able to operate the telegraph in 1851, and in 1852 it was complained of another that he "had not learnt to work the telegraph, or at all events paid no attention to it".

This railway, like the others, continued to operate with the older forms of signals until increased literacy made the use of the so-called "speaking" telegraphs possible – or until the development of other telegraphs, such as the one in use between Norwich and Yarmouth, made it possible for signalmen to communicate their intentions by one movement of a handle. The single-stroke bell system, devised by Charles Vincent Walker (1812–1882) and first applied on the South Eastern Railway in 1851, went some way towards solving this problem, since it made communication possible by a code of bell strokes.

For the most part, however, railways used the simplest forms of signalling that the nature of their traffic would allow. Until 1852 the North Eastern Railway made use of revolving disc signals mounted on short posts, and it was not until then that the semaphore signal was first installed on this railway. For a long time the Great Western relied on its disc and crossbar signals. In this design the disc was mounted above the bar and at right angles to it, so that when, say, the bar was displayed the disc would be edge-on and invisible to drivers. This was the "line blocked" signal: "line clear" was shown by a reversal of these positions. To prevent the wind affecting signals both the bar and disc were perforated, a precaution that was made especially necessary by the great size of these appliances. Some posts were between forty and sixty feet high, the disc was three or four feet in diameter, and the bar was eight feet long and one foot three inches wide. The size and height of these signals widely recommended them. Another advantage was that they gave a *positive* "line clear" signal. The earlier revolving boards, and the discs of the North Eastern, when turned edge-on to the drivers seemed to signal not "line clear" so much as a mere absence of danger. Despite the advantages of the disc and crossbar, however, the signals were difficult to group in busy sections and drivers felt an additional need for a signal which would give them a clearer indication of the state of the line ahead.

What was needed was a three-position, or three-aspect, signal – one which would signal "clear" and "danger" and also "caution". Brunel produced an early three-aspect signal for the Great Western, a flag signal which became known as a "fantail" or "kite". Two cloth shutters, one red and the other green, were hung from a hooped rail and signalled "clear" when both shutters were drawn up to the post, "caution" when the green shutter dropped, and "danger" when the red shutter was exposed. The experiment with "fantails" did not last very long, however, because it was found the wind quickly reduced shutters to rags and made their efficient operation impossible. A compromise was reached by attaching independently operated arrow-shaped caution boards to the existing disc and crossbar signals, so that "caution" could be signalled if necessary on the display of the "clear" disc. Disc and crossbar signals remained in general use on this railway until November, 1869, when the Great Western ordered them to be replaced by the slotted-post semaphore signals which previously (since 1863) had been confined to their West Midlands District and the lines North of Prestfield Junction at Wolverhampton.

Before it became the practice to mount fishtail "distant" semaphore signals in the rear of "home" (or "stop") semaphores, in order that the state of the latter might be reproduced by the former, which thereby served as "caution" signals, most semaphores were operated on a three-aspect system. The arm in a horizontal position signified "stop", depressed at an angle of 45 degrees it signalled "caution", and when it was dropped out of sight (the "normal" position), usually into a slot in the signal post, it signalled "clear". This method of semaphore signalling remained in general favour until 1876. On January 21st of that year a double collision occurred on the Great Northern Railway at Abbotts Ripton through the failure of signals whose slotted-posts had become choked with snow. After this the three-aspect signal in a slotted-post began to disappear. . . .

On Friday, January 21st, 1876, a coal train composed of thirty-three vehicles left a station just north of Peterborough for London. The rain which had been falling most of the day had changed to sleet and snow, but despite these conditions trains on the line were running pretty well to time. The coal train ran about seven miles to Holme, and there the signalman attempted to stop it in order that it might shunt and allow a following Scottish express to pass. The signalman had moved his lever to set his semaphore to danger, but was amazed to see the mineral train run through. The driver of the train said subsequently that he had seen no danger signal. The Holme signalman, on seeing the train pass against his signals, as he thought, immediately telegraphed Abbotts Ripton, the next box where the train could shunt. Here also the semaphores failed to work, though the signalman succeeded in stopping the train with a hand lamp. As the express was by now overdue the driver of the coal train was ordered to shunt immediately and the signalman set his home and distant levers to danger against the express whilst this was going on. But snow and sleet had again choked the semaphore slots, and the last four trucks of the coal train were still foul of the running line when the express bore down on them at about fifty miles an hour. Rescue work was started immediately and another engine was dispatched along the line to warn oncoming traffic of the obstruction and to lay detonators. An approaching down passenger train received a warning from this engine when it was only 800 yards from the wreckage. Handbrakes were applied immediately (no continuous brakes were fitted) but the momentum of the train could not be arrested. Firing off the detonators on the greasy rails, on a down grade of 1 in 200, it ploughed into the previous wreck at 15 m.p.h. In this disaster thirteen people lost their lives and over fifty were injured. Among the dead was the eldest son of Dion Boucicault, the actor and dramatist. Another distinguished passenger, the

Russian Ambassador, was rescued without hurt, as were three directors of the railway.

After this accident the danger of working with slotted-post semaphores in conditions of snow and ice was readily appreciated. In September of the next year Edward French introduced his centrally-balanced semaphore arm – the "somersault" semaphore – and this type of signal was installed on the Great Northern as well as on some other railways – among them the Taff Vale, the Rhymney and Barry, the Lancashire, Derbyshire and East Coast, and the Belfast and Northern Counties Railway.

The somersault signal, however, while it gave a very clear indication, was not popular. It was expensive both to install and maintain, and it gradually gave way before subsequent standardization which brought semaphores closer to the design we know today.

The accident at Abbotts Ripton had effects on signalling which were more far-reaching than the introduction of the somersault signal. As a result of a Board of Trade recommendation after the collision it became accepted practice to counterweight signal arms so that they would automatically swing to the "on" position if anything went wrong with their control wires. This accident, moreover, started a change in the normal position of semaphore arms: previously signals had stood at "clear" when normal. After Abbotts Ripton "danger" gradually superseded as a normal position. . . .

During the 1850s an increasing number of companies began to operate their stretches of single line on the block or space interval system with telegraphs. The difficulty of operating a railway efficiently without some such equipment had long been realized and may perhaps best be illustrated by an incident which occurred on the Newcastle and Carlisle Railway in the late 1830s. The locomotive *Hercules* broke an axle near Milton and blocked the down line, forcing the railway the next day to operate the up line as a single-line running road in both directions. An up train was delayed at Milton while a man was dispatched ten miles along the line to warn an oncoming train from Carlisle to cross over to the down line in order to let the up train pass. But the messenger and the signalman at Milton were both playing for safety, and though the trains finally occupied different lines, they stood for three hours, ten miles apart, while the confusion was being sorted out.

A considerable number of inventions in the 1850s made it possible for the railways to operate block systems efficiently with their existing staffs. One man who was typical of the signal engineers of the period was Edward Tyer (1830–1912), who in 1851 first made considerable improvements in the design of existing telegraph instruments – principally by reducing the number of wires and batteries required. On January 22nd, 1852, Tyer, who was then only 22 years old, took out his first patent for a block telegraph instrument which, by means of a treadle rail, allowed trains to signal their approach automatically to a signalman into whose section the train was passing. Similarly, a "line clear" indication could be given by the same means to a rear signalman whose section the train was leaving. This invention not only made it possible for trains to give their own warning to signalmen, but also made it possible for the latter to send a signal to the engine driver in his cab whether to proceed or stop. This apparatus was first installed on the Brighton Railway and on some sections of the South Eastern Railway. In later years Napoleon III showed considerable interest in Tyer's invention, and caused an indicator based on its principles to be erected in his private saloon.

The improvements in safe railway working in the second half of the last century were made possible by a number of inventors who were undoubtedly encouraged by the growth of public and official interest in signalling and safety systems. Edward Tyer continued his work of the 1850s up to as late as 1910. In November, 1861, he patented an alphabetical telegraph (the Step-by-Step telegraph) which improved his previous arrangements for interchanging signals between two stations by the concurrence and manipulation of both signalmen involved. In 1865 Tyer brought out yet further improvements to this telegraph and also produced apparatus which made it possible for the guard of a train which had broken down (in a tunnel, say) to signal the fact to the stations on each side of him. This patent also covered apparatus designed for the last vehicle of a train which would signal automatically to a station in the rear that all vehicles composing the train had cleared a section, tunnel or junction. This was an important contribution to safety, since the block system, while otherwise nearly foolproof, could fail when a train became divided and left a vehicle or a number of vehicles in a section. . . .

Another important aspect of signalling which was covered by [an 1869] patent was the electric interlocking of signals. A signalman who was "passing on" a train had an instrument in his box which repeated the condition of the signals in the section in advance, into which he was sending the train. Thus he could be sure that the signals for the train had been set ahead in the proper positions. He could not be sure, however, that the advance signalman would not alter the aspect of the signals after the train had passed his box, when it would be too late for him to do anything to prevent disaster. Tyer's patent of 1869 made it possible for the signalman, on seeing from his indicator that the distant signals were properly set, to lock them so that the signalman who otherwise controlled them could not alter their aspect until the train was safely passed into the (third) section beyond. Also, of course, a signalman could lock the signals of a box in the rear of his section, so as to assure himself that they could not be set to "clear" and so endanger from behind a train running through his section. . . .

Tyer produced a great number of other instruments accessory to the main purpose of controlling traffic by block telegraph. Among them [was] a bay indicator which allowed a signalman at a terminus where a single main line diverged into several bays or platforms to warn a distant station which bay it was necessary for an approaching train to take. Another apparatus was Tyer's train starter, which allowed a platform inspector to signal electrically to the main signal box when a particular train was ready to leave and could be signalled out as soon as the line was ready for it.

No less than twenty British railway companies were using Tyer's apparatus in the 1870s, some of them having used the equipment for nearly twenty years. Two railways in France were operated by Tyer's methods, one in Russia, and one in India.

The success of his instruments did not mean, however, that Tyer had the field of railway signalling all to himself. Other inventors were producing work of equal importance.

Charles Ernest Spagnoletti (1832–1915) was appointed Telegraph Superintendent to the Great Western in 1855 when he was only twenty-three years old. It was he who produced for block telegraph instruments the disc indicator which was first used on the Metropolitan Railway in 1862 and which was introduced to the Great Western system, where it is still in use, in 1864 and 1865. . . . He experimented with electrically-operated signals and also tried out in 1875, at Queen's Road and Praed Street stations on the Inner Circle, an early device for operating semaphore signals by electricity instead of by hand. He was an advocate of electric as opposed to mechanical locking on signal and point lever frames, and successfully produced an electric interlocking system between block instruments and levers which was put into general use on the Metropolitan Railway. To the general public he may yet prove to be a famous figure – for in 1878 Sir William Preece recorded Spagnoletti's vocal rendering of *God save the Queen* on an early Edison phonograph. The idea was to preserve the records and have them played again in 1978.

W. H. Preece was himself an important figure in railway signalling at this time. It was he who suggested in 1862 that the difficulty some signalmen had in understanding needle indicators on block telegraphs might well be overcome if the indicators were made to resemble the familiar semaphore arms, both in appearance and operation. Edward Tyer and Charles Vincent Walker both took up this idea; Tyer in the form Preece had suggested, and Walker

L*

as an adjunct to his bell system. It is said, however, that Walker had used some such indicator as early as 1854. One of Preece's most outstanding contributions to railway safety was a "check" apparatus which he incorporated into the signalling bell of block telegraph instruments. By means of this apparatus a signalman was able to know not only that his bell signal had been received at a distant box, but that it had been understood and acted upon. In circuit with the operator's bell-key was a make-and-break device on the arms of the distant electric block indicator, and the movement of the distant signals in response to a bell call was repeated on an indicator on the sender's bell-key.

John Imray, W. R. Sykes, John Saxby, Edwin Clark and others, all made important contributions and many of their inventions, particularly those of Saxby and Sykes, are in use to this day. [Sykes] perhaps made his greatest contributions to safety in his early work on automatic and power signalling. John Saxby followed his pioneer interlocking work at the Bricklayer's Arms Junction (1856) with other successes in the manual signalling field. In 1867 he brought out his catch handle lock for signal and point levers. This lock actuated lever locking gear whenever the intention of the signalman to move the lever into a conflicting relationship with other levers was expressed by the grasping of the lever release catch. The prototype of the lever frame locking system in use to-day was not brought out until 1870, when Messrs. J. J., J. J. F. and W. A. Stevens patented their system of tappet interlocking – which involved longitudinally sliding bolts engaging in notches in the bars projecting from levers. To move a lever it was necessary to force its locking bolt sideways where it would engage the notches of conflicting levers, locking them till the first lever was replaced and would allow the bolt to travel back and re-engage its own notches.

In 1875 James Edward Annett devised a key and lock for little-used siding connections. When the siding was not in use its point lever was locked by a key kept separately on the locking frame of the rear box. In the event of the key being withdrawn, to unlock the siding points for traffic, the signals of the main running lines affected by traffic on the siding became automatically locked to danger. This was an economical arrangement which did away with the necessity for signals at the sidings.

In addition to the great amount of inventive genius that was dedicated to what might be called the "first principles" of signalling, there were in the 1870s and thereabouts a number of other inventions whose importance at the time must not be underestimated simply because modern practice has far outstripped their early beginnings. There was, for instance, the signal light which relit itself if for some reason it became extinguished. The lamp was carried in the centre of a revolving drum which was turned back against a spring and held in position by clips. The clips gripped the drum when the heat of the lamp expanded the metal. If the lamp went out the drum was released and was spun round by the spring, causing matches fixed to it to burn against a striking surface and relight the lamp. There was also an early lamp "repeater" which gave an electrical warning if the lamp went out. Here the principle was the same as in the revolving lamp, the contraction of metal when the lamp cooled causing an electrical bell circuit to be completed.

The dangers attendant upon operating traffic in both directions on a single line (as well as the dangers arising from unpunctuality) were well brought out by an accident which occurred on September 10th, 1874, on the Great Eastern Railway, which was then operating the Norwich to Yarmouth line. Twenty-five were killed and forty-four injured when the 5 p.m. London to Yarmouth express met the 8.40 p.m. mail running in the other direction. The trains were scheduled to pass at Brundall, but as the express was late the Inspector at Thorpe issued orders for Brundall to send the mail on. After giving these instructions to his signal clerk he saw the London express approaching and returned to countermand his order. It was not until the express left Thorpe for Brundall that the clerk remembered to cancel his previous signal to the latter place. But by then the mail was on its way and, in the words of a local contemporary, "a railway accident of most fearful character took place . . . which has thrown the whole neighbourhood into consternation".

The mode of working this single line had not altered since the route was opened thirty years before. It was the first accident on this railway, and by an ironic chance it occurred when a double track had just been laid and was awaiting Board of Trade approval before being opened. In the matter of unpunctuality, which was one of the prime causes of the accident, the Board of Trade noted in its report that during 1874 the London express had been on time on only seven occasions, and the Yarmouth mail on only four.

The simplest way, in theory, to work a single line is to adhere strictly to a time-table. But, as the Thorpe collision shows, theory did not always work out in practice. Some railways used pilotmen whose duty was personally to conduct trains over stretches of single line, but for the most part the pilot system was superseded by the staff system. In the latter case a single baton of authority was kept at one of the stations at each end of a single line, and no single line section could be entered by a train or engine unless the driver was in possession of the baton or staff. This was perfectly workable, of course, so long as trains ran in both directions alternately, but when trains were required to follow one another in the same direction there was often great delay while someone was dispatched to a distant station to pick up the baton left there by the last train. The rigidity of the staff system was modified by a ticket system, which allowed a station master to dispatch trains along a single line section, *so long as he held the staff at his station,* by giving the drivers written permission. No driver, however, could enter a single line section with a ticket unless he first saw for himself that the staff was at the station he was about to leave. In some cases the staff was composed of two or three unscrewable sections. The driver of the first train running over a single line from station *A* to station *B* would be shown the whole staff and would then be given a part of it as his authority. Similarly, the driver of the second train in the same direction would be shown the staff and given another portion of it. No conflicting train could be dispatched by the stationmaster at *B* until the whole staff was in his possession.

Edward Tyer felt a deep concern in the matter of safety on single lines, and it is perhaps for his work after the wreck of 1874 that he will be best remembered. In March, 1878, he patented his tablet system. The patent was for two electrically interlocked slot-machine instruments, to be installed one at each end of a single line stretch. The machines contained tablets or tokens, which in themselves constituted permission to proceed when a driver was given one into his possession. Each machine contained a number of tablets, but as soon as a tablet was removed from one machine, the issuing machine, as well as its counterpart at the next station, was automatically locked and no further tablets could be withdrawn from either until the tablet which had been issued was replaced in one or other of them. For sections where "permissive" working was desirable, Tyer produced modified apparatus so that, if a signalman wanted to send another train into the single stretch to follow one which had gone before, he could, by obtaining the concurrence of the signalman at the other end, open his own machine and extract another tablet. But this meant that the machine at the other end would not become unlocked for the issue of a tablet until *two* tablets were placed in it. Tyer brought out a number of improvements to the design and operation of these machines, providing for the interlocking of points and signals with his apparatus, and later producing machines from which up to forty-eight tablets could be withdrawn. This improvement allowed "permissive" working over long stretches of line where there would be considerable delay if following trains had to wait until those preceding them had reached the end of a section. For lines where there was heavy traffic in both directions Tyer produced modified tablet-crossing apparatus to enable two or more trains to pass at an intermediate crossing loop.

When fast running was required and there was danger to train crews in exchanging tokens by hand, automatic exchangers were installed so that tablets could be picked up from lineside standards on arms swung out from the engine. Before this, tokens used to be placed in a bag with a large hooped leather handle and collected by engine firemen on the forearm. Firemen used to boast of the high speeds at which they were accustomed to do this, but the danger involved must have been considerable – especially when one reads of a fireman who missed the token bag altogether and caught instead the leather pipe of a water tower which hauled him off his engine. In the colonies, where a large proportion of track consisted of single lines, Tyer's "permissive" apparatus was of immense benefit and importance. During the Boer War the military authorities especially commended it since it allowed them to send large numbers of troop trains up to the fighting without having to wait for each separate train to clear the line before another was dispatched.

from DANGER AHEAD *1951*

The First Fatality

LIVERPOOL, half-past 8 o'clock, Wednesday night.

I have just returned from our journey along the rail-road from
Liverpool to Manchester, and back again; and although I had
intended to give you some faint description of this astounding
work of art, of the crowds which lined almost every inch of our
road, of the flags and banners, and booths and scaffoldings, and
gorgeous tents, which have enlivened even the dullest parts of our
journey, I am obliged, on account of the lateness of the hour, to
defer that description as comparatively uninteresting, owing to the
fatal accident that has befallen Mr Huskisson. . . .

Mr Huskisson was discoursing with Mr Joseph Sandars, one of
the principal originators and promoters of this railroad, and was
congratulating that gentleman as one of the happiest men in the
world, in having seen a work of such importance and magnitude
happily brought to a conclusion under his auspices, when he was
called away to speak with some other gentlemen, who were
anxious to hear his opinion on some of the details of the road.
Before he left Mr Sandars, he said to that gentleman, "Well, I
must go and shake hands with the Duke [of Wellington] on this
day at any rate." The gentlemen who had called him away
detained him some time, and whilst he was standing with them,
the *Rocket* engine, which, like the *Phoenix* had to pass the Duke's
car, to take up its station at the watering place, came slowly up,
and as the engineer had been for some time checking its velocity,
so silently that it was almost upon the group before they observed
it. In the hurry of the moment all attempted to get out of the way.
Mr Holmes M.P. who was standing by the side of Mr Huskisson,
desired the gentlemen not to stir, but to cling close by the side of
their own car – most excellent advice, had it been followed – for as
no engine can move off the rail, any person who stands clear of it,
is perfectly safe from danger. Unfortunately, in the hurry and
agitation of the moment, Mr Huskisson did not pursue this
advice. He hesitated, staggered a little as if not knowing what to
do, then attempted to run forward, found it impossible to get off
the road, on account of an excavation of some 14 or 15 feet depth
being on that side of it on which he was, attempted again to get

334

into the car, was hit by a motion of the door as he was mounting a step, and was thrown down directly in the path of the *Rocket,* as that engine came opposite to the Duke's car. He contrived to move himself a little out of its path before it came in contact with him, otherwise it must have gone directly over his head and breast. As it was, the wheel went over his left thigh, squeezing it almost to a jelly, broke the leg, it is said, in two places, laid the muscles bare from the ankle nearly to the hip, and tore out a large piece of flesh as it left him. Mrs Huskisson, who, along with several other ladies, witnessed the accident, uttered a shriek of agony, which none who heard will ever forget. As soon as Mr Huskisson could be raised from the ground, he asked where Mrs Huskisson was, and in the most cool and collected manner gave such directions as he thought best fitted for the situation in which he was placed. Mrs Huskisson was immediately by his side to attend to his wishes, but was soon obliged to give way to Dr Brandreth, who applied a tourniquet to stop the dreadful effusion of blood under which Mr Huskisson was suffering. In a few minutes afterwards Mr Huskisson fainted away, and in that condition was removed, as carefully as circumstances would allow, into the car, in which the band of music preceding the Duke's car had been placed. The musicians were immediately turned out of it, and Mrs Huskisson, Mr Wainewright (Mr Huskisson's private secretary), and several other of Mr Huskisson's friends took their places. The Duke's car was detached from the *Northumbrian* engine and fastened laterally to the two engines *Phoenix* and *North Star.* The *Northumbrian* engine then having no other weight to draw but the car which had carried the band, and was now occupied by Mr Huskisson and his party, proceeded at a rapid rate to Manchester to procure medical assistance. As it passed by our car Mr Huskisson was laid at the bottom of it, pale and ghostly as death, and his wife was hanging over him in an agony of tears.

from THE TIMES, *Friday, 17 September 1830*

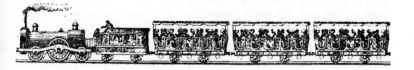

Dickens in Danger

CHARLES DICKENS

Gad's Hill Place, Higham by Rochester, Kent.
Tuesday, Thirteenth June, 1865.

MY DEAR MITTON,

I should have written to you yesterday or the day before, if I had been quite up to writing.

I was in the only carriage that did not go over into the stream. It was caught upon the turn by some of the ruin of the bridge, and hung suspended and balanced in an apparently impossible manner. Two ladies were my fellow-passengers, an old one and a young one. This is exactly what passed. You may judge from it the precise length of the suspense. Suddenly we were off the rail, and beating the ground as the car of a half-emptied balloon might. The old lady cried out "My God!" and the young one screamed. I caught hold of them both (the old lady sat opposite and the young one on my left) and said: "We can't help ourselves, but we can be quiet and composed. Pray don't cry out." The old lady immediately answered: "Thank you. Rely upon me. Upon my soul I will be quiet." We were then all tilted down together in a corner of the carriage, and stopped. I said to them thereupon, "You may be sure nothing worse can happen. Our danger *must* be over. Will you remain here without stirring, while I get out of the window?" They both answered quite collectedly "Yes" and I got out without the least notion what had happened.

Fortunately I got out with great caution and stood upon the step. Looking down I saw the bridge gone, and nothing below me but the line of rail. Some people in the two other compartments were madly trying to plunge out of the window, and had no idea that there was an open swampy field fifteen feet down below them, and nothing else! The two guards (one with his face cut) were running up and down on the down side of the bridge (which was not torn up) quite wildly. I called out to them: "Look at me. Do stop an instant and look at me, and tell me whether you don't know me." One of them answered, "We know you very well, Mr

336

Dickens." "Then," I said, "my good fellow, for God's sake give me your key, and send one of those labourers here, and I'll empty this carriage." We did it quite safely, by means of a plank or two, and when it was done I saw all the rest of the train, except the two baggage vans, down in the stream. I got into the carriage again for my brandy flask, took off my travelling hat for a basin, climbed down the brickwork, and filled my hat with water.

Suddenly I came upon a staggering man covered with blood (I think he must have been flung clean out of his carriage), with such a frightful cut across the skull that I couldn't bear to look at him. I poured some water over his face and gave him some drink, then gave him some brandy, and laid him down on the grass, and he said: "I am gone," and died afterwards. Then I stumbled over a lady lying on her back against a little pollard-tree, with the blood streaming over her face (which was lead colour) in a number of distinct little streams from the head. I asked her if she could swallow a little brandy and she just nodded, and I gave her some and left her for somebody else. The next time I passed her she was dead. Then a man, examined at the inquest yesterday (who evidently had not the least remembrance of what really passed), came running up to me and implored me to help him find his wife, who was afterwards found dead. No imagination can conceive the ruin of the carriages, or the extraordinary weights under which the people were lying, or the complications into which they were twisted up among iron and wood, and mud and water.

I don't want to be examined at the inquest and I don't want to write about it. I could do no good either way, and I could only seem to speak about myself, which of course I would rather not do. I am keeping very quiet here. I have a – I don't know what to call it – constitutional (I suppose) presence of mind, and was not in the least fluttered at the time. I instantly remembered that I had the MS. of a number with me and clambered back into the carriage for it. But in writing these scanty words of recollection I feel the shake and am obliged to stop.

Ever faithfully,

CHARLES DICKENS

from LETTERS OF CHARLES DICKENS 1893 edn.

Abergele, 1868

JOHN PENDLETON

The disaster at Abergele [on August 20] stands out conspicuously in English railway history, not only because of its extent, but because of the piteous helplessness of its victims. . . . The Irish limited mail started from Euston at a quarter past seven o'clock in the morning, as it had done with almost invariable punctuality for eight years. The run to Chester was safely accomplished, and the train, after attaining some local carriages, started out on the North Wales track on its eighty-five mile run to Holyhead. Near Abergele the mail had got into full swing, and was making high speed on what the driver believed was a clear track, when it crashed into some trucks. A man sitting on a rail by the line side, and smoking his pipe reflectively, saw the waggons come down the incline. They were oil-laden and should have been shunted at Llandulas, but the siding would not take the entire goods train. The driver and brakesmen knew the time the mail was due, and, aware that they had not the regulation ten minutes for making up the train aright, in the hurry of the operation they gave too much speed to the kick-off trucks, and these, knocking against the paraffin-laden waggons, impelled them on to the main line. Arthur Thompson, the driver of the mail, did not notice the obstruction till his train was almost on it. He had just time to give a warning signal, shout to his mate, and leap off the footplate, when the crash came. A hiss of steam, a cloud of smoke, and a loud noise heralded the disaster. The mail engine, dashing into the trucks, broke many of the oil barrels in pieces, and drove on through the wreckage till it was disabled, and three carriages were thrown across the line. Seventeen hundred gallons of paraffin were liberated by the force of the collision, and the fore part of the train, as by a lightning flash, was wrapped in flame.

The train consisted of thirteen carriages. Next to the front guard's van was a composite carriage, then two first-class carriages, a second-class carriage, the travelling post office, the mail tender, a parcel van, a first-class carriage, three composite carriages, and a guard's van in the rear. The guard's van, next the engine and all the carriages down to the post office were consumed. So quick and intense was the heat that scarcely a cry was heard, or a struggle noticed, in the doomed carriages, about which the fire leapt. No fewer than thirty-three persons lost their lives; and of these, twenty-eight were burned to death, some of the remains being so thoroughly charred that it was impossible to identify them. Lord and Lady Farnham were among the victims; but the Duchess of Abercorn, who, with her family, occupied a carriage near the end of the train, escaped injury.

One passenger, who crept out of the carriage window after the collision, said he saw a sight never to be forgotten. With the violence of the concussion some of the petroleum barrels had been thrown on the embankment, and others rolled under the carriages, but all exploded together. The engine, the coaches, and the luggage van were enveloped in fire. When a portion of the train had been pushed away from the burning mass, there were among the broken timbers and the hot ironwork smoking skeletons, all that was left of men, and women, and children, and they moved horribly along with the wreck.

A curious story was told by Catherine Dickens, a platelayer's wife. When the accident occurred she ran on the line from her cottage, and, going to one of the carriages towards which the fire was leaping, urged a lady to throw her child out, and she held up her frock to catch the little one; but the mother to whom she pleaded seemed indifferent, and declined her help. The story was discredited, though the platelayers' wife adhered to her tale, and said the carriage handle was so hot when she first sought the child's safety that she instantly relinquished her grasp.

The heat around the train was unbearable, the vapour from the unconsumed oil suffocating, and the flame of the paraffin terrible in its devastation. An expert said the awful stillness which characterized the occupants of the leading carriages was due to the shock caused by the sudden exposure of the entire body to fire. No one, at all events in the fore part of the train, seems to have made any very determined attempt to escape. The passengers, as they sat at ease, perhaps admiring the landscape, or looking out across the pebbly beach to the sea, or reading, or sewing, or anticipating, in thought and chat, a pleasant voyage across the Irish Channel, gave one startled cry, and then, by anaesthesia or asphyxia, were deprived of sensation. The salvage taken from the wreckage was remarkable. In the heap of human dust, diamonds, rubies, opals, and emeralds were found. The furnace fire had robbed them of their settings, of their gold and filigree; but they sparkled, and glittered, and gleamed impervious to the heat amid their ghastly surroundings. Twenty-four watches were picked out of the ashes; and strewn about the line were the remnants of bracelets, brooches, rings, smelling-bottles, scissors, and many half-calcined ornaments.

The inquiry concerning the disaster lasted many days. The jury found that most of the victims died from suffocation before the fire touched them; they suggested a drastic reform in shunting operations; they censured the Llandulas stationmaster, and found the brakesmen in charge of the goods waggons guilty of man-slaughter – but at the assizes these men were acquitted. Colonel Rich, in his report of the disaster, pointed out the unwisdom of locking the carriage doors, strongly condemned passengers for their thoughtlessness in treating railway officials, and, making sarcastic reference to the management of the line, said:

"I fear that it is only too true that the rules printed and issued by railway companies to their servants, and which are generally very good, are made principally with the object of being pro-duced when accidents happen from the breach of them, and that the companies allow many of them to be broken daily, without taking the slightest notice of the disobedience."

The accident caused a profound sensation throughout the country, and comment upon it was continually revived, particu-larly when the mail engine-driver died from his injuries, and when the brakesmen were put on their trial. The railway company revised their instructions, and set about making better siding accommodation; but the travelling public were not easily pacified. The taunt was thrown out that the directors ought to make a siding all the way from Chester to Bangor, and there was an emphatic demand that passenger and goods trains should run on different sets of metals, "that the two services should be separate, and conducted on lines of their own".

The passenger, quitting the bustle and noise of the enlarged station at Chester, on his leisurely way by the sand-banked Dee,

and quaint Flint, and thriving Rhyl, to some more remote Welsh
watering-place, seldom thinks as he goes along the line that nurses
the shore, looking out of the carriage window at the pastoral and
wooded beauty of Abergele, that beyond the shadowed roadway,

in the graveyard, by the village, lie the remains of those who on
this memorable day had their life's journey so abruptly checked.
In the summer of 1893 the author, visiting Abergele, found that
the railway accident of a quarter of a century ago was the talk of
the village still. The disaster is the great historic event of the
locality. It is a grim calendar in the records of the place. This
villager died about a year before the railway smash; that woman
was married three years after it. Nearly everything is reckoned
from the day the Irish mail was wrecked and partially destroyed by
fire. "Would you like to see the grave, sir?" said the old verger,
who was full of reminiscences of the dread time. It was on the far
side of the churchyard, near the tomb of the men who were cast
ashore after the burning of the emigrant ship *Ocean Monarch* in the
bay in 1848. A large granite monument marks the spot where the
victims of the railway disaster are buried, and it bears an inscription "sacred to the memory" of the thirty-three persons who
perished.

from OUR RAILWAYS *1894*

Thorpe, 1874

L. T. C. ROLT

In the events at Thorpe station, Norwich, on September 10th, 1874, which culminated in the worst head-on collision in the history of British railways there is no light relief. A mundane railway platform became, for sixteen critical minutes, a stage for high tragedy in which no dramatic ingredient was lacking. Unknown to the actors, we, their audience, can watch error upon trivial error leading in remorseless sequence to their terrible conclusion. And only when it is too late, when disaster becomes inevitable, does there come the sudden overwhelming realization of guilt and error.

Before beginning the action the stage must be set. The single line of the Great Eastern Railway between Norwich and Yarmouth was one of the first in the country to be controlled by electric telegraph. The installation of five-needle Cooke and Wheatstone instruments on the Norfolk Railway . . . in 1848 was considered at the time to be a model of its kind. For twenty-six years it had controlled the traffic over the line without a single mishap. Now, the Great Eastern Company proposed to double the line and by the irony of fate a second set of metals had already been laid between Thorpe and the East Norfolk Junction at Whittingham, the very section upon which the collision occurred, and was only awaiting inspection and approval by the Board of Trade. The movement of trains through this section was controlled by the telegraph instruments at Thorpe and at Brundall, the next station east of Norwich. At Brundall the stationmaster worked the telegraph himself. At Thorpe the instruments were worked by a telegraph clerk acting under the instruction of the station inspector. If late running made it necessary to alter the normal crossing arrangements, the procedure at Thorpe was as follows. The telegraph office had a window with a sliding wicket, like a booking office, which faced the platform. At this window was kept a message pad for the use of the station inspector. The inspector would write his instruction on the pad, sign it, and hand it to the telegraph clerk who would then transmit it to Brundall exactly as

written with the signature as proof of its authority. Brundall
would then acknowledge it in the same form and both the message
sent and the reply received would be entered by the clerk in a
record book. At the same time the station inspector would hand
a signed instruction to the driver of the train concerned.

The 5 p.m. express from Liverpool Street to Yarmouth was
normally booked to cross the 8.40 p.m. up Mail train at Brundall
but on this occasion the express was running late. The drama
began at 9.16 when Cooper, the night inspector, who had just
come on duty, went to the stationmaster's office as usual to
receive his orders for the night.

"What about having the Mail up, sir?" Cooper asked. Sproule,
the stationmaster, consulted his watch and inquired what time the
Mail was due to arrive at Brundall. "Nine-twenty-five," Cooper
told him. "We will not have the Mail up," Sproule replied,
"certainly not." "You know, sir," Cooper reminded him, "there is
an order allowing us to detain the 9.10 down as late as 9.35." To
this the stationmaster made an ambiguous reply. "All right," he
said, "we will soon get her off." Now it seems clear that Sproule's
"All right" was delivered in a tone of impatient dismissal and that
by "her" he was referring to the express and not to the Mail. But
evidently Cooper thought that Sproule had conceded his point.
He left the office, walked straight to the telegraph office, tapped
on the wicket and said to the young clerk, Robson, "Tell Brundall
to send the Mail on to Norwich." Robson wrote the message down
on the pad but Cooper had hurried away without stopping to
sign it. The time was then 9.22.

One minute later the express drew in to the down platform
drawn by the four-coupled mixed traffic engine No. 218. She was
met by the day inspector, Parker, who, thinking the train might
arrive punctually, had already made out an order authorizing her
driver to proceed. He was standing by the engine when Cooper
came up and he asked him whether he had arranged for the Mail
to come on. Inexplicably, Cooper answered, "No, certainly not;
let us get the train away as soon as possible." Parker then handed
the order to the driver and told him to proceed to Brundall. Events
now moved swiftly. Parker gave the express the "right away" at
9.30 and from his office window the stationmaster watched it pull
away. It had scarcely cleared the platform when Edward Trew, an

inspector of railway police, wishing to speak to the telegraph clerk upon some other business, knocked on the office wicket. Robson immediately opened it and asked where the express was.

"She has just left," Trew replied. "What, left the yard?" asked Robson. He seemed about to make some exclamation when Cooper hurried up. "You haven't ordered the Mail up, have you?" he asked. "You told me to order her up," Robson retorted. The clerk at once went to his instrument and signalled "Stop Mail" to Brundall. Immediately the deadly reply came back: "Mail left." He returned to the wicket, put the pad with its fatal message in front of Cooper and asked him to sign it. "No," cried the wretched man, "No. I never gave you that message. I did not, I did not." Robson's reply was unanswerable. "Why, if you did not, have you now come back to cancel it?" At this moment Hayden, the ticket collector came up. "What's the matter?" he asked, and Cooper answered, "The Mail is coming up." "Good God," said Hayden, "this is a frightful thing." The stationmaster, overhearing the raised voices and the word "Mail", guessed that something was wrong and rushed out of his office. He described the scene at the inquiry. "What about the Mail?" he asked. Cooper was standing against the window with his back to him as he said this. When he turned towards him his face was as white as chalk; "he had the appearance," said the stationmaster, "of a man paralysed." "I have ordered the Mail up," he answered. Both men knew very well what these words meant. They meant that on this dark and rainy autumn night with visibility down to 300 yards Cooper had sent two trains to certain destruction. No power on earth could save them now. Sproule was so unstrung that he said he scarcely knew what happened after this. He felt so deeply for Cooper that he could hardly speak, but he remembered suspending him and telling Hayden to take his place.

While this little stricken group of men stood helplessly upon the platform at Norwich in the overwhelming knowledge of what they had done, the tragedy was being played out in the blackness beyond the station lights where the express and the Mail were speeding towards each other. They met between the Yare Bridge and the East Norfolk Junction, and the noise of their collision, said those who heard it, was like a great clap of thunder. Of the last few terrible moments of that drama there was no witness for both engine crews perished. But on the engine of the up Mail, the 7-foot single No. 54, they found the regulator shut and the tender brake screwed hard down. In all, twenty-five lives were lost in the Thorpe disaster and seventy-three were injured.

from RED FOR DANGER *1955*

Penistone, 1884

JOHN PENDLETON

The disaster on the Manchester, Sheffield and Lincolnshire Railway at the Bullhouse curve, near Penistone, on July 16 almost rivalled the Abergele catastrophe in the number killed and the damage done to rolling stock; but the accident fortunately had not the dread accompaniment of fire. Sam Cawood, who had driven the newspaper train for years, got on the footplate of his engine at London Road Station, Manchester, for the return journey to town, and went out with the express, which was crowded with passengers, at half-past twelve o'clock, noon. He ran without mishap, at the rate of nearly fifty miles an hour, till he had passed Hazlehead, and then the crank axle of the leading wheels of the four-wheeled bogie engine broke. The driver applied the brake with all his might, but the impetus of the train forced the carriages off the line. With the exception of the engine, tender, and a horsebox, all the vehicles were flung from the permanent way. The first and second carriages were hurled down the steep embankment into a field, and the next two coaches were pitched into the country lane and smashed, their occupants being killed or fearfully injured. The other five vehicles were overturned, with their wheels in the air, and the guards in the brake van had remarkable escapes from death.

The broken carriages were heaped in almost inextricable tangle; and out of the wreckage on the embankment and near the bridge nineteen bodies – ten women, six men, and three children – were taken. A passenger cut his way out of a shattered compartment, but many others were so grievously injured that they could do nothing to help themselves, and their cries and moans were heartrending. There was some element of romance and superstition in the accident. One traveller was delayed on his way to a wedding party, and the silence that reigned for a moment after the disaster was disturbed by the crowing of a cock that had escaped from the darkness of a hamper in the van, and thought it was morn. No fewer than twenty-four persons were killed instantaneously or died from the effects of the accident, and the number of injured was never accurately known. The Queen expressed her deep sympathy with the relatives of the killed and with the injured; and in every part of the country the wreck of the express was the chief topic of conversation for many days.

There was much inquiry, and from the mass of evidence two simple stories stand out clearly. The signalman said the express passed his box at twenty minutes past one o'clock in the afternoon, and three minutes afterwards the train was a wreck. He had only just time to readjust his signals, when he heard a crash; and looking out of the window, he saw the engine, tender, and horse-box staggering along the line – the rest of the train was down the embankment and over the bridge. The driver's account was even more dramatic. At Manchester he went beneath his engine, examined the crank axle, and was confident it was thoroughly sound. At Bullhouse he noticed something wrong with the motion of the wheels, heard a crack, and felt the locomotive lurch. He put on the brake, but the engine scrambled somehow beyond the bridge. Then, looking back, he exclaimed: "Oh, dear me! wherever is the train?"

The outside web of the right-hand crank of the driving axle had broken, causing the engine partially to leave the rails. The draw hook at the end of the horsebox had snapped, and the remainder of the train had fallen pell-mell down the bank, making havoc and death. The crank axle that caused the mischief had only run fifty thousand miles, one-sixth the ordinary life of an axle, and was made of solid steel; but inside the web was "an invisible flaw, which had matured, by continual vibration, into an absolute fracture". Major Marindin said the accident to the crank was not one that could have been foreseen or prevented, though a powerful continuous brake ought to have so reduced the speed that the consequences would have been far less fatal. He held that not the smallest fault could be found with the servants of the company for the manner in which they had performed their duty; and the jury returned a verdict of accidental death, recommending, however, that some more searching mode of testing axles should be adopted.

from OUR RAILWAYS *1894*

Armagh, 1889

L. T. C. ROLT

After the rear collision at Straffan in 1853 no major disaster occurred in Ireland until June 12th, 1889, when the Armagh collision took place. This was not only Ireland's worst accident but it caused greater loss of life than any accident that had occurred on any British railway up to that time. . . .

The Newry & Armagh line began life as an independent concern which had only been absorbed by the Great Northern in 1879 and it possessed its own station at Armagh. From this terminus the railway climbed almost continuously on gradients of 1 in 75 and 1 in 82 for three miles to Dobbins Bridge Summit. The single line was worked by staff and ticket but not on the absolute block system, trains being despatched at a ten minute time interval, or twenty minutes for a passenger train following a goods. Thomas McGrath, a driver with very little experience of the

Newry road, was sent from Dundalk to Armagh with a four-coupled engine to work the [school] excursion. Knowing the gradients he had to face he was somewhat disconcerted to find himself called upon to haul a train of fifteen vehicles packed with no less than 940 passengers. He sought out John Foster, the Armagh stationmaster, and said that according to his instructions, given to him at Dundalk, his maximum load would be thirteen vehicles. If he was to take more he must have pilot assistance over the bank. "I did not write those instructions for you," Foster replied. "No," said McGrath, "Mr Cowan (the Superintendent) did." To this Foster retorted: "Any driver who comes here doesn't grumble about taking an excursion train with him." "Why didn't you send proper word to Dundalk?" the driver retorted, "then I should have had a proper six-coupled engine with me." With this McGrath turned on his heel and returned in high dudgeon to his footplate. A few moments later Superintendent Cowan's chief clerk, James Elliot, who was in charge of the running of the excursion and proposed to travel on the engine, joined McGrath on the footplate. He had heard about the brush between the driver and the stationmaster and suggested that, in default of a pilot, Patrick Murphy, who was in charge of the regular train which was due to follow the excursion at 10.35 a.m., should provide banking assistance in the rear. But McGrath was still nettled by the stationmaster's remarks. He refused the offer and a few moments later, with steam roaring from the safety valves and his reversing lever in full forward gear, he opened his regulator and put his engine at the bank.

Although the rail was dry and his engine was steaming well, McGrath gradually lost speed on the long gradient. They were within sight of the summit at Dobbins Bridge when the labouring locomotive finally stalled. It was a case of so near and yet so far, for there was 125 lb. of steam on the gauge, only five pounds below the full working pressure, and McGrath knew that it was hopeless to attempt to restart. McGrath and Elliot then debated the question of what was to be done. There were two alternatives. Either they could protect the train in the rear and then wait for Murphy to arrive with the lightly loaded regular train to push them over the summit, or they could divide the train. Although it would have been somewhat irregular practice, the first course would not only have been the simpler and safer but would also have involved less delay to both trains. Yet Elliot decided to divide and McGrath agreed. It was a fatal decision. Elliot called to a porter named William Moorhead who was acting as guard in the front van and asked him how many carriages he thought the siding at Hamilton's Bawn (the first station over the summit) would hold. Moorhead replied that it was already partly filled with wagons but that he thought it should take five. After the leading five had been shunted there the engine could return for the rest of the train. Elliot therefore instructed Moorhead to uncouple between the fifth and sixth carriages.

Now the excursion train was fitted with a vacuum brake of the old "simple" or non-automatic type which worked in the opposite fashion to the automatic brake, the vacuum applying the brake and the admission of air to the train pipe releasing it. This meant that as soon as a flexible brake pipe was disconnected the brakes would cease to function. All the men in charge of the train knew this. Thomas Henry, the rear guard, was wedged in his brake compartment with no less than fifteen passengers when Elliot ran back down the train to tell him what they were about to do. He ordered Henry to screw his handbrake down hard and then to come down and scotch some of the wheels with stones. By giving such an order, Elliot completely disregarded the Company's rule which stated: "With a heavy train the guard must not leave his van until perfectly satisfied that his brake will hold the train securely. . . ." But Henry did as he was bid. Meanwhile Moorhead had placed stones under the wheels of the sixth carriage and now proceeded to uncouple, undoing the screw coupling to its full extent so that he could do so without calling upon McGrath to ease back. No sooner had he lifted the link off the hook, than McGrath did ease back. It was not much, but it was enough. With a lurch and a crunch the coach wheels rode over the stones and the long, crowded train began slowly to move back down the gradient. Panic ensued. Henry leapt back into his crowded van and, urged on by Elliot who was standing on the step, attempted with the assistance of two passengers to get another turn on the handbrake. It was useless. The brake would not hold. The van wheels continued to revolve. Elliot leaped off the step crying, "Oh, my God, we will all be killed", and rushed forward. "My God," he shouted to McGrath, "what did you come back against the carriages for?" McGrath was now setting back on Moorhead's instructions and the latter was vainly trying to re-couple the two portions of the train. Twice he managed to get the link raised ready to drop over the drawhook of the sixth coach; twice at the crucial moment he tripped and fell over some old rails which were lying by the lineside. No one thought of lifting one of these rails and thrusting it through a wheel as a sprag. Instead they stumbled along making futile efforts to stop the runaways by putting more stones from the ballast under the wheels. They slipped aside or were crushed to powder. The runaways rapidly gathered speed and soon outpaced their pursuers. "We went so fast," said Henry, "that we could not see the hedges as we passed." To prevent unauthorized entry, as the Company phrased it, all the compartment doors had been locked before the train left Armagh. Except for those in the van with Henry, not a soul could escape from the train.

While these events were taking place at the top of the bank, Patrick Murphy had left Armagh with the regular train and, with only a horse-box, two vans and three coaches on his drawbar, he was forging up the gradient at a steady thirty miles an hour. They were approaching a point one and half miles from Dobbins Bridge when Murphy's fireman suddenly yelled, "Hold! Hold! Hold!" Rocking down the track towards them at frightful speed came the ten carriages of the excursion. The leading van was empty. Its occupants had already jumped for their lives. As soon as his fireman shouted, Murphy shut off steam and applied the vacuum brake so that at the moment of impact his speed was reduced to five miles an hour. In the terrific collision which ensued the first three vehicles of the excursion were completely destroyed, their shattered, twisted fragments being scattered down the 40-foot embankment, while those behind them piled in crazy confusion, some on the metals and some on the steep embankment sides. The locomotive fell over on to its side but its following train broke away and began to run back towards Armagh in two portions, first the three coaches and two vans and then, some distance behind it, the horse-box and the engine tender. The guard managed to pull up the first portion on his screw brake a quarter of a mile further down the bank and a second violent collision might then have followed but for a lucky chance. As the tender broke away from his engine, Patrick Murphy contrived to cling to the coal plate. Dazed and shocked after his terrible experience, Murphy none the less managed to scramble to his feet and screw down the tender brake. By doing so he stopped the tender and horse-box three carriage lengths short of his train. Eighty lives were lost in this appalling catastrophe, many of the casualties being young children, while the roll of those seriously injured was equally high.

from RED FOR DANGER *1955*

Grantham, 1906

L. T. C. ROLT

No simple solution can suffice to explain the cause of the disaster which occurred at Grantham on September 19th [1906]. Of all the major accidents that have occurred in our railway history it remains the most mysterious. The train involved was the 8.45 p.m. semi-fast mail from King's Cross to Edinburgh which was booked to stop at Peterborough and Grantham. On this occasion it consisted of twelve vehicles, five of them, including two sleeping cars, being twelve-wheeled East Coast Joint Stock. It was usual on this run for engines to be changed at Peterborough, and when the train arrived there No. 276, one of the famous Ivatt "Atlantics", then only two years old, was waiting to work it forward. On the footplate were Driver Fleetwood of Doncaster and Fireman Talbot. Several of the station staff at Peterborough spoke with them before the train arrived and declared afterwards that both men were perfectly sober and in normal health. Fleetwood knew the road intimately. He had had eighteen years driving experience and had been in sole charge of No. 276 since she first came out of the shops. His fireman was a highly competent and intelligent young man who was perfectly capable of taking over the controls from the driver should the need arise. He had served a premium apprenticeship at Doncaster works and was now working under the district locomotive superintendent, firing on various types of locomotive for the purpose of taking notes on their behaviour under working conditions. Both men had booked on duty at

Doncaster that afternoon. They had worked the 2.55 p.m. train to
York and the 6.50 p.m. express from York to Peterborough. Now
they were returning to Doncaster where they would book off.
They had worked precisely the same rota the previous day.

The train was due to stop at Grantham at 11 p.m. and Henry
Pile, the night station inspector, was standing on the down platform ready to receive it together with three postmen who were
waiting to load mails. Alfred Day, who was on duty in Grantham
south signal box had his own distant signal at "caution". Richard
Scoffin in the north box had all his down main line signals at
"danger" to protect the Nottingham line junction where he was
crossing the 10.57 p.m. up Leicester goods train from the up
Nottingham line to the up main. This meant that the goods had
to cross over the down main, so the down line facing points at the
junction were, very properly, set for the Nottingham line also. It
was a dark night with occasional scuds of rain which made the rail
greasy but it was perfectly clear and the red eyes of the Junction
signals glowed brightly. Suddenly, Cecil Cox, one of the postmen,
stepped to the platform edge and looked up the line. "It's coming
in," he called. His mate joined him, took one look at the swiftly
approaching headlights and shook his head. "It's a run through,"
he said. A moment later the train was thundering through the
platform and Cox was shouting above the din, "It isn't, it has our
mail carriage on it." Inspector Pile estimated the speed of the train
as forty miles an hour, others thought more, but all agreed that the
brakes were not applied. None of them noticed the driver and
fireman. The only man at Grantham that night who did so was
Alfred Day in the south signal box. He said he saw them both
standing motionless, one on either side of the footplate, each
staring ahead through his cab spectacle glass. The bewildered
little group on the platform turned to watch the train disappear
into the darkness under the red danger lights. A moment later
they heard a great noise like an explosion and then the night sky
over the north yard was lit with flames. They ran then, stumbling
over the network of rails and point rods, to give what help they
could.

The "Atlantic" rode the points on to the Nottingham line and
the reverse curve which followed it, but on this second curve the
tender, with its long fixed wheelbase, was derailed and swept away

the parapet wall of an underbridge for a length of 65 yards. It then broke away and fell over the side of the bridge. In doing so it derailed the locomotive which slewed broadside across the tracks with the leading three vehicles piled against it. The following six vehicles plunged down the embankment just beyond the bridge and only the last three remained upright and unharmed. Fire broke out almost immediately in the wreckage both above and below, the one being started by coals from the engine firebox and the other by escaping gas. Driver Fleetwood and Fireman Talbot were killed instantly and their locomotive was so badly damaged that it was impossible to determine the position of the regulator and brake lever at the time of the accident. Fortunately three brake vans and the mail coach were at the front of the train otherwise casualties might have been much heavier, but even so eleven passengers and a postal sorter lost their lives.

The Grantham disaster produced an unprecedented crop of rumours and fantastic theories. The driver was drunk. The driver had gone mad. As the train approached Grantham the driver and fireman had been seen struggling desperately with one another on the footplate. The driver was accustomed to join the train at Grantham, had thought he had done so on this occasion and believed that he faced a clear run to Doncaster. All these stories were either disproved at the inquiry or else the facts made them quite preposterous. The theory most favoured and most credible was that Fleetwood was suddenly taken ill and that Talbot was so concerned in aiding him that he did not realize the position of the train until it was too late. Certainly Fleetwood had complained of illness which he had said was sciatica. He had been taken ill on the footplate in the previous June and was off duty for a week. He was not given a medical examination when he returned to work and the inspector, Colonel Von Donop, gave his opinion that all drivers should in future be so examined before being allowed to resume footplate duty. Yet, convincing though this theory is, it cannot be reconciled with the evidence of Signalman Alfred Day. His claim to have seen Fleetwood and Talbot standing on the footplate, and the fact that the train did not whistle in accordance with invariable custom on approaching Grantham both seem to suggest that the men mistook their whereabouts. But here again, such an extraordinary aberration on the part of

M

two intelligent men, both of whom knew the road intimately and had worked over it with the same train on the previous night, seems incredible. Not only was it a clear night, but a number of Great Northern footplate men testified at the inquiry that the approach to Grantham was quite unmistakable under any conditions. What precisely took place on the footplate of Ivatt "Atlantic" No. 276 on this September night forty-eight years ago is a question that Sherlock Holmes himself could not answer. It remains the railway equivalent of the mystery of the *Marie Celeste*.

from RED FOR DANGER *1955*

Ais Gill, 1913

L. T. C. ROLT

On the night of September 1st, 1913, two four-coupled Midland express locomotives were coaling up at Carlisle preparatory to working the night Scots expresses on their way south to St Pancras. The first was No. 993, Driver Nicholson and Fireman Metcalf, who were booked to work the Stranraer and Glasgow train which was due out of Carlisle at 1.35 a.m. No. 446, Driver Caudle and Fireman Follows, would come after with the Inverness and Edinburgh portion, due out at 1.49 a.m. Their tenders were being filled up with South Tyne coal. It was a good quality steam coal, but it had not been screened and contained a very large proportion of small coal and slack. Driver Caudle stirred it critically with his boot and was heard to remark: "If she'll steam on this she'll steam on anything."

Driver Nicholson had the same misgivings which were by no means relieved when he found that his train consisted of ten coaches, three of them twelve-wheeled sleeping cars, weighing 243 tons. This was 13 tons over the maximum rated load for his engine on "the long drag" up to Ais Gill summit. He therefore asked for pilot assistance, but was told that no pilot was available.

When No. 993 pulled out alone with her train at 1.38 a.m. – three minutes late – she had to lift her load from near sea level to a height of 1,167 feet in forty-seven miles, the last nine of which

from Crosby Garret tunnel to Ais Gill summit were on an almost
continuous gradient of 1 in 100. To make things more difficult, it
was, needless to say, typical Pennine weather – a pitch dark night
of rain with a strong wind blowing from the north-east. No. 993
was soon in trouble. Fireman Metcalf did his best and Nicholson
himself took a turn with the shovel but with such small coal they
could not keep a lively fire and, despite all their efforts, when the
gradient stiffened, so the needle of the steam pressure gauge
remorselessly crept back. Over the eight and a quarter miles
between Ormside and Kirby Stephen they were able to average
only twenty-nine miles an hour as against the scheduled forty. At
Mallerstang the speed of the labouring engine had dropped to
twenty miles per hour and they were running ten minutes late.
By this time steam pressure had fallen so low that Nicholson had
to put on his large ejector to maintain the vacuum and so prevent
the brakes on the train from rubbing. Three miles south of Mallerstang box, pressure had fallen to 85 lb. and No. 993 came to a
stand. She was only half a mile short of Ais Gill summit and,
incidentally, but two miles away from Grisedale Crossing where,
less than three years before, disaster had befallen the down Scotch
express.

As soon as the train stopped, Donelly, the front guard, jumped
down and asked Nicholson what was the matter. "We'll be a few
minutes, we're short of steam," shouted Nicholson above the dull
roar of the blower. He stood in the glare from the open firedoor as
Metcalf, wielding his long pricker, was cleaning the bars. The
rear guard, Whitley, had also got out of his compartment, and
now Donelly turned and called to him: "Only a minute." Whitley
therefore took no steps to protect the train by placing detonators
in the rear. Meanwhile Signalman Sutherland at Mallerstang was
wondering why he had received no "out of section" signal from
Clemnet at Ais Gill box. Clemnet told him on the telephone that
he had no information, so Sutherland kept his signals at danger
when he was offered the Inverness and Edinburgh train.

Driver Caudle was making better progress with No. 446 for he
had only six bogies weighing 157 tons behind his tender. But his
engine, too, was steaming badly owing to the small coal. As they
were approaching the short Birkett tunnel near Mallerstang,
Caudle left the footplate and went out on to the framing to oil the

left-hand driving axle box. Owing to the force of the wind it took him longer to make his perilous way round the framing than he had expected and by the time he got back to the footplate the train had run past the Mallerstang distant signal which was just over 1,000 yards from the south end of the tunnel. Neither man saw it. There was a minor crisis on the footplate when Caudle returned. Water was short; it was out of sight in the bottom fitting of the gauge glass and Follows was trying in vain to get the right-hand injector to work. Caudle immediately went to his aid. "Injectors need humouring sometimes," said the driver. Delicately he manipulated the steam and water controls until at last the coughing and hissing of the obstinate injector ceased and it broke into its reassuring song. But by this time they had run past all the Mallerstang signals without observing them. The next thing that happened was that Follows suddenly shouted: "Look out, Sam, there's a red light in front of us."

Signalman Sutherland at Mallerstang was watching Caudle's train approach. At first he thought it was slowing down and that Caudle had seen the distant signal at "Caution". He therefore lowered his "home" with the idea of stopping the train at his starting signal. The next instant he realized that the locomotive was still steaming hard. Immediately he flung the home signal back to danger, grabbed his red handlamp and waved it from the box as the train went past. It did not stop and Sutherland sent the "Train running away on right line" signal to Clemnet at Ais Gill. A minute or so later he heard the distant sound of an engine whistle followed by a sinister rumbling noise.

Signalman Clemnet, too, was wondering what was happening down the line and, just as Sutton at Hawes Junction had done two years before, he was staring northwards into the darkness through the rain bleared windows of his lonely cabin. It had just turned 3 o'clock when he saw what he afterwards described as a red mist rising and falling away in the night sky beyond his up distant signal. Five minutes afterwards he heard someone stumbling up the steps to his box. It was Fireman Metcalf in a state of collapse bringing the news of disaster. Clemnet at once stopped a down goods train which was just about to pass.

Driver Nicholson was the first to see the Edinburgh express approaching. Glancing back down the line he saw in the sky the moving glare from an open fire door. At once he sent Metcalf running back and opened both his whistle and his regulator. But No. 993 still could not move her heavy train. Guard Whitley rushed down the line waving a red lamp and blowing a whistle but it was of no avail. Driver Caudle's engine crashed into the rear van of the stationary train, demolished it completely, and buried itself in the third-class coach next to it. The roof of the wrecked van slid over the top of No. 446 and cut through three compartments of the first carriage behind the tender. Fire caused by escaping gas broke out instantly in the rear of the leading train, completely consuming the remains of the van, the partially demolished third, and the sleeping car which was coupled next to it. It was a funeral pyre for fourteen passengers who perished almost without trace. In addition, thirty-eight passengers in the second train were seriously injured. It was as though the ancient gods of this high, wild country, still unappeased, had demanded a second sacrifice.

from RED FOR DANGER *1955*

The Tay Bridge Catastrophe

JOHN PREBBLE

All arguments for and against the building of the [Tay] bridge in the twenty years that preceded its erection can be viewed only in the perspective of the long struggle between the Caledonian and the North British. They fought for the domination of Scotland. It was a ruthless, worthless and sometimes comic war.

Both companies had been born in the mid-forties, distant spawn from the fertile genius of that rogue speculator George Hudson who, whatever else might be said of him, at least had a vision of a great central railway system instead of a cloud of gadflies trying to run their railways like stage-coach lines.

When the two companies settled down to fight, the Caledonian was swinging up from the Border to Glasgow. The North British curved up the east of the Lowlands to Edinburgh. They held Scotland between finger and thumb, pinching out the smaller lines, and the only fault in this analogy is that the thumb and finger were not members of the one hand.

When the North British acquired the Edinburgh, Perth and Dundee it was already reaching for the north-eastern Highlands. And there it was blocked, for the Caledonian, in one of the most brutal struggles in railway history, had swallowed many of the little lines and now sat smugly across the path of the North British. . . .

Through the 'fifties the North British watched the growth of the Caledonian with much uneasiness. Once the Caledonian's influence reached the cities of Perth, Dundee and Aberdeen, and it began to live off the land north of them, the North British knew that its chance of reaching across the Tay and sharing the plunder was hopeless. The holders of Ordinary stock in the company were impatient men, and this is understandable in view of the fact that they often went without a dividend. They were Englishmen for the most part, and were beginning to wonder who it was that had advised them to invest in railways. . . .

Consequently, when Thomas Bouch first deposited his plans for a bridge across the Tay, the directors of the North British may have thought it excellent, but were halted by the realization that they had not got the £200,000 to pay for it.

The argument for the bridge was indisputable. To travel from Edinburgh to Dundee was an experience which, once attempted, was not repeated if the passenger could think of an alternative. Between him and his destination lay two wide estuaries to be crossed by ferry, and in winter this part of the journey needed a strong stomach and a lethargic imagination.

With that malignant sadism, of which only the compilers of railway time-tables seem capable, the best train of the day left Waverley Station, Edinburgh, at 6.25 a.m. The whole journey was no more than forty-six miles, but it took three hours and twelve minutes to complete it, or more if there were storms on the Tay or the Forth.

If the travellers had not eaten before leaving home they stood in shivering groups in the buffet room at Waverley, where . . . the coffee, according to William Morris, was "ineffably bad." The train, ill-heated and trailing two fish trucks, then took them to Granton on the Forth where they boarded a ferry. These were graceful boats, low in the hull with beating paddles on either side, raking masts, and high, slender smoke-stacks. From the shore they appeared to be resting lightly on the water like dragon-flies, but aboard them, in a half-gale, the passengers leant sickly against the bulkheads with their ears full of the remorseless splash of the paddles, and their nostrils full of the stench of fish.

At Burntisland a train took them the thirty-six miles northward to Tayport on the south shore of the Tay estuary. There another boat took them across to Broughty Ferry, where a third train took them into Dundee, and very happy they all were to be done with the whole wretched business.

Thus it did not require a dreamer like Thomas Bouch to see that a fast express, running uninterrupted from Edinburgh to Dundee, crossing the Forth and the Tay by bridge, was infinitely preferable to the agony of the ferry system.

But the building of bridges costs money, and whenever the directors of the North British thought about money they thought of their English shareholders and the problem of an Ordinary dividend. Many of these shareholders also held Caledonian stock, and were not above pointing out at the half-yearly meetings that whereas they received some return from their Caledonian holdings they could not always say the same for their North British [which] . . . was sick in the limbs. At its half-yearly meetings shareholders shouted angrily from the floor, the meaning of their words lost in apoplectic indignation, and the chairman's gavel beat uselessly against the noise they made. Once, in lieu of a dividend it would appear, the Ordinary shareholders received a tastefully-printed map of the Company's network, a work of some delicacy admired by the directors and by no one else.

In one year the Caledonian was able to increase its profits by £23,461, against a loss of £3,009 by the North British.

Thomas Bouch, in his forties now, and appearing older behind his greying beard, continued his practice of calling on North British directors to talk about his bridge. He was listened to with more politeness, for the Company was now like a sick man who gets some comfort from thinking of his remedy, although he may be in no position to pay for it.

Thomas Bouch came carrying long rolls of cartridge paper tied with pink tape, figures of stress and strain, figures of rivets, and

bricks and cement and river-borings. But he did not know where
to find the money.

Yet the answer was simple. If the jute and flax merchants of
Dundee, the farmers of Forfar were to be connected with the Fife
shore, and to be set within reach of Edinburgh, why should they
not pay?

In Dundee there was a solicitor called Thomas Thornton, an
intelligent man who had none of Bouch's extravagant dreams but
who was jealous of his city's prosperity and aware of the great
industrial earthquake that was roughly changing the contours of
Britain. He called a meeting in his office.

It was a Friday, and it was October, and the Tay was a still sheet
of yellow metal indistinguishable from the fog that hung down
Dundee Law like a shawl. In the lawyer's office was Provost
Parker and a sprinkling of jute and flax manufacturers, bleachers
and dyers, who did not care one way or the other about the
irritating squabble between the two railway companies, except in
so far as it affected their businesses. They listened to Thomas
Bouch, and perhaps yawned through his talk of malleable iron
girders, and the relationship between the height of a span and its
length. What they wanted to know was *could* such a bridge be
built, and if it could what would it cost them and what return
could they expect? None of these questions seems to have been
answered satisfactorily.

That was in 1863, and although it was a meeting of some significance, in that it was the first time that the proposed bridge had
moved from Thomas Bouch's imagination to a committee table,
it proved nothing and proposed nothing.

A year passed to another October and to a public meeting in the
Council Chamber at Dundee, presided over by Baillie Yeaman, but
inspired and planned once more by Thomas Thornton. It was a
larger meeting, now in addition to the big merchants there were
small shopkeepers like Mr Phin, the grocer of Perth Road, who
thought he owed his presence to his civic pride.

Bouch stood up before them all, flanked by a water carafe and
his roll of designs, and tried to answer such questions as: *will it fall
down as Mr Matthew says?* and *How much will it cost?*

"It is a very ordinary undertaking," said Bouch, not, perhaps,
because he believed this but perhaps because constant opposition

to his dream had forced him to understate its magnitude when speaking of it, "and we have several far more stupendous and greater bridges already constructed." He did not say where, and it is strange that no one thought of asking him.

"I have estimated the cost at £180,000," he said, "I will stake my professional reputation that the cost will not exceed this amount." This was a very high stake, and placing it was one of those wild misjudgments of which Bouch was capable.

There was generous applause. There was even more applause when James Cox, who was one of Dundee's richest citizens, and its largest employer of labour, was suddenly warmed by Bouch's enthusiasm and declared his support for the scheme, declaring it in a most convincing manner. He said that he was prepared to put his money into it. This was something that the men of Dundee could understand.

"RESOLVED . . ." agreed the Town Councillors and the bankers and the jute merchants and the flaxspinners and the grocer from Perth Road ". . . that it would be for the public advantage, and tend greatly to the traffic of the North of Scotland and specially the town and trade of Dundee, were the present inconvenient and expensive route to the south improved by the construction of a bridge across the River Tay, and were suitable provision made for a general passenger station at Dundee; and that a Committee be appointed to consider and promote the scheme."

A week later the public was offered the prospectus of the Tay Bridge and Dundee Union Railway Undertaking. It had a proposed capital of £350,000 in 14,000 shares of £25 each. . . . On the fifteenth day of November, 1864, Parliamentary notice was given of a Bill to provide for the incorporation of the company. The Bill also provided for the construction of the bridge and its connecting lines, and, *inter alia*, it gave power to the North British Railway Company to subscribe to the capital. The North British appears to have appreciated this gesture without making any promises.

At once the Caledonian awoke to the danger. Flushed with its little victories over the North British, it had believed this plan for a bridge would never get beyond Thomas Bouch's drawing table. Now, suddenly, it was blossoming quickly. The directors of the Caledonian sat down to assess the opposition to the scheme.

It was formidable. The Dundee Harbour Board, many of the

Trustees of which were Town Councillors, not unnaturally resented a future in which goods might be brought in and out of the city by rail instead of by sea. The Harbour dues were high, and the Board was prosperous, and this was a state of affairs they wished to keep unchanged.

The Scottish Central and the Scottish North Eastern Railways, who controlled the north of the Tay, with a future already darkened by the spreading wings of the Caledonian, had no wish to see the claret and cream carriages of the North British coming across the river also.

Finally there was the City of Perth, ancient capital of Scotland, and, like all those with threadbare dignity, quick to take offence. The rivalry between Perth and Dundee was old, and if it was no longer expressed by the ring of broadsword on targe, or the dust-trail of pikemen, it was still deep-rooted and bitter. The tide turned at Perth, but yet the city looked upon itself as a sea-port. The bridge would be a dam that destroyed it.

The Caledonian lobbied enthusiastically among such opposition. On the Dundee Council it found many headshakers and lip-curlers, many men with heavy investments in the Caledonian itself. Suitably stimulated they began to voice their opposition to the scheme with some heat. They said, cannily, that they liked fine the idea of a bridge, but did not believe it was possible to build one two miles long. Or, if it were possible, why should it be the monopoly of one railway only, why should not others have interest? They were afraid that the desire to build such a bridge sprang more from pride than common sense. . . .

The sustained clamour of disapproval set up vibrations of uneasiness among the supporters of the Undertaking. It became apparent to Cox and to Lawyer Thornton that most of them would defect at the slightest pressure. Thornton called another meeting at which it was agreed to withdraw their skirmishing line and entrench. The Bill fell through.

The North British, realizing that it must now make some positive move or see the whole idea of a bridge lost, agreed to promote its own bridge. Thomas Bouch, working very hard through the winter of 1864–1865, changed his plans and deposited new designs for a bridge 300 yards west of the original one. He proposed a ribbon of iron reaching out from Wormit Bay on the south bank to a point west of the Binns of Blackness. From there the line was to be carried to the high ground over the Dundee and Perth Railway, curving and reaching eastward to the west flank of the city.

The second Bill was to come before Parliament in the session of 1865–1866.

The Caledonian seemed to experience a change of heart. Its directors met the directors of the North British and worked out their joint financial responsibility once the North British line crossed the Tay. The Caledonian could afford to be this magnanimous. If the river was going to be bridged they felt it essential to protect their rights and privileges. Meanwhile they continued to take steps to make sure that this Bill too would be withdrawn.

They took over the Scottish North Eastern and they transferred their lobbying to the House of Commons. They knew that the North British, impoverished, unsettled by dissension, would break down if the opposition in the House was strong enough. They based their opposition on the fact that the North British could not afford to pay for the bridge.

And indeed when the North British loosened its pursestrings it found that this was so. It withdrew its Bill.

Now the Caledonian, with the smile of a tiger, talked peace with the North British, and suggested an armistice in the bitter price war. But the Caledonian had won a great victory, and in industry there is no compassion for the vanquished. . . .

At the moment of its defeat, however, the Undertaking received the support of the one man who was to drive it through to success.

In November, 1866, a few months after the Bill foundered, John Stirling of Kippendavie became chairman of the North British Railway. In an industry that was dominated by such picaresque characters as George Hudson he was a man of unusual breeding and gentility. He had become Laird of Kippendavie and Laird of Kippenross before he was ten years old, and although he was rich enough to grow and enjoy a life of rustic leisure, his astute and agile mind drove him into railway politics.

He became one of the most powerful men in the Scottish North Eastern Railway, and he struck a hard bargain with the Caledonian when that octopus took over the line. Perhaps the cruel nature of the struggle that preceded the surrender left him with a gentlemanly distaste for the tactics and behaviour of the big company. Certainly when he became chairman of the North British he was determined to break the Caledonian's hold on Scotland.

Moribund, frightened though it was, the North British was the only other company that could do this, and the Tay Bridge would be its only successful weapon.

Stirling was fifty-five, and he had been engaged in the long, atrophying warfare of railway politics for the whole of his adult life. He was at an age when most men would have been content to let their life unreel itself in its own way, with the least entanglement.

But Stirling chose to fight for the Tay Bridge. Perhaps he knew that, for all its breast-beating, the heart was going out of the Caledonian. The bridge was inevitable. It would be built. The Caledonian could not stop it, it could only halt it. . . .

So once again the supporters of the scheme met, in the Council Room at Dundee on September 7, 1869. There was James Cox, now a Baillie, there was Lawyer Thornton, and there was a representative sprinkling of Councillors and Harbour Trustees. There was Thomas Bouch, the uncommon denominator of them all.

Stirling spoke to them amiably, suggesting that he thought there would be little difficulty in bringing his company behind the Undertaking. With what must have been an ironical smile he referred to the one factor that should convince the most violent of opponents among his shareholders. The North British Railway was paying £9,000 a year for the use of the short stretch of railway between Broughty Ferry and Dundee. The building of a bridge would save the North British this money.

His directors, he said, would recommend the company to guarantee $5\frac{1}{4}$ per cent on the stock in the Undertaking.

The meeting ended in expressions of mutual goodwill, and Thomas Bouch took the Tay Ferry, and took the Fife train, and then took the Forth Ferry to Edinburgh, his strangely remote spirit uplifted.

But when Stirling called a meeting of North British shareholders they received him uneasily. They said his proposal was an outright declaration of war on the Caledonian.

"We are not declaring war . . ." said Stirling gently, but he and his board, and every shareholder in the room knew that they were. Once the North British secured a foothold across the Tay it would carry much of the passenger and goods traffic now wholly carried by the Caledonian or its allies.

Exactly, said Stirling. But was that not why they *must* build the bridge? Without it and the trade it would bring the North British would die.

For how much?

For, perhaps, £250,000.

"Build it for that and I am content," said one shareholder, "and the sooner the better. But it is in my mind that it will cost double that sum." To emphasize what he meant, he voted against the proposal.

But Stirling carried the majority with him, which he must have done as much by force of personality as by argument. Perhaps, in his own long struggle with the Caledonian, he had discovered that company's breaking-point, and knew that it would be the bridge.

Certainly the Caledonian almost crippled itself in a last attempt to destroy the North British, cutting goods rates and passenger fares still further. Out on the roads plate-laying gangs of the rival companies, Irishmen for the most part, came to blows and on one occasion to murder. Booking-clerks flailed their fists on Waverley station and disgusted a public who now did not care which railway controlled Scotland, so long as it meant that they would be able to travel in carriages that were well-furnished, well-heated, and well-ventilated, something which could not be said for the North British stock.

In the year 1869, the North British Railway Company came as close to collapse as it had ever been.

"We have three hundred stations," said Stirling bluntly, "yet our traffic per mile is £1,058, while the Caledonian, with fewer lines and fewer stations, is £1,458."

Survival rested on the bridge, the rainbow bridge of Thomas Bouch.

Stirling realized that the opposition was weakening. Although it was noisy it was not strong enough to defeat the new Bill in Parliament. He was sure of this when the Tay Navigation Commissioners travelled down to Edinburgh to see him. Speaking for

Perth, they said they now had no objection to a bridge, provided its central girders were a hundred feet from the water, high enough to permit the passage of sea-going ships. Stirling smiled, and charmed them, exacting from them a promise of no further opposition should he make the bridge as high as they wished.

The City of Perth needed much charming. Its dignity had been injured by the ribald humour of the Dundee Press which had described it as "a rest-and-be-thankful spot, whose fleet upon the Tay consists chiefly of some sand-sloops, not so large as Tyne wherries".

Bouch needed charming, too. He knew that the truck of the largest ship likely to go up-river was not more than 70 feet from the water, and consequently his designs had allowed for a clearance of no more than 80 feet. But Stirling talked him into making the figure 100. Bouch was too busy that year to argue much. He was worrying about the river-bed. He had commissioned "a thoroughly experienced borer, Mr Wylie" to take soundings from bank to bank. Mr Wylie did so, and reported the happy news that there was solid rock foundations all the way across, with the exception of some 250 yards on the north shore. His figures were accepted, which later proved most unfortunate.

Stirling's charm was needed again when the Dundee Harbour Trustees, under Provost Yeaman, received their copy of the new North British Bill. They read the small print and were horrified to discover two clauses sanctioning a subscription of £50,000 on their part. Yeaman set off for Edinburgh to tell Stirling that someone had "acted most impertinently". It was true that the Harbour Trustees were no longer placing any obstacle in the way of the bridge, but that did not mean they were putting all this money behind it. Stirling politely withdrew the clauses, and Provost Yeaman left with a lasting admiration for the railway laird.

In the last week of March, 1870, the North British defended its Bill before Committee in the House of Commons. Its opponents, the only opponents left now, were the Tay Navigation Commissioners and the Caledonian Railway. The men from Perth were making a token opposition only, Stirling having bought them off with his promise of the High Girders. The Caledonian, left thus isolated, facing the charge of deliberately halting the natural progress of the industry, declared no opposition to the bridge in principle, but reserved doubts about the financial strength of its proposers.

Had the public not grown enthusiastic about the bridge the Caledonian's lobbying might have had stronger effect than it did. [But] on July 15, 1870, the Bill received the Royal Assent. . . .

[One evening nine years later] John Watt, a foreman surface worker in the employ of the North British Railway Company, went to share a can of tea with his friend Thomas Barclay.

It was not far from his cottage to the signal cabin, but the path led up the Fifeshire bank of the Tay and he found it hard to climb the wet earth against the pull of a south-westerly gale. This was a stronger wind than any Watt could remember. He felt it beating against his ears, taking the air from his mouth before he could suck it into his lungs. When he reached the shelter of the cabin he heard a restless thrumming along the latticed iron of the new bridge. Heavy clouds were fast-racing down the firth to the German Sea, and in the darkness below them the bridge was a thread of tiny lamps only, looped across the throat of the Tay. Now and then the wind tore a hole in the clouds, and a full moon shone on the black water and the black girders and the black nipple of Dundee Law.

Thomas Barclay's signal cabin was held in a fork where the single line left the bridge and turned eastward and westward. It was high in the wind and its northern windows faced across the Tay to the city of Dundee over a mile away.

The two men greeted each other and agreed that the weather

was bad. The cabin was vibrating uneasily, and John Watt stood with his back to the stove and looked out of the window and said again that the weather was bad.

At eight minutes past seven o'clock the signal bell rang, and John Watt asked if this came from St Fort. Barclay said that it did, and that the 5.20 from Burntisland had left St Fort and would soon be at the bridge. He signalled the cabin on the northern bank, and within fifteen seconds his signal was acknowledged by one beat of the bell, and then two, and then a final beat. It was nine minutes past seven and Thomas Barclay recorded these times in his log book.

They felt the push of the gale against the cabin, and because it could be as bad as this in the lee of Wormit Bay where they were, they knew that it must be very bad out in the firth.

At twelve minutes past seven the train came along the westward turn. They saw it first as a flare against the darkness, a string of sparks drawn taut, and then smudges of uncertain light from six carriages. Barclay took a baton from its hole, and he opened the door of the cabin and went down the steps to the boarding.

The train passed him slowly, moving, as the regulations insisted, at no more than three miles an hour. Barclay walked alongside the engine for a few paces, and he saw the glare of the fire on the driver's white moleskin trousers, the black mark of a grin as the stoker leant out to take the baton. Then Barclay halted and watched the carriages pass, and saw a face here and there looking down at him from the windows. Once it was a child's face.

He went back to the cabin, glad to be out of the wind. It was thirteen minutes past seven and he signalled to the northern box that the train was on the bridge. The acknowledgment came back promptly – one beat of the bell, and then two, and then a final beat. Thomas Barclay gave the clear signal to Wormit and he recorded the times in his log book.

The tension had passed, and he squatted down before the fire and raked out the dead coals.

From the north window of the cabin John Watt said "There is something wrong with the train." He said it calmly and without excitement.

John Watt had served the Company for twelve years against the three years and eight months of Barclay's service. But Barclay was a young man and jealous of his work, and proud that he had been signalman at the south cabin since the opening of the great bridge. He was quick to resent any suggestion that Watt might know more about the bridge than he. He said "Nothing has happened to the train, John."

Standing by the window of the closed door Watt had watched the train as it gathered speed on the bridge. He saw the retiring sway of its three red tail-lamps, and then, suddenly he saw a spray of sparks from its wheels that grew and merged into a steady flame pulled eastward by the wind. He watched this curiously for three minutes until there were three distinct flashes and then one great flash. Then there was darkness. He could not see the tail lamps now.

He said "The train's gone over, Thomas."

Barclay got up from the fire and came to the window, holding his face against it and frowning.

"Her tail lamps have gone," said Watt.

Barclay looked across the dark river and at last he said "Of course her tail lamps have gone. She's gone down the incline to the north side. We'll see her again soon."

They waited, and Watt said "I'm afraid something's happened to her, Thomas."

"Wait," said Barclay, "Wait, we'll see her soon."

He was impatient with the older man, and he took the scuttle and went down the steps for more coal. When he returned Watt was still watching the river and he said that he had not seen the train again. It was three minutes since he had said that the train had gone over, and Barclay now knew that something must be wrong.

He rang the bell to the north box and there was no acknowledgment. He tried both his speaking instruments and there was no reply.

Watt and Barclay looked at each other and did not know what to do, or how to say what they were thinking. Then, because they felt alone in this box of light and because they could not imagine what had happened outside in the darkness, they opened the door and ran down the steps. They stood on the boarding and the wind tore at them.

Instinctively they began to walk out along the bridge, and they halted after twenty yards for the wind had already forced them to their knees. They were afraid of being blown into the river, so they went back, and ran along the eastward turn and struggled down the bank to the shore of the Tay. They walked up and down, to the east and to the west side of the bridge, shielding their eyes from the wind and staring out across the river, and when they shouted at each other the wind snatched the sentences and broke them into meaningless words.

They saw nothing, until the moon came out, and then they saw. The centre of the bridge was no longer there. The High Girders, thirteen spans through which the line had passed as through a tunnel, were gone, and the twelve iron columns that had supported them were gone too. One thousand and sixty yards of the great Tay Bridge were gone, and with them an engine, five carriages and a brake van belonging to the North British Railway Company. Gone also were seventy-five men, women, and children.

This happened at approximately twenty minutes past seven on the evening of Sunday, December 28, 1879. It was the night of the Great Storm.

from THE HIGH GIRDERS *1955*

An American Heroine

J. A. SWISHER

Late in the afternoon of July 6, 1881, heavy black clouds rolled up from the horizon and the gloom presaging a violent storm swept over the Des Moines Valley. Farmers hastened their evening chores while anxious housewives hurried to bring in their washing and see that the chickens had found shelter. As the dense cloud-veil spread over the sky, twilight deepened into the darkness of night, which was made blacker in contrast to the vivid illumination of the lightning flashes. Nearer and nearer came the ominous rumble and crash of the thunder until it made the windows rattle. Then down came the rain in sheets.

In a little cottage up the valley of Honey Creek beside the Chicago & Northwestern Railroad about half a mile from the Des Moines River, the Shelley children watched the appalling storm until "fright took possession" and drove them from the window, "through which the lightning flashed dreadful pictures of destruction". The creek became a raging torrent, and the turbulent waters rose until they threatened the stable halfway down the slope where the stock had taken refuge. Something had to be done. Kate, who was fifteen, the oldest of the children, dashed out into the rain, waded through the water that was pouring down the hillside, let out the horses and cows to take care of themselves, and rescued some little pigs that had climbed on a pile of hay for safety.

The storm continued with unabated violence during the long evening and on into the night. At the Shelley home there was no inclination to retire. While the younger children dozed, Kate and her mother remained alert and vigilant – apprehensive of danger. Honey Creek, filled with fence posts and uprooted trees, was still rising. They feared that the railroad bridge across the creek a quarter of a mile up the track could not withstand the flood, and they knew the long wooden trestle across the Des Moines River must be under a terrific strain.

The spring and early summer had been unusually rainy, so that the river had stood for days at high-water mark. Railroad embankments had been undermined and bridge piling had loosened. M. J. Shelley, an immigrant from Tipperary, Ireland, had been section foreman before he died in 1878, and well his family knew the perils of the railroad on such a night as this. . . .

It must have been after eleven o'clock when Kate and her mother heard the rumble of a train crossing the Des Moines River bridge. It was the "pusher", an engine stationed at Moingona to serve as an auxiliary in pulling heavy trains up the grade on either side of the river. The crew, consisting of Ed Wood, George Olmstead, Adam Agar, and Patrick Donahue, had been ordered to "run to Boone and return to Moingona regardless of all trains". The engine came backing down the track with the brakeman and section foreman standing on the running board behind the tender looking for washouts. Past the Shelley house they went and onto the swaying Honey Creek bridge. Twice Kate heard the engine bell toll distinctly, and "then came the horrible crash and the fierce hissing of steam" as the engine plunged down with her crew into twenty-five feet of rapid, swirling water.

"Oh, Mother," Kate exclaimed, "they have gone down." The storm and all else was forgotten. "It seemed as still as death, as silent as the grave." Kate decided that she must go to help the men and stop the passenger train that would soon be due at Moingona – the midnight express from the west. Many lives were in her hands that night. The remonstrances of her mother were of no avail. She felt she simply had to go. Attired in an old skirt and jacket, she caught up a straw hat, improvised a lantern by hanging a little miner's lamp in an old lantern frame, and started out into the night and the storm to do her duty as she saw it, knowing that Mother and the children were praying God to keep her from harm.

The entire valley was flooded by that time, and the yard of the Shelley home resembled the "inside of a huge oval bowl" filled with water which extended to the railroad track. Unable to go directly to the railroad and thence up the track to the wreck at the bridge, Kate climbed the bluff back of the house, made a semi-circular detour to the southwest until she reached a place where the wagon road came through a cut in the bluffs and crossed the railroad. Once on the track, she ran to the broken bridge.

Upon arriving at the scene of the wreck, she saw by the lightning that two of the men, Wood and Agar, had chanced to clamber upon some convenient trees in the midst of the swelling flood and thus escape drowning for the time being. The other two were lost. One of the men called to her again and again, but in the tumult she could not understand what he said.

Unable to render aid to the ill-fated crew and realizing that the midnight train would soon be due, she turned westward and hastened as fast as she could go toward Moingona in an effort to save the lives of the passengers on board the approaching train. Moingona was only a mile and a quarter away, but the Des Moines River with its long wooden bridge trembling from the incessant rush of the high water lay between her and the little village.

After a temporary lull the storm had burst out anew. The thunder and lightning were frightful, while the rain came in gusts and torrents. The attempt to reach Moingona across the raging Des Moines seemed almost certain death: to hesitate might mean the death of hundreds of passengers on the train speeding to destruction. That was the thought that kept pounding at Kate's consciousness as she ran along the track. If she could only get there on time. What if the train should catch her on the bridge? What if the train should go thundering by in the darkness? She pictured the engine plunging into Honey Creek, the coaches piling up in the water. In imagination she could almost hear the screams of the people. She must hurry – hurry! How hard the wind blew! Sometimes it almost took her off her feet. There seemed to be no strength left in her. But she must go on!

Drenched to the skin, trembling and breathless, she reached the river. Never before had she seen the water so high. It was roaring by almost level with the track. The muddy river was filled with debris – even big trees uprooted by the wind and carried away by the water were sweeping headlong toward Des Moines. Across the seething flood stretched the long bridge that seemed just on the point of joining the general rush down stream.

Pedestrians had never been invited to use the bridge and as a method of discouraging such a practice some of the planking had been removed. The ties were a full pace apart and studded thickly with twisted rusty spikes. There was danger in crossing during fair weather and in daylight, but to attempt the feat in pitch darkness with the wind blowing a gale, rain pouring on the slippery ties, and a raging torrent below was an exploit to daunt the courage of any man.

Unchecked by the timbered bluffs of Honey Creek Valley, the wind swept the river bridge with terrific force. As Kate hesitated a moment to catch her breath and appraise the situation, a gust more violent than usual extinguished the feeble light of her lantern and left her in inky darkness relieved only by the lightning. A feeling of terror seized her, but at the thought of the drowning men back at the broken bridge and the oncoming express, she dropped to her knees and began to crawl slowly, laboriously, across the long wind-swept trestle. Guided by the rails, she felt her way from tie to tie. Again and again her skirt caught on a nail and she all but lost her balance. Now and then a sharp pain shot through her hands and knees as a protruding spike or splinter gouged into her flesh. As each flash of lightning displayed the angry swirling water only a few feet below, she almost fell beneath the ties from dizziness.

Halfway over a piercing flash of lightning revealed an enormous tree rushing down upon the very spot where she was clinging. In the instant of vision she noticed that the earth was still hanging to the roots of the tree. Momentary panic brought her upright on her knees as she clasped her hands in terror and in prayer, for it seemed inevitable that the shock would carry away the bridge. But the monster glided between the piers with a rush, the branches scattering foam and water over the girl as they passed.

Finding herself still unharmed, she resumed her painful progress. It seemed as though she had been on that bridge for hours.

She could scarcely remember when she started, while the beginning of the storm and her rescue of the little pigs earlier in the evening seemed years ago. Each minute stretched out interminably and the impression grew upon her that the end of the bridge was constantly receding. At last, however, she felt the solid ground beneath her. Standing erect, she stopped to breathe for a moment and then set out on the run to the station a quarter of a mile away. It was getting late and her strength was failing fast.

How she finally arrived and told her story, Kate Shelley could never remember. She only recalled that some one said, "The girl is crazy". Then one of the railroad men recognized her and the dreadful import of the message was realized. The whistle of an engine in the yards aroused the town. [A red lamp halted the midnight express.] In a few minutes men with ropes and other equipment were ready to go to the rescue of Wood and Agar at the Honey Creek bridge. Kate accompanied the rescue party across the river on the engine, guided them along the bluff to the track above the washout, and thence back to the scene of the disaster on the east bank of the creek, where the survivors of the wreck could be helped. After many efforts a rope was cast to Wood, who made it fast to his tree and then came ashore hand over hand. Agar could not be rescued until the water began to subside when he too was taken from his refuge, completely exhausted from his long exposure. . . .

[Afterwards Kate was] showered with letters filled with testimonials of gratitude and praise. Some contained verses in her honour, others eulogized her in prose, while there was no end of hair-raising, heart-throbbing descriptions of the adventure. There were letters of sympathy, letters requesting a photograph, a fragment of her dress, or a splinter from the bridge, and letters offering glowing opportunities for investing her fortune.

Numerous gifts and tokens of esteem were bestowed upon her. The school children of Dubuque gave her a medal. The Chicago *Tribune* raised a fund to help the Shelley family out of debt. . . . A drinking fountain erected in a Dubuque park was dedicated to her. The employees of the North Western Railroad gave her a gold watch and chain while the company issued her a life pass over the road. . . .

In 1903 [Kate] accepted employment as station agent at

Moingona – a position which she held until a short time before her death on January 21, 1912. Twice each day during all these years she went from her home to the little depot, crossing the new iron bridge that had replaced the one over which she crawled on that fateful July night so many years before. Trains always stopped at her little cottage when she was on board. At the time of her funeral the company sent a special train to her home for the convenience of the family and hundreds of friends.

On the main line of the North Western Railroad between Boone and Ogden and about four miles north of the village of Moingona, a fine new bridge now spans the Des Moines River. This structure, one of the longest and highest of its kind, is widely known as the Kate Shelley Bridge.

from THE PALIMPSEST, *Vol. VI, 2, 1925*

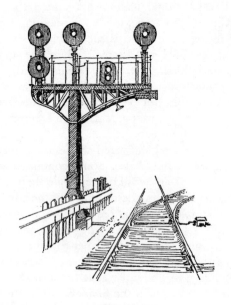

PART VII

Services and Specials

Sleeping-Car

ROGER LLOYD

Half of the fascination [of rail travel] is in the sense of exciting incongruity, in eating breakfast *not* in one's own dining-room, in *not* being asleep in bed at midnight but pacing Crewe or Cambridge stations instead, waiting for the 1.10 or the 12.56.

For this reason, and other things being equal, a night journey is better rewarded by memorable sensations than is a day journey. But the most thrilling incongruity of all is undoubtedly the act of undressing and getting into bed *not* in one's own bedroom but in a train while being hurled through the countryside at a mile a minute.

I feel sure that if they would openly confess what is in their minds, practically every sleeping-car passenger approaches the train and clutches his special tickets with a real thrill. There is the attendant who quickly identifies and always welcomes his guests, addressing them by name and title. It may no doubt be very childish, and perhaps even a trifle snobbish, to be pleased when greeted by name, but it does undoubtedly light a little glow inside not to be treated as just an anonymous bit of the travelling public. Down a deeply padded and soft-footed corridor the attendant takes you to your own tiny cabin, and you think – this time with a rather anti-social satisfaction – that it cannot matter to you how crowded the train is, since this kingdom is for that night your very own, and nobody else can get into it. Admittedly the kingdom is minute, but it is marvellously ingenious and comfortable. It has two dropping tables, three racks, three different lights – one of them exactly over your head, a soft bed, a venetian blind over the window which you can raise or lower as you like, many hooks and a few coat hangers – and all that in about the space of less than half an ordinary compartment. Yet there is ample room. It is a masterpiece of modern domestic architecture, and the genius who designed it must have had by heart the nursery admonition, a Place for Everything and Everything in its Place.

But having parted with considerable sums of money to procure this private miniature bedroom on the non-stop 10.30 p.m. from Glasgow to Euston, it would be just as well actually to sleep in it. That is the part which my perversity makes so difficult. Knowing that it would be so, I did not begin to undress until we had started. Until then I walked up to the front of the train to see what engine we had, which that night was *City of Sheffield,* and to read the lists in the sleeping-car windows to see if I recognized any of the names of my fellow passengers. At 10.30 we began to move, and telling myself that we stopped nowhere until Euston (except for the stop at Upperby engine shed south of Carlisle to change the driver and fireman) so that there would be nothing to see or to hear to keep me awake, I undressed and got into bed and firmly put out the light.

I actually got quickly to a light sleep too, which was marvellous for someone interested in railways. For the trouble is of course that people who have this infirmity are much too interested in what is going on to let themselves fall properly asleep. My own Waterloo in the battle for the sort of steady slumber which, thank God, always blesses me at home, is to start wondering where we are. It is hopeless to let yourself do this on a line you know really well, for you start testing yourself to see if you can discover your whereabouts by the clues of sound alone. My light sleep is instantly dissipated into wakefulness by a slowing of the train and the changed rhythm of the wheels.

Then the mind comes back to the wakefulness of consciousness with a jerk. Why are we slowing? Is it a signal? No, for we aren't stopping dead. Well, then, perhaps we're climbing Beattock. Now I come to think of it there was a lighted station a few miles back, and I suppose it must have been Carstairs. Yes, I think that must be right because I can now hear the engine laboriously and steadily puffing, and obviously we are climbing a long incline. It must be the Beattock Bank. Or no! it might be Shap Fell. I might have slept longer than I suppose. If it is, that lighted station must have been Carlisle. But then if it was we should have stopped for a minute at Upperby shed to change the engine crew, and I'm pretty sure we didn't. By this time there is nothing for it but to switch on the light and look at my watch. That settles it. It's only just midnight, so we couldn't possibly have passed Carlisle. This must be Beattock after all.

Well, now that I know that, perhaps I can go to sleep again; and in fact I do so at once, and, as the event showed I stayed asleep for quite a long time. What next wakes me is a sudden pressure at my feet as the train swings round a curve. Once more, speculation drowsily starts working. It was my feet, not my head, that felt it, so it must be a right-hand curve; and here is a biggish station full of lights. It must be Preston, for the entry to it from the north is a sharp right-hand curve. But as we run through it, I am doubtful, for if it is really Preston we should now be running over the Ribble Bridge, and certainly we are not. Then where are we? I curse myself and try to sleep again, refraining from putting on the light. Once more I am comfortably dozing, when we swing round another curve, over many points, and pass a busy engine shed. This time I get up, slide the louvre from the window, and look out. Yes, this is certainly Preston, and the time is 3.15 a.m., so we must be well on time so far. The false alarm, then, must have been Lancaster; and I must have slept steadily the whole way from Beattock and missed Carlisle altogether.

Having thoroughly yielded to this nosey inquisitiveness I really go to sleep this time, but even in sleep I am vaguely conscious of the geographical messages of noise. We rattle over a bridge – obviously the Sutton Weaver viaduct, so we are near Warrington. A little later comes the characteristically cavernous sound of Crewe, which cannot be mistaken for anywhere else. Then comes a station where a train thunders over our heads as we pass beneath it – probably Lichfield, or it might be Tamworth. Either way it is nowhere near time for that cup of tea which the attendant is going to bring as we run through Bletchley, so go to sleep again, and this time do it properly. And oddly enough I do so, for I hear nothing whatever of Rugby or the Crick Tunnel, or the noisy cutting where the line from Northampton joins us.

The next thing I know is the attendant's knock, and a cup of tea, and his greeting, "Good morning sir. We're just through Bletchley and only five minutes late." This is the magic moment, but it is not only the tea that makes it so. The night is far spent and the day is at hand. Or may be it is more than at hand: the full light has already come. But the mist is not yet shifted from the fields, and, sitting on the bed and then slowly shaving while watching the countryside slip past, one can see the sun gently dissolving the low cloud of vapour, and thrill to the peculiarly beautiful greenness of the grass when seen in that fresh light. Not until Willesden does that magic fade, but then before there is time to regret its passing we are running by the Camden engine sheds, where the engines for the morning procession of expresses between 10 and 11 are out in the yard being prepared for duty. It is the journey's end, for in a moment we are running into Platform 3 at Euston at 7.30.

from THE FASCINATION OF RAILWAYS *1951*

Dining-Car

PAUL JENNINGS

Sometimes it almost seems as if the diesel has had the same effect on our railways as Comte had on philosophy. The mysterious felt essence, the unspeakable but powerful spirit, the god of steam, gave place to an abstract system; a merely human plan of lines, trains, signals, at its grandest merely the nervous system of a huge body, Britain, to be compared scientifically and classified with the systems of other bodies like France, America, Italy (very good stations). Here, on this foggy island (and what is steam but very hot fog?) where the very god or devil of Motion first came among men between Stockton and Darlington (the names themselves show man's dual nature; Stocktown, material, full of things – boots, wagons, timber, bundles, *stock* and Darlington, spiritual, as one might say Angeltown, Lovetown, Soultown) – here, too, a cold and positive science reigns.

Unremarkable men [have now pulled] down that noble structure of which [I] wrote only eleven years ago "fundamentally Euston is a temple, complete with Propylaeum . . . or sacred arch. When we look at early prints of Euston, showing it in all the glory of cream stone against a Canaletto sky, it is easy to imagine the people coming through the Propylaeum with their gifts to the old railway gods. The houses that now huddle round Euston were a later development, as innkeepers and traders moved in to cater for the pilgrims."

The wild cry of the steam whistle blown through the night,
piercing the soul with the poetry of journeys, tears, embarkations,
lost loves, change, wars, laughter, happiness on the wind, tiny
cameos of long-ago meetings in sunlight, solitude, decisions,
accidents, time, has given place to this matter-of-fact parping:

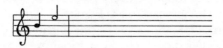

At best all that this suggests is the continuation

– "Tannhaüser", an alien idea nothing to do with the mystery of
British travel.

Steam engines had *names*: I have often been carried to Liverpool
Street by *John Milton,* and there was another one called, mys-
teriously, *Stindon Hall.* You might think that diesels would at least
have names like Jones, Smith, Robinson, Jenkins, Bartlett: but
they have only numbers.

Yet there is one department where, perhaps as a compensation,
they are getting *more* mysterious all the time: the restaurant cars.
In them is gradually becoming concentrated all that strongly
corporate, withdrawn, *other* life that the whole system once had.
You get the feeling that they listen to this modern diesel executive
only when they want to, they are directed from some secret headquarters of their own, possibly static, in old tunnels in Northamp-
tonshire, possibly mobile (why does that tremendous smell of stale
bread come from the grilles under Platform 9 at Waterloo?). A
train is now the only place where you can get a huge, comfortable
bulging British tea – sandwiches with the crusts cut off, toast,
strange sweet jams, meticulously jarred, bread and butter, *toasted
tea-cakes*, plum cake, chocolate biscuits, one after the other (you
try and get that in one of those fluorescent scampi parlours).
Surely *that* menu isn't drawn up by these diesel chaps? It wouldn't
be surprising if the train turned down a weedy disused branch line,

velvet curtains were drawn, the gas lit, and ladies like Mrs
Dalloway came in with three-tiered cakestands.

When they do go along with the executive – public-relations-
minded, modern, comparative – they show more than ever a self-
confident, irrational life of their own. *The Hungry Traveller*, a smart
pamphlet recently found at every passenger's table, said that we
had more restaurant cars than France, Belgium, Italy, Spain,
Western Germany, Scandinavia, the Netherlands and Luxembourg
put together. They didn't actually say so, but the feeling was that
it was fine (well, about £2 a meal) if you were going from Paris to
Lyons, but if you wanted to go from, say, Nantes to Grenoble
you'd be lucky to get a train, let alone a meal. Lines fizzle out,
trains rust away, stationmasters sell the rails, passengers are lost
for ever in rainy hills. . . .

But *our* restaurant cars nurse the secret inner life of our railway
shires, where lonely George Eliot farmhouses stand in tufted
meadows and small roads curve away round low green hills. Never
mind about London–Birmingham; there is a restaurant car on a
train that every day makes the unimaginable journey from Ipswich
to Liverpool. And if a train doesn't have a full restaurant car, such
as serves those great teas, the time-table footnote says RB – buffet
car, or the even smaller MB – miniature buffet, just one man
serving from a little kind of pantry. Doubtless on very minor
routes there are even smaller sub-divisions, tiny waiters going
round with little boxes containing mouse sandwiches, noggins of
soup, thimbles of lemonade.

French railway waiters seem solitary individuals among a society
of diners all spooning it up: but here it is the passengers who eat
alone, isolated, while the waiters continuously pass messages to
one another in undertones, in their mysterious railway fellowship.
Not that they disregard the passengers; they are forever trying to
draw them in. Only last week one of them said to the grim-faced
lady in a flower-pot hat sitting opposite me, "steak, tender as a
lady's heart, madam". They seem to be always on the verge of
drawing us into their great secret.

On the little card showing trains from Hull to London there is
one scheduled to arrive at "4.38K". In the footnotes it says "K –
Commencing July 1st second-class passengers can arrive King's
Cross 4.18 p.m. *without restaurant car*" (my italics). One day I shall

make that journey. I shall make a special effort. I shall go first class. I shall have only just got through the caviar, turtle soup and *steak au poivre* when the misty suburban hills, fag ends of the Chilterns, begin to close in; and *then,* I hope, the waiter will murmur in my ear "let the second-class rabble get on, to their dull appointments, sir. What is time to people like us? There is *poire Hélène,* coffee, brandy, cigars. Let us stop the restaurant car, here, now, in this beech wood. Why don't you *stay* on this train, with us. Let us show you. . . ."

from THE OBSERVER *29 October 1962*

Buffet-Car

BRYAN MORGAN

This is not about drinking in ships, which is much the same as drinking on land only cheaper. It is not about drinking in aircraft, and still less about such Victorian pleasures as drinking in balloons. . . . It is not even about drinking in trams, though that can be done on three lines in Germany, one of which had a purple-and-yellow buffet-car till they thought better of it.

No. It concerns drinking in trains.

I take it as axiomatic that you can only be said to be drinking in a train if both you and the train are going somewhere. An exhibition Pullman at a British Industries Fair, or a *wagon-lits* diner waiting immobile in a siding of Dunkirk quay, may serve meals but are sad, brittle, earthbound affairs. And similarly the man who commutes from Victoria to East Croydon and back with a glass on the table through the terrible hours between When They Close and When They're Open is not so much a traveller as an absorbent character with an alternative to the Soho basement club for which the admission is – if you take the broad view – only a penny platform ticket.

Finally, I would exclude all private drinking from this thesis. You can take a snifter from a hip flask anywhere, and I have been driven to this sort of thing myself in a jolting, all-stations kind of

train between Shrewsbury and Welshpool (it never stopped long
enough for a quick one in the buffet, and by the time we got to
Wales it would probably be Sunday, and so we had to pick up
miniatures of gin from every progressive station). But I, as one
who loves both drinking and trains beyond the call of duty,
believe the combination to need the smell (physical and meta-
phorical) of the Dining-Car.

Diners are much-loved things, for we never quite outgrow our
childhood amazement at the idea of refreshment on wheels. The
moving sunlit countryside; the strange cries from the hell-hole of
the galley; the stewards trying to steer a steady course (in Germany,
I am told, they learn their trade by walking along white lines in the
sealed-off cars of trains moving rapidly: the initiates have to do
things blindfold and it all sounds rather like a party game); the
times when you hit facing points too fast and everything *almost*
goes for a Burton; all these add a glow even to a British Railways
"only-'am-salad-sir" and light ale, and even for the business man
who breakfasts and dines on the Manchester expresses twice a
week. It was Mr Raymond Postgate who confessed to me that
dining-cars inclined him towards euphoria and eupepsia: and Mr
Postgate's senses are not easily bamboozled.

We all, of course, have disappointing memories and resentments
of things other than the high price of railway refreshment. We
recall the race gang who made life intolerable on the "Queen of
Scots", the garrulous GI escaping from Iceland on the Gjedser –
Copenhagen ferry train, the wines which have been stored on hot
axle-boxes, the beer which takes ten minutes to convert itself from
the gaseous to the liquid phase, the B.R. steward snarling "Sherry",
the *wagon-lits* men twirling brandy bottles like Indian clubs in a
last attempt to seduce the homebound British, the waiters everywhere who have manifestly not been trained to walk down even
a static white line. But as against these there are the unforgettable
moments, such as. . . .

Such as the hour when you get up from tea on the 5.10 out of
Paddington, and watch them drop the Bicester slip-coach, and
then settle down to the first evening drink: such as a lightweight
diner suddenly turning up at Kreiensen on a July afternoon when
all Germany lies like a dog in the sun: the soft-running "Sørland
Express" adding its last benison to a holiday spent on the haunted

isles of Oslo Fjord: Listrac as the Barcelona train sights the great
purple line of the Massif: the weedy Royal Canal watched through
the front observation window of that Dublin – Sligo diesel which
they will throttle back to 5 m.p.h. if you let the driver know that
a man wants to finish his glass in peace: and, moment of moments,
the morning flash of Léman as dawn and the "Direct-Orient" ride
on together and, after the night's agonies of a day-car, the smell
of coffee steals down the corridor and tempts you to tot up the
big, creamy, inward-bent bowls with a rum.

I do not normally drink rum for breakfast, but diners incline one
to extravagance. Is that, one wonders, because of the décor within
and without? Because one uses them so comparatively rarely? Or
because, even more than under licensing laws, time is against you,
gentlemen?

For drinks in trains are elusive. I was once at a wedding where,
asking for a second glass of champagne, I was loftily told by the
caterer's man that "That stuff ain't to be drunk indiscriminate".
Similarly, one cannot drink indiscriminate on trains. One may be
ordered – or at least blarneyed – into indulgence on such machines
as the "Brighton Belle", encouraged to drink on such unexpected
lines as the Newcastle and Carlisle and the King's Cross to
Cambridge, and granted a quick one standing up on the way to
Basle or Bognor. But as against these there are the day-long, dry,
cross-country runs from (say) Liverpool to Plymouth on a
Sunday, when every wayside pub passes like a mirage in a desert
and one reaches journey's end two minutes after they've closed
(and usually, too, when you suspect they're still open in the county
you've just left).

So often too, when there *is* a diner, one is allowed in only
between meals. Since train hours tend to be breakfast 8–11, lunch
11–3, tea 3–6, dinner 6–they-take-the-thing-off, this restricts the
railborne imbiber – though B.R.'s experiment in getting over the
trouble, which was to provide windowless diners of supreme discomfort coupled to ye-olde-worlde tavern cars, was far from a
success. This habit of concentrating on food rather than drink,
incidentally, is economically odd: every train in the world makes
more money from its drinkers than its eaters, with the sole exception of pilgrimage excursions. Carmelites, it seems, yield small
returns even on mineral waters.

Yet, despite all handicaps, there is a deep and mystical harmony between drinking and rail-faring. It is not for nothing, one feels, that below London Bridge slumber pipes and puncheons of wine, or that the gothic vaults of St Pancras constitute a beer warehouse. It is not for nothing that the only London theatre in which you can drink in the auditorium lies under the arches of Charing Cross. It is not for nothing that many Continental branch-line stations are virtually pubs with platforms where tickets are sold across the bar, or that when the Lough Swilly line in Ireland closed they left the stations open since every one had a buffet and the bhoys were still thirsty if now immobile.

The subject of railway drinking, then, is ancient, honourable, complex and many-faceted. One could meditate on the characteristics of divers lands – the curious, English and almost amiable *seediness* of B.R., the sharp eye to the main chance of the *wagon-lits* company with its night club on the "Blue Train", or the fact that Denmark is probably the happiest land for the parched passenger, since you are always jumping from trains to boats and back and there is time on both for a quick one. One could consider the *entente* which seems to exist between underground trains and Dubonnet, the customs formalities which dictate that strange rituals be performed with lead-sealed lockers when international expresses cross frontiers, the transatlantic frou-fra when you enter a state which honours the eighteenth amendment, or the orgies in NAAFI troop-trains. One could go up a mountain and brood for years on vital statistics, asking oneself whether the *wagon-lits* company really needs those 650,000 bottles in reserve and what accounts for the fact that, whereas a German diner carries 80 beer and 90 wine and spirit glasses (which seems generous enough), we hit back with over 200 of each. Or, of course, one could devote a thesis to the subject to which a film has already been largely devoted – the subject of drinking on *light* railways.

Switzerland is the obvious country for this, with its half-dozen trim little *elektrischebahnen* running trim little buffet-cars. But I prefer to consider more exotic specimens – the narrow-gauge lines of Yugoslavia and Newfoundland and Spain, the Réseau du Vivarais in France where you used to be joined at a wild way-halt in the Cevennes by a girl in a white coat who discovered a drink-filled ice-box in the tiny autorail, the deliciously Tyrolean

Zillertalbahn with its old teak diner and its steward wearing a large silver shield saying "I speak English", the Rotterdam steam tram and its pea-green refreshment cars. . . . And then one remembers too that a man could once have fortified himself on the narrow-gauge in Britain – on the old Welsh Highland railway, of all places.

But that was long ago; for railway drinking is not what it was in the days when on a *wagon-lits* express even the driver wore a white coat. Lines, like man, are losing their individualities: and the tarty, unsoothing murals of today's air-conditioned diesels are no substitute for the lovely aura of mahogany, plush, brass and cut glass which the Pullman company still honours if nobody else does. Still, train-drinking will hold its fascination for several reasons.

One will go on doing it because one is enjoying the journey or because one is not: because one is alone or because one is in company: because one is thirsty or because there is always time for another. Or because the only alternative may be to drink in refreshment rooms.

from THE COMPLEAT IMBIBER *1956*

Station Hotel

C. BRUYN ANDREWS

The London Station Hotels had, and still have, a distinct position of their own. Surrounded by so many other hotels in every direction, they lack the predominating importance of many of the Station Hotels in provincial towns: they are not, like the hotels at Bradford, Leeds, Sheffield or York, well-known meeting places for commercial travellers. They are more like the Station Hotels at Edinburgh or the smaller hotels at Perth or Inverness, and from the beginning each hotel had a peculiar social atmosphere of its own. As a fashionable resort the Grosvenor Hotel at Victoria Station took the lead; its noble hall, with its classical pillars, fine staircase and gallery above, all painted in pale "Adams" colours, is a feminine version of the Reform Club. The Charing Cross Hotel had a more cosmopolitan air, but its atmosphere reflected the tone given it by its beautiful and stately staircase, with its finely graduated steps.

The Great Western Royal Hotel at Paddington was managed, when it was opened in 1854, by the late Steward of the Union Club, and to this day it in some respects resembles a West End Club. The hall porter and the head waiter, in spite of the impersonality of modern innovations, still recognize many of the visitors and greet them with something of the dignified deference of an accomplished butler. There were habitués and casual but well-known visitors, recognized by all the staff, the servants stayed there most of their lives, and took a pride in the hotel and in those who used it. It was not exactly that the Station Hotels were exclusive, but there were certainly people who were very much at their ease in them, and there were classes who would never have dreamt of using them even for light refreshment.

In its quiet Victorian sedateness, the Great Western Hotel at Paddington was unique. Before the recent alterations there lingered about it an atmosphere of serenity and security, that belonged to a gentler and more self-assured age. Those like myself who knew it well, especially at Christmas when a child, will never forget its Victorian comfort, what it meant to lie in bed with the distant whistle of the trains outside: to feel that the bustle of the station was there when you had the need of it, but that in the meantime it was none of your concern; to hear the confused murmur of life and activity in the station grow less as the evening turned into night. To light the little coloured candles of the Christmas tree on the same solid white bedroom mantelpiece on which it had stood each year, to see the glistening globes doubly beautiful in the mirror behind, seems to belong more to a dream than a memory. What a mature beauty the mirror's heavy gilt frame gave to the whole scene! How nobly it showed off the Christmas cards, pushed precariously into the gap between the beading and the glass, and the presents clustered temptingly at its base! And, when through the heavily braided curtains the morning came with its yearly excitements of carols and pantomimes, was not the renewal of life on the platforms outside, and that familiar smell of trains that came gently in, a perfect prelude to the bacon and eggs downstairs under the great semi-draped allegorical ladies with their arms full of the good things of the earth? Year after year one knew that everything would be the same, from the slowly moving, quietly smiling waiter and the bill of fare, with its sedate mixture of French and English, to the sprig of holly stuck jauntily into the ham. It would be a pity if the British Railways, the largest hotel owners in the world to-day, lost that subtle atmosphere, which in the past has made their hotels a temporary residence rather than a restaurant and a sleeping place.

from THE RAILWAY AGE *1937*

Bradshaw, 1885

F. S. WILLIAMS

The legal historian records a remarkable judicial opinion. It appears that some years ago a witness observed that he had on a certain occasion examined the pages of *Bradshaw's Guide* for some twenty consecutive minutes; whereupon the judge declared that the evidence of such a person must not be relied upon – that he was a fit subject for a commission *de lunatico inquirendo*. We are so unfortunate as to differ from the learned gentleman. We are of the opinion that one of the most valuable, if one of the most uncon-nected, periodicals issued from the monthly press, is that which bears the name of *Bradshaw,* and that it contains data which even the statesman, the philosopher, and the humorist may ponder. The name itself is suggestive. "Some men," it has been said, "are born to greatness, others achieve greatness, and others have greatness thrust upon them;" and to one of these orders of fame we must assign a position for the author of the work in question. It is something to leave behind us a title which posterity will ponder; it must be more to win contemporaneous renown; what must it not be to write our name upon both the present and the future literature of our country? To insert his name in the almanacks of his empire was an honour Julius Caesar laboured to deserve, and Augustus intrigued to share. But to make one's name a necessity in the language of our country, and every month to have it proclaimed and reproclaimed amid the busiest haunts of men, must be a triumph the Caesars never won. Sneering critics may extinguish ambitious enemies by the mere use of an indefinite article, when they recount that "*a* Mr So-and-so then addressed the meeting;" but that which is the marring of one man may be the making of another; the insertion of the article may turn a surname into a noun, and be the means of spreading it on every side and of handing it down to coming centuries. Thus our reader may muse, in mood more grave or gay, when he next stands at a railway book-stall and buys "*a Bradshaw*".

But though month by month tens of thousands peruse the pages of this most popular of all the monthlies, even fame so great is not without alloy. Ill-natured people declare that the volume is as unintelligible as a book of logarithms to a school-girl, and that its study is as exacting a mental toil as the mastery of the integral calculus. Still we venture to think that after all there may be something worth pondering in a sixpenny *Bradshaw*.

It is not long since our journeyings were regulated, not by a volume that contains nearly half a million items, but by a few coachmen's "way-bills". It is not long since – as Mr Oliver Heywood remarked at the opening of the Eccles, Tyldesley, and Wigan line – that railway passengers "had to give their names, and spell them, in order to their being written on a large green paper ticket; when between Liverpool and Manchester there was a long stay at Newton in order that passengers might refresh themselves with Eccles cakes; and when 'a guide' to the line to London cost five shillings, with a cheap edition at half a crown." Nor are we aware of any better means by which to give vividness to our conception of the greatness of this peaceful revolution than to hold in our hand a time-table as it was years ago and as it is today.

The *Railway Companion*, as it was then called, was less than half the size of a page of *Bradshaw*, and contained only about six leaves of railway information. Some cab fares, some little plans of towns, and maps of the counties through which the railways ran, were added. The book was enclosed in a cloth cover, upon which was a small gold label, and it was sold for a shilling. Subsequently two editions of the "Guide" were published at threepence and sixpence; these have grown in their proportions with the growth of what is called by courtesy "our railway system", until we have now a volume of hundreds of pages, telling us of the movements of the thousands of passenger trains that daily run along our great iron thoroughfares, or wind their course along the innumerable byeways that cross and re-cross the land.

from OUR IRON ROADS *6th Edn. 1885*

Bookstall

HENRY MAYHEW

Although the sale of newspapers at the railway termini, &c., cannot strictly be classed as a street-sale, it is so far an open-air traffic as to require some brief notice, and it has now become a trade of no small importance.

The privilege of selling to railway-passengers, within the precincts of the terminus, is disposed of by tender. At present the newsvendor on the North Western Line, I am informed, pays to the company, for the right of sale at the Euston-square terminus, and the provincial stations, as large a sum as 1,700*l*. per annum. The amount usually given is of course in proportion to the number of stations, and the traffic of the railway.

The purchaser of this exclusive privilege sends his own servants to sell the newspapers and books, which he supplies to them in the quantity required. The men thus engaged are paid from 20*s*. to 30*s*. a week, and the boys receive from 6*s*. to 10*s*. 6*d*. weekly, but rarely 10*s*. 6*d*.

All the morning and evening papers are sold at the Station, but of the weekly press, those are sent for sale which in the manager's judgment are likely to sell, or which his agent informs him are

N*

"asked for". It is the same with the weekly unstamped publications. The reason seems obvious; if there be more than can be sold, a dead loss is incurred, for the surplusage, as regards newspapers, is only saleable as waste paper.

The books sold at railways are nearly all of the class best known as "light reading", or what some account light reading. The price does not often exceed 1*s.*; and among the books offered for sale in these places are novels in one volume, published at 1*s.* – sometimes in two volumes, at 1*s.* each; "monthly parts" of works issued in weekly numbers; shilling books of poetry; but rarely political or controversial pamphlets. One man, who understood this trade, told me that "a few of the pamphlets about the Pope and Cardinal Wiseman sold at first; but in a month or six weeks, people began to say, 'A shilling for that! I'm sick of the thing.'"

The large sum given for the privilege of an exclusive sale, shows that the number of books and papers sold at railway stations must be very considerable. But it must be borne in mind, that the price, and consequently the profit on the daily neswpapers, sold at the railways, is greater than elsewhere. None are charged less than 6*d.*, the regular price at a news-agent's shop being 5*d.*, so that as the cost price is 4*d.* the profit is double. Nor is it unusual for a passenger by an early train, who grows impatient for his paper, to cry out, "A shilling for the *Times*!" This, however, is only the case, I am told, with those who start very early in the morning; for the daily papers are obtained for the railway stations from among the earliest impressions, and can be had at the accustomed price as early as six o'clock, although, if there be exciting news and a great demand, a larger amount may be given.

from LONDON LABOUR AND THE LONDON POOR *1851*

Boat Train

ROGER LLOYD

When the [Channel Islands] train comes down from Clapham at about 8.30 p.m. Waterloo Station always seems to be enjoying one of its few spacious and leisurely moments. Vast crowds are not there and so queues do not form. There is room to move, and the loudspeaker is dispensing more light music than announcements.

Although the train stops at Basingstoke and Winchester, few people use it except for those who are bound either for the Channel Islands or for Le Havre, and the language of the passengers is almost as likely to be French as English. The whole train in fact has a pleasantly continental and holiday air. Two vans at the back carry the mail, and the mail bag labels have half the towns in France stencilled on them. The French passengers generally bring continental newspapers with them, and the Channel Islanders show by their talk that either they have been making holiday on the mainland or that they hope to enjoy much sailing and yachting round the coasts of the islands. Their talk is mostly of the sea and its ships, and of the merits of whatever boat it is which is to be on the Jersey run that night, and of whether the sea will be rough or calm. There is a dining-car, but not many have dinner. The hour is too late, and besides, the experienced traveller to Le Havre or St Peter Port knows well that the railway boats have an excellent restaurant, where they serve a far more ample and varied supper before the boat sails than can be had anywhere ashore.

At nine o'clock out into the darkness and round the double curve into Vauxhall the train runs behind its "Lord Nelson" or its "King Arthur" engine, and by Clapham Junction it has worked up to full speed. At Basingstoke it picks up a few passengers, and those waiting for it at Winchester hear the most stirring announcement of the day there, "Channel Islands Boat Train. Only passengers for Jersey, Guernsey and France travel by this train. The next stop will be inside Southampton Docks." They enter and the train sweeps on, working up again to full speed before Shawford, and rushing through the maze of lines at Eastleigh at nearly seventy miles an hour. Not for another mile or two, when it comes to St Denys, does it begin to slacken speed, and for me this is the signal to find a corridor window looking out on the right-hand side of the train, and to lean out of it for the rest of the way. We slow down steadily until Southampton Terminus Station comes into sight, where a tank engine is shunting rolling stock ready for the morning trains, and it seems almost as if we were going to enter it, but at the last moment we lurch to the left, and slowly glide round the outside of it. By now we are crawling at no more

than walking pace, and we go across what is in daytime a very
busy road, our passage being guarded by a man with a bell and a
red lamp. Then the train passes through the dock gates, and
grinds round a left-hand curve so sharp that one wonders so large
an engine can negotiate it. In less than a minute more we pass out
of the darkness and into the glaring, metallic light of the dock
shed, where at last we come to rest.

from THE FASCINATION OF RAILWAYS *1951*

Ferry Train

PAUL JENNINGS

Many Victorians thought that steam and the electric telegraph
were going to unite mankind, but of course really there is a very
subtle and close connection between railways and nationalism. A
country may exist as a formless dreaming embryo for centuries,
but it becomes vertebrate, definite, self-conscious, a great mad
national *person,* only when it has this co-ordinated steel skeleton.

Many of the great nineteenth-century national writers knew this
and more besides, often with foreboding. Mr Dombey was merely
going to Leamington, but to Dickens the train that took him there
"the power that forced itself upon its iron way – its own – defiant
of all paths and roads, piercing through the heart of every obstacle
and dragging living creatures of all classes, ages and degrees
behind it, was a type of the universal monster, Death." *The Idiot*
opens in a train. *Anna Karenina* is full of the sad hiss of steam. In
Dr Zhivago the railway almost seems to be one of the characters;
almost as soon as the lines were laid in Russia they bore fatal
electric rumours of unrest, soldiers, refugees who never knew
whether the next station would be friendly.

Possibly, if we get through the next fifty years, the seething,
undeniable atomic unity of our science will have forced a parallel
unity on us, and we shall look back, from that age of the air, of
fluid frontiers, of international policing, to the *armoured* train as the
high point of lunatic, self-contained nationalism, with its mysterious, *other* soldiers in long coats lurking behind their iron

frontiers, always looking as if they were about to fire their huge
cannon but actually subject to ludicrous civilian mishaps, derail-
ments, running out of coal. . . .

Everyone experiences moments on a railway when his own
private journey suddenly seems trivial, for he hears the nation's
heart drumming through this iron stethoscope; he *knows* those
great triangular stacks of timber, that woman, glimpsed for a
second in a yard, pegging washing, those dumps of old iron
drums, those lone figures in hopeless-looking allotments; that
line, curving off and away over unknown canals, invites him into
a secret part of the national mind. Held up at a level-crossing,
waiting at some windy junction set above derelict meadows, or in
a waiting-room like a vestry, with a great coal fire and long
ecclesiastical benches and pictures of cathedrals, he may see some
extraordinary thing; a *fast* goods train, flashing by at sixty miles
an hour, as though to a disaster.

As the fireman hurls on more coal, somewhere men are wringing
their hands, taking out their watches, waiting with desperate impatience for this great load of – what? Pumps for floods, rams to
shore up a collapsing stadium, hundreds of booming steel bins to
catch the spawning output of some factory run mad?

He may see a lone engine racing wildly backwards (just discovered the coupling broken, rushing back to rescue the marooned
carriages?). And on a really lucky day he may see, in one of those
slow goods trains that simply go slowly up and down outside
stations, *bing bong bang* all day long, two or three wagons labelled

Societe Anglo-Belge des Ferryboats

There is something about the way these dreamy wagons pass
that instantly causes the mind to jump from the actual *Société* and
its perfectly normal business to another *Société,* totally unreal, born
of the railway trance. *This* organization has something static,
almost legendary about it. Once, doubtless, it did a bustling, real
trade. Bolts of actual cloth, early cog-wheels, English harness,
were carried by Puffing Billys to Harwich, loaded on to *le ferryboat*
with its paddle-wheel and great brown sail, welcomed at Zee-
brugge by bishop and burgomaster; and the return journey would
bring us cargoes of lace and great Belgian pies and sausages.

Perhaps, because the dreamer on the platform (and who is

awake on a platform?) has never seen an actual Anglo-Belgian ferryboat operated by the real *Société,* he drifts into a world where the *Société* is heraldic, and all physical business is prosaically handled by British Railways and their Belgian equivalent, to which the *Société* has the same relationship as those accountants and insurance managers from Croydon and Gerrards Cross in the Worshipful Company of Carriage Makers have to a production line in Coventry.

He sees dress uniforms with a faintly marine character, and the eating of great dinners in Gothic cloth halls, alternately in England and Belgium. He sees the ancient gold loving-cup brought out every seven years, at the installation dinner of the new Admiral-Manager, and passed round as the old toast is roared out yet again:

> Oy! Par terre! Et oy! Par mer!
> Ut hoy! Les grands chemins de fer!
> Oy! Buvez qui voudray
> Oy! Vivent les ferryboats anglais!

How pleasant if those trundling wagons simply contained the food for the *Société's* dinners. On their side, vast Belgian *pâtés* and buns and cakes and monster dishes made of pork and owls and veal and sour cream and wine and butter; on ours, noble sirloins, Stiltons, traditional Railway Pudding, strong ale. How pleasant, above all, if this were how the railway became international!

from THE OBSERVER *12 February 1961*

Excursion Train

THOMAS COOK

I was an enthusiastic temperance man, and the secretary of a district association, which embraced parts of the two counties of Leicester and Northampton. A great meeting was to be held at Leicester, over which Lawrence Heyworth, Esq., of Liverpool – a great railway as well as temperance man – was advertised to preside. From my residence at Market Harborough I walked to Leicester (fifteen miles) to attend that meeting. About midway between Harborough and Leicester – my mind's eye has often reverted to the spot – a thought flashed through my brain, what a glorious thing it would be if the newly-developed powers of railways and locomotion could be made subservient to the promotion of temperance! That thought grew upon me as I travelled over the last six or eight miles. I carried it up to the platform, and, strong in the confidence of the sympathy of the chairman, I broached the idea of engaging a special train to carry the friends of temperance from Leicester to Loughborough and back to attend a quarterly delegate meeting appointed to be held there in the two or three weeks following. The chairman approved, the meeting roared with excitement, and early next day I proposed my grand scheme to John Fox Bell, the resident secretary of the Midland Counties Railway Company. Mr Paget, of Loughborough, opened his park for a gala, and on the day appointed about five hundred passengers filled some twenty or twenty-five open carriages – they were called "tubs" in those days – and the party rode the enormous distance of eleven miles and back for a shilling, children half-price. We carried music with us, and music met us at the Loughborough station. The people crowded the streets, filled windows, covered the house-tops, and cheered us all along the line, with the heartiest welcome. All went off in the best style and in perfect safety we returned to Leicester; and thus was struck the keynote of my excursions, and the social idea grew upon me.

from LEISURE HOUR *1860*

Courier's Train

ANTHONY CARSON

Once I worked as a clerk in an office and I grew thinner and my suits fell to bits and I watched the seagulls out of the window. The months passed and I knew I had taken the wrong road. "You're not paid to watch seagulls," said the manager. In my spare time I went to Victoria Station and bought cups of tea and watched the trains. The ceiling of the station shook with the thunder of wheels, and men with fur collars and attaché cases disappeared in clouds of steam. There was a faint imported smell of sea, a catch in the throat, a volley of shouts, and an explosion of children like fireworks. The Golden Arrow drew in. Out came the eternal over-wrapped exiles from operas and roulette, pampered ghosts from Anglo-French hotels, lovers, swindlers, actresses, impostors, believers, bores and magicians. But all that mattered to me was the gold and blue of the places they had been to, the singing names, like Leman, Maggiore, Garda, Ischia, Ibiza.

Eventually I joined a travel agency. I almost lived in trains, pushing hordes of people round monuments, cramming them into cathedrals, and winkling them out of gondolas. Once, on the Paris–Vallorbe run, my train split in two. Half my clients disappeared down a gradient. The runaway carriages reappeared half an hour later at Vallorbe station and were greeted by hysterical shouts, as though they had come back from Siberia. But the train didn't pull up. It puffed off busily in the general direction of Italy, and I found it quite impossible to control the pandemonium on the station platform. Even I, the courier, wasn't aware that this divided train was returning to another platform.

I lived in a world of smoke, station buffets, Customs offices and rattling corridors; the antiseptic rush through the Simplon tunnel; the gleaming run beside the lake of Geneva; carriages of priests, soldiers, Chianti and garlic between Pisa and Rome; and the eternal stolid caravanserai of British clients getting constipated from pasta and ruins. I was still a prisoner entangled in a web of questions, complaints and prejudices. But through the carriage window, past the vacuum flask and the knitting needles, I could see the running rainbow feet of beauty.

After a time I began to weary of trains and to long for London. But I could not escape. The demon which had haunted me in the office and dragged me to Victoria Station to gape at the expresses would not release me. It was my living. Sleeping past Lyons, breakfast at the frontier, loving past Stresa, eating past the Apennines. Eventually I broke up a highly organized tour of Italy by running off with one of the clients, was sacked by the agency and took up writing.

A summer and a winter passed and London lay on my stomach like a lobster supper. I was making no money. The current was turned off, and I dreamed of the Continental railroads like swallows whose wings flutter in their sleep. Somewhere, someone was waving to me. "You should be here!" Again I haunted Victoria Station. Then I paid a visit to another travel agency. "I am a railway expert," I said. "Can you speak Spanish?" asked the manager. "Certainly," I replied. "We are experimenting with a place called Sitges in the north of Spain. We would like you to take about fifty clients there from London. Would you be prepared to do that?" "Yes," I said. "Be careful with them," said the manager. "Some of them are old ladies and not used to travel. You start in a fortnight, and if you call in tomorrow I will give you the list."

We went on the Newhaven–Dieppe–Paris route, and left for Port Bou from the Gare d'Austerlitz. So far it was an uneventful journey, except that four of the old ladies recognized me from my last Italian tour, and I could see them rustling up and down the corridors with scandal. The next morning we steamed into Cerbère, and I was smoked out of my carriage with questions. Do we change here? Is this Spain? Is Franco here? Shall we change our money? Can we use the lavatories in this station or would they arrest us? Can we get coffee? Tea? Aspirins?

Before I need answer all the questions the train slid through a tunnel and we arrived in Port Bou, Spain. Directly we got down on to the platform it was obvious that all the officials hated us on sight. Many of them were armed to the teeth. We were driven into a gloomy barrack-like Customs shed, our suitcases were wrenched open and the contents scattered right and left. One of my old ladies burst into tears. Have you any drugs, firearms, or porno-graphic literature? an official was asking her.

There were six ticket-windows operated by six dour, sadistic railway employees. When you presented a form to be stamped each one said "Wrong window". Finally, at the risk of being shot, I got out on to the Port Bou–Barcelona platform and made inquiries about my agency reservations. A very old man in a peaked cap with RAILWAY SERVICES written on it pointed at a carriage. "They are there," he said. The carriage was bursting with people. "But I have fifty clients," I shouted. The old man looked at me with terrible patient sadness. "That which has to be . . ." he said and crept away.

Finally we arranged ourselves on the train. I stood next a plump Spaniard in the corridor who was looking out of the window at the embittered tourists flapping about the platform like intolerably harassed poultry. "In an odd way it pays," he said, offering me a cigarette. "All of you foreigners, after this ghastly experience at the frontier, are expecting the worst from us. But when you find how friendly we are, and how much we hate our railways, it will seem all the better. Where are you going to?" "I am taking fifty English people to Sitges." "Be prepared for the worst," said the Spaniard, "and beware of the tunnels." He gave me details of the journey.

We reached Barcelona in the afternoon. Three of my old ladies had fainted, and there were ten cases of diarrhoea. ("You should have told us about the water.") There were two trains to Sitges. One said "Very Fast" and the other "Highly Rapid." I chose the Highly Rapid and chased my party into two or three amazingly empty carriages. There was another train which I had not noticed. It was called "Supremely Quick." This left almost immediately. We waited in our train, starving, for about an hour, while it gradually filled up. When it was obviously crammed it left for the next Barcelona station, Paseo de Gracia.

Here was a waiting cargo of fresh passengers. Women lay on the floor like threshed wheat, suckling babies. Aerated-water sellers climbed through a trellis of arms and legs and half the station got on to the train to say goodbye. At the next station the beggars were waiting followed by the lottery sellers carrying dolls and bags of sweets.

An hour later, remembering what the Spaniard at Port Bou had advised me, I squeezed my way through the train and warned all my party to take down their luggage and put it on to the outside platform. "The train only stops for a minute at Sitges," I told them. In the middle of this operation we entered the first tunnel. The carriages filled with smoke and the lottery sellers, coughing with rage, stumbled over their dolls, aerated water rolled over the floor and pickpockets got to work. In all, there were nine tunnels and they were very long and the train was slow. Finally we came into the light, and the town of Sitges, white as ice-cream, glimmered into view.

We poured out of the carriages, the fists of the lottery sellers pistoning through the windows, grappling with a cascade of luggage. Suddenly, with horror, I remembered I had placed some old ladies on the front carriage. I could see no sign of them. I ran forward to the platform behind the engine.

They were there. Five of them. Their faces were quite black. From one desperate feathered hat I could distinctly see a little spiral of smoke ascend, like the aftermath of Red Indian massacre. "This is Sitges," I said in a small voice. But they just looked at me.

And the train, with no warning, as much as to show it *was* a train, made off towards Valencia.

I am back at Victoria Station again. Meet me at Platform Eight.

from PUNCH *2 June 1954*

Emigrant Train

ROBERT LOUIS STEVENSON

It was about two in the afternoon of Friday that I found myself in front of the Emigrant House, with more than a hundred others, to be sorted and boxed for the journey. A white-haired official, with a stick under one arm, and a list in the other hand, stood apart in front of us, and called name after name in the tone of a command. At each name you would see a family gather up its brats and bundles and run for the hindmost of the three cars that stood awaiting us, and I soon concluded that this was to be set apart for the women and children. The second or central car, it turned out, was devoted to men travelling alone, and the third to the Chinese. The official was easily moved to anger at the least delay; but the emigrants were both quick at answering their names, and speedy in getting themselves and their effects on board.

The families once housed, we men carried the second car without ceremony by simultaneous assault. I suppose the reader has some notion of an American railroad-car, that long, narrow wooden box, like a flat-roofed Noah's ark, with a stove and a convenience, one at either end, a passage down the middle, and transverse benches upon either hand. Those destined for emigrants on the Union Pacific are only remarkable for their extreme plainness, nothing but wood entering in any part into their constitution, and for the usual inefficacy of the lamps, which often went out and shed but a dying glimmer even while they burned. The benches are too short for anything but a young child. Where there is scarce elbow-room for two to sit, there will not be space enough for one to lie. Hence the company, or rather, as it appears from certain bills about the Transfer Station, the company's servants, have conceived a plan for the better accommodation of travellers. They prevail on every two to chum together. To each of the chums they sell a board and three square cushions stuffed with straw, and covered with thin cotton. The benches can be made to face each other in pairs, for the backs are reversible. On the approach of night the boards are laid from bench to bench, making a couch wide enough for two, and long enough for a man of the middle height; and the chums lie down side by side upon the cushions with the head to the conductor's van and the feet to the engine. When the train is full, of course this plan is impossible, for there must not be more than one to every bench, neither can it be carried out unless the chums agree. It was to bring about this last condition that our white-haired official now bestirred himself. He made a most active master of ceremonies, introducing likely couples, and even guaranteeing the amiability and honesty of each. The greater the number of happy couples the better for his pocket, for it was he who sold the raw material of the beds. His price for one board and three straw cushions began with two dollars and a half; but before the train left, and, I am sorry to say, long after I had purchased mine, it had fallen to one dollar and a half.

The match-maker had a difficulty with me; perhaps, like some ladies, I showed myself too eager for union at any price; but certainly the first who was picked out to be my bedfellow, declined the honour without thanks. He was an old, heavy, slow-spoken man, I think from Yankeeland, looked me all over with great timidity, and then began to excuse himself in broken phrases. He didn't know the young man, he said. The young man might be very honest, but how was he to know that? There was another young man whom he had met already in the train; he guessed *he* was honest, and would prefer to chum with *him* upon the whole. All this without any sort of excuse, as though I had been inanimate or absent. I began to tremble lest everyone should refuse my company, and I be left rejected. But the next in turn was a tall, strapping, long-limbed, small-headed, curly-haired Pennsylvania

Dutchman, with a soldierly smartness in his manner. To be exact, he had acquired it in the navy. But that was all one; he had at least been trained to desperate resolves, so he accepted the match, and the white-haired swindler pronounced the connubial benediction, and pocketed his fees.

The rest of the afternoon was spent in making up the train. I am afraid to say how many baggage-waggons followed the engine, certainly a score; then came the Chinese, then we, then the families, and the rear was brought up by the conductor in what, if I have it rightly, is called his caboose. The class to which I belonged was of course far the largest, and we ran over, so to speak, to both sides; so that there were some Caucasians among the Chinamen, and some bachelors among the families. But our own car was pure from admixture, save for one little boy of eight or nine who had the whooping-cough. At last, about six, the long train crawled out of the Transfer Station and across the wide Missouri river to Omaha, westward bound.

It was a troubled uncomfortable evening in the cars. There was thunder in the air, which helped to keep us restless. A man played many airs upon the cornet, and none of them were much attended to, until he came to *Home, sweet home*. It was truly strange to note how the talk ceased at that, and the faces began to lengthen. I have no idea whether musically this air is to be considered good or bad; but it belongs to that class of art which may be best described as a brutal assault upon the feelings. Pathos must be relieved by dignity of treatment. If you wallow naked in the pathetic, like the author of *Home, sweet home*, you make your hearers weep in an unmanly fashion; and even while yet they are moved, they despise themselves and hate the occasion of their weakness. It did not come to tears that night, for the experiment was interrupted. An elderly, hard-looking man, with a goatee beard and about as much appearance of sentiment as you would expect from a retired slaver, turned with a start and bade the performer stop that "damned thing". "I've heard about enough of that," he added; "give us something about the good country we're going to." A murmur of adhesion ran round the car; the performer took the instrument from his lips, laughed and nodded, and then struck into a dancing measure; and, like a new Timotheus, stilled immediately the emotion he had raised.

The day faded; the lamps were lit; a party of wild young men, who got off next evening at North Platte, stood together on the stern platform, singing *The Sweet By-and-bye* with very tuneful voices; the chums began to put up their beds; and it seemed as if the business of the day were at an end. But it was not so; for, the train stopping at some station, the cars were instantly thronged with the natives, wives and fathers, young men and maidens, some of them in little more than nightgear, some with stable lanterns, and all offering beds for sale. Their charge began with twenty-five cents a cushion, but fell, before the train went on again, to fifteen, with the bed-board gratis, or less than one-fifth of what I had paid for mine at the Transfer. This is my contribution to the economy of future emigrants.

A great personage on an American train is the newsboy. He sells books (such books!), papers, fruit, lollipops, and cigars; and on emigrant journeys, soap, towels, tin washing dishes, tin coffee pitchers, coffee, tea, sugar, and tinned eatables, mostly hash or beans and bacon. Early next morning the newsboy went around the cars, and chumming on a more extended principle became the order of the hour. It requires but a copartnery of two to manage beds; but washing and eating can be carried on most economically by a syndicate of three. I myself entered a little after sunrise into articles of agreement, and became one of the firm of Pennsylvania, Shakespeare, and Dubuque. Shakespeare was my own nickname on the cars; Pennsylvania that of my bedfellow; and Dubuque, the name of a place in the State of Iowa, that of an amiable young fellow going west to cure an asthma, and retarding his recovery by incessantly chewing or smoking, and sometimes chewing and smoking together. I have never seen tobacco so sillily abused. Shakespeare bought a tin washing-dish, Dubuque a towel, and Pennsylvania a brick of soap. The partners used these instruments, one after another, according to the order of their first awaking; and when the firm had finished there was no want of borrowers. Each filled the tin dish at the water filter opposite the stove, and retired with the whole stock in trade to the platform of the car. There he knelt down, supporting himself by a shoulder against the woodwork or one elbow crooked about the railing, and made a shift to wash his face and neck and hands; a cold, an insufficient, and, if the train is moving rapidly, a somewhat dangerous toilet.

On a similar division of expense, the firm of Pennsylvania, Shakespeare, and Dubuque supplied themselves with coffee, sugar, and necessary vessels; and their operations are a type of what went on through all the cars. Before the sun was up the stove would be brightly burning; at the first station the natives would come on board with milk and eggs and coffee cakes; and soon from end to end the car would be filled with little parties breakfasting upon the bed-boards. It was the pleasantest hour of the day.

There were meals to be had, however, by the wayside: a breakfast in the morning, a dinner somewhere between eleven and two, and supper from five to eight or nine at night. We had rarely less than twenty minutes for each; and if we had not spent many another twenty minutes waiting for some express upon a side track among miles of desert, we might have taken an hour to each repast and arrived at San Francisco up to time. For haste is not the foible of an emigrant train. It gets through on sufferance, running the gauntlet among its more considerable brethren; should there be a block, it is unhesitatingly sacrificed; and they cannot, in consequence, predict the length of the passage within a day or so. Civility is the main comfort that you miss. Equality, though conceived very largely in America, does not extend so low down as to an emigrant. Thus in all other trains, a warning cry of "All aboard!" recalls the passengers to take their seats; but as soon as I was alone with emigrants, and from the Transfer all the way to San Francisco, I found this ceremony was pretermitted; the train stole from the station without note of warning, and you had to keep an eye upon it even while you ate. The annoyance is considerable, and the disrespect both wanton and petty.

Many conductors, again, will hold no communication with an emigrant. I asked a conductor one day at what time the train would stop for dinner; as he made no answer I repeated the question, with a like result; a third time I returned to the charge, and then Jack-in-office looked me coolly in the face for several seconds and turned ostentatiously away. I believe he was half ashamed of his brutality; for when another person made the same inquiry, although he still refused the information, he condescended to answer, and even to justify his reticence in a voice loud enough for me to hear. It was, he said, his principle not to tell people where they were to dine; for one answer led to many other questions, as what o'clock it was? or, how soon should we be there? and he could not afford to be eternally worried.

As you are thus cut off from the superior authorities, a great deal of your comfort depends on the character of the newsboy. He has it in his power indefinitely to better and brighten the emigrant's lot. The newsboy with whom we started from the Transfer was a dark, bullying, contemptuous, insolent scoundrel, who treated us like dogs. Indeed, in his case, matters came nearly to a fight. It happened thus: he was going his rounds through the cars with some commodities for sale, and coming to a party who were at *Seven-up* or *Cascino* (our two games), upon a bed-board, slung down a cigar-box in the middle of the cards, knocking one man's hand to the floor. It was the last straw. In a moment the whole party were upon their feet, the cigars were upset, and he was ordered to "get out of that directly, or he would get more than he reckoned for". The fellow grumbled and muttered, but ended by making off, and was less openly insulting in the future. On the other hand, the lad who rode with us in this capacity from Ogden to Sacramento made himself the friend of all, and helped us with information, attention, assistance, and a kind countenance. He told us where and when we should have our meals, and how long the train would stop; kept seats at table for those who were delayed, and watched that we should neither be left behind nor yet unnecessarily hurried. You, who live at home at ease, can hardly realize the greatness of this service, even had it stood alone. When I think of that lad coming and going, train after train, with his bright face and civil words, I see how easily a good man may become the benefactor of his kind. Perhaps he is discontented with himself, perhaps troubled with ambitions; why, if he but knew it, he is a hero of the old Greek stamp; and while he thinks he is only earning a profit of a few cents, and that perhaps exorbitant, he is doing a man's work, and bettering the world. . . .

It had thundered on the Friday night, but the sun rose on Saturday without a cloud. We were at sea – there is no other adequate expression – on the plains of Nebraska. I made my observatory on the top of a fruit-waggon, and sat by the hour upon that perch to spy about me, and to spy in vain for something new. It was a world almost without a feature; an empty sky, an empty earth; front and back, the line of railway stretched from horizon to horizon, like a cue across a billiard-board; on either hand, the green plain ran till it touched the skirts of heaven. Along the track innumerable wild sunflowers, no bigger than a crown-piece, bloomed in a continuous flower-bed; grazing beasts were seen upon the prairie at all degrees of distance and diminution; and now and again we might perceive a few dots beside the rail-road which grew more and more distinct as we drew nearer till they turned into wooden cabins, and then dwindled and dwindled in our wake until they melted into their surroundings, and we were once more alone upon the billiard-board. The train toiled over this infinity like a snail; and being the one thing moving, it was wonderful what huge proportions it began to assume in our regard. It seemed miles in length, and either end of it within but a step of the horizon. Even my own body or my own head seemed a great thing in that emptiness. I note the feeling the more readily as it is the contrary of what I have read of in the experience of others. Day and night, above the roar of the train, our ears were kept busy with the incessant chirp of grasshoppers – a noise like the winding up of countless clocks and watches, which began after a while to seem proper to that land.

To one hurrying through by steam there was a certain exhilara-tion in this spacious vacancy, this greatness of the air, this discovery of the whole arch of heaven, this straight, unbroken, prison-line of the horizon. Yet one could not but reflect upon the weariness of those who passed by there in old days, at the foot's pace of oxen, painfully urging their teams, and with no landmark but that unattainable evening sun for which they steered, and which daily fled them by an equal stride. . . .

To cross such a plain is to grow homesick for the mountains. I longed for the Black Hills of Wyoming, which I knew we were soon to enter, like an ice-bound whaler for the spring. Alas! and it was a worse country than the other. All Sunday and Monday we travelled through these sad mountains, or over the main ridge of the Rockies, which is a fair match to them for misery of aspect. Hour after hour it was the same unhomely and unkindly world about our onward path; tumbled boulders, cliffs that drearily imitate the shape of monuments and fortifications – how drearily, how tamely, none can tell who has not seen them; not a tree, not a patch of sward, not one shapely or commanding mountain form; sage-brush, eternal sage-brush, over all, the same weariful and gloomy colouring, grays warming into brown, grays darkening towards black; and for sole sign of life, here and there a few fleeing antelopes; here and there, but at incredible intervals, a creek running in a cañon. The plains have a grandeur of their own; but here there is nothing but a contorted smallness. Except for the air, which was light and stimulating, there was not one good circumstance in that God-forsaken land.

I had been suffering in my health a good deal all the way; and at last, whether I was exhausted by my complaint or poisoned in some wayside eating-house, the evening we left Laramie, I fell sick outright. That was a night which I shall not readily forget. The lamps did not go out; each made a faint shining in its own neighbourhood, and the shadows were confounded together in the long, hollow box of the car. The sleepers lay in uneasy attitudes; here two chums alongside, flat upon their backs like dead folk; there a man sprawling on the floor, with his face upon his arm; there another half seated with his head and shoulders on the bench. The most passive were continually and roughly shaken by the movement of the train; others stirred, turned, or stretched out their arms like children; it was surprising how many groaned and murmured in their sleep; and as I passed to and fro, stepping across the prostrate, and caught now a snore, now a gasp, now a half-formed word, it gave me a measure of the worthlessness of rest in that unresting vehicle. Although it was chill, I was obliged to open my window, for the degradation of the air soon became intolerable to one who was awake and using the full supply of life. Outside, in a glimmering night, I saw the black, amorphous hills shoot by unweariedly into our wake. They that long for morning have never longed for it more earnestly than I.

And yet when day came, it was to shine upon the same broken and unsightly quarter of the world. Mile upon mile, and not a tree, a bird, or a river. Only down the long, sterile canons, the train shot hooting and awoke the resting echo. That train was the one piece of life in all the deadly land; it was the one actor, the one spectacle fit to be observed in this paralysis of man and nature. And when I think how the railroad has been pushed through this

unwatered wilderness and haunt of savage tribes, and now will
bear an emigrant for some £12 from the Atlantic to the Golden
Gates; how at each stage of the construction, roaring, impromptu
cities, full of gold and lust and death, sprang up and then died
away again, and are now but wayside stations in the desert; how
in these uncouth places pigtailed Chinese pirates worked side by
side with border ruffians and broken men from Europe, talking
together in a mixed dialect, mostly oaths, gambling, drinking,
quarrelling and murdering like wolves; how the plumed here-
ditary lord of all America heard, in this last fastness, the scream
of the "bad medicine waggon" charioting his foes; and then when
I go on to remember that all this epical turmoil was conducted
by gentlemen in frock coats, and with a view to nothing more
extraordinary than a fortune and a subsequent visit to Paris, it
seems to me, I own, as if this railway were the one typical achievement of the age in which we live, as if it brought together into one
plot all the ends of the world and all the degrees of social rank,
and offered to some great writer the busiest, the most extended,
and the most varied subject for an enduring literary work. If it be
romance, if it be contrast, if it be heroism that we require, what
was Troy town to this? . . .

At Ogden we changed cars from the Union Pacific to the
Central Pacific line of railroad. The change was doubly welcome;
for, first, we had better cars on the new line; and, second, those in
which we had been cooped for more than ninety hours had begun
to stink abominably. Several yards away, as we returned, let us
say from dinner, our nostrils were assailed by rancid air. I have
stood on a platform while the whole train was shunting; and as
the dwelling-cars drew near, there would come a whiff of pure
menagerie, only a little sourer, as from men instead of monkeys.
I think we are human only in virtue of open windows. Without
fresh air, you only require a bad heart, and a remarkable command
of the Queen's English, to become such another as Dean Swift;
a kind of leering, human goat, leaping and wagging your scut on
mountains of offence. I do my best to keep my head the other
way, and look for the human rather than the bestial in this Yahoo-
like business of the emigrant train. But one thing I must say, the
car of the Chinese was notably the least offensive.

The cars on the Central Pacific were nearly twice as high, and so proportionately airier; they were freshly varnished, which gave us all a sense of cleanliness as though we had bathed; the seats drew out and joined in the centre, so that there was no more need for bed boards; and there was an upper tier of berths which could be closed by day and opened at night. . . .

A little corner of Utah is soon traversed, and leaves no particular impressions on the mind. By an early hour on Wednesday morning we stopped to breakfast at Toano, a little station on a bleak, high-lying plateau in Nevada. . . .

From Toano we travelled all day through deserts of alkali and sand, horrible to man, and bare sage-brush country that seemed little kindlier, and came by supper-time to Elko. As we were standing, after our manner, outside the station, I saw two men whip suddenly from underneath the cars, and take to their heels across country. They were tramps, it appeared, who had been riding on the beams since eleven of the night before; and several of my fellow-passengers had already seen and conversed with them while we broke our fast at Toano. These land stowaways play a great part over here in America, and I should have liked dearly to become acquainted with them.

At Elko an odd circumstance befell me. I was coming out from supper, when I was stopped by a small, stout, ruddy man, followed by two others taller and ruddier than himself.

"Ex-cuse me, sir," he said, "but do you happen to be going on?"

I said I was, whereupon he said he hoped to persuade me to desist from that intention. He had a situation to offer me, and if we could come to terms, why, good and well. "You see," he continued, "I'm running a theatre here, and we're a little short in the orchestra. You're a musician, I guess?"

I assured him that, beyond a rudimentary acquaintance with "Auld Lang Syne" and "The Wearing of the Green", I had no pretension whatever to that style. He seemed much put out of countenance; and one of his taller companions asked him, on the nail, for five dollars.

"You see, sir," added the latter to me, "he bet you were a musician; I bet you weren't. No offence, I hope?"

"None whatever," I said, and the two withdrew to the bar, where I presume the debt was liquidated.

This little adventure woke bright hopes in my fellow-travellers, who thought they had now come to a country where situations went a-begging. But I am not so sure that the offer was in good faith. Indeed, I am more than half persuaded it was but a feeler to decide the bet.

Of all the next day I will tell you nothing, for the best of all reasons, that I remember no more than that we continued through desolate and desert scenes, fiery hot and deadly weary. But some time after I had fallen asleep that night, I was awakened by one of my companions. It was in vain that I resisted. A fire of enthusiasm and whisky burned in his eyes; and he declared we were in a new country, and I must come forth upon the platform and see with my own eyes. The train was then, in its patient way, standing halted in a by-track. It was a clear, moonlit night; but the valley was too narrow to admit the moonshine direct, and only a diffused glimmer whitened the tall rocks and relieved the blackness of the pines. A hoarse clamour filled the air; it was the continuous plunge of a cascade somewhere near at hand among the mountains. The air struck chill, but tasted good and vigorous in the nostrils – a fine, dry, old mountain atmosphere. I was dead sleepy, but I returned to roost with a grateful mountain feeling at my heart.

When I awoke next morning, I was puzzled for a while to know if it were day or night, for the illumination was unusual. I sat up at last, and found we were grading slowly downward through a long snowshed; and suddenly we shot into an open; and before we were swallowed into the next length of wooden tunnel, I had one glimpse of a huge pine-forested ravine upon my left, a foaming river, and a sky already coloured with the fires of dawn. I am usually very calm over the displays of nature; but you will scarce believe how my heart leaped at this. It was like meeting one's wife. I had come home again – home from unsightly deserts to the green and habitable corners of the earth. Every spire of pine along the hill-top, every trouty pool along that mountain river, was more dear to me than a blood relation. Few people have praised God more happily than I did. And thenceforward, down by Blue Canon, Alta, Dutch Flat, and all the old mining camps, through a sea of mountain forests, dropping thousands of feet toward the far sea-level as we went, not I only, but all the passengers on board, threw off their sense of dirt and heat and weariness, and bawled like schoolboys, and thronged with shining eyes upon the platform and became new creatures within and without. The sun no longer oppressed us with heat, it only shone laughingly along the mountain-side, until we were fain to laugh ourselves for glee. At every turn we could see farther into the land and our own happy futures. At every town the cocks were tossing their clear notes into the golden air, and crowing for the new day and the new country. For this was indeed our destination; this was "the good country" we had been going to so long.

By afternoon we were at Sacramento, the city of gardens in a plain of corn; and the next day before the dawn we were lying to upon the Oakland side of San Francisco Bay. The day was breaking as we crossed the ferry; the fog was rising over the citied hills of San Francisco; the bay was perfect – not a ripple, scarce a stain, upon its blue expanse; everything was waiting, breathless, for the sun. A spot of cloudy gold lit first upon the head of Tamalpais, and then widened downward on its shapely shoulder; the air seemed to awaken, and began to sparkle; and suddenly

The tall hills Titan discovered,

and the city of San Francisco, and the bay of gold and corn, were lit from end to end with summer daylight.

from ACROSS THE PLAINS *1892*

Hobo's Train

W. H. DAVIES

Brum informed me of a freight train that was to leave the yards at midnight, on which we could beat our way to a small town on the borders of the hop country. Not knowing what to do with ourselves until that time arrived, we continued to drink until we were not in a fit condition for this hazardous undertaking – except we were fortunate to get an empty car, so as to lie down and sleep upon the journey. At last we made our way towards the yards, where we saw the men making up the train. We kept out of sight until that was done and then in the darkness Brum inspected one side of the train and I the other, in quest of an empty car. In vain we sought for that comfort. There was nothing to do but to ride the bumpers or the top of the car, exposed to the cold night air. We jumped the bumpers, the engine whistled twice, toot! toot! and we felt ourselves slowly moving out of the yards. Brum was on one car and I was on the next facing him. Never shall I forget the horrors of that ride. He had taken fast hold on the handle bar of his car, and I had done likewise with mine. We had been riding some fifteen minutes, and the train was going at its full speed when, to my horror, I saw Brum lurch forward, and then quickly pull himself straight and erect. Several times he did this, and I shouted to him. It was no use, for the man was drunk and fighting against the over-powering effects, and it was a mystery to me how he kept his hold. At last he became motionless for so long that I knew the next time he lurched forward his weight of body must break his hold, and he would fall under the wheels and be cut to pieces. I worked myself carefully towards him and woke him. Although I had great difficulty in waking him, he swore that he was not asleep. I had scarcely done this when a lantern was shown from the top of the car, and a brakesman's voice hailed us. "Hallo, where are you two going?" "To the hop fields," I answered. "Well," he sneered, "I guess you won't get to them on this train, so jump off, at once. Jump! d'ye hear?" he cried, using a great oath, as he saw we were little inclined to obey. Brum was now wide awake. "If you don't jump at once," shouted this irate

brakesman, "you will be thrown off." "To jump," said Brum
quietly, "will be sure death, and to be thrown off will mean no
more." "Wait until I come back," cried the brakesman, "and we
will see whether you ride this train or not," on which he left us,
making his way towards the caboose. "Now," said Brum, "when
he returns we must be on the top of the car, for he will probably
bring with him a coupling pin to strike us off the bumpers, making
us fall under the wheels." We quickly clambered on top and in a
few minutes could see a light approaching us, moving along the
top of the cars. We were now lying flat, so that he might not see
us until he stood on the same car. He was very near to us, when
we sprang to our feet, and unexpectedly gripped him, one on each
side, and before he could recover from his first astonishment. In
all my life I have never seen so much fear on a human face. He
must have seen our half drunken condition and at once gave up
all hopes of mercy from such men, for he stood helpless, not
knowing what to do. If he struggled it would mean the fall and
death of the three, and did he remain helpless in our hands, it
might mean being thrown from that height from a car going at the
rate of thirty miles an hour. "Now," said Brum to him, "what is it
to be? Shall we ride this train without interference, or shall we
have a wrestling bout up here, when the first fall must be our last?
Speak!" "Boys", said he, affecting a short laugh, "you have the
drop on me; you can ride." We watched him making his way back
to the caboose, which he entered, but every moment I expected to
see him reappear assisted by others. It might have been that there
was some friction among them, and that they would not ask
assistance from one another. For instance, an engineer has to take
orders from the conductor, but the former is as well paid, if not
better, than the latter, and the most responsibility is on his shoulders, and this often makes ill blood between them. At any rate,
American tramps know well that neither the engineer nor the
fireman, his faithful attendant, will inform the conductor or brakesman of their presence on a train. Perhaps the man was ashamed of
his ill-success, and did not care to own his defeat to the conductor
and his fellow brakesmen; but whatever was the matter, we rode
that train to its destination and without any more interference.

from THE AUTOBIOGRAPHY OF A SUPER-TRAMP *1908*

Ammunition Train

PETER FLEMING

I forget which of us it was who found the ammunition train. There were two of them, as a matter of fact, lying forlornly in a railway siding outside the town of Larissa. Larissa in the great empty plain of Thessaly was [the] main supply base in Northern Greece from which, in April 1941, the British Expeditionary forces were withdrawing under heavy German pressure.

The town had been bombed by the Italians, then it had been badly damaged by an earthquake, and now it was receiving regular attention from the Luftwaffe. It was an awful mess. The Greek railway staff had run away, and it was pretty obvious that the two ammunition trains had been abandoned. I knew that we were seriously short of ammunition further down the line so I went to the Brigadier in charge of the base and asked permission to try and get one of the trains away. It was given with alacrity.

I don't want you to think that this action on my part was public spirited, or anything like that. My motives were purely selfish. *We wanted a job.* We were a small unit which had been carrying out various irregular activities further north; but now the sort of tasks for which we were designed had become impossible, and we were in danger of becoming what Civil Servants call redundant. We felt that if we could get this train away we should be doing something useful and justifying our existence. Besides, one of us claimed that he knew how to drive an engine.

This was Norman Johnstone, a brother officer in the Grenadier Guards. One of our jobs earlier in the campaign had been to destroy some rolling-stock which could not be moved away. Norman had a splendid time blowing up about twenty valuable locomotives and a lot of trucks, but towards the end we ran out of explosives. At this stage a sergeant in the 4th Hussars turned up, who was an engine-driver in civilian life. With Norman helping him, he got steam up in the four surviving engines, drove them a quarter of a mile down the line, then sent them full tilt back into the station where they caused further havoc of a spectacular and enjoyable kind.

These were perhaps not ideal conditions under which to learn how to drive an engine, especially as the whole thing was carried out under shell-fire; and all we really knew for certain about Norman's capabilities as an engine-driver was that every single locomotive with which he had been associated had become scrap metal in a matter of minutes. Still, he was a very determined and a very methodical chap, and there seemed no harm in letting him have a go. So early in the morning we made our way to the railway station, just in time for the first air-raid of the day.

Except for occasional parties of refugees and stragglers from the Greek army the station was deserted. There were two excellent reasons for this. First of all there were no trains running, so there was no point in anybody going there anyhow. Secondly, the station was practically the only thing left in the ruins of Larissa that was worth bombing; we had ten air raids altogether before we left in the afternoon, and they always had a go at the station.

The first thing we had to do was to get steam up in a railway engine. There were plenty of these about but all except two had been rendered unserviceable by the Luftwaffe. We started work on the bigger of the two.

After having a quick look round Norman explained to us that one of the most popular – and probably in the long run the _soundest_ – of all methods of making steam was by boiling water; but we, he said, might have to devise some alternative formula, as the water mains had been cut by bombs and there was very little coal to be found. However, in the long run we got together enough of these two more or less essential ingredients, and all was going well when one of the few large bombs that came our way blew a hole in the track just outside the shed we were working in – thus, as it were, locking the stable door before we had been able to steal the horse. Greatly disgusted, we transferred our attention to the only other sound engine.

There were more air-raids, and it came on to rain, and two Greek deserters stole my car, and altogether things did not look very hopeful, especially when somebody pointed out that there was now only one undamaged and navigable set of tracks leading out of the battered marshalling yard.

But the needle on the pressure-gauge in the cabin of our engine was rising slowly, and at last, whistling excitedly, the ancient machine got under way. It was a majestic sight, and it would have been even more majestic if she had not gone backwards instead of forwards.

It was at this point that a certain gap in Norman's education as an engine driver became evident. The sergeant in the 4th Hussars had taught him how to start a locomotive and how to launch it on a career of self-destruction; but Norman's early training in how to stop an engine had been confined entirely to making it run violently into a lot of other rolling stock. We trotted anxiously along the cinders, hanging, so to speak, on to Norman's stirrup leathers. "Do you know how to stop?" we shouted. "Not yet", replied Norman, a trifle testily.

But he soon found out and presently mastered the knack of making the engine go forwards as well as backwards, and we steamed rather incredulously northwards towards the siding where the ammunition trains lay.

We chose the bigger of the two. It consisted of 26 trucks containing 120 tons of ammunition and 150 tons of petrol. It was not what you might call an ideally balanced cargo from our point of view, and nobody particularly wanted the petrol, but the train was made up like that and we had to lump it. . . .

Almost as soon as we had left Larissa we began to climb up a long, gentle slope; and we had only done about five miles when the needle on the pressure gauge began slowly but firmly to fall. We stoked like mad. Norman pulled, pushed and twiddled the various devices on what we quite incorrectly called the dashboard. Pressure continued to fall, and the train went slower and slower. At last it stopped altogether.

"We'd better get out," said Norman, "and have a look at the injector-sprockets". He may not actually have said "injector sprockets" but anyhow it was some technical term which meant nothing to us and may not have meant a very great deal to him. It was at this point that we realized that the train was not merely stopped but was beginning to run slowly backwards down the hill. The thought of free-wheeling backwards into Larissa was distasteful to all of us. In the hurry of departure we had had no time to organize our ten brakemen, who were confined in the guard's van instead of being dispersed along the train so that they could operate the brakes on individual goods wagons.

There was only one thing to do. I leapt off the engine and ran back down the train as fast as I could, like an old lady running for a bus, jumped on the back of the nearest goods van, swarmed up a little ladder on to its roof and feverishly turned the wheel which put the brake on. The train continued to go backwards, but it seemed to have stopped gathering speed and at last, after I had repeated this operation several times, it came reluctantly to a stop.

We were really getting a great deal of fun out of this train. We had got a tremendous kick out of starting it, and now we were scarcely less elated at having brought it to a standstill. But we had to face the facts and the *main* fact was that as engine-drivers, though we had no doubt some excellent qualities – originality, determination, cheerfulness and so on – we were open to the serious criticism that we didn't seem to be able to drive our engine very far. A run of five miles, with a small discount for going backwards unexpectedly, is not much to show for a hard day's work.

At this point, moreover, it suddenly began to look as if we were going to lose our precious train altogether. As we tinkered away at the engine, the air grew loud with an expected but none the less unwelcome noise, and a number of enemy bombers could be seen marching through the sky towards us. We were a very conspicuous object in the middle of that empty plain and I quickly gave orders for the ten men in the guard's van to go and take cover five hundred yards from the train. In point of fact there was no cover to take but they trotted off with alacrity and sat down round a small tree about the size of a big gooseberry bush in the middle distance. We could not very well leave the engine because the fire might have gone out (or anyhow we thought it might) and we should have had to start all over again.

But if we had our troubles the enemy, as so often happens, had his too. The bombers were obviously interested in us, but it soon became equally obvious that they had no bombs, having wasted them all on the ruins of Larissa earlier in the day.

They still, however, had their machine guns and three or four of the aircraft proceeded to attack us, coming in very low one after the other. But they all made the same mistake, which they might not have made if we ourselves had taken evasive action and left the train. They all attacked the engine, round which they could see signs of life, instead of flying up and down the twenty odd wagons full of petrol and H. E. and spraying them with bullets, which could hardly have failed to produce spectacular results. They concentrated on putting the engine out of action; and the engine, as we ourselves were just beginning to realize, was out of action already, all the water in the boiler having somehow disappeared.

We used the engine in much the same way as one uses a grouse-butt. Whichever side the attack was coming from, we got the other side. The flying machine, making a terrible noise and blazing away with its machine-gun, swept down on us and as it roared overhead – much bigger, much more malevolent but not really very much *higher* than the average grouse – we pooped off at it with our Tommy gun, to which the German rear-gunner replied with a burst that kicked up the dust a hundred yards away or more. It got rather silly after a bit. I am quite sure we never hit the Luftwaffe, and the only damage the Luftwaffe did to us was to make a hole in a map somebody had left in the cab. And one of the things about driving a train is that you do not need a map to do it with.

They gave it up quite soon – it was getting late anyhow – and went home to Bulgaria. We climbed back into our engine again, and as I looked at our only casualty – the map, torn by an explosive bullet and covered in coal dust – I could not help rather envying the Luftwaffe who believed that they had succeeded in doing what they set out to do. It was only too obvious that we had not. Night fell and it was fairly cold.

Then all of a sudden, out of the darkness, another train appeared, full of Australian gunners whose guns were supposed to have come on the road. They towed us back to the next station. Here we picked up a good engine with a Greek driver and set off for the south.

Forty-eight hours after we had started work on this unlikely project we reached our – or rather the ammunition's – destination. It was a place called Amphykleion and here I formally handed over the train – twenty-six coaches, one hundred and fifty tons of petrol, one hundred and twenty tons of ammunition – to the supply people. Everyone was delighted with it. "This really will make a difference," they said. We felt childishly pleased. The sun shone, it was a lovely morning. And this marked improvement in the weather made it comparatively easy for a small force of German dive-bombers, a few hours later, to dispose of the train and all its contents with a terrible finality.

from B.B.C. BROADCAST *1949*

Deportation Train

ANDREW KARPATI

The day before we were deported I went down to the tracks by our camp to take a close look at the cattle trucks then being assembled into a long train. I was not much more than thirteen, not particularly brave, but I had always taken risks to satisfy my curiosity.

In the event, the few S.S. men and Hungarian gendarmes who were around paid no attention to me, and I kept walking up and down along the train with the excitement anything connected with a journey always aroused in me. What fear I had seemed to come from the metalwork and the rails; but the wooden part fascinated me. For many of the wagons were painted in colours different from the usual brick red of Hungarian goods trains.

I started deciphering letters and names I had never seen before. "Italia" was easy, so was the German "D.R.B."; but "S.N.C.F." and "B" took longer because I knew very little French; in the end, I even guessed some of the Slavonic names – and I was pleased with this. "An international train! I must tell my parents at once" – they had been abroad a lot – "but perhaps better not – it would only. . . ."

When we knew that families were not going to be separated, being put into the wagons frightened us less than we expected. Our turn came in the evening, and there was even a certain relief in this, after having stood all day in lined-up groups of about ninety in the oppressive heat, after the improvized latrines of the over-crowded camp, the shouting and the whip-cracking, the beatings by Hungarian fascists in search of valuables, the uncertainty about our immediate fate.

Now something definite was happening at last, perhaps the worst was over – and did not the very fact that they bothered to get all this transport organized, that they counted us, show that the pessimists may be, must be, wrong? Mrs E. need not have poisoned herself. Mrs E. was a close friend of my parents, and I kept thinking of her: the livid face, the lolling tongue, the hair falling back as she lay dying in pain.

Before climbing up into the trucks, I looked at the S.S. officer who counted us, half-muttering. Again the same double feeling: terror in the thick protruding lower lip, pouches under bored eyes, riding boots, holster, death's-head cap – but some reassurance in being checked in the required quantity on a sort of bill of lading, in the smooth way things were ordered. At least he stopped people from pushing – to be crushed to death was a recurrent fear – if people don't panic there's no cause for panic: instead of a stampede, a silent procession.

Inside the truck there was still a little light from the small air-holes. My parents, my sister and I succeeded in getting quite near to one of these "windows", near one of the corners: a privileged position, I at once realized. As the others kept pressing in – about ninety of them – we somehow still had some space left: I sat on top of my rucksack with my legs drawn up, facing an old man, who sat propped up against the side of the wagon. I soon learned to loathe this man as no one before: he was far too big and he took up far too much room, he shouted in a raucous voice when in distress, his bony giant's fingers shaking with palsy only an inch away; between his trembling legs a half-full demijohn that held not a drop of water for others – except his wife.

My family was somewhere to my right, but increasingly distant, partitioned by bundles of things and limbs, the distinction between these two finally obscured by the darkness. (The late nightfall of summer solstice. Our watches had been taken away; the light through the airholes was our timekeeper.) And if in the dark this huge old man dominated the narrow space before me, I had at first no notion of what went on behind me and to my left: that was outer space whose events I tried to guess by the sounds that came from it.

Somewhere, very far, a child started to cry, then someone called for light, several people, one after the other, called for a doctor. All was vague and unreal, deadened by futile attempts at sleep and

by my boyish determination to detach myself from it all. But one
of the cries was answered, and I recognized with a certain joy the
voice of a doctor I knew: "Be patient, I am coming, I still have
some opium," or something like that – the word opium stuck in
my mind. . . .

Meanwhile the train had started, and I must have slept a little
because when it stopped again somewhere, no one knew where –
there were guards shouting outside and some people shouting in
the dark within – I woke up to a dry numbness and to my first bad
thirst.

In the two-and-a-half-day journey that followed, the outline in
the wagons became clearer – there was even a sense of settling
down, of organization – but the numbness and the thirst grew all
the time. The need for water was the hardest to bear, then there
was the need to dispose of refuse, urine and faeces, and the need to
know where we were.

Our thirst was so bad that I at least could not take any food at
all throughout the journey despite the fact that we still had some
reserves. But we had no water left in the heat known as "dog
days", and thirst became both chronic and obsessive: in paying
attention to this particular condition one forgot the general condition. I don't remember anything else of these long hours! I
didn't even realize how ill my father was (so ill that he was to die
soon after arrival).

The dryness in the mouth gradually absorbed the rising stench;
only saliva, getting rarer, offered some refreshment. But once,
when the train halted in the middle of some fields, a peasant woman
ran to our wagon and, with astonishing speed and skill, handed in
a big jug of water; there was enough to be shared out with considerable fairness among those near the airhole. Again, when we
reached the frontier area, we stopped in line with a military train;
a German soldier leant across and pushed up his billy-can full of
cold tea. That was enough for some of us; I think I must have had
an unfairly large share, thanks to my age.

These unknown helpers restored one's sense of humanity; the
experience is now linked in my mind – perhaps arbitrarily – with
the Samaritan woman at Jacob's well and the promise of living
water; I am certain that such people are the wellspring of hope in
a time of troubles.

The second need, the disposal of excrement, was organized by the most active members of our congested community. Saucepans and all sorts of other cooking utensils were produced from the luggage, and these were relayed from person to person till they reached the airhole where their contents were emptied with some difficulty. Of course, they could not be washed out, and the fact that many people were suffering badly from diarrhoea made things worse. But although all this spread squalor, it also seemed to rouse people from their torpor – it called for energy and even humour.

Finally, the mind's greatest need: the need to know where we were. Soon after the dawn of the first day we found out that we were heading west; later in the day we realized that we were passing Budapest, and even houses were recognized with a strange excitement; the first day had passed and we were still heading west. This was generally interpreted as a good sign. Although nobody at the time knew about the death camps – if people had known many would have escaped – there was a dread connected with the north and north-east: the way to Poland.

There had been rumours of previous deportations. . . . certainly, people felt the west could not be so bad. I think this was partly based on a general – unfounded – belief that people could not be killed in the Budapest area, or – as the train rumbled on towards Vienna – in such a "civilized" place as Greater Germany; partly on the rumour that someone had seen a postcard sent by a deportee from Thuringia saying "We are safe". Someone else had heard that an important bridge to the north had been blown up; someone else that there might be exchanges.

On such rumours and speculations our whole structure of hope was founded – mingling with the knowledge that the allies were advancing towards Northern Italy, that they had landed in Normandy, that the Russians had broken through the front west of Vitebsk, and *might* soon be advancing through the Carpathians; the Yugoslav partisans were also said to be doing well. And the slowness of the Eighth Army in Italy was thought of with impatience even as we suffered from the slowness of the train. Yet every glimpse through the airholes, every recognized station, helped to make the worst part of the journey – when some became hysterical and many wholly apathetic – bearable to those who "followed the news".

o*

By the time the doors were opened, at a camp that turned out to be in Lower Austria, most of us were so lifeless that the sun and the air were welcomed only in theory, because one knew, from memory, that they were beneficent; but exposure to this change, after clambering down and trying to stand on one's feet, weakened the body and confused the mind.

I remember staring, for a long time, at the filth of the wagon we had left behind, with a renewed and sickly sense of unreality: waiting to be moved like a parcel and prepared to be thrown back, to stay in the train for good. In the wagon next to ours there was a corpse, the first I had ever seen, but I looked at it with indifference: big yellow feet, a woman, not very old – what did it matter? This lack of feeling and wanting anything was also a new experience.

I think it was the thirst that helped me to recover myself; I saw a man from the camp carrying a bucket of water, ran up to him and, without asking or warning, dipped my mug into the bucket. An S.S. man roared at me, but by then I had drunk. Then only did I feel it was better to be out of the cattle truck.

from THE OBSERVER *16 July 1961*

PART VIII

Foreign Parts

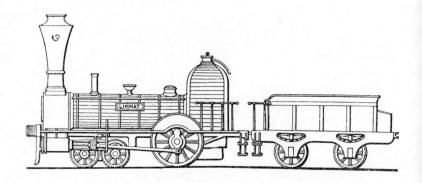

Comments on Three Nations

BRYAN MORGAN

The system of the Société Nationale des Chemins de Fer Français is in many respects admirable. Its trains are generally uncrowded, outstandingly punctual, comfortable if prison-bleak in the main-line second class . . . not dilatory (though the claim that *"Les Chemins de Fer français sont les plus rapides du monde sur les longs parcours"* is a sentiment open to doubt) and visually passable apart from some idiotic modern coaches which look like drain-pipes. Further, though the nationalization of 1938 destroyed much local colour on their main lines, the French railways retain more regional character than those of the majority of countries. Above all they have a largeness, a majesty of spirit and a sense of huge spaces which make them for me the most heart-stirring in the world. It is from the viewpoint of one *qui se passionne pour* the lines of France, great and small, that I here admit that for practical purposes they are the most inadequate of any important country.

It is not that, even after years of decline, the Republic is short of track: thinly-populated as it is, it has the highest ratio of track-miles per inhabitant in Europe, and its figure of track-miles per square mile is not a lot below average. But it *is* very short of trains. When things are going well it is fine sport to work out routes which defeat the thinness of French transport, but when you are behind schedule or have struck dull country and bad weather it is a fearful thing to force a passage to some important-looking junction and then find that there is no transport at all for six hours and none going the way you want for fifteen.

Part of the trouble is that the whole rail system of the Republic – the dozen great trunk routes radiating from Paris, the inner and outer circles of *relations interrégionales* – works on the assumptions that the main reason for travel is to commute with Paris, and that a day-train and a night-train will suit everybody. So the *directs* leave the capital at about 8 a.m. and 10 p.m.: at major stations down the line a fatuous game of train-making-and-train-taking, based on the theory that one prefers to spend hours being biffed and buffeted around rather than quietly change platforms, is played: and at the dimmest way-junctions little moves save in relation to a once-daily event. For even the French rarely put on a local connection at 3 a.m.

This would not matter so much had France buses: but it has them only very patchily. There are some well-served roads, but there are vast areas where the only buses of the day are tied to the Paris trains. Somehow this always means that they run at 6.30 a.m., which is fine for the farmers, marketers and relation-visitors of a nation which keeps peasant hours, but less satisfactory for a traveller who dislikes early rising and wants to cover more than thirty miles a day.

Still, a theorist could claim that if French transport is inadequate it is at least "planned". It is, of course; and that means that it is ruthlessly inflexible. On the large scale it is vulnerable to acts of God and the Republic's enemies: on the small scale it falls to pieces whenever it is tested. On national holidays, for instance, dozens of trippers crowd on buses for which no reliefs exist, and by the time they have all stowed their cauliflowers and had their argument with the driver you are hours late and the few who really were aiming for the Paris express resign themselves to an over-night vigil at the junction.

This inflexibility and *limitation des parcours kilométriques* exists today by Act of Parliament: for around 1938 the French decided that what they wanted was rationalized transport. They suppressed many existing bus services which theoretically duplicated railways, excluded four-fifths of them from the timetables, and got booking-office officials into a state where they would swear that nowhere in France did a bus supplement a railway – whilst just across the square there were two departing before the next train.

But on the whole the planners made a good job of immobilizing the country. As to new routes, it was regulated that none could even be considered without the approbation of the prefect, the P.T.T. bosses and a whole gaggle of bureaucrats for every Département through which the projected service was to pass – and then, of course, it was only an application for Paris to consider. Finally, this rigmarole had to be gone through whenever a company felt it could run two buses daily instead of one.

All this is A Moral To Planners. Today France offers the sight of what was amongst the finest transport systems of Europe but is so no more. Its services have moved so far backwards that in many areas it is almost impossible to travel – and, in fact, a fair proportion of the French have only taken a train during their conscription period.

Now, public transport is one of those things which not only evolves from national habits but helps to form them: just as the desire to travel breeds means of travel, so do lack of facilities encourage lack of enterprise. Since France . . . is not much less populous than Germany and certainly no poorer than Italy, since even Spain and Ireland, sunk in their broad-gauge darkness, are little worse off for trains than it is, one must look for a psychological explanation of this descending spiral of too little transport too little patronized. The French spirit has always suffered from a chauvinism and insularity, both national and provincial, which is a tough and healthy thing within reason but is now in danger of paralysing the nation. It is admirable that a man should know where his home is, but appalling that he should be as unable to leave it as he is in most of rural France today. Even the narrowed intellectual horizons of Paris – its loss, not perhaps of creativeness, but certainly of influence – could be correlated with the fact that between it and the provinces the crossing of one ridge of hills is an enterprise and of two an adventure. If Paris becomes another Dublin, the fault will be partly that of the Ministry of Transport.

France, in fact, provides the paradox of a country which, though it takes its transport with Latin seriousness (even amateur clubs have headquarters in places like the Gare de l'Est and one feels there that railways, like *l'amour*, are not a pleasure to be taken lightly), is in retreat from a railway age which it once accepted perhaps over-enthusiastically. One does not have to look far for evidence of this rusting of wheels: to travel by train in France today is to see branch-line after branch-line torn up, or burying itself in grass between the passage of rare goods-trains, or used as a sad graveyard for junked locomotives. Such lines are called – and there is a bitter irony in the term – *lignes coördonnées*. . . .

The backward swing of the pendulum began about 1925, and reached its nadir when the new decrees came into force. In a year or so 7,000 miles of SNCF track – nearly a quarter of the whole – were abandoned, severing cross-country links and changing the map of the country: from the outskirts of Paris to Tours, for instance, a stretch of line which had once twenty-one junctions found itself with one. Then came the war, with destructions which were never made good. And on top of this, many route-miles have been cut from double to single track, while the last indignity is being reached today when on several main lines, including the proud P.L.M. *ligne impériale*, the local services are provided, not by train nor even autorail, but by S N C F bus . . . .

ITALY

The calumny is still abroad that Mussolini made the Italian railways run to time, but they were punctual long before the March on Rome. Just before and after the nationalization of 1905 they were certainly wayward, but today it is hard to believe that. There is no hint in the services of the Ferrovie dello Stato Italiano of that siesta-charmed, *dolce far niente* Italy of English imagination: they are instead the services, Milanese rather than Neapolitan in inspiration, which one would expect from an efficient and hard-working industrial nation.

Yet Italy not only has trains in a big way: it believes in trains. Its bus and coach services are unrepressed and extremely good, once one has found out where they start from. . . . But the Italian railways remain very active. . . . Densely populated as Italy is, the amount of passenger traffic on its roads and rails – the hourly long-distance buses, the frequent ten- and twelve-car trains running regularly on dim branch-lines where France would make do with two autorails on selected Thursdays – remains something of a mystery in a country not rich, and one can only resort to a psycological explanation – that that restlessness of the Latin heart which finds outlet in night-long strollings and counter-strollings of the streets can only be fully assuaged by a journey on wheels.

So the Italian railways – even the obscurest ones – are very adequate and there-when-you-want-them. But they have more than adequancy. They have, thank God, some *style*.

One does not find it everywhere. The local steam train can be a decrepit and charmless thing: the standard electric locomotive is as unbeautiful as its equivalent everywhere; and as for Italian suburban trains, they are just like suburban trains in Italian films. At the other extreme, the F.S.'s Fiat railcars and almost indistinguishable *autotreni* and *elettrotreni* are bulbous and flashy in a khaki-and-red livery which looks none the better for being mirror-bright. . . . But the average fast train – not very old and not very new, running on a line where traffic is insufficiently dense to warrant electrification but too dense to be served by railcars – does have an indefinable presence.

It is largely due to the red velvet. An Italian first-class *direttissimo* has an air which makes one forget what an abomination class-limitation is, an air of deep plush and gilt and Florians'; while a good many second-class cars, including some of those which find their way to international trains, are not merely comfortable but recall an age when the ideal was not comfort but luxury. Even the business-like modern steel coaches have a decided charm to them, with their roofs silvered against the sun and with diamond panes to their toilets; they look like *trains*, and that is not so common these days.

There are, of course, some deplorable points about the Italian railways. Their booking-offices follow the Latin practice of opening only five minutes before a train is due, which is all right at a sleepy Spanish halt but idiotic when handling several thousand passengers daily (and when, furthermore, there is always a buffet open day and night to sell half a dozen coffees). This would not matter so much were it not that the same woman is always before me in the queue. She is a war-widow, poor dear, remarried to the victim of an industrial accident, having fifteen children and visibly expecting another, going on her annual holiday and with a brother-in-law working on the railways. She has a horrible little card to prove that all this entitles her to a 95 per cent reduction, but she is standing out for 100 per cent and is prepared to argue the point until we have all missed the express. . . . I have met that woman in half the stations of Italy, and I would wish that she were dead were not I certain that all her sixteen children would then line up in front of me to apply for their orphan's reductions.

Equally annoying are Italian travelling habits. The national idea of the proper use of a train is to distribute the great piles of luggage necessitated by the southern love of *things* all over the seats, suspend the *bambini* in hammocks from the luggage-racks, settle Grandma in the corner, draw the curtains and then go and stand in the corridor, occasionally tossing beer-bottles and orange-peel back into the compartment. One sometimes feels that the Italian people have better transport than they deserve. . . .

A final black mark against the F.S. is for its secrecy. In the great concourses of its stations there is everything that the traveller can desire except timetable-bills. In all Italy I doubt if there are thirty stations with anything more than a misleading departures-board, and in those the sheets will cover only the nearby State main lines. Everybody in Italy hence carries a pocket timetable (it is a great day for the bookstalls when they change), but consults it as furtively as if it were pirated or on the Papal Index.

There is a parallel to this in the Italian reluctance to display menus; but a closer parallel, I think, is with those French and Italian banks where so many *opérations sur fonds et titres*, so many *transactions diverses* with adding-machines go on, that anybody merely wanting to cash a cheque feels an intruder. Similarly in an Italian station one surveys the dozens of offices down the long arcades, the archivists and the statisticians and the telegraph-operators (what the devil are all those tape-machines *for*?) at work in their great marmoreal halls, and feels one's own little journey an impertinence. At any rate, nothing could be more typical of the private world of the Italian railways than that when the custombuilt, streamlined, air-conditioned, supplement-charging, observation-car-equipped Milan–Naples *elettrotreno* was introduced, the publicity told you everything about it except when it left and when it arrived. . . .

One could not approve the M.N., but it leads one back to Italian railway faith. It is, in fact, a bit of Latin panache, a gesture of the type which led to the building, as late as 1934, of the last and second-longest of the world's mountain tunnels. Just as Italy had been there at the start, so was she there at the end, when right down her spine they carved the $11\frac{1}{2}$-mile Apennine Gallery and so built the final master-work of the railway age simply to lop twenty miles from the Florence–Bologna run.

Yet it is not this, nor all the new lines and tunnels projected, but the modern stations of Italy which represent her greatest contribution to the railways – and perhaps to the whole culture – of the twentieth century.

Apart from a few flamboyant mistakes such as those motortrains and new blocks of flats as uninspired as their equivalents everywhere, most things made in modern Italy look very good, especially in comparison with their French counterparts. It has no mosaic *Bureaux des Postes* or furniture which even the Tottenham Court Road would disown, and there will be no more Milan Centrals. It is rebuilding everything well, but there are two things which it is rebuilding supremely.

These are churches, and railway stations. Both rise above bombed cities, clean and cool and *right*: both carry some sense of being built beyond immediate demands, of being made because it is a good thing to make, an act of faith needing no utilitarian justification. In the face of them one feels that Pugin was not wholly wrong in holding that only a decent Catholic could build a decent station.

They were constructed, of course, with E.R.P. funds: and the Americans, who were willing to pay for industrial reconstruction and willing to pay for art, have blinked a little at getting both for the same money. But now the blinking is done the stations remain, representing between them the one major and indisputable work of architecture to emerge from our post-war barrenness. From the calm and comfortable majesty of Roma Termini to the provincial good taste of Siena, they have nothing out of place: they pay no more heed to the clichés of "functional" austerity than to the clichés of the past: they seem always a gasp better than they had to be. And when, at home, every nameboard testifies to how desperately British Railways need a Frank Pick, one wonders if our own reconstructions might not be handed over to the builders of those stations along the Emilian Way. . . .

GERMANY

By "Germany" I mean Western Germany. Those who knew the country in days when the Hamburg–Berlin line occupied sixteen timetable pages, when through cars to Prague were more than a gesture and when the going was good to the holy cities on the edge of the map like Cracow and Czestochowa, may rest on memories – memories of halycon journeys through the woods of Brandenburg and the orchards of Silesia, memories of adventures in the deep Harz, memories of the 750 mm. network of Saxony and the vast 600 mm. one of Mecklenburg which survive national-ized and unapproachable. But to me these are as unknown as Muscovy itself.

It makes sense, however, to consider the lines of the West alone, as it does not make sense in Austria. With Berlin and all about it blotted out, the railway map of Germany still does not strike one as a thing of loose ends, for Frankfurt and Munich and the rest gather their systems – denser than those of the East – about them in shapely fashion. This, perhaps, is only to be expected, for although the German railways were early national-ized they are, in most instances, older than Germany: in any case the Deutsche Bundesbahn gives the impression of being an entity.

And a splendid entity it is, resurgent in pride, organizing most of Europe's expresses, convinced that Rome and Copenhagen are German stations and, for all its unpunctualities and all its deplor-able branch-line stock, again the finest of the major national rail-ways of Europe. It is not an unfamiliar entity, either, for the shape of the Western Republic and of her railways is not so different from the British. There is the same density on the ground, the same duplications, the same long branches in networks and short ones with dead ends; even station customs seem familiar. Cross-country running is better organized than in Britain, but in the huge, heartening, ever-expanding if sometimes inaccurate Kurs-buch an English railway-lover feels much at home until the sections start dropping to pieces through sheer German overweight.

The German attitude to railways is, of course, a very serious one. That they are the arteries of national economy far more than in most countries is shown by a dozen phenomena – the learned publications, the social status and high pay of the railwayman, the fact that bomb-damage has not been used as the excuse for closing a single line, the centrally-sited stations, the teaching of railway-lore in schools, the transport of lorries by rail and so on, right down to the fact that when a German contractor has a job to do he starts by building a 600 mm. line. But it is also true that the national respect for the things is tinged with that amused affection characteristic of our own attitude to railways. Latin nations may passionately defend them: but only north of the Alps, I think, does one commonly find love, only there could there exist an *Arbeits-gruppe Sterbende Bahnen,* a working-party on dying railways. . . .

So familiar does the German system feel to me that there are only two sentiments of which I want to deliver myself before leaping upon it. The first concerns that unpleasant matter of

. *Zuschlag* [for] I object to having to pay a supplement to travel on an ordinary train which happens to be going a long way. Germany has a rather obstructionist record in the matter of making comfortable travel cheaper, and the *Zuschlag* is an anachronism and an illogicality in a country so well served by trains. But as the beastly thing is being tidied-up, if not dropped, let us say here only that it provides an invitation to the hardy to explore the length and breadth of the country by all-stations trains.

Complementary to this survival of an old bad thing there is the appearance of a new good one. The traditional passenger stock of the D.B. is very green-drab and unbeautiful: but in the revival of Germany, as of Italy, many handsome things have been made: and though its streamlined diesel-trains are as meretricious as such things always are (I like the glassy local *Schienenbusse*, however, with their way of turning a main line into a light railway), the new steam stock is really good-looking.

The close-coupled lightweight trains are pleasing enough though in the old livery, but – class distinctions apart – give me those superbly comfortable royal blue cars with the silver legends. They work mainly on Germany's numerous, often really fast, but ever-changing internal name-trains, for the D.B. gets rather unhappy when as much as a broken-down third-class coach leaves its borders. (On return, anyway, there are maddening delays as they make sure that no Frenchman has walked off with an ash-tray and no Dane broken a light-bulb.) But you can see whole rakes of them from The Hook to Basle, and when clean they put everything else to shame.

from THE END OF THE LINE *1955*

Through the Alps

CECIL J. ALLEN

To the railway engineer there might well seem to be few more unpromising fields for the exercise of his art than Switzerland. The great mountain chains of the Alps and the Jura, riven in all directions by deep gorges, offer the most formidable problems in the laying of evenly graded lines capable of operation by normal means. Many of the higher-lying mountain resorts, not to mention the lofty passes and the mountain summits themselves, might appear at first sight to be completely inaccessible by rail. Further, the extent of snowfall at the high altitudes and the dangers of the avalanche might well threaten to make railway operation impossible in the depth of the winter. Yet the railway network of Switzerland today witnesses to the fact that in the mind of the railway engineer the word "impossible" does not exist; and its operation, notwithstanding all the difficulties imposed by Nature, is an object-lesson in efficiency to many countries in which railway working is of a far simpler order.

Many problems of special difficulty confront an engineer in planning a railway in mountainous country. Simply put, he has to preserve an even balance between constructional cost, operating cost and probable traffic receipts. A main line, from which the maximum receipts may be expected, must be laid out in such a way as to permit the operation of heavy trains at reasonable speeds. Loads and speeds, however, are governed by the steepness of the gradients and the sharpness of the curvature, and when the limits of both have been fixed, the major problem of the engineer, in the narrow and irregular confines of an Alpine valley, is to preserve his evenness of gradient and curvature without unduly increasing his costs of construction. In general, the flatter the gradient of a mountain line, so much the greater will be the amount of bridging and tunnelling needed to maintain it.

When the traffic prospects are on a more moderate scale, it is possible to contract the track gauge from the standard 4 feet $8\frac{1}{2}$ inches to 1 metre or less, which permits sharper curvature. This in its turn enables the engineer to follow the contours of rugged mountainsides with a minimum of tunnels, bridges, cuttings and embankments, using every foothold that Nature offers him. But the sharper curvature, and the steeper gradients with which it is often associated, restrict both speed and carrying capacity. With every increase in the steepness of inclination, there is further restriction, until we come to the purely mountain railways ... with gradients as steep as from 1 in 2 to 1 in $1\frac{1}{8}$, carrying capacity limited to single cars of the lightest possible construction, and speeds of 5 m.p.h. or even less.

Not until the first attempts had been made to penetrate the heart of the Alps was the art of railway location called into play in its most extreme forms. It was decided in general that for main-line work which would involve the working of heavy loads at reasonable speeds, gradients should be kept down to a maximum of 1 in 40 or slightly steeper; the maximum gradients on the Gotthard line, for example, rule at between 1 in 37 and 1 in 40, and on the Lötschberg at 1 in 37 also. But the difficulty confronting the engineer is that in carrying railways up valleys such as those of the Reuss and the Ticino, on the Gotthard line, or the Kander, on the Lötschberg, inclinations such as these are nothing like sufficient to keep pace with the rapid rise of the valley floors.

An even greater difficulty is found in the extremely irregular inclinations of many of the Alpine valleys. Owing to glacial action in past ages, stepped valley formations are common; a valley basin, mountain-walled but with a fairly level floor, will be separated from another valley basin some hundreds of feet higher in level by a deep gorge down which the river forces its way by a series of falls, so facing the engineer with an immense step, from the one basin to the other, up which his railway must climb. This is seen in striking fashion on the Lötschberg line, in the ascent that the railway is compelled to make in a very short distance from the flat lower basin of the Kander valley at Frutigen up to the basin in which lies the village of Kandersteg, 1,200 feet higher in altitude.

Where no other expedient is possible, the railway is turned into the mountainside and carried round in a complete corkscrew turn, to emerge, if a gradient of 1 in 40 is being used, at a level higher by some 120 feet or so. Or, to avoid the stoppage and reversal of trains that is necessary if a zigzag route is laid up a mountain slope – as, for example, on the great climb of the Central Railway of Peru into the Andes – semi-spiral tunnels are used to enable the railway to reverse its direction, so that the line curves to and fro on a mountainside without any interruption of the continuous running.

This is the plan which has been followed at Mitholz to get the Lötschberg line up from the Kandergrund to the Kandersteg basin of the Kander valley, and a similar expedient may be found on the Gotthard line opposite the village of Wassen. . . . In carrying the southern slope of the Gotthard down the Biaschina ravine, the engineers have used four completely spiral tunnels in succession between Rodi–Fiesso and Giornico. The chief disadvantage of this principle is the amount of curvature introduced into the line, which has to be compensated; that is to say, the nominal gradient must be flattened in order to allow for increased flange-resistance of the trains in travelling round the curves. Thus the amount of height gained or lost by the spiral tunnel is reduced correspondingly.

In many cases the engineers have anticipated abrupt rises in valley floors by carrying their lines, with the help of steep continuous gradients, high up the sides of mountain valleys well in advance. This is a procedure of great advantage to the passenger, as it affords him magnificent ranges of view that would be denied to him if he were travelling by road along the floor of the same valley. The most outstanding Alpine example of location-work of this description is the ascent of the Lötschberg line from Brigue up the north wall of the Rhone valley until, at Hohtenn, just before it turns into the Lonza gorge, it is some 1,300 feet above the valley floor. But this method also has its engineering problems, as it makes it necessary for the railway to cross, often at a great altitude, every ravine coming down from the mountains to join the main valley.

The steepest gradient on any narrow-gauge line carrying substantial traffic is the 1 in 29 that has been necessary, together with some most remarkable spiral development, to get the Rhaetian main line up the higher part of the Albula valley on its way to St Moritz. Trains of up to ten coaches of corridor stock, restaurant car included, are worked up this gradient. Gradients as steep as 1 in 20 may be found on some of the smaller standard-gauge lines, such as the South-Eastern in its climb eastwards out of the Gotthard junction of Arth-Goldau, but passenger-train loads over this section rarely exceed four or five coaches. On the metre gauge the maximum steepness for adhesion working in Switzerland is 7·3 per cent, or 1 in 13¾, and a long stretch at this inclination may be found on the Montreux–Oberland–Bernois Railway as it climbs from the Lake of Geneva up to the tunnel under the Col de Jaman. Another line with similar gradients is the Bernina, which is laid with many miles of 1 in 14 and some more most amazing curved location-work . . . in order to make the abrupt descent of 3,500 feet from Alp Grüm to Poschiavo.

Where steeper gradients are necessary . . . rack-and-pinion working is brought into operation. As this method of operation slows down the trains very considerably, however, it is confined to lines on which traffic is relatively light, and speed is of less importance. In Switzerland, also, it is found, with few exceptions, on narrow-gauge lines only. . . . Well-known examples of such lines are the Brünig, the Furka-Oberalp and the Visp-Zermatt. But rack-and-pinion and the even steeper funicular railways come rightly in the mountain-railway category. . . .

There is scarcely a single town or village of any size in Switzerland that is without railway communication; the only important exception is the holiday resort of Adelboden, reached by postal motor-coach from the station of Frutigen, on the Lötschberg line. On the other hand, there are several high-lying villages of note which have their railway access but none by road; notable examples are Zermatt, Mürren and Wengen. One railway at least – the Jungfrau line – carries passengers up to a world of snow and ice that they could never have reached otherwise, unless competent snow and ice climbers. And even more startling mountain conquests have been planned, such as the fantastic schemes for carrying passengers to the summit of the proud Matterhorn.

from SWITZERLAND'S AMAZING RAILWAYS *1959*

Belgian Branches

PETER ALLEN and P. B. WHITEHOUSE

Belgium, being by nature rather flat (except for the Ardennes and the countryside around Liège and Brussels) was an ideal country for the light railway, and in due course many tramway systems grew up in the larger towns. But there were few rural lines during the early days in spite of the fact that neighbouring Holland had taken the rural tram to its bosom. Holland, however, made the mistake of building many small lines of different gauge, some light railways, some tramways, and all with differing types of rolling stock. This mistake was not made in Belgium. Only in odd cases were there private lines and for the most part the whole network was a national undertaking, though it was the policy to administer everything through a system of semi-autonomous companies, each with its own area, making end-to-end connections with branches of neighbouring units. This was called the *Société Nationale des Chemins de fer Vicinaux*. The organization had the task of building tramways (not light or narrow gauge railways) where necessary in Belgium. Originally the S.N.C.V. provided only the rolling stock for these lines and the working was by the private companies, but about 1920 a change of economic circumstances gradually altered this and with few exceptions all the lines were taken over, thus producing a real network of some considerable importance. Even then there were little or no through running arrangements, and though one could get, on paper, from one end of the country to the other, it was in fact still necessary to change from system to system so many times that much of their value as through routes was never exploited. As some of the links of the organization were standard gauge, a third rail was sometimes laid on such sections to enable the metre gauge locomotives to deal with the traffic.

This short explanation of the growth of the metre gauge network will show just how the steam tramway developed. By the end of 1913 there were no fewer than 3,650 km. operated by steam locomotives (against 410 km. of electrified routes, excluding the large city tramways lines). In the north there was originally a 3 ft. 6 in. gauge system connecting with the Dutch steam tram lines of the same gauge. Later these Belgian lines were converted to metre gauge. For this huge system 750 steam engines, 2,460 passenger trailers and 7,470 vans were available. The engines were, in the main, of the standard tramway pattern, 0–6–0s with side sheets covering the wheels and motion, and capable of being driven from either end. The narrow gauge tram engines varied from about 12 to 23 tons in weight. The coaches were mostly four wheelers built as cheaply as possible. Superficially, the rolling stock was standardized but there were some slight differences between the systems. The standard livery was perhaps best described as "weathered primrose" with black or chocolate lining and lettering. Later the steam stock was painted green.

During the First World War when the whole railway system

was used for military purposes, coal for civilian use was conveyed almost entirely by tramway, and, as electric traction was still very much in its infancy and restricted to the large towns and their vicinity, it was the steam tramway which did most of the work. It suffered accordingly from lack of maintenance and from the attentions of the Germans who destroyed a good part of it, leaving only 1,865 km. intact.

There was a period of reconstruction after the war and steam traction had a further short period of glory. In 1925 the steam-operated system had grown to 3,938 km. and many new steam engines had been built. The peak post-war year for steam loco-motives was 1925 (as perhaps it was in France). From then on the modernization continued and many lines were closed to steam, the routes being taken over by *autorails* or becoming electrified. Later even these began to give way to the bus, but the system as a whole survived. The steam tram engines were still kept mainly for freight but also for a few passenger services, especially when traffic was heavy. As late as 1940 over 500 of these engines remained in service.

The last war prolonged their life still further, and many trains were hauled by steam, largely because of petrol and oil rationing and the consequent restriction of bus and *autorail* services. Inci-dentally, some of the sections of the *Vicinal* passed over the border into Holland and smuggling became a national occupation at the time of the liberation and after. From 1945 onwards steam as a motive power began to disappear rapidly, as better roads were built. Even the freight traffic lost a great deal of its former importance, and the last passenger steam tram ran in 1952. Some of the lightly patronized electric and most of the *autorail*-served lines have also disappeared, but, generally speaking, the whole of the remaining system is fairly sound.

In spite of our remarks concerning the solidarity and efficiency of the remaining S.N.C.V. lines, it is rather depressing to travel across Belgium and follow mile after mile of metre gauge track on the side of the road rusting away and waiting for the demolition men. In the industrial areas of Flanders there is plenty of evidence of lines that have gone, with traces of queer track-work where there used to be important junctions, but where single through service alone survives. The coastal system from

La Panne to Knocke is now but a shadow of its former self. We well remember using this shortly before the last war when it was quite an adventure to travel to Blankenberghe by the last tram from Ostend, for someone a little the worse for wear would always be sure to try and jump on one of the little four-wheeler trailers as the long "train" swung out of the *Place du Commerce*. His acrobatics as he tried to climb on the scrolled ironwork gates which rattled on every rail-joint were worth watching.

At about the same period the S.N.C.V. operated a very smart excursion service to Middelburg on the Dutch island of Walcheren. The chromium-plated luxury coach offered a parallel excursion at a much higher fare, but those in the know used the tram. The service operated to Retranchement, where a transfer was made to the Dutch steam tram which carried the passengers to Breskens. The quay at Breskens was always a sight, for long lines of coaches waited their turn to go aboard the car ferry while passengers on the steam tram rode to the front of the queue, quietly walked on board the ferry and sailed, taking the Dutch train from Flushing to Middelburg. It was no uncommon thing to be making one's way back to the station at Middelburg after a full and happy day and meet friends from the same hotel who had but just arrived and were due to return to their coach in half-an-hour.

Let us finish with one last glimpse of the steam trams. They served scores of the little towns, storming in from a track alongside the roads and polders, bells ringing and steam everywhere, to pull up in what passed for the centre. These trams knew their place for they kept to the side of the road in the towns and villages just as in the open country. As a result all the houses down one side of the street had tall narrow mirrors fitted to the doorposts so that the occupants could see if it was safe to cross the threshold. It never seemed that the expense was justified for so few trams ran, though when they did the town suddenly came to life and, just as suddenly, as the tram departed, lapsed into slumber again.

from NARROW GAUGE RAILWAYS IN EUROPE *1959*

Hardships in Jugoslavia

PETER ALLEN and P. B. WHITEHOUSE

It was Jan and Cora Gordon, in one of their enjoyable travel books of the nineteen-twenties, who years ago gave us our first taste for Asiatic Europe in general and for the Jugoslav narrow gauge in particular in describing every refinement of discomfort experienced in a nightmare journey from Slavonski Brod all through the dark hours to Sarajevo, ending thus:

"At Sarajevo station we looked out into the face of the smiling Orient. Below us, for there was no platform, stood a man with a welcoming gesture, welcoming our baggage and tips rather than us. He was a swarthy fellow, half-darkened by the sun, half-lacquered by grime, a dirty shirt of pink cretonne clothed the upper hemisphere of him, his equator was a dirty red sash, his antarctic regions were covered with baggy knee breeches and Turkish shoes; over his beady-eyed bulbous-nosed face he wore a filthy fez; a large brass plate pierced with a number gave him some official recognition. He was the porter, probably Jewish.

"The train had run in and had halted in an open space before a restaurant, which looked rather more like a ramshackle riverside restaurant of the *banlieue* of Paris than a railway station; a low building or verandah stretched at length and shrouded in green creeper. The engine, a strange-looking construction which had dragged us from Brod, was running back along a parallel line. Topped by a fat bonneted funnel, with tiny wheels and an elaboration of complex and ingenious external machinery, it made one think of some illustration of African entomology, one of those long-legged beetles of the Congo, for it moved with a ridiculous agitation of mobile members compared with the visible motion achieved."

Ever since then, although many years and war and upheaval intervened, it was a matter of looking for the chance to test these things for ourselves. Sarajevo always remained a romantic and remote place in our imagining, the spot where the fatal shots were fired that altered all the world, an outpost of Islam in Europe with its sixty-seven mosques, where the muezzins called the faithful to prayer, with veiled women, and with all the squalor and colour and life of the bazaar.

Slavonski Brod did in fact provide our first sight of the narrow rails of Jugoslavia in the course of a journey across Europe from Paris to Istanbul in the "Simplon–Orient Express" in 1949. At the junction our express had rested for a while to change engines, the hideous tall Hungarian 4–8–0 which had hauled us down the Sava valley from Zagreb coming off, and a big German Pacific had backed down to take us on to Belgrade, the top-booted, peak-capped fireman standing high on top of the tender, raking down the pungent brown coal. But it was the little train with the soft smoke at the other end of the platform that we really wanted to see, so elbowing our way through the great crowd on the platform we just had time to take a flying shot of the 2–6–6–0 tank engine at its head, hoping that the red-starred Communist officials wouldn't object, before we had to board the big express again.

Then later that day, while we were waiting to rejoin our sleeper in Belgrade, a small unlit narrow gauge train was quietly backed into the main station, a little country train, its locomotive liberally sprinkled with domes and sandboxes, and in an instant its ancient dark coaches filled with a silent crowd of passengers waiting to return to the back country, women in trousers, women with head-cloths, some held in the teeth so as to deputize for the now forbidden Moslem veil, and men in breeches and long black stockings, men in long tight trousers like jodhpurs, some in breeches with a centre bag, ready, they say, to receive the Prophet should he be, as legend foretold, born again of a man, short coats like Eton jackets, curling slippers of an old Turkish design, cummerbunds and little round caps, fierce moustaches and altogether a great air of country and mountain life. It made one want to abandon the great train with its blue sleepers for Nish and Skoplje, Sofia and Istanbul and join the little one just to find out where it was going and what manner of wild land it would end up in by next dawn. . . .

Not till 1955 were we in Jugoslavia again, and then we were a lot more knowing. We had by then become aware that the Jugoslav narrow gauge system is a significant part of the national railway network, especially in the mountainous provinces of Bosnia, Hercegovina and Dalmatia, where, dating from the time of the Austrian protectorate decreed by the Berlin Congress of 1878 and after the annexation of the provinces in 1907, the Austrians built lines as military railways.

Being on holiday on the Dalmatian coast in 1955, we were able to plan to visit Sarajevo and also Mostar and to go by train too. This undertaking meant rising at the formidable hour of 5 a.m. in the pearly summer dawn to catch the 6.10 steam train out of Dubrovnik. This consisted of half-a-dozen assorted coaches including a 2 ft. 6 in. dining car, headed by a 2–8–2 of fairly modern Austrian design originating between the wars and banked by a grotesque 0–8–2 two-cylinder compound with a vast spark-arresting Austrian chimney which accompanied us for three or four miles up the first slope of the coastal mountain range. From then on we were engulfed in one huge panorama of upland scenery, wild bare stony hills like Old Crome's quarry, with long descents along the sides of valleys, the train clinging to the contours, incessantly on curves and plunging in and out of tunnels.

After the first great heave over the coastal mountains which scowl above Dubrovnik, pressing it tight against the sea, the line passes through the junction of Uskoplje, where another 2 ft. 6 in. gauge line runs south down the coast past Cavtat to Hercegnovi on the beautiful and spectacular gulf of Kotor. Then continuing on the main line comes Hum, a second junction, with a line through to the fast-growing new city of Titograd. Then the line begins its descent of the long Trebišnica valley, a narrow fertile plain in a wilderness of mountains, where, when we passed, the crops were being harvested and threshed on the hard threshing floors by sledges drawn by teams of horses. On then to Gabela, where the train joins the Neretva Valley. From here through to Mostar the country is most attractive, with a blue swirling river in a valley and high hills all around it. We reached Mostar, capital of Hercegovina, just after 11 o'clock, five hours and ninety miles from home. Mostar was something of a disappointment, with many old decaying mosques, some disused and all locked up save one. The new buildings in the city, dreary cement blocks of typical Peoples' Republic type, did not encourage us to think that they would survive for as many years as the mosques. Only the old medieval bridge across the rocky gorge of the Neretva came up to expectation, even if this was in splints for repairs, so while the hot afternoon oozed away we sat dejected and uncomfortable – we never found a comfortable chair in all Jugoslavia – waiting to pick up another train to carry us on to Sarajevo. This was a much more attractive conveyance – a three-car *automotrice* built just before the war by Ganz of Hungary to speed up the running on this narrow and difficult line, which it did to such a tune that it was soon nicknamed "The Mad Sarajevan". The diesel certainly gave us a much more enjoyable run, although the bar and accommodation were not quite as majestic as in the old narrow-gauge diner which we had used in the first part of the journey. Nevertheless, all was made good by the wonderful scenery, as the line climbed up the ever-narrowing gorge of the Neretva River, with its massive crags, rocks and cliffs dominating the line while the waters rolled and tumbled over great stones beside the track.

Near the head of the valley is the old Moslem town of Jablanica, where a large hydro-electric project was under construction, including the creation of a huge man-made lake. As we ran along the edge of this in the waning evening light, it looked a greener and more attractive landscape, with woods and farms with steep, pitched roofs and brown rocks after all the miles of harsh grey limestone. Then just as it got dark we had a stretch of about six miles on the rack section at about 1 in 17, although the Ganz railcars go up without rack assistance. Finally, we came to the saddle of the pass at Bradina, where we had some time to wait to cross another train, a wait made memorable by the fireflies dancing and darting in the dark trees, switching their little lights on and off, on and off. Then we ran down through a two-mile tunnel full of stinking smoke and emerged nearly at Sarajevo, revealed soon after as a mass of lights, sidings, locomotives, wagons and all the paraphernalia of a big city. The second stretch of 79 miles from Mostar had taken us four and a half hours, and, taking stock that evening of the whole day's journey, we felt that, beautiful as it had been, it was something to have done rather than something to do.

from NARROW GAUGE RAILWAYS IN EUROPE *1959*

The Road to Samarkand

PETER FLEMING

The Russian train was called an express train. It left the small
Caspian port of Krasnovodsk, within an hour or two of the
advertised time, one evening in the autumn of 1934 and in a
somewhat irresolute manner set off eastwards.

It was not a very good train; and although some trains, like some
ladies, can be not very good and still have considerable charm, this
was not one of those trains. There was one soft-class coach, with
four berths to a compartment more or less on the lines of our own
third class sleepers, but very much more austere and also extremely
dirty and verminous. The rest of the carriages were hard-class,
with the passengers lying on three tiers of wooden shelves which
ran the whole length of the coach. There was no dining car.

It was a three or four day journey to Samarkand. Night fell soon
after we had started . . . and it was discouraging to find that the
electric light on the train was not working. My fellow-passengers
in the soft-class coach all turned out to be fairly senior railway
officials bound for a conference in Tashkent. It was to be what the
Russians call a self-criticism conference at which the delegates,
theoretically, take it in turns to explain the appalling blunders for
which each of them has been responsible and to suggest how these
blunders can be avoided in the future. One of the possible reme-
dies is so obvious that I cannot believe that these conferences are
much fun, and if I had been going to one I know that I should not
have felt at my best; but I cannot say that I was much impressed
by the reaction of the twenty or thirty railway officials to the
complete failure of the electric lighting system on a train in which
they had to spend three long nights. All this happened, you must
remember, in the 1930s, and in those distant days to be deprived
without warning in one's own country of some essential service
or amenity was looked on by the British, not as another thorn in
an outsize martyr's crown which it is their duty to wear with as
good a grace as possible, but as a cue for action or at least for
vigorous protest. If nothing came of the protest, one improvized.
The Russians neither protested nor improvized.

As the deserts turned from gold to dove-grey and the dusk closed in across them on the thin black line of the Trans-Caspian Railway, my fellow-passengers put their soup-stained memoranda back into their portfolios of imitation leather and let the darkness flow over them till it obscured everything in the compartment except the glowing tips of their cigarettes, eternally agitated in debate.

Nobody tried to mend the dynamo, nobody tried to buy candles when we stopped at the occasional villages and the still more occasional towns. "Oriental fatalism" is perhaps the explanation that suggests itself to those of you who know the Russians; and I agree that there is something in it. But no nation is more Oriental or more fatalistic than the Chinese, and I remember thinking that if the other passengers in that coach had been senior Chinese railway officials, or even ordinary Chinese, some poor station-master would have been intimidated or bribed into providing us with lamps and we should have travelled in a blaze of light.

Still, we travelled, which was the main thing. I think I have said that there was no dining-car on the train; nor was any other source of food or drink provided. This added greatly to the interest of a slow and rather tedious journey. It meant that one depended entirely for victuals on the stations at which the train stopped; and although I say "one depended" I really mean that about three hundred depended, for of course everybody on the train was equally anxious to avoid starvation.

Imagine for a moment that you were a passenger on a slow train without a dining-car, travelling through Russian central Asia. Tomorrow morning you wake up as soon as it gets light. You have an upper berth. The three other men in the compartment are inert, untidy molehills of humanity. Soon they will wake up too, and make themselves once more into mountains, full of self-importance and statistics and full perhaps also of an abstruse charm. But now they are huddled with their knees up to their chins. They are clenched like a fist against the cold, and although the cold is not all that severe they are not as well equipped to meet it as the peasants in the hard-class carriages mostly are. Those three molehills are important people, senior officials of a national-ized service in a socialist State. Being important people, they are entitled to certain privileges and priorities. As a result, instead of wearing sheepskins and felt boots like most of the hard-class passengers, they are dressed in European-style suits and shoes, and although these clothes make them feel *ochin kulturni* (or very cultured) they also make them feel the cold much more than their social inferiors. . . .

As you peer down from your upper berth the first thing that strikes you is what a terrible mess the compartment is in. The whole floor is carpeted, like the floor of a parrot's cage, with the husks of sunflower seeds. The spittoon has become a sort of cornucopia, over flowing with melon-rind and bread-crusts and grapeskins and egg-shells and cigarette ends.

You climb down from your berth and pick your way through the debris into the corridor. The sun is rising over the desert and on the southward horizon you can see a line of blue mountains beyond which lies Persia. The express train is tearing along at a steady twenty-five miles an hour. Presently it begins to slow down, whistling in that rather hysterical way to which so many foreign trains are addicted, and at length comes convulsively to a stop in a small wayside station, where with any luck you can buy something to eat for breakfast – sour milk, grapes, bread, perhaps the carcase of a chicken.

At last the train, by now in an indescribably filthy state, reaches Samarkand, only about twelve hours late. However blasé you may be, it is no good pretending that there is not something romantic about the sound of Samarkand; and I got out of the train in a state of pleasurable curiosity. The road had not been exactly golden. But here at any rate, I thought, was Samarkand. . .

It turned out that I was mistaken, for the railway station is some five miles from the city.

from B.B.C. BROADCAST *November 1949*

Japanese Journey

C. S. SMALL

Between Osaka and Tokyo, the largest city in Japan, if not in the world, one can make the journey in eight hours on a mainline express, or in three days by local lines.

If you elect the more interesting roundabout route you start your trip from Uenomachi, the Osaka terminal station of the Kinki Nippon Railway. This private electrified line owns some 2,000 pieces of rolling stock, carries over 300,000,000 people per year and is staffed by 9,423 employees. The Osaka to Nagoya run is quite pleasant and there are many points of interest.

The first is the girls. One thing that every visitor to Japan notices immediately is the abundance of girls. They are everywhere. Restaurants have more waitresses than customers. A theatre in Tokyo has a modest chorus line of a mere three hundred girls. Every bus has one as a conductor. Salesgirls in the department stores outnumber the customers.

The J.N.R. is one of the few exceptions. This establishment swarms with men, and the girls are restricted to operating dining cars and being "candy butchers". This American slang expression might be defined as an itinerant pedlar plying his or her trade of vending comestibles in the aisles of coaching stock equipped with corridors.

The Kinki Nippon follows the Japanese practice of providing three girls on the Owari express that leaves their Uenomachi station in Osaka every day at 3.50 p.m. The Number One Girl is clad in an air hostess uniform. This charmer affects a bored and slightly dispeptic look and has no visible reason for being aboard. The Number Two Girl, who rates not such glamorous attire, and therefore feels free to present a cheerful mien to the paying customers, is the hot towel dispenser.

A hot towel is an old Oriental custom and quite a pleasant one. In hot weather it removes the sweat and grime, and in cold weather thaws icicles that form on one's person in unheated Japan. The towel is dispensed on the narrow gauge train in the Osaka–Nagoya direction or on the standard gauge train in the opposite direction. Among the ironmongery at the gauge change point is the towel boiler.

Girl Three fulfils the traditional post of the candy butcher. The Kinki Nippon follows the system widely established by air-lines, which rely on the presence of pretty girls to take the passengers' minds off such trivia as late arrivals, insufficient room, noise, bumps, dust and square wheels.

The distance from Osaka to Nagoya by the K.N.R. is 121 miles and the express takes three hours and five minutes. The initial journey is made on a standard gauge train of four multiple unit cars. Among the delights of this railroad are the folding chairs placed in the ends of the cars. All seats are reserved and these camp chairs are for the overflow. In the front car the glass in the motorman's compartment is clear and you can draw up one of the folding chairs and thus secure an unimpeded view of the line.

The line is of typical inter-urban construction with a minimum of cut and fill. The ruling grade is 3·5 per cent and it is interesting to watch the speedometer in the cab in conjunction with the gradient posts. On the flat or downhill the maximum speed often reaches 60 miles per hour.

After the soot and grime of Osaka has been left behind, the train lopes through the rice fields of a pleasant valley. It is a peaceful scene and quite pretty. The sum of the ups and downs is positive as the track rises to the mountains which run down the Kii peninsula. Although the builders would avoid a fill at the expense of a three per cent grade they did not shrink from tunnelling. There are a considerable number of short tunnels before the train plunges into a long bore, pops out for a moment at a passing siding and then enters another long tunnel. It is then but a short distance downgrade to Nakagawa where you disembark from the standard gauge train and cross the platform to the waiting narrow gauge.

You get your hot towel and then the narrow gauge is off like a scared rabbit. Sixty miles per hour seem quite natural on the wide track, but is rather frightening on 3 ft. 6 in. gauge iron. The narrow gauge portion of the line looks more like a railroad for, being the same gauge as the J.N.R., it is in a position to carry interchange freight traffic. The freight locomotives are of the box and steeple cab types and look quite powerful. Your faith in the railroad aspect is soon shaken.

At Yokkaichi the line takes a ninety degree bend. It is not a curve; it is a genuine right-angle bend. The track then proceeds through a gent's clothing store, if not literally, then at least figuratively, for on both sides there are open shops but a few feet away. Crawling down the alley, the track comes to the next station of Suma where there is a super dilapidated Toonerville Trolley which oscillates off to some implausibly named village.

A great straightening project is under way, and by the time these words appear in print, the narrow gauge rails will no longer file between the hat counter and the rack of odd-sized pants. The Yokkaichi Bend will then enter into folklore. This is as it should be, for it is fitting and proper that a railroad should have a past. The bend will grow sharper each year and the pants counter will move closer to the track with each telling.

While today those in the know ride the K.N.R. between Osaka and Nagoya, there is no particular *esprit de corps* among the alumni of this route. It is a pleasant ride and that is all. There is little doubt that the Yokkaichi Bend will separate the men from the boys. When global rail fans foregather and fall to reminiscing there will be someone who rode the K.N.R. after they removed the bend. He will tell the assemblage that the K.N.R. is the only electric railroad having a station called "Fuse". To top this piece of information a real veteran has but casually to mention that when he rode the K.N.R. there was a bend at Yokkaichi.

There are some other minor wonders including two bridges, one of fifteen and another of fourteen spans. A minor triumph are the flowers in four vases in each second-class car.

The final wonder is that the line ends up at Nagoya in a subway which terminates under a department store and is connected by a subterranean passage way to the rival station of the J.N.R. The total cost of riding the express is Yen 630, . . . or 12s. 6d.; which is inexpensive for a three-hour ride with a hot towel thrown in.

from FAR WHEELS *1959*

Short Line, U.S.A.

LUCIUS BEEBE

The definition of a short line is precisely what its name implies, and it is not to be confused with the branch lines of a main-line railroad. It is independently operated with motive power and rolling stock bearing its own name or insigne, even though it may in some cases be owned or controlled through stock ownership by a great railway system. Almost invariably short lines connect and exchange traffic with a main-line railroad and in some cases they are themselves fed and nourished by other connecting short lines. The Southern Railway, traversing as it does a territory more opulent than any other in short lines, connects with no fewer than fifty-seven, all various, like the pickles, all operated independently and in patterns of the individual devising, while the Rock Island and Northern Pacific, operating in regions where feeders are few and far between, connect with but one each, and the Boston and Albany with none! A short-line map of the United States reveals that independence and individuality, so long considered essentially Yankee qualities, in the field of railroading at least, flourish most luxuriously in the Deep South, overflowing in eccentric and florid abundance into Texas, Arkansas, and North Carolina.

But the happy hunting ground of the ultimately sophisticated connoisseur of short-haul railroading is in Colorado, Nevada, and California, where the little roads are fewer and farther apart than in Georgia, Alabama, South Carolina, and Mississippi, but are richer than any others in fragrant souvenirs of the heroic youth of the land.

The historian or minstrel, as the case may be, is warmed by the names of the Smoky Mountain or the Live Oak, Perry and Gulf, and he will shed an unhappy tear for the little Lawndale or other tragic abandonments, but his pulse quickens at the mention of the Virginia and Truckee, the Midland Terminal, the Rio Grande Southern [all now abandoned] or the narrow-gauge division of the Southern Pacific.

In the most general imagining the railroad is a country thing. Its operations are rural and the vistas from the windows of its cars are those of fields and fertile meadows, grazing cattle, tall trees, barns, silos, and homesteads. Within the memory of almost all Americans, the railroads of their youth skirted the streams of boyhood, penetrated delightfully through shady woods, and paused briefly in their going at forgotten crossroads and improbable and isolated spots.

The railroads of later worldly experience may thunder through tall stacked factories, past steel mills and the massed refineries of giant industry, but it was not always so. The first railroads were part of remote landscapes and country backgrounds, and the first train brigades swam gently through the rank grass of meadow-

lands and under the curving branches of groves of friendly trees.
In the distance thunderheads piled up in summer skies and in the
evening their headlamps shone yellow and wavering in the
gathering darkness. Their bells were a country sound, one with
the church bells that are so intimately and dearly involved in the
lines and imaginings of country people.

So, to achieve its ultimately proper setting, the short-line railroad must be removed and essentially divorced from the contriv-
ings of industrialization. Its concern must be with agriculture or
with the resources of nature even as the dominant traffic of the
Durham and Southern is Carolina tobacco, of the Clarendon and
Pittsford the quarried marble of Vermont, and of the Bath and
Hammondsport the wine grapes of upper New York. The Unadilla
Valley lives almost alone by the dairy products of its region, and
the Atlantic and East Carolina is known as "The Mullet Line" by
reason of the quantities of fish it carries. The East Broad Top is a
coal railroad, and without the peanut crop of rural Georgia the
Sylvania Central would have scant reason for being. The tally is
a long one and would of necessity include the Louisiana and North
West, whose freight is almost exclusively lumber, the Frankfort
and Cincinnati, whose lifeblood is the bourbon whisky of
Kentucky, and the Prescott and Northwestern, which annually
hauls out the richest portion of Arkansas' peach crop. . . .

Thus it is apparent that the archetypal little railroad is predomi-
nantly a country concern. It may be the Smoky Mountain or the
San Luis Central or the Arcade and Attica or the Moscow, Camden
and San Augustine. Or it may be the Weatherford, Mineral Wells
and Northeastern, which deals largely with Crazy Water, a product
of Texas mineral spas, or the Sumpter Valley, which carried
nothing but the pine of Oregon.

But its right of way will run through cornlands or orchards or
past meadows and grazing lands fenced with wooden rails and
through grass which in some places will grow so tall as to hide the
flashing cross heads in their guides and the radius bars of its locomotives in passing. The smoke of its going will roll richly from
the stacks of its engines, uninhibited by fear of operating execu-
tives, and there will be the personal touches of the crew visible in
the form of stag horns on the headlamp, a braided bell cord or a
bronze eagle with wings spread on the top of the smokebox. Its

rails will in no way resemble those of main lines, and here and there the ties will have merged themselves with the elemental earth on which they are laid. The whistle posts will have known their most recent coat of paint when Taft was in the White House, its trestles will be of wood and very susceptible to fire, and its passenger coaches will be of at least Edwardian origin, perhaps Victorian, with stained glass in their clerestory windows, open platforms, Pintsch lamps, and wood-burning stoves of the type long since outlawed for interstate commerce.

Here is the Happy Valley Railroad, the legendary short line of Never Never Land which is to railroaders the mythical equivalent of the Big Rock Candy Mountain of hobo dreams. And it is the Happy Valley Railroad of which we sing. . . .

The short line is the negation of regimented uniformity and it survives as a triumph of individualism and even eccentricity in a world grown gray from the breath of assembly-line efficiency. Largely, the employees of short lines shun the collectivist infamies as well as the forged and fictional usufructs of unionism; mostly their operations are innocent of the trammeling devices of signaling, dispatching and traffic control of any save the most primitive sort. They run on the basis of a sort of synthesis of whim of their immediate operatives and shippers and passengers without too much hindrance from the fiat idiocies of the I.C.C. and other and allied super-nuisance agencies. And in their rolling stock and motive power may be discerned the ultimate triumph of individuality, of ingenuity combined with caprice and the evolution of character from the circumstance of necessity.

Short-line operations in themselves offer a fruitful field for the amateur of heterodoxy. There are, for example, the roads which run only at night, such as the Yreka Western in California, the Oregon and Northwestern in southern Oregon, whose handsome black and gold 2–8–2s with tender cabs for the head brakeman will never be photographed in the main line, since their run from Hines to Seneca and back is over before daybreak, and the Trona, a mining road in the most desolate reaches of the Mojave Desert which only ventures out of the ore tipples to meet the Southern Pacific at Searles, California, in the darkest hours of early morning. Most such roads occupy their daylight shifting cars within the premises of mills, lumber yards, mines, smelters and manufactories.

P*

There are the roads, like the Chestnut Ridge in Pennsylvania, the Manistee and Northeastern in northern Michigan and the Trinidad Division of the Colorado and Wyoming, a property of the mighty Colorado Fuel and Iron Company, which possess neither wye nor turntable, with the result that an even fifty per cent of their operations are accomplished backward while the other half of the time their engines run pilot first as their builders intended. The Tooele Valley, only passenger-haul short line in Utah, although it might well turn its motive power at either end of its run, always heads its engines east and pushes its passenger coaches ahead of them. The reason is that from Tooele, where its rails run down the main street of the town, to the Anaconda Copper Company's smelter at International five miles away, the grade is a steady two and a half per cent. "We run 'em like this," the conductor told us of his three aged wooden coaches, "because if they ever got away on the grade they'd take most of Old Town and New Town with 'em and jump the whole kit 'n' caboodle over the U.P. rails down in the valley."

The foibles and eccentricities of individualism, to which the short lines, even at the advanced date of this survey, are subject, are almost as numerous as their separate entities. There is, for example, the Roscoe, Snyder and Pacific in Texas, which was built less as a common carrier than as a spite railroad or nuisance value to interfere with the Santa Fe by crossing its right of way a maximum number of times instead of paralleling it; there is the Colorado and Wyoming, which operates in three separate and unconnected divisions, the farthest from each other being several hundred miles apart in two states; there is the White Sulphur Springs and Yellowstone Park in Montana, which unaccountably turned up in the estate of John Ringling North, the circus heir; there is the Narragansett Pier Railroad in Rhode Island which operates highway buses with rubber tires combined with flanged wheels and which leaves the rails for the highway when fancy dictates; and there is the East Washington, the old "Chesapeake Beach line", which was originally built by Otto Mears, who was a good deal better known for his Rio Grande Southern in the Colorado San Juan.

Connoisseurs are familiar with the Norwood and St Lawrence in upper New York State, which is so attached to its single passenger coach that it is never uncoupled from it even during yard operations; with the Kelley's Creek and Northwestern which advertises freight service only but nevertheless carries passengers; with the Wyoming Railway running between Clearmont and Buffalo, Wyoming, whose train crews stop their trains and open gates whenever the right of way crosses the pastures; and with the Apache in Arizona, which makes a practice of starting its trains about an hour ahead of schedule to preclude the possibility of any passenger business whatsoever.

On the Grasse River Railroad in the north woods of New York the authors discovered a stoutly built little Black Maria coach in which the lumber company which controls the road is accustomed to bring back its timber workers from town on Saturday night after the saloons close, first taking the precaution of locking them in. The Hartwell Railroad in Georgia is owned and operated by the proprietor of the local newspaper who contrives to make a good thing out of both, while on several roads, notably the Warren and Oachita Valley in Arkansas, the Huntingdon and Broad Top Mountain in Pennsylvania and the Ferdinand in southern Indiana, there are one-time self-propelled gasoline-motor coaches with their engines removed in service as passenger cars. On the Rockdale, Sandow and Southern Railroad in Texas, passengers who once rode in the caboose when the trains were steam powered now ride in the operating cab of a gas-electric along with the crew, and the same is true of the Stewartstown in Pennsylvania.

Probably no portion of the country is so fertile in the business of trading locomotives as the Pacific coast, from the tall-timber lands of Oregon and Washington as far as the border of Old Mexico. Among the short lines and lumber-dominated railroads of the region there can scarcely be found an engine in service on the road for which it was originally built, and many have changed hands so often that their pedigree is lost in the mists of comparative antiquity.

Some short-line trains have never achieved the final terminal of their last run. Judgment Day will dawn to find them still unreported at Okay Depot crossover and they will spend all eternity half way between nowhere and nowhere, in the ditch or through the weakened trestle, as the case may be. There were savage wrecks in the high ramparts of the Colorado Rockies in the narrow-gauge seventies and eighties from which the debris has never recovered and whose traces in the form of rusted trucks and shattered engine frames are visible to this day.

In June of 1933, Engine No. 8 of the Wiscasset, Waterville and Farmington Railway, a narrow-gauge pike still surviving in Maine, on the down run from Albion broke a rail just below Whitefield and went over the fill for the last time. That afternoon the railroad, which . . . dated [its charter] back to 1854, suspended operations and closed its books forever.

Six miles from Eagle Gorge, Washington, on the Northern Pacific, a fir tree grows through the tender of the last train over the right of way of the Buffellen Lumber and Manufacturing Company which jumped the tracks on the trestle a quarter of a century ago, never to be rerailed. A once-resplendent combine from the New York Central, during the presidency of Chauncy M. Depew, and a few twisted remains of the boiler of a Mason-built engine at Steadman in the Mojave Desert are all that exists today to show where once the Ludlow and Southern Railroad's last train in 1925 burned with the mines it served before its engineer could crack the throttle. The annals of the little railroads are freighted with the records of last runs which were never made.

from MIXED TRAIN DAILY *1947*

Oxygen in the *Andes*

C. S. SMALL

So much has been written about the Central Railroad of Peru that to describe the five per cent grades, the twenty-one switchbacks, the sixty-six tunnels, the fifty-nine bridges and the fantastic altitudes reached, to dwell further on these marvels, would be sheer repetition. There are, however, several sidelights on this line which seem not to have received much attention.

One of the things which used to amuse me in the days when I regularly rode on the Ferrocarril Central was the doctor and the free oxygen. At Gasapalca Station the doctor would get aboard with his crew of assistants and they would load the oxygen cylinder into the baggage car alongside the fish which was destined for the mining camps. The doctor was a merry little man and as soon as the train left Casapalca which was at some 13,625 feet, he would patrol the train looking for passengers who were turning that delicate shade of green which ushers in a bout of sirochee, the local name for mountain sickness.

Behind the doctor would come the helpers carrying the oxygen in ordinary rubber balloons which had been filled from the cylinder. All this nonsense about sirochee was quite baffling to the assistants who were Quetchua Indians and who had been born in the high sierra. They had enormous barrel-like chests and at each breath took in twice as great a volume of air as the normal sea-level creature.

The briskest business was always done between Ticlio and Oroya. The actual main line summit at 15,693 feet was in a tunnel which certainly did not help those gasping like fish out of water. Even when the train had breasted the summit and was rapidly dropping into Oroya at the modest altitude of 12,225 feet there would be calls, for some did not seem to get sick until the worst was over.

The free oxygen service was only furnished on the two main line trains. The rail car that traversed the Morococha branch and thus reached 15,800 feet had no such luxury service. It was assumed that only hardened local inhabitants and damn fool

Yankee miners would be stupid enough to go to Morococha in the first place, and neither of these two classes counted with the railway officials.

The atmospheric pressure at the summit was about nine pounds per square inch absolute in contrast to 14·7 pounds at sea level. This incontrovertible fact has often led me to wonder why the equipment was fitted with vacuum brakes. This type of brake is applied by the atmospheric pressure and thus at the summit there was only 60 per cent of the force which was available at sea level.

The Ferrocarril Central had been built by an American, and at the time I was familiar with the line, there was quite a bit of American made rolling stock left. The engines had been rebuilt with red buffer beams, vacuum brakes and English type smoke box doors and cabs. It required careful scrutiny to find the unmistakable bar frames and guy rods from the smoke box to the pilot. Underneath all this camouflage was an old Rogers 2–8–0.

The freight equipment at this time had no power brakes at all. So on both the freight and the passenger trains they had genuine brakemen with stout brake clubs and when the engineer whistled for the brakes these worthies swung into action. When they were dropping a train down the five per cent grade through the switchbacks the brakemen earned their pay.

If you ever ride this line be sure to sit on the right hand side of the coach when you leave Lima. From this side you will see the scenery instead of the blank rock walls and will end up in Oroya or Huancayo on the left side since the switchback reversals do not come out even.

There is one way to ride downhill on the F.C.C. which will probably not be approved by the management and for which no tickets are issued. Preceding the daily passenger train downhill is the gravity car which is an ordinary four-wheel hand car fitted with a bench-like seat and a giant hand brake lever. The track inspector who rode the car on one memorable day was dressed in native homespun over which he wore a poncho. His head was wrapped in a scarf and to top the assembly he had a home-made felt hat.

Lying at eleven degrees south latitude the F.C.C. is in the tropics but the altitude results in biting cold weather in the Sierra.

Flying downhill on a hand car exposed to the elements is cold and dangerous work.

The whole purpose of the gravity car is to find slides and rocks on the tracks. In the rainy season these are a common occurrence and the road may be out of service for considerable periods while the track is dug out or the road-bed put back under the track. In theory, at least, the car can stop when it finds an obstruction. The passenger train is not admitted to the block until the gravity car emerges at the other end.

To slide down a five per cent grade through innumerable tunnels, many of which emerge into daylight on a bridge far above the canyon floor, on a four-wheel unsprung hand car, is a breath-taking experience. While in theory it is the ideal way to see the scenery, and should be ideal for pictures, if you could take them, most of the few who have taken this illicit trip could do little but hang on and wonder why they had come.

from FAR WHEELS *1959*

PART IX

Fact and Fiction

Mixed Passengers

LEWIS CARROLL

"Tickets, please!" said the Guard, putting his head in at the window. In a moment everybody was holding out a ticket: they were about the same size as the people, and quite seemed to fill the carriage.

"Now then! Show your ticket, child!" the Guard went on, looking angrily at Alice. And a great many voices all said together ("like the chorus of a song", thought Alice), "Don't keep him waiting, child! Why, his time is worth a thousand pounds a minute!"

"I'm afraid I haven't got one," Alice said in a frightened tone: "there wasn't a ticket-office where I came from." And again the chorus of voices went on. "There wasn't room for one where she came from. The land there is worth a thousand pounds an inch!"

"Don't make excuses," said the Guard: "you should have bought one from the engine-driver," and once more the chorus of voices went on with "The man that drives the engine. Why, the smoke alone is worth a thousand pounds a puff!"

Alice thought to herself, "Then there's no use in speaking." The voices didn't join in this time, as she hadn't spoken, but, to her great surprise, they all *thought* in chorus (I hope you understand what *thinking in chorus* means – for I must confess that *I* don't), "Better say nothing at all. Language is worth a thousand pounds a word!"

"I shall dream about a thousand pounds tonight, I know I shall!" thought Alice.

All this time the Guard was looking at her, first through a telescope, then through a microscope, and then through an opera-glass. At last he said, "You're travelling the wrong way," and shut up the window and went away.

"So young a child," said the gentleman sitting opposite to her (he was dressed in white paper), "ought to know which way she's going, even if she doesn't know her own name!"

A Goat, that was sitting next to the gentleman in white, shut his eyes and said in a loud voice, "She ought to know her way to the ticket-office even if she doesn't know her alphabet!"

There was a Beetle sitting next the Goat (it was a very queer set of passengers altogether), and, as the rule seemed to be that they should all speak in turn, *he* went on with "She'll have to go back from here as luggage!"

Alice couldn't see who was sitting beyond the Beetle, but a hoarse voice spoke next. "Changes engines —" it said, and there it choked and was obliged to leave off.

"It sounds like a horse," Alice thought to herself. And an extremely small voice, close to her ear, said, "You might make a joke on that—something about 'horse' and 'hoarse', you know."

Then a very gentle voice in the distance said, "She must be labelled 'Lass, with care', you know —"

And after that other voices went on ("What a number of people there are in the carriage!" thought Alice), saying, "She must go by post, as she's got a head on her —" "She must be sent as a message by the telegraph —" "She must draw the train herself the rest of the way —" and so on.

But the gentleman dressed in white paper leaned forwards and whispered in her ear, "Never mind what they all say, my dear, but take a return-ticket every time the train stops."

"Indeed I shan't!" Alice said rather impatiently. "I don't belong to this railway journey at all – I was in a wood just now – and I wish I could get back there!" "You might make a joke on *that*," said the little voice close to her ear: "something about 'you *would*, if you could', you know."

"Don't tease so," said Alice, looking about in vain to see where the voice came from; "if you're so anxious to have a joke made, why don't you make one yourself?"

The little voice sighed deeply: it was *very* unhappy, evidently, and Alice would have said something pitying to comfort it, "if it would only sigh like other people!" she thought. But this was such a wonderfully small sigh, that she wouldn't have heard it at all, if it hadn't come *quite* close to her ear. The consequence of this was that it tickled her ear very much, and quite took off her thoughts from the unhappiness of the poor little creature.

"I know you are a friend," the little voice went on; "a dear friend, and an old friend. And you won't hurt me, though I *am* an insect."

"What kind of insect?" Alice inquired a little anxiously. What she really wanted to know was, whether it could sting or not, but she thought this wouldn't be quite a civil question to ask.

"What, then you don't—" the little voice began, when it was drowned by a shrill scream from the engine, and everybody jumped up in alarm, Alice among the rest.

The Horse, who had put his head out of the window, quietly drew it in and said, "It's only a brook we have to jump over." Everybody seemed satisfied with this, though Alice felt a little nervous at the idea of trains jumping at all. "However, it'll take us into the Fourth Square, that's some comfort!" she said to herself. In another moment she felt the carriage rise straight up into the air, and in her fright she caught at the thing nearest to her hand, which happened to be the Goat's beard.

from ALICE THROUGH THE LOOKING-GLASS *1871*

The Vanishing Train

ARTHUR CONAN DOYLE

The confession of Herbert de Lernac, now lying under sentence of death at Marseilles, has thrown a light upon one of the most inexplicable crimes of the century – an incident which is, I believe, absolutely unprecedented in the criminal annals of any country. ...

On the 3rd of June, 1890, a gentleman, who gave his name as Monsieur Louis Caratal, desired an interview with Mr James Bland, the superintendent of the London and West Coast Central Station in Liverpool. He was a small man, middle-aged and dark, with a stoop which was so marked that it suggested some deformity of the spine. He was accompanied by a friend, a man of imposing physique, whose deferential manner and constant attention showed that his position was one of dependence. This friend or companion, whose name did not transpire, was certainly a foreigner, and probably from his swarthy complexion, either a Spaniard or a South American. One peculiarity was observed in him. He carried in his left hand a small black, leather dispatch-box, and it was noticed by a sharp-eyed clerk in the Central office that this box was fastened to his wrist by a strap. No importance was attached to the fact at the time, but subsequent events endowed it with some significance. Monsieur Caratal was shown up to Mr Bland's office, while his companion remained outside.

Monsieur Caratal's business was quickly dispatched. He had arrived that afternoon from Central America. Affairs of the utmost importance demanded that he should be in Paris without the loss of an unnecessary hour. He had missed the London express. A special must be provided. Money was of no importance. Time was everything. If the company would speed him on his way, they might make their own terms.

Mr Bland struck the electric bell, summoned Mr Potter Hood, the traffic manager, and had the matter arranged in five minutes. The train would start in three-quarters of an hour. It would take that time to insure that the line should be clear. The powerful engine called Rochdale (No. 247 on the company's register) was attached to two carriages, with a guard's van behind. The first carriage was solely for the purpose of decreasing the inconvenience arising from the oscillation. The second was divided, as usual, into four compartments, a first-class, a first-class smoking, a second-class, and a second-class smoking. The first compartment, which was nearest to the engine, was the one allotted to the travellers. The other three were empty. The guard of the special train was James McPherson, who had been some years in the service of the company. The stoker, William Smith, was a new hand.

Monsieur Caratal, upon leaving the superintendent's office, rejoined his companion, and both of them manifested extreme impatience to be off. Having paid the money asked, which amounted to fifty pounds five shillings, at the usual special rate of five shillings a mile, they demanded to be shown the carriage, and at once took their seats in it, although they were assured that the better part of an hour must elapse before the line could be cleared. In the meantime a singular coincidence had occurred in the office which Monsieur Caratal had just quitted.

A request for a special is not a very uncommon circumstance in a rich commercial centre, but that two should be required upon the same afternoon was most unusual. It so happened, however, that Mr Bland had hardly dismissed the first traveller before a second entered with a similar request. This was a Mr Horace Moore, a gentlemanly man of military appearance, who alleged that the sudden illness of his wife in London made it absolutely imperative that he should not lose an instant in starting upon the journey. His distress and anxiety were so evident that Mr Bland did all that was possible to meet his wishes. A second special was out of the question, as the ordinary local service was already somewhat deranged by the first. There was the alternative, however, that Mr Moore should share the expense of Monsieur Caratal's train, and should travel in the other empty first-class compartment, if Monsieur Caratal objected to having him in the one which he occupied. It was difficult to see any objection to such an arrangement, and yet Monsieur Caratal, upon the suggestion being made to him by Mr Potter Hood, absolutely refused to consider it for an instant. The train was his, he said, and he would insist upon the exclusive use of it. All argument failed to overcome his ungracious objections, and finally the plan had to be abandoned. Mr Horace Moore left the station in great distress, after learning that his only course was to take the ordinary slow train which leaves Liverpool at six o'clock. At four-thirty-one exactly by the station clock the special train, containing the crippled Monsieur Caratal and his gigantic companion, steamed out of the Liverpool station. The line was at that time clear, and there should have been no stoppage before Manchester.

The trains of the London and West Coast Railway run over the lines of another company as far as this town, which should have been reached by the special rather before six o'clock. At a quarter after six considerable surprise and some consternation were caused amongst the officials at Liverpool by the receipt of a telegram from Manchester to say that it had not yet arrived. An inquiry directed to St Helens, which is a third of the way between the two cities, elicited the following reply —

"To James Bland, Superintendent, Central L. & W. C., Liverpool. – Special passed here at 4.52, well up to time. – Dowser, St Helens."

This telegram was received at six forty. At six fifty a second message was received from Manchester —

"No sign of special as advised by you."

And then ten minutes later a third, more bewildering –

"Presume some mistake as to proposed running of special.

Local train from St Helens timed to follow it has just arrived and has seen nothing of it. Kindly wire advices. – Manchester."

The matter was assuming a most amazing aspect, although in some respects the last telegram was a relief to the authorities at Liverpool. If an accident had occurred to the special, it seemed hardly possible that the local train could have passed down the same line without observing it. And yet, what was the alternative? Where could the train be? Had it possibly been sidetracked for some reason in order to allow the slower train to go past? Such an explanation was possible if some small repair had to be effected. A telegram was dispatched to each of the stations between St Helens and Manchester, and the superintendent and traffic manager waited in the utmost suspense at the instrument for the series of replies which would enable them to say for certain what had become of the missing train. The answers came back in the order of questions, which was the order of the stations beginning at the St Helens end —

"Special passed here five o'clock. – Collins Green."

"Special passed here six past five. – Earlestown."

"Special passed here 5.10. – Newton."

"Special passed here 5.20. – Kenyon Junction."

"No special train has passed here. – Barton Moss."

The two officials stared at each other in amazement.

"This is unique in my thirty years of experience," said Mr Bland.

"Absolutely unprecedented and inexplicable, sir. The special has gone wrong between Kenyon Junction and Barton Moss."

"And yet there is no siding, so far as my memory serves me, between the two stations. The special must have run off the metals."

"But how could the four-fifty parliamentary pass over the same line without observing it?"

"There's no alternative, Mr Hood. It *must* be so. Possibly the local train may have observed something which may throw some light upon the matter. We will wire to Manchester for more information, and to Kenyon Junction with instructions that the line be examined instantly as far as Barton Moss."

The answer from Manchester came within a few minutes.

"No news of missing special. Driver and guard of slow train

positive no accident between Kenyon Junction and Barton Moss. Line quite clear, and no sign of anything unusual. – Manchester."

"That driver and guard will have to go," said Mr Bland, grimly. "There has been a wreck and they have missed it. The special has obviously run off the metals without disturbing the line – how it could have done so passes my comprehension – but so it must be, and we shall have a wire from Kenyon or Barton Moss presently to say that they have found her at the bottom of an embankment."

But Mr Bland's prophecy was not destined to be fulfilled. Half an hour passed, and then there arrived the following message from the station-master of Kenyon Junction —

"There are no traces of the missing special. It is quite certain that she passed here, and that she did not arrive at Barton Moss. We have detached engine from goods train, and I have myself ridden down the line, but all is clear, and there is no sign of any accident."

Mr Bland tore his hair in his perplexity.

"This is rank lunacy, Hood!" he cried. "Does a train vanish into thin air in England in broad daylight? The thing is preposterous. An engine, a tender, two carriages, a van, five human beings – and all lost on a straight line of railway! Unless we get something positive within the next hour I'll take Inspector Collins, and go down myself."

And then at last something positive did occur. It took the shape of another telegram from Kenyon Junction.

"Regret to report that the dead body of John Slater, driver of the special train, has just been found among the gorse bushes at a point two and a quarter miles from the Junction. Had fallen from his engine, pitched down the embankment, and rolled among bushes. Injuries to his head, from the fall, appear to be cause of death. Ground has now been carefully examined, and there is no trace of the missing train."

The country was [then] in the throes of a political crisis, and the attention of the public was further distracted by the important and sensational developments in Paris, where a huge scandal threatened to destroy the Government and to wreck the reputations of many of the leading men in France. The papers were full of these events, and the singular disappearance of the special train attracted less attention than would have been the case in more peaceful times. The grotesque nature of the event helped to detract from its importance, for the papers were disinclined to believe the facts as reported to them. More than one of the London journals treated the matter as an ingenious hoax, until the coroner's inquest upon the unfortunate driver (an inquest which elicited nothing of importance) convinced them of the tragedy of the incident.

Mr Bland, accompanied by Inspector Collins, the senior detective officer in the service of the company, went down to Kenyon Junction the same evening, and their research lasted throughout the following day, but was attended with purely negative results. Not only was no trace found of the missing train, but no conjecture could be put forward which could possibly explain the facts. At the same time, Inspector Collins's official report (which lies before me as I write) served to show that the possibilities were more numerous than might have been expected.

"In the stretch of railway between these two points," said he, "the country is dotted with ironworks and collieries. Of these, some are being worked and some have been abandoned. There are no fewer than twelve which have small gauge lines which run trolly-cars down to the main line. These can, of course, be disregarded. Besides these, however, there are seven which have, or have had, proper lines running down and connecting with points to the main line, so as to convey their produce from the mouth of the mine to the great centres of distribution. In every case these lines are only a few miles in length. Out of the seven, four belong to collieries which are worked out, or at least to shafts which are no longer used. These are the Redgauntlet, Hero, Slough of Despond, and Heartsease mines, the latter having ten years ago been one of the principal mines in Lancashire. These four side lines may be eliminated from our inquiry, for, to prevent possible accidents, the rails nearest to the main line have been taken up, and there is no longer any connection. There remain three other side lines leading —

(*a*) To the Carnstock Iron Works;
(*b*) To the Big Ben Colliery;
(*c*) To the Perseverance Colliery.

"Of these the Big Ben line is not more than a quarter of a mile long, and ends at a dead wall of coal waiting removal from the mouth of the mine. Nothing had been seen or heard there of any special. The Carnstock Iron Works line was blocked all day upon the 3rd of June by sixteen truckloads of hematite. It is a single line, and nothing could have passed. As to the Perseverance line, it is a large double line, which does a considerable traffic, for the output of the mine is very large. On the 3rd of June this traffic proceeded as usual; hundreds of men including a gang of railway platelayers, were working along the two miles and a quarter which constitute the total length of the line, and it is inconceivable that an unexpected train could have come down there without attracting universal attention. It may be remarked in conclusion that this branch line is nearer to St Helens than the point at which the engine-driver was discovered, so that we have every reason to believe that the train was past that point before misfortune over-took her.

"As to John Slater, there is no clue to be gathered from his appearance or injuries. We can only say that, so far as we can see, he met his end by falling off his engine, though why he fell, or what became of the engine after his fall, is a question upon which I do not feel qualified to offer an opinion." In conclusion, the inspector offered his resignation to the Board, being much nettled by an accusation of incompetence in the London papers.

A month elapsed, during which both the police and the company prosecuted their inquiries without the slightest success. A reward was offered and a pardon promised in case of crime, but they were both unclaimed. Every day the public opened their papers with the conviction that so grotesque a mystery would at last be solved, but week after week passed by, and a solution remained as far off as ever. In broad daylight, upon a June after-noon in the most thickly inhabited portion of England, a train with its occupants had disappeared as completely as if some master of subtle chemistry had volatilized it into gas. Indeed, among the various conjectures which were put forward in the public press, there were some which seriously asserted that supernatural, or, at least, preternatural, agencies had been at work, and that the defor-med Monsieur Caratal was probably a person who was better known under a less polite name. Others fixed upon his swarthy companion as being the author of the mischief, but what it was exactly which he had done could never be clearly formulated in words.

Amongst the many suggestions put forward by various news-papers or private individuals, there were one or two which were feasible enough to attract the attention of the public. One which appeared in *The Times*, over the signature of an amateur reasoner of some celebrity at that date, attempted to deal with the matter in a critical and semi-scientific manner. An extract must suffice, although the curious can see the whole letter in the issue of the 3rd of July.

"It is one of the elementary principles of practical reasoning," he remarked, "that when the impossible has been eliminated the residuum, *however improbable,* must contain the truth. It is certain that the train left Kenyon Junction. It is certain that it did not reach Barton Moss. It is in the highest degree unlikely, but still possible, that it may have taken one of the seven available side lines. It is obviously impossible for a train to run where there are no rails, and, therefore, we may reduce our improbables to the three open lines, namely the Carnstock Iron Works, the Big Ben, and the Perseverance. Is there a secret society of colliers, an English *Camorra,* which is capable of destroying both train and passengers? It is improbable, but it is not impossible. I confess that I am unable to suggest any other solution. I should certainly advise the company to direct all their energies towards the obser-vation of those three lines, and of the workmen at the end of them. A careful supervision of the pawnbrokers' shops of the district might possibly bring some suggestive facts to light."

The suggestion coming from a recognized authority upon such matters created considerable interest, and a fierce opposition from those who considered such a statement to be a preposterous libel upon an honest and deserving set of men. The only answer to this criticism was a challenge to the objectors to lay any more feasible explanations before the public. In reply to this two others were forthcoming (*Times,* July 7th and 9th). The first suggested that the train might have run off the metals and be lying submerged in the Lancashire and Staffordshire Canal, which runs parallel to the railway for some hundreds of yards. This suggestion was thrown out of court by the published depth of the canal, which was entirely insufficient to conceal so large an object. The second correspondent wrote calling attention to the bag which appeared to be the sole luggage which the travellers had brought with them, and suggesting that some novel explosive of immense and pulverizing power might have been concealed in it. The obvious absurdity, however, of supposing that the whole train might be blown to dust while the metals remained uninjured reduced any such explanation to a farce. The investigation had drifted into this hopeless position when a new and most unexpected incident occurred.

This was nothing less than the receipt by Mrs McPherson of a letter from her husband, James McPherson, who had been the guard of the missing train. The letter, which was dated July 5th, 1890, was posted from New York and came to hand upon July 14th. Some doubts were expressed as to its genuine character, but Mrs McPherson was positive as to the writing, and the fact that it contained a remittance of a hundred dollars in five-dollar notes was enough in itself to discount the idea of a hoax. No address was given in the letter, which ran in this way:

"MY DEAR WIFE, —
"I have been thinking a great deal, and I find it very hard to give you up. The same with Lizzie. I try to fight against it, but it will always come back to me. I send you some money which will change into twenty English pounds. This should be enough to bring both Lizzie and you across the Atlantic, and you will find the Hamburg boats which stop at Southampton very good boats, and cheaper than Liverpool. If you could come here and stop at the Johnston House I would try and send you word how to meet, but things are very difficult with me at present, and I am not very happy, finding it hard to give you both up. So no more at present, from your loving husband,

"JAMES MCPHERSON."

For a time it was confidently anticipated that this letter would lead to the clearing up of the whole matter, the more so as it was ascertained that a passenger who bore a close resemblance to the missing guard had travelled from Southampton under the name of Summers in the Hamburg and New York liner *Vistula,* which started upon the 7th of June. Mrs McPherson and her sister Lizzie Dolton went across to New York as directed and stayed for three weeks at the Johnston House, without hearing anything from the missing man. It is probable that some injudicious comments in the Press may have warned him that the police were using them as a bait. However, this may be, it is certain that he neither wrote nor came, and the women were eventually compelled to return to Liverpool.

And so the matter stood, and has continued to stand up to the present year of 1898. Incredible as it may seem, nothing has transpired during these eight years which has shed the least light upon the extraordinary disappearance of the special train which contained Monsieur Caratal and his companion. Careful inquiries into the antecedents of the two travellers have only established the fact that Monsieur Caratal was well known as a financier and political agent in Central America, and that during his voyage to Europe he had betrayed extraordinary anxiety to reach Paris. His companion, whose name was entered upon the passenger lists as Eduardo Gomez, was a man whose record was a violent one, and whose reputation was that of a bravo and a bully. There was evidence to show, however, that he was honestly devoted to the interests of Monsieur Caratal, and that the latter, being a man of puny physique, employed the other as a guard and protector. It may be added that no information came from Paris as to what the objects of Monsieur Caratal's hurried journey may have been. This comprises all the facts of the case up to the publication in the Marseilles papers of the recent confession of Herbert de Lernac, now under sentence of death for the murder of a merchant named Bonvalot. This statement may be literally translated as follows:

"It is not out of mere pride or boasting that I give this information, for, if that were my object, I could tell a dozen actions of mine which are quite as splendid; but I do it in order that certain gentlemen in Paris may understand that I, who am able here to tell about the fate of Monsieur Caratal, can also tell in whose interest and at whose request the deed was done, unless the reprieve which I am awaiting comes to me very quickly. Take warning, messieurs, before it is too late! You know Herbert de Lernac, and you are aware that his deeds are as ready as his words. Hasten then, or you are lost!

"At present I shall mention no names – if you only heard the names, what would you not think! – but I shall merely tell you how cleverly I did it. I was true to my employers then, and no doubt they will be true to me now. I hope so, and until I am convinced that they have betrayed me, these names, which would convulse Europe, shall not be divulged. But on that day . . . well, I say no more!

"In a word, then, there was a famous trial in Paris, in the year 1890, in connection with a monstrous scandal in politics and finance. How monstrous that scandal was can never be known save by such confidential agents as myself. The honour and careers of many of the chief men in France were at stake. You have seen a group of ninepins standing, all so rigid, and prim, and unbending. Then there comes the ball from far away and pop, pop, pop – there are your ninepins on the floor. Well, imagine some of the greatest men in France as these ninepins and then this Monsieur Caratal was the ball which could be seen coming from far away. If he arrived, then it was pop, pop, pop for all of them. It was determined that he should not arrive.

"I do not accuse them all of being conscious of what was to happen. There were, as I have said, great financial as well as political interests at stake, and a syndicate was formed to manage the business. Some subscribed to the syndicate who hardly understood what were its objects. But others understood very well, and they can rely upon it that I have not forgotten their names. They had ample warning that Monsieur Caratal was coming long before he left South America, and they knew that the evidence which he held would certainly mean ruin to all of them. The syndicate had the command of an unlimited amount of money – absolutely unlimited, you understand. They looked round for an agent who was capable of wielding this gigantic power. The man chosen must be inventive, resolute, adaptive – a man in a million. They chose Herbert de Lernac, and I admit that they were right.

"My duties were to choose my subordinates, to use freely the power which money gives, and to make certain that Monsieur Caratal should never arrive in Paris. With characteristic energy I set about my commission within an hour of receiving my instructions, and the steps which I took were the very best for the purpose which could possibly be devised.

"A man whom I could trust was dispatched instantly to South America to travel home with Monsieur Caratal. Had he arrived in

time the ship would never have reached Liverpool; but alas! it
had already started before my agent could reach it. I fitted out a
small armed brig to intercept it, but again I was unfortunate. Like
all great organizers I was, however, prepared for failure, and had
a series of alternatives prepared, one or the other of which must
succeed. You must not underrate the difficulties of my undertaking, or imagine that a mere commonplace assassination would
meet the case. We must destroy not only Monsieur Caratal, but
Monsieur Caratal's documents, and Monsieur Caratal's companions also, if we had reason to believe that he had communicated his secrets to them. And you must remember that they were
on the alert, and keenly suspicious of any such attempt. It was a
task which was in every way worthy of me, for I am always most
masterful where another would be appalled.

"I was all ready for Monsieur Caratal's reception in Liverpool,
and I was the more eager because I had reason to believe that he
had made arrangements by which he would have a considerable
guard from the moment that he arrived in London. Anything
which was to be done must be done between the moment of his
setting foot upon the Liverpool quay and that of his arrival at the
London and West Coast terminus in London. We prepared six
plans, each more elaborate than the last; which plan would be used
would depend upon his own movements. Do what he would, we
were ready for him. If he had stayed in Liverpool, we were ready.
If he took an ordinary train, an express, or a special, all was ready.
Everything had been foreseen and provided for.

"You may imagine that I could not do all this myself. What
could I know of the English railway lines? But money can procure
willing agents all the world over, and I soon had one of the
acutest brains in England to assist me. I will mention no names,
but it would be unjust to claim all the credit for myself. My English
ally was worthy of such an alliance. He knew the London and
West Coast line thoroughly, and he had the command of a band
of workers who were trustworthy and intelligent. The idea was
his, and my own judgment was only required in the details. We
bought over several officials, amongst whom the most important
was James McPherson, whom we had ascertained to be the guard
most likely to be employed upon a special train. Smith, the stoker,
was also in our employ. John Slater, the engine-driver, had been

approached, but had been found to be obstinate and dangerous, so we desisted. We had no certainty that Monsieur Caratal would take a special, but we thought it very probable, for it was of the utmost importance to him that he should reach Paris without delay. It was for this contingency, therefore, that we made special preparations – preparations which were complete down to the last detail long before his steamer had sighted the shores of England. You will be amused to learn that there was one of my agents in the pilot-boat which brought that steamer to its moorings.

"The moment that Caratal arrived in Liverpool we knew that he suspected danger and was on his guard. He had brought with him as an escort a dangerous fellow, named Gomez, a man who carried weapons, and was prepared to use them. This fellow carried Caratal's confidential papers for him, and was ready to protect either them or his master. The probability was that Caratal had taken him into his counsels, and that to remove Caratal without removing Gomez would be a mere waste of energy. It was necessary that they should be involved in a common fate, and our plans to that end were much facilitated by their request for a special train. On that special train you will understand that two out of the three servants of the company were really in our employ, at a price which would make them independent for a lifetime. I do not go so far as to say that the English are more honest than any other nation, but I have found them more expensive to buy.

"I have already spoken of my English agent – who is a man with a considerable future before him, unless some complaint of the throat carries him off before his time. He had charge of all arrangements at Liverpool, whilst I was stationed at the inn at Kenyon, where I awaited a cipher signal to act. When the special was arranged for, my agent instantly telegraphed to me and warned me how soon I should have everything ready. He himself under the name of Horace Moore applied immediately for a special also, in the hope that he would be sent down with Monsieur Caratal, which might under certain circumstances have been helpful to us. If, for example, our great *coup* had failed, it would then have become the duty of my agent to have shot them both and destroyed their papers. Caratal was on his guard, however, and refused to admit any other traveller. My agent then left the

Q

station, returned by another entrance, entered the guard's van on the side farthest from the platform, and travelled down with McPherson the guard.

"In the meantime you will be interested to know what my movements were. Everything had been prepared for days before, and only the finishing touches were needed. The side line which we had chosen had once joined the main line, but it had been disconnected. We had only to replace a few rails to connect it once more. These rails had been laid down as far as could be done without danger of attracting attention, and now it was merely a case of completing a juncture with the line, and arranging the points as they had been before. The sleepers had never been removed, and the rails, fish-plates and rivets were all ready, for we had taken them from a siding on the abandoned portion of the line. With my small but competent band of workers, we had everything ready long before the special arrived. When it did arrive, it ran off upon the small side line so easily that the jolting of the points appears to have been entirely unnoticed by the two travellers.

"Our plan had been that Smith, the stoker, should chloroform John Slater, the driver, so that he should vanish with the others. In this respect, and in this respect only, our plans miscarried – I except the criminal folly of McPherson in writing home to his wife. Our stoker did his business so clumsily that Slater in his struggles fell off the engine, and though fortune was with us so far that he broke his neck in the fall, still he remained as a blot upon that which would otherwise have been one of those complete masterpieces which are only to be contemplated in silent admiration. The criminal expert will find in John Slater the one flaw in all our admirable combinations. A man who has had as many triumphs as I can afford to be frank, and I therefore lay my finger upon John Slater, and I proclaim him to be a flaw.

"But now I have got our special train upon the small line two kilometres, or rather more than one mile, in length, which leads, or rather used to lead, to the abandoned Heartsease mine, once one of the largest coal mines in England. You will ask how it is that no one saw the train upon this unused line. I answer that along its entire length it runs through a deep cutting, and that, unless someone had been on the edge of that cutting, he could not have seen it. There *was* someone on the edge of that cutting. I was there. And now I will tell you what I saw.

"My assistant had remained at the points in order that he might superintend the switching off of the train. He had four armed men with him, so that if the train ran off the line – we thought it probable, because the points were very rusty – we might still have resources to fall back upon. Having once seen it safely on the side line, he handed over the responsibility to me. I was waiting at a point which overlooks the mouth of the mine, and I was also armed, as were my two companions. Come what might, you see, I was always ready.

"The moment that the train was fairly on the side line, Smith, the stoker, slowed-down the engine, and then, having turned it on to the fullest speed again, he and McPherson, with my English lieutenant, sprang off before it was too late. It may be that it was this slowing-down which first attracted the attention of the travellers, but the train was running at full speed again before their heads appeared at the open window. It makes me smile to think how bewildered they must have been. Picture to yourself your own feelings if, on looking out of your luxurious carriage, you suddenly perceived that the lines upon which you ran were rusted and corroded, red and yellow with disuse and decay! What a catch must have come in their breath as in a second it flashed upon them that it was not Manchester but Death which was waiting for them at the end of that sinister line. But the train was running with frantic speed, rolling and rocking over the rotten line, while the wheels made a frightful screaming sound upon the rusted surface. I was close to them, and could see their faces. Caratal was praying, I think – there was something like a rosary dangling out of his hand. The other roared like a bull who smells the blood of the slaughter-house. He saw us standing on the bank, and he beckoned to us like a madman. Then he tore at his wrist and threw his dispatch-box out of the window in our direction. Of course, his meaning was obvious. Here was the evidence, and they would promise to be silent if their lives were spared. It would have been very agreeable if we could have done so, but business is business. Besides, the train was now as much beyond our control as theirs.

"He ceased howling when the train rattled round the curve and they saw the black mouth of the mine yawning before them. We had removed the boards which had covered it, and we had cleared the square entrance. The rails had formerly run very close to the shaft for the convenience of loading the coal, and we had only to add two or three lengths of rail in order to lead to the very brink of the shaft. In fact, as the lengths would not quite fit, our line projected about three feet over the edge. We saw the two heads at the window: Caratal below, Gomez above; but they had both been struck silent by what they saw. And yet they could not withdraw their heads. The sight seemed to have paralysed them.

"I had wondered how the train running at a great speed would take the pit into which I had guided it, and I was much interested in watching it. One of my colleagues thought that it would actually jump it, and indeed it was not very far from doing so. Fortunately, however, it fell short, and the buffers of the engine struck the other lip of the shaft with a tremendous crash. The funnel flew off into the air. The tender, carriages, and van were all smashed up into one jumble, which, with the remains of the engine, choked for a minute or so the mouth of the pit. Then something gave way in the middle, and the whole mass of green iron, smoking coals, brass fittings, wheels, wood-work, and cushions all crumbled together and crashed down into the mine. We heard the rattle, rattle, rattle, as the debris struck against the walls, and then, quite a long time afterwards, there came a deep roar as the remains of the train struck the bottom. The boiler may have burst, for a sharp crash came after the roar, and then a dense cloud of steam and smoke swirled up out of the black depths, falling in a spray as thick as rain all round us. Then the vapour shredded off into thin wisps, which floated away in the summer sunshine, and all was quiet again in the Heartsease mine.

"And now, having carried out our plans so successfully, it only remained to leave no trace behind us. Our little band of workers at the other end had already ripped up the rails and disconnected the side line, replacing everything as it had been before. We were equally busy at the mine. The funnel and other fragments were thrown in, the shaft was planked over as it used to be, and the lines which led to it were torn up and taken away. Then, without flurry, but without dealy, we all made our way out of the country, most of us to Paris, my English colleague to Manchester, and

McPherson to Southampton, whence he emigrated to America. Let the English papers of that date tell how thoroughly we had done our work, and how completely we had thrown the cleverest of their detectives off our track.

"You will remember that Gomez threw his bag of papers out of the window, and I need not say that I secured that bag and brought them to my employers. It may interest my employers now, however, to learn that out of that bag I took one or two little papers as a souvenir of the occasion. I have no wish to publish these papers; but, still, it is every man for himself in this world, and what else can I do if my friends will not come to my aid when I want them? Messieurs, you may believe that Herbert de Lernac is quite as formidable when he is against you as when he is with you, and that he is not a man to go to the guillotine until he has seen that every one of you is *en route* for New Caledonia. For your own sake, if not for mine, make haste, Monsieur de —, and General —, and Baron — (you can fill up the blanks for yourselves as you read this). I promise you that in the next edition there will be no blanks to fill.

"P.S. – As I look over my statement there is only one omission which I can see. It concerns the unfortunate man McPherson, who was foolish enough to write to his wife and to make an appointment with her in New York. It can be imagined that when interests like ours were at stake, we could not leave them to the chance of whether a man in that class of life would or would not give away his secrets to a woman. Having once broken his oath by writing to his wife, we could not trust him any more. We took steps therefore to insure that he should not see his wife. I have sometimes thought that it would be a kindness to write to her and to assure her that there is no impediment to her marrying again."

from THE COLLECTED STORIES *1924*

Journey to the Summit

R. B. CUNNINGHAME-GRAHAM

The bustle on the Euston platform stopped for an instant to let the men who carried him to the third-class compartment pass along the train. Gaunt and emaciated, he looked just at death's door, and, as they propped him in the carriage between two pillows, he faintly said, "Jock, do ye think I'll live as far as Moffat? I should na' like to die in London in the smoke."

His cockney wife, drying her tears with a cheap hemstitched pocket handkerchief, her scanty town-bred hair looking like wisps of tow beneath her hat, bought from some window in which each individual article was marked at seven-and-sixpence, could only sob. His brother, with the country sun and wind burn still upon his face, and his huge hands hanging like hams in front of him, made answer.

"Andra'," he said, "gin ye last as far as Beattock, we'll gie ye a braw hurl back to the farm, syne the bask air, ye ken, and the milk, and – but can ye last as far as Beattock, Andra'?"

The sick man, sitting with the cold sweat upon his face, his shrunken limbs looking like sticks inside his ill-made black slop suit, after considering the proposition on its merits, looked up, and said, "I should na' like to bet I feel fair boss, God knows; but there, the mischief of it is, he will na' tell ye, so that, as ye may say, his knowlidge has na' commercial value. I ken I look as gash as Garscadden. Ye mind, Jock, in the braw auld times, when the auld laird just slipped away, whiles they were birlin' at the clairet. A braw death, Jock . . . do ye think it'll be rainin' aboot Ecclefechan? Aye . . . sure to be rainin' aboot Lockerbie. Nae Christians there, Jock, a' Johnstones and Jardines, ye mind?"

The wife, who had been occupied with an air cushion, and, having lost the bellows, had been blowing into it till her cheeks seemed almost bursting, and her false teeth were loosened in her head, left off her toil to ask her husband "If 'e could pick a bit of something, a porkpie, or a nice sausage roll, or something tasty," which she could fetch from the refreshment room. The invalid having declined to eat, and his brother having drawn from his pocket a dirty bag, in which were peppermints, gave him a "drop", telling him that he "minded he aye used to like them weel, when the meenister had fairly got into his prelection in the auld kirk, outby".

The train slid almost imperceptibly away, the passengers upon the platform looking after it with that half foolish, half astonished look with which men watch a disappearing train. Then a few sandwich papers rose with the dust almost to the level of the platform, sank again, the clock struck twelve and the station fell into a half quiescence, like a volcano in the interval between the lava showers. Inside the third-class carriage all was quiet until the lights of Harrow shone upon the left, when the sick man, turning himself with difficulty, said, "Good-bye, Harrow-on-the-Hill. I aye liked Harrow for the hill's sake, tho' ye can scarcely ca' yon wee bit mound a hill, Jean."

His wife, who, even in her grief, still smarted under the Scotch variant of her name, which all her life she had pronounced as "Jayne", and who, true cockney as she was, bounded her world within the lines of Plaistow, Peckham Rye, the Welsh 'Arp ('Endon way), and Willesden, moved uncomfortably at the depreciation of the chief mountain in her cosmos, but held her peace. Loving her husband in a sort of half-antagonistic fashion, born of the difference of type between the hard, unyielding, yet humorous and sentimental Lowland Scot and the conglomerate of all races of the island which meet in London, . . . there had arisen between them that intangible veil of misconception which, though not excluding love, is yet impervious to respect. Each saw the other's failings, or, perhaps, thought the good qualities which each possessed were faults, for usually men judge each other by their good points, which, seen through prejudice of race, religion, and surroundings, appear to them defects.

The brother, who but a week ago had left his farm unwillingly, just when the "neeps were wantin' heughin' and a feck o' things requirin' to be done, forby a puckle sheep waitin' for keelin'," to come and see his brother for the last time, sat in that dour and seeming apathetic attitude which falls upon the country man, torn from his daily toil, and plunged into a town. Most things in London, during the brief intervals he had passed away from the sick-bed, seemed foolish to him, and of a nature such as a selfrespecting Moffat man, in the hebdomadal enjoyment of the "prelections" of a Free Church minister, could not authorize. . . .

The moon shone brightly into the compartment, extinguishing the flickering of the half-candle-power electric light. Rugby, the station all lit up, and with its platforms occupied but by a few belated passengers, all muffled up like racehorses taking their exercise, flashed past. They slipped through Cannock Chase, which stretches down with heath and firs, clear brawling streams, and birch trees, an outpost of the north lost in the midland clay. They crossed the oily Trent, flowing through alder copses, and with its backwaters, all overgrown with lilies, like an aguapey in Paraguay or in Brazil.

The sick man, wrapped in cheap rugs, and sitting like Guy Fawkes, in the half comic, half pathetic way that sick folk sit, making them sport for fools, and, at the same time, moistening the eye of the judicious, who reflect that they themselves may one day sit as they do, bereft of all the dignity of strength, looked listlessly at nothing as the train sped on. His loving, tactless wife, whose cheap "sized" handkerchief had long since become a rag with mopping up her tears, endeavoured to bring round her husband's thoughts to paradise, which she conceived a sort of music hall, where angels sat with their wings folded, listening to sentimental songs.

Her brother-in-law, reared on the fiery faith of Moffat Calvinism, eyed her with great disfavour, as a terrier eyes a rat imprisoned in a cage.

"Jean wumman," he burst out, "to hear ye talk, I would jist think your meenister had been a perfectly illeeterate man, pairadise here, pairadise there, what do ye think a man like Andra' could dae daunderin' aboot a gairden naked, pu'in soor aipples frae the trees?"

Cockney and Scots conceit, impervious alike to outside criticism, and each so bolstered in its pride as to be quite incapable of seeing that anything existed outside the purlieus of their sight, would soon have made the carriage into a battle-field, had not the husband, with the authority of approaching death, put in his word.

"Whist, Jeanie wumman. Jock, dae ye no ken that the Odium-Theologicum is just a curse – pairadise – set ye baith up – pairadise. I dinna' even richtly ken if I can last as far as Beattock."

Stafford, its iron furnaces belching out flames, which burned red holes into the night, seemed to approach, rather than be approached, so smoothly ran the train. The mingled moonlight and the glare of iron-works lit the canal beside the railway, and from the water rose white vapours as from Styx or Periphlegethon. Through Cheshire ran the train, its timbered houses showing ghastly in the frost which coated all the carriage windows, and rendered them opaque. Preston, the catholic city, lay silent in the night, its river babbling through the public park, and then the hills of Lancashire loomed lofty in the night. Past Garstang, with its waterlily-covered ponds, Garstang where, in the days gone by, catholic squires, against their will, were forced on Sundays to "take wine" in Church on pain of fine, the puffing serpent slid.

The talk inside the carriage had given place to sleep, that is, the brother-in-law and wife slept fitfully, but the sick man looked out, counting the miles to Moffat, and speculating on his strength. Big drops of sweat stood on his forehead, and his breath came double, whistling through his lungs.

They passed by Lancaster, skirting the sea on which the moon shone bright, setting the fishing boats in silver as they lay scarcely moving on the waves. Then, so to speak, the train set its face up against Shap Fell, and, puffing heavily, drew up into the hills, the scattered grey stone houses of the north, flanked by their gnarled and twisted ash trees, hanging upon the edge of the streams, as

Q*

lonely, and as cut off from the world (except the passing train) as if they had been in Central Africa. The moorland roads, winding amongst the heather, showed that the feet of generations had marked them out, and not the line, spade, and theodolite, with all the circumstance of modern road makers. They, too, looked white and unearthly in the moonlight, and now and then a sheep, aroused by the snorting of the train, moved from the heather into the middle of the road, and stood there motionless, its shadow filling the narrow track, and flickering on the heather at the edge.

The keen and penetrating air of the hills and night aroused the two sleepers, and they began to talk, after the Scottish fashion, of the funeral, before the anticipated corpse.

"Ye ken, we've got a braw new hearse outby, sort of Epescopalian-lookin', we' gless a' roond, so's ye can see the kist. Very conceity too, they mak' the hearses noo-a-days. I min' when they were jist auld sort o' ruckly boxes, awfu' licht, ye ken, upon the springs, and just went dodderin' alang, the body swingin' to and fro, as if it would flee richt oot. The roads, ye ken, were no high hand so richtly metalled in thae days."

The subject of the conversation took it cheerfully, expressing pleasure at the advance of progress as typified in the new hearse, hoping his brother had a decent "stan' o' black," and looking at his death, after the fashion of his kind, as it were something outside himself, a fact indeed, on which, at the same time, he could express himself with confidence as being in some measure interested. His wife, not being Scottish, took quite another view, and seemed to think that the mere mention of the word was impious, or, at the least, of such a nature as to bring on immediate dissolution. . . . She endeavoured to persuade her husband that he looked better, and yet would mend, once in his native air.

"At Moffit, ye'd 'ave the benefit of the 'ill breezes, and that 'ere country milk, which never 'as no cream in it, but 'olesome, as you say. Why yuss, in about eight days at Moffit, you'll be as 'earty as you ever was. Yuss, you will, you take my word."

. . . Just at the Summit they stopped an instant to let a goods train pass, and, in a faint voice, the consumptive said, "I'd almost lay a wager now I'd last to Moffat, Jock. The Shap, ye ken, I aye looked at as the beginning of the run home. The hills, ye ken, are sort o' heartsome. No that they're bonny hills like Moffat hills,

na', na', ill-shapen sort of things, just like Borunty tatties, awfu'
puir names too, Shap Fell and Rowland Edge, Hutton Roof Crags,
and Arnside Fell; heard ever ony body sich like names for hills?
Neathing to fill the mooth; man, the Scotch hills jist grap ye in the
mooth for a' the world like speerits."

They stopped at Penrith, which the old castle walls make even
meaner, in the cold morning light, than other stations look. Little
Salkeld, and Armathwaite, Cotehill, and Scotby all rushed past,
and the train, slackening, stopped with a jerk upon the platform
at Carlisle. The sleepy porters bawled out "change for Maryport",
some drovers slouched into carriages, kicking their dogs before
them, and, slamming-to the doors, exchanged the time of day with
others of their tribe, all carrying ash or hazel sticks, all red-faced
and keen-eyed, their caps all crumpled, and their greatcoat tails all
creased, as if their wearers had lain down to sleep full dressed, so
as to lose no time in getting to the labours of the day. The old red
sandstone church, with something of a castle in its look, as well
befits a shrine close to a frontier where in days gone by the priest
had need to watch and pray, frowned on the passing train, and on
the manufactories, whose banked-up fires sent poisonous fumes
into the air, withering the trees, which, in the public park, a
careful council had hedged round about with wire.

The Eden ran from bank to bank, its water swirling past as
wildly as when "The Bauld Buccleugh" and his Moss Troopers,
bearing "the Kinmount" fettered in their midst, plunged in and
passed it, whilst the keen Lord Scroope stood on the brink amazed
and motionless. Gretna, so close to England, and yet a thousand
miles away in speech and feeling, found the sands now flying
through the glass. All through the mosses which once were the
"Debateable Land" on which the moss-troopers of the clan
Graeme were used to hide the cattle stolen from the "auncient
enemy", the now repatriated Scotsman murmured feebly "that
it was bonny scenery" although a drearier prospect of "moss hags"
and stunted birch trees is not to be found. At Ecclefechan he just
raised his head, and faintly spoke of "yon auld carle, Carlyle, ye
ken, a dour thrawn body, but a gran' pheelosopher", and then
lapsed into silence, broken by frequent struggles to take breath.

His wife and brother sat still, and eyed him as a cow watches a
locomotive engine pass, amazed and helpless, and he himself had

but the strength to whisper "Jock, I'm dune, I'll no' see Moffat, blast it, yon smoke, ye ken, yon London smoke has been ower muckle for ma lungs."

The tearful, helpless wife, not able even to pump up the harmful and unnecessary conventional lie, which after all, consoles only the liar, sat pale and limp, chewing the fingers of her Berlin gloves. Upon the weather-beaten cheek of Jock glistened a tear, which he brushed off as angrily as it if had been a wasp.

"Aye, Andra'," he said, "I would hae liket awfu' weel that ye should win to Moffat. Man, the rowan trees are a' in bloom, and there's a bonny breer upon the corn – aye, ou aye, the reid bogs are lookin' gran' the year – but Andra', I'll tak' ye east to the auld kirk yaird, ye'll no' ken onything aboot it, but we'll hae a heartsome funeral."

Lockerbie seemed to fly towards them, and the dying Andra' smiled as his brother pointed out the place and said, "Ye mind, there are no ony Christians in it", and answered, "Aye, I mind naething but Jardines", as he fought for breath.

The death dews gathered on his forehead as the train shot by Nethercleugh, passed Wamphray, and Dinwoodie, and with a jerk pulled up at Beattock just at the summit of the pass.

So in the cold spring morning light, the fine rain beating on the platform, as the wife and brother got their almost speechless care out of the carriage, the brother whispered, "Dam't, ye've done it, Andra', here's Beattock; I'll tak' ye east to Moffat yet to dee."

But on the platform, huddled on the bench to which he had been brought, Andra' sat speechless and dying in the rain. The doors banged to, the guard stepping in lightly as the train flew past, and a belated porter shouted, "Beattock, Beattock for Moffat", and then, summoning his last strength, Andra' smiled, and whispered faintly in his brother's ear, "Aye, Beattock – for Moffat?" Then his head fell back, and a faint bloody foam oozed from his pallid lips. His wife stood crying helplessly, the rain beating upon the flowers of her cheap hat, rendering it shapeless and ridiculous. But Jock, drawing out a bottle, took a short dram and saying, "Andra', man, ye made a richt gude fecht o' it", snorted an instant in a red pocket handkerchief, and calling up a boy, said, "Rin, Jamie, to the toon, and tell McNicol to send up and fetch a corp". Then, after helping to remove the body to the waiting-room, walked out into the rain, and, whistling "Corn Rigs" quietly between his teeth lit up his pipe, and muttered as he smoked "A richt gude fecht – man aye, ou aye, a game Jin Andra', puir felly. Weel, Weel, he'll hae a braw hurl onyway in the new Moffat hearse."

from SUCCESS *1902*

The Great Locomotive Chase

JOHN BUCHAN

The time is the spring of 1862, the second year of the American Civil War. The scene is the State of Tennessee; the Confederates are concentrating at Corinth, Mississippi, and the two Northern forces of Grant and Buell are moving on that spot. A month before Grant had won the important action of Fort Donelson. A month later he was to win the battle of Shiloh.

In Buell's army was General O. M. Mitchel, commanding the Northern forces in Middle Tennessee and protecting Nashville with a force of some 17,000 men. Now, President Lincoln especially desired that Eastern Tennessee should be cleared of the enemy, since it was one of the latter's chief supply grounds. General Mitchel believed that Corinth would soon fall, and that the next movement would be eastward towards Chattanooga, that key-point on the Tennessee river which was later the scene of one of Grant's most famous victories. He thought, rightly, that if he could press into the enemy's country and occupy strategical points ahead, he would pave the way for Grant's march eastward.

On the 8th of April the Northerners won the battle of Pittsburg Landing. Next day Mitchel marched south from Shelbyville into Alabama and seized Huntsville. From there he sent a detachment westward to open up communication with the Northern troops at Pittsburg Landing. On the same day he himself took another detachment seventy miles by rail and arrived without difficulty within thirty miles of Chattanooga, two hours from the key position in the West. There, however, he stuck fast, and the capture of Chattanooga was delayed for two years. He failed because another plan had failed. . . .

Chattanooga at the moment was practically without a garrison; but in Georgia there were ample Confederate troops, and the Georgia State Railway and the East Tennessee Railway could bring them up in great force at short notice. If Mitchel was to seize and hold Chattanooga, these lines must be cut for long enough to enable him to consolidate his position. Now, in his army was a certain spy of the name of James J. Andrews, one of those daring adventurers who, in the civil war of volunteers, many of whom were as yet without regular uniforms, could perform exploits impossible in a normal campaign. Andrews conceived the idea of a raid on the Confederate railways, and Mitchel approved. Before he left Shelbyville he authorized Andrews to take twenty-four men, enter the enemy's territory and burn the bridges on the vital railways.

The men were selected from three Ohio regiments, and told only that they were required for secret and dangerous service. They exchanged their uniforms for the ordinary dress worn by civilians in the South, and carried no arms except revolvers. On the 7th of April, by a roadside a mile east of Shelbyville, in the late evening, they met Andrews, who told them his plan. In small detachments of three or four they were to go east into the Cumberland Mountains and work southward, and on the evening of the third day rendezvous with Andrews at Marietta in Georgia, more than 200 miles distant. If any one asked them questions they were to declare that they were Kentuckians going to join the Confederate army.

The weather was bad and the travellers were much delayed by swollen streams. This led Andrews to believe that Mitchel's column would also be delayed, so he sent secret word to the different groups that the attempt would be postponed one day, from Friday to Saturday, 12th April. Of the little party one lost his road and never arrived at the destination; two reached Marietta, but missed the rendezvous; and two were captured and forced into the Confederate army. Twenty, however, early on the morning of Saturday, 12th April, met in Andrews' room at the Marietta Hotel.

They had travelled from Chattanooga as ordinary passengers on the Georgia State Railway. The sight of that railway impressed them with the difficulties of their task, for it was crowded with trains and soldiers. In order to do their work they must capture an engine, but the station where the capture was to be made – Big Shanty – had recently been made a Confederate Camp. Their job was, therefore, to seize an engine in a camp with soldiers all round them, to run it from one to two hundred miles through enemy country, and to dodge or overpower any trains they might meet – no small undertaking for a score of men. Some were in favour of abandoning the enterprise, but Andrews stuck stubbornly to his purpose. He gave his final instructions, and the twenty proceeded to the ticket office to purchase tickets for different stations on the line to Chattanooga.

For eight miles they rode in comfort as passengers, till at Big Shanty they saw the Confederate tents in the misty morning. It had been a drizzling April dawn, and a steady rain was now beginning. The train stopped at Big Shanty for breakfast, and this gave them their chance, for the conductor, the engine-driver, and most of the passengers descended for their meal, leaving the train unguarded.

Among the twenty were men who understood the stoking and driving of railway engines, and it did not take long to uncouple three empty vans, the locomotive, and the tender. Brown and Knight, the two engineers, and the fireman climbed into the cab, and the rest clambered into the rear goods van – no easy job, for the cars stood on a high bank. A sentry with rifle in hand stood not a dozen feet from the engine, watching the whole proceedings, but no move was made until it was too late. Andrews gave the signal, the wheels slipped at first on the greasy metals, and then the train moved forward; and before the uproar in the station behind began it had gathered speed.

The first and worst problem was the passing of trains coming from the north. There were two trains on the time-table which had to be passed at certain stations, and there was also a local goods train not scheduled, whigh might be anywhere. Andrews hoped to avoid the danger of collision by running according to the schedule of the train he had captured, until the goods train was passed, and then to increase to topmost speed till he reached the Oostenaula and Chickamauga bridges, burn them and pass on through Chattanooga to Mitchel as he moved up from Huntsville. He hoped to reach his chief early in the afternoon.

It was a perfectly feasible plan, and it would almost certainly have been carried out but for that fatal days' delay. On Friday, the day originally fixed, all the trains had been up to time, and the weather had been good; but on that Saturday, as luck would have it, the whole railway was in disorder, every train was late, and two "extras" had been put on, of which the leader had no notion. Had he known this, even a man of his audacity would scarcely have started, and the world would have been the poorer by the loss of a stirring tale.

The party had to make frequent stops, particularly between stations, to tear up the track, cut the telegraph wires, and load on sleepers to be used for bridge burning; and also at wayside stations to take on wood and water. At the latter Andrews bluffed the officials by telling them that he was one of General Beauregard's officers, and was running a powder train through to that General at Corinth. Unfortunately he had no proper instruments for pulling up the rails, and it was important to keep to the schedule of the captured train, so they tore light-heartedly past towns and villages, trusting to luck, and exhilarated by the successful start of their wild adventure.

At a station called Etowah they found the "Yonah", an old engine owned by an iron company, standing with steam up; but their mind was all on the local goods train, so they left it untouched. Thirty miles on from Big Shanty they reached Kingston, where a branch line entered from the town of Rome. On the branch a train was waiting for the mail – that is to say, their captured train – and Andrews learned that the local goods was expected immediately; so he ran on to a side track, and waited for it.

Presently it arrived, and to the consternation of the little party it carried a red flag to show that another train was close behind it. Andrews marched boldly across to its conductor and asked what was the meaning of the railway being blocked in this fashion, when he had orders to take the powder straight through to General Beauregard? In reply he was told that Mitchel had captured Huntsville and was said to be marching on Chattanooga, and that everything was being cleared out of that town. Andrews ordered him to move his train down the line out of the way, and he obeyed.

It seemed an eternity to the party before the "extra" arrived, and to their dismay when it turned up they saw that it bore another red flag. The reason given was that it was too heavy for one engine and had therefore to be made up into two sections. So began another anxious wait. The little band – Andrews with the engine-drivers and fireman in the cab, and the rest taking the place of Beauregard's ammunition in the goods vans – had to preserve composure as best they could, with three trains clustered round them and every passenger in the three extremely curious about the mysterious powder train into which the morning mail had been transformed. For one hour and five minutes they waited at Kingston, the men in the goods vans being warned by Andrews to be ready to fight in case of need. He himself kept close to the station in case some mischief-maker should send an inquiring telegram down the line. At long last came the second half of the local, and as soon as it passed the end of their side track the adventurers moved on.

But the alarm had now been raised behind them. From the midst of the confusion at Big Shanty two men set out on foot along the track to make some effort to capture the Northerners. They were railwaymen – one the conductor of the train, W. A. Fuller, and the other a foreman of the Atlanta railway machine shops, called Anthony Murphy. They found a hand-car and pushed forward on it till they reached Etowah, where they realized that the line had been cut by pitching headforemost down the embankment into a ditch. A little thing like this did not dismay them, and at Etowah they found the "Yonah", the iron company's old locomotive, which, as we know, was standing with steam up. They got on board, filled it up with soldiers who happened to be near, and started off at full speed for Kingston, where they were convinced they would catch the filibusters. The "Yonah" actually entered Kingston station four minutes after Andrews had started, and was of course immediately confronted with the three long trains facing the wrong way. It would have taken too long to move them, so the "Yonah" was abandoned, and Murphy uncoupled the engine and one coach of the Rome train, and con-tinued the chase. It was now any one's race. Andrews and his merry men were only a few minutes ahead.

Four miles north from Kingston the little party again stopped and cut the wires. They started to take up a rail and were pulling at the loosened end, when to their consternation they heard behind them the whistle of an engine. They managed to break the rail and then clambered in and moved on. At the next station, Adairsville, they found a mixed goods and passenger train waiting, and learned that there was an express on the road. It was a crazy risk to take, but they dared not delay, so they started at a terrific speed for the next station, Calhoun, hoping to reach it before the express, which was late, could arrive.

They did the nine miles to Calhoun in less than nine minutes, and saw in front of them the express just starting. Hearing their whistle it backed, and enabled them to take a side track, but it stopped in such a manner as to close the other end of the switch. There stood the trains side by side, almost touching each other. Naturally questions were asked, and Andrews was hard put to it to explain. He told the powder story, and demanded in the name of General Beauregard that the other train should at once let him pass. With some difficulty its conductor was persuaded, and moved forward.

They were saved by the broken rail. The pursuit saw it in time and reversed their engine. Leaving the soldiers behind, Fuller and Murphy ran along the track till they met the train which Andrews had passed at Adairsville. They made it back in pursuit, and at Adairsville dropped the coaches and continued with only the locomotive and tender, both loaded with a further complement of armed soldiers. They thought that their quarry was safe at Calhoun, but they reached that place a minute or two after Andrews had moved out.

Everything now depended on whether the band of twenty could make another gap in the track in time, for if they could the road was clear before them to Chattanooga. A few minutes ahead of them was the Oostenaula bridge, and if that could be burned they would soon be safe in Mitchel's camp.

But the mischief was that they had no proper tools, and the taking up of the rails was terribly slow. Once again they heard the whistle of a locomotive behind them and saw their pursuer with armed men aboard. Another minute would have removed the rail, and their victory would have been assured; but they could do nothing more than bend it, and were compelled to hurry back to their engine.

Now began one of the most astounding hunts on record. At all costs Andrews must gain a little time so as to set fire to the Oostenaula bridge; so he dropped first one car and then another. The pursuing engine, however, simply picked them up and pushed them ahead of it. There was no time to do anything at the bridge. Over its high trestles they tore, with Fuller and his soldiers almost within rifle shot.

Soon it appeared that there was no difference in the pace of the two engines. The Confederates could not overtake the filibusters, and Fuller's policy was therefore to keep close behind so as to prevent Andrews damaging the track and taking on wood and water. Both engines were driven to their last decimal of power, and Andrews succeeded in keeping his distance. But he was constantly delayed, for he was obliged to cut the telegraph wires after every station he passed, in order that an alarm might not be sent ahead; and he could not stop long enough to tear up rails.

All that man could do in the way of obstruction he did, for at all costs he must gain enough ground to destroy the Chickamauga bridges. He broke off the end of their last goods van and dropped it and various sleepers behind him, and this sufficiently checked the pursuit to enable him on two occasions to take in wood and water. More than once his party almost succeeded in lifting a rail, but each time Fuller got within rifle range before the work was completed. Through it all it rained, a steady even-down deluge. The day before had been clear, with a high wind, and a fire would have been quick to start, but on that Saturday, to burn a bridge would take time and much fuel.

On went the chase, mile after mile, past little forgotten stations and quiet villages, round perilous curves, and over culverts and embankments which had never before known such speed. Hope revived whenever the enemy was lost sight of behind a curve, but whenever the line straightened the smoke appeared again in the distance, and on their ears fell the ominous scream of his whistle. To the men, strung to a desperate tension, every minute seemed an hour. If the Northerners' courage was superb, so also was the pursuit's. Several times Fuller only escaped wreck by a hairbreadth. At one point a rail placed across the track at a curve was not seen until the train was upon it, when, said Fuller, "the engine seemed to bounce altogether off the track, and to alight again on the rails by a miracle." A few of the soldiers lost their nerve and would have given up the chase, but the stubborn resolution of their leader constrained them.

Some of Andrews' party now proposed that they should turn and ambush the enemy, getting into close quarters so that their revolvers would be a match for his guns. This plan would probably have succeeded, but Andrews still hoped to gain sufficient ground to achieve his main purpose; and he feared too, that the country ahead might have been warned by a telegram sent round to Chattanooga by way of Richmond. He thought his only chance was to stake everything on speed. Close to the town of Dalton he stopped again to cut wires and confuse the track. A Confederate regiment was encamped a hundred yards away, but, assuming that the train was part of the normal traffic, the men scarcely lifted their eyes to look at it. Fuller had written a telegram to Chattanooga and dropped a man with orders to send it. Part of the telegram got through before the wires were cut and created a panic in that town. Meantime, Andrews' supply of fuel was getting very low, and it was clear that unless he could delay the pursuit long enough to take in more, his journey would soon come to an end.

Beyond Dalton the adventurers made their last efforts to take up a rail, but, as they had no tools except an iron bar, the coming of the enemy compelled them to desist. Beyond that was a long tunnel, which they made no attempt to damage. Andrews saw that the situation was getting desperate, and he played his last card.

He increased speed so that he gained some considerable distance. Then the side and end boards of the last goods van were broken up, fuel was piled upon it, and fire brought from the engine. A long covered bridge lay a little ahead, and by the time they reached it the van was fairly on fire. It was uncoupled in the middle of the bridge, and they awaited the issue. If this device was successful there was sufficient steam in their boiler to carry them to the next woodyard.

But the device did not succeed. Before the bridge had caught fire Fuller was upon them. He dashed right through the smoke and drove the burning car before him to the next side track.

Left with very little fuel and with no obstructions to drop on the track, the position of the adventurers was now hopeless. In a few minutes their engine would come to a standstill. Their only chance was to leave it and escape. The wisest plan would probably have been to desert the train in a body, move northward through the mountains by tracks which could not be followed by cavalry, and where there were no telegraphs. But Andrews thought that they should separate. He ordered the men to jump from the engine one by one and disperse in the woods. So ended in failure a most gallant enterprise.

Melancholy is the conclusion of the tale. Ignorant of the country and far from their friends, the fugitives were easily hunted down. Several were captured the same day, and all but two within the week. As the adventurers had been in civil dress inside the enemy's lines they were regarded as spies, court-martialled, and Andrews and seven others condemned and executed. The advance of the Northern forces prevented the trial of the rest, and of the remainder, eight succeeded in making their escape from Atlanta in broad daylight, and ultimately reaching the North. The others, who also made the attempt, were recaptured and held captive till March 1863, when they were exchanged for Confederate prisoners.

from A BOOK OF ESCAPES AND HURRIED JOURNEYS *1925*

Dickens and the Railway

ROBIN ATTHILL

By tradition Dickens fathered the white Christmas and immortalized the stagecoach: Christmas at Dingley Dell, with the huge codfish and half a dozen barrels of oysters being stowed in the boot, hot brandy and water for all, Sam Weller jumping up behind, the Pickwickians pulling their coats round their legs and their shawls round their noses, "and away they go". That was 1836, when Dickens was twenty-four. He had grown up in the late Georgian world of stage-coaches and coaching inns: the England of Cobbett, not yet smothered by what Edmund Wilson has called the "industrial-commercial civilization" which we know today.

Pickwick Papers (1836), *Oliver Twist* (1838), *Nicholas Nickleby* (1839); *The Old Curiosity Shop* (1841), *Barnaby Rudge* (1841): all these describe the Old England. In *Martin Chuzzlewit* (1844) Mrs Gamp inveighs against steam engines as liable to interfere with her practice by causing premature child-births but *David Copperfield* (1850) is firmly set in the stage-coach era, there is one reference to the coming of the railway in *Bleak House* (1853), and none in *Great Expectations* (1861). . . . When Mr Pickwick visited Bath in 1836, we must suppose him blissfully unaware that a young man called Isambard Kingdom Brunel had already planned a railway from Bristol to London. The last mail-coach on the Bath road ran in 1841, and Mr Weller senior could think about hanging up his whip for good and all.

With *Dombey and Son* (1848), however, Dickens revealed himself fully cognizant of the railway. The date is significant: 1847–8 marked the peak of the Railway Mania and George Hudson's spectacular failure; and in 1844, Turner, in his seventieth year, had exhibited his *Rain, Steam and Speed*, in which the hare, the old natural symbol of speed, vainly tries to outdistance the racing train. Both painting and novel salute the beginning of a new epoch.

Dombey and Son marks the emergence of Dickens as artist rather than entertainer, with greater singleness of mind and concentration of purpose, controlling his many talents towards the expression of a coherent artistic vision. He was to become increasingly concerned with the social malaise of the new industrial-commercial world around him, which was remote indeed from the carefree Regency days to which Pickwick really belonged, when stage-coaches bowled gaily along them acadamized turnpike roads. Mr Gradgrind and Mr Bounderby, Mr Veneering and Mr Podsnap were now in the saddle, and the iron horse was tearing and snorting its way along the iron road, the highway of the new iron age, "with your hammering and roaring and hissing and lamp-iling, you brute!" as Mrs Gamp observed with a shake of her umbrella. As a novelist, Dickens was to develop into an imaginative artist of the first rank, who strove to organize his vision within the limits of the art-form he was using, and to express the core of that vision by means of a poetic use of symbols: of these the railway was one – a symbol of the power and ruthlessness of the new era.

"I left Dullborough (says the Uncommercial Traveller) in the days when there were no railroads in the land, I left it in a stage-coach . . . I was cavalierly shunted back into Dullborough the other day by train . . . and the first discovery I made was that the Station had swallowed up the playing-field.

"It was gone. The two beautiful hawthorn-trees, the hedges, the turf, and all those buttercups and daisies had given place to the stoniest of jolting roads: while beyond the station an ugly dark monster of a tunnel kept its jaws open, as if it had swallowed them and were ravenous for more destruction."

Dullborough was Rochester, which for Dickens was full of the *Associations of Childhood*. Elsewhere he describes the actual coming of the railway: in Lincolnshire (*Bleak House*, chapter 55) "preparations are afoot, measurements are made, ground is staked out . . . fragments of embankments are thrown up, and left as precipices with torrents of rusty carts and barrows tumbling over them; tripods of tall poles appear on hill-tops where there are rumours of tunnels; everything looks chaotic" – just as it does in the drawings of J. C. Bourne, or where the new motorways slash their way through the twentieth-century landscape.

Dombey and Son contains Dickens's description of the entry of the railway into London: the London and Birmingham Railway, opened in 1837–8 and depicted in many of Bourne's finest drawings. Toodle, the railway fireman whose wife is engaged as wet-nurse for little Paul Dombey, lives in Staggs's Gardens, a squalid row of houses in Camden Town, which had just been rent by the "first shock of a great earthquake . . . with carcases of ragged tenements, and fragments of unfinished walls and arches, and piles of scaffolding, and wildernesses of bricks, and giant forms of cranes, and tripods straddled above nothing" (chapter 6). This was the great cutting between Camden Town and the new terminus at Euston, conceived and executed by Robert Stephenson on the heroic scale. . . .

A few years later, when Paul Dombey is dying, and a servant is dispatched to fetch his old nurse, "there was no such place as Staggs's Gardens. It had vanished from the earth." Instead, there were palaces, and tiers of warehouses, and streets swarming with passengers and vehicles of every kind.

"There were railway hotels, coffee-houses, lodging-houses, boarding-houses; railway plans, maps, views, wrappers, bottles, sandwich-boxes, and time-tables; railway hackney-coach and cab stands; railway omnibuses, railway streets and buildings. . . . There was even railway time observed in clocks as if the sun itself had given in. . . . Night and day the conquering engines rumbled at their distant work, or advancing smoothly to their journey's end, and gliding like tame dragons into the allotted corners grooved out to the inch for their reception, stood bubbling and trembling there, making the walls quake, as if they were dilating with the secret knowledge of great powers yet unsuspected in them, and strong purposes not yet achieved" (chapter 15).

Toodle, the fireman, is one of the New Men, dressed in a canvas suit abundantly besmeared with coal-dust and oil, with cinders in his whiskers and a smell of half-slaked ashes all over him. But certainly not a bad-looking fellow, and certainly a warm-hearted human being, deliberately contrasted with the inhumanity of Dombey, who regards him as a "presumptuous raker among coals and ashes", merely for wearing a piece of crêpe in mourning for little Paul. "The ashes sometimes gets in here," says Toodle, touching his chest, "and makes a man speak gruff, as at the present time. But it is ashes, sir, not crustiness." And in the description of a footplate journey on the mail from London Bridge to Dover and back (*Household Words*, 12 December 1857), the quality of the driver, "steady Tom Jones . . . at all hours of the day and night ready to ride on the whirlwind and direct the storm . . . for the very humble reward of from forty to fifty shillings a week", is singled out for praise. "As he stands there before me in the glare of the coke oven, or the flickering light of the station in the middle of the night, carefully oiling the joints of his engine, he is the model of an honest, conscientious workman, dutiful, orderly and regular."

Toodle works the train on which Dombey and Major Bagstock travel down to Leamington, and the description of the journey is a remarkable piece of virtuoso writing, achieving in words the kaleidoscopic effect of speed that Turner had achieved in paint. De Quincey in *The English Mail Coach* had caught the exhilaration of going down with the mail, elated with the news of victory in the French wars; but the mails only averaged 8–9 m.p.h., whereas by 1848 the Great Western Railway had timed *The Flying Dutchman* to Didcot at an average speed of 57 m.p.h. . . . . No wonder that there is an almost delirious excitement in Dickens's prose when confronted by this new phenomenon of speed.

The effect of speed is achieved by the overwhelming accumulation of detail, as the train cleaves its way across the English landscape, "through the chalk, through the mould, through the clay, through the rock". Away with a shriek, and a roar, and a rattle goes the train, and for two pages and more Dickens concentrates on the pounding rhythm of the wheels in a carefully paragraphed prose-poem (chapter 20). Humphry House has criticized the refrain as blatant and overdone, but shrewdly notes the subtle variations and counterpointed rhythms, suggestive of the changing lengths of rail and the shifting stresses at points and crossings.

"Through the hollow, on the height, by the heath, by the orchard, by the park, by the garden, over the canal, across the river, where the sheep are feeding, where the mill is going, where the barge is floating, where the dead are lying, where the factory is smoking, where the stream is running, where the village clusters, where the great cathedral rises, where the bleak moor lies, and the wild breeze smooths or ruffles it at its inconstant will; away with a shriek, and a roar, and a rattle, and no trace to leave behind but dust and vapour; like as in the track of the remorseless monster, Death!"

. . . In *Dombey and Son* the railway is thus integrated with the story as a symbol of the power and ruthlessness of the new means of locomotion: Dickens is describing the impact of the railway upon early Victorian society. In *Hard Times* (1854) the railway has become as it were absorbed into the landscape, as well as into the pattern of the industrial society depicted; but although it plays a less individual and spectacular part in the story, we are always aware of the railway in the background.

Coketown was "a town of machinery and tall chimneys . . . and vast piles of building full of windows, where there was a rattling and a trembling all day long, and where the piston of the steam-engine worked monotonously up and down, like the head of an elephant in a state of melancholy madness" (the melancholy mad elephants are another recurrent symbol of the power and inhumanity of the industrial age). The great factories looked, when they were illuminated, like fairy palaces—or the travellers by express train said so, as they whirled past over the arches nearby, hardly felt or heard above the crash and rattle of the machinery. There are many hectic journeys in these expresses: Mr Bounderby's country house is fifteen miles from Coketown, accessible "by a railway striding on many arches over a wild country, undermined by deserted coal-shafts, and spotted at night by fires and black shapes of stationary engines at pits' mouths". Bitzer comes down by train, "shrieking and rattling over the long line of arches", with the news of Mrs Gradgrind's illness, and Louisa rumbles back to Coketown and is whirled into its smoky jaws.

At the crisis of Louisa's tragedy, Mrs Sparsit dives into the train, and is borne down into the country in her evil attempt to compromise Louisa and her supposed lover. As darkness falls, a thunderstorm breaks, and Louisa and Mrs Sparsit, whom she does not recognize in her limp and streaming state, sit in the station waiting-room, listening to the storm and watching the lightning as it quivers and zigzags on the iron tracks.

"The seizure of the station with a fit of trembling, gradually deepening to a complaint of the heart, announced the train. Fire and steam, and smoke, and red light; a hiss, a crash, a bell, and a shriek; Louisa put into one carriage, Mrs Sparsit into another; the little station a desert speck in the thunderstorm" (chapter 11). The technique is impressionist; we are again reminded of Turner's *Rain, Steam and Speed*. The scene is depicted with a minimum of words and a maximum of effect. The short nervous sentences are typical of *Hard Times,* an intensely poetic piece of writing, with its compact structure of interwoven plots, its taut style and the recurring images of which the railway is one of the most effective. Dickens is in fact using the railway to a double purpose: it emphasizes the swiftness of communication now made possible by the railway network – mention is even made of the electric wires "which ruled a colossal strip of music-paper out of the evening sky"; and it also serves to intensify the emotional excitement, though Dickens had shown himself capable of achieving this in the pre-railway world of *Bleak House,* where Inspector Bucket makes his breathlessly controlled dash in the carriage with Esther, through snow and rain, in search of Lady Dedlock.

Quite apart from the imaginative truth of such descriptive passages, one cannot fail to be impressed by Dickens's extraordinary powers of accurate observation. Dickens was a great journalist as well as a great novelist, and much of the effectiveness of his writing derives from his ability to get his facts right, and, if possible, at first-hand. When he wanted to know what engine-driving was like, he obtained a footplate pass from the Secretary of the South Eastern Railway for his young contributor, John Hollingshead. Both the weekly journals which Dickens edited, *Household Words* (1850–9) and *All the Year Round* (1859–70), are full of the railway: the contributions range from serious articles on railway policy to descriptions of journeys, stories, and humorous poems. The railway refreshment room is a perennial object of attack: the *locus classicus* is Mugby Junction, which was really Rugby (*All the Year Round*, 1866, reprinted in *Christmas Stories*), but this was only renewing the attack initiated in *The Uncommercial Traveller* (chapter 6): there are twenty minutes for dinner before you go, and you want your dinner, and like Dr Johnson you like to dine; but (says Dickens), "I cannot dine on stale sponge-cakes that turn to sand in the mouth. I cannot dine on shining brown patties, composed of unknown animals within, and offering to my view the device of an indigestible star-fish in leaden pie-crust without. I cannot dine on a sandwich that has long been pining under an exhausted receiver. I cannot dine on barley-sugar. I cannot dine on toffee." And the year is 1860.

The junction itself – the all-too-familiar punctuation-mark of a cross-country journey – is described vividly and memorably in *The Lazy Tour of Two Idle Apprentices* (*Household Words*, 3 October 1857) (chapter 3). It is all there: the cross-lines of rails zigzagging into it, "like a congress of iron vipers"; sidings with cattle-trucks full of frightened animals; warehouses in which goods "seemed to have taken the veil (of the consistency of tarpaulin), and to have retired from the world without any hope of getting back to it"; an elevated signal-box where a pointsman "was constantly going through the motions of drawing immense quantities of beer at a public-house bar"; and on the walls at night, under the glaring gaslights, lurid advertisements for sauces and bedsteads, patent safes and umbrellas, thrust themselves on the eye. The station itself is either totally unconscious or wildly raving; the change is effected by one awkward shave of the air from a wooden razor – a vivid Dickensian image for the signal arm. A bell rings and bedlam ensues.

"Simmering, whistling, trembling, rumbling, thundering. Trains on the whole confusion of intersecting rails, crossing one another, bumping one another, hissing one another, backing to go forward, tearing into distance to come close. People frantic. Exiles seeking restoration to their native carriages, and banished to remoter climes. . . . Then, in a minute, the station relapsed into stupor, as the stoker of the Cattle Train, the last to depart, went gliding out of it, wiping the long nose of his oil-can with a dirty pocket-handkerchief."

It is this eye for significant detail, and an extraordinary sensibility to atmosphere, that makes Dickens's writings about the railway so convincing. Both these qualities recur in his short story, *No. 1 Branch Line: The Signalman* (*All the Year Round*, 1866, reprinted in *Christmas Stories*), a little masterpiece of the macabre. The setting is a solitary signal-box in a deep and murky cutting that leads to a yet murkier tunnel-mouth, where a red signal-light

looms out of the drifting vapour left by passing trains. Twice the signalman has been haunted by the ringing of his electric bell (inaudible to any ears but his own), and by the appearance of a spectral figure at the tunnel-mouth, on each occasion a supernatural prelude to a disaster on the line. For a week he has been subjected to a third visitation, but "What is the danger? Where is the danger? There is danger overhanging, somewhere on the Line. Some dreadful calamity will happen." His strained imagination does not allow him to entertain any premonition of his own death, and just at dawn, when he has struck the signal-light, he is himself cut down by an engine and killed at the mouth of the tunnel.

from ENGLISH *Spring 1961*

Belloc Breaks a Vow

HILAIRE BELLOC

In Como I bought bread, sausage, and a very little wine for fourpence, and with one franc eighty left I stood in the street eating and wondering what my next step should be.

It seemed on the map perhaps twenty-five, perhaps twenty-six miles to Milan. It was now nearly noon, and as hot as could be. I might, if I held out, cover the distance in eight or nine hours, but I did not see myself walking in the middle heat on the plain of Lombardy, and even if I had been able I should only have got into Milan at dark or later, when the post office (with my money in it) would be shut; and where could I sleep, for my one franc eighty would be gone? A man covering these distances must have one good meal a day or he falls ill. I could beg, but there was the risk of being arrested, and that means an indefinite waste of time, perhaps several days. . . . I had nothing to sell or to pawn, and I had no friends. The Consul I would not attempt; I knew too much of such things as Consuls when poor and dirty men try them. Besides which, there was no Consul. I pondered.

I went into the cool of the cathedral to sit in its fine darkness and think better. I sat before a shrine where candles were burning, put up for their private intentions by the faithful. Of many, two had nearly burnt out. I watched them in their slow race for extinction when a thought took me.

"I will," said I to myself, "use these candles for an ordeal or heavenly judgement. The left hand one shall be for attempting the road at the risk of illness or very dangerous failure; the right hand one shall stand for my going by rail till I come to that point on the railway where one franc eighty will take me, and thence walking into Milan – and heaven defend the right."

They were a long time going out, and they fell evenly. At last the right hand one shot up the long flame that precedes the death of candles; the contest took on interest, and even excitement, when, just as I thought the left hand certain of winning, it went out without guess or warning, like a second-rate person leaving this world for another. The right hand candle waved its flame still higher, as though in triumph, outlived its colleague just the moment to enjoy glory, and then in its turn went fluttering down the dark way from which they say there is no return.

None may protest against the voice of the Gods. I went straight to the nearest railway station (for there are two), and putting down one franc eighty, asked in French for a ticket to whatever station that sum would reach down the line. The ticket came out marked Milan, and I admitted the miracle and confessed the finger of Providence. There was no change, and as I got into the train I had become that rarest and ultimate kind of traveller, the man without any money whatsoever – without passport, without letters, without food or wine; it would be interesting to see what would follow if the train broke down.

The train rolled on. I noticed Lombardy out of the windows. It is flat. I listened to the talk of the crowded peasants in the train. I did not understand it. I twice leaned out to see if Milan were not standing up before me out of the plain, but I saw nothing. Then I fell asleep, and when I woke suddenly it was because we were in the terminus of that noble great town, which I then set out to traverse in search of my necessary money and sustenance. It was yet but early in the afternoon.

from THE PATH TO ROME *1902*

Strike Service

SPIKE HUGHES

To this day I have little idea of what the General Strike was about; I was too young at the time to take much interest in its political causes and now I am twice as old the whole thing is rather stale. As one who has since joined a Trade Union I am usually rather reticent in referring to my activities during the Strike; I fear they might be misunderstood and my principles questioned.

The truth is, of course, that I and some 2,000 other young men at Cambridge went to work in the General Strike with no thought of strike-breaking, of being "patriotic", saving the country from Bolshevism or anything like it. We saw in the whole business nothing more or less than a heaven-sent opportunity to run a railway.

To begin with I reported at six o'clock every morning dressed in a blazer and plus-fours and worked as a porter; my picture was taken and appeared as the personification of "The Lighter Side" in the local Press. I had a bottle of beer in my hand at the time, for we were generously supplied with quantities of free drink and food. I did not greatly relish moving boxes of ageing fish, so I ceased to be a porter after a day or so and became a guard.

I was lectured on a guard's duties and responsibilities by an old retired railwayman, given a whistle, red and green flags, a handful of fog detonators and told to report for the 6.30 a.m. to Ely the following morning.

When I arrived at the train I found that I was by no means the only guard in the van. There were sixteen others, each of whom had been instructed to report at the same time and place. Our train consisted of two or three coaches and was driven by an engine-driver and a stoker who were rowing Blues. During our maiden voyage the stoker unwisely stood up on the tender as we went under a bridge; but he came back next day, with his head bandaged and helped us to keep our record of having the only engine on the line that didn't go off the boil.

Our main job on a round trip to Ely and back was to collect the milk. At the first stop I understood why seventeen guards were considered necessary. I approached a churn on the platform and prepared to roll it in the casual manner I had seen porters employ. We needed every one of seventeen guards to collect the milk; the churns which are rolled so easily are the empties. Full churns weigh like lead.

The Ely milk train carried no passengers even though accommodation was provided for them and the train's schedule was advertised in the Press. We used our flags and whistles, even the fog signals were exploded on the line to hear what kind of noise they made; but none of us ever punched a ticket.

At last, one morning as we drew into a country station we saw two elderly women standing on the platform waiting for the train. Our engine driver overshot the station by fifty yards in his excitement and if a public-spirited small boy had not previously opened them we would have shattered the level-crossing gates ahead of us. When the train had been manoeuvred into position, seventeen guards scrambled out with ticket-punches in hand to show our first passengers into the best first-class seats (nobody had provided us with forms for excess fares, so we couldn't have taken any extra money if we'd wanted to).

All our invitations were refused. Imagining that perhaps the two women had been unable to buy tickets and were shy of boarding a train without paying, we assured them that they could pay the other end. We were still anxious to have passengers even if they had no tickets for us to punch.

We asked the women where they wanted to get to.

"Oh," replied one of them sweetly, "we're not travelling anywhere. We've just come to say how *wonderful* we think you boys are!"

It was a dejected whistle which gave the right-away to the driver, and on the return journey our van echoed to coarse and bitter words on the subject of public ingratitude. On my return to Cambridge I gave up being a guard and became a signalman, though not until I had worked as guard behind 52 trucks of rotting cabbages which had to be taken to Tottenham.

To the layman the guard of a goods train appears to have an easy life spent in brewing tea or toasting kippers over the stove in his van. In reality it is an energetic existence. British goods trains do not as a rule have Westinghouse brakes, so that when the train goes down hill you hear the clanking of buffers getting near you as the engine puts on its brakes. The guard then turns his own brake-wheel furiously and holds on for dear life as the full force of 52 trucks hits the brake-van a tremendous crack.

A signalman's life provides more opportunity for tea and kippers, though my first spell in a signal box during the Strike offered a little too much leisure. I had the misfortune to be posted to a box just outside Cambridge station, where I found a young viscount (now a Tory M.P.) already installed and resentful of the idea that he needed an assistant. He refused to allow anybody but himself to touch the signals, and after a few hours of inactivity, my mates and I (the authorities considered every job on the railway should be done in triplicate at least) bade his lordship a good day and left.

We were then sent to another box at the junction near Shelford, where one line goes from Cambridge to Liverpool Street, another to King's Cross and a third to some small market town in Suffolk.

We were much happier in this box. Every day at one o'clock the only passenger train of the day passed, bound for Liverpool Street, and the guard would throw our lunch and a bottle of beer on the grass verge as the train went by.

One day, though, the guard was careless; our lunch landed on the grass, but the beer bottle hit the side of the signal box and was broken.

The next day the 1 p.m. Up never got to Liverpool Street at all; or if it did, it wasn't the fault of anybody in our box, for we set the points so that the train went along the line to some unknown destination in Suffolk. And for all we know or care, that train is still there.

Shortly afterwards the General Strike ended; we were all paid handsomely for many hours of overtime and I was a little disappointed when, drawing my money at the Labour Exchange, I was not allowed to have a card entitling me to draw the dole as an out-of-work railwayman. I have been told by strikers who were "out" during the General Strike that they felt they had lost something when it was all over. They were not the only ones; those few days in May, 1926, were, for thousands of us, pure, ecstatic wish-fulfilment.

from OPENING BARS *1946*

R

The Harebell Hunters

RICHARD COLLIER

"Careful," my Uncle Victor whispered, "Keep low. Someone's coming back."

I made no answer, only swallowed with my heart like a pounding engine against my ribs, shrinking deeper still into hot dry grass.

August sun dazzled raw white and blinding on the metals of the railway line but from where we lay, in head-high grass on the cutting above, we could not see the track, vanishing into blue distance between the line of hills. We could hear only the steady crunching on the gravel beside the rails as a ganger made his way back along the track to where we were lying. We had been lying there for an hour now and we were hot and thirsty but excited too because the gangers were looking for us.

No sabotage was in our minds but the possession of a wild flower – one single spike of blooms, the shape of bells that grew in purple drifts along the cutting not a hundred yards from where we lay. Often we had seen it from the train in passing but this morning we meant to have a sprig of it, to be identified later from one of the old dog-eared flower books that Uncle Victor kept in his study.

Wild flowers, wild birds, all manner of fish and fowl – to search out these we had braved every imaginable danger, Uncle Victor and I. . . .

The gangers had caught only one glimpse of us on this cutting an hour back but if they did not know where we were hiding or why they were determined to find out.

An uncomfortable business that could have been, to be caught trespassing on railway property with a flimsy excuse. It might mean detention until the local bobby arrived to sort things out, perhaps a summons and a fine.

Worse, it would mean my parents knowing that the nature rambles which Uncle Victor and I took almost every day of the school holidays, winter and summer – a whole four months of the year, remember – were often fraught with peril to life and limb. . . .

They said that Uncle was wonderfully agile for his age but if they knew just how agile I think our walks might have ceased altogether.

Now the footsteps had died away along the railway track. Beside me there was a stealthy rustling as Uncle Victor drew from his pocket – a time-table.

"There's a train due in the station up there just after midday," he whispered. "But remember the gradient sign down the track – the train has to whistle then. And that's a mile away. See our chance?"

"No," I said obtusely.

"Why, you addle-pated troglodyte," hissed Uncle Victor fiercely. "When the train whistles, the gangers'll clear the track, won't they? They'll stand well to one side to let the train go past. There's a curve in the bank that'll screen us from view and that'll just give me time to nip along in cover, grab the plant and get back here."

"But what about me?" I objected, "I could go."

"You stay here and keep your old eyes peeled for the other one. It's my belief he's gone up the line to report to the station. You must cover my retreat."

It seemed to me that Uncle Victor was taking on more than his due share of danger. But it made sense. The station lay only three hundred yards up the line to our right and it needed watching. The old steam train which still ran between these wild chalk hills which were our hunting ground would be coming from our left and would take a good two minutes to cover the mile that lay between us and the start of the gradient. So Uncle Victor stood a chance.

A second passed, then we stiffened. A mile away on the hot still morning we heard the train cry.

"I'm off," Uncle Victor breathed and suddenly he had gone, snaking away through scrub and high grass in the way that only he could – head low, as flat on his belly as a grass snake, using only his elbows to propel him. He said he had learned it from a poacher and it was easy to believe him.

Minutes passed in the hot stillness. I could hear the faint far-off pulsing as the train drew nearer. At the same time I heard footsteps coming hard from the direction of the station. Round the bend in the track, red-faced and sweating in a shirt open to his waist and corduroy pants, came one of the biggest, toughest gangers I had ever seen.

At that moment, from up the track, came a wild swelling roar of triumph, such as the field will give when a fox breaks cover. The big ganger passed me at a trot, not seeing me. Unable to bear it any longer I jumped up.

And then I saw – they had Uncle Victor cornered. As tough as whipcord he was and running hard, his old fishing hat set squarely on his silver head, the purple flower clutched tightly in his grasp. But a whole line of gangers streamed after him, yelling, the distance narrowing every second. Next instant he would run full tilt into the big ganger's arms.

With a shout I dashed to the edge of the cutting, seizing a clod of earth and pitching it clean at the big man's head.

Wonder of wonders, it worked! With a snarl he swung away from Uncle Victor and began clawing his way up the crumbling chalk shelf towards me. I had not heard such interesting words since the milkman fell headlong over my scooter in the drive.

And in that minute the train came round the bend three hundred yards away and both Uncle Victor and I saw at the same moment what we must do. With a great sweep of his arm Uncle Victor signalled "Over!"

So over it was. After all those months in his company I was as bronzed and wiry and agile as a chimpanzee and the ganger was hampered by his bulk. In one roaring white cascade of chalk I was down the cutting and on to the track with the big man marooned up on the bluff like a treed squirrel and bawling to make the heavens fall.

And now the train came on, bulking enormously, little darts of steam licking round its piston, a great plume of smoke bannering away behind, thundering on the hot metals so close that as we darted across its path we were only feet away from the flying wheels. But we were across, Uncle Victor and I, though the hot breath of the train scorched our cheeks like a desert wind, and as coach after coach rumbled in its wake the gangers were left behind cheated of their prey.

But we were running still, along the opposite cleft of the cutting, down a twisting track carved for the railway workers, though there was one bad moment at the station level crossing when the stationmaster and one of his porters tried to bar our way. But we dodged them as easily as two-year-olds among the milk churns and the rolling stock and were away on to a country bus at the bottom of the road.

"Well, well," Uncle Victor said when we were nicely settled on the top deck and the bus was bearing us from the scene of our crime towards the nearest market town, "we must take care of this when we risked the wrath of the Philistine hordes to get it."

And he cradled the spike of purple bells very gently inside an empty tobacco tin and shut tight the lid, so that the plant would be hermetically sealed and would not wither. . . .

It was a Canterbury Bell, one of seven varieties that grew wild in our county, though I had not known there was more than one kind until Uncle Victor told me.

"Perhaps by tonight," he said, "we'll be famous because we've discovered a new species. Perhaps we won't. The main thing is, you know, we tried."

In the end, I think, it turned out to be one of the commonest varieties of all, but of course he was right. We had done our best. We had tried.

from A HOUSE CALLED MEMORY *1960*

PART X

Railway Verse

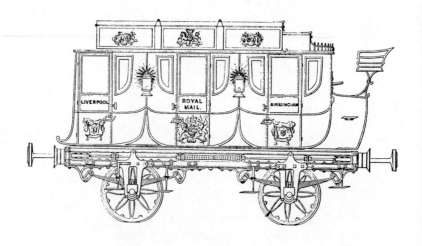

Opening Hymn

If you will listen to my song
I'll not detain you long.
On the 1st of May the folks did throng
To view the Oxford Railway.
And to have a ride – what a treat,
Father, mother, son, and daughter
Along the line like one o'clock,
By fire, steam, and water.

CHORUS: Rifum, Tifum, mirth and fun,
Don't you wonder how it's done,
Carriages without horses run
On the Hampton and Oxford Railway.

From village, and from the towns,
The gents and ladies flocked around.
And music through the air did sound,
Along the Oxford Railway.
There was bakers, butchers, nailers too,
Lots of gentlemen in blue,
And all did strive to get a view
Along the Oxford Railway.

An old woman peeping at the line
Said I wouldn't care a farthing,
But they destroyed my cottage fine
And cut away my garden,
Where I so many years did dwell
Growing lots of cabbages and potatoes,
But worse than all my daughter Nell
Went off with the navigators.

In Alcestor lives a bonny lass,
I think they call her Nancy,
Says she a trip upon the line
Greatly would please my fancy.

I will ride by steam and work by steam,
By steam I'll on be hurried,
And when I can a husband find
By steam I will be married.

And when the line is finished at both ends,
You may send your cocks and hens
And go and visit all your friends,
Your ducks and turkeys, pigs and geese,
To any part wherever you please –
You may also send your butter and eggs,
And they can ride who've got no legs
By the Hampton and Oxford Railway.

                                        ANON

Tragic Incident

The trains are stopp'd, the MIGHTY CHIEFS OF FLAME
To quench their thirst the crystal water claim;
While from their post the great in crowds alight,
When, by a line-train, in its hasty flight,
Through striving to avoid it, Huskisson
By unforeseen mischance was over-run.
That stroke, alas! was death in shortest time;
Thus fell the great financier in his prime!
This fatal chance not only caused delay,
But damped the joy that erst had crown'd the day . . .

At length the Steam-Chiefs with replenish'd force
To Manchester pursued their pageant course;
A grand reception there secure they found;
And though acclaim still made the air resound,
The blithe response was clogg'd with grief's alloy,
The fate of Huskisson still chill'd their joy.
The mutual greetings and the banquet o'er,
The Steam-Chiefs, in procession as before,
With equal pomp and eight-fold gorgeous train,

Forthwith returned to Liverpool again:
While still the eager crowds, we scarce need say,
Their progress hail'd with plaudits all the way.
Now in conclusion, 'twould be vain to tell,
How high at Liverpool was rapture's swell!
How rich the banquet and how choice the wines,
Where thus in state the mighty Arthur dines!
While eloquence, like the occasion, rare,
May be inferr'd, since Peel and Brougham were there!

T. BAKER

(*from The Steam Engine*)

King Steam

Hurrah for the rail! for the stout iron rail,
    A boon to both country and town,
From the very first day that the permanent way
    And the far-famed fish-point was laid down.
'Tis destined, you'll find, to befriend all mankind,
    To strew blessings all over the world;
Man's science, they say, gave it birth one fine day,
    And the flag of King Steam was unfurled.

CHORUS:

    Then hurrah for King Steam, whose wild whistle and
        scream
        Gives notice to friends and to foes,
      As he makes the dust fly, and goes thundering by,
    So stand clear, and make room for King Steam.

Aye! a monarch, I say, hath he been from the day
    He was born; on that glad happy hour,
Until now, when we know the vast debt that we owe
    To his daring, his speed, and his power!
See the birds left behind, as he outstrips the wind
    By the aid of key, sleeper, and metal.
Great Watt little thought what a giant he'd caught,
    When the infant was boiling a kettle.

They may tell, if they will, that our monarch can kill,
  'Tis a fact, I admit, and well know,
But fairly inquire, and there's this to admire,
  The fault is but rarely his own.
With the high and the low he's his failings, we know,
  And his moments of weakness, no doubt.
Since the world first began there were spots on the sun,
  Then why should King Steam be without?
      Then hurrah (etc.)

NED FARMER

The Speculators

The night was stormy and dark,
  The town was shut up in sleep:
Only those were abroad who were out on a lark,
  Or those who'd no beds to keep.

I pass'd through the lonely street,
  The wind did sing and blow;
I could hear the policeman's feet
  Clapping to and fro.

There stood a potato-man
  In the midst of all the wet;
He stood with his 'tato-can.
  In the lonely Haymarket.

Two gents of dismal mien,
  And dank and greasy rags,
Came out of a shop for gin,
  Swaggering over the flags:

Swaggering over the stones,
  These shabby bucks did walk;
And I went and followed those seedy ones,
  And listened to their talk.

Was I sober or awake?
    Could I believe my ears?
Those dismal beggars spake
    Of nothing but railroad shares . . .

Their talk did me perplex,
    All night I tumbled and tost,
And thought of railroad specs,
    And how money was won and lost.

"Bless railroads everywhere,"
    I said, "and the world's advance;
Bless every railroad share
    In Italy, Ireland, France;
For never a beggar need now despair,
    And every rogue has a chance."
                    W. M. THACKERAY

Casey Jones

Come all you rounders, if you wanta hear
Story about a brave ingineer.

Now, "K. C." *Jones* was this rounder's *name*,
On a six-eight-wheeler, boys, he won his fame.
Caller called K.C. at a half-past *four*,
Kissed his wife at the station *door*,
Mounted to the cabin with his orders in his hand,
Took his farewell trip to the Promised Land.

> *Casey Jones! Mounted to the cabin,*
> *Casey Jones! with his orders in his hand.*
> *Casey Jones! Mounted to the cabin,*
> *Took his farewell trip, to the Promised Land.*

"Put *in* yo' water, an' a-shovel in yo' *coal*,
Stick yo' head *out* the winda, watch them drivers *roll*,
I'll *run* her *till* she *leaves* the rail,

'Cause I'm, eight hours *late* with that western mail."
Looked *at* his *watch*, an his watch was *slow*;
Looked *at* the water, an' the *wat*er was low.
Turned to the fireman, an' then he *said*,
"We're gonna reach Frisco, but we'll all be dead."

> *Casey Jones! Gonna reach Frisco,*
> *Casey Jones! but we'll all be dead.*
> *Casey Jones! Gonna reach Frisco,*
> *Gonna reach Frisco, but we'll all be dead.*

K. C. pulled *up* that Reno *hill,*
Whistled for the crossin' with an *aw*ful shrill.
Switchman *knew* by the ingine's *moans*
That the man *at* the throttle *was* K. C. *Jones.*
Pulled up within two *miles* of the place
Number *Four starin'* him right in the face!
Turned to the fireman says, "Boy, better *jump,*
'Cause the's *two* locomotives that's a-gointa *bump.*"

> *Casey Jones! Two locomotives,*
> *Casey Jones! that's a-gointa bump,*
> *Casey Jones! Two locomotives,*
> *Two locomotives that's a-gointa bump.*

K.C. *said* jes' befo' he *died,*
"*Two mo'* roads, that I wanted to ride."
Fireman says "What *can* they be?"
"It's the Southern Pa*c*ific, an' the Santa Fe."
Missis *Jones* sat *on* her *bed,* a sighin',
Jes' received a message that K.C. was dyin',
Says, "*Go* ta bed, chillun, an' *hush* yo' cryin',
'Cause you got another poppa on the Salt Lake Line."

> *Missis Casey Jones! Got another poppa,*
> *Missis Casey Jones! on the Salt Lake Line.*
> *Missis Casey Jones! Got another poppa,*
> *Got another poppa on the Salt Lake Line.*

ANON

The Little Red Caboose behind the Train

Conductor he's a fine old man, his hair is turning gray,
 He works on in the sunshine and the rain.
And the angels all are sober, as he rides all alone,
 In that little red caboose behind the train.
'Twas many a year ago, his hair was black as jet,
 It's whiter now, his heart has known such pain
And I'll tell you all a story, a story that is true,
 Of that little red caboose behind the train.

He met her in September, she was so fair and sweet.
 Oftimes together they'd walk lovers' lane.
Never was a girl more fair, no sweeter ever rode
 In that little red caboose behind the train.
'Twas on a frosty morn, the cold north wind did blow.
 The cold had frozen up the window pane.
They were riding to the city, it was on their honeymoon,
 In that little red caboose behind the train.

The engineer had ridden that line for many years.
 He said the cold was driving him insane.
But he held on to that throttle, his pal was in the rear,
 In that little red caboose behind the train.
The fast express came roaring at ninety miles an hour.
 The brakie tried to see, but it was in vain,
For his fingers all were frozen. He said a silent prayer
 For that little red caboose behind the train.

'Twas after that collision, among the wreckage there,
 They found her body crushed amid blood stain.
Many were the tears and heartaches, and many were the
  prayers,
 For that little red caboose behind the train.
They laid her in the graveyard beside the railroad track.
 He still works in the sunshine and the rain.
And the angels all are sober, as he rides all alone
 In that little red caboose behind the train.

ANON

The Tay Bridge Disaster

Beautiful Railway Bridge of the Silv'ry Tay!
Alas! I am very sorry to say
That ninety lives have been taken away,
On the last Sabbath day of 1879
Which will be remember'd for a very long time.

When the train left Edinburgh
The passengers' hearts were light and felt no sorrow,
But Boreas blew a terrific gale,
Which made their hearts for to quail,
And many of the passengers with fear did say –
"I hope God will send us safe across the Bridge of Tay."

So the train mov'd slowly along the Bridge of Tay,
Until it was about midway,
Then the central girders with a crash gave way,
And down went the train and passengers into the Tay!
The Storm Fiend did loudly bray,
Because ninety lives had been taken away,
On the last Sabbath day of 1879,
Which will be remember'd for a very long time.

It must have been an awful sight,
To witness in the dusky moonlight,
While the Storm Fiend did laugh, and angry did bray,
Along the Railway Bridge of the Silv'ry Tay.
I must now conclude my lay
By telling the world fearlessly without the least dismay,
That your central girders would not have given away,
At least many sensible men do say,
Had they been supported on each side with buttresses,
At least many sensible men confesses,
For the stronger we our houses do build,
The less chance we have of being killed.

WILLIAM MCGONAGALL

Are ye right there, Michael?

Ye may talk of Columbus's sailing
Across the Atlantic sea
But he never tried to go railing
From Ennis as far as Kilkee
You run for the train in the mornin'
The excursion train starting at eight,
You're there when the clock gives the warnin',
And there for an hour you will wait
And as you're waiting in the train
You'll hear the guard sing this refrain;

"Are ye right there, Michael? are ye right?
Do ye think that ye'll be there before the night?
Oh, ye've been so long in startin';
That ye couldn't say for sartin';
Still ye might now, Michael, so ye might!"

They find out where the engine's been hiding,
And it drags you to sweet Corofin;
Says the guard, "Back her down on the siding,
There's the goods from Kilrush comin' in."
Perhaps it comes in in two hours,
Perhaps it breaks down on the way;
"If it does," says the guard, "be the powers,
We're here for the rest of the day!"
And while you sit and curse your luck,
The train backs down into a truck!

"Are ye right there, Michael? are ye right?
Have ye got the parcel there for Missus White?
Oh, ye haven't! Oh, begorra!
Say it's comin' down tomorra
And it might now, Michael, so it might!"

At Lahinch the sea shines like a jewel,
With joy you are ready to shout,

S

When the stoker cries out,
"There's no fuel,
And the fire is taytotallay out.
But hand up that bit of a log there
I'll soon have ye out of the fix;
There's a fine clamp of turf in the bog there;"
And the rest go a-gatherin' sticks.
And while you're breaking bits off trees,
You hear some wise remarks like these:

"Are ye right there, Michael, are ye right?
Do ye think that ye can get the fire to light?
Oh, an hour you'll require,
For the turf it might be dryer,
Well it might now, Michael, so it might."

Kilkee! Oh, you never get near it!
You're in luck if the train brings you back,
For the permanent way is so queer, it
Spends most of its time off the track.
Uphill the ould engin' is climbin'
While the passengers push with a will;
You're in luck when you reach Ennistymon,
For all the way home is downhill.
And as you're wobbling through the dark,
You hear the guard make this remark:

"Are ye right there, Michael? are ye right?
Do ye think that ye'll be home before it's light?
'Tis all dependin' whether
The ould engin' howlds together
And it might now, Michael, so it might!"

PERCY FRENCH

The Iron Steed

In our black stable by the sea,
Five and twenty stalls you see –
Five and twenty strong are we:
The lanterns tossed the shadows round,
Live coals were scattered on the ground,
The swarthy ostlers echoing stept,
But silent all night long we slept.
Inactive we, the steeds of the day,
The shakers of the mountains, lay.
Earth's oldest veins our dam and sire,
Iron chimeras fed with fire.
All we, the unweary, lay at rest;
The sleepless lamp burned on our crest;
And in the darkness far and nigh,
We heard our iron compeers cry . . .

From a Railway Carriage

Faster than fairies, faster than witches,
Bridges and houses, hedges and ditches;
And charging along like troops in a battle,
All through the meadows the horses and cattle:
All of the sights of the hill and the plain
Fly as thick as driving rain;
And ever again, in the wink of an eye,
Painted stations whistle by.

Here is a child who clambers and scrambles,
All by himself and gathering brambles;
Here is a tramp who stands and gazes,
And there is the green for stringing the daisies!
Here is a cart run away in the road
Lumping along with man and load;
And here is a mill, and there is a river:
Each a glimpse and gone for ever!

ROBERT LOUIS STEVENSON

Faintheart in a Railway Train

At nine in the morning there passed a church,
　At ten there passed me the sea,
At twelve a town of smoke and smirch,
At two a forest of oak and birch,
　And then, on a platform, she:

A radiant stranger, who saw not me.
　I said, "Get out to her do I dare?"
But I kept my seat in my search for a plea,
And the wheels moved on. O could it but be
　That I had alighted there!

THOMAS HARDY

Romance

"Romance!" the season-tickets mourn,
"*He* never ran to catch his train,
"But passed with coach and guard and horn –
"And left the local – late again!"
Confound Romance! . . . And all unseen
Romance brought up the nine-fifteen.

His hand was on the lever laid,
His oil-can soothed the worrying cranks,
His whistle waked the snowbound grade,
His fog-horn cut the reeking Banks;
By dock and deep and mine and mill
The Boy-god reckless laboured still!

Robed, crowned and throned, He wove his spell,
Where heart-blood beat or hearth-smoke curled,
With unconsidered miracle,
Hedged in a backward-gazing world:
Then taught His chosen bard to say:
"Our King was with us – yesterday!"

RUDYARD KIPLING
(from The King)

Cyclopean

This circled cosmos whereof man is god
  Has suns and stars of green and gold and red,
And cloudlands of great smoke, that range o'er range
  Far floating, hide its iron heavens o'erhead.

God! Shall we ever honour what we are,
  And see one moment ere the age expire,
The vision of man shouting and erect,
  Whirled by the shrieking steeds of flood and fire?

Or must Fate act the same grey farce again,
  And wait, till one, amid Time's wrecks and scars,
Speaks to a ruin here, "What poet-race
  Shot such cyclopean arches at the stars?"

G. K. CHESTERTON

Broad-gauge Farewell

So! I shall never see you more,
You mighty lord of railway-roar;
The splendid stroke of driving-wheel,
The burnished brass, the shining steel,
Triumphant pride of him who drives
From Paddington to far St Ives.
Another year, and then your place
Knows you no more; a pigmy race
Usurps the glory of the road,
And trails along a lesser load.
Drive on then, engine, drive amain,
Wrap me, like love, yet once again,
A follower in your fiery train.

Drive on! and driving, let me know
The golden West, its warmth, its glow.
Pass Thames with all his winding maze;
Sweet Clifton dreaming in a haze;
And, farther yet, pass Taunton Vale,
And Dawlish rocks, and Teignmouth sail,
And Totnes, where the dancing Dart
Comes seaward with a gladsome heart;
Then let me feel the wind blow free
From levels of the Cornish sea.

Drive on! let all your fiery soul,
Your puissant heart that scorns control,
Your burnished limbs of circling steel,
The throb, the pulse of driving-wheel,
O'erflood the breast of him whose gaze
Is set to watch your perilous ways. . . .

HORATIO F. BROWN

Dawn

Opposite me two Germans snore and sweat.
   Through sullen swirling gloom we jolt and roar.
We have been here for ever: even yet
   A dim watch tells two hours, two aeons, more.
The windows are tight-shut and slimy-wet
   With a night's foetor. There are two hours more;
Two hours to dawn and Milan; two hours yet.
   Opposite me two Germans sweat and snore. . . .

One of them wakes, and spits, and sleeps again.
The darkness shivers. A wan light through the rain
Strikes on our faces, drawn and white. Somewhere
A new day sprawls; and, inside, the foul air
Is chill, and damp, and fouler than before. . . .
Opposite me two Germans sweat and snore.

RUPERT BROOKE

Morning Express

Along the wind-swept platform, pinched and white,
The travellers stand in pools of wintry light,
Offering themselves to morn's long, slanting arrows,
The train's due; porters trundle laden barrows.
The train steams in, volleying resplendent clouds
    Of sun-blown vapour. Hither and about,
Scared people hurry, storming the doors in crowds.
    The officials seem to waken with a shout,
Resolved to hoist and plunder; some to the vans
Leap; others rumble the milk in gleaming cans.
Boys, indolent-eyed, from baskets leaning back,
    Question each face; a man with a hammer steals
Stooping from coach to coach; with clang and clack
    Touches and tests, and listens to the wheels.
Guard sounds a warning whistle, points to the clock
With brandished flag, and on his folded flock
Claps the last door: the monster grunts: 'Enough!'
Tightening his load of links with pant and puff.
Under the arch, then forth into blue day,
Glide the processional windows on their way,
And glimpse the stately folk who sit at ease
To view the world like kings taking the seas
In prosperous weather: drifting banners tell
    Their progress to the counties; with them goes
    The clamour of their journeying; while those
Who sped them stand to wave a last farewell.

A Local Train of Thought

Alone, in silence, at a certain time of night,
Listening, and looking up from what I'm trying to write,
I hear a local train along the Valley. And "There
Goes the one-fifty," think I to myself; aware
That somehow its habitual travelling comforts me,

Making my world seem safer, homelier, sure to be
The same to-morrow; and the same, one hopes, next year.
"There's peacetime in that train." One hears it disappear
With needless warning whistle and rail-resounding wheels.
"That train's quite like an old familiar friend," one feels.

SIEGFRIED SASSOON

Railway Note

The station roofs curve off and line is lost
In white thick vapour. A smooth marble sun
Hangs there. It is the sun. An ermine frost
Edges each thorn and willow skeleton
Beyond the ghosts of goods-yard engines. Who
On earth will get the big expresses through?
But these men do.
We ride incredulous at the use and eyes
That pierce this blankness: like a sword-fish flies
The train with other trains ahead, behind,
Signalled with detonation, whistle, shout;
At the great junction stops.
Ticket-collectors board us and fling out
Their pleasantry as though
They liked things so,
Answering the talkative considerate kind,
"Not so bad now, but it's *been* bad you know."

Two Wars

Professing loud energy, out of the junction departed
The branch-line engine. The small train rounded the bend
Watched by us pilgrims of summer, and most by me, –
Who had known this picture since first my travelling started,
And knew it as sadly pleasant, the usual end
Of singing returns to beloved simplicity.

The small train went from view behind the plantation,
Monotonous, – but there's a grace in monotony!
I felt its journey, I watched in imagination
Its brown smoke spun with sunshine wandering free
Past the great weir with its round flood-mirror beneath,
And where the magpie rises from orchard shadows,
And among the oasts, and like a rosy wreath
Mimicking children's flower-play in the meadows.

The thing so easy, so daily, of so small stature
Gave me another picture: of war's warped face
Where still the sun and the leaf and the lark praised Nature,
But no little engine bustled from place to place;
When summer succeeded summer, yet only ghosts
Or to-morrow's ghosts could venture hand or foot
In the track between the terrible telegraph-posts, –
The end of all things lying between the hut
Which lurked this side, and the shattered local train
That.
   So easy it was; and should that come again –.
EDMUND BLUNDEN

Adlestrop

Yes, I remember Adlestrop –
The name, because one afternoon
Of heat the express-train drew up there
Unwontedly. It was late June.

The steam hissed. Someone cleared his throat.
No one left and no one came
On the bare platform. What I saw
Was Adlestrop – only the name

And willows, willow-herb, and grass,
And meadowsweet, and haycocks dry,
No whit less still and lonely fair
Than the high cloudlets in the sky.

And for that minute a blackbird sang
Close by, and round him, mistier,
Farther and farther, all the birds
Of Oxfordshire and Gloucestershire.

EDWARD THOMAS

The Everlasting Percy

I used to be a fearful lad,
The things I did were downright bad;
And worst of all were what I done
From seventeen to twenty-one
On all the railways far and wide
From sinfulness and shameful pride.

For several years I was so wicked
I used to go without a ticket,
And travelled underneath the seat
Down in the dust of people's feet,
Or else I sat as bold as brass
And told them "Season", in first-class.
In 1921, at Harwich,
I smoked in a non-smoking carriage;
I never knew what Life nor Art meant,
I wrote "Reserved" on my compartment,
And once (I was a guilty man)
I swopped the labels in guard's van.

From 1922 to 4.
I leant against the carriage door
Without a-looking at the latch;
And once, a-leaving Colney Hatch,
I put a huge and heavy parcel
Which I were taking to Newcastle,
Entirely filled with lumps of lead,
Up on the rack above my head;
And when it tumbled down, oh Lord!
I pulled communication cord.

The guard came round and said, "You mule!
What have you done, you dirty fool?"
I simply sat and smiled, and said
"Is this train right for Holyhead?"
He said "You blinking blasted swine,
You'll have to pay the five-pound fine."
I gave a false name and address,
Puffed up with my vaingloriousness.
At Bickershaw and Strood and Staines
I've often got on moving trains,
And once alit at Norwood West
Before my coach had come to rest.
A window and a lamp I broke
At Chipping Sodbury and Stoke
And worse I did at Wissendine:
I threw out bottles on the line
And other articles as be
Likely to cause grave injury
To persons working on the line –
That's what I did at Wissendine.
I grew so careless what I'd do
Throwing things out, and dangerous too,
That, last and worst of all I'd done,
I threw a great sultana bun
Out of the train at Pontypridd –
It hit a platelayer, it did,
I thought that I should have to swing
And never hear the sweet birds sing.
The jury recommended mercy,
And that's how grace was given to Percy.

                                   E. V. KNOX

The Express

After the first powerful plain manifesto
The black statement of pistons, without more fuss
But gliding like a queen, she leaves the station.
Without bowing and with restrained unconcern

She passes the houses which humbly crowd outside,
The gasworks and at last the heavy page
Of death, printed by gravestones in the cemetery.
Beyond the town there lies the open country
Where, gathering speed, she acquires mystery,
The luminous self-possession of ships on ocean.
It is now she begins to sing – at first quite low
Then loud, and at last with a jazzy madness –
The song of her whistle screaming at curves.
Of deafening tunnels, brakes, innumerable bolts.
And always light, aerial, underneath
Goes the elate metre of her wheels.
Steaming through metal landscape on her lines
She plunges new eras of wild happiness
Where speed throws up strange shapes, broad curves
And parallels clean like the steel of guns.
At last, further than Edinburgh or Rome,
Beyond the crest of the world, she reaches night
Where only a low streamline brightness
Of phosphorus on the tossing hills is white.
Ah, like a comet through flame she moves entranced
Wrapt in her music no bird song, no, nor bough
Breaking with honey buds, shall ever equal.

STEPHEN SPENDER

Night Mail

This is the night mail crossing the border,
Bringing the cheque and the postal order,
Letters for the rich, letters for the poor,
The shop at the corner and the girl next door,
Pulling up Beattock, a steady climb –
The gradient's against her but she's on time.

Past cotton grass and moorland boulder,
Shovelling white steam over her shoulder,
Snorting noisily as she passes
Silent miles of wind-bent grasses;

Birds turn their heads as she approaches,
Stare from the bushes at her blank-faced coaches;
Sheepdogs cannot turn her course
They slumber on with paws across,
In the farm she passes no one wakes,
But a jug in a bedroom gently shakes.

Dawn freshens, the climb is done.
Down towards Glasgow she descends
Towards the steam tugs, yelping down the glade
    of cranes
Towards the fields of apparatus, the furnaces
Set on the dark plain like gigantic chessmen.
All Scotland waits for her;
In the dark glens, beside the pale-green sea lochs,
Men long for news.

Letters of thanks, letters from banks,
Letters of joy from the girl and boy,
Receipted bills and invitations
To inspect new stock or visit relations,
And applications for situations,
And timid lovers' declarations,
And gossip, gossip from all the nations,
News circumstantial, news financial,
Letters with holiday snaps to enlarge in,
Letters with faces scrawled in the margin,
Letters from uncles, cousins and aunts,
Letters to Scotland from the South of France,
Letters of condolence to Highlands and Lowlands,
Notes from overseas to the Hebrides;
Written on paper of every hue,
The pink, the violet, the white and the blue,
The chatty, the catty, the boring, adoring,
The cold and official and the heart's outpouring,
Clever, stupid, short and long,
The typed and the printed and the spelt all wrong.
Thousands are still asleep
Dreaming of terrifying monsters

Or a friendly tea beside the brand at Cranston's
    or Crawford's;
Asleep in working Glasgow, asleep in well-set
    Edinburgh,
Asleep in granite Aberdeen.
They continue their dreams
But shall wake soon and long for letters.
And none will hear the postman's knock
Without a quickening of the heart,
For who can bear to feel himself forgotten?

W. H. AUDEN

The Railway Cat

There's a whisper down the line at 11.39
When the Night Mail's ready to depart,
Saying "Skimble where is Skimble has he gone to hunt the
    thimble?
We must find him or the train can't start."
All the guards and all the porters and the stationmaster's
    daughters
They are searching high and low,
Saying "Skimble where is Skimble for unless he's very nimble
Then the Night Mail just can't go."
At 11.42 then the signal's nearly due
And the passengers are frantic to a man –
Then Skimble will appear and he'll saunter to the rear:
He's been busy in the luggage van!
    He gives one flash of his grass-green eyes
      And the signal goes "All Clear!"
    And we're off at last for the northern part
      Of the Northern Hemisphere!

You may say that by and large it is Skimble who's in charge
Of the Sleeping Car Express.
From the driver and the guards to the bagmen playing cards
He will supervise them all, more or less.
Down the corridor he paces and examines all the faces

Of the travellers in the First and in the Third;
He establishes control by a regular patrol
And he'd know at once if anything occurred.
He will watch you without winking and he sees what you are
    thinking
And it's certain that he doesn't approve
Of hilarity and riot, so the folk are very quiet
When Skimble is about and on the move.
      You can play no pranks with Skimbleshanks!
        He's a Cat that cannot be ignored;
    So nothing goes wrong on the Northern Mail
      When Skimbleshanks is aboard.

Oh it's very pleasant when you have found your little den
With your name written up on the door.
And the berth is very neat with a newly folded sheet
And there's not a speck of dust on the floor.
There is every sort of light – you can make it dark or bright;
There's a handle that you turn to make a breeze.
There's a funny little basin you're supposed to wash your
    face in
And a crank to shut the window if you sneeze.
Then the guard looks in politely and will ask you very brightly
"Do you like your morning tea weak or strong?"
But Skimble's just behind him and was ready to remind him,
For Skimble won't let anything go wrong.
      And when you creep into your cosy berth
        And pull up the counterpane,
    You ought to reflect that it's very nice
    To know that you won't be bothered by mice –
    You can leave all that to the Railway Cat,
      The Cat of the Railway Train!

In the watches of the night he is always fresh and bright;
Every now and then he has a cup of tea
With perhaps a drop of Scotch while he's keeping on the watch,
Only stopping here and there to catch a flea.
You were fast asleep at Crewe and so you never knew
That he was walking up and down the station;

You were sleeping all the while he was busy at Carlisle,
Where he greets the stationmaster with elation.
But you saw him at Dumfries, where he speaks to the police
If there's anything they ought to know about:
When you get to Gallowgate there you do not have to wait –
For Skimbleshanks will help you to get out!
   He gives you a wave of his long brown tail
      Which says: "I'll see you again!
   You'll meet without fail on the Midnight Mail
      The Cat of the Railway Train."

                                        T. S. ELIOT

Incident in August

When the Circle train was held up by a signal
   Between Gloucester Road and High Street (Ken)
In the battering dog-day heat of August
   We sweated and mopped our brows. And then
We saw in the cutting, amid the loosestrife
   And butterflies looping through bindweed trails,
A boy who lay drinking, straight from the bottle,
   When, of course, he was paid to look after the rails.

High stood the sun and the heat-haze shimmered,
   The crickets shrilled to the burnished tracks;
But our minds and the motors throbbed together,
   Insisting "You're late. You mustn't relax,
You mustn't look backward, you mustn't look . . .
   Southward?"
   (Oh, the linemen stood by in the hills of Var
And leaned on their spades as the trains went past them
   And swigged red wine from a great stone jar.)

Now, the boy in the sunlight was drinking water –
   Or beer at the best. It might have been Beaune
Or Chateauneuf, but a London embankment.
   Was not the slopes of the Côtes-du-Rhône.

Still, a Mistral blew out of dry Vaucluse,
  A Mistral blew over South-West Ten . . .
Till the train pulled out from Mondragon-sur-Lez
  As the points changed back towards High Street
    (Ken).

BRYAN MORGAN

Harviston End

I looked out of the train,
  And I suddenly saw the empty station
  As we hurtled through, with a hollow roar . . .
"Harviston End" . . . It was dark and dead;
Thick dandelions choking the flower-bed,
Torn posters that flapped on the porter's shed,
  A broken window-pane,
    The waiting-room's shuttered desolation,
      The padlock on the booking-office door. . . .

    Rrring . . . Rrring . . . Rrring . . .

I remember that platform bell,
  Which started the quiet station once an hour.
"Harviston End" . . . White pebbles used to spell
  The name along the borders, all in flower
With fierce geranium, lobelia and stocks;
  Sweet alyssum, and a golden privet hedge . . .
There was always a labelled bicycle, or a box
Of seedlings at the platform's edge
When a train was expected;
  Or a basket of pigeons in the shade,
Drawling and crooning, waiting to be collected . . .
  In the luggage office (where I was sometimes
    weighed
As a great treat, on the station scales)
  There was a musky smell of bran, and paraffin;
While, outside, sunlight dazzled upon the rails
  And on the bright advertisements (enamelled tin –

Three pen-nibs, and a splash of inky blue);
And the air soft with tar, the summer smell . . .
And the chuff of a steam-train drowsing through
The hazy hills . . . And the sound of the bell . . .

Rrring . . . Rrring . . . Rrring . . .

And now the platform bell will ring no more.
They will not come again,
Those summers of youth and exultation;
New trains must run, and new tracks must wind,
And a place out of sight is soon out of mind –
And "Harviston End" has been left behind . . .
As we hurtled through, with a hollow roar,
I looked out of the train,
And I suddenly saw the empty station.

PETER LING

Exploring

. . . Great was my joy with London at my feet –
All London mine, five shillings in my hand
And not expected back till after tea!
Great was our joy, Ronald Hughes Wright's and mine,
To travel by the Underground all day
Between the rush hours, so that very soon
There was no station, north to Finsbury Park,
To Barking eastwards, Clapham Common south,
No temporary platform in the west
Among the Actons and the Ealings, where
We had not once alighted. Metroland
Beckoned us out to lanes in beechy Bucks –
Goldschmidt and Howland (in a wooden hut
Beside the station): "Most attractive sites
Ripe for development"; Charrington's for coal;
And not far off the neo-Tudor shops.
We knew the different railways by their smells.
The City and South reeked like a changing-room;

Its orange engines and old rolling-stock,
Its narrow platforms, undulating tracks,
Seemed even then historic. Next in age,
The Central London, with its cut-glass shades
On draughty stations, had an ozone smell –
Not seaweed-scented ozone from the sea
But something chemical from Birmingham. . . .

JOHN BETJEMAN

Nostalgia

You loved them too: those locos motley gay
That once seemed permanent as their own way? –
The Midland "lake", the Caledonia blue;
The Brighton "Stroudleys" in their umber hue;
North Western "Jumbos", shimmeringly black,
That sped, shrill-whistled, on their "Premier" track;
And all a forest's tints of green – G.C.,
G.N., G.W., L.T.S., H.B.,
South Western, Highland, "Chatham": many more
Both on our own and on the Emerald shore?
Did you, beneath a sooty Oldham sky,
Think dour the "Aspinalls" of L. and Y.,
Or, in the gloom of the Five Towns, admire
The cheerful, sturdy, red North Staffordshire?
Do you remember how the Suffolk sun
Gleamed on a blue Great Eastern "Hamilton"?
In Wessex did you keep slow company
With the "tanks" (royal) of the S. and D.,
That waited, as it seemed, for crack of doom
(While they performed strange rites) at Templecombe?
Across the Fens and Broadland did you reach,
And come – in course of time – to Cromer (Beach)
Behind a khaki M. and G.N.J.,
And was the "pea soup" to your liking – say! –
Of the N.B. that took us over Forth
On our first wizard journey Further North?

The Johnson "singles", Drummond 4–4–os!
Were ever engines lovelier than those?
What treasured names they bore – *Sir Francis Drake,*
Swallow, Lysander, Lady of the Lake,
Courier, Gladstone, Glowworm, Lorna Doone,
Titan, Apollo, Jeanie Deans, Typhoon . . .
And in their wake what rainbow splendour ran:
The bronze-green coaches of the Cambrian;
G.N.S. red and white; North Eastern "plum";
"Salmon" that struck one young observer dumb
At grim old Waterloo; the varnished teak
That, North or South, was never far to seek,
But had for apogee East Coast Joint Stock
That left King's Cross each morning, ten o'clock –
Though many held this did not equal quite
The West Coast purple-brown and (spilt-milk) white.

Those Furness trains – red, white, and blue – at Grange?
That "orange" touch at Manchester (Exchange);
At Central the dark oak of Cheshire Lines?
Or – what the memory most of all enshrines:
The crown and consummation of our dreams! –
Those great "joint" hubs where many colour-schemes
Converged to hold us under such a spell:
York, Cambridge, Perth, or Carlisle (Citadel)? . . .
The high "bird-cages" of L.C. and D.?
Those dismal Broad Street arks one used to see
Above one ere (in hardly prouder state!)
One trundled up the bank at Bishopsgate? . . .
Those little Emett lines which "also ran,"
Saucily mocking at the march of man –
Festiniog, Southwold, Wantage, Isle of Wight,
Lynton and Barnstaple, East Suffolk Light? . . .
Yes, I remember! But I will not flog
My muse to furnish the whole catalogue.

"Each to his choice." Although my youth was bred
Amid the comfortable Midland red,
And though for long, wherever I might roam,

M.R. to me spelled certitude and home,
Yet all my exiled Western blood took fire
When – a small boy, in snowy-starched attire –
I first changed trains at Bristol (Temple Meads).
Awhile my tastes were fickle; but the seeds
Sown there have proved the stubbornest by far:
Upon my heart is graved G.W.R.
And when I came to live near Brunel's wall,
Between the red cliffs and the rise and fall
Of Devon waves, I thought long years to see,
In ever-more-familiar livery,
The "Dutchman" or the "Limited" swing by,
Washed by the Channel spray.
                    Hope born to die!*

                                        R. P. LISTER

                        *Laus Deo, it was not!—Ed.

A Prayer

As the through-train of words with white-hot whistle
Shrills past the heart's mean halts, the mind's full stops,
    With all the signals down; past the small town
    Contentment, and the citizens all leaning
And loitering parenthetically
    In waiting-rooms, or interrogative on platforms;
Its screaming mouth crammed tight with urgent meaning,
– I, by it borne on, look out and wonder
    To what happy or calamitous terminus
I am bound, what anonymity or what renown.

O if at length into Age, the last of all stations,
It slides and slows, and its smoky mane of thunder
    Thins out, and I detrain; when I stand in that place
On whose piers and wharves, from all sources and seas,
Men wearily arrive – I pray that still
I may have with me my pities and indignations.

                                        W. R. RODGERS

Acknowledgements

Acknowledgements and thanks are due to the following authors
and publishers for permission to use copyright material:

To Canon Roger Lloyd and Allen & Unwin Ltd. for four extracts from *The Fascination
of Railways*

To Mr Alvin F. Harlow and Crown Publishers, Inc., for "The Collector" from
A Treasury of Railroad Folklore

To Rev. E. Beal and Thomas Nelson & Sons Ltd. for "The Modeller" from *The
Craft of Modelling Railways*

To Mr L. T. C. Rolt and Constable & Co., Longmans Green & Co. and The Bodley
Head respectively, for three extracts from *Lines of Character*, for "The Royal Albert
Bridge" from *Isambard Kingdom Brunel*, and for four extracts from *Red for Danger*

To Mr W. A. Tuplin and Allen& Unwin Ltd. for two extracts and one drawing from
Great Western Steam

To Mr C. Hamilton Ellis and Allen & Unwin Ltd. for two extracts from *The Trains
We Loved* and five extracts from *British Railway History 1877–1947*

To Mr Clifford Dyment and J. M. Dent & Sons Ltd. for the extract from *The
Railway Game*

To Miss Marjorie Whitelaw and the Review of the Hunting Group of Companies for
"Preview"

To John Murray Ltd. for "Railways in 1843" from *The Railways of England* by the
late Sir Wm. Acworth; as also to John Murray Ltd. for the late Sir Arthur Conan
Doyle's story *The Lost Special* (titled here "The Vanishing Train")

To Professor Jack Simmons and Routledge and Kegan Paul Ltd. for five extracts
from *The Railways of Britain*

To Mr Roger Fulford and the B.B.C. for "Racing to Scotland"

To Cassell & Co. Ltd. for three extracts and numerous drawings from *Our Railways*
by John Pendleton

To Mr O. S. Nock and the respective publishers for two extracts from *The Railway
Engineers* (Batsford), for "Patrick Stirling" and "Nigel Gresley" from *Steam Loco-
motive* (British Transport Commission), for "The Heyday of Steam" from *Steam
Locomotive* (Allen & Unwin), and for one extract from *Scottish Railways* (Nelson)

To Longmans Green & Co. for "Henry Ivatt" from *The Book of the Locomotive* by
G. Giffard Jackson

To Mr Geoffrey Freeman Allen and Ian Allan Ltd. for "The Twilight of Steam"
from *British Railways Today and Tomorrow* (1959)

To Mr Michael Robbins and Routledge & Kegan Paul Ltd. for the extract from
The Railway Age

To Mr Christian Barman for the extract from *An Introduction to Railway Architecture*
(Art & Technics)

To Mr John Betjeman and John Murray Ltd. for the extract from *First and Last
Loves* and "Exploring" from *Summoned By Bells*

To Mr H. Shirley Smith & Phoenix House Ltd. for the extract from *The World's
Great Bridges*

To Mr Cecil J. Allen, and Ian Allan Ltd. and Thomas Nelson & Sons Ltd. respectively, for one extract from *Titled Trains of Great Britain*, and one extract from
Switzerland's Amazing Railways

To the Proprietors of Punch for permission to reprint "London Extension"
(originally *Steam Train to Kensington*) by John Betjeman; for "Courier's Train"
(originally *Railway Networks*) by Anthony Carson; and for the poems *Harviston End*
by P. Ling, *Nostalgia* by R. P. Lister, *The Everlasting Percy* by E. V. Knox, and
Incident in August by Bryan Morgan

551

To Mr R. C. Robertson-Glasgow and the Sunday Times for "Farewell to a Branch"

To Mr Richard Blythe and Newman Neame Ltd. for "Signalling grows up" from *Danger Ahead* and for two illustrations

To Mr John Prebble and Secker & Warburg Ltd. for the extracts on The Tay Bridge Disaster from *The High Girders*

To Mr J. A. Swisher and State Historical Society, Iowa, for "An American Heroine"

To Mr Paul Jennings and The Observer for "Dining-Car" and "Ferry Train"

To Country Life Ltd. for the extract from *The Railway Age* by the late C. Bruyn Andrews

To Mrs W. H. Davies and Jonathan Cape Ltd. for the extract from *Autobiography of a Super-Tramp* by the late W. H. Davies

To Colonel Peter Fleming and the B.B.C. for "Ammunition Train" and "The Road to Samarkand"

To Mr Andrew Karpati and The Observer for "Deportation Train"

To Mr Peter Allen, Mr P. B. Whitehouse and Ian Allan Ltd. for two extracts from *Narrow Gauge Railways in Europe*

To Mr C. S. Small and Cleaver-Hume Ltd. for two extracts from *Far Wheels*

To Mr Lucius Beebe and Dutton & Co. Inc. for "Short Line, U.S.A." from *Mixed Train Daily*

To the Literary Executors of the late R. B. Cunninghame-Graham for the extract from *Success*

To Thomas Nelson & Sons Ltd. for "The Great Locomotive Chase" from *A Book of Escapes and Hurried Journeys* by the late John Buchan

To Mr Robin Atthill and the English Association for "Dickens and the Railway" from *English, No. 76.*

To Allen & Unwin Ltd. for the extract from *The Path to Rome* by the late Hilaire Belloc

To Mr Spike Hughes and Pilot Press for the extract from *Opening Bars*

To Mr Richard Collier and Wm. Collins Sons Ltd. for the extract from *A House Called Memory*

To Gerald Duckworth & Co. Ltd. for "The Tay Bridge Disaster" by William McGonagall from *Poetic Gems*

To Keith Prowse Ltd. for "Are Ye Right There, Michael?" from The Percy French Song-Book

To Macmillan & Co. Ltd. for "Faintheart in a Railway Train" by the late Thomas Hardy

To Mrs George Bambridge, and to Methuen & Co. Ltd. and the Macmillan Company of Canada, for three verses (called here "Romance") from *The King* by the late Rudyard Kipling from *The Seven Seas*

To J. M. Dent & Sons Ltd. for "Cyclopean" by G. K. Chesterton

To Sidgwick & Jackson Ltd. for "Dawn" by Rupert Brooke

To Mr Siegfried Sassoon and Faber & Faber Ltd. for "Morning Express" and "A Local Train of Thought"

To Professor Edmund Blunden and Wm. Collins Sons Ltd. for "Railway Note" and "Two Wars"

To Mrs Helen Thomas for "Adlestrop" by the late Edward Thomas

To Mr Stephen Spender and Faber & Faber Ltd. for "The Express"

To H.M. Postmaster General for "Night Mail" by W. H. Auden

To Mr T. S. Eliot and Faber & Faber Ltd. for "Skimbleshanks, The Railway Cat" from *Old Possum's Book of Practical Cats*

To Mr W. R. Rodgers and Secker & Warburg Ltd. for "Awake"

Finally the Editor would like to thank Cleaver-Hume Ltd. for permission to reproduce "Comments on three Nations" from *The End of the Line*, and to express gratitude to Putnam & Co. for permission to reproduce "Buffet Car" from *The Compleat Imbiber*.

Acknowledgements for the Illustrations

Acknowledgement is made to the following publications for
the reproduction of the illustrations on the pages shown:

Our Railways by John Pendleton (Cassell, 1894): 19, 21, 22, 60, 102, 149, 150, 158,
169, 212, 232, 234, 245, 274, 277, 278, 302, 322, 328, 341, 346, 367, 370, 377, 378,
393, 519, 550
The Railway Age by C. Bruyn Andrews (Country Life, 1937): 59, 222, 236, 254, 466
A Handbook of Early Advertising Art (3rd Edition) by Clarence P. Hornung: 414,
427
The Railway Gazette: 428
A Treasury of Railroad Folklore (Crown Publishers, Inc., 1956): 460, 463
Souvenir Booklet of Great Western Railway Museum, Swindon: 486

Special acknowledgements are also due:

To Mrs J. N. Maskelyne and Percival Marshall & Co. Ltd. for three drawings from
Locomotives I Have Known by the late J. N. Maskelyne
To St. Pancras Public Library for "Camden Town Circular Engine House" on page
177
To British Railways for the drawing of the diesel locomotive which appears on page
210
To George Newnes & Co. Ltd. for the illustration from *Silver Blaze* on page 465

The unattributed reproductions are taken from *Specimen of Printing Types of the
Caslon and Glasgow Letter Foundry* (1854) and *Printing Type Specimens of Miller and
Richard* (1927).

Index of Authors